T0311190

# FIGHTING for AMERICA

This book is a publication of

INDIANA UNIVERSITY PRESS
Office of Scholarly Publishing
Herman B Wells Library 350
1320 East 10th Street
Bloomington, Indiana 47405 USA

iupress.indiana.edu

Telephone   800-842-6796
Fax   812-855-7931

First paperback edition 2014
© 2011 by Jeremy M. Black

All rights reserved

No part of this book may be reproduced
or utilized in any form or by any means,
electronic or mechanical, including
photocopying and recording, or by
any information storage and retrieval
system, without permission in writing
from the publisher. The Association of
American University Presses' Resolution
on Permissions constitutes the only
exception to this prohibition.

∞ The paper used in this publication meets
the minimum requirements of the American
National Standard for Information
Sciences – Permanence of Paper for Printed
Library Materials, ANSI Z39.48-1992.

Manufactured in the
United States of America

The Library of Congress has cataloged
the original edition as follows:

Black, Jeremy.
  Fighting for America : the struggle
for mastery in North America,
1519–1871 / Jeremy Black.
    p. cm.
    Includes bibliographical
references and index.
    ISBN 978-0-253-35660-4 (cloth : alk.
paper) 1. United States – Territorial
expansion. 2. Manifest Destiny.
3. Geopolitics – North America – History.
4. Geopolitics – United States – History.
5. North America – History, Military.
6. Great Britain – Colonies – America –
History. 7. France – Colonies – America –
History. I. Title.
    E179.5.B66 2011
    970.01 – dc22

                                    2011008159

ISBN 978-0-253-01481-8 (paperback)
ISBN 978-0-253-00561-8 (ebook)

2 3 4 5   19 18 17 16 15 14

# FIGHTING
## for
# AMERICA

### THE STRUGGLE FOR MASTERY
### IN NORTH AMERICA
### 1519-1871

JEREMY BLACK

INDIANA UNIVERSITY PRESS    *Bloomington & Indianapolis*

*For*

DENNIS SHOWALTER

# CONTENTS

# PREFACE & ACKNOWLEDGMENTS

The United States had an undoubted right to settle wherever they pleased on the shores of the Pacific Ocean without being questioned by the English government, and he had really thought that they were at least to be left unmolested on their continent of North America.

*Stratford Canning to Robert, Viscount Castlereagh, Foreign Secretary, 28 Jan. 1821*

John Quincy Adams, the Secretary of State, was particularly blunt in January 1821 when repulsing the attempt by Stratford Canning, the British envoy, to discuss whether the American government was seeking to establish a new settlement on the Columbia River. Adams asserted Manifest Destiny before the term was devised and was not interested in Canning's discussion of British rights or the 1818 convention between the two powers.[1] Adams's account was to triumph as his work and the efforts of others created a state that spanned the continent. Yet, this process was far from inevitable and this book is a story of conflict, diplomacy, geopolitics, and politics. The prize was mastery in North America, and the eventual result the invention of a United States of America that stretched from ocean to ocean and achieved this mastery. To that end, this book offers a one-volume sweeping geopolitical history of North America from the landing of Spanish troops under Hernán Cortés in modern Mexico in 1519 until 1871 when, with the Treaty of Washington and the withdrawal of most British garrisons, Britain in effect accepted American mastery in North America and the North American Question was thereby settled.

Benefiting from adopting the long approach and from studying continuities and discontinuities in this time scale, this history serves to offer an analytical narrative and has, as its central theme, the argument that the fate of North America was not a matter of manifest destiny but was affected by contingencies and, moreover, was fairly unclear until quite late. The purpose, in part, of this book is to undermine exceptionalist and determinist narratives that project the inevitability of U.S. domination over North America, and, instead, to reconceptualize "American space" from an international perspective. By doing so, and adopting the long-term perspective, Manifest Destiny emerges not as American providence or predestination, but rather as a concept used by a number of competitors and as a descriptor of struggle in history. Moreover, the outcome of U.S. domination seems more contingent throughout the period covered than is suggested by any reference to Manifest Destiny.

Furthermore, this outcome was largely decided only as a result of events in the 1860s, developments that seemed highly unpredictable to contemporaries, both American and foreign. Indeed, the decade 1861–71 was not a coda but a decisive culmination, with the eventual outcome of the American Civil War (1861–65) ensuring the maintenance of American unity, and the end both of the prospect of Southern independence and of the reality of Southern autonomy. Secondly, the 1860s were very important because the absence of European intervention in the Civil War helped to secure the results of the Civil War, as well as reflecting, and ensuring, a sense of relative American power. Thirdly, the American intimidation of Emperor Napoleon III and the resulting withdrawal of French forces from Mexico (also a response to European power politics in the shape of Prussian success against Austria in 1866), was, in part, a consequence of Union victory and strength. In Mexico, the other North American civil war of the 1860s, one that was longer than its more famous counterpart and is overly neglected other than by specialists on Mexican history, ended with the conservative, monarchist, pro-French side defeated, and with the liberal, republican, anti-French cause that the Union had wished to win triumphant. Fourthly, "Seward's Folly," the American purchase of Alaska and the Aleutian Islands in 1867, marked the effective end of Russian interest in North America and brought America a great expanse of territory and an increased presence in the North Pacific, while also locating British Columbia between two areas of American territory. Lastly, the withdrawal of most British garrisons from Canada after

1871 was in part a result of the Union victory, and marked the effective end of the North American Question, with America clearly dominant in North America and the defense of Canada essentially left to local forces. Canadian Confederation in 1867 was another testimony to the importance of this decade, to the concerns raised by American power, and to the interactions that were so important to developments both across the continent and more widely because Confederation also involved British concerns, priorities, and responses.

This book relates traditional political history from an imperial perspective, but is also an outgrowth of newfound interest in trans-Atlantic perspectives. The geopolitical trajectory of North America cannot be divorced from international and domestic politics, and its relationship with both was dynamic. In short, American exceptionalism has to be reconceptualized to take note of the pressures and impact of international competition, and this competition provides the context within which to consider the struggle for the future of Canada, Mexico, and the successive Wests of America.

From its inception as an independent state in 1776, America was the largest and most powerful republic in the world, and it swiftly became a democratic empire that challenged the prejudices and suppositions of European commentators. There was an obvious contrast between America and the geopolitics of dynastic imperial "space" represented by the Family Compact between the branches of the Bourbon dynasty in France and Spain, notably the Third Family Compact of 1761.[2] The likely course of the development both of America and of North America, however, were far from clear. Furthermore, this geopolitical uncertainty had a major impact on the development of American identity, constitutionalism, and politics, as well as providing important topics for the last. The same was also the case for Mexico and Canada.

Not only did the struggles between Britain, France, and Spain mold the processes prior to 1775, but they were also influential down till 1815, being, however, joined from 1783 by the impact of the tension between Britain and the United States – tension that led to war in 1812. Moreover, Anglo-American tension continued to play a major role until the 1860s, with American-French and American-Spanish tension also at times being important.

Furthermore, the independent "players" within the American space included not only politicians and political movements with different concepts of how the country should respond to the perceived anxieties, exigencies, and opportunities of its geopolitical position, but also Native Americans.[3] Whatever the sovereignty as far as European and American governments were concerned, Native Americans had their own sense of Manifest Destiny, were autonomous and able to take initiatives in their own right, and were also an element at issue in confrontations between the British and French or Spaniards, and, subsequently, the Americans and Britain, Spain, and Mexico.

The role of Native Americans dramatized, but did not exhaust, the impact of the "frontier." In the United States, as in other empires, there was a struggle for control over imperial expansion between center and periphery. "Adventurers" or projectors, notably the filibusters who sought to seize non-American territory,[4] were important in the latter (and deserve attention), as, more generally, was a practice of independence and defiance of government by Americans, albeit one which, by the close of the period, had been greatly lessened in importance. Prior to that, the very presence of an advancing frontier both attracted the "marginals," who were unhappy with governmental authority, and also moved them further away from centers of settlement and power. Shays Rebellion (1786–87) and the Whiskey Rebellion (1794), in Massachusetts and Pennsylvania respectively, were early instances of hostility to governmental authority, and had significant consequences for the development of the American constitution and for political ideas and practice. Moreover, it is important to consider what these rebellions and other tensions could have led to. There might well have been pressure for a stronger federal force capable of enforcing government power or, conversely, there might have been a "balkanization" of America, akin to that in Mexico where local militias and strongmen enjoyed great and disruptive power from the 1820s, a pattern also seen elsewhere in Latin America, notably in Argentina.

The dispatch of American troops to overawe the Mormons in Utah in 1857–58 was another aspect of the process of dealing with frontier opposition. With the exception of Utah, however, there were no significant problems with autonomous groups moving beyond the bounds of American control nor adopting an independent position within those bounds. Nor, prior to 1861, was sectional rebellion a serious issue. There was no equivalent to the frontier rebellions Mexico had faced in Texas and California (nor the separatism in Central America), nor those that the British were to face in Manitoba. The nullification crisis of 1832–33 in South Carolina and the border wars in Kansas and Missouri in the 1850s were less significant than these crises.

Although less so than Native Americans, African Americans were also "players" in the struggle for mastery in North America, with slavery motivating a great deal of violence. Aside from the conflict involved in the slave trade, both in Africa and in the struggle to control European plantation colonies in the New World, it is also necessary to consider the active roles played by African Americans in the American Revolution and the Civil War. The Caribbean played a direct role in this dimension: the revolution in Saint-Domingue (later Haiti) in the 1790s was connected to the fact that Afro-Caribbeans fought in the French forces in the American Revolution in which France intervened in 1778, while, in turn, developments in Saint-Domingue greatly influenced U.S. policy toward France and Britain in the 1790s, as well as American expansionist ambitions thereafter. As a consequence of these players and factors, this book will neither be a conventional diplomatic history nor a conventional military study, but will contain elements of both, albeit each understood in their broadest sense and given a political context.

Authorship by a non-American helps ensure that the important role played by European powers in the struggle for mastery in North America receives due attention, and this European history sheds a better light on the predicament of republican America. Nevertheless, it would be wrong to suggest that there are not longstanding, shrewd, and valuable works by distinguished American scholars in the field, as well as pertinent studies by British academics.

The subject of this book, obviously, is a topic that could be covered in several volumes but, for the sake of comprehension and in order to focus on the main themes, there is a determination to produce just one volume. The starting point is open to debate, debate that has been politicized as an instance of the more general contentiousness of the public history that is an important adjunct of this study. In the early 1920s, when the large-scale "New Italian" immigration from southern Italy (not of the earlier northern Italians who could be seen as more "European," even Alpine) was under attack, the Viking origin of America in about 1000 became more popular as a theme, and Columbus's role in "discovering" the New World and beginning European links with the Americas was played down. Moreover, by 1992, the five-hundredth anniversary of his arrival in the New World, there was savage criticism of the consequences of his voyages for Native Americans, criticism that represented a marked contrast to the celebrations in 1892.[5] Alternatively, it was tempting, notably for WASP (White Anglo-Saxon Protestant) commentators, to begin the history with the foundation of the first permanent English settlement in North America – at Jamestown in Virginia in 1607. Ironically, such an approach itself led to controversy in 2007 over the consequences of English colonization for Native and African Americans.[6]

However, any focus on English settlement underplays the role of Spain. What became the United States was not central to Spanish concerns, as, indeed, was shown by the Spanish willingness to part with Florida in 1763 in order to regain the far more valuable and strategically significant colony of Cuba from Britain, and also by the delay until the eighteenth century in pursuing the prospect of expansion into California. Nevertheless, Spain devoted efforts to preserving its position from European interlopers in Florida and the Gulf coast from the 1560s on, while Mexico, a key Spanish colony, is, geographically, in North America (as opposed to South America), as is all of what became the southwest part of the United States. There, Spain, and, later, and more clearly, Mexico, was a major "player," particularly from the 1770s to the 1840s. Furthermore, again considering the perspective from the south, the Caribbean is an essential context for comprehending continental events until the close of the eighteenth century.

American exceptionalism is an important instance of the way in which history has served in the Atlantic world (as elsewhere) to provide a distinctive patriotic account of direct relevance to the present.[7] Nevertheless, geopolitical competition is a key context for, and qualification of, this exceptionalism, and there is a need, as for other states, to understand the political development of the United States in part in this context of international competition and, in particular, to relate political contention to debates over foreign policy and military goals and structure. The rise of American power from 1776 therefore is best explored as a consequence of interaction with other powerful and expansive empires, both European and also New World in the shape of Native Americans and Mexico.

I am most grateful for opportunities to develop ideas provided by lectures at West Point, the University of Virginia, the College of William and Mary, Roger Williams University, and the Naval War College. I have also benefited greatly from the comments made on all or part of earlier drafts by Kristofer Allerfeldt, John Beeler, David Brown, Matthew Brown, Duncan Campbell, Howard Fuller, Irving Levinson, Phillip Myers, Michael Neiberg, Walter Nugent, Peter Onuf, Tim Shannon, Dennis Showalter, Sam Watson, Don Yerxa, and Neil York. None is responsible for any errors that remain. I would like to thank Joyce Rappaport, the copyeditor. It is a great pleasure to dedicate this book to Dennis Showalter, a historian of enormous resource who is held in great affection by all who know him and who has been a great inspiration, a major encouragement, and a good friend to me.

# ABBREVIATIONS

| | |
|---|---|
| Add | Additional Manuscripts |
| A E | Ministère des Relations Extérieures, Paris |
| Ang. | Angleterre |
| A S | All Souls College Library, Oxford |
| AST. | Turin, Archivio di Stato |
| B B | Bland Burges papers |
| B L | British Library, London |
| Bodl | Bodleian Library, Oxford |
| C P | Correspondance Politique |
| DRO | Devon Record Office, Exeter |
| Farmington | Farmington, Connecticut, Lewis Walpole Library, Weston papers |
| FO | Foreign Office |
| HL. | San Marino, California, Huntington Library |
| Ing. | Inghilterra |
| LM. | Lettere Ministri |
| NA | National Archives, Kew |
| os | old style dates |
| PCC | Papers of the Continental Congress, National Archives, Washington |
| Penn. | Pennsylvania Historical Society, Philadelphia |
| SP | State Papers |

FIGHTING for AMERICA

# INTRODUCTION

America was the object of the war; the sentiments of the nation before the war, and during the war, were fixed upon America only.

*Anon.,* A Full and Free Enquiry into the Merits of the Peace *(1765)*

If there is no one way to present the past, then that is particularly the case for the topic of this book. There are key differences in context and approach, conceptualization and methodology, and the sounds range from the funeral laments for the indigenous cultures of North America, to the brash triumphant clarion calls of a supposed destiny for the American republic as it came to span the continent. History as the accounts of the past is more than the silent spectator to our tale, for part of its value is to make overt what are often implicit choices of approach and analysis. In making the implicit overt, we must turn first not to the actors in the tale, but rather to the writer and readers who clothe them with meaning. The readers are the key, for it is you who decide what to take from this book, but, by the nature of this book, you are unknown at this moment of the author's creation. It is most unclear how many readers will be American, how many British, and how many from other countries; how much the readers will have prior knowledge of the subject, or indeed, more pertinently, relevant assumptions; and, lastly, the values of the readers, and their impact on their assessment of the subject, are unknown.

The writer is less important, but clearer in focus. Frequently, it is helpful reviewers who clarify this focus by drawing attention to the assumptions that can be seen in the work. These are assumptions that the author downplays in the Anglophone tradition, because of the intellectual, pedagogic, and cultural preference in academic life for concealing the role of the author and, in particular, for letting the material dictate the treatment. That, however, is not the stance here, in part because I want to explain why I am adopting the approach that I am taking, and without pretending that this is the sole approach that can be followed. The Introduction is a more appropriate format than the Preface for doing so, because the latter tends to be more detached from the text. The key point of departure is that of sequence, a historian's note, but also a contribution that helps explain the author's role. The writing of this book followed soon on that of my *Geopolitics* (2009), and, in part, is a case study for the discussion in that book, notably the probing there of the conceptual problems of geopolitics and of its application. Geopolitics is clearly crucial to the history of North America; the development of American power occurred in large part as a territorial phenomenon and was expressed in terms of territorial expansion. Moreover, this process was understood with reference to a developing appreciation of the political and ideological significance of space. Thus, Manifest Destiny created North America.

American expansion was part of the general current of nineteenth-century imperialism, a current not restricted to Western powers as it was also seen later in the century with Japan and Ethiopia. An aspect of this imperialism was a widespread interest in geography, not least in the sense of the spatial encoding of information. Geography, as the acquisition of spatially linked information and, even more, its organization and analysis, was, in the nineteenth century, an aspect of the systematization of knowledge also seen in subjects such as ethnography and geology. The physical geography of the world was understood in terms of measurement, and was measured accordingly. Seas were charted, heights gauged, depths plumbed, and rainfall and temperature recorded; and all was integrated, so that the world, its parts and its dynamics, were increasingly understood in terms of a Western matrix of knowledge. Areas were given an aggregate assessment that reflected and denoted value and values to Westerners.[1] Similarly, regions were grouped together, most prominently as continents, in response to Western ideas. Thus, the South Atlantic world of the west coast of Africa, Brazil, the Guianas and the West Indies, was subordinated to a Western model in which Africa and the New World were separate,[2] a model that made no sense of the large-scale enforced movement of Africans across the South Atlantic from the sixteenth to the nineteenth century.

North America did not have a pre-(European) contact identity as the societies of the period there had only limited knowledge of each other.[3] Instead, as a separate space, North America owed something to the conceptual process by which Westerners arranged the world, although there was also the powerful political drive from within the United States, a drive that helped separate North America from the varied ideas of Latin, Central, and South America. The impetus to rethink both America and North America in terms of (and in advance of) American territorial expansion had an important domestic political dimension as well as that of the geopolitics of international competition. This domestic dimension reflected tensions and dynamics in American politics, notably that between the interior and the coastal littoral. The rejection of metropolitan values associated with the latter by those laying claim in a nativist fashion to values that were presented as inherently American was particularly important. If Americans thus rejected the coast, it was as one with a rejection of European values, and was frequently in part driven by this factor.

Need and opportunity also played a part. It was necessary for Americans to reconceptualize their country, its regional setting, and the wider hemispheric, Atlantic, and global contexts, in response to, and in terms of, the Louisiana Purchase of 1803, and the unfinished business this gave rise to over Oregon and the Texas frontier, and relations concerning Native Americans over an unprecedented area. This process was taken forward as each of the latter issues became more pressing; opportunity, need, and ideas proving mutually energizing. Moreover, the establishment of American power on the Pacific, in aspiration from the 1800s and in practice from the late 1840s, provided the opportunity for justifying a complete rethinking of the North American space, one in which transcontinentalism came to the fore.

America as a Pacific power was a direction for expansion that was not brought to fruition until the mid-nineteenth century when, in 1850, California swiftly became a state after its conquest from Mexico in 1846. However, in terms of international power politics, transcontinentalism

was, from the second quarter of the nineteenth century, more important than the frontier, which was a notion more valuable for relations
with Native Americans and for American political culture, and related
academic analysis, than for a sense of America in the wider world. The
latter was readily supplied by the linkage of transcontinentalism to the
notion of America as a Pacific power, an idea discussed by Benjamin
Franklin and William Pitt the Elder, Earl of Chatham, the former British first minister, in August 1774.[4] Once independent, Americans looked
to China and Japan across the Pacific and not, as the British did, as an
extension of India and an application of India's economic and military
power. Linked to this, Central America as an isthmus route between
Atlantic and Pacific America, an aspiration that came to completion with
the Panama Canal in 1914, was, from the 1850s, a key geopolitical axis
for the United States, as the Suez Canal, opened in 1869, was for Britain.
This was one direction of American geopolitics, that of the country in
the wider world.

Another, and a related, direction was that of geopolitics within
North America, and here the situation changed radically with American independence in 1776. No longer constrained by British power, the
newly independent Americans were able to define and pursue a distinctive geopolitics within North America. This geopolitics was as much a
matter of the specific tone of the relations with the Native Americans as
of particular geographical considerations. In addition, the spatial consequences of American political culture were also significant, not least
a strong desire for territory and influence that manifested itself as land
hunger.

This desire was explicable in terms of American development but
also became an important aspect of a more general Western power projection into the heart of continents, a tendency that led to the creation
and reordering of frontiers across the world in the nineteenth century as
the Western matrix of knowledge, as well as Western equations of force,
were employed in ordering the world on Western terms and in Western
interests, at the same time that the spread of agrarian settlement transformed environments. Force and legitimacy were brought together, for
example in the drawing of straight frontier and administrative lines on
maps, without regard to ethnic, linguistic, religious, economic, and po-

litical alignments and practices, let alone drainage patterns, landforms, and biological provinces, which was very much the American pattern. The reconceptualization of the frontier and the redrawing of frontiers were thus crucial aspects of the expression of Western power as norms and conventions were applied. In the case of America, this process was eased by the subjugation of the Natives and their enforced allocation to reservations, which were both a physical reality and an expression of segregationalist attitudes.

The development of geopolitics as a formal discourse, system of analysis, and call for action, can all be located in this process of power projection and the reconceptualization of space. Indeed, geopolitics, whether formal or, more commonly, informal, was a response to the conceptual and policy problems posed by the rapid changes in world power in the nineteenth century. Key changes included the rise of the British empire to superpower status, its competition with Russia in Asia, the rise of America, and the impact on sea and land, space and power, of steamships and railways.

The explicit development of the subject did not begin until the close of the century, when the Swede Rudolf Kjellén (1864–1922), professor of political science at Uppsala, coined the term *Geopolitik* in 1899. To Kjellén, it was necessary to understand geopolitics in order to appreciate the true nature of national interests. Emphasizing the value and application of scientific methods, Kjellén presented the state as taking on particular significance in terms of its existence and effectiveness as a geographical entity. To him, both rested in part on the state's relationship with other states as geographical entities.

This approach took forward the work of Friedrich Ratzel (1844–1904), Germany's leading political scientist, who had stressed the close relationship of people and environment in his *Politische Geographie* (1897). Ratzel presented the territorialization of space as an expression of conflicting political drives, and one held in tension by them. Trained in the natural sciences, Ratzel, like many American politicians of the nineteenth century, conceived of international relations in the Darwinian terms of a struggle for survival, although arguing that Charles Darwin had failed to devote due attention to the issue of space. Ratzel also saw states as organic and thus ignored divisions within them, let alone the play of individual political and military leaders, who, in practice, provide a key level for understanding geopolitical pressures.

Ratzel emphasized territorial expansion as both product and cause of a state's success as an organic phenomenon. This was an analysis eminently suited to America, a state that had spread from ocean to ocean, and that was then projecting its power overseas. To Ratzel, the union of expansion and strength, the two being crucial to the state's existence, rather than simply controlling space itself, was expressed in terms of its pursuit of *Lebensraum* (living space), a term devised in 1860 by the biologist Oscar Peschel in a review of Darwin's *The Origin of Species*, and deployed in 1902 by Ratzel in his *Die Erde und das Leben* [The Earth and Life]. Success in this pursuit, Ratzel argued, would guarantee, as well as define, power, and thus permit the pursuit of great-power status.[5] The idea of living space made sense of the expansionist drive of America for new land for settlement.

The emphasis, as in other intellectual fields, was on a universal law that would apparently provide both explanation and a key to reordering circumstances; and, to Kjellén, such an advance in understanding was necessary because of the pronounced flux in world affairs, one of transformative international political and economic changes, notably the rise of the United States. In explaining them, Kjellén argued that geopolitics took precedence over the other forms of politics, an argument that represented a departure from historicist accounts of states in terms of particular constitutional, legal, diplomatic and political legacies, rationalizations and legitimations, and one that is pertinent given the emphasis on the latter in American discussion. Kjellén argued that these conventional accounts were overly narrow and drew on a particular political and intellectual strand, that of French bourgeois republicanism and Enlightenment ideas. Instead, Kjellén pressed for a wider concept of states as communities, communities that were geographically grounded. This approach enabled him to measure the relative power of states, putting aside what he presented as subjective approaches and views, notably those focused on ethical standards.[6]

Geopolitics, in practice, rested on broad currents of nineteenth-century thought. Trained mostly in the natural sciences, nineteenth-century geographers assumed a close relationship between humanity and the biophysical environment, and sought to probe it in terms of the environmental control that they took for granted. Seeking a justification that was not based on historical legitimacy, environmentalism proved an attractive method for the geographers and historians of successful and expanding states, notably the United States and Germany.[7] Aside from justifying a place in the sun for these states, acting as a physical dimension of notions of the Manifest Destiny about ineluctable expansionism, environmentalism played a crucial role in the organic theory of the state.

In the United States, this approach was adapted to the country's territorial expansion. Key works were produced by Albert Perry Brigham – *Geographic Influences in American History* (1903), and by Ellen Churchill Semple, who was linked to the University of Chicago although, because she insisted on time for herself and her writing, she did not have a full-time post there. Semple had studied under Ratzel in Leipzig in 1891–92 and 1895, and she popularized the idea of anthropogeography, the geography of environmental influences, in her *American History and Its Geographic Conditions* (1903) and her *Influences of Geographic Environment on the Basis of Ratzel's System of Anthropo-Geography* (1911). In contrast to the more cautious and less determinist Brigham, Semple argued the relationship between the physical environment and historical movements.[8]

So also did the historian Frederick Jackson Turner, most famously in a paper "The Significance of the Frontier in American History," which he read at the Chicago meeting of the American Historical Association in 1893. Turner emphasized the importance of free land on the western edge of America's advancing settlement and saw the moving frontier as a key element in America's development, one that gave Americans particular characteristics.[9] This was scarcely an apolitical approach, and it was unsurprising that Turner praised Senator Thomas Hart Benton of Missouri, a prominent expansionist of mid-century who argued for America's westward destiny and pressed hard for America to occupy the Oregon Country. Benton also sponsored his son-in-law, John Frémont, a bellicose self-publicizing army topographical engineer who disobeyed orders so as to support rebellion by American settlers in 1846 in California against Mexican rule.

Turner's frontier thesis, particularly influential in the 1910s and 1920s, though less so in the 1930s and 1940s, was taken forward by his students, for example Frederick Merk at Harvard, who wrote *American Expansion in the Nineteenth Century*, and, in turn, taught and influenced Ray Billington, whose book on *Westward Expansion: A History of the American Frontier* (1949) went through several editions and was dedicated to Merk for perpetuating Turner's traditions. In presenting the frontier environments as putting a stamp on America, not least by creating different American civilizations that, in turn, underlay sectional conflicts, Turner left relatively little role for the geopolitics of the international tensions and, at times, struggle for dominance in North America. This approach was not one that would have made much sense to commentators in the eighteenth and early nineteenth centuries who were prone both to link issues with Native Americans to wider currents of international rivalry and to consider the governmental response in this light. An article by "Americanus" in the *St James's Chronicle* of 10 January 1764 accusing the French of inspiring attacks by Native Americans on British colonists (a frequent theme)[10] was typical in its paranoia, accusations, and strident tone. In practice, Pontiac's War was not due to French instigation:

> The incapacity of the peace-making ministry is nowhere more evident than in the affairs of America; our conquests there seem plainly to have been the chief object of their peace; yet so poorly did they provide for their security that we see the French are wresting from us, by mere artifice, what we have purchased with millions of men, and ten millions of treasure. How long will the British government be the dupe of French policy? How long will it suffer in fatal supineness their sly encroachments? Will it not reflect that a similar conduct gave birth to the late war, with all its expenses and horrors? Let the ministers, who slumber on the bed of down, or riot in the feast of affluence and luxury, for a moment think on the miserable state of those who fondly trusting to their protection, are now devoted to the murderous knife of savage Indians, or to the cruel perfidy of the insinuating, and yet as murderous, Frenchmen; the father and the son, the mother and the tender infant, weltering in each others' blood.

Arguments from the late nineteenth century about the relationship between environment and westward movement were read back into the century to help make expansion seem necessary and inevitable. Yet, this approach can be qualified on geographical and historical grounds, and the two should be discussed together. Historical geography, however, is largely shunned by historians and written by geographers. Indeed, the most important work on the subject covered in this book is by an

American geographer, Donald Meinig, whose multivolume *The Shaping of America* began with *Atlantic America, 1492–1800* (1986). Meinig was not alone. Another geographer, Stephen Hornsby, pushed the discussion forward in his *British Atlantic, American Frontier: Spaces of Power in Early Modern British America* (2005). These, and other works, drew on the longstanding interest of American and Canadian historical geographers in the frontier, a subject that can still be profitably probed,[11] as well as in settlement, and in the creation and impact of economic links, and profitably located these topics in a world that was not restricted to the frontier but, instead, spanned the Atlantic. In doing so, these works provided a valuable geographical dimension for the Atlanticist approach that is newly fashionable among many historians. Greatly influenced while a teenager by Fernand Braudel's study of the Mediterranean,[12] and always engaged by geography, I have found this geographical work of great interest and importance, not least because it provides the spatial dimension that is underplayed, at best, in so many historical works.

Yet, geographical and geopolitical studies tend to neglect the specifics of politics, and, indeed, often lack archival references of any type. The contrast between Meinig and Braudel is particularly apparent, as the latter's Mediterranean work contained many such references. However, Braudel's work also indicated the problem facing studies such as this, because the structural, more geographical, dimension of his work, with its emphasis on long-term factors, does not readily cohere with the chronological political section dealing with the late sixteenth century, the *Age of Philip II*. In the preface to the first French edition, written in 1946, he described the history of events as the "crests of foam that the tides of history carry on their strong back," while his preface to the second edition, written in 1963, asked "Is it possible somehow to convey simultaneously both that conspicuous history which holds our attention by its continual and dramatic changes – and that other, submerged, history, almost silent and always discreet, virtually unsuspected either by its observers or its participants, which is little touched by the obstinate erosion of time?"[13] This problem, a fundamental one for scholarship, provides a historiographical context for my book because there is a similar tension in geopolitical accounts between structure and agency, although structural factors are not, of course, "little touched" by time.

This tension is worth noting when considering how far the discussion of North American history can be fitted into any of the standard analyses employed by geopoliticians. These analyses have focused on Eurasia, with Halford Mackinder's core-periphery thesis[14] reinterpreted for later circumstances, including, notably, the Cold War,[15] while Samuel P. Huntington's "clash of civilizations" similarly focused on Eurasia, albeit with a different analysis and prospectus. The degree to which North America was fitted into these analyses varied, although such an incorporation was central to the Cold War analyses.

This incorporation, however, was irrelevant as far as the earlier North American Question was concerned. For that, as already noted, there was a different analysis and language, that of the frontier, a practice and concept of longstanding relevance, but how far the frontier created America is less clear. Instead, there was a tension between an advancing frontier creating new territory to incorporate, politically, economically, and psychologically, and existing views of country and people, state, and nation. Political divisions, overt and latent, in the latter affected the process of incorporation. For example, there is considerable evidence of the role of geographic literacy in helping influence identity formation in America,[16] but it has also been argued that there was a major contrast between the world of print and rhetoric in which the idea of America was advanced,[17] and a reality in which there was not a consolidated national sphere or a unified economy but, rather, a set of localities that was best represented by the federalism of the political system.[18] These localities, moreover, contributed to sectional more than national views, and both political movements, such as Federalism, and regional presentations of the country reflected this sectionalism.[19] Diplomats very much presented politics in regional terms, as in 1810 when Francis Jackson, the perceptive British envoy, described both support for Britain and Federalist politics as being strongly held in the north.[20] Localism was noted throughout the period, as in April 1865 when Sir Frederick Bruce, the British envoy, suggested that Virginia troops were "averse to undertaking a campaign in the South" and, of Robert E. Lee, the commander of the Confederate Army of Northern Virginia, of whom it was said that "strong local attachment . . . may have induced him to hold Richmond to the last, at the risk of being unable to effect a retreat in safety."[21] The regionalism of perception was to be overcome by Union success in the Civil War (1861–65), but, prior to that, there was always a tension for foreign observers when looking at America as an expanding power, between presenting regional differences and, instead, and far more commonly, discussing it in terms of a strong and forceful presence without any emphasis on such differences. The latter approach became far more common after the Civil War.

Spatial issues were mentioned in the diplomatic correspondence when considering American expansionism. Sometimes the images were simplistic, though not the less potent for that, as in 1851 when John Crittenden, the attorney general and acting secretary of state, told the British envoy that, although he had been against the acquisition of Texas and the lands from Mexico, he would be pleased to win Cuba by honorable means "lying as it did across the mouth of the great commercial artery of the United States," the Mississippi River.[22] This was very much an account of North America that presented the Caribbean as integral to the north–south route offered by the Mississippi and, in doing so, ignored the alternative of west–east rail links as a means to integrate Trans-Appalachia. A belief in the ability of railways to express as well as to overcome geographical links and constraints represented a new version of earlier comments on rivers and roads. The presence or absence of these had, indeed, been important in the interaction of patterns of economic exchange with political identity.[23]

Rail links reflected the dynamic character of applied technology, but such technology also had other applications to geopolitics. For example, six years later, Frederick, Lord Napier, the British envoy in Washington, argued that the maritime strategic value of Cuba had been transformed by steam-power that defied both storms and currents, adding, "The passages of Cuba will not be closed and opened by the fluctuations of wind and weather, they will be patrolled and governed by the navy which possesses a general ascendancy. The accidents and vicissitudes of local war at sea are superseded by the steady predominance of steam."[24]

In 1867, Bruce, the British envoy, presented the spatial issues of American expansionism in a fashion that assumed a familiarity with geography. His dispatch is worth quoting at length because it offers an important text for geopolitics before the term:

As population and industrial development increase in Minnesota, Montana, and other North Western states which adjoin the British frontier,[25] it is not difficult to foresee that the demand will arise for communication by the line of the Saskatchewan River which is said to offer the greatest facilities for reaching the Pacific. And if the Provinces,[26] aided by Great Britain are unable to meet it when it becomes necessary, and show themselves incapable of providing greater facilities for the transit of produce from the Lake region through the St Lawrence to the Atlantic, the desire of the United States to drive their British rivals off this continent will be powerfully reinforced by the material interests of the North West[27] which will be enlisted in favor of conquest or annexation. Whether therefore the policy adopted by Great Britain in the Northern part of this continent contemplates provincial connection with the mother country as a permanent relation, or looks to it merely as a step towards provincial independence in the future, its success will materially depend upon our ability to deal in a sufficiently liberal and comprehensive manner with the transit question. It may be hopeless to think at present of opening up a route to the Pacific.[28] But the formation of a government over the region that extends from Canada west towards British Columbia including the fertile valley of the Saskatchewan River, ought not to be delayed.[29] The population of the United States are pushing with great rapidity up the territories of Nebraska and Montana to the northern frontier, attracted by the great mining wealth of those regions, which extends, I am told, across the boundary into North America.[30]

Thus economics was linked to spatial factors, not least with the relationship suggested by the settlement of Saskatchewan in order to provide food for the mining regions. Geography and economic benefit were both related by commentators such as Bruce to rail links, and the latter lent much energy and direction to geopolitical analyses and arguments, as in discussion of the prospect of railways and/or canals across the Central American isthmus, the projected routes of which were particularly important to international politics there in the 1850s. These routes were linked to reports that naval bases would be established for protection and power projection.[31]

American politicians thought that their influence in the Canadian West would be increased by rail links to Wisconsin and on to Chicago, and British diplomats sought to offer alternatives. In part, their suggestions were based on competition, protecting the Canadian West from absorption by America, but there was also the idea that links, by canal and river as well as rail, between the American West and the St. Lawrence would create a connection between America and Canada that would prevent war and be more useful than investment on fortifications.[32] Bruce argued that the British needed to learn from the way in which America was financing its transcontinental railway, and thus overcoming geography in the cause of geopolitics: "we must show something of the same spirit of enterprise in dealing with great distances and physical obstacles, if we are to maintain British North America as a counterpoise to this Republic." He went further by arguing that, unless Canada could be shown to benefit from British rule, there would be pressure for annexation. Bruce, indeed, offered a stark and deterministic materialism: "No mere sympathy will be sufficient to outweigh these material considerations."[33] In 1870, Hamilton Fish, the American Secretary of State, followed suit by telling Edward Thornton, the British envoy, that British Columbia, Saskatchewan, and the Canadian West should logically join America as it alone could provide them with the necessary outlets.[34] Without transport links, territory was regarded as of limited value.

By the 1860s, the pressures of competitive imperialism, expansionism, and nation-building were encouraging arguments that accorded with elements of the classical geopolitics that were soon to be explicitly advanced as a theory. Yet, aside from the question of how far such arguments were valid earlier,[35] it is also clear that this analysis underplays the role of individuals and groups, the extent to which they have agency, the limited purchase of material considerations, and the extent to which the latter were themselves subject to perception and contention, points that emerge in this study.

Linked to what can be seen as a Clausewitzian triad of geopolitics, strategic cultures, and public policy, tension between structure and agency also emerges in another of the set of interests that illuminate this work, that in military history, power politics, and international relations. Again, there is the difference between the broad sweep of the long term, with its deterministic characteristics, and the short term of the contingent. There is the question whether the specifics of conflict and power politics, notably campaigns and alliances, should take precedence over the structural character of the systemic dimension, and how best they can be integrated.

As far as the systemic dimension is concerned, it is instructive to consider how far Paul Schroeder's presentation of the European international dimension of the period,[36] or, alternatively, European-dominated geopolitical analysis, can, or should, be extended to include North America, and, if so, how far such an integration affected contemporary options. These options were those of both Americans and Europeans. For example, a key objective for European powers was to keep other European powers out of North America, and one way to do this was to cede territory or interests to the United States. The sale of Louisiana by Napoleon I in 1803 was the crucial instance as it provided a way to keep it out of British hands, both permanently and during the war between Britain and France that was resuming after the failure of the Peace of Amiens of the previous year. Moreover, even though they were not at war, France was scarcely going to help Britain gain Oregon or California in the 1840s, while the British were repeatedly unwilling to back Napoleon III in Mexico in the 1860s. A reluctance to make America an enemy also played a role and also helped explain the lack of European intervention in 1898 when America defeated Spain and took over (directly or indirectly) much of its empire.

Yet, it is too easy to write with hindsight, not only of American expansion but also of the lack of serious conflict with European powers after 1815. Hindsight and geopolitical analysis are frequently linked as with that of Anglo-American cooperation in the two world wars and the Cold War which can be expressed in terms of an oceanic bond. In contrast, a critical edge is provided by counterfactualism, notably how far the struggle for mastery in North America would have been different had there been conflict with European powers or differing outcomes in the wars in which America did engage; and, indeed, whether such outcomes were possible.

Counterfactuals considered by contemporaries are valid because they affected options.[37] Thus, the counterfactual of what would have happened had the Oregon Question remained a possible cause of war with Britain at the time when the Americans attacked Mexico in 1846 is pertinent because this issue was raised at the time. Indeed, President James K. Polk's decision in 1846 to accept a Canadian frontier on the 49th N Parallel, which was not the frontier he had vociferously pursued at the time of the 1844 presidential election, owed much to his concern about the prospect of just such a combination. Equally, counterfactuals have to take note of the views of the time. Thus, British policymakers in

1846 believed that it would be wrong to try to exploit the growing crisis between America and Mexico. It is instructive to consider the extent to which, in this and other cases, more than one factor played a role, as it is all too easy to argue that only one factor played a role and requires explanation. Aside from prudential considerations in 1846, the British believed that such conduct would be dishonorable, as well as foolish in the event of American victory; the latter was a factor also cited in the debate over intervention in the Civil War.

Sequencing emerges again in the focus of this book on the period 1815–71, for it is designed as the third of a trilogy beginning with *Crisis of Empire,* my treatment of the Anglo-American relationship in the eighteenth century, and continuing with my *War of 1812.* Yet, because my focus is geopolitical, I do not begin this book with the end of that war in 1815 but, instead, look to longer-term continuities and discontinuities. Indeed, the latter only emerge clearly in the long-term because that provides a complicating context for causal relationships that are too readily drawn when the frame of reference is short term.

Other historiographical facets are offered in the coverage of North America, first, by the tension between Atlanticist[38] and Continental accounts of its history, each of which can be considered in geopolitical terms; and, secondly, by the question of how far recent American policy is helping to drive the scholarship. The former tension adds the comparative dimension because an aspect of the Atlanticist approach is that which compares British, Spanish, and other European imperial expansion,[39] as well as the subsequent fate of their colonies once independent. This approach considers the New World refraction of Old World drives and legacies, but, necessarily, draws attention to that relationship as the dynamic one.

A related, but different, Atlanticist account is one that focuses on the slave trade. That relationship was a key one spanning the Atlantic, and again one that provides a comparative context, so that, for example, it is helpful to contrast the end of slavery in the United States with that in Brazil. Yet, far more than a cruel trade and the subsequent history of the slaves are involved. Geopolitics and politics are about people as much as territory, and, in many cases, more so, because land is given meaning by the people who settle and work it. The slave trade transformed the politics of the eastern seaboard of America. Control within the settler community had been a factor from the outset, as had the use of force to despoil or overawe Native peoples, but the slave trade and slavery added a crucial new dimension of coercion. That this was not innate to the New World experience of the Europeans was suggested by the relatively limited experience of slavery in New England (although Rhode Island merchants were prominent slavers), let alone Nova Scotia and Newfoundland, but slavery cannot be divorced from the geopolitics and politics of the New World. Indeed, the prominent role slavery played in divisions within America from the 1820s, helping both to cement a sense of separate and particular Southern identity and to give it an expansionist dynamic, was more than poetic justice; it was also inherent to the geopolitics of North America.

Racial issues were not restricted to relations with African and Native Americans but also played an important, indeed growing, role in the response to the Hispanic world. John Crampton, the British envoy, reflected on the total failure of an American filibustering attempt on Cuba in 1851:

> The ease with which Texas was wrested from Mexico [1836], and the feeble resistance of the Mexicans in the last war have created an overweening notion of the superiority of the "Anglo-Saxon" over the "Spanish" race in America, and the impossibility of any effectual resistance being made by the latter if attacked by the former. This impression would have continued unimpaired if Cuba had been preserved to Spain by the intervention of a foreign force, or even by a strict execution of the laws of the United States.[40]

Six years later, another envoy, but this time reflecting a sense of racial destiny:

> The English Race whether by direct movement from the Mother Country or by transmission through the United States will undoubtedly spread to the Central American Region . . . emigrants of Anglo-Saxon blood.[41]

National stereotyping linked to racial and religious prejudices and cultural assumptions were also to affect scholars, as in the views of Turner and of Francis Parkman on the defeat of the French by the Anglo-Saxons in the French and Indian or Seven Years War of 1754/6–63.[42]

In contrast to Atlanticist accounts, the Continental approach places more emphasis on relations between European settlers and others, and, on the other hand, Native Americans, and does so by noting the agency of the latter.[43] Albeit, this agency was affected by European requirements as with the geographical information provided to Europeans which was generally of larger areas than would normally have been necessary intra-culturally,[44] because the Europeans wished to fit their frontier into their wider world. With the Continental approach, the dynamic becomes that of the frontier and the related and changing "middle ground" between European and Native Americans, especially if the former were traders rather than settlers. In this space, which was conceptual as much as spatial, individuals and groups have been seen as playing an active role in organizing relations and affecting each other, instead of being in conflict, or, indeed, simply victims of a distant imperial power. This approach is part of an understanding of empire, and geopolitics more generally, in terms not of structures but of processes in which not only those immediately engaged in colonization played a crucial role, but also those affected by imperialism.[45]

A Continental approach ensures that geopolitics are reconceptualized, not only with the understanding of the distribution of power and the forces involved but also in the case of the subsequent scholarly emphasis. Thus, a treatment of the War of 1812 from this perspective would devote more attention to the American conflicts with Tecumseh and with the Creek, than to the conflict on the Lake Champlain axis and the British campaign in the Chesapeake in 1814, not least because the first had greater consequence in terms of altering the geopolitics of North America by gravely weakening Native strength and resistance east of the Mississippi. As a related, but different, point, a Continental approach can also lead to a downplaying of the international dimension after 1815, not least to a tendency to treat confrontation then with Britain as of limited importance. Thus, with this approach, the North American Question becomes that of slavery and relations with the South, and it is essentially treated as one within the United States. The international dimension of the Civil War is generally underplayed.[46]

This approach is an aspect of what is often termed exceptionalism: the sense of a unique national history, and thus destiny and identity.[47] In such an account, there is a tendency to neglect other states and forces, for example Britain and the Oregon Question or France in Mexico, or to treat them as an "other" that was predestined to fail and that was of limited consequence for this and other reasons. These tendencies play a major role in public myth, but they are highly misleading. Yet, exceptionalism in a different context may be pertinent, as with the argument that the United States in the nineteenth century had customs and interests distinct to that of Europe (although similar to Brazil) because of slavery, Native Americans, and a ready expansionism borne of its frontier status. The British ability to accommodate these different interests and assumptions has been presented as an aspect of the solution of the North American Question.[48]

Lastly, there is the extent to which much recent literature on American history has been shaped by present-day concerns with American foreign policy.[49] In particular, the invasion of Iraq in 2003, and the attitudes and policies linked with, or attributed to, the Neoconservatives, led to plentiful discussion of the extent to which America has long had imperial tendencies, and, indeed, was an imperial republic from its inception.[50] In such an account, the expansionism of the colonial period flows into that of independent America. Both can be seen in terms of an "empire of liberty,"[51] and, speaking at the United States Military Academy at West Point in November 2009, President Barack Obama differentiated American power from that of other states by saying that Americans did not come to conquer. There is, however, the important caveat that this expansion was repeatedly at the expense of the Native population, who were displaced with considerable brutality and great suffering. Moreover, such displacement was also seen in the case of many other imperial states, which helps limit American exceptionalism. Only a portion of the historical literature makes points that are directly relevant to the debate on modern America, but there is a common theme of the importance of power and conflict in American history, which has implications for the present and the future.

There is no intention here to take part in the discussion of American policy over the last decade. Indeed, the habit of readily reading from present to past, and back again, is one that is as ahistorical, and potentially misleading, as the earlier tendency to neglect the role of the past in American developments.[52] Instead, there is a need to consider particular periods and questions with reference to their specific contexts.

This point is discussed in the concluding chapter, but, briefly, the struggle for mastery that is the subject of this book closed in the 1860s with the Anglo-American Treaty of Washington of 1871 marking the close of the international dimension to this struggle. It was followed by a very different period in which the United States, clearly dominant in North America, did not need to fear the other great powers, but, instead, increasingly saw itself in global terms and as a global force.[53] Moreover, as is discussed in chapter 16, there was an important shift in American geopolitics in the 1860s, from a concern with territory to a greater interest in markets. Such geoeconomic factors had been significant earlier, but they became more central as a goal than territorial expansion. Economic strength, and, in particular, industrial primacy, helped ensure that from the 1890s, and, even more clearly, the latter stages of the First World War, the United States acted as a leading state on the world stage, a situation made brutally clear in 1898 with the sweeping defeat of Spain in both Cuba and the Philippines.

From 1940, initially with the crisis dramatically created by the fall of France and the apparently imminent fall of Britain, the United States was challenged, first by the Axis powers and then, from the late 1940s, by the Soviet Union, but the nature of this challenge was very different to that in the period discussed in this book. The same point can be made about the current "War on Terror," whatever it may result in, and also, in contrast, the possibility that the rise in Chinese power will lead to a resumption of great power confrontation. Thus, the tendency to search for historical lessons can be unhelpful, as indeed is the process of reading the past in terms of the present. What, however, is valuable from the past is the reminder of discontinuities, the unexpected, the play of contingency, and the extent to which governmental (and other) choices play a major role. The relationships between these and the potent geopolitics of power are a central theme of this book.

# 1

# SIXTEENTH-CENTURY BACKGROUND

North America was created as a geopolitical issue by Europeans. Such a stark remark is subject to criticism on the grounds of Eurocentricity, and certainly risks underplaying the vitality of Native American states and peoples, let alone the extent to which the overwhelming majority of those who lived in North America in 1700 still had their origins in the Americas, with a more distant source in those who had once crossed from Asia across a Bering Strait land bridge. Yet, once in the Americas, these peoples had not interacted with the outer world. Instead, they had followed their own course of development, with distinctive outcomes in terms of religions, technological bases, and military methods. Exceptionalism is an overused concept, but, if the Americas were exceptional, in the sense of different, then this was far more the case in 1450 than in 1870.

Crucially, the Americas did not see long-range maritime activity, and certainly not activity comparable to some of the Pacific peoples, or Indian Ocean, East Asian, and European traders and states. Instead, American states were centered inland, as with the Aztec and Inca empires or the less-famous North American peoples that left extensive settlements reflecting a considerable degree of organization, notably in the Mississippi Valley, such as Cahokia. The same was true of areas of dense village settlement as in Huronia, the region of Huron settlement north of Lake Ontario where the results of archaeological work do not challenge Samuel de Champlain's estimate of a population of about 30,000 in 1615.

There were a number of probable reasons for this inland focus, including the tendency of coastal lowlands, for example near the Caribbean to the east of the Aztec heartland, to attract the vectors of disease, such as mosquitoes, as well as the difficulty of working many of these lowlands for farming. Environmental determinism, however, will not suffice, as such conditions do not describe all of the American coastlines. More significantly, there was also a lack of maritime activity and infrastructure that reflected the nature of economic development, specifically the absence of large-scale, long-range trade, as well as of polities capable of developing naval forces.

As a result, the geopolitics at the oceanic level was a case of Europeans reaching the Americas, and not vice versa, a case of expansion and pressure between continents that continued to be an issue until the close of our period. Moreover, the other key aspect was that East Asian maritime links with the Americas were very restricted. Their extent is controversial, but the key point is that whatever knowledge of the Americas existed in East Asia, it was not exploited. There was no inherent reason for this. The northeastern quarter of the Pacific is particularly empty as far as islands were concerned, thus limiting the potential for island-hopping across the ocean, but the Russians were to show in the eighteenth century that it was possible to develop maritime links in the Aleutian chain and along the Alaskan coast, links that eventually reached modern California. Earlier, China, Japan, and Korea each had large navies, and long-range naval and maritime activity had proved possible, notably for the Chinese into the Indian Ocean. However, China abandoned this naval activity in the fifteenth century,[1] and in the 1590s the East Asian powers concentrated on a major struggle for dominance centered on Korea.

There was no inherent reason why this struggle should have prevented power projection into the Americas. Indeed, Portugal's (eventually unsuccessful) commitment in Morocco and, even more, Spain's central role in European conflict in the sixteenth century did not prevent their conquest of a large part of the Americas. This ability existed despite the extent to which Spain also played the leading role in confronting the deteriorating position created by the rise, from the 1520s, of Ottoman naval power and capability in the central and western Mediterranean. The manpower for activity in the Americas could certainly have been spared by the East Asian powers. Yet, this was not a prospect, and that is central to the geopolitics of our story. It is a geopolitics read from east to west and not vice versa, and this point remains the case throughout. In the seventeenth century, Japan abandoned power projection completely, while, once the Manchu had conquered Ming China, the Chinese power projection was directed into Central Asia.[2]

The priorities and roles of outside powers are also at stake when considering the geopolitics of European commitment. Although the Iberians greatly benefited in their location from the direction of the ocean currents when crossing the Atlantic to the Caribbean, it was not inevitable that they should lead this commitment. Indeed, leaving aside fictional accounts, for example Barry Fell's series beginning with *America B.C.* (1976) or Clive Cussler's depiction of a Roman voyage to the Americas, the Vikings, in about 1000, were the first to cross the Atlantic, benefiting from the way stops provided by Iceland and Greenland, where settlements had been established in about 860 and in 986 respectively. Such stops were valuable not only for the functional reasons of providing water and sustenance for the crew, but also because they created successive stages of possibilities for future voyages. The same was to be true for the Iberians and their use of islands, notably the Canaries, Madeira, the Cape Verde Islands, and the Azores. The sagas indicate that there were four expeditions to North America, two of which carried settlers. A settlement was established new L'Anse aux Meadows at the northern tip of Newfoundland in about 1000. However, although the expedition stayed at least a year, the remote and forested coast was not suitable for the creation of a pastoral economy able to trade with Greenland. The native population was also unfriendly. After the Vikings left, L'Anse aux Meadows was reoccupied by Natives.[3]

Viking voyages show what could be achieved with maritime technology prior to the fifteenth century and indicate that, although the technology was an important constraint, it did not prevent long-range activity. However, these voyages were peripheral to the main thrust of Viking activity which, instead, focused on nearby targets, such as invasions of England in the 1010s (successful) and 1060s (unsuccessful), and of Scotland in the 1260s (unsuccessful). Moreover, the peripheral character of the North Atlantic, with both the Faroe Islands and Iceland under the distant Danish crown, was accentuated by the deterioration in climate and related problems with food supplies and disease that hit the Viking settlements and acted as a structural change. Combined with attacks by the native population, and the fall in trade in Europe, these problems led to the end of the Viking settlements on Greenland in about 1500.

The contrast in scale with subsequent developments in North America is readily apparent, but there are interesting questions as to why the Greenland natives were more successful than their Native American counterparts in the early seventeenth century. The key feature appears to have been the ability of the Europeans, in the face of a hostile ecology, to sustain new settlement, an ability that reflected both the availability of settlers and the extent to which they could readily trade with Europe. In the case of Greenland, the hostile demographic regime in both Europe and the North Atlantic settlements stemming from climatic deterioration and disease ensured that these push-and-pull factors were absent, while Greenland drew on the very limited population resources of Iceland, in contrast to the far more plentiful resources of France, England, the Netherlands, and Spain in the seventeenth century.

Nor were push-and-pull factors revived for the Scandinavians in the fifteenth and sixteenth centuries. Instead, internal Scandinavian power politics linked to the collapse of the Union of Kalmar and the Protestant Reformation played a central role, and, although both Denmark (the kingdom that ruled Norway and Iceland) and its rival Sweden each pursued transoceanic schemes, they did not do so with the energy or resources seen from the other Western European maritime states. Denmark was a major naval power in the sixteenth and seventeenth centuries, and was to establish bases in West Africa, India, and the West Indies, but Danish interests in the North Atlantic did not lead to the pursuit of a North American destiny. Explaining a negative is problematic, but, in the Danish case, the commitment to alternative goals does appear to have crowded out North Atlantic interests, in part because there were fewer spare resources, less entrepreneurial mercantile enterprise, and more central control than in the case of the other maritime states. Yet, these factors did not prevent Sweden in 1638, at a time when it was heavily involved in the Thirty Years' War in Europe, from establishing a colony, New Sweden, in the lower Delaware valley on the mid-Atlantic coast of North America, a colony, however, that was to be conquered by the Dutch in 1650.

The Vikings were not the sole Northern Europeans interested in the Atlantic. Seafarers from the British Isles also sailed far in pursuit of fish, although the extent of their voyages is unclear.[4] In part, this lack of clarity reflected their limited ability to disseminate whatever knowledge they acquired. Moreover, although profitable, fishing generally did not attract the government attention, or large-scale investment, necessary to develop initiatives. Crucially, fish did not lead to commitment by the metropolitan interests that were so significant in aligning political support with necessary investment.

Thus, a key factor in the geopolitics of European interest was to be that European knowledge of North America developed from south to north, with the initial contact coming first from Christopher Columbus's arrival in the West Indies in 1492. His voyages were part of a pattern of Iberian expansion, with, as an important element, non-Iberian navigators and economic interests taking advantage of the support of the expansionist crowns of Portugal and Castile. These rulers, in turn, sought to supplement their own resources with those they could recruit to their service.

This expansionism was territorial and religious as well as economic. Drawing on their longstanding role in driving the Moors and Islam from Iberia, a task apparently achieved with the fall of the last Moorish kingdom, Granada, in 1492, the crowns of Portugal and Castile had already taken the fight into North Africa and also had seized the islands of the eastern Atlantic, the Canaries, Madeira, the Azores, and the Cape Verde Islands which served as important stopping places on the route to the West Indies and South America and were therefore important to the geopolitical history of the New World. Portugal, moreover, established bases in West Africa, from which it obtained gold and slaves and sought allies against the Moors, and went on to explore the route around southern Africa into the Indian Ocean.

In contrast, following Columbus, Castile made the running in the Americas, with, as a result, Portugal restricted there to Brazil. Moreover, Portugal did not seek to establish a territorial presence in North America to the north of the Castilian zone; although Portuguese interests were to play a role there, notably in fishing. More recent Portuguese influence is readily found in maritime New England. In the Papal division of the

New World by the Treaty of Tordesillas in 1494, North America was allocated to Castile, or Spain as it can be termed after the union of the inheritances of Castile and Aragon. North America's relative lack of appeal to contemporaries was shown by the absence of Portuguese attempts to circumvent this restriction, although, in addition, Portugal was not well placed to defy neighboring Spain in this, while from 1580 to 1640, after a successful invasion, the kings of Spain were also kings of Portugal.

The Spanish conquest of the Caribbean was incomplete, with only some of the larger islands, principally Hispaniola, Cuba, and Puerto Rico seeming attractive for seizure and settlement, which left later opportunities for other European powers, notably France, England and the Dutch. However, the Spaniards brought European diseases, and the inroads of disease helped ensure that the demographic balance in the West Indies rapidly changed, and also greatly demoralized the native population. Once seized, these islands, especially Cuba, where a harbor was developed at Havana from 1511, became important bases for Spanish activity, fulfilling a role that was lacking as far as the Atlantic seaboard of North America was concerned: offshore islands, such as Newfoundland and Bermuda, played only a minor part as far as English settlement was concerned. In contrast, Cuba provided Spain with a springboard for the invasion of Mesoamerica.

In 1519, Hernán Cortés landed at Veracruz with about 450 soldiers, 14 small cannons, and 16 horses. His overthrow of the Aztec Empire, based in Mesoamerica in what is now Central Mexico, was rapidly achieved. Montezuma, the panicky Aztec leader, was fascinated by Cortés, worried that he might be a god or an envoy from a powerful potentate, and was unwilling to act decisively against him. Cortés reached Tenochtitlán, the Aztec capital, without having to fight his way there. In 1520, the situation deteriorated from the Spanish point of view. A massacre of Aztec nobles in the courtyard of the Great Temple helped lead to an Aztec rising. Cortés had to flee Tenochtitlán having had Montezuma killed. Cortés had to fight his way back into Tenochtitlán in 1521.

In some respects, this was a remarkable achievement, but it was also part of a wider pattern of territorial change in 1515–30. The Ottoman Turks, under Selim the Grim, conquered the Mamluk Empire of Egypt and Syria, while Selim's son, Suleiman the Magnificent, pressed on to

overthrow Hungary, capturing Belgrade in 1521 and defeating Louis
II of Hungary at Mohács in 1526. That year in India, the Mughals conquered the Lodi Sultanate of Delhi. Earlier in the century, the Safavids
had conquered Persia. Each, in its way, was a remarkable achievement,
and, together, they serve as a reminder of the possibility of change and,
in particular, of the extent to which states that lacked any real grounding
comparable to the engaged and mobilized mass publics of the nineteenth
and twentieth centuries could readily fall when their rulers and élites
were overthrown. This process was eased, and, in part, achieved, by recruiting part of the existing élite and reconciling it to the new rulers.
Thus, the Rajputs were recruited by the Mughals. The Spanish conquest
of much of Central and South America in the early and mid-sixteenth
century fits into this pattern. The Spaniards exploited existing divisions
within central Mexico, notably forming an alliance with the Tlaxcaltecs,
a people surrounded by Aztec territory, subordinated to the Aztecs, and
resentful. They and allies provided significant numbers to help in the
conquest of Tenochtitlán in 1521. Native support was essential in order
to match the massive numerical superiority of the Aztecs, who learned
to alter their tactics to counter European arms, especially firepower.[5]

There were significant contrasts with the situation in North America and Africa. Whereas Mexico, Peru, and Hindustan were populous
and had a well-developed agricultural system that could provide plenty
of resources for an invader, much of North America and Africa lacked
comparable storehouses, food for plunder, and roads. The population in
the Middle Mississippi which had been a major center of activity from
about 1000, fell dramatically in about 1450. Mexico, Peru, and Hindustan
were also more centralized politically, and thus easier to take over once
the ruler had been seized, whereas North America and Africa were more
segmented, and new chiefs could readily emerge.

But there were also significant differences between North America
and Africa. The inroads made by disease in the Americas were very different to the case of the conquests in Eurasia, and this pattern was to
be repeated in the seventeenth century: the Manchu conquest of Ming
China was not accompanied or secured by a disease onslaught. In contrast, disease made major inroads on the Natives of North America in
the seventeenth century, just as it had had a terrible impact in the West

Indies and Central America in the sixteenth. To search for an equivalent to the inroads in the Americas, it is necessary to turn to sub-Saharan Africa, but there the demographic gradient was very different, as disease helped weaken the European presence, for example in Portuguese Mozambique, greatly affecting the ability to advance into the interior. In 1400, Europe and the much less densely populated Americas each had about 42–44 million people, but the situation was very different, as far as native populations were concerned by 1650.

In the West Indies, European diseases hit the Native population hard, but the diseases' local counterparts, such as yellow fever, also had a devastating impact on European officials, troops, and settlers. Without these losses, the West Indies would have been relatively far more important demographically as far as the European New World was concerned, and, correspondingly, the North American colonies would have been less significant. Moreover, a more benign ecological situation in the Caribbean would have encouraged more settlers to go there, and thus would have ensured a different emphasis in English/British activities, with more effort devoted possibly to Central America and to islands unoccupied by Europeans such as St. Vincent.

The second major contrast between the New World and the position across much of Eurasia relates to religion. It is possible to paint a benign account of the Spanish conquest and, in particular, to discuss the Christianity of Spanish America as syncretic, drawing on local roots and practices[6] as well as being European in its origins. This account of a melded sacred space can then serve as a key indicator of a more general pattern of cooperation, as consensus was elicited, and this pattern can then be seen as the basis for the politics of Spanish America. In particular, a causal line can be drawn from syncretism and consensus to stability, and this stability can be seen as a central characteristic of Spanish America, as well as a possible reason why its society proved less dynamic, both then and subsequently, than that of British America.

Yet, that account ignores both much of the process by which the Spaniards established their presence and also the comparative dimension. There was a destruction of native religious sites and an extirpation of practices deemed unacceptable, these practices being employed by commentators to demonstrate the superiority of Spanish rule. Christian worship in Spanish America might contain elements of compromise, but there was no compromise about Christianity. The Inquisition became important to the campaign to end Native religion, as with the issue of burning of idols.[7] The situation was different from the position in Eurasia where there were important confessional tensions, but without conquest by the Ottomans, Mughals, and Manchus leading to the ending of other religious practices. Yet, the Spaniards and their descendants never outnumbered the indigenous or mixed population, so, although the Spaniards could make unremitting war on the pagan deities, as well as use control over native labor to lessen the position of the indigenous nobility, they left large tracts of land in the hands of cooperative Natives, particularly those who had readily allied themselves with the conquest.[8]

Spanish practice was to be followed by other Europeans. Proselytism was regarded as a product of superiority, a justification for conquest, and a way to secure control. The net outcome was an assault on native culture far greater than that seen, for example, in India, and, as a consequence, a disruption of native society that contributed, alongside disease, to its breakdown. The result, established from the outset, was a pattern of conquest that was more total than that generally seen elsewhere. It was a pattern that looked in particular to the Iberian Reconquista, but it was one strengthened by key aspects of European history and public culture in the sixteenth century, namely the assault by a revived Islam in the shape of the Ottoman (Turkish) Empire, an assault that also involved the enslavement of Christians, and the marked increase in religious violence within Christendom due to the Reformation.

In the Americas, there was also a typecasting of native societies as harsh, primitive, and uncivilized, and this encouraged not only total war and cruelty on the part of the conquerors, as in Mexico, but also a determination to extirpate their society.[9] In part, this activity can be seen as arising from a belief in manifest destiny, and the history of North America can be presented in terms of a number of competing such destinies that were finally all subordinated to that of nineteenth-century America.

The argument that the pattern of British imperialism in North America and, notably, treatment of the Native Americans, was set by the treatment of the (Catholic) Irish, is well established in the literature, but this was also part of a more general practice of post-Reformation treatment of the heterodox, not least their dehumanization by presentation as animals. This violence extended to the response to other Europeans in the New World, despite, and, in part due to, the extent to which all Europeans were heavily outnumbered, especially in what became the United States. Thus, in 1565, a Spanish force slaughtered Huguenots (French Protestants) who had established a presence in Florida. The difficulty of controlling and caring for captives was a factor in prisoner massacres, but the central drive was that of a deliberate destruction of those held to be threats. Sacred space was at issue both in terms of relations between Europeans and with regard to those with Natives.

The treatment of the defeated raises a question about the more structural use of geopolitical ideas, or, rather, suggests that they have to be understood in a flexible fashion. The extremely varied conduct of conquerors on the world scale in the sixteenth and seventeenth centuries introduces a powerful element of agency. Moreover, countering any simplistic usage of a form of geopolitics "plus," in this case geopolitics plus demographics, demographic imbalance was not the sole factor in the case of Spanish policy, as later also with that of the British; for, as already indicated, similar imbalances can be seen elsewhere, notably with Muslim invaders of Hindustan, but without comparable results in terms of the treatment of local religions.

Cultural dominance and the destruction of independent indigenous activity was not the only situation in the Americas, not least because of the significance of the frontier, a "middle ground" of great depth. This "middle ground" was not so much a zone or region as, for long, a description of much of the area of European activity in North America, especially in British and French North America, but also with important instances for Spain and (in Brazil) for Portugal. Moreover, alongside the role of the frontier, the French, who had far fewer settlers than the British, displayed a greater willingness, alongside proselytism, to try to adapt to native societies, in large part because they were not driven by a lust for land comparable to that shown by British settlers and speculators. Thus, the practice of European activity was not fixed and, indeed, partly arose and was reconfigured as a result of competition between the powers. At the same time, the role of the "middle ground" was to become different, and, in some respects, less important, from the late seventeenth century as British control was extended, and as the total extent of their colonies' core areas became interspread, and thus more similar to the presence established by the Spaniards in central Mexico.

This presence in Mexico and that of Spain in South America brought great wealth, notably of bullion, wealth that was far more significant in the sixteenth century than is the case today, because currency was based on metallic value, and state resources therefore owed much to the availability of specie. Bullion, indeed, was a theme in the geopolitics of the Americas, and notably of the great importance of what became Latin America. Indeed, the continued economic value of bullion permits a rereading of the standard account of New World power politics in 1700–1850, for the major new source of bullion in that period was not what became the United States, but rather the Portuguese colony of Brazil. Indeed, the United States proved a singular disappointment, including to those pressing in Europe for colonial development, until the California Gold Rush in the mid-nineteenth century, followed by the exploitation of the Rockies and Sierras, for example the Comstock Lode in the latter.

The discovery and utilization of gold in the province of Minas Gerais in the early eighteenth century made Brazil a key colonial asset and helped explain the attraction of Portugal as an ally of Britain, and also the need to defend Portugal against Spanish and French attack. Britain might lose the Thirteen Colonies, but it crucially protected Portugal against invasion in 1762 and 1808–1812, and the Royal Navy was the basic guarantor of Brazil. Indeed, British naval power was the crucial offshore element or hidden hand in the struggles for Latin American independence in the 1820s and in the subsequent conflicts between Latin American powers, notably Brazil and Argentina.

Rumors of bullion encouraged Spanish expeditions north from Mexico into the American interior, such as that of Francisco Vásquez de Coronado into what is now New Mexico and thence into the Great Plains in 1540. The rumors proved erroneous, just as English explorers such as Martin Frobisher in the 1570s did not find the bullion they sought in North American waters, in his case the Canadian Arctic.[10] There were certainly no benefits to match those found in Mexico. Similarly, there was no follow-up to the expedition of Hernando do Soto who, between

1539 and 1542, brutally pillaged the Lower Mississippi and nearby lands. In 1541, he won a battle with the Choctaw at Mabila (Selma, Alabama), in which his cavalry was able to dominate the open ground without competition. After Soto's death, de Moscoso pressed on in 1542–43 into what is now eastern Texas. The diseases brought by this expedition proved devastating for the local people.

The lack of benefit is not the sole reason why European interest in America north of Mexico was limited, but it was important, while, within Mexico itself, northward expansion was impeded by the Chichimeca in 1550–90.[11] However, in 1598, the Spaniards were able to press north to establish a position in what they called New Mexico. Nevertheless, Santa Fe was very much to be an outlier, not least because it did not have the Pacific access that had been anticipated.

The Spaniards, moreover, encountered problems in Central America, although Panama, established in 1519, became the base for Francisco Pizarro's expeditions to Peru in 1524, 1526, and 1531–33. Cortés himself led a costly campaign in Honduras in 1524 and Guatemala was conquered by 1542, but, although, helped by the malaria the Spaniards introduced, much of the Yucatán, the center of Mayan civilization, was conquered in 1527–41, the Itzás of the central Petén were not defeated until 1697,[12] and opposition in the Yucatán was to be a major problem for Mexico when it succeeded Spain, with resistance being particularly vigorous in the 1840s and 1990s.

It also proved difficult to maintain royal authority in the areas that were under Spanish control. Aside from important practical difficulties, there were also problems in intellectually grasping the new territories; these problems may have been related to a Spanish focus on the conquest of peoples compared to an English one on land.[13] Philip II's government sought maps to reveal, understand, and display what had been seized, and to help support further expansion, Philip entrusted the task to two prominent cartographers, Alonso de Santa Cruz and Juan López de Velasco, but neither visited the New World. Instead, they sent questionnaires to local officials, but the replies were far fewer than had been anticipated, and this helped cause the abandonment of the mapping.[14]

Unlike Mexico, Florida proved to be a sphere of European competition. With coasts on the Atlantic and the Gulf of Mexico, it was readily accessible, and, in many respects, was equivalent to the major islands of the West Indies. Thus, Florida was part of the Caribbean. This helped explain Spanish interest, but the scale was far less than that in Mexico and Venezuela. Spain established bases in Florida, although the first fort at St. Augustine, built in 1565, was burned down by the Timucua the following spring. Spain also made a major effort at proselytism among the Native population. Settlements that were Spanish-Native were founded. This was an extension of the Spanish world that would have been probably robust enough to see off Native attacks, although the destruction wrought by British-encouraged Native attacks in the 1700s is noteworthy.

In the event, Huguenots established a base in Florida in 1564, in part in order to threaten the route back to Europe taken by the Spanish treasure ships from Veracruz, and in part as a consequence of the French Wars of Religion, as Philip II of Spain was a key supporter of the Guise faction, the main opponent of the Huguenots. Florida also represented French attempts to benefit from the Atlantic, at least in the shape of the entrepreneurial energy of Atlantic and Channel ports such as Dieppe and La Rochelle, the latter the key Huguenot strongholds.

Just as the French failed in Brazil in the 1550s, so French Florida rapidly fell victim to Spanish counterattack, and, in particular, to the greater ability of Spain to deploy power from nearby Cuba, a key capability as Spain was under considerable pressure in Europe in the 1560s, notably from the Turks in the Mediterranean. Deployment from Cuba was an impressive display of Spanish effectiveness and resilience, and one that set a pattern that was seen up to the Spanish ability to reconquer West Florida from Britain in 1779–81, and to the initially successful attempts in the 1810s to resist the Latin American Wars of Independence.

The Spaniards reestablished their position in Florida in 1565, but it was less extensive than prior to the French arrival. Indeed, after the 1560s, Florida was very much a marginal colony and, as such, not an effective base for Spanish power projection further north, nor a source of profit or lobbying that provided encouragement for such action. There was some Spanish activity further north, including missionaries in the Chesapeake, but it was not sustained.

This situation set an effective limit to Spanish America, and thus provided the English with a margin of opportunity when they attempted (unsuccessfully) to establish a colony on the North Carolina Banks in the 1580s and (successfully) in Virginia from 1607. Moreover, as Carolina was only established in the 1660s and Georgia in the 1730s, the lack of Spanish interest in northward expansion was also significant in creating what was, from the European perspective, a vacuum into which the British could expand. This view was mistaken, in that there were many Native Americans in the region, but correct insofar as the future was to lie with the European powers.

The failure of French Florida was also instructive because it indicated the extent to which colonial enterprise that might otherwise have succeeded could be cut short by European action, a lesson that was to be underlined by the failure of the Swedes in the Delaware Valley, and by that of the Dutch in Brazil and the Hudson Valley in the mid-seventeenth century, at the hands of Portugal and England respectively. The extent to which respective success and failure can be explained in geopolitical terms is unclear as the ability and willingness to deploy superior resources, and to do so successfully, was the key issue.

French interest in North America was also to be seen in the valley of the St. Lawrence, a region free from any Spanish presence, but one that was to prove difficult for settlement due to the impact of the harsh climate on agriculture. Contact began in 1534 when Jacques Cartier did not find the route to the Orient he pursued. As with much European activity elsewhere, a quest for precious metals became important. Cartier sought them from his second voyage in 1535 and he returned from his 1541 expedition with what he thought was gold and diamonds, only for it to be pyrites and quartz. The basic French configuration in North America was apparent from the 1560s: a presence in what became Canada and another on the southern littoral, although Louisiana, eventually, and not Florida, was to be the colony in question. This geography of French settlement was both a response to, and opportunity for, the eventual pattern of English settlement.

English interest in North America in the sixteenth century proved episodic, especially in the first half. John Cabot's voyages were not followed up, and whereas Henry VII (r. 1485–1509) had taken a role in European diplomacy while avoiding serious conflict, and supported Cabot, Henry VIII (r. 1509–47) was far more concerned about Continental power politics and was eager to spend much of his wealth, and as much of that of his subjects as he could grab, on war. Entrepreneurial merchants in mid-century were more interested in the opportunities offered by the slave trade from West Africa to the West Indies, and then, as relations deteriorated with Spain from the 1560s, in the loot to be gained from the Spanish Empire, than they were in North America. Lands beyond the Spanish Empire could be claimed, with Francis Drake claiming California as New Albion in 1579 during his circumnavigation of the world, and colonists landed on Roanoke Island in what is now North Carolina in 1585 and 1588 only to fall victim to disease, starvation, or Native Americans.[15] However, despite growing interest in the idea of an English Protestant Atlantic empire,[16] English overseas settlement focused on Ireland while commercial expansion looked to the East Indies, the Mediterranean, and Russia.

The situation was to change in the early seventeenth century, and it is easy to trace a line from sixteenth-century ideas and initiatives to later settlements. There is much basis for this analysis, not least with the growth in geographical knowledge of, and speculation about, the North Atlantic. However, the striking point by 1600 was the contrast between England or France, and Spain, the king of which, from 1580 to 1640, was also ruler of Portugal. As yet, the English Atlantic was very limited as a territorial reality. Seafarers sailed in numbers to the rich fishing grounds off Newfoundland and established temporary settlements on the island that were closely linked to the fisheries. While economically significant, this presence, however, did not measure up in terms of power politics. The role of the English state in transoceanic activity was greatly restricted, and this was even more the case of that of Scotland: attempts in the 1620s to establish a colony in what became Nova Scotia failed.

Other features of European North America also lay mostly in the future, including large-scale African slavery. This point requires underlining as an important aspect of geopolitics was/is that of power over people, and a crucial dimension of this power was to be provided by enslavement and the movement of slaves. Initially, the labor force for the European colonies appeared provided by the Native population of North America, and this element remained the key element in Mexico and Peru. However, the inroads of disease hit this Native population hard,

particularly smallpox, which broke out in Mexico in 1520, the year after
the invasion force under Cortés arrived. Smallpox appears to have killed
at least half the Aztecs, including Montezuma's brother and successor,
the energetic leader Cuitlahuac, and to have greatly hit the morale of the
survivors. Disease weakened potential resistance to European control in
the Americas, and acted like enslavement in disrupting social structures
and household and communal economics, leading to famine. From the
European perspective, however, disease also had a savage effect on the
potential labor force.

More generally, Spanish colonial policies and practices, including
the end of Native religious rituals, affected local society and limited the
possibility of post-epidemic population recovery. The resulting problem
was compounded by the commercial opportunities created by plantation
agriculture and by mining, each of which required large workforces. The
obvious solution was to obtain slaves from the Native population outside
the span of European territorial control, and slave raiding and purchase
were to be important, not least, but not only, in Brazil, New France, and
in the southern English mainland colonies in the late seventeenth and
early eighteenth century. The Spaniards carried out large-scale slaving
in the sixteenth century among Natives in Honduras and Nicaragua.[17]
The benefits gained from the sale of slaves helped to destabilize Native
society by encouraging conflict between tribes in order to seize people
for slavery, which was a process also seen in West Africa. People were
commodified as a result, which proved a central aspect of the way in
which the slave trade affected relations between Europeans and Native
Americans.

Despite the benefits gained from the internal slave trade, there were
also problems for the colonists, including the availability and cost of slaves,
with Native resistance and flight proving key factors. Moreover, control
over Native labor within the area of Spanish control was affected by royal
legislation, which sought to address clerical pressure to treat the Natives
as subjects ready for Christianization, rather than as slaves. Indeed, Native slavery was formally abolished in the *Leyes Nuevas* of 1542. However,
the implementation of edicts took time and was frequently ignored by
local officials and landowners. Furthermore, systems of tied labor, especially the *encomienda* (land and Native families allocated to colonists), and

forced migration, notably the *repartimiento,* under which a part of the male population had to work away from home, represented de facto slavery.[18]

Native slaves remained important in frontier regions distant from the points of arrival of African slaves, such as northern Mexico. Nevertheless, the equations of opportunity and cost were to favor the purchase of slaves in West Africa and their shipment across the Atlantic. Initially, Africans were shipped into Spanish America via Spain, but, from 1518, *asientos* or licenses were granted for their direct movement. As it was initially more expensive to supply Spanish America with African slaves than with Native slaves, the Africans were often used as house slaves, a form of high-value slavery that indicated their cost. As a reminder from the outset of the variety of roles that Africans were to take in the Americas, some fought as *conquistadors.*[19] Such variety undercut racial typecasting, but far less so than it should have done.

By the mid-sixteenth century, the situation had changed and, rather than providing a marginal part of the labor force, Africa was becoming steadily more important as a source of slaves, not least because it was believed that Africans were physically stronger than Natives. Nevertheless, African slaves remained more expensive than Native labor who could be controlled in various ways, including by making service an element of debt repayment. In 1570, there were probably only 20,000 African slaves in Spanish America,[20] although the numbers increased over the following century, and in many areas, including a large number on the Pacific coast of Guatemala.[21] Labor control and slavery were a key background to the economic rationale of some of the territorial struggles discussed in the next chapter, and slavery helped make West Africa part of the trans-Atlantic world created by the establishment of European colonies in the Americas.

# 2

# CREATING NEW FRONTIERS
# 1600-74

Much of the seventeenth century was not a great age of European expansion, and certainly did not compare with that seen in the first seventy years of the sixteenth century. Indeed, there were some important European failures in the seventeenth century, with bases lost, including Fort Zeelandia (on Taiwan), Candia (Crete), Tangier, Albazin (in the Amur valley), and Mombasa, by the Dutch, Venetians, English, Russians, and Portuguese respectively, and with the Portuguese unsuccessful in the Bay of Bengal and the Zambezi Valley. In South America, expansion was limited, and notably so in the case of the southern border of Spanish expansion in Chile. From 1683, a very different overall impression was to be created when the disastrous failure of the Turkish siege of Vienna was followed by major inroads into the Turkish Empire. However, prior to that, the two major areas of European expansion in the seventeenth century, European understood as Christian European, were Siberia and North America. Of the two, the former was the most impressive in scale and provides an instructive comparison for activity in North America. The Russians expanded from the 1580s through the Urals and across Siberia, reaching the Pacific in the 1630s, a formidable distance greater than that of the Europeans in North America, either in that period or, indeed, in total by 1846 when America stretched to the Pacific.

In doing so, the Russians benefited from the inroads of disease and from the ability to secure assistance and allies from among the divided local population. Moreover, Siberia, a more hostile environment than North America, supported a smaller population, and was therefore able to mount less resistance and to cope with less disruption. The Russians also benefited from superior technology, in the shape of gunpowder weaponry, and crucially from the extent to which they were not challenged by any other European power. Islamic khanates that might have sought to encourage resistance were overcome, while Manchu China acted (eventually) in the 1680s as an effective restraint on Russian expansion in the Amur Valley region, rather than as a player in Siberia itself. Having obliged the Russians, by the Treaty of Nerchinsk of 1689, to abandon their plans for the Amur Valley, the Chinese focused from the 1690s to the 1750s on the Dshungars of Xinjiang and on Tibet, a focus that was fostered by good Chinese relations with Russia.

Emphasizing this factor might suggest that the key contrast with North America was provided by the competition there between the European powers, with their rival political and commercial interests leading them both to supply Native allies with firearms, and to take more direct steps to weaken European opponents and their Native allies. That was indeed a factor, but stressing it risks placing excessive weight on the European ability to direct the Native Americans.

There was a consistent attempt to do so, but it was also the case that Europeans were used by the latter in order to serve their own interests, a pattern that matched that seen with the slave trade from West Africa and, more generally, with European imperial activity. Alliance was therefore a complex process in which advantage was contested and support in part purchased, notably by the European provision of goods. The acquisition of land by settlers proved part of this process, and, again, contrasting understandings of terms and symbols between Europeans and Natives played an important role both in easing acquisition and in making it contentious.

The habitual account of the period covered in this chapter would begin with the English establishment of Jamestown in Virginia in 1607, their first permanent base, and would follow an account of the development of English North America with a discussion of the four-party confrontation between English, French, Dutch, and Native Americans that ended with the confirmation in 1674, at the end of the Third Anglo-Dutch War, of the English acquisition of New Amsterdam (renamed New York), and the consequent end of New Netherland. Part of the settlement of Anglo-Dutch differences at the end of the three mid-century Anglo-Dutch wars was therefore an endorsement of the English view of power on the eastern seaboard of North America.

This verdict, moreover, was not to be overturned in 1688 when William III of Orange successfully invaded England at the head of a Dutch army and overthrew James II (and VII of Scotland), a victory swiftly followed by the overthrow of James's officials in North America, which underlined the dependence of developments there on European power politics. However, a key aspect of the Glorious Revolution was that, although it served Dutch interests, it did so by forwarding those of William III, who became William III of Britain. As such, he might initially depend in part on foreign, notably Dutch, troops, but he grounded his position by being King of England. There was no attempt to reverse the earlier Dutch failure in North America. Instead, Dutch colonial expansion ceased in the New World (it had failed against Portugal in Brazil in the 1650s) and was now focused on the East Indies, the sphere of the Dutch East India Company.

These developments were indeed crucial to the future trajectory of North America, but, looking from 1600, it is more appropriate to begin with the European power that was already established on the North American mainland, Spain. The opportunity for Spanish expansion was clearly present, but the seventeenth century was a period of grave difficulties for the Spanish state, society, and economy, and Spain was involved in difficult wars in Europe for most of it, notably until 1609, and from 1621 to 1668, 1673 to 1678, 1683 to 1684, and 1689 to 1697. Spain's opponents, each for part of the period, included France, England and the Dutch. There were also serious rebellions in Spain's European empire, notably, but not only, in the 1640s.

Spain's warfare greatly lessened the resources available for transoceanic expansion (as well as leading to conflict there with the forces of European rivals, especially in the Caribbean), although that point should not have been too serious as the demographic and economic resources of Spanish America were themselves considerable. However, both were affected by the general downturn of the global economy in the seventeenth century, a downturn that owed much to the impact on agriculture of the Little Iron Age, a period of cooling that may have been related to sun spots. Alongside these general problems, there were specific difficulties for Spain and the Spanish state that, together, contributed to the extent to which Spain suffered most gravely from the "General Crisis of the Seventeenth Century." The relationship between this crisis and both developments and potential in Spanish America, and the consequences of the latter for the New World as a whole, have not attracted sufficient attention, as discussion of North America in the seventeenth century tends to focus on England and France.

It is notable that Spain did not display the vigor seen over the previous century. The economic strains of the period combined with the pressures created by the fiscal needs of the Crown, contributing to periodic crises, notably the violent overthrow in Mexico City in 1624 of the Marquis of Gelves, the Viceroy of New Spain. Moreover, as with the British colonies in the 1770s, the reality of control from the metropole challenged ideas of colonial rights and practices of colonial autonomy.

Settlement from Spain in the New World was limited and the bulk of the population continued to be Native. For example, in central Mexico, the Native percentage of the population in 1646 was 87.2, while Spaniards, whether born in Mexico or immigrants, amounted to 8 percent, *mestizos* (mixed) were 1.1, and *pardos* (wholly or partly black) 3.7.[1] Such figures are open to qualification, not simply in terms of counting numbers but also of categorization, as it is important to give due weight to the extent and impact of mixed unions. Thus, many listed as Spaniards and many *pardos* contained some Native blood, while racial concepts were cultural as much as biological.

Nevertheless, despite the disastrous effects of disease on the Native population, the Spaniards remained a marked minority and this ethnic mix was very different from that of English North America. There, although the numbers of mixed-race people rose, their overall impact was lessened by the scale of migration from Europe and by a relatively high survival rate among these migrants, which ensured a reasonable gender balance, which, in turn, increased the European population.[2] Colonial history would have played out very differently if the majority of the population in Philadelphia had been Delaware or *mestizos,* and the majority of New Yorkers had been Mohawk.

Expansion was not a theme that meant much in Florida nor along the northern frontier of New Spain, which can be seen as a missed opportunity, but the subsequent history of Louisiana as a French colony showed the difficulty of developing a presence in the absence of a large population. However, Louisiana also served as the basis for a wide-ranging trading system in the hinterland while, in the mid-eighteenth century, France managed to deploy power along the axis between Louisiana and Canada, a deployment that Spain could not match from its colonies. The Spaniards could have established bases along the northern shore of the Gulf of Mexico, but there was no obvious threat to their interests there until the 1680s, and no real incentive for them to act. Instead, Spain had to protect its Caribbean possessions from English, Dutch, and French attacks, for example Oliver Cromwell's Western Design of 1654–55, which failed against the key colony of Hispaniola (now Haiti and the Dominican Republic), but succeeded against Jamaica, then a far less important island, establishing a British colonial presence that lasted until 1962.

These attacks reflected power politics, not least the English attempt to wreck the articulation of the Spanish Empire, especially by cutting the movement of its bullion. As a reminder of the role of multiple factors, the attacks were also a product of the geopolitics stemming from the economic development of the period, notably the expansion of New World exports to Europe. The profit derived from the production of plantation crops, particularly sugar, tobacco, and coffee, led to pressure for control over both territory and people, for these crops required much labor. Moreover, the export of these crops, together with that to the Americas of European manufactured goods that this helped finance, played a major role in restructuring much of the European economy. This two-way trade powerfully developed and accentuated the role of Europe's Atlantic seaboard, and crucially strengthened the importance of port cities, especially Bordeaux and Bristol, Liverpool and Nantes, and Charleston and Havana. The import of plantation crops also greatly affected the material culture of Europeans, their diet, and health. By supplying new products, or providing existing ones at a more attractive price, or in new forms, this trade both satisfied and encouraged consumer demand. Moreover, transoceanic trade provided goods designed to stimulate, and, as none of these was "necessary," this process was very much consumerism and one linked to shifts in taste.[3]

The history of English, French, and Dutch North America in this period indicated that state action, while important, and notably so with the deployment of warships and troops, was less so than the ability to provide settlers, and then to link them into a trans-Atlantic trading pattern. Prominent settlements founded by Europeans included Jamestown (1607) and Plymouth (1620) by the English, Quebec by the French (1608), and New Amsterdam (1614) and Albany (1624) by the Dutch.

One result of the growing presence of Europeans, and the greater commercial opportunities they provided for the Native Americans, was an increase in warfare between the tribes as they sought to control contact with the Europeans, and also growing European involvement in the warfare, not that warfare was solely due to the Europeans. Indeed, such an argument underplays the role of Native agency.[4] The diseases brought by the Europeans, which hit the Atlantic coast from the 1600s and the St. Lawrence–Great Lakes area from the mid-1630s, also encouraged conflict as the Iroquois launched "mourning wars" from the 1640s to rebuild numbers through adopting captives.

The French originally refused to supply firearms, but, after an initial prohibition, the Dutch began trading arms as part of their commercial strategy to use trade to underpin their colony, and as warfare increased in scope, restrictions on the supply of firearms decreased. In the early 1640s, the French also began to send muskets to baptized native allies to strengthen them against the Mohawk, who themselves traded freely for Dutch muskets after agreements in 1643 and 1648. By 1648, the Mohawk had amassed at least eight hundred muskets. In the 1650s, the Swedes even provided the Susquehannock of the Delaware Valley, on whom they were dependent, with cannon and they used them against both Iroquois and the English. However, this transfer of artillery was unusual and, without cannon, the Native Americans had little impact on European forts. The transfer of firearms to allies was an echo of the processes by which, during the Thirty Years' War (1618–48), the major European powers, including France, Spain, and the Dutch, provided arms and support for their European allies in return for support.

The Native Americans were well attuned to fighting in the hinterland and their general lack of fixed battle positions made it difficult for opposing Europeans to devise clear tactical goals and ensured that there was no role for volley fire. Furthermore, as experts with bows and arrows, they were adept in missile warfare, and thus were more readily able to make the transition to muskets, which were easier to aim, and the bullets of which, unlike arrows, were less likely to be deflected by brush and could not be dodged. These factors combined to reduce any significant advantage in military technology the settlers might have possessed.

In the Pequot War of 1637, it was first the overwhelming superiority in firearms of the English that brought them victory in the Connecticut River valley, but also the degree to which their opponents were not supported by other tribes.[5] The latter was repeatedly a factor in the absence of revivalist religious movements among Native Americans such as that in the 1800s. The opportunities and pressures stemming from contact with Europeans exacerbated tensions between tribes such as that between the Mohawk and the Dutch-allied Algonquian Mahican in the Hudson valley in the late 1620s. The clash of English and Native military cultures proved a challenge to each, encouraging a high level of violence.[6] There were also crossovers, notably scalping, which was pursued prior to the European arrival and then used by the Europeans and allied Natives to develop relations.[7]

From the 1640s, the spread of firearms among Native Americans made them even more effective opponents of European colonists,[8] and, as a result, the power balance was shifted less by weaponry than by demography. The latter reflected the extent to which the Europeans came to North America to colonize rather than to trade, and they came in increasing numbers. By contrast, Native American numbers did not grow and, instead, were devastated by European diseases, notably smallpox. For example, the population of Huron and Petun in what is now Ontario fell from 20,000–30,000 in 1634 to 12,000 in 1639.[9] The rise in the European population led to a land hunger that drove the politics of spatial control, a hunger accentuated by the significance to the colonial economy of large numbers of imported livestock. The use of these livestock focused tensions over subsistence practices, land use, property rights, and control.[10]

English North America had the vital edge in people because it drew on a number of different settlement streams, a process that was encouraged by the highly diverse nature of the English colonies, and the absence of any uniformity, notably religious practice. However, there was no real settlement stream associated with the Hudson's Bay Company that, in 1670, was granted, by Charles II, exclusive trading privileges in Rupert's Land, the areas drained by rivers flowing into Hudson Bay. At that time, there was no idea about the extent of this area. A base was established at Rupert House, on James Bay, the southeastern extension of Hudson Bay, that year.

The prime settlement streams were, first, those disaffected with the English ecclesiastical system, who settled in New England from 1620, and largely consisted of families. This stream expanded rapidly as a result of the high birth rate among settlers and their limited exposure to hostile diseases in New England; and the settlers established a series of largely autonomous self-governing communities in which men worked their own land and followed their own trades. Religious differences encouraged the establishment of Rhode Island and Connecticut, which became fresh centers for activity.

Secondly, Virginia developed as a more hierarchical society, one that was a closer approximation to that of England. Economic opportunity, crucially land ownership, varied greatly in Virginia, and much labor was provided by indentured workers who were given their passage across the Atlantic in return for being obliged to work for, usually, seven years. The long terms of service that were exacted and "the extreme demand for labor" encouraged dealing in servants, and their hiring was harsher and more degrading than in England.[11]

Tobacco became the major crop in both Virginia and Maryland. Its limited capital requirements and high profitability encouraged settlers and investment. Because it was an export crop, the links with England were underlined. The needs and difficulties of tobacco cultivation and trade, however, created serious problems for farmers, and this situation ensured a particular sensitivity to labor availability and cost that encouraged a shift to slavery, which, in turn, became normal. Social differentiation was marked, in contrast, in quasi-egalitarian New England where the amount of land received by the first colonists was more uniform than was the case in Virginia where there were particular differences between Tidewater planters and their up-country rivals. The return, on terms, of monarchy in England and its colonies, with the Restoration in the person of Charles II in 1660, added a clear political dimension, as the king recognized the rights of resident landowners to land ownership and political participation.[12]

Thirdly, Carolina (later South Carolina), which was founded as a separate colony in 1663, became, from the outset, a plantation economy reliant on slave labor. Founded from Barbados, the colony looked to the West Indies in economic, social, and political terms. As a reminder, however, that similar environmental circumstances could lead in different directions, Georgia, which was chartered as a colony in 1732, initially sought a very different spatial character in that the Trustees, seeking to create a colony of virtuous small farmers, banned slavery both because they were concerned about slave risings and because they were opposed to aristocratic slave plantations and their impact on the yeoman farmers. Thus the spatial nature of settlement was to be different to that in neighboring South Carolina, and this was seen as integral to a contrasting spatial dynamic of local power. In the event, poor sandy soils, the cost of white labor, and the example of successful South Carolina, combined to ensure the end of the slavery ban in 1750 and the Trustees' surrender of their Charter in 1752. Plantation cultivation then spread from South Carolina.

The struggle between England and the Netherlands in North America was but a facet of the wider conflict between the two powers, and was a relatively minor aspect of it. Nevertheless, the easy conquest, in 1664 at a time of peace, of poorly fortified New Amsterdam, which became, as a result, New York, left England with a fourth strand of settlement, a more mixed one drawing on Germany, Scandinavia, and the Low Countries as well as the British Isles. This strand occupied the Middle Colonies, initially what became the colonies of New York, New Jersey, and Delaware, and, subsequently, Pennsylvania, the colony founded by William Penn in 1681, not that these colonies should be understood as controlling the territory now covered by these states. Most of New York and

Pennsylvania was still under the control of Native Americans, and this remained the case into the late eighteenth century.

The geographical position of these colonies underlined the importance of their acquisition by England. Control over New Amsterdam was seen as a way to enforce English protectionist legislation.[13] Moreover, the population of these colonies contributed to the extent to which that of the British colonies greatly outnumbered the population of those of France. The coherence of English North America would have been very different had New York and New Jersey remained under Dutch control, let alone passed under that of France. The latter was not a strong option, but France and the Dutch allied against Spain from 1635 to 1648, both opposed the Commonwealth regime established by Parliamentary victory in the Civil War in 1642–46, and they cooperated at the time of the Second Anglo-Dutch War (1665–66). Moreover, the possibility of further cooperation was created both by French intervention in domestic Dutch politics and by the fate of the related conflicts between the two powers. Thus, the French invasion of the United Provinces (Dutch Republic) in 1672, an invasion only thwarted by the breaching of the dykes holding back the waters, led to the possibility of a very different settlement of the future of the Dutch colonial position, one in which France and a pliant United Provinces were allied. In 1672, however, Charles II of England was allied to Louis XIV of France against the Dutch, and thus French victory would not have compromised England's position in New York. The Dutch recaptured the city in 1673, but, in 1674, it was returned to England by the Peace of Westminster that ended the Third Anglo-Dutch War. Moreover, the Dutch and the French did not cooperate against Britain until 1780.

The issue of France's role in Anglo-Dutch relations underlines the importance of chronological conjuncture as well as of contingency, and the extent to which they took precedence over geopolitical considerations, not least by lending point to the counterfactuals of alternative developments. Alternatively, this issue can be represented in terms of France's lesser interest in transoceanic matters. In particular, Louis XIV's focus was very much on land power and European power politics and, largely as a result, France did not make a lasting transition to being a successful naval power, although this point has to be matched by an understanding of the degree to which France was one of the leading naval powers in the world between 1670 and 1900, and usually the second one.

European power politics helped frame the context for developments in North America, not least by setting and changing diplomatic alignments, and thus the power politics of the colonies and, indirectly, their relationships with Native allies. More than government policy, however, was involved as the French also proved more reluctant than the British to settle as emigrants, although, again, the role of government was significant because, unlike in Britain, there was no encouragement to foreign and heterodox settlers in France's colonies. Thus, the Huguenots, France's Protestants, many of whom fled France in the 1680s as their rights were eroded and then, in 1685, extinguished, ended up strengthening the British colonies. The major French acquisition in the New World in the second half of the seventeenth century was Saint-Domingue, the western half of Hispaniola, and it is significant that France pursued the option of a plantation rather than a settlement colony.

The disposal of forces in the New World owed much to local resources based on settlers, as well as to the availability of Crown forces overseas. From that perspective, thanks to the much greater number of British settlers, the future of North America, in terms of British victory in 1760 and the peace settlement of 1763, already seemed apparent. Notably, there was the development of significant militia forces in the British colonies.[14] Yet, under Louis XIV (r. 1643–1715), and notably in the mid-1660s, there was also an increase in the allocation of French forces to North America and a determined attempt to strengthen Canada. This effort helped ensure an increase in the tempo of European competition in the continent, a tempo that became readily apparent from the 1690s and that already, in 1686, had led to the French capture of the English bases on James Bay. Moreover, the short-lived establishment of the French base of Fort St. Louis on the Texan coast in the 1680s provoked a series of Spanish expeditions into Texas and along the Gulf of Mexico.

However, alongside this European competition, the Native American dimension remained highly significant. For example, the Spaniards were forced out of the Santa Fe region of New Mexico between 1680 and 1692 by the Pueblo rebellion, which reflected the pressures created by disease, drought, Spanish fiscal demands, and Apache and Navajo raiding, and which was led by a victim of Spanish attempts to suppress Native religion. Santa Fe itself resisted Native siege in 1680, but had then had to be evacuated. Across North America, there was no suggestion in this period of inevitable European triumph, while the developing clash between French and British interests did not define European interest in the continent.

# 3

# BRITAIN, FRANCE,
# AND THE NATIVES
# 1674-1715

By 1715, the pattern of Anglo-French confrontation down to eventual British success in 1760 had been fairly clearly set. French North America was heavily outnumbered in terms of settlers, while its military resources were also weaker. As a result, French success against the British in the Yorktown campaign of 1781 was to be as part of a coalition, with the American Patriots providing crucial troops and bases. In contrast, British efforts in earlier conflicts had drawn on more numerous settlers as well as on regular forces sent from Britain. The willingness of the British to deploy a considerable force in an (unsuccessful) amphibious attempt to capture Quebec in 1711[1] prefigured the more consistent attempt on French North America that was to be considered in 1746–47 and to be pursued in 1757–60, and ultimately to total success as far as French Canada was concerned.

The 1711 attempt, in turn, was the latest stage in a series of British attempts mounted on Canada in the 1690s and 1700s,[2] a series that had begun in the 1620s: Quebec had been captured in 1629, only to be returned in 1632 as part of the peace settlement. These attempts did not succeed insofar as the St. Lawrence center of French power was at issue, but the situation was very different in Nova Scotia. The capture of French positions there, notably Port Royal in 1690 and 1710, did not end the question of its future, as the British were to become concerned about the position of the Acadians (French settlers) and of the local Native Americans. However, this capture altered the strategic situation for Canada by greatly lessening the British task in future conflicts and also by providing bases for future operations against Canada. The latter advantage was not fully realized until the development of the fortress-port of Halifax, but the first advantage was already apparent by the time of the next conflict in the 1740s.

These advantages underlined the significance of the decision to press, in the negotiations that led to the Peace of Utrecht in 1713, for the retention of the British gains, as well as for the affirmation of the British position in Newfoundland and around Hudson's Bay. The practice in negotiations was that only some wartime gains were retained, the situation also seen in Anglo-French treaties in 1763, 1802, and 1814–15. As a result, it was the British decision to press for the gains in North America that was significant as, although the government was more concerned in the early 1710s with the situation in Europe than with that in North America, it was more interested in the latter than Louis XIV. Conversely, he was willing to yield his claims as part of the cost for detaching Britain from Austria, which did not make peace until the following year.

Yet, as a reminder that government was not an abstract force, and, instead, that the goals and policies of the British government were refracted through the prisms and pressures of politics, the greater focus on North America in the early 1710s was not to be maintained in the next war with France – the War of the Austrian Succession, in which Britain fought France in 1743–48 and was formally at war from 1744; the conflict is known as King George's War in the United States. The key factor in the early 1710s was the gain of power by Tory politicians by Robert Harley and Henry St. John, later Viscount Bolingbroke, and their commitment to "blue water" policies of naval strength and imperial expansion. These policies were followed in an explicit rejection of the earlier Whig commitment to European power politics, and their military counterpart, the large-scale deployment of troops in the Low Countries.

The Tories, however, fell from power in 1714 with the accession of the Hanoverian dynasty in the person of George I (r. 1714–27), who relied on the Whigs, albeit with frequent clashes over personnel and policy. This situation was also seen under his son, George II (r. 1727–60). As a party, the Tories did not subsequently return to office, but Tory ideas played a role in the return to interest in North America under William Pitt the Elder in the 1750s. In the meanwhile, there was no consistent governmental interest in weakening France in North America, not least because the two powers were allies from 1716 to 1731. As a result, there was a degree of disconnect between British expansion on the ground in North America, which was notable insofar as the extension of settlement was concerned, and a more cautious governmental policy; and this contrast was certainly the case up till the mid-1740s, and, in a very different context, was to be seen in the decade that closed with the outbreak of the War of American Independence. A counterfactual is readily posed, notably the extent to which the furtherance of Tory policies would have led to a more assertive government stance in North America, both in wartime, notably in 1745–48, and in peacetime. This question can also be read back to ask whether (if constituted) Tory ministries in the 1690s and 1700s would have devoted a fraction of the large sums spent on the Continent by the Whigs to attacking Canada.

Expenditure was certainly not the sole issue, although governors, such as Colonel Joseph Dudley of Massachusetts, were worried about the "great cost" of defending their colonies.[3] The campaigns of these years also indicated the importance of planning, command, logistics, and disease, and greater resources could complicate, rather than solve, these issues. At the same time, there was no inherent reason why the British forces deployed in North America in 1708 and 1711 should not have been employed earlier, at least after 1692 when the French fleet was heavily defeated at Barfleur, leaving the British navy clearly stronger and lessening the risk of an invasion of Britain.

Thus, the political factor cannot serve in a deterministic fashion, any more than the drawing of smooth connections linked to demographical weight and geopolitical drives. This point is underlined if British North America is read from the south rather than the north or as well as the north. Such a reading places greater emphasis on relations with Spain and also on the question of Louisiana, and serves as a reminder that the three powers, Britain, France, and Spain, were in a complex as well as dynamic relationship, a point further underlined when they went to war in 1719.

Yet, the shifting pattern of European politics reflected more than geopolitical drives or the pursuit of interests in what might be regarded as modern "realist" terms. Instead, dynasticism was a key factor, and, with the end of the Spanish Habsburg line, dynastic advantage took Louis XIV's second grandson, Philip, Duke of Anjou, to the throne of Spain, as Philip V, in 1700, a position he held until 1746. This dynastic gain was challenged in the War of the Spanish Succession by an alliance led by Austria, Britain, and the Dutch, an alliance that supported Charles III, an Austrian Habsburg claimant to the Spanish Empire who, in 1711, became Charles VI, Holy Roman Emperor and ruler of Austria. A direct descendant, Archduke Maximilian, was to fail in the 1860s in his quest to retain his contested Emperorship of Mexico. Maximilian in Mexico had more success than Charles in Spain in holding the center of power, but both faced serious domestic opposition.

As a result of the failure of Charles's challenge, a failure that owed much to Louis's expensive support for his grandson, the relationship between the French colonial position and that of Spain, and thus the geopolitics of the New World, altered greatly. Moreover, France benefited, and sought to benefit, from the integrity of the Spanish Empire by drawing on the bullion of the latter and by seeking to penetrate its markets.

Conflict between France and Spain in 1719–21 was to indicate that this new pattern was far from fixed, and, instead, was dependent on princely strategies and factional politics; but, nevertheless, the dynastic reconfiguration of Western Europe in 1700 greatly altered the geopolitics of North America. The change is a reminder of a central theme of this book, the dependence on North America on the outside world. French concern with the integrity of the Spanish Empire exemplified that dependence, as in 1740 when France threatened conflict in order to restrain Britain's ambitions in the Caribbean in the war with Spain begun in 1739, the War of Jenkins' Ear.[4]

Dependence on European events was accentuated by the increased ease of crossing the Atlantic. The Atlantic "shrank" between 1675 and 1740 as a result of significant improvements, such as the development of postal services and the introduction of the helm wheel soon after 1700 that dramatically increased rudder control on large ships by removing the need to steer with the tiller. The number and predictability of Atlantic crossings increased,[5] although seasonal weather factors still greatly affected plans for the movement of troops across the Atlantic.[6]

The dependence on Europe does not imply that the relationship was all one-way. French concern in North America was focused on Britain, in large part due to the dynamics of European power politics and dynasticism, not least George II's support for Austria in 1731–32 and 1742–48, and France's determination to weaken Austria in wars launched in 1733 and 1741. Nevertheless, this concern was also, by the early 1750s, a product of British expansionism into the North American interior, or rather the extension of British–Native networks and the challenge they apparently posed to their French counterparts. The latter reading of North American power politics has become more common in recent decades and is linked to an understanding of the relations between Europeans and Native Americans as dynamic. Moreover, a sense of the Europeans as weak and vulnerable, which was certainly the case with Louisiana, but also of the Spaniards in Florida and Texas, detracts from the presentation of North American history in terms of geopolitics directed from the capitals of Europe. Any mapping of power on the ground in 1690 or 1720 would suggest a situation different to that of European claims and pretensions, for these were of scant interest to Native Americans. An appreciation of the deficiencies of European war making contributes to an understanding of weakness, but these deficiencies were not grasped in these capitals. Instead, there was a confidence that decisions taken would have corresponding results or at least important consequences. At times, the contrasting reality was starkly apparent, as with the bold territorial claims made when colonies such as Carolina were chartered. The contrast was underplayed in Europe (as opposed to on the ground), because the power and role of the Native Americans were not appreciated. Instead, there was a tendency to emphasize limits in the shape of the pretensions of other European powers.

This difference between claims and ambitions, and the reality on the ground, can be taken further by considering the limitations of imperial ambition and colonial power as a system of governance, not least the restricted amount of information enjoyed by metropolitan governments when considering choices, but also, more significantly, these limitations of colonial power as a source of policy. Clashing colonial interests led Britain and France to war in the 1750s, but it is mistaken to read this situation back to earlier conflicts between the two powers. To do so underplays the primacy of politics in Europe. Yet, despite the focus of governmental policies on Europe, their consequences in North America were also important. Thus, the French decision to send troops to Canada in the 1660s greatly affected Native American power politics. The latter were scarcely unchanging, but, as with the very different case of the African slave trade, European pressure had an impact on local political patterns and in a highly disruptive fashion.

As far as geographical span was concerned, France was more active in the interior of North America away from the settlements near the Atlantic littoral than Britain was, although, in 1671, Thomas Batts and Robert Fallam, traveling west from Virginia, became the first Europeans to cross the Appalachians and reach the Mississippi watershed. Two years later, James Needham and Gabriel Arthur followed the Occaneechee Path across the Appalachians. Combined with Britain's success in consolidating and expanding its position on the Atlantic, a position which by 1720 extended between Cape Breton Island and Florida, French expansion led to an increasingly contrasting geopolitical position: in place of two largely similar transoceanic empires, came one, France, that was clearly inferior in naval strength and coastal position, but that was markedly stronger in the interior. To the west of New France, the journeys of Jesuit missionaries and of *coureurs du bois* (fur traders) had greatly extended French influence and knowledge. Trading bases were established at Sault-Ste-Marie and St. Ignace in 1668, giving the French an important presence in the strategic region where Lake Huron joined lakes Michigan and Superior (to use the subsequent English names).

There were hopes that waterways, and thus trade routes, would lead from Lake Superior to Hudson Bay and to the gulfs of Mexico and California, so that control of the interior would bring a French presence on all the coasts of the continent, to which the interior was subordinate in European geopolitical thought. Achievements did not match these hopes, but were still impressive. Traveling into Wisconsin in 1669, Father Allouez heard of the Mississippi. Two years later, at a ceremonial meeting of Native Americans at Sault-Ste-Marie, French officials laid claim to North America as far as the "South Sea," the Pacific. In 1673, a seven-strong mission led by Louis Jolliet, a fur trader, and Father Jacques Marquette, set off to find the Mississippi and to travel to its outlet. They traveled as far as the confluence with the Arkansas River and, on their return, used a shorter route via the Illinois River and the Chicago Portage. Marquette reported that a route from the Great Lakes to the Gulf of Mexico had been discovered. Further north, an expedition from the St. Lawrence reached Hudson Bay in 1672, but the English Hudson's Bay Company was already established there and developing its fur-trading network, with its combination of oceanic supply and river routes across large parts of the interior. Also in the 1670s, the governor of New France, Louis de Buade de Frontenac, strengthened the French position on Lake Ontario by building Fort Frontenac in 1673.

His protégé, René-Robert Cavalier, Sieur de la Salle, founded a series of trading posts on the Illinois River. However, closer to the heart of French power, Frontenac's attempt to crush the Western Iroquois in 1682 led to a humiliating climbdown after influenza and logistical problems weakened the French force. Yet this did not stop the spread of the system of trading posts. Further west, positions were established at Fort St. Joseph (1679), Fort Crèvecoeur (1680), and Fort St. Louis (1682), consolidating France's presence between Lake Michigan and the Mississippi. North of Lake Superior, bases were founded at Fort Kaministiquia (1678), Fort Népigon (1679), and Fort La Tourette (1684). In 1682, La Salle canoed down the Mississippi to its mouth. On 9 April, he planted the cross, raised the arms of France, and claimed the river, its tributaries, and the lands they watered, for Louis. Angered by the failure to defeat the Iroquois, the distant Louis XIV disgraced Frontenac in 1683 and criticized La Salle's discoveries as worthless; but his opinion on the latter was changed by clerics eager to extend the Catholic Church. An energetic new governor, Jacques-René de Brisay de Denonville, arrived in 1685 with 500 troops, part of the force of 1,750 men sent in 1683–88. He successfully attacked the villages of the Seneca in 1687 and negotiated an acceptable peace with the Iroquois in 1688. Further west, the network of French posts extended with the foundation of Fort St. Croix (1683), St. Antoine (1686), and Fort La Point (1693) south of Lake Superior.

La Salle had found little support in Quebec for his plan for a series of forts down the Mississippi, but he met with a better reception in France in 1684, in large part because Louis was then at war with Spain and the opportunity of challenging its position in the Caribbean was welcome. La Salle was sent to the Gulf of Mexico with four ships and three hundred settlers but, missing the Mississippi delta, landed four hundred miles to the desolate west. His enterprise collapsed into recriminations that cost him his life, and Louis Hennepin's 1697 map put the mouth of the Mississippi too far west, but La Salle's initiative swiftly bore fruit with the foundation of a colony in Louisiana, named after Louis XIV, just as New Orleans was named after Philip, Duke of Orléans, Regent from 1715, for the infant Louis XV. The establishment of the French position in Louisiana, where Fort Maurepas in Biloxi Bay was founded in 1699, followed by Mobile in 1702 and New Orleans in 1718, was directed against Spain, rather than England, and breached the Spanish hold on the northern shore of the Gulf of Mexico, as well as adding to the French presence in the Caribbean, a presence that already encompassed Martinique, Guadeloupe, and, most significantly, Saint-Domingue. For more than a century, Spain had been France's foremost enemy, with only brief periods of alliance; and this pattern was readily apparent in 1673–86, when the two were at, or close to, war for most of the period, a situation that recurred from 1689 to 1697.

Louisiana was less accessible to British attack than Acadia (Nova Scotia), in part because of its greater distance from British naval bases, and in part because of the lack of a nearby British colony like Massachusetts capable of providing substantial military assistance for any expedition. However, the conflicts in the Caribbean in the 1690s and 1700s indicated that British limitations in the region were not restricted to the surrounding coasts but were more generally a reflection of the difficulties of employing amphibious power successfully in a situation in which Britain lacked the capabilities it had developed by the 1750s. Yet, in most of the West Indian islands it was a case of European states fighting each other (rather than Natives), which ensured that naval strength and amphibious power could offer a lot. On the Continent, in contrast, there was the further issue of the Native Americans. This problem was less apparent if operations were a case of attacking or defending ports such as St. Augustine in Florida, but even then, Native assistance could be highly significant. Such assistance was far more significant in the interior, and provided an opportunity to protect and advance interests. Nevertheless, at the same time, the pressure to provide assistance helped create tension between and among Native groups, for example the powerful Iroquois League. As a result, while some Natives eagerly sought cooperation with Europeans, others pursued neutrality, as with the Iroquois' Grand Settlement of 1701.[7]

The foundation of Louisiana and the retention of Canada were impressive French achievements in the face of greater British naval power, although the sugar plantations of (French) Saint-Domingue or (British) Jamaica produced far more profit than did the fur trade of the entire Mississippi Basin. Moreover, meanwhile, British North America had considerably expanded its demographic lead over its French rival. This development was readily apparent in the attempts launched on French positions from the 1690s to 1710s, notably the contributions made by New England in manpower, ships, supplies, and money, and these indicated the extent to which colonial autonomy was already a significant part of the geopolitics of the British Empire. Much of this colonial power, however, was directed not against the French Empire but rather against Native Americans judged hostile. Moreover, a key way to elicit colonial support for action against France was to present it as the inspiration of Native hostility. King Philip's War in 1675–76 gave the British colonists clear control of southern New England, and, although the war saw significant cooperation between colonists and Natives, the conflict also helped link a sense of colonial identity with a military self-sufficiency.[8]

Whatever the problems of using colonial military forces, British officials benefited from the greater stability in political relations in and with their colonies from the 1690s compared to the tumultuous late 1670s and 1680s, the period of Bacon's Rebellion in Virginia (1676), the "Huy and Crye" rebellion in Maryland (1676), and the disruption linked to the authoritarian schemes of James, Duke of York, later James II, and their eventual overthrow.

By 1730, there were fewer than 42,000 French colonists in North America compared with 400,000 British Americans: the former a reflection of the exclusionary nature of French immigration policy as opposed to the British decision to use its colonies as a refuge for the unwanted. The role of government in this contrast represented a sacrifice of the colonial option by France as great as Louis XIV's willingness to cede

colonial claims in 1713 as an aspect of his focus on dynastic and continental interests.[9]

The buoyancy of the British colonies reflected their rapidly rising population and a degree of economic liberalism. Neither was true
of their French rivals. For example, the fur-trading network of the Hudson's Bay Company competed with the French who, from 1632 until 1681,
prohibited travel without permission in the Canadian interior, leading
to the illegal trade of the *coureurs de bois,* unlicensed fur traders. In addition, monopolistic practices and taxation were burdens on the fur trade,
making French products in Canada more expensive. The interior trade
was not liberated until 1681, although it was still regulated thereafter by
means of a system of permits. Liberalization led to a large supply of beaver in Montreal, but the response was not an acceptance of the opportunities and problems of the free market, but rather more regulation. In
1696, a royal edict closed most interior trading posts and ended the permit system, and the angry *coureurs de bois,* unable to trade with Montreal,
instead sold their furs to the British. The permit system was restored in
1716, a liberalization in French terms, but still one that restricted the fur
trade and also made it easier to force the traders to pay taxes.[10]

Whereas company controls over British activity such as those of the
Hudson's Bay Company became less significant, not least with the decline of proprietary powers in the settlement colonies such as Maryland,
the situation was different in the French colonies. There, alongside the
royal powers seen with mercantilist practices and ethos, there was also
profiteering and clientage by officials. None helped the development
of France's colonies.[11] The latter were heavily dependent on an ability to
benefit from relations with the Native Americans, linking France's transoceanic networks to the riverine systems that channeled exchange in the
interior of the continent. As a result, French imperialism and dynamics, in part, was inserted into the continuities of Native development.
The same was true of the British colonies, but their rapid demographic
growth and the related development of agrarian society created a different pattern to that of dependent links with the Natives.[12] This contrast
was to be important in the development of an independent America.

# 4

## MULTIPLE CURRENTS
## 1715-53

The success we met with in trade was principally owing to the
settlement and improvement of our colonies which are now become a
fountain of wealth and the only branch of commerce, except that with
Portugal, which gives a balance in favour of the British nation.

Old England, *18 February (os) 1744*

The lure of the interior coexisted with the pressures arising from transoceanic links; there was coexistence but only at times close interaction.
It is possible to present an account suggesting some sort of seamless link
between frontiers and metropoles, provinces and capitals, but the reality was of a far more episodic and complex relationship both then and
in other periods: links existed, but there were cross-currents including
those arising from different priorities.

French policy provided a good example of this situation. The French
were particularly active in the interior of North America, and their activities were far-flung. Fort Niagara was rebuilt in the 1720s. In the 1730s,
Pierre Gaultier de La Vérendrye built a series of posts toward the sea
then believed to be in what is now western Canada: Fort St. Charles
(1732) on the Lake of the Woods was followed by Fort Maurepas (1734)
at the southern end of Lake Winnipeg, and by Fort La Reine (1738) on
the Assiniboine River. Fort Bourbon (1739) took the French presence to
the northwest shore of Lake Winnipeg, Fort Dauphin (1742) established
their presence on the western shore of Lake Winnipegosis, and Fort La
Corne (1753) was founded near the Fords of the Saskatchewan. These
fords were a crucial node of Native trade routes first reached by French

explorers in 1739–40, and part of a geography of influence and power very different to that of the later world of roads and railways.

These explorations enhanced the French position in the fur trade, but did not bring the hoped-for route to the Pacific. In 1738, La Vérendrye set off from Fort La Reine to find the "great river" reported to run west to the Pacific from near the headwaters of the Missouri. The expedition reached the Missouri near modern Bismarck in North Dakota. In 1742–43, he sent two of his sons on a further search for the Pacific. They crossed much of Dakota before turning back short of the River Platte because their Native companions feared attack.

Activity on the Pacific coasts had no links with those of Europeans in the interior, reflecting an aspect of the way in which North America was not yet a unit. In the North Pacific, the impulse to Russian territorial expansion and scientific development provided by Peter the Great bore fruit. In 1724, he ordered the Dane Vitus Bering to discover a serviceable sea route from Siberia to North America. Sailing from Okhotsk in 1728, Bering navigated the strait separating Asia from America that now bears his name, although he failed to sight Alaska due to the fog. In 1733, Bering was told to follow a different route, sailing across the North Pacific. He did so with Aleksey Chirikov in 1741. The two were separated at sea. They explored the Alaskan coast and the Aleutians, but storms, scurvy, and an inability to work out his location led Bering's ship to winter in the Komandorskis where Bering died.[1]

Such activity did not involve clashes with other states. In contrast, near and on the Gulf of Mexico, war with Spain in 1719 led to the French capture of East Texas and of Pensacola, the major Spanish base in West Florida, both to surprise attacks. Spain was vulnerable as a result of the costs incurred in the recent War of the Spanish Succession, because Philip V was more concerned about the conflict in Spain itself (attacked by British and French forces) and in Sicily (invaded by Spanish forces in 1718), and because France had more military possibilities as a consequence of Britain's active encouragement and support. The situation prefigured that in 1818–19 in that Britain then was unwilling to provide backing for Spanish Florida against the United States.

Returning to the war begun in 1719, Pensacola was recaptured by an expedition from Havana, the key Spanish base for the Gulf, before being taken again by the French and their local allies, the Choctaw. The Spaniards, however, regained it at the subsequent peace negotiated in 1720, while an expeditionary force reestablished their position in East Texas in 1721.

This rivalry encouraged the French to look north from Louisiana. In 1719, Bénard de La Harpe reached modern Oklahoma in his search for Native trade and a new route to New Mexico with which the French wished to develop trade links independent of Spanish control, an aspiration that looked toward the expansionism of the Republic of Texas in the early 1840s. Further north, interest in the Missouri and the nearby lands in 1719 led to a treaty-making expedition that reached the Pawnee of southern Nebraska, and, five years later, to the establishment of Fort d'Orléans on the north bank of the Missouri near its confluence with the Mississippi. A mission westward from there reached the Padouca, possibly the Comanche, in modern central Kansas, in 1724, and found them willing to trade, but the initiative could not be sustained from distant Louisiana, a colony then in serious difficulties, and, in 1728, Fort d'Orléans was abandoned.

Eleven years later, a group of nine from New France led by Pierre Mallet crossed Kansas en route from the Missouri to the Spanish base at Santa Fe. They opened up a precarious trade route, but that was unwelcome to the Spanish authorities, although their power was limited. In 1766–68, when the Marqués de Rubí inspected northern New Spain, he came to the conclusion that much was occupied by Spain only in theory and that the frontier line was imaginary.[2]

The French were dependent on the cooperation of Native Americans. They traded with them extensively, while their settlements relied on local allies, such as the Choctaw near Louisiana. Agreements and alliances, in turn, drew the French into local rivalries, for example supporting the Potawatomi against the Fox tribe of modern Illinois. A series of French–Native attacks were launched against the Fox in 1712, 1715, 1716, 1728, 1730, 1731, and 1734. Indeed, the governor, Charles Beauharnais, sought to exterminate the Fox. By 1738, the tribe, once 10,000 strong, numbered only a few hundred.

In Louisiana, French territorial expansion was an issue. Fort Toulouse, founded on the Alabama River system in 1717, was designed to limit British expansion from the Carolinas, and the alliance with Britain from 1716 to 1731 did not prevent concern about British intentions toward Louisiana, especially approaches to the Native population and the provision of arms to them. The French competed with the British to win Native allies, and both this competition, and a belief in it being more central and extensive than was in fact the case, encouraged this activity and led to diplomatic representations.[3] Similarly, the French and Spaniards competed among the Alabama and the Creek in the late 1710s, establishing a regional pattern that was to last, with important variations in participants, until the end of Spanish Florida in 1819–21.

Non-Native powers, and the goods and opportunities they provided, were thus fed into local antagonisms, helping to fuel them at the same time that the powers were affected, if not manipulated. Dependence on European goods increasingly affected Native household economies and political alignments.[4] This process continued until America became the sole effective power after the War of 1812, with neither Britain nor Mexico willing to challenge this power by means of Native Americans who themselves were weakened and, in part eventually, forcibly driven away.

Further west, on the Mississippi, upstream from New Orleans, the Natchez initially accepted French trade and expansion and the French were able to establish a fortified trading base at Fort Rosalie (Natchez) in 1716. Nevertheless, in 1729, a French land fraud led to a Natchez attack in which Fort Rosalie was destroyed and more than two hundred settlers killed. Repeating the situation for the Yamasee and Tuscarora in Carolina, the Natchez, however, did not receive the support of other tribes, and in 1731 were crushed by the French and the Choctaw in a campaign of systematic extermination. The French began a practice of burning prisoners alive.[5]

Nevertheless, the cost of the rebellion hit the colony's proprietor, the Company of the Indies, leading the Crown to resume control of Louisiana in 1731. The uprising showed the weakness of the colony, as it had been necessary to call in troops from France. The larger population base of the British colonies made them more robust. In his *Description de la Louisiane* (Paris, 1688), Louis Hennepin, a missionary who had accompanied La Salle, described Louisiana as the future breadbasket for the French Empire, a fertile area able to produce wine and foodstuffs for the

French West Indies. Reality proved otherwise. Fort Rosalie had been the center of the tobacco industry, and its destruction greatly harmed attempts to develop economic links with France and the French West Indies, and this contributed to Louisiana's marginal character, a character only really ended after the development of American settlement in Kentucky and Tennessee, when it became the outlet for a buoyant economic region.

The war with the Natchez led to a spread of French commitments. Having been driven back by the Natchez in an attempt to reach the Arkansas country in 1731, the French established a garrison at Arkansas Post in 1732 in order to keep an eye on the Chickasaw. The remnants of the Natchez had taken refuge with the Chickasaw, who were both rivals of the pro-French Choctaw and who, partly as a result, traded with the British and looked to their assistance.[6] Chickasaw independence concerned the French, who in 1736 launched attacks from New France and Louisiana. Both were ambushed and defeated, and a large number of French captives were burnt to death. However, in 1739, a larger force was concentrated, again from both New France (Canada) and Louisiana. Intimidated, the Chickasaw agreed to a truce, but they remained aligned with the British, and, in 1749, drove the French from their position at Arkansas Post, an aspect of the instability in European–Native relations after the War of the Austrian Succession.[7] This instability contributed to French moves against both pro-British Natives and the prospect of British expansion, moves that led to renewed conflict with the British colonists in 1754.

The campaigns of the 1720s–40s in the American interior were far from the concern of most French policymakers, and indeed the cause of the colonies was patronized by Maurepas, the active and talented Minister of the Marine, but not a figure central to foreign policy. The marginal economic nature of French North America did not help. Grain, fish, and timber from Canada and Newfoundland helped support the French West Indies, but agricultural exports from Canada were limited, while, although the "Illinois Country" – the mid-Mississippi valley – was more suitable for grain, it was too distant to spur large-scale immigration.[8]

The attention of French policymakers, such as the octogenarian Cardinal Fleury, the head of the ministry from 1726 until his death in 1743, remained focused on Europe, and the principal exception, as far as the New World was concerned, was the Caribbean. Thus, Britain and Spain went to war in 1739 over trade there. In contrast, the likely consequences of the new British colony of Georgia for the Spaniards in Florida was a secondary issue, although it was one that led to frequent Spanish complaints in the late 1730s,[9] as well as encouraging the Spaniards to improve the fortifications of St. Augustine.

A focus on Georgia can encourage the idea that it was a key issue, but both the British and Spanish governments and British public opinion were more concerned with Caribbean trade. Yet, establishing the primacy of other power politics does not lessen the role of competition in North America. Instead, this understanding shifts attention in North America to local agents, both officials and the settler population. At this level, relations with the Native Americans tended to bulk larger as an issue than to policymakers in Europe. Thus, many New Englanders were more troubled by the Abenaki, and by the French as their allies, than by Anglo–French relations outside this context.

The challenge from the Native Americans came first as far as Spain was concerned beyond the Gulf of Mexico. The pressure the Spaniards suffered reflected both the deficiencies of European warfare and developments among their opponents. As far as the former was concerned, the Spanish attempt to create an impregnable cordon of *presidios* (fortified bases) to protect their northern possessions lacked adequate resources. It was hoped that the *presidios* would provide protection, and thus an incentive, for those Natives considering a shift from their nomadic existence to a fixed agricultural life. In turn, such cultural and religious converts would become loyal subjects who might serve as an example to others. This prospectus proved overly optimistic. Moreover, the strategic role of the *presidios* was anyway vitiated by the ability of Native American war parties to bypass them without difficulty. There was no equivalent to the role of deep-water anchorages for warfare between European states, a role that made fortification worthwhile along coastlines.

Moreover, population shifts on the Great Plains, especially the southward movement of the Comanche and the Ute, put pressure on the Spaniards, and this pressure was accentuated by the impact of the spread of firearms and horses. As earlier in the northeast in the seventeenth century, this spread reflected not only competition between European powers but also lack of certainty on the part of individual powers as to how appropriate it was to trade with firearms.

Those living near Spanish settlements in the southwest in the early seventeenth century had been the first Native Americans to acquire horses, and their use spread northward, by trade and theft, to the Rocky Mountains and the Great Plains. The Apache and Comanche had the horse before the end of the century, and the Cheyenne and Pawnee by 1755. In the eighteenth century, more horses were acquired from Europeans trading from the St. Lawrence Valley. A major equestrian culture developed on the Great Plains, and the combination of firearms and horses made the tribes of the Plains a formidable military challenge to each other and to Europeans.

The spread and use of firearms and horses forced the Spaniards to reconsider their military methods, as the Native tribes were able to respond with considerable flexibility to Spanish tactics. Spanish expeditions, such as those against the Apache in 1732 and 1775, were hindered, in turn, by the lack of fixed points for them to attack. Punitive expeditions were, at best, of limited value. These expeditions were dependent anyway on support drawn from a shifting pattern of Native alliances; thus Opata were recruited for expeditions against Apache. Moreover, rebellions, such as that of the Pima of Arizona in 1751, underlined the fragility of Spanish achievement.

There was no expansion of New Spain in the early eighteenth century comparable to that of Portuguese Brazil where new Captaincies were founded for São Paulo (1709), Minas Gerais (1720), Goiáz (1746), and Mato Grosso (1748). These represented a major advance into the interior, and one that was encouraged greatly by the mining profits obtained from Minas Gerais. Had the northward expansion of New Spain matched that of Portugal in Brazil, or even the growth of the Spanish presence east of the Andes, then the geopolitics of North America would have been very different. However, the higher density of the Native population in central Mexico and their generations-long experience as residents of sedentary agricultural communities made that area far more attractive to commercial agriculture. Further north, the terrain was hostile, not least with the lack of water, while Native American strength was a major factor and was more significant than in much of Brazil, although the Portuguese experienced serious problems there, and were unable to overcome the Mura of Amazonia.

Moreover, the distance from the Gulf and Pacific coasts to Santa Fe, the main center of Spanish activity, was great, and, as yet, there was no northward movement into California and no effective development of Texas. There was Spanish activity, as with the foundation of Tucson in 1695, but nothing to compare with that of the French or British in North America in this period. Moreover, much activity was defensive, with the expansion of the presidial system in Sonora designed to protect northern Mexico from raiding by Apache and by Hokan-speaking nomads from the desert coast on the Gulf of California.[10] However, the establishment of missions on the coast of lower California led to the search for a land route from Mexico around the head of the Gulf of California in the 1690s and 1700s. Father Eusebio Kino, a Jesuit missionary, who in 1687 founded the mission of Nuestra Señora de los Doloros, was responsible for a large number of expeditions for both proselytizing and geographical ends.[11]

Religious energy was important to the Spanish imperial mission, and helped justify it. When Santa Fe was regained in 1692 after the Pueblo rebellion in 1680, there was a reimposition of Catholic control: Franciscan priests absolved Natives for their apostasy and baptized those born after 1680, with the governor serving as godfather for the children of the prominent. In 1697, in the first clash for control of lower California, the battle of Loreto Conchō, a well-armed Spanish missionary party, fought off a Native attack, and victory was followed by the spread of Christianity; as elsewhere during the Iberian conquest of Latin America, smaller, weaker, Native groups proved more receptive to conversion.[12]

Also in 1697, when Nojpeten, the capital of the Maya people known as Itza, was stormed, Martín de Ursúa, the interim governor of Yucatán, ordered his men to plant the flag with the royal arms of Spain and religious standards among the Itza temples "in which the majesty of God had been offended by idolatries." Ursúa thanked God for his victory and then joined soldiers and Franciscans in destroying a large number of "idols." This was religious war against opponents presented as guilty of human sacrifice, cannibalism, and killing priests, and there were very heavy losses among Nojpeten's defenders.

This, however, was no easy conquest, for the Spaniards found it difficult to support their new position. They were helped, however, by the rapid decline of the Itza under the pressures of Spanish seizures of food, terrible epidemics, probably influenza and later smallpox, the capture of much of their leadership by the Spaniards, and subsequent disputes among the Itza. An Itza rebellion in 1704 was ultimately unsuccessful, and the Spaniards were able to impose a measure of control thanks to moving the population into towns and Christian missions. Those who evaded the control lived in isolated forest areas, but were no longer able to challenge Spanish dominance.[13]

The conquest of the Itza took place almost two centuries after Cortés arrived in Mexico, which indicates the incompleteness and difficulty of the Spanish conquest there. There was no lack of Spanish governmental effort and drive in the late seventeenth century,[14] but, under Charles II (r. 1665–1700) and Philip V (r. 1700–46), this activity was very much focused on Europe, while, in the New World, the Vice-Royalty of New Spain was unable to provide the necessary impetus. Indeed, its obligations were far-flung, including responsibility for modern Venezuela until 1739. Venezuela was a source of cacao, tobacco, cotton, coffee, sugar, and indigo; Cuba of tobacco, sugar, and hides; and Mexico of sugar, dyestuffs, cacao and, in particular, silver. There were no equivalent exports from Florida or New Mexico.

Furthermore, New Spain had to focus on defense against British attack in the Caribbean, especially with the Wars of the Spanish Succession (1702–13), the Quadruple Alliance (1718–20), and of Jenkins' Ear (1739–48). Important episodes included Admiral Vernon's seizure of Porto Bello in 1739, and the earlier British blockade there in 1726–27 when the two powers fought a quasi-war, and also the large-scale, but unsuccessful, British expedition against Cartagena in 1741. Already, in 1672–87, in response to an unsuccessful attack in 1668 by Robert Searles, an English pirate, the Spaniards had constructed at St. Augustine the Castillo de San Marcos, a massive stone fortress with a permanent garrison that saw off British sieges in 1702, 1728, and 1740.

Later in the eighteenth century, the Spaniards were to make a greater effort, developing a position in California, exploring further north, and recovering Florida from Britain.[15] Had comparable activity been seen in the early decades, then it is likely that a very different impression would have been gained about Spanish capabilities and, moreover, one that would have affected not only the impression of dynamics across North America, but also of Spanish potential before and after. However, Ferdinand VI (r. 1746–59) resisted French pressure to act against Britain and warnings that, otherwise, the Spanish colonies would follow those of France in being attacked. Far from being driven to align with France by fear of British expansion or by dynastic links, Ferdinand was reasonably close to Britain. In contrast, his more active half-brother and successor, Charles III (r. 1759–88) was concerned about a fundamental shift of oceanic power toward Britain and, largely as a consequence, was far readier to cooperate with France, which led to a major change in the geopolitics of the Atlantic world.

Despite the challenges from Britain and, later and more indirectly, Russia to Spanish control in its northern American borderlands, Spain was helped by the extent to which most of its Latin American empire was not under external pressure. While Portugal was ruled by Philip IV of Spain, Brazil had been successfully attacked by the Dutch in 1630, leading to the establishment of New Holland, a colony regained by Portugal in 1654. Spain and Portugal also clashed over control of the northern shore of the Plate estuary, in the area of modern Uruguay, with Portugal holding the Colónia do Sacramento from 1680 to 1705, 1715, 1750, and 1762 to 1777. Compared to the struggle between France and Britain in North America, this was a small-scale and contained dispute.

As with the French and British, it is inappropriate to focus on hostility between Spain and the Native Americans if that leads to an overlooking of the important rivalries between the Native Americans. Indeed, these rivalries helped the Spaniards reoccupy Santa Fe in 1692. Moreover, the Comanche defeated the Penxaye Apache in the 1700s, and, in the second half of the century, had a lengthy struggle with their former allies, the southern Ute, who had themselves defeated the Navajo in the 1710s to 1750s.

Although they benefited from Native American support, for instance from the Catawba,[16] the British also faced determined resistance. The Yamasee, with Creek support, nearly destroyed the colonies in the Carolinas in 1715, while guerrilla warfare by the Abenaki in Dummer's War (1722–27) kept British settlers out of Vermont. These conflicts underline the role of Native agency and the complexity of relations, with traditional Native rivalries playing an important role, but also diplomacy, as when both the Creek and Carolinians sought to influence the Cherokee during the Yamasee war; in the end, the Cherokee hoodwinked the Carolinians into the war with the Creek.[17]

These conflicts become more prominent in this period because of the lack of sustained warfare between the European powers. Yet, the latter remained in the background, which helped ensure that a major dimension of the geopolitics of North America was latent. Moreover, the geopolitical and military significance of the Atlantic littoral was downplayed because of the lack of this warfare. Instead of ports, such as Pensacola, which the French indeed captured from Spain in 1719, the focus for contention was on river routes. Nevertheless, the significance of the ports was shown by the major difference between the forts designed to fend off Native American attacks, which were based on simple palisade designs, and the more elaborate fortresses built to resist European-style sieges, such as Charleston and Halifax where the British followed the models of Vauban's fortifications. To take these fortresses, it was necessary to have an artillery train and thus the related transport and protection systems: roads and troops or warships. The latter provided both transport and firepower.

Halifax anchored Britain's presence in Nova Scotia, providing a key military and governmental base that helped support an often complex, and in the end harsh, policy of controlling both Natives and French settlers.[18] For some commentators, Nova Scotia, moreover, offered a control on Britain's other colonies. A memorandum in the papers of Sir Robert Walpole, head of the ministry from 1720 to 1742, presented Nova Scotia as a province that would "raise a considerable revenue to the Crown, make a frontier against our French neighbours, and drain a great number of inhabitants from New England where they are daily aiming at an independency and very much interfere with the trade of their mother kingdom."[19] Halifax also became important as a naval base, and, as such, provided Britain with a capability both south along the Atlantic seaboard, and north into the Gulf of St. Lawrence.[20]

One impressive European-style fortress, Louisbourg on Cape Breton, played a major role in the geopolitics of the period as it was seen as the linchpin of France's forward defense for Canada, as well as a threat to Britain's North American colonies. Yet, as a reminder of the need to understand the wider Atlantic logic of developments in North America, Louisbourg, founded in 1720, was designed to support the French presence in the Newfoundland fisheries against the British. These fisheries remained important to France, with large quantities of dry cod exported to Europe. Louisbourg also served as a halfway port between the French West Indies and France. Thus, the construction of this fortress, on which large sums were spent from the 1720s, should be seen in a global context, a concept for which Atlantic history serves a short hand. Much to the pleasure of New England and of London mercantile circles,[21] Louisbourg was captured in 1745 by a Massachusetts force supported by British warships, only to be controversially returned as a result of the Treaty of Aix la Chapelle (1748) that ended the war formally begun in 1744.

Far less was sent by France on fortifications in the North American interior, although they were seen as important to anchoring a presence. Moreover, this process accelerated with time, so that the British built more forts in the 1720s to 1740s than earlier. These forts were more formidable than the defenses created by the Native Americans, although the Fox fort on the Illinois Grand Prairie had a heavily fortified palisade and maze of trenches that offered protection from French gunfire in 1730. However, the Fox lacked cannon.

Fortresses were important because their garrisons could resist and harass raiding parties, but they did not guarantee control of the interior. Moreover, the European presence was weakened because, after the unsuccessful 1711 Quebec expedition, the British sent few regulars to North America until the 1750s. French fears in 1735, when war seemed a prospect, of British attacks on Quebec and Louisiana,[22] were not realized. Moreover, the ability of the Europeans to travel by sea, an ability anyway challenged by storms such as those that helped wreck the French amphibious attempt to regain Louisbourg in 1746, became less valuable once they moved away from coastal regions. In addition, European success in frontier warfare depended in part on adaptation to the way of war of the Native Americans and/or on their assistance. Similarly, Natives were able to learn from their own failures and those of other tribes, and to adapt accordingly.[23]

The power balance was shifted less by weaponry than by demography. The Europeans came in increasing numbers, especially in the British colonies. By contrast, Native American numbers did not grow. Moreover, although themselves in flux as new settlers, immigrants had settled ideas of government and social organization. In contrast, traditional Native American cultural and religious beliefs and imperatives were lost with conversion to Christianity. Many Native Americans converted, and then tended to support the Europeans.

Alongside rising numbers, advantages of mobility, logistical support, and reinforcement enabled Europeans to concentrate forces at points of conflict. This ability was to be seen most clearly, however, in warfare between European powers, and was less effective in the interior. Less, rather than ineffective, is a key distinction, but this point opens up parallels between the difficulty in controlling the interior in the first half of the century and the problems encountered by the British when operating into the interior during the American War of Independence. Yet, this was not an undifferentiated interior; instead, there were interiors, regions distant from the coastal littoral, although scarcely separate to it; and these regions were in a dynamic situation.

The varying experience of the interior owed most to the complexity in relations with the Native Americans, relations that differed both in peace and in war. In confronting this challenge, there was a degree of adaptability by both regular troops and by colonists,[24] although the extent to which the regulars needed to adapt has been questioned as there was already considerable familiarity with irregular warfare in Europe. In short, the American interior might have been unknown space to the regulars, but its strangeness should not be exaggerated.[25]

There has also been debate about the extent to which the colonists did or were able to adapt. As a result, North America has been presented as a space where European-style tactics continued to prevail.[26] It has also been argued that the interior was overcome in part due to the devising of a distinctive way of war based on irregular and total warfare directed against hostile populations, as in the destruction of Native crops and villages.[27]

The key change in this period was the demographic revolution caused by large-scale settlement by Europeans, as well as the enforced settlement of African slaves, both linked to a stronger racial consciousness that also affected the British colonists' perception of Native Americans.[28] European and African settlement changed the geography of North America and, with it, its geopolitics. Change was most modest in Mexico as new settlement there was limited. In the mid-1740s, the respective percentages in central Mexico of Natives, Spaniards (whether born in Mexico or immigrants), *mestizos* (mixed), and *pardos* (wholly or partly black) were 74 and then about 9 each.[29] Racial distinctions extended to those of mixed blood, with individuals who looked European more likely to receive favorable treatment than those who looked African or Native. There was a tendency to social allocation based on pigment that reflected racist assumptions and influenced the different access of mixed-blood individuals to economic and other opportunities. Thus, in Santa Fe, Spaniards of pure blood were the top stratum of society.

In contrast to Mexico, the slave population became more important in British North America as a result of a transformation in the economy of the southern colonies. The number of slaves in British North America rose from about 20,000 in 1700 to more than 300,000 by 1763, particularly as South Carolina and, later, Georgia were developed as plantation economies, supplementing those on the Chesapeake. In both, rice became an additional plantation crop, reflecting the particular opportunities of the tidewater environment.

Yet the crucial development was the rise in the European population, a population that helped provide Britain with a key margin of advantage. In 1750, François-Marie Durand, the perceptive French chargé d'affaires in London, urged his government to pay attention to the large number of emigrants going to British North America.[30] This rise ensured that the racial politics could be one in which the British settlers dominated not only the slaves but also the Natives on whom they had earlier been dependent.[31] The numbers of the latter continued to be hit by disease, with smallpox wiping out about half the Cherokee in the late 1730s. The demographic context changed for good from the 1740s from which there was a marked upward trend in the population of Europe, and thus more people available as migrants. American dependence on European developments was very much shown in this geopolitics of population growth and movement.

# 5

# WAR FOR DOMINANCE
# 1754-64

With regard to the war in America, he said, he could not help wondering
at the absurdity of both nations, to exhaust their strength, and wealth,
for an object that did not appear, to him, to be worth the while, that
he was persuaded, by next year, both nations would be sick of it.

*Frederick the Great of Prussia, 1756*

The French and Indian War takes central place in this period, although
most British readers will know it better as the Seven Years' War. This war
left Britain the dominant power in North America and its consequences
inadvertently helped prepare the way for the War of American Independence, prefiguring the relationship between the Mexican War and the
Civil War, and serving as a reminder that unforeseen results powerfully
subvert deterministic accounts of developments.

Yet, like other periods, these years should not simply be seen in terms
of rivalry between the European powers. Instead, Native Americans play
a major role, not least because their relationship with the rivalry between
Britain and France helped lead the two powers to war in the mid-1750s.
Furthermore, this episode, and the eventual role of the Native Americans in at least one key British operation, the advance on Fort Duquesne
in 1758, did not exhaust their importance. Instead, conflict in the early
1760s between them and the British, both Cherokee War and Pontiac's
War, underlined the extent to which victory over France did not end the
challenge posed by North America to British power. If the Native Americans were unsuccessful in ending the British advance, so also were the
French, but the measure of British success was more complex than sug-

gested by this remark. Moreover, the extensive warfare with the Native Americans helped increase colonial sensitivity about the policies of the British government, as well as the latter's concern about the military presence in North America. The financial implications of this presence played a major role in causing crisis between colonists and government.

As a reminder that the last issue did not only involve Britain, it is instructive to consider the situation facing Spain. On 16 March 1758, about two thousand Comanche and allies, armed with at least one thousand French muskets, attacked the San Sabá mission, eighty miles northwest of modern Austin, Texas, killing all but one of the missionaries, beheading the effigy of Saint Francis, and forcing the soldiers to leave the nearby *presidio*. More significantly, this blow, and the defeat two years later of a Spanish attack on the Taovaya village in the Red River valley, led the Spaniards to abandon efforts to convert the Apache and, in 1769, the *presidio* was removed from the San Sabá valley. By the end of the century, most of the missions and *presidios* in the north had been abandoned.

When superior resources could be brought to bear in the New World, the situation could be very different. For example, firepower – cannon and muskets – was responsible for the victory of Caibaté in 1756, by which a joint Portuguese–Spanish army smashed a Native force attempting to block its advance on the Jesuit missions of Paraguay and Brazil. However, firepower capability could only achieve so much. In some areas, both in Latin America and in North America, hostile terrain, determined opposition, or the absence of major European pressure ensured success for Native forces. The British defeat in 1755, in the first key battle in the French and American War, fits into this pattern, at least in demonstrating the potential of regular European forces for failure. This defeat arose because of a British attempt to use force to settle what appears to be the Gordian knot of North American problems by establishing a strong presence in the Ohio Valley. The British and French commissioners, to whom disputes over the Canadian frontier had been referred by the peace conference at Aix-la-Chapelle in 1748, had failed to settle them and, as the local agents of both powers jockeyed for advantage, fighting broke out.

The Marquis de la Galissonière, interim governor-general of New France in 1749–50, had pressed for strengthening Canada and for the containment of the British colonies. To that end, Fort St. Jean was re-built in 1748 to strengthen the French position near Lake Champlain and a new wagon road linked the fort to Montreal. Niagara was also rebuilt, and in 1750 the French erected Fort Rouillé (Toronto). In 1749, the French had sent a small force into the Ohio Valley under Céleron de Blainville, although it had little effect, bar burying lead plates asserting French sovereignty. In 1752–54, however, the French sent more troops, drove out British traders, intimidated Britain's Native allies, and con-structed forts. Both sides were convinced that the other was stirring up the hostility of Native Americans and was acting in an aggressive fashion. Contributing to the volatility, there were also commercial in-terests, notably the fur trade, which interacted with Native alliances, and the pursuit of land claims by British colonial interests. Exploration, meanwhile, was leading the British to new possibilities, as in 1750 when Thomas Walker, traveling from Virginia, reached Cumberland Gap, the gateway to Kentucky. Two years later, John Finley realized that the Gap indeed opened the way to these lowlands.

It is important to set policies in context, as they indicate a greater assertiveness on both sides. In the French case, there was a dynamic stra-tegic policy. For example, aside from the drive into the Ohio Valley, the French presence north of Lake Superior was strengthened by the build-ing of Fort-à-la-Carpe on the Albany River in 1751 and the taking of the Hudson's Bay Company post of Henley House in 1755. This assertiveness was not simply directed against the British: the destruction of villages and crops forced the Chickasaw to terms in 1752.

Furthermore, in India, Joseph-François Dupleix, the governor of the main French base at Pondicherry from 1742, followed an expansionist and interventionist policy. In a parallel with North American geopoli-tics, this policy entailed an interaction with Indian potentates in which the French, having proved their prowess, sought to profit from the situ-ation, while at the same time they served the purposes of Indian allies. As, however, with the situation in North America, this emphasis can be counteracted with a view stressing the alien character of French expan-sion and the discontinuities and disruption it caused. In India, as in North America, moreover, the French eventually failed. Drawn into the politics of several Indian states, the French eventually found the local warfare intractable. Dupleix's demands for men and money led to his recall in 1754 and a provisional peace was reached with the British that winter. In North America, it proved harder for both sides to disengage. Royal authority was more directly involved than in India, where it was largely a case of the two East India Companies hiring out troops to rival Indians. Instead, it was the French determination to rely upon establishing forts, rather than on alliances with Native Americans held together by trade, that led to the war with Britain. As was to be repeatedly the case with European expansion, the attempt to increase the degree of control over native peoples, and to make it concrete through fortified positions, led to a reaction not only from these peoples but also from other European powers.

As the crisis of 1754–55 resulted in transformative changes in North America and the British Empire, it is worth considering in some detail, not least from the geopolitical angle. On 3 July 1754, a force of Virginia militia under George Washington, dispatched to resist French moves in the Ohio Valley, was forced to surrender at Fort Necessity in the valley of the River Monongahela, which, in practice, was a vulnerable stockade. Far from making the British government cautious, as the French hoped,[1] British countermeasures, that owed much to concern about domestic criticism of the ministry, increased tension, and negotiations, about what had initially appeared a "bagatelle,"[2] collapsed on the incompatibility of territorial demands.

A particular aspect of geopolitics was related to the competing claims in British and French maps. Maps and the politics of space were closely linked, and indeed led to contention, not only between British and French tracts and maps, but also among the former. For example, one of the tracts, Lewis Evans's *Geographical, Historical, Political, Philosophical and Mechanical Essays: The First Containing an Analysis of a General Map of the Middle British Colonies in America and of the Country of the Confederate Indians* (1755) was criticized in New York, especially by the *New York Mercury,* for acknowledging too many French claims, although it was used by General Braddock in 1755. Criticism of Evans's map led in 1756 to the publication of a second essay by Evans. John Cleveland, the Secretary to the Admiralty, left a volume with relevant tracts dealing with the geography of North America supported by maps, and it also included Ellis Huske's *The Present State of North America* (1755), which backed the cartographer John Mitchell in his pro-British *Map of the British and French Dominions in North America*,[3] and Thomas Jeffery's *Explanation for the New Map of Nova Scotia . . . with the Adjacent Parts of New England and Canada* (1755), which took issue with the accuracy of Mitchell's map. Public interest can be gauged from the fact that two editions of Huske appeared in Boston in 1755 and two in London.[4]

There were also tensions in the politics of British imperial expansion. Enthusiasm for such expansion reflected both political positioning and the strengthening of the public engagement with such expansion as a way to ensure commercial strength and maritime destiny,[5] but, however much linked by opposition to France, the running together of "an empire of the seas," the traditional idea of British power, with the new goal of territorial empire in North America, represented a geopolitical conflation that posed serious problems in policy as well as conception. Partly as a result, it is appropriate to be cautious in presenting an undifferentiated account of British public attitudes and geopolitics, not least because it is unclear how extensive was prewar commitment to territorial expansion. Various government officials in both the colonies and London were very interested in British claims to land in the Ohio Valley prior to the outbreak of fighting,[6] but the war, like many other conflicts, for example the American Civil War, helped foster ambitions that preceded the war, and powerfully so, not only at the governmental level but also in terms of public discussion. Thus, the geopolitics of North America and British ambitions, and the related strategic culture, were changed, indeed transformed, during and by the war, as much as causing it, or setting its alignment. This process does not deny the value of relating expansionism and other geopolitical themes to longer-term sociocultural developments, including, in the case of the mid-eighteenth century, a growing assertiveness on the part of the expanding middling orders in Britain,[7] but the relationship between these developments and policy was complex. Opposition to France, popular opinion, and a geopolitics of North American conquest can all be linked, and the focus on France in British foreign policy from the 1670s certainly encouraged an important shift in the public imagination of Britain as an imperial power toward a greater role for transoceanic interests and concerns.

However, it was not inevitable that this concern should center on North America, still less the Ohio Valley. In the event, the geography of anxiety owed much to a perception of French aggression being concentrated there.

In Britain, as in America both in the colonial period and, even more, when it became independent, the goals of policy were crucial themes in public debate, and geopolitics and strategic culture were thus centrally linked to questions of public politics. The politics of strategy helped provide a considerable measure of continuity to order debate, but, in turn, issues and problems were interpreted and debated in terms of the experience of conflict. As later with independent America, this experience was perceived through the perspective of collective (and contentious) public myths, and thus geopolitics served as an idiom of public debate and policy. In the case of British policy at this juncture – an instance of the situation on other occasions – debate, politics, and policy were in a complex relationship, and shaping this relationship in terms of geopolitics and strategic culture, or rather a particular understanding of them, may lead to an underplaying of this complexity. The clash with the French in the Ohio Valley in 1754 transformed the situation so that, whereas at the start of the year the impact on British politics of the shift in public consciousness toward a greater concern over colonial disputes with the Bourbons, especially with France in North America, was limited, by late 1754, the prevalent opinion in political and governmental circles expressed a need to stand up to France in these disputes.

As a reminder of a question that would recur in the mid-nineteenth century, there was no clear relationship between Britain's North American policy and the more general issues of Britain's diplomatic standing toward France and other European powers. The latter, indeed, were less acute in 1754 than they had been earlier in the decade. In one light, that provided Britain with a window of opportunity for action in America, although as a reminder of the difficulty of drawing conclusions, the evidence for this as a causal relationship is problematic. Moreover, while North America had been a cause of diplomatic activity and ministerial anxiety for a number of years, its sudden rise to prominence in the summer of 1754, with the outbreak of fighting in the Ohio Valley that April, was a surprise to many in London (although not to colonial officials such as Virginia's influential lieutenant-governor, Robert Dinwiddie) and Paris, rather than the product of readily apparent geopolitical forces. This point underlines the nonlinear character of geopolitics: geographical factors may have a long-term role, but they are operative in particular political circumstances, which is a different emphasis to that offered by Fernand Braudel.

The prominence of North American issues in 1754 was enhanced because it matched with a potent and politically loaded theme of public debate, the French threat. In turn, the responses of British ministers were shaped by their own very different attitudes and experience, and here the notion of a geopolitics and strategic culture can appear unduly hegemonic and based on an unsubtle concept of influence. Instead, ministers in 1754–63 were divided over what policies to pursue and how best to pursue them, and notably over the balance of commitments to Europe or America. This argument can be repeated for other episodes discussed in this book, and provides an important element of complexity in considering the struggle for mastery in North America, although issues were not always considered in those terms.

In 1754–55, however, the crisis rapidly escalated in both America and Anglo-French relations, indicating not only the potential linkage between the North American interior and the wider currents of international relations, but also the extent to which this interior could seem sufficiently important to prompt conflict. Thus, in September 1754, William Murray, one of the key government spokesmen in the House of Commons, argued that French successes threatened the future of the tobacco trade, which was, he pointed out, a major source of British customs revenue.[8] This overreaction linked the interior to the coastal littoral to a misleading extent that testified to the sense of threat. The *Monitor*, one of the leading London newspapers, in its issue of 6 September 1755, claimed that "the voice of the people" cried loudly for war "to restrain the ambitious views of the French . . . whose deep concerted schemes, for many years, to drive us out of the American colonies, had almost succeeded." However, there were differences then within the British ministry over policy, while as the crisis of 1754–55 in North America was linked, in 1756, to the outbreak of war between Britain's ally Prussia and France's ally Austria, British ministerial priorities shifted to Europe.

The largely unsuccessful British attempt to intercept French reinforcements for Canada in June 1755 led the French government to recall its
diplomats. On 9 July, an advancing force of British regulars and Virginia
militia under General Edward Braddock was defeated at the Monongahela River close to Fort Duquesne. The well-aimed fire of a smaller
French and Native American force using forest cover proved devastating to a column that simply did not know how to respond. The absence
of Native American allies and of experience in forest warfare was crucial
to Braddock's defeat, a defeat that made a considerable impact on contemporaries, notably in North America where it suggested that the frontier areas lacked security and that the French–Native alliance might carry
all before it. At the same time, the defeat was to have less of an impact on
British domestic opinion than Admiral Byng's failure the following year
to relieve the British garrison on the Mediterranean island of Minorca.
The instances were far from identical, not least as Byng did not show the
fortitude displayed by Braddock, but the greater concern about naval
engagements and events nearer home was readily apparent.

Just over five years after Braddock's defeat, the governor-general
of New France surrendered with the French force in Montreal, bringing
New France to an end. This result reflected both features specific to North
America and those more generally pertinent for the Anglo-French struggle during that war as a whole. Thus, comparisons emerge and deserve
attention. In 1757, poor weather and the presence of a French squadron
ensured that the planned British attack on Louisbourg, and then Quebec,
the sole means to strike a "decisive" step,[9] was not mounted, while the
attack on the port of Rochefort on France's Atlantic coast also failed,
due to inadequate cooperation between naval and army commanders,
and indifferent and hesitant generalship. Similarly, in 1758, British commitments broadened out, not only with troops sent to Germany to help
Frederick the Great (II) of Prussia, but also with a massive three-pronged
offensive against New France.

In Europe as in North America, there was an availability of resources
for the British and a determination to apply them; these helped take the
initiative from the French. The consistent willingness of the government
to send more troops to North America despite commitments elsewhere
is readily apparent.[10] Moreover, the dispatch of troops was linked to na-

val predominance. James, Lord Kilkerran, writing in 1756, noted, "It is with pleasure observed that our new ministry appear to lay the affairs of America so much to heart that so great numbers of troops are going over, which must have considerable convoy, and it is to be hoped that our marine will keep a more sharp look out to prevent the French from adding to their number in that country."[11]

In North America, separate expeditions in 1758 attacked Louisbourg, Carillon (Ticonderoga), and Fort Duquesne. This "vigorous American plan"[12] represented an unprecedented effort at this distance for any world power, one that both changed the geopolitics of North America and yet which can also be discussed in terms of the specifics of political decisions in particular conjunctures, notably the commitment by William Pitt the Elder, one of the two leading British ministers in 1757–61, to a policy of transoceanic expansion and to the argument that this policy was integral to Britain's wider strategy, with Germany and North America interrelated. Pitt was readily persuaded that the idea of "a defensive war in America" was "fruitless and impracticable."[13]

Alongside the stress on the short term in the 1750s, on victory as having transformed the geopolitics of the British Empire, the basis for this transformation had already been laid by the development of British North America, both in itself and as an economic world linked to the West Indies more successfully than the French colonies on the mainland were to their islands. The colonists were regarded as a significant military resource, able to assist the operations of British regulars,[14] although there were also complaints about their divisions.[15] The growing sophistication of British naval strength, particularly an ably managed amphibious capability,[16] was also very important.

In addition, earlier British successes against Nova Scotia and Cape Breton Island had indicated potential and paved the way for further success. A sense of unfinished business was important to the politics and strategy of the war, both in Britain and in its American colonies, especially Massachusetts. That colony had played a key role in the successful 1745 attack on Louisbourg, only to see the fortress handed back in the subsequent peace treaty, not so much to secure British goals elsewhere but as an aspect of a treaty concluded on the basis of the status quo ante bellum: a return to the prewar situation.

Lastly, the British were helped by the sequential nature of their war making: in the Seven Years' War, it was possible to focus on France because conflict with Spain did not begin until 1762, while Britain was not at war with Austria or Russia, despite their being allied to France in conflict with Frederick II of Prussia, who, in turn, was allied to Britain. Charles III of Spain indeed feared such a sequence, with the conquest of Canada making Britain more arrogant and leading it to turn against Spain.[17] The focus on just one opponent brought Britain advantages not only in 1754–61 but also in other circumstances: in taking the initiative in North America in 1814 and 1815 (the latter stages of the War of 1812), and in the possibility of war with the United States over the Oregon question in 1846. In contrast, there was no success for Britain in 1775–78, even though Britain fought the American colonists alone until France's entry into the war in mid-1778.

Had conflict with Spain begun earlier, then it would not have been possible to focus so many military resources on fighting France in North America. Conversely, the course of the conflict there might have been very different as there would have been targets of opportunity in Spanish America, as well as the need to take them in order to compensate for possible Spanish gains at the expense of Britain or of Britain's ally Portugal, which Spain indeed invaded in 1762. That year, Arthur Dobbs, governor of North Carolina, pressed John, 3rd Earl of Bute, George III's favorite adviser, on the value of freeing the Spanish colonies and transforming them into free states allied to Britain, with the latter also gaining Florida and a number of key sites, including Veracruz and the isthmus of Darien.[18] War with Spain earlier would also have had major implications for the Southern colonies, especially neighboring Georgia, while, had French-ruled New Orleans been captured as a result of the war, there would have been pressure to retain it. Thus, the primacy of European power politics emerges clearly. It also had a politico-cultural dimension. The loss of Canada in 1760 and of Louisiana in 1763 was criticized in France by merchants in the Atlantic ports, but had only limited impact elsewhere, not least because these colonies were seen in fashionable circles as barren and profitless. Aristocratic families had scant presence in French North America. In contrast, America was far more important in British public debate.

The deployment of massive British force to America underlined the extent to which the war there with France was an aspect of Atlantic history, and thus undermines the argument that conflict in America should be seen as radically different to that in Europe. Frontier warfare with Native Americans posed particular challenges,[19] but the British army was the key template for colonial military institutions and commanders, and this point qualifies the idea of American exceptionalism as far as conflict was concerned. In 1758, the advance on Carillon, by a force of 6,400 British regulars and 9,000 American provincials, an army that would have been inconceivable in the interior a half-century earlier, became a "stupid"[20] frontal assault, and was a costly failure. Yet, underlining the major British effort in North America,[21] this was not the sole attacking force, and, despite failure in one operation, it was possible to press on. The successful attack on Louisbourg that year involved 13,000 troops and indicated the importance of naval superiority[22] and of army–navy cooperation in the amphibious deployment of striking power. That on Fort Duquesne, by an army of 7,000 men, mostly American provincials, showed the value of experience. Braddock's mistakes were avoided and the French position was weakened when Pennsylvania authorities promised the Native Americans that they would not claim land west of the Appalachians.[23] The consequent shift of Native support, especially of Shawnee and Delaware, obliged the French to give up the Ohio region. Viewed from Europe, this was still a two-sided conflict, whereas, on the ground in the interior, the shifting support and fears of Native American groups could be decisive. A lack of interest in the backcountry was shown by some British commentators, Charles, 3rd Duke of Richmond, a lieutenant-colonel and later a prominent supporter of the American Patriots, writing to his brother George, another officer, that the expedition against Fort Duquesne was "a needless business; it is a difficult job, and when got not worth the taking."[24]

In 1759, however, in a well-prepared campaign,[25] the British concentrated on the St. Lawrence valley, the center of French power, and the sphere where British naval capability, including logistical support, could be used most effectively. The navy convoyed a force of 8,600 troops under James Wolfe to near Quebec. Eventually, Wolfe moved his troops past the city, scaled the cliffs from the river, and, on 13 September, defeated the French outside the city. British defensive firepower hit the French charge and then the British successfully advanced at bayonet point.[26] The events of that day played a key role in the history of North America, although the subsequent capture of Quebec had to be maintained in 1760 in the face of a subsequent French attempt to recapture it. Moreover, the sensitivity of this conflict in modern public history was indicated in 2009 when concerns over Québecois views led to a marked downplaying of the anniversary in Canada. Furthermore, a loss of confidence in the national past, and specifically in the imperial experience, had the same consequence in Britain.

As a reminder of the key interrelationship of events in North America with those in Europe, the British garrison in Quebec was relieved in 1760 by a naval squadron. This naval range owed much to the far smaller size of the French navy, its heavy losses of ships and manpower in 1758, largely to weather and disease, its serious financial problems, the impact of the British blockade, and the British defeat of French fleets in European waters in 1759: at Lagos on the Portuguese coast on 18–19 August and, more decisively, in Quiberon Bay on 20 November. In 1760, the fate of Canada was finally settled, with the three-pronged advance converging on Montreal where the French surrendered. The campaign was an impressive triumph of resources and planning, and indicated the accumulated skill of the British army in North America.[27]

Campaigning was not so much a verdict as a preliminary report, for the results of war were judged by governments and mediated by diplomats. In Britain, there was a debate over which French conquests should be retained and which returned as part of the peace settlement. The territorial clauses of the Peace of Paris of 1763 reflected the decisiveness of Britain's victory in the naval and colonial struggle. There was no possibility of equivalence, as there had been after the War of the Austrian Succession, when Louisbourg was returned in order to regain Madras, which had been captured by the French in the war. Nor was it necessary to destroy Louisbourg and Quebec so that they should be less valuable when returned.[28] Public views played a role, Newcastle commenting in 1758, "the Nation (and, as I hear from Lord Kinnoull, the considerable manufacturers etc. in Yorkshire) are so set upon keeping Louisbourg, that it will be difficult to part with it. . . . Minorca is now despised, and will certainly not be thought any equivalent for Louisbourg."[29] Nevertheless, a debate in Britain as to whether to retain Canada or the conquered West Indian islands of Guadeloupe and Martinique provides an abrupt lesson on the need to put the struggle for mastery in North America in context. Greater economic benefit was seen to derive from the West Indies, but it was also argued that these islands in British hands would cause serious competitive damage to the earlier British sugar islands. In 1761, François de Bussy, the experienced French diplomat (and sometime spy for the British) sent to probe the possibility of peace, reported that the British were readier to return Caribbean gains than Canada.[30] He described the latter as the object of the war and the prime concern of the nation.[31]

A further comparative context is obtained by noting what appeared most significant to the ministers of the day. Thus, in the abortive peace talks of 1761, the French offered Britain the cession of all Canada bar Cape Breton Island, which was to be retained unfortified so that French fishermen could dry their catches from the valuable Newfoundland fishery. This issue had already been raised in 1760.[32] In the event, the Peace of Paris left the French a part of the valuable Newfoundland fishery. Etienne, Duke of Choiseul, the leading French minister, had proved adamant in the negotiations both on Newfoundland[33] and on the West Indies, but not on Canada. The retention of the Newfoundland fishery ensured that, as British critics of the measure predicted,[34] the French had a crucial resource of mariners from which they could recruit for the navy, and this helped them greatly in the War of American Independence.[35] Pitt, who had been firm on the point in 1760–61,[36] attacked the measure in the debate on the Peace Preliminaries in the House of Commons on 9 December 1762. Moreover, Pitt's concern about North American matters had led him to press in 1761 that the plenipotentiaries for any peace talks should include one informed of North American and commercial issues.[37]

The French willingness to cede territory in North America was also shown with Louisiana, for Choiseul had to bring into the peace a disappointed Spain, heavily defeated by Britain in 1762. The key operations in the war occurred in Cuba, the Philippines, and Portugal, but North America served to help adjust the result. Choiseul was determined to maintain the alliance with Spain, and, in October 1762, the Spaniards were offered New Orleans and Louisiana west of the Mississippi as an inducement, and also were advised to cede Florida to Britain in order to regain Cuba, which the British had successfully invaded earlier that year, successfully besieging Havana and thus wrecking Spanish naval power in the West Indies.[38] The bulk of Louisiana for Spain was a return for Britain's insistence on regaining the Mediterranean island of Minorca (Spanish until 1708), which it had lost to French forces in 1756, and which was to have been a Spanish gain from the war. This exchange proved the basis of the eventual settlement and, with Florida, Britain gained Louisiana east of the Mississippi, which became part of the new colony of West Florida. These changes were a challenge to Native Americans, such as Choctaw and the Chickasaw, who relied upon trade with France or Spain. The boundary of Louisiana offered another problematic issue for the future,[39] not least as the watersheds that defined river basins were as yet unknown.

In 1763, there was no equivalent of the 1748 return of Louisbourg to France to outrage British colonists, but the peace negotiations thus underlined the continued salience of European interests and decision makers. The terms were seen there as a triumph for Britain, one that French commentators warned overturned any balance of power overseas. The *Universal Magazine* of March 1763 provided a map of the extent of territory Britain now controlled in North America; it was both a triumphant display of British achievement and a response to reader interest.

This salience of Europe, however, was to be challenged in the Americas over the following decades; and these challenges, although very different in character, reflected the difficulty of setting policy from distant capitals, let alone of maintaining control. At the outset, the end of conflict between the British and French in North America was accompanied in 1759–61 by war with the Cherokee, in which the British deployed regulars, colonial troops, and allied Native Americans such as the Chickasaw, forcing the Cherokee to terms. This bland remark, however, provides no indication of the difficulty of the struggle, nor of the extent to which this war was, in effect, followed by a compromise peace.[40]

Nevertheless, the conflict indicated two, linked, aspects of British strength. First, it proved possible to move troops from elsewhere within what, therefore, was an integrated military system. In one respect, this was a system spanning the entire British Empire but, in practice, there were sectors within this, first the North Atlantic as a whole, in other words including Britain and, crucially, the European commitments sustained from Britain, and, secondly, the Western Atlantic from Canada to the West Indies. Thus, victory in Canada was followed by the southward movement of British military resources, although, in a key indication of needs and opportunities, this process did not mean large-scale operations into Continental America against the Native Americans, nor attacks on Louisiana, Florida, or Mexico. There would have been grave logistical problems for the former, and it would not have been clear what they were designed to achieve. Neither point, however, would have been true of amphibious operations against New Orleans or against St. Augustine, Pensacola, or Veracruz once the war had broadened out to include Spain in 1762. Fuentes, the Spanish envoy in London, pressed the need for preparations against such attacks, Bussy was concerned about Louisiana, and Choiseul was worried that Britain might conquer Mexico, which, he feared, would provide a market for their manufactures and ruin much of France's.[41] The latter outcome would hit the French balance of payments and, in particular, lessen the silver obtained from Veracruz, silver that was used to finance France's imports from India, and much else. As a reminder of the human cost behind such abstractions, the harshness of conditions in Mexican silver mines led in 1766 to an organized withdrawal of labor in order to obtain change, a novel practice.[42]

The movement of silver was an aspect of another key way to conceptualize geopolitics, that of spaces of financial resource. Mexico, Spain, and France were in one such space, competing with Britain, whose fiscal supports rested much more on the gold of the Brazilian colony of its client state Portugal[43] and on the profits of the East India Company than on North America. The Franco-Spanish attack on Portugal in 1762 was thus an assault on Britain's entire imperial system, including its Atlantic dimension. The ability to raise money and at a favorable rate of interest was seen by both domestic and foreign commentators, such as the well-informed Sardinian envoy Count Viry, as crucial to British success.[44]

The British focus in 1762 was not on the mainland but on attacks in the West Indies, first, and successfully, against French islands, and then the costly capture of Havana, an impressive operation made especially deadly for the British by the inroads of yellow fever. The second aspect of British strength seen in the Seven Years' War and in the Cherokee War was their ability to renew operations, notably with new forces, after initial setbacks, and this ability reflected the articulation of forces within the imperial military system.

The Peace of Paris proved a key episode in North American history, both in terms of great power relations and also within the bounds of British North America as understood by the British.[45] The peace was followed by conflict with the Native Americans, because the negotiations had not taken note of their views, while tensions rose as the British failed to provide the Native Americans with anticipated presents, and colonists moved into Native lands. This situation led to Pontiac's War (1763–64), which involved a number of tribes in the Ohio River system, especially the Ottawa under Pontiac, who tried to subordinate tribal rivalries to pan-Native action. Successful attacks were made on a series of British forts while the British were forced to abandon others, and field forces were also ambushed. The British proved less effective at fighting in the woodlands of the frontier zone than their opponents, and the army's dependence on supply routes made it more vulnerable to ambush.

Owing, however, to the British conquest of Canada, the Native Americans had no access to firearms other than those they had captured. The Anglo-French rivalry that had given a measure of opportunity to the Native Americans, providing, for example, French arms and ammunition to the Abenaki of Vermont for use against New England, had been ended. This situation prefigured that which was to face the Native Americans once Anglo–American relations were settled in and after 1815. Furthermore, in 1763–64, large numbers of British troops were deployed. The capacity of the regulars and colonists to respond to Native successes and to mount fresh efforts was indicative of the manpower resources they enjoyed, and the situation was stabilized anew.

This stabilization of relations with the Native Americans, however, entailed the British accepting the limitations of the use of force. Instead, they turned back to diplomacy. Thus, the difficulties of imperial expansion were revealed rapidly after the success over France. These difficulties were seen not only with the Natives[46] but also with the British colonists. Pontiac's War indicated the extent to which mid-century conflict produced both changes and strain in the Native and European societies of eastern North America, strains that increased anxiety and tension over governmental policies.[47] Conflict with Natives tested both regulars and colonials and encouraged the development of experience with what was termed small war, as well as a process of brutalization and fear through conflict in a challenging cultural context.[48] In 1765, nevertheless, despite the enhanced capability represented by experience of small war, most of North America was still under the control of Native Americans and both the Cherokee War and Pontiac's War had indicated their resilience in regions reasonably close to centers of British settlement. In the southeast, moreover, the Creek Confederacy was a potent element, not least adept at playing off different European powers.[49]

The situation was to change radically, however, in part because the colonists, from 1776, gained independence, freedom of action, and greater numbers, but it would be misleading to treat independence as the factor explaining America's development and the subjugation of Native Americans. Indeed, the indigenous populations of Russia, Australia, New Zealand, and Canada were also brought under control while those areas were ruled as part of great imperial states. Yet, in the case of what became the United States, the attitude of the imperial government was significant, as it entailed, alongside the pressure on Native interests, a degree of protection of Native lands.[50] This protection, however, was to be swept aside as part of the overthrow of the British Empire in the Thirteen Colonies.

# 6

# BRITAIN TRIUMPHANT TO
# AMERICA INDEPENDENT
# 1765-76

The empire of America may be said to be the renovation
of youth to the kingdom of Great Britain.

*Anon.*, A Full and Free Enquiry into the Merits of the Peace *(1765)*

Oft told, the story of the breakdown of the imperial link is generally presented in political terms, although Stephen Hornsby has recently advanced a geopolitical thesis. Arguing that profound and longstanding differences existed between the American eastern seaboard and the Atlantic regions of eastern Canada and the West Indies, he sees these differences as being pushed to the fore after the conquest of Canada: "In attempting to govern the enlarged spaces of the British Atlantic, the British government had tightened imperial authority over the seaboard colonies, which, in turn, had provoked a fierce political backlash.... The strength of British power over its Atlantic empire reinforced the imperial government's desire to rein in the continental colonies, while at the same time spurring the colonists to throw off the imperial harness."[1] The attempt by the British government to control the interior threw this issue to the fore. There was no consistent master plan of control, but the determination, with the controversial Royal Proclamation issued on 7 October 1763, to stop settlement, and indeed surveying, in areas seen as rightly Native American, was followed by the Quebec Act of 1774, which allocated much of the interior with the lands west of the Alleghenies and north of the Ohio River going to the Canadian colony. This was a step that affected both settlers and the speculators who had invested in land, a group that included influential circles in

America, notably in Virginia, as well as back-country groups, such as Pennsylvania's Paxton Boys, that rejected the idea of Friendly Natives and that were ready to resort to violence.[2]

The weakness of the British regular forces in the interior[3] was such that control or, rather, influence, depended on cooperation with the Natives, but in a situation made unstable by the expansion of the colonists. The expansion helped explain the British failure to pacify the region when compared with their far greater success in controlling and winning over the Scottish Highlands, their conquest in 1746 following the suppression of the Jacobite rising,[4] although the Highlands covered far less territory and were also subject to British naval action. The pressure of American settlement in Trans-Appalachia gathered pace in the 1770s, in part because the impact of the resistance seen in Pontiac's War in lessening expansion was diminished with time, but also due to the rapid rise in the colonial population, an increase reflecting both immigration and inherent growth: American colonial society had a higher rate of family formation than its British counterpart.

This rise led to land hunger, although, alongside that hunger stemming from a wish and need to cultivate land, came the ambition and concern about social status and personal worth that was integral to speculation, with land claims proving a key currency. Thus, for example, the tensions of Virginian society were played out across the Appalachians, notably in Kentucky in 1774: Lord Dunmore's War was in part a grab for territory from the Shawnee, one in which initial military failure was followed by success as more troops were deployed.[5] In 1766, the Chickasaw reserve in South Carolina, granted in 1737, was cut from 20,000 to 800 acres. Individual careers reflected the quest for land. George Washington had started out as a surveyor in the 1750s, while Robert Dinwiddie was lieutenant-governor of Virginia and a shareholder in the Ohio Company. In part, the American Revolution was a quest for personal independence and fulfillment in which control of land on the frontiers played a key role.[6]

Control of land was also a prime feature in the expansion and improvement of communications, as these were seen as a key means to derive benefit. This purpose could link officials, speculators, and settlers, as in East Florida where Lieutenant-Governor John Moultrie decided in 1773 to build roads from St. Augustine to facilitate the movement of crops to market and thus to encourage immigration. By 1776, roads had been constructed to Georgia and south past New Smyrna to Eliot's Plantation.[7] Other plans, such as that for the Iberville canal in the Mississippi valley,[8] were abortive, but knowledge of Trans-Appalachia improved thanks in particular to the mapping of Philip Pitman, who published *The Present State of the European Settlements on the Mississippi* (London, 1770), and Thomas Hutchins, whose *A New Map of the Western Parts of Virginia* was published in London in 1778. Such knowledge, however, simply increased sensitivity about British policy.

That the Quebec Act was also seen as a pro-Catholic step was unwelcome to American colonists who took in anti-Catholicism as a key aspect of their political as well as religious heritage. Indeed, the argument that the political ideas in America that helped inspire the rejection of George III drew heavily on oppositionist thought in Britain, especially earlier in the century, needs to give due weight to the role of "religious space," in the sense that anti-Catholicism was a key aspect of both British and American thought, and that this anti-Catholicism had a geopolitical dimension, both providing unity and an expectation of unity to the British Empire and opposition to others.[9] If, to the British and Americans, Catholicism helped describe the illegitimate (because arbitrary) exercise of power, anti-Catholicism also had meaning in North America both in terms of hostility to French and Spanish power (as well as for proselytism among Native Americans), but also with regard to territory acquired by Britain.

This situation made the Quebec Act doubly sensitive, for the British government's attempt to mollify the Catholics of Quebec, a group who were not going to be expelled like the Acadians of Nova Scotia, but also to control them by creating a provincial government without an elected legislature,[10] threatened to reopen New England anxieties about the threat from the north. Moreover, the allocation of Trans-Appalachia to the colony of Quebec meant a political solution in which American religious concerns about Catholics were linked to questions of expansion and settlement. This geopolitics of religious anxiety ignored the real intentions of George III and his ministers, although it captured their sense of the empire as a pluralist enterprise and one in which the acceptance of diversity was key to imperial stability, and thus strength. In effect, this governmental policy represented an imperial federalism, but one directed from the center, which was not welcome in the thirteen North American colonies that rebelled in 1775.

British steps were not abstract measures of territorial allocation on an apparently empty map, but, rather, were attempts to control a situation made volatile by the pace of claim and settlement on what was seen as an open frontier by many colonists. Such a concept meant little to government with its attempt to control space, but the very act of governmental control was unwelcome to those for whom control, instead, meant a presence on the spot. Thus, there was a psychological as well as a political tension, both focused on the frontier.[11]

This geopolitical account, focused on the dynamics of the frontier, offers much of value, but it does not explain why the revolution broke out in Massachusetts, with the key steps occurring in a port, Boston. This point captures a central element of crisis and its spatiality, namely the challenging of British control over the imperial commercial system that it sought to police with the Navigation Acts.[12] This challenge reflected the linkage through commercial regulation of commerce and governance, a linkage that was put under great stress from the tensions in the Atlantic economy, not least the pressures on credit systems within the empire (and in the colonies) caused by economic ups and down, the shortage of specie, and the insecure nature of paper money and credit. These problems helped result in colonial opposition to imperial governance and British merchants, leading to pressures for the nonimportation of British goods as well as to the nonpayment of debts, notably by Virginia tobacco planters, both policies that hit the entrepreneurial, commercial side of the London economy. Yet, these economic and financial pressures within the trans-Atlantic empire were also related to longstanding tensions within the colonies, especially between farmers and merchants.[13] Moreover, there was also strong interest in strengthening economic links within the empire, for example importing North American rather than Swedish iron.[14]

The spatial dynamics or geopolitics of the American Revolution suggests that the contesting of authority and power in North America has to be approached with a sense of multiple frontiers for both. However, although that idea might work in an American context, the degree to which George III's government also faced opposition in the British Isles raises questions about the extent to which spatial considerations explain causes, as opposed to what happened when conflict began, related to the effectiveness of authority and power in particular locations. If, for example, the Stamp Act of 1765 was unpopular in the colonies, the Cider Excise of 1763 led to popular opposition in England. If there was a deadly riot in Boston in 1769, a similar disruption had occurred in London in 1768.

Thus, empire raised questions of authority and power, secular and ecclesiastical,[15] anew, as government was inscribed in, and through, new territories, but these questions were scarcely unique to the colonies. Nor did the colonists or British commentators see them as unique. There was great interest in North America in Wilkesite and other opposition to government in Britain, and a strong feeling of community and commonality. Colonists fought to defend their vision of the rights of Englishmen, and did so in opposition to their conception of the policies of the British government, regarded as a disruptive force. Indeed, the Liberty of Englishness was seen as under threat from an imperial Britishness in which Scottish interests associated with John, 3rd Earl of Bute, George III's first favorite, bulked large. As far as the American Patriots were concerned, this British force had to be rebutted in the American colonies, but, if that colonial challenge failed, a new independent state was to be created, a situation that prefigured that in the South in the run-up to the Civil War.

Yet, the habit, in both the colonies and Britain, of looking to George III for redress reflected the strong cross-currents at play. If psychological, political, and legal contractualism between authority and the subordinate was well developed, for example among the Massachusetts' soldiers, and helped link the Seven Years' War to the American Revolution,[16] it was a contractualism that still left a major role for the appropriate use of authority. This contractualism played a part not only in encouraging opposition to British legislation, notably the Stamp Act (1765), the Townshend Duties (1767), and the Coercive Acts (1774). It also helped ensure that there was an assumption that the British government would response positively to the agitation in 1775, just as it had earlier repealed the Stamp Act and some of the Townshend Duties, in 1766 and 1770 respectively.

Combined with the difficulty in ensuring cooperation between the colonies, this mistaken assumption helped ensure that there was a significant gap between the outbreak of hostilities in April 1775, a step seen as a response to British action at Concord and Lexington, and the declaration of independence on 4 July 1776. Given the extent of petitioning in Britain in favor of the conciliation of American opinion, as well as the attitudes and role of the parliamentary opposition, led by Charles, 2nd Marquess of Rockingham, who, when in government, had repealed the Stamp Act, it is easy to appreciate that this belief was not only convenient but also plausible.[17] Moreover, the Glorious Revolution of 1688 and Union with Scotland in 1707 indicated the extent to which constitutional change was crucial to recent British history.

Such cross-currents on both sides of the Atlantic, or interpenetrations (to employ faddish language), indicate the problem with the ready application of geopolitical analysis, as with the claim that "the full consequences to the French empire of the proximity of British North America to the Caribbean can never be known because, after 1763, successive British governments threw away the advantages that this proximity offered by pursuing what was from a geopolitical standpoint an extremely ill-judged policy," that of trying to raise American taxes for British garrisons.[18] In fact, this policy did not have to lead to the outcome of independence. Indeed, the radicalism and violence associated with the Patriots offended many Americans, helping ensure a fall in Patriot popularity in Boston after 1770 as well as the radical city's isolation from much opinion elsewhere.

Another geopolitical perspective was provided by the wider struggle between Britain and the Bourbons. There was no renewal of conflict until 1778, and indeed there was a marked growth in British trade with Spanish America via free ports in the British West Indies,[19] while the French government sought cooperation with Britain in response to the First Partition of Poland in 1772 by Austria, Prussia, and Russia. This search for cooperation, however, rested on brittle support in Britain and soon fell victim to clashing European interests. Moreover, rivalry and a sense of struggle between Britain and the Bourbons were crucial backgrounds to the crisis in the British colonies, and also to the French and Spanish attempt to strengthen their colonies and, eventually, their response to the problems in the British Empire.

War came closest in 1770, in the Falkland Islands crisis, a crisis arising from competing Anglo-Spanish territorial claims near the southern
end of the Americas. The Falklands were regarded as a key staging post
on the route to the Pacific round Cape Horn. This path was not used by
Spain, as it preferred to rely on cross-isthmus routes in Central America.
Thus, British interest in the Falklands was unwelcome, and had indeed
led to controversy in the 1740s, with Spain complaining about British
interests there. There would have been a comparable strategic interest
in North America had the Northwest Passage been viable, and the hope
that it was continued to play a role in British exploration, for example in
the 1740s and 1770s. Yet, successive disappointments meant that there
was no comparable strategic need to acquire staging posts in the far
north. As a result, the Spanish defense of the Pacific focused on the
Falklands, with the important addition of attempts to thwart British efforts to develop a presence in Central America, notably on the Mosquito
Coast, the Atlantic coast of modern Nicaragua. Insofar as the northern
Pacific appeared under threat to Spanish observers, it was primarily from
Russia, not Britain, and this anxiety encouraged Spanish expansion into
California.

War over the Falklands in 1770 would probably have led to British
action against Louisiana, in both New Orleans and in its hinterland, but
an Anglo-Spanish conflict in the New World would have focused on
the West Indies, while the key naval engagements would have been in
European waters. In the event, Choiseul was dismissed on 24 December,
a ministerial change that reflected France's unwillingness to support
Spain in war with Britain as had initially seemed likely. France's backing
down was followed by that of Spain, and this led, on 22 January 1771, to a
peaceful resolution of the crisis, with British honor satisfied,[20] but there
were other crises, for example over the French acquisition of Corsica in
1768 and, earlier, over competing interests in the West Indies and West
Africa. In 1774, there was concern about Spanish preparations for an
attack on Brazil.[21]

These crises underlined the significance of naval power, but also
suggested that it would be necessary for Britain, France, and Spain to
protect their New World possessions by force. Such a goal might be seen
as jeopardized by Britain's colonial policies, which led to an upsurge

in opposition there, but these policies were designed to strengthen the empire. Trade, its profits, and the ability to tax them appeared the key in any future clash with the French and Spaniards, not land. In contrast, the open frontier in the interior seemed a strategic irrelevance, as any likely conflict in the New World would probably focus on the West Indies.

The significance of the coastal littoral and of naval power projection was shown by the effort devoted to the production of charts. For example, after the Seven Years' War, the Swiss-born Joseph Frederick Wallet DesBarres, who had been trained at the Royal Military College, Woolwich, and who served as a military engineer in North America, was instructed to survey the coastlines of Nova Scotia, Newfoundland, and the Gulf of St. Lawrence. His work served as a basis for his *The Atlantic Neptune,* a survey of the east coast of North America.[22]

At the same time, knowledge of the interior increased, with the army taking a role in mapping,[23] while the Hudson's Bay Company benefited greatly from the end of French Canada in order to expand its commercial penetration of the interior. The inland treks of the 1740s and 1750s served as the basis for subsequent trading expeditions, and, in 1774, Cumberland House became the Company's first inland trading post. The French traders who continued to develop the rival river routes from the Great Lakes were now working for British entrepreneurs.

The most impressive aspect of the expansion of Spanish power was an indirect product of competition with Britain, as concern about British activity in the Pacific, as well as about Russian ambitions in the northeast Pacific, led to an upsurge in Spanish naval activity, launched from San Blas in Mexico. The Russians were extending their power along the Aleutian Islands. The Aleut had initially posed few problems for the Russians in their quest for furs, but in 1761 effective resistance on the Fox Islands began. This was overcome in 1766 by an amphibious force deploying cannon organized by Ivan Solovief, a merchant from Okhotsk. Massacre and disease secured the Russian "achievement."

Spanish activity, which included naval expeditions, notably in 1775 and 1779,[24] and overland activity, led to rapid expansion into California, with San Francisco founded in 1776 and Los Angeles five years later. The pace of Spanish exploration north from Mexico had slackened considerably in the seventeenth century after a major burst in the sixteenth, but, in the eighteenth century it revived, in large part in response to real and threatened moves by other European powers, but also in an effort to find overland routes to the new settlements on the upper Californian coast. In 1775–76, Father Francisco Garcés explored what is now Arizona and Colorado and was the first European to enter the Great Basin; he was thus able to refute the belief that there was a large inland sea there. In 1776, Fathers Silvestre de Vélez de Escalanto and Francisco Atanasio Domínguez traveled further north in what is now Colorado and Utah.

However, in 1775, the Ipai burnt the Spanish mission at San Diego. Moreover, the Yuma rebellion of 1781, in which Spanish positions were destroyed, thwarted plans for expansion through the Colorado Valley and into Central Arizona. Indeed, the extension of Spanish control was largely restricted to Lower California and the coast of California north from San Diego. Further east, Spain reorganized the defenses of Louisiana as part of the process of imperial renewal seen under Charles III (r. 1759–88). This reorganization did not initially threaten the British, although it greatly helped Spain when the two powers went to war in 1779. Britain, then, was already vulnerable in West Florida due to conflict elsewhere with American revolutionaries and France.

Ironically, Spanish renewal also led to colonial opposition. Opposition to Spanish rule, after trade outside the Spanish imperial system or in non-Spanish ships was banned, led to a rebellion in New Orleans in 1768. Mindful of its ally's determination to restore authority, France rejected this attempt to return to its rule, and Spanish forces reimposed control. The rebellion's ringleaders were executed. Spanish rule in Louisiana and the arrival of British control in West Florida also changed, if not disrupted, relations with, and among, the Native Americans,[25] contributing to a general situation of stress that was not restricted to the British Atlantic colonies and their hinterland.

On a very different scale, and amid a number of rebellions in South America, the rigorous collection of taxes led to a general insurrection in Peru in 1780–81, headed by Túpac Amaru, a descendant of the last Inca rulers. More than 100,000 people died in the subsequent conflict, but the uprising was suppressed. At Arequipa in Peru in 1780, superior Spanish firepower helped ensure the defeat of local rebels armed with lances, sticks, and the traditional Andean weapon, the sling. Yet, Spain's colonies were not solely characterized by disaffection, while their economies were not simply subordinated to the requirements of metropolitan Spain. Thus, Mexico was not only a source of raw materials for Europe. Instead, Mexico City was the center of a major trading network within Latin America, which, in part, involved the sale of food. There was a development in industrial production for sale within the colonies, for example of Mexican textiles. This development increased wealth and employment within the colonies. Industrial production also helped fund the demand for food, and thus improved the prospects of the rural economy, and, notably, trade in food and specialization in particular crops. Thus, demand in the New World for cacao was greater than in Europe, and Mexico in particular consumed a large quantity. The prosperity of parts of Latin America was to be gravely affected by the European wars of 1793–1815 and, even more, by the Latin American Wars of Independence.

The wider comparative context, probed recently by John H. Elliott,[26] serves as a reminder that the 1950s' idea of an Atlantic revolution, a thesis advanced by Jacques Godechot and Robert Palmer,[27] still has life in it. Indeed, part of the interest in Atlantic history[28] can be seen as a vindication of this work on a broad current of major change, although its scope is no longer restricted to the Atlantic.[29] Comparative perspectives also underline the wide-ranging commitments of the major powers, and thus the complexity of their geopolitical concerns. The Atlantic linkages that brought range and strength to these powers, moreover, also ensured vulnerability, as the extent of their commitments presented problems. In addition, difficulties in one area were transmitted round the imperial system, weakening it as far as its rivals were concerned.

# 7

# BRITAIN DEFEATED
# 1775-83

Civilization acting across space was the aspect of geopolitics captured by Edward Gibbon in the fourth volume of his *Decline and Fall of the Roman Empire*, written in 1782–84 and published in 1788. He claimed that, in what was seen as the unlikely event of civilization collapsing in Europe in the face of new barbarian inroads, which he assumed would come from Central Asia: "Europe would revive and flourish in the American world, which is already filled with her colonies and institutions.... America now contains about six millions of European blood and descent; and their numbers, at least in the North, are continually increasing. Whatever may be the changes in their political situation, they must preserve the manners of Europe."[1]

This consolation might well be vindicated in a geopolitical light in the long term of the twentieth century, with Wilhelmine and Nazi Germany and Soviet Russia cast in these barbarian roles, both culturally and geopolitically, but Gibbon's argument was an after-echo of a bitter war of independence (1775–83) and one that poses the question of how best to link strategy with geopolitics. A member of Parliament, Gibbon himself had supported government policy.

The discussion of strategy itself faces two main conceptual problems. First, there is the question of the viability of any discussion of the concept of strategy for an age that had at best an uncertain grasp of the very idea of strategy, let alone of what the concept entailed. Secondly, there is the issue that strategy is usually discussed by military historians in terms of war-winning. That, however, is to misunderstand strategy or, rather, to operationalize it in terms of military activity when, in fact, the key to strategy is the political purposes that are pursued. In short, strategy is a process of understanding problems and determining goals, and not the details of the plans by which these goals are implemented by military means. This conceptual point helps ensure that domestic policies can be as significant in the implementation of strategy as their military counterparts. Thus, for example, in the case of the current "War on Terror," measures taken to try to secure the support of the bulk of the Muslim population of countries threatened by terrorism are as germane as the use of force against known or suspected terrorists.

British strategy in the War of Independence has to be understood in this light because this strategy was very different in type to that which was followed during the French and Indian or Seven Years' War. As far as British policy, let alone colonial attitudes in 1754–63, were concerned, the focus had been on conquest, and not on pacification. The latter, indeed, was very much subservient to the former, although different policies were pursued for the purpose of pacification. These included an eighteenth-century equivalent of ethnic cleansing in the expulsion of the Acadians from Nova Scotia, as well as the very different post-conquest accommodation of the French Catholics of Quebec.

In the War of Independence, in contrast, pacification was the British strategy, and the question was how best to secure it. The purpose of the war was clear – the return of the Americans to their loyalty – and the method chosen was different to that in response to the Jacobite rebellions in Scotland and northern England in 1715–16 and 1745–46. In the latter cases, as later in the face of the unsuccessful Irish rebellion in 1798, the remedy had been more clearly military and there was a higher degree of violence, notably in the treatment of the defeated. However, in making that argument, it is necessary to note postwar policies for stability through reorganization, most obviously in the introduction of new governmental systems for the Scottish Highlands and Ireland, particularly the 1801 Act of Union that united Ireland and Britain constitutionally and especially their parliaments.

This point raises the question of whether comparable methods for the American colonies might have been devised and successfully implemented, creating new geopolitical relationships. The stress on conciliation from 1776 and its failure suggests not, although timing was an important issue. What was offered to the Patriots by the Carlisle Commission in 1778 might have averted revolution in America in 1775, or opposition earlier. In the case of America, there was not the sequencing seen in Scotland and Ireland but, instead, a willingness to consider not only pacification alongside conflict but also a new governmental system as an aspect of this pacification. Indeed, in one sense, pacification began at the outset, with the misconceived and mishandled attempt to seize arms in Massachusetts, although the coercive character of this step and the authoritarian nature of British policy in New England after the Boston Tea Party ensured that the pacification then sought was scarcely conciliatory. The most prominent instances of pacification through conciliation were the instructions to the Howe brothers (the British commanding general and admiral) in 1776 to negotiate as well as fight, and, even more clearly, the dispatch of the Carlisle Commission in 1778, while opposition politicians sought to "save America" by advancing their own ideas, although William Pitt the Elder, now Earl of Chatham, refused to countenance American independence.[2]

The restoration of colonial government in the South that followed the beginning of a Southern strategy in late 1778 was a concrete step indicating, during the war, what the British were seeking to achieve to end the conflict. There was a military edge to this policy, as it was hoped that it would lead to the raising of additional forces of Loyalists, as well as lessening support for the Patriots. Alongside that, and more insistently, were the practices of British commanders. Although the Americans were traitors, they were treated with great leniency, and suggestions of harsher treatment were generally ignored by the British. In part, there were military reasons, notably concern about the position of British prisoners, of which there were large numbers after the surrender of an invading force at Saratoga in 1777, but the political dimension was also significant.

This emphasis on pacification provides an essential continuity to British strategy, but there were, of course, differences in emphasis. An attempt at evaluation faces the classic problem in that history occurs forward, 1775 preceding 1776, but is analyzed from posterity with 1775 understood in the light of 1776. This approach is unhelpful because it is teleological and because the course of the war was affected by discontinuities that transformed its parameters. The usual one given concerns the internationalization of the war with France's entry in 1778, but, prior to that, the declaration of American independence in 1776 transformed the situation. Whether or not geopolitics is seen in terms of structural fundamentals or of shorter-term spatial factors, independence was a key moment affecting geopolitics both within North America and as far as its wider significance was concerned. Independence was both a political act that helped create a nation and an act that ensured that the conflict would prove a lengthy war. The war showed foreign powers that the Americans would fight, could fight, could fight well, and could fight with success.

Alongside the transformation of independence came unpredictable military events, such as the unsuccessful American invasion of Canada in 1775–76, and the British failures at Saratoga (1777) and Yorktown (1781), each of which led to the surrender of an army. These events were not secondary to the military operationalization of strategy but, instead, helped direct it. The wider political dimension was also affected by events. Thus, the British Southern strategy – which both militarily and politically from 1778 aimed to regain the support of the South – arose in large part from the impact of French entry. This entry ended the relatively unusual situation in which Britain was at war solely in North America, and therefore was able to concentrate attention and resources on it, although that had been the case in 1755. Britain was essentially pushed in 1778 into a bifurcated effort, with a struggle for pacification continuing in the Thirteen Colonies (albeit being complicated by the French presence there), while a straightforward military conflict began elsewhere. Again, this apparently clear distinction can be qualified by noting that Britain had political options to consider that affected its war with France.

The general impression is of progressive moves toward such a bifurcated effort, but, in practice, the political dimension again came first, and was made more complex by the need to consider not only Britain, France, and the Americans, but also the goals and moves of various powers, including unpredictable responses to the actions of others. Thus, aside from Britain's relations with the states with which it eventually went to war (France, Spain from 1779, and the Dutch from 1780), there were those with neutral powers, both friendly and unfriendly, the last headed by the League of Armed Neutrality organized by Catherine II (the Great) of Russia. These relations were linked to the military operationalization of strategy, not least with the possibility that alliances in Europe would yield troops for North America.

Furthermore, the European crisis of 1778, which led to the War of the Bavarian Succession of 1778–79 between Prussia and France's ally Austria, created opportunities for Britain (notably of France becoming involved in the war and/or of Britain gaining German allies), and indeed was seen in this light. There has since also been scholarly discussion on the lines that a more interventionist European policy from the early 1760s would have provided Britain with allies and have distracted France from taking part in the American war, with key consequences for British options there.[3] This point covers a fundamental aspect of British strategy in the 1770s. Britain was acting as a satisfied power, keen obviously to retain and safeguard its position, but not interested in gaining fresh territory. Representing a satisfied power, British ministers were not interested in seeking to strengthen the status quo by alliances with powers that wished to overturn it and were accordingly wary of becoming involved in European power politics. Here the American war fitted into a pattern that had begun with George III's rejection of the Prussian alliance in 1761–62 and had continued with a subsequent refusal to accept Russian requirements for an alliance (requirements that included support in conflict with Turkey), as well as with the rejection of French approaches for joint action against the First Partition of Poland of 1772.

Thus, there was to be no recurrence of the situation during the Seven Years' War (1756–63), namely war in alliance with a Continental power (in that case, Prussia), a situation that, however unintentional, had proved particularly potent, or, at least, had been shaped thus in political terms by William Pitt the Elder with his presentation of British policy in terms of conquering Canada in Europe: forcing France to commit itself heavily in Europe, and thus making it easier for Britain to win in North America. In the War of American Independence, there would be no alliance with Prussia (nor anyone else) to distract France, and, thus no commitment of the British army to the Continent, as had occurred in 1758, lessening the numbers available for operations in North America. Even more, subsidized German troops, such as those deployed in 1757 in an unsuccessful attempt to defend the Electorate of Hanover against French attack, would not be used for "German," or European, power-political purposes. Some subsidized troops would be retained in Europe, Hanoverians for example being sent to serve in the Gibraltar garrison, but most, notably the Hessians, were sent to America where, at peak strength, they comprised nearly 40 percent of the British army. Britain's fundamental strategy therefore rested on a cohesion that had military consequences: passivity in Europe combined with the preservation of the status quo in America.

This strategy was not dictated by geopolitical imperatives. Instead, it rested on policy choices. Consideration of alternatives is instructive as it highlights not the apparent determinism of the standard use of geopolitics, but the extent of choice and the intelligence of the policy chosen. The thesis that post-1763 Britain should have supported Russian demands on Turkey,[4] with which Russia was at war from 1768 to 1774, or, subsequently, Poland, which Russia helped despoil in the partition of 1772, discounts the problems that would have been created by such an alliance. This thesis also exaggerates what the British state could afford to do, and that at a time when it was struggling, as a result of the Seven Years' War, with the burden of unprecedented debt and facing serious political problems in Britain and North America over attempts to raise taxation. Indeed, given the problems posed by the latter, it is curious to note scholarly claims that the government should have embraced policies that would have entailed considerable expense. This prefigures the situation in 1814–15, in that fiscal and political pressures then made any continuance of the War of 1812 with America unwelcome.

Secondly, even had Britain allied with Austria, Prussia, or Russia after 1763, there is little reason to believe that it would have enjoyed much influence with its ally or allies, or even been consulted by them. This conclusion was suggested by Britain's experience with Austria in 1731–33 and 1748–55, and with Prussia in 1756–63, and is taken further by the personalities involved, a feature generally underplayed in geopolitical discussion. It was not a case of alliance with Prussia or Russia, but with Frederick the Great and Catherine the Great, and each of them both despised George III and had poor relations with him. This issue looks toward the potential problems of British cooperation with the quixotic Napoleon III of France over Mexico and the American Civil War in the 1860s.

Moreover, as the three major Eastern European powers were at, or close to, war in 1768–74, 1778–79 and 1782–83, the caution of George III and his British ministers was vindicated. Not only were these conflicts in which Britain had only limited interest, but it was also unlikely that these powers would have been able or willing to provide appropriate support to Britain in confrontations with the Bourbons. Even had they done so, the transferability of resources was limited, not least because these powers lacked fleets able to influence the struggle at sea, while more auxiliaries backing Britain in North America in 1775–83 might have made little more difference than a greater number of French troops supporting Emperor Maximilian in Mexico in the 1860s. In each case, there was a powerful domestic opposition able to sustain resistance: the "output" of success in conflict between regular forces was unlikely to lead to the "outcome" of a victorious end to the war with the end of the revolution.

What about the "What if?" of Austrian or Prussian pressure on France, or the possibility of this pressure, deterring the latter from help-ing the Americans from 1778, and thus justifying interventionist Brit-ish diplomacy? It is pertinent to ask, however, whether such an alliance would not have led, instead, to a highly damaging British commitment to one side or the other, both in the Austro-Prussian War of the Ba-varian Succession (1778–79) and in other possible confrontations. The Seven Years' War, in which Britain had allied with Prussia, was scarcely encouraging in this respect, as it was, initially, far from clear that Brit-ain's involvement in the conflict on the Continent then would work out as favorably as, in the event, happened. It is only in hindsight that the strategy appears successful. The relationship between crises in Europe in 1863–64, over Poland and Schleswig-Holstein, and the ability of Britain and France, had they wished, to take an assertive role in the Civil War (see pp. 333–36) is instructive in this context.

In addition, had Britain allied with Austria or Prussia in the War of the Bavarian Succession, then George III's German territory, the Elec-torate of Hanover would presumably have been exposed to attack by its opponent. Hanover was vulnerable, as was repeatedly demonstrated, and had it been overrun, as had happened by the French in 1757 and was to happen with Prussia in 1803 and France in 1806, then its recovery might have jeopardized the military, diplomatic, and political options of the British government.

Furthermore, the War of the Bavarian Succession was restricted to two campaigning seasons, but could have been longer, like the Seven Years' War, or could have speedily resumed, as with the two Austro-Prussian conflicts of the 1740s: 1740–72 and 1745–76. Either result would have posed problems for Britain had it been involved. Unpredictability entailed risk, and it is instructive to note a comment in the *Manchester Courier* of 1 October 1864 on the range of international issues in Europe: "There was something more than mere dogmatism on the part of those who undertake to play the oracle in such matters, when it was said that the first shot fired in anger within the confines of Europe would make the stones of every capital rattle."

Moreover, as another critique of the interventionist counterfactual, and, in this case, specifically the argument that it could have deterred French action, and thus ensured British victory, the British had, prior to French entry into the war, already failed to translate victories in North America, such as the battle of Long Island and the capture of New York in 1776, or the battle of Brandywine and the capture of Philadelphia in 1777, into an acceptable political verdict. Thus, the question "What if no French entry into the war?" is of less moment than might be suggested by a focus on the major French role in the Franco-American defeat of the British at Yorktown in 1781. This point underlines the need to locate speculation about diplomatic options in a context of understanding strategic possibilities, although, as also with the Civil War and other nineteenth-century crises, the latter in turn were affected by these options.

Imperial overreach can be presented as lying in part in a failure to create and sustain effective alliances, but while this thesis sounds obvious, it lacks ready measurement. It may be easier to assess overreach in terms of financial problems, or a lack of adequate military resources, but both are true for most combatants in history. Moreover, far from being opposites, reach and overreach were part of the same process, while the very success of Britain as an imperial power for so long suggested that overreach was not a terribly helpful concept.

There was also no significant domestic constituency for an interventionist diplomacy, and notably none for any particular interventionist course of action. Aside from the practicalities of British power, and the nature of British politics, the Western Question, the fate of Western Europe, more particularly the Low Countries, the Rhineland and Italy, had been settled diplomatically in the 1750s, by the Austrian alliances with Spain (1752) and then France (1756), removing both need and opportunity for British intervention. This shift in power politics was crucial, for British public support for interventionism on the Continent was fragile, if not weak, unless the Bourbons (the rulers of France and Spain) were the target, a situation also seen in the 1860s. Indeed, the domestic coalition of interests and ideas upon which public backing for foreign policy rested in the eighteenth century was heavily reliant on the consistency offered by the resonance of the anti-Bourbon beat. Thus, British military strategy in the War of American Independence cannot be separated from wider currents of political preference and engagement. Looked at differently, the North American Question was not separate from concerns that were domestic as much as foreign, and "European" as much as "Atlantic."

What British strategy appeared to entail in North America, however, varied greatly. The mistaken initial British impression was of opposition largely only in Massachusetts, and this impression, which drew on a longstanding belief that New England was different from the other colonies, suggested that a vigorous defense of imperial interests there would save the situation. This view led to British legislation in 1774 specific to this colony and to a concentration of Britain's forces in North America there. The initial military operationalization of strategy continued after the clashes at Concord and Lexington on 19 April 1775, both because the stress on Massachusetts appeared vindicated and because there were not enough troops for action elsewhere.

British policy failed both in Massachusetts and elsewhere. In the former, the military presence was unable to prevent rebellion or to contain it. Heavy casualties at the battle of Bunker Hill on 17 June 1775 discouraged the British garrison from leaving Boston and eventually, on 17 March 1776, the British had to evacuate it when the harbor was threatened by American cannon. Elsewhere in North America, the lack of troops stemming from the concentration on Boston ensured that British authority was overthrown in the other twelve rebellious colonies, while the Americans were able to mount an invasion of Canada that achieved initial success, bottling up the British in Quebec.[5] Thus, the original geography of the revolution was very important. The decision to focus on Massachusetts reflected the political perception that it was the core of the revolution and that successful action there would deter opposition elsewhere, but this proved an erroneous assumption, although one that was understandable given the troop numbers available.

As a result of the events in the first stage, the second stage of the war, a stage expected neither by most of the American Patriots nor by the British government, led to a major British effort to regain control, a policy that entailed both a formidable military effort and peacemaking proposals. Here, again, it is necessary to look at the military options in terms of the political situation. The end of the rebellion/revolution could not be achieved by reconquering the Thirteen Colonies (and driving the Americans from Canada). The task of such a reconquest was too great, while the Declaration of Independence altered the situation because it ensured that the conflict ceased to be a rebellion and, instead, became the first instance of a European settler colony seeking independence, which was a radical step. This step was taken in order to encourage foreign support by making it less likely that the conflict would end in a reconciliation within the British Empire. This outcome made foreign support more worthwhile both to the foreign powers and the American Patriots.[6] It became necessary for the British to secure military results that achieved the political outcome of an end to rebellion, an outcome that was likely to require both a negotiated settlement and acquiescence in the return to loyalty and in subsequently maintaining obedience. This outcome rested on a different politics to that of the conquest of New France (Canada) during the Seven Years' War, a step secured by the governor's surrender in 1760 and the subsequent peace negotiations in 1762–63.

The determination of the Americans to have relations with the European states was significant as it entailed not only a striving for legitimacy seen in asserting a right to statehood among other states, but also a practical desire to acquire resources. In particular, France and Spain were key sources of arms and funds, while America came to play a role in public politics in France. This role focused the interest in geographical information about America that stemmed from the war and that was also seen in the individual American colonies. Atlases and maps were produced in considerable numbers.[7] War ensured a particular interest in accurate maps. Although combatants, the French, including the navy, in order to make up for their lack of knowledge and access to the North American shoreline, relied on the availability of British printed maps sold through the map trade.[8]

The American need for support produced a new geopolitics, with the diplomatic recognition of the new state, in turn, becoming a fundamental issue in relations between Britain and other European states. The British government sought to block recognition, and treated the reception of American diplomats as an hostile act, prefiguring the response by the Union in the Civil War to the treatment of Confederate representatives as belligerents rather than rebels. Indeed, the signature of treaties between Louis XVI and the Americans in 1778 was correctly regarded as a sign of imminent hostilities with Britain.

What was unclear was which military results would best secure the desired outcomes, a question that went back to the beginning of the revolution when British ministers had debated whether they could rely on naval power alone, or whether it would be necessary to deploy an army large enough to defeat opposition.[9] A key factor encouraging the latter was the conviction that it was necessary not to abandon the Loyalists and the belief that there were large numbers of them.

Yet, even sending an army left policy unclear. Was the priority for the British the defeat, indeed destruction, of the Continental Army, as it represented the Revolution, not least its unity, or was it the capture of key American centers? Each goal appeared possible, and there was a mutual dependence between them, one that was different from the situation during the Civil War. The British would not be able to defeat the Americans unless they could land and support troops, and for this capability to be maintained it was necessary to secure port cities: the Champlain–Hudson axis could be invaded from Canada in 1777 and 1814, but these invasions were unsuccessful and only affected a limited part of America. In contrast, amphibious forces could address the centers of American power.

Yet, as for the Union in the Civil War, captured port cities could best be held if opposing field forces were defeated. The equations of troop numbers made this clear, not least the problems posed for finite military resources by maintaining large garrison forces. Indeed, the latter issue lent further military point to the political strategy of pacification, as such a strategy would produce local Loyalist forces as well as diminishing the number of Patriots. The British emphasis possibly should have been on destroying the Continental Army, which was definitely a prospect in 1776–77, but, instead, was on regaining key centers, not least as this policy was seen as a way of demonstrating the return of royal authority, notably by ensuring that large numbers of Americans again came under the Crown. Indeed, from the period when the Empire struck back, the summer of 1776, the British gained control of most of the key American points, either for much of the war (New York from 1776, Savannah from 1778, Charleston from 1780), or, as it turned out, temporarily (Newport from 1776, Philadelphia from 1777).

Yet this policy faced difficulties, with Charleston falling neither in 1776 nor in 1779, and still left important centers, most obviously Boston from 1776, that were not under British control. This point indicated the fundamental political problem facing the British and, more generally true in military history: whatever they achieved in the field it would still be necessary to achieve a political settlement, at least in the form of a return to loyalty. The understanding of this issue was an achievement for the British, but also posed a problem, while, correspondingly, this understanding was also both achievement and problem for the Patriots.

This point helps explain the attention devoted by Patriot leaders throughout the war to politics, in order to secure the persistence and coherence of the war effort. Political engagement entailed support for independence but also an opposition to Britain that drew part of its vigor from a paranoia that saw British policy as directed to a new ethnic prospectus and geography. Prewar anxieties about Native Americans and blacks were given renewed energy. In South Carolina, as in Virginia, the cause of liberty was advanced with a clear racist inflection. Thus, in 1775, Thomas Jeremiah, a harbor pilot in Charleston and a wealthy "Free Negro," was falsely accused of acting as a British agent in encouraging a slave insurrection, a charge advanced by Henry Laurens, the city's foremost patriot and later president of the Continental Congress. Though free, Jeremiah was tried in a slave court, convicted, and hanged.[10] In a section in the Declaration of Independence that was deleted, Jefferson accused George III of inciting a slave rebellion, and the willingness of slaves to respond to encouragement by John, 4th Earl of Dunmore, the last royal Governor, made this issue particularly sensitive for Virginians.[11] A paranoid sensibility contributed to Patriot resolve, as it gave meaning to more abstract feelings about liberty. This situation prefigured that in South Carolina in 1861. Yet, liberty was also more than an abstract issue. Instead, the constitutionalism seen in the new state constitutions was linked to local struggles for power and about policy.

The British, in turn, could try, by political approaches and military efforts, to alter these political equations within the Thirteen Colonies, prefiguring Confederate attempts to affect the situation in the North during the Civil War. At times, the British succeeded in doing so, as in the New York campaign of 1776 when British victories led many of Washington's men to return home while Loyalists came forward in numbers. The porous nature of the allegiance of many[12] provided a clear political benefit to victory. Thus, a new political prospectus was offered in South Carolina, after the successful siege of Charleston in 1780. Indeed, in tidewater South Carolina, British authority was swiftly recognized. On 5 June, more than two hundred of the more prominent citizens of Charleston congratulated the British commanders on the restoration of the political connection with the Crown. A loyal address came from Georgetown, South Carolina, the following month, while several of the leading politicians of the state returned to Charleston to accept British rule. These developments appeared to be a vindication of the British policy of combining military force with a conciliatory policy, offering a new imperial relationship that granted most of the American demands made at the outbreak of the war.

It was scarcely surprising that Northern politicians, such as Ezekiel Cornell of Rhode Island, came to doubt the determination of their Southern counterparts, but there were also many Loyalists further north. Thus in Monmouth County, New Jersey, a "frontier" county only nominally under Patriot control, 605 of the fewer than 6,000 adult males enlisted in Loyalist and other British units, while 580 provided long-term service to the Patriots. An additional 1,374 Patriots served in the militia and 252 served as Loyalist irregulars.[13] Many of those who chose to stay in Newport when the British occupied it in 1776 were Loyalists.[14]

To treat this conflict, on either side, therefore simply as a military struggle is to underplay the key role of political goals, and similar points can be made about the Civil War and, albeit to a lesser extent, the War of 1812. Indeed, in the case of the War of Independence, these goals affected not only the moves of armies (a conventional but overly limited understanding of strategy), but even the nature of the forces deployed by both sides. The British use of German "mercenaries," and, even more, Native Americans and African Americans, provided opportunities for hostile political mobilization on the part of the Patriots, who, for example, inaccurately presented the British as encouraging Native allies to scalp Americans. The American reliance on France correspondingly increased domestic support for war in Britain, stiffening, for example, the resolve of Gibbon, and also hit sympathy for the Patriots, who could now be presented as hypocrites, willing to ally with a Catholic autocracy (two when Spain joined in 1779), and with Britain's national enemy as well.

These alliances brought the war to a new stage as there was no clear guide to the allocation of British resources between the war with the Bourbons and that with the Americans. It was relatively easy for the Patriots to abandon the Greater American plan of conquering Canada after American failure there in 1776 was followed by British military efforts in the Thirteen Colonies that had to be countered. In contrast, there was no such agreement over policy in Britain. Partisan politics came into play, not least the politics of justification, with the Opposition pressing for a focus on the Bourbons and the ministry unwilling to follow to the same extent, not least because it neither wished nor thought it appropriate to abandon hopes of America.

Yet, although the American–French treaties led the British government in 1778 to order the evacuation of Philadelphia and to send an expedition that captured the Caribbean sugar island of St. Lucia, it would be mistaken to present war against France and war in America as alternatives. Instead, there was a belief that Bourbon entry linked the two conflicts, and that the Bourbon system had a cohesion, such that the application of British power at appropriate points would have a major impact. West Indies' trade was seen as a crucial source of French government revenue, thanks to the profit derived from the re-export of colonial goods in Europe and to the possibility of raising loans on this trade. Thus, for Britain to seize colonies and interrupt trade was regarded as a way to harm France's ability to wage war. This strategy had been employed against Spain, but essentially, as in 1726, to affect its ability to pursue objectives in Europe. The key element from 1778 was an attempt to affect France's ability to pursue its objectives in North America.

The West Indies were also important to British strategy in North America: one of the reasons for the focus on the South from late 1778 was the belief that it provided a key source of supplies for the British West Indies, and especially of food, without which the viability of the slave economy, and thus the trade, prosperity, and security of the British colonies, was limited.[15] If, therefore, the compromise that ended the war was to lead to a partition of British North America, as indeed occurred in 1783, with Britain retaining Canada, then it was hoped that Britain could also retain South Carolina and Georgia, if not North Carolina. Moreover, such a retention would accord with the concentration of Loyalists in the region, as well as the potential to win Native American and African American support to the cause of counterrevolutionary kingship; and would also strengthen the case for holding onto Florida, which had not rebelled. This strategy appeared both politically and militarily viable in 1780.[16] Despite the anxieties expressed in 1778, French entry had not obliged the British to abandon New York nor had it led to another attack on Canada nor to the permanent postponing of British operations in the South. The American effort was in difficulties. In January 1781, short of pay, food, and clothes, and seeking discharge, both the Pennsylvania Line and three New Jersey regiments mutinied. The Pennsylvania mutiny was ended only by concessions, including the discharge of five-sixths of the men. This episode is a reminder of the precarious nature of the Revolution militarily, and the extent to which the situation did not improve as the Revolution continued. It also provides a different perspective on the war. As any consideration of the correspondence of Nathanael Greene and Charles, 2nd Earl Cornwallis, the rival commanders in the Carolinas in the winter of 1780–81, would indicate,[17] both sides faced serious difficulties and experienced major drawbacks. Militarily, this meant both that there was everything to play for, and that managing limitations was as important as grasping opportunities. Politically, these drawbacks also ensured not only that there was everything to play for, but also that whichever side was better able to accept its weaknesses and persist was likely to win the struggle of will.

Similarly, the British position had not collapsed outside America. In turn, although winning the alliance, a success to which Benjamin Franklin greatly contributed, greatly increased Patriot confidence,[18] American relations with the French government were often difficult, as French assistance was rarely as unreserved as required, while there was justified concern about France's pursuit of its own national interests, particularly in terms of French territorial goals in the West Indies. John Adams proved a perspicacious diplomat in understanding the differences in French and American interests and the dangers of dependence on France.[19] Moreover, alongside the customary tensions of any alliance, especially one that linked two powers with such dissimilar objectives, there were also the problems of introducing a new revolutionary state into the world of *ancien régime* diplomacy, and of acting as military and financial agent for America.[20]

In 1781, however, French naval power provided a crucial factor in forcing the surrender of the British army in Virginia. The French expeditionary force also played a significant role. The surrender of the besieged army at Yorktown on 19 October 1781 settled the debate over British policy because its political consequences led to the fall of the Lord North ministry in March 1782. The collapse of the wartime ministry was made more significant because it was not succeeded by a similar one following royal views, as would, for example, have been a ministry under Lord Thurlow, the Lord Chancellor, a close ally of George III. Instead, the opposition, under Charles, 2nd Marquess of Rockingham, came to power. As a result of this governmental revolution, 1782 was a key year of the war, even though it was a year in which the Patriots had singularly little success, Washington, in particular, getting nowhere with his plan to capture New York, which reflected the extent to which Yorktown led to a new stalemate in the fighting rather than a close, a stalemate that interacted with continuing tensions on the American side, political, fiscal, and economic.[21] Moreover, this American failure was more generally significant as it marked the decline in the Franco-American alliance. This decline reflected both the problems of pursuing very different military priorities and, far more significantly, a war weariness on the part of the French government.

This war weariness arose not only from the cost of the conflict, but also from the priorities of European power politics, specifically the concern of Charles, Count of Vergennes, the influential Foreign Minister, that Russian expansion posed a threat to the European system. Indeed, Vergennes, earlier a long-serving envoy in Constantinople (Istanbul), sought cooperation with Britain, albeit a Britain that was no longer the dominant colonial power and that was willing to heed the French lead.[22] This situation looked toward the centrality of European considerations in French policy during the Napoleonic years (those of Napoleon I), notably in 1803 and 1812, and subsequently to Napoleon III's willingness to subordinate New World ambitions to European concerns, especially in 1866–67 when he abandoned his Mexican commitment.

Moreover, on 12 April 1782, the French fleet in the West Indies was defeated by Admiral Rodney at the battle of the Saintes. Thus, militarily, the war was going Britain's way. New warships were being launched, public finances were robust, and fears of rebellion in Ireland and of disaffection in Britain were largely assuaged, in part as a result of conciliation in Ireland comparable to that which had been unsuccessfully attempted in America with the Carlisle Commission. In addition, in 1782, the Bourbons were increasingly unable to attempt another invasion of Britain such as that which had failed in 1779, Gibraltar had been held, and the British position in both India and Canada was more resilient than had been feared.

Yet, despite the reluctance of George III, who considered abdicating, the politics in 1782 was now of peace and a settlement that were not focused on a return of America to its loyalty. Instead, the priority was the disruption, if not destruction, of the coalition of powers fighting Britain and, it was hoped, better relations with an independent America. Paradoxically, this British strategy was to be successful, which simply underlines the conceptual problems of conceiving of strategy in terms of its military operationalization, and thus of geopolitics in terms of such strategies. America's willingness to settle without its allies was instrumental to the destruction of this coalition, and that event was important for postwar geopolitics and politics. It opened the way to an Atlantic world defined by an Anglo-American partnership, however uneasy, and with France very much a lesser player.

However, to fuel the paranoia of many Americans, the potential remained for the coalition that Britain had seemed to be seeking during the war, that with both the Native Americans and the blacks; although the British call to the slaves to arms (understandably) was focused on military benefit, not social change, and the British scarcely pursued a full-fledged slavery strategy.[23] Many Natives supported the British during the war, and pressed hard on the frontier of European settlements, especially in New York and Pennsylvania in 1778, and New York in 1780 and 1781. Their ability to do so in part reflected the American failure in 1776 to sustain their position in Canada, and thus to repeat the British success in 1760 in lessening Native options.

Expeditions by the Patriots against the Natives were often unsuccessful, but, despite the fighting quality of the Natives, the cumulative pressure of sustained conflict damaged their societies and disrupted their economies, and indeed proved devastating for many, notably – but not only – the Iroquois in 1779 whose homes and cornfields were burnt in order to force them onto the defensive. The willingness of the Americans to engage in savage anti-societal violence, for example the slaughter of captives, including children, as with the Gnadenhutten massacre of Wyandot in Pennsylvania in 1782, as well as in the destruction of crops, inflicted enormous damage on Native societies. The war also proved disruptive for Native societies that were not devastated, for instance for the Creek,[24] and for their relations with British traders who had acted as intermediaries.[25] The Chickasaw lost their reservation in Carolina. The Natives were to be those who suffered most from the new geopolitics of North America.

Opposition by both Natives and blacks continued after the war, contributing to the bellicose character of many Americans. Calling themselves the King of England's soldiers, some blacks fought on from the swamps by the River Savannah after the British had evacuated Charleston and Savannah. In May 1786, a combined force of militia and Catawba (Native Americans) defeated them, but, a year later, a governor's message mentioned serious depredations of armed blacks "too numerous to be quelled by patrols" in southern South Carolina.[26] It was also unclear whether the Loyalist diaspora would prove the basis for action against America. Alongside these threats came that from the dissolution of the pro-American wartime coalition, which both made Britain more menacing and raised the threat that it might find European allies.

# 8

# FLEXING MUSCLES
# 1783-1811

*A New and Correct Map of the United States of North America* "agreable to the Peace of 1783" was published in New Haven in 1784. Produced by Abel Buell, a silversmith there, it was advertised by him as "The first ever published, engraved and finished by one man, and an American," and as designed for the "patriotic gentleman." The map presented a new land reaching to the Mississippi, and offered a potent prospectus of American independence followed by national expansion. The two concepts, independence and expansion, were clearly linked, notably with the British cession of the "Old Northwest," Trans-Appalachia, to America in 1783, a cession that greatly increased the land mass offered by the thirteen colonies. America obtained Trans-Appalachia without having either conquered or peopled it because of what might be called Franklin's geopolitical sensibility about American destiny. Of the three American negotiators in Paris in 1782, he held out most firmly for the Mississippi boundary on the most, more than Jay or Adams. Franklin argued that, otherwise, the new nation would be cooped up between the Appalachians and the sea. In fact, few Americans, possibly only 25,000, lived in Trans-Appalachia in 1782, most of them in central Kentucky. Franklin's emphasis on a need for Trans-Appalachia traced back at least as far as his essay "Observations on the Increase of Mankind," written in 1751, in which, arguing against British mercantilist policies, he maintained that natural increase among the American colonists was causing their population to double roughly every quarter-century, and, before very long, they would require Trans-Appalachia or else would become as poverty-ridden as British people. It is unclear how far Franklin's personal involvement in western lands influenced his geopolitical thinking, and the relationship may have worked the other way: his ideas about the need for western living space may have induced him to speculate.

Franklin also argued in his "Observations" that the American population would outstrip Britain's, but that this young and agrarian population would be consumers of British manufactures rather than competitors. He claimed that the Americans would not go into manufactures themselves, as they were doing better economically and in family-building as farmers, compared to British wage laborers, so that Britain had nothing to fear on behalf of its own industry and did not need to be protectionist.

The Americans had strengthened their claim to Trans-Appalachia thanks in part to the actions of George Rogers Clark, a Virginian who had settled in Kentucky and persuaded the governor of Virginia to support his attempt to overcome the French settlements in the Illinois country that had come under British rule as a result of the Seven Years' War. Advancing down the Ohio River in 1778, Clark had occupied Kaskaskia, Cahokia, and Vincennes. Two years later, he provided support to Spanish-ruled St. Louis when it was threatened by British attack. Such activity limited the sway of the British forces based in Detroit, who were defeated at Vincennes in 1779 after they had recaptured the position.

Made without mention of, or the consent of, the Native population, the cession of Trans-Appalachia, or the old Northwest, was followed by American claims, warfare, and settlement in the region. These, in turn, looked toward the background of the resumption of conflict between Britain and America in 1812, because American politicians argued that Britain was behind continued Native resistance. In particular, Canada in British hands, a verdict the Americans had threatened with invasion in 1775, only to be totally defeated the following year, was regarded as both the unfinished business of independence and a challenge to America's settlement of the interior and its ability to defeat the Native Americans. Franklin unsuccessfully argued during the peace negotiations that it would benefit Britain to give Canada to the United States. That Canada proved the destination of many Loyalists exacerbated the situation. Thus, Canada in British hands underlined past failure and present threat.

A similar analysis was presented for the southern borderlands. Independence was seen as providing good title to lands occupied by Native

Americans, and their continued opposition was linked by Americans to real or potential encouragement by European powers, notably Spain, the colonial power in Louisiana, and, more seriously, Florida. As well as acknowledging West Florida as Spanish, Britain ceded East Florida as part of the peace settlement. In the mid-1780s, the Creek were not opposed to expansion by Georgia but also had treaties with Spain. There was also concern about relations between the Native Americans and British commercial interests in the Spanish colonies, notably in Pensacola.

Thus, ambition and anxiety combined to drive forward American expansion. Expansion was achieved, with both territorial cessions by Native Americans, and the Louisiana Purchase of 1803, which vastly increased the area recognized by European powers as American, and also transformed its visual representation.[1] Trans-Appalachia was linked to the Atlantic world by and through America.[2] The new area was organized by the establishment of new states and territories.

This process seemed necessary and appropriate because stadial models of social development led to the view that Natives, as hunter-gatherers, were at an earlier stage of human development and could only share in the future of North America if they changed "into civilized republicans and good Americans."[3] Jefferson was very interested in Native American linguistics and displayed Native artifacts in the hall of his home at Monticello, but he was also insistent that the "merciless Indian savages" of the Declaration of Independence (1776) make way for settlers, in furtherance of America's destiny,[4] a view held throughout the period covered by this book. In 1865, the report by the Senate Committee on Indian Affairs referred to "the same uncompromising, eternal, irrepressible conflict between savage and civilized life which we have always found in the history of settlement and colonization of the United States from the beginning."[5] Jefferson also regarded the Natives as a tool for British revenge. This opinion was widely held, leading to suspicion of links between Britain and the Natives, for example with the Creeks who opposed American expansion in the southeast.[6]

Moreover, the very American conception of appropriate governance encouraged expansion. In response to their perception of mistreatment as part of the British Empire, Americans both before and after independence pressed for an eventual equality within a federalism that was seen as the means and ideology necessary to combine liberty with strength, and locality with extent. This approach proved a way to deal with the bold territorial claims of the seven "landed" colonies that had extensive western lands. The federal approach led, as a consequence of these western land cessions to Congress, and, following the Ordinances of 1784, 1785, and 1787 (the last the Northwest Ordinance), to the rapid spread of the state system and thus made expansion appear normative without threatening the imperial excess associated with Rome and Britain. Instead, Americans came to believe not only that their territory should expand, but also that, to survive, the Union had to be dynamic. There was to be no equivalent to the expansion of the French republic in the 1790s, for it created allied republics, such as the Rauracian, Batavian, Ligurian, and Cisalpine, only to manipulate and direct them, rather as Napoleon subsequently treated the new principalities he created or enhanced, although his means of operation was dynastic.

The federal government, rather than the states, gained responsibility for running the vast lands at stake both from 1783 and subsequently. As a stage to statehood for the resulting territories, however, these territories were understood as American. Native American sovereignty and rights were ignored or subordinated. Taxation was part of the equation, as federal land sales provided revenue that did not need to be raised by direct taxation.

The new states were to be equal and uniform, as far as their government and the federal government were concerned, and this solution was regarded as a way to ensure republican ideals as well as to avoid the divisive characteristics associated with British imperial government and the risk that these territories would become breakaway nations. This uniformity was given spatial form when the Ordinance of 1784 for the government of the Western Territory, the product of a Congressional committee chaired by Jefferson, proposed that all states have boundaries based on the precision of mathematics, rather than the variations of topography. This idea was taken further in the Land Ordinance of 1785, which proposed a grid system for the allocation of land, an allocation designed to fulfill Congressional hopes that the rapid development of the frontier and the spread of commercial connections would strengthen the Union and prevent separatism.[7]

An account of independence followed by expansion, while indeed important, presents less than the full picture, and, consequentially does not really explain why foreign policy proved so contentious in American politics. Instead, it is necessary to appreciate the concerns of American politicians of the period and, in particular, their fear of conflict with the European great powers. There was also a wish to assert the value and importance of America that reflected an anxious concern about what was seen as European condescension. In contrast to assumptions that America benefited from being a land of freedom,[8] the theory of degeneracy advanced by the influential French intellectual Georges, Count of Buffon was especially challenging as, in a variant of the Enlightenment's interest in environmentalism, it argued that the climate of the New World naturally ensured that its plants, animals, and, indeed, people were enfeebled. This thesis was challenged by American politician-intellectuals, notably Franklin, Hamilton, and Jefferson in his *Notes on the State of Virginia* (1784),[9] but, by extension, the fate of the new state appeared a test of the argument.

Fear of conflict with the European great powers might seem misguided given that France and Britain themselves came close to conflict with each other in 1787, in the Dutch crisis, and again, with France allied to Spain, in the Nootka Sound Crisis of 1790, while, from 1793 to 1815, with two brief exceptions in 1802–1803 and 1814–15, Britain and France were at war in the French Revolutionary and Napoleonic Wars. Moreover, Spain was a principal in these conflicts for most of that period, and, indeed, a battlefield from 1808 to 1814.

It is easy, therefore, to suggest that the European powers had so exhausted themselves by conflict that America was able to enjoy security to profit from large-scale economic growth, and to pursue its interests, a view offered by contemporaries.[10] This account thus prefigures the idea that the exhaustion of the European powers in the two world wars helped ensure that the United States became the great world power. Yet again, there is considerable weight in the popular account, and it largely conforms to the idea that America enjoyed "free security" after 1820, but this account is not without problems for the period 1783–1815. In particular, war between the European powers in 1793–1815 threatened America both in the short term and, even more, in the long term.

In ranging ahistorically through American history, there is an obvious point of comparison with 1865, when victory by large, well-resourced, and experienced Union forces resulted in a situation in which other powers feared attack. This was the case with Britain in Canada and France in Mexico. One obvious danger, therefore, in 1793–1815 was that overwhelming victory by Britain (and its allies) or, more probably prior to late 1812, by France (and its allies) would leave the victor free to pursue their interests in the New World. Indeed, the British did so in 1814–15, as victory over Napoleon enabled them to transfer troops and ships to North America, and thus to ratchet up greatly the pace of attack on America with which Britain had been at war since 1812. Had, in contrast, Napoleon been victorious, there was the prospect of his resuming his pursuit of a Western Design or intervening in Latin America in support of his brother, Joseph, whom he had made King of Spain in 1808, albeit at the cost of beginning a large-scale rebellion. The pursuit of interests by European powers did not have to mean direct intervention of this type at the expense of America, but the actual or threatened seizure of the colonies of European rivals represented a threat. This was particularly the case as far as the fates of Louisiana and Florida were concerned, as Britain might seize either or both, and particularly their ports. The British capture of Havana in 1762 provided a relevant instance.

Moreover, the control of trade routes was thrown to the fore in conflict between the European powers as economic warfare became a more significant factor, leading to restrictions, if not attacks, on neutral trade. This warfare was the case from the outset but became more significant as the failure of Britain's alliance system on the Continent in 1795 led to increased British reliance on the blockade not only of France but also of France's allies and conquests. This blockade, which rested on the unparalleled strength of the Royal Navy, compromised American trade and economic independence, and threatened to undo the American achievement of using independence in order to break free of the constraints of British economic controls and management.

Conversely, any reliance on taking a role in the British commercial world was challenged by French attacks on trade with this world. These attacks were a threat because of French power and the possibility of extending this into the colonies of allied states, notably Spain. France had important Caribbean bases until 1810, when Guadeloupe fell to the British (Martinique and Santo Domingo were taken in 1809), while the United States lacked the naval strength and experience to know best how to deal with such attacks. In 1805, to Jefferson's concern, the French were able to concentrate warships from Europe at Martinique before sailing back for Europe.[11]

Thus, a picture of the international system as less threatening from 1793 due to war thereafter involving Britain, France, and Spain is overly simplistic, although that view does capture the problems posed for America when the three powers were at peace in 1802–1803, as Napoleon was then able to pursue his Western Design, which was intended to strengthen and transform France's New World position. Far from conflict between the European powers making the situation necessarily less difficult for the United States, the very outbreak of large-scale war made it easier, as well as more risky, for Britain and France to consider a resort to wider hostilities, not least because their military preparedness was enhanced, and particularly so in the case of Britain. There was also a sense that these conflicts were the latest in a sequence between Britain and France. That sense placed America in the frame both as a participant in conflict and as a sphere for action.

Yet, America as a state was not well prepared for war. First, it was only an embryonic state, and certainly very different to new-republican France in 1792. Although by the Declaration of Independence in 1776 Americans joined in expounding an ideology that did not know territorial boundaries, reality proved more troubling. The American constitution took time to negotiate, let alone bed down. The national federal settlement presented by the ratification of the Constitution was one that was made more necessary by the troubling international situation and the difficulties of conducting foreign policy,[12] but it was also more relevant, as well as possible, thanks to the extent to which it acknowledged serious sectional differences. Edward Thornton, the British Secretary of Embassy, commented in 1791 on the

> jealousy which exists between separate states. . . . The inhabitants of Massachusetts, of Connecticut, of New York has each some anecdote to relate of public artifice and chicanery in the others, or turns into ridicule their private customs; and I have heard it asserted of the Virginians, who from the events

of the war, I believe, are more averse from a connection with us than any other state, that they would rather form an alliance with Old than New England. The cause of this jealousy I should be inclined to refer to their division into separate states.[13]

Jefferson was readier to see a division between North and South, based on their "two characters" that, he claimed, blended in Pennsylvania.[14] Thus, from the outset, geopolitics became a matter of tensions and divisions within America as well as within the wider situation in North America. Alongside regional differences, there were longstanding tensions between individual states over boundaries and the allocation of territory, for example between Virginia and Pennsylvania around Pittsburgh. There also were secessionist pressures. The latter took on particular force when linked to threats to negotiate with foreign powers, as with both Delaware and Nantucket.

Sectional differences were linked to foreign policy. Thus, regional interests were at stake in the Jay–Gardoqui negotiations of 1786 when the states of New England and New York were willing for America to forego the right to trade on the Mississippi, thereby selling out the then interests of Trans-Appalachia, in exchange for favorable trade relations with Spain. Anxiety about the possibility of foreign support for Native Americans, whose lands were eagerly sought, played an important role in increasing political tension within America and giving it bite in terms of regional animosity; and violence on the frontier, notably in the Ohio Valley and Tennessee, kept the issue to the fore.

The recent struggle against George III was deployed in an effort to create a nationalism[15] and national history, and this effort contrasted with the lack of much sense of a national American character in the colonial period. Instead, in the late colonial period, there were many local histories. Jefferson's *Summary View of the Rights of British America* (1774) was a history of Virginia. The new national postwar memory was useful, but it largely only highlighted the question of how to secure independence, a question accentuated by the widespread belief in the 1780s that Confederation had failed.

Secondly, the new state was very weak militarily. After independence, its navy was dismantled and its army savagely cut back. In part, these reductions reflected the financial crisis left by the war, notably heavy debts, which helps explain the importance of the establishment of public credit in 1789 when Congress assumed the war debt. Moreover, between the end of the War of Independence and the adoption of the Constitution, there was a critical absence of a federal revenue base. There were also a series of linked political issues that discouraged the maintenance of military strength. These included not only the anti-army ideology derived from the British background and the colonial experience, but also the extent to which the unsettled governmental situation left any basis for military arrangements unclear, irrespective of the political controversies bound up in issues of army size and command. In 1783, the Continental Congress rejected the plan, supported by Washington and Alexander Hamilton, for a national army.

The removal of British power as an issue in domestic American politics helped ensure that these politics focused instead on differences within America. These politics related not only to policy issues but also to the problems of constitutionalism, notably of ensuring that a system based on suffrage could, and would, be secure, stable, and successful. Americans sought in their future to solve the longstanding problem of how to create an effective mixed government. The Federal constitution was regarded as a key ingredient as it was seen to have overcome the consolidation of power in the executive in Britain. Thus, the American constitution righted that of Britain, just as America had defeated Britain, and local government was regarded as a key barrier against despotism. Yet, the stability of this solution was unclear, not only in terms of domestic differences but also with reference to its impact on America's international competitiveness. Moreover, the very expansion of the state accentuated this question as well as that of regional differences, as this expansion provided issues for contention, both domestically and with foreign powers, and also injected an element of volatility into politics that increased concerns. In particular, new states meant more congressmen, and thus challenged existing balances of political power. This expansion proved important also to questions of political identity that related to more wide-ranging issues of foreign policy. The result between 1783 and 1812 was a closer linkage of politics and foreign policy than was to be seen in the decade after the War of 1812 ended in 1815. This linkage provided part of the dynamic in the complex and contentious relations between George Washington, John Adams, Thomas Jefferson, and Alexander Hamilton, and, as such, helped ensure that the unity Washington had sought to foster collapsed, leading, in particular, to the bitter presidential election of 1800.

Yet, it is all too easy to describe American politics in terms of these clashes of personalities, and the related ideas, without giving due weight to the extent to which they were under pressure from events and circumstances that engendered fears. Thus, the Nootka Sound Crisis of 1790, which arose from clashing British and Spanish interests in Vancouver Island, was one that threatened to determine the fate of much of North America but without the Americans playing any role in its settlement. The varied background to this crisis included the collapse of the wartime alliance that supported American independence, a collapse that increased the seriousness of the question of how Britain was to respond to the new American state, and especially to outstanding issues arising from the implementation of the recent peace treaty with America. These issues created problems for both Britain and America. Aside from the possible domestic reaction within Britain if the implementation was too unfavorable or humiliating, there was the question of the security of Canada and of Britain's Caribbean possessions.

In a report from Paris of 1786, William Eden, a well-connected British diplomat who had visited America as a member of the abortive Carlisle (peace) Commission in 1778, struck a prophetic note about the possibility that the New World would challenge the interests and power of Europe: "there are strong appearances here of a disposition to believe that Great Britain and France ought to unite in some solid plan of permanent peace: and many of the most considerable and efficient people talk with little reserve of the dangers to be apprehended from the revolted colonies if they should be encouraged to gain commercial strength and consistency of government."[16] Eden, however, was unusual in his commitment to good relations with France, and this forecast was not seen as a serious prospect in London. Indeed, Eden's prospectus had few echoes, although in 1787 the new French foreign minister, Armand, Count of Montmorin, expressed his hope that the Americans would not be able to establish a new constitution and his fear that, if they did, they would be able to develop a strength that they would probably be eager to abuse.[17]

In Britain, instead, American–French cooperation was still feared, there was no interest in an Anglo-French alignment directed against the Americans, and better relations with the last were sought. In July 1784, John, 3rd Duke of Dorset, the envoy in Paris, a critic of Eden, and very much an aristocrat, thought it "worth our while to sooth the Americans as no pains are spared by the French to render us still odious in their eyes."[18] Postwar bitterness and suspicion on both sides, however, proved a major hindrance to the improvement of Anglo-American relations, and the rapid and profitable recovery of commercial links was not matched in the political sphere, nor, as the Americans suggested,[19] with a trade treaty.

In order to break the tripartite situation and limit French influence, the British government insisted that Anglo-American negotiations must take place in London, not Paris. John Adams, the first American diplomat accredited to the British court, was presented to George III on 1 June 1785, but the draft treaties he submitted to Francis, Marquess of Carmarthen, the Foreign Secretary, in July 1785 and April 1786 were unacceptable as they challenged the protectionism of the British imperial trading system as outlined in the Navigation Act. British anger about the American refusal to pay debts, a point that William Pitt the Younger, the prime minister, stressed in December 1785,[20] and to compensate Loyalists, led to a British refusal to evacuate posts near the Canadian frontier, a step seen by Americans as stirring up Native American opposition.

In the event, war between the major powers in North America came closest not due to America's unwillingness to accept such an infraction of the peace terms, but, rather, as a result of Spanish unwillingness to accept British action. The history of Spain's American empire between 1783 and 1826 is such that it is easy to understand why the country tends to be seen as a victim, and indeed, as a result, a means to American greatness. This approach is reasonable from the perspective of the 1820s when the empire collapsed, but it underrates Spain's earlier position, and the strong statecraft of Charles III (r. 1759–88). Spanish participation in the War of American Independence revealed the importance and effectiveness of its military, which conquered West Florida from Britain in 1779–81.

The subsequent peace saw Spain gain West and East Florida, as well as the Mediterranean island of Minorca, and, in 1787, the British evacu-

ated the Mosquito Coast of Nicaragua as part of a settlement of their
Central American differences with Spain. This was scarcely an instance
of America dominating the Caribbean. Indeed, Spain remained an important naval power, not only in European waters but also based in Havana where durable ships were built using tropical hardwoods. Massive
112- and 120-gun three-deckers, as well as 74-gun two-deckers of high
quality, were launched by Spain in the 1780s, and, although postwar
cuts in naval estimates were followed by a substantial cut of 11 percent
in 1788, training and seamanship improvements were begun in 1785, and
the Americans had nothing to match the Spanish navy.

Spanish policy did not focus on North America and, in 1776, there
were only 1,900 troops to defend the 1,800-mile frontier of Spanish North
America. Goods and trade were used to keep the peace with the Natives,
but the idea of Comanche subjugation through external manipulation
by Spanish officials in the 1780s ignores the nature of Comanche political culture.[21] The Comanche cooperated with the Spaniards in attacks
on the Apache in the late 1780s, but only to suit their own goals. Spanish
attempts to direct and manipulate Comanche war making were repeatedly unsuccessful. In the mid-1780s, Spanish attention focused on the
Mediterranean and on European power politics. Attacks on Algiers were
launched (unsuccessfully) in 1783 and 1784, and Spanish ministers were
concerned about Russian advances into the Turkish Empire in the war
that began in 1787, concerns that reflected the deployment of Russian
naval power in the Mediterranean from 1769.

When conflict came near for Spain over North America, it was with
Britain, not America. In 1789, there was Spanish concern about a reported
plan for the dispatch of a British fleet to the Caribbean, British worries
about Spanish naval preparations, and tension in the Bay of Honduras.[22]
In the event, the Pacific coast proved the key issue. As the United States
did not play a role, it is easy to leave this episode out of this book, but it
is important because of what it shows about the situation soon after the
War of American Independence and also to demonstrate a clear contrast
with the situation in the 1840s, at the time of the Oregon crisis and the
Mexican War, when the United States took the leading role.

Initially, the international crisis began as a consequence of Spanish action designed predominantly to block a reported Russian plan to

occupy Nootka Sound on Vancouver Island. In 1784, the Russians had established a permanent base on Kodiak Island in the Aleutian Islands, and, thereafter, started to expand their activities along the Alaskan coast, helped by the impact of European diseases, which, alongside Russian massacres, led to a dramatic fall in the population of the eastern Aleutians. Mass conversions of the Kodiak Aleut began in 1794. In February 1789, Eden wrote from Madrid, "Accounts have been received here from Mexico of several settlements of Russians being made on the coast of California between the 49 and 68 Degrees,"[23] in modern terms the coasts of British Columbia and Alaska.

The Spanish government had already decided to act, as part of a general pattern of asserting Spanish interests along the Pacific coast. From the 1770s, Spanish explorations had sailed north of colonizing activity in California. The surveying voyage of Bruno de Hezeta in 1775 led to the sighting of the estuary of the Columbia River, although the currents were too swift for his scurvy-weakened crew to enter the river. Earlier, seven of the crew had been killed by Natives when they put ashore for water. Francisco de la Bodega y Quadria, who had sailed on when Hezeta turned back, reached 58°30'N, despite scurvy affecting most of the crew, and his surveying voyages led to a far better map of the coast from the Columbia northward. The viceroy of New Spain, Antonio María de Bucareli, speculated that the Columbia might be the outflow of the (nonexistent) inland sea marked on maps, and, in 1793, Guesmes-Pachecoy Paddila, Count of Revillagigedo, his successor, suggested that the river might cross the continent, which would give it considerable commercial and strategic importance. This belief led to an unsuccessful attempt to establish a settlement at the mouth of the Columbia and to penetrate up-river: it was thwarted by the difficulty of the river channel and the hostile attitude of the Natives.[24]

Meanwhile, the Spaniards had made efforts further north to discover a Northwest passage. In 1788, Estéban José Martínez explored what is now the Pacific coast of Canada; in 1790 Salvador Fidalgo explored Prince William Sound and Cook Inlet, and Manuel Quimper the Strait of Juan de Fuca; in 1791–92 Alejandro Malaspina surveyed the coast to 60°N; and in 1792 Dionisio Alcala Galiano and Cayetano Valdes surveyed the last unmapped portion of the Pacific coast of North America, part of California. No navigable Northwest passage had been found and no river proved to give access to an inland sea.[25]

In May 1789, a Spanish warship anchored in Nootka Sound asserted Spain's right to the area and, on 5 July, in response to the claim of Nootka Sound on behalf of George III by a British merchantman, arrested the captain and his crew. The Spanish commander proclaimed that the coast from Cape Horn to 60° North was possessed by the Spanish crown; the coast further north being left to Russia.

Neither government wished to push the matter, but the British government asserted rights to trade and make settlements on the coast, and both sides began naval preparations. John Meares, the entrepreneur largely responsible for the British presence in Nootka Sound, reported that Spanish actions had been taken despite the presence of a British settlement flying the flag built on land purchased from the local Native American chief, the latter's acknowledgment of British overlordship, the Native agreement that the British should enjoy the exclusive right to trade, and Meares's prior claim to territory on behalf of George III.

In an instructive instance of the role of domestic politics that was to be fully seen in American history, the imminence of a general election in Britain in 1790 probably played a role in the government's decision to prepare for war, but it is unclear what this role was.[26] As preparations for war developed, the military and strategic salience of the European sphere was shown by the shelving by Britain of a small proposed expedition to the Pacific coast of America in favor of the prospect of fleet action in European waters where British naval power could be brought to bear most effectively, both militarily and politically. Such an allocation of strength would not have been so valid had Britain, France, or Spain been involved, in alliance or enmity, with America.

Pitt told the House of Commons that Spanish claims would prevent Britain from extending its navigation and fishery in the Pacific.[27] This issue was also relevant for America, whose traders had been taking a growing role in the Pacific. So also was the British government's interest in hoping to realize oft-held aspirations to support revolution in Spanish colonies. On 6 May 1790, Pitt and William Grenville, the home secretary, had a meeting with Francisco de Miranda, a Spanish American seeking British support for an independent federated empire in Spanish America.

There were to be several more meetings over the next month, and, like much British planning for war, they indicated the extent to which Britain was willing to envisage major changes if war were to break out with Spain.[28] These changes were designed to leave Britain far more powerful in the Americas, as it was assumed that independent states freed from Spanish rule would look to Britain. Such an outcome was both worrying to America in general, and also had specific consequences in terms of the possibility that Britain itself would regain the Floridas from Spain and therefore be in a position to meddle in relations further north, notably between the American government and the Native Americans.

There was also consideration on the British part of more direct intervention in America, notably of using the Vermont separatists and other American frontiersmen, especially those of Kentucky, in order both to prevent America from joining Spain and to attack the Spanish positions on the Gulf Coast, especially New Orleans.[29] Grenville subsequently argued that the possibility of Native Americans and "American back settlers" being used to attack Spanish colonies had been exaggerated, but, in a glance at the possible volatility of developments in the New World, he emphasized the need for Britain to retain their help in case of an American attack on British positions: "It is unquestionably true that the Americans have for these last two or three years been mediating attempts against our posts."[30]

At the same time as it was considering military options, the British government was also negotiating for the maintenance of peace with Spain and its key ally, France, but the American state was of no consequence in such discussions. In May 1790, the British outlined terms that included not only reparation for the seizures at Nootka but also a refusal to accept both Spanish claims to American territories that they did not occupy and Spanish claims to the exclusive navigation of the Pacific. As Spain was not actually in occupation of the American coastline north of San Francisco, where a base had been founded in 1776, the British position opened up a large extent of coastline to settlement, especially if it could be made clear that Spain had no right to Nootka Sound. Moreover, Spain ruled few of the Pacific island groups, with the exception of the Philippines, Marianas, and Carolines in the western Pacific. The British position, although presented as a defensive step designed to prevent future clashes, was pregnant with possibilities for new British establishments, and this was important given current and growing British interest in the Pacific. Furthermore, in rebutting Spanish claims, both to the American mainland and to the exclusive navigation of the Pacific, the instruction by Francis, Marquess of Leeds, the Foreign Secretary, to Alleyne Fitzherbert, the British envoy in Spain, referred to the "principles of the Law of Nations," as well as "the plain sense" or "fair construction" of existing treaties,[31] a disruptive thesis that looked toward arguments that were later to be made by America. Spanish fears over many years of British colonial intentions seemed to be realized, and it has been claimed that the British argument gave "a gloss of respectability to a ruthless act of expropriation,"[32] a point that could be made about American expansionism.

Poor Anglo-American relations might seem to have made America a feasible ally for Spain, but the two powers were in dispute, especially over the northern frontier of West Florida.[33] In addition, Anglo-American relations were eased by suggestions about the possibility of an alliance. George Beckwith, a British agent in New York, although not an accredited minister, explored the possibilities in discussions with Alexander Hamilton, the secretary of the treasury. The two powers, however, had different views about the fates of any conquests from Spain, especially New Orleans.[34] This issue captured a prime problem in any cooperation with the United States, namely the extent to which the Americans were unwilling to see European powers established or indeed influential in the New World, let alone North America. As a consequence, the nature of any alliance with America was heavily conditional, while an important aspect of such an alliance was that foreign powers would be expected to support American expansion. American vulnerability on this head was demonstrated in October 1790 in the Ohio Valley, when more than two hundred soldiers were killed in a failed invasion of Native territory designed to end violence stemming from Native hostility to what were seen as extorted land cessions in treaties of 1785–89. The following year, a Native army killed 647 men when they successfully attacked an American force under Arthur St. Clair, the territorial governor, at Kekionga on 4 November. The Native capacity to mount a major attack was abundantly demonstrated.[35]

In 1790, the likely response of America to the outbreak of war between Britain and Spain was an imponderable for the other powers, but
the French envoy, who saw New York more as a London suburb than
an American town, reported that America needed ten years of peace
to settle its government.[36] Moreover, Britain displayed a strength that
the Americans could not match: not only a major naval armament but
also an ability to sustain it despite the heavy cost. On 1 May 1790, the
Admiralty was ordered to fit out a fleet of forty ships of the line to be
assembled at Spithead as soon as possible, while the allied Dutch added
a squadron of ten of the line. By 8 October, the fleet at Spithead, the major British anchorage, consisted of forty-three ships of the line and ten
frigates, while there were also warships on other stations. At that stage,
the Americans had no ships of the line. The French National Assembly
threatened to arm forty-five ships of the line on behalf of Spain, and,
if they proved unable to do so due to their political crisis, the numbers
again were significant.

British diplomatic instructions indicated the extent to which North
America was being planned out without reference to America. On 17
August 1790, Fitzherbert was sent fresh instructions: the Spanish claim
of sovereignty over the coast of America must be dropped as part of a
settlement in which Britain and Spain agreed to those limits of latitude
and territorial waters within which British merchants could not settle or
trade freely, while, outside those limits, they should have the same rights
of navigation, fishing and settlement on unoccupied territory. Fitzherbert was told to suggest territorial waters of five, or at the most ten,
leagues from the coast, and the latitudes of 31°N–45°S, from Little (Baja
or Alta) California in northern Mexico to the fjord coastline of modern
southern Chile. If necessary, 40°N was to be accepted as the northern
limit: about 170 miles north of San Francisco, which would still have left
the coastline of modern Canada and the Pacific Northwest of the United
States open to British activity.[37]

There were high hopes in Britain about the economic possibilities
of the region, especially over the long-sought Northwest Passage.[38] One
of the major purposes of Commander George Vancouver's voyage to the
northeastern Pacific, which began in April 1791, was to discover such a
passage as well as to strengthen the British position on the coast by ad-

vancing the linkage of knowledge and control.[39] Suggesting the way in which the geopolitics of North America was still open to the imagination because its geography was unknown, Robert Liston, a British diplomat, wrote of a possible Northwest Passage from near Nootka Sound to Hudson's Bay and of a large inland sea like the Baltic or the Mediterranean, adding, "if the coasts of this new Mediterranean are of a rich sort, producing ship-timber, and peopled with a race of men wishing to exchange furs for our woollens and other manufactures, we cannot give up such an extensive prospect for the increase of our trade."[40]

On the Pacific coast, European and American traders wanted sea-otter pelts, and offered the Natives trinkets, beads, copper, iron, firearms, textiles, and alcohol. Trade brought the Natives much prosperity, but also the disruption and suffering of alcoholism, firearms, and smallpox. Initially cordial, relations soon became strained, with mutual distaste periodically exploding into violence, mainly owing to fraud and kidnapping by white traders. Hostilities usually ended in a stand-off, although the Natives suffered more casualties thanks to the greater firepower of American, British, and Russian ships.[41] This trade was part of the new energetic dynamic of American commerce, a dynamic that was part of the long-term linkage between the activities of private individuals aggressively pursuing free enterprise and the global expansion of American influence. Obtaining furs, Captain Robert Gray, in the first circumnavigation (1787–90) of the globe by an American ship, sold them in Canton, and, in turn, bought tea, which he sold in Boston where the voyage was organized.[42] Fifty fur-trade voyages to the northwest coast were made by Americans between 1795 and 1804, while Boston and Salem became major bases for the China trade.

In an instructive indication of the disruptive role of representative assemblies in diplomacy, one that looked toward later foreign concern about Congress, the French National Assembly unexpectedly complicated affairs on 26 August 1790 by pressing Louis XVI to negotiate a "national" treaty between France and Spain and to arm a large fleet, which suggested the possibility of war with Britain. The British response indicated the possibilities posed by such assemblies, but offered a contrast with American history as there was scant foreign intervention in Congress. In part, this was because there was a lack of such a practice in America as opposed, for example, to Sweden, but the case of France shows that it was possible to see such intervention without this experience. The British sent two agents to Paris, William Augustus Miles and Hugh Elliot, and they made approaches to prominent politicians, notably Talleyrand, Mirabeau, and Lafayette, and seem to have succeeded in lessening suspicion of Britain in these circles.

Meanwhile, reports about British ambitions in the New World increased, throwing light on current and later American anxieties. Thus, in September 1790, the French envoy in London warned that Britain was after French colonies in the West Indies and claimed that the British had secret agents in Saint-Domingue.[43]

In the event, a compromise of Anglo-Spanish differences was reached in October 1790. Spain provided compensation for the Nootka losses, territorial waters were to be ten leagues from the coast, and the possible latitudinal limit in the north was rejected, in favor of allowing free settlement to the north of the area occupied by Spain in April 1789. However, British merchants were not to be allowed to trade directly with Spanish America. Spain had backed down, and the crisis prefigured the weakness that it was to show when confronted with American pressure, not least because of the failure of the Franco-Spanish alliance that had been so important in Anglo-Bourbon relations and the Atlantic world since 1700. Yet, that weakness also posed a problem for America, because it was Britain that seemed best placed to exert pressure and to benefit from Spanish problems. In 1790, it was a question of British warships possibly being sent to the Gulf of Mexico, and not American ones. Thus, American relations with Spain more clearly became a matter of a tripartite relation with Britain, explicitly or implicitly, whereas earlier it had been France that was also a key player when Britain was opposed to Spain.

Trade, rather than territory, was most at stake for the British in the Pacific. Negotiations in the late 1780s for Manila (in the Spanish Philippines) to become a free port and those for the opening of British diplomatic relations with China in the early 1790s, the MacCartney mission of 1793–94, both of which proved abortive, were indicative of British attitudes, although another, far more territorial, strand was provided by the establishment of a British settlement in Australia in 1788. The

British flag was hoisted at Nootka when the Spaniards handed over the site of Meares's house in 1795, but the position was left to the Native Americans.

There were other players on the Pacific coast, although not Japan nor China. In 1802, the Russian-American Company's base at Novo Arch-angel'sk (Sitka), established in 1799, was taken by the Tlingit Chief Ska-yutlelt, but in 1804 it was recaptured and then well fortified. Alaska was integrated into the Russian orbit in part as a result of the establishment in 1789 on the Maley Aniui River in Siberia, eight hundred miles west of the Bering Strait, of a trade fair that became a focus for exports of furs by Alaskan natives.[44]

In 1812, the Russians were to leapfrog to the south, establishing Fort Ross, one hundred kilometers north of Spanish-held San Francisco, in order to acquire the fur of sea otters. The Pomo who lived nearby reacted violently, but disease and Russian firepower cut their numbers. Explorers also sought to extend the Russian presence in the Arctic, exploring the coast of Alaska and making unsuccessful attempts to discover a north-west passage from the west in 1815–18 and 1820–21.[45] Moreover, in 1815, an independent initiative by George Sheffer, an employee of the Russian-American Company, nearly led to the acquisition of Hawaii.[46]

In the face of British and American protests, Tsar Alexander I claimed all of North America's Pacific coast down to 51°N in 1821. How-ever, this thinly populated Russian empire was to be short-lived. An American–Russian treaty of 1824 and an Anglo-Russian one of 1825 fixed the southern limit of Russia's claim at 54°40, the southern extent of to-day's Alaskan panhandle, and the northernmost limit of the Spanish claims that America inherited by the Transcontinental Treaty of 1819. The 1825 treaty, which brought to a close negotiations started in 1820, also established 141°W as the eastern boundary of Alaska and gave the British the right to navigate rivers that crossed Alaska's borders, a clear means to commercial penetration. Alaska was sold in 1867, but this episode was a reminder of the far-flung nature of Russian power.

An emphasis on the Nootka Sound Crisis has value but also under-plays the extent to which the international situation influenced Ameri-can domestic politics, because the latter factor did not come to the fore until the outbreak of war between Britain and France in 1793. Before then, there had been great concern about British policy and supposed plans, as well as anxiety about Spanish views, notably the role of New Orleans as the outlet for Mississippi trade and, therefore, the key point for the settlements west of the Appalachians. These interests had led to differences within America, not least because they interacted with regional political identities, but there was nothing to compare with the raw emotion and anger that came to the fore as the increasingly radical French Revolution became a divisive feature of American politics.

Initially, the French Revolution could be readily welcomed as it was comprehensible in American terms, and, indeed, could be presented as a second stage to the American Revolution and a reflection of the way in which the Declaration of Independence was a global document speaking to, and for, the world.[47] The prominent role of the Marquis de Lafayette in the early stages of the French Revolution encouraged this elision of difference, as he had become a hero through participation in the War of American Independence; but so also did a degree of naïve optimism in America that reflected not only francophilia but also a delight that the more unwelcome aspects of French politics and society were being overthrown. This development represented a potent justification of the wartime alliance with France and also suggested anew that America was on the side of progress and the future, and, indeed, a model for both, which enhanced its significance.

Moreover, the achievement of change initially without war within or involving France was an important factor as it thus became not only simpler to praise French developments but also for America to adjust to a new and more benign international order. Furthermore, such progress in France made it easier to hope that British politics would take a favorable turn for America, a hope that had seemed very close to fruition when the opposition Whigs nearly gained power in the Regency Crisis of 1788–89, for many of them had supported the American cause during the War of Independence.

The outbreak of the French Revolutionary War, first with Austria and Prussia in 1792, and then with Britain, the Dutch, and Spain in 1793, changed the situation. So, even more, did the growing radicalism and violence of the revolution, violence that culminated with the Terror of 1794, and radicalism with the abandonment of Christianity, a step that was unwelcome to Americans whatever their views on Catholicism and established churches. These changes did more than make France's American friends uncomfortable; they also shattered the political peace in America. Already, in 1793, President Washington's Neutrality Proclamation, which annulled the eleventh article of America's treaty with France in 1778, had led to a debate between Alexander Hamilton, the secretary to the treasury, and James Madison about the roles of the executive and legislature in the conduct of foreign policy.[48]

More directly, any hope that America might be free from European conflicts, ideological as much as political and military, seemed implausible as revolution and the emancipation of slaves in Saint-Domingue produced a violent cataclysm that terrified Southerners (and others); as French diplomats in America, most prominently Edmond Genet, planned to use America as a base for conflict with France's European opponents, and also intervened in American politics to further their goals; and as France's many successes in 1792–97 left it the most powerful state in Western Europe, and one apparently able to pursue its ambitions more widely. The volatile situation in America's borderlands appeared to give France the opportunity of shared interests. There was both pull, from America, and push, from France and its agents. In 1792, James Cole Mountflorence approached the French government on behalf of settlers in what is now Tennessee, seeking help in gaining Louisiana from Spain. The following year, George Rogers Clark accepted a commission from France as a general. Genet, himself, was instructed to dispatch agents to Kentucky, which had been established as a state in 1792, in order to arrange an invasion of Louisiana, while Michel-Ange-Bernard Mangourit, the French Consul in Charleston, was ordered by Genet to organize the invasion of Florida and Louisiana in order to drive Spain out, with support in South Carolina to be obtained by the offer of land and trade. Genet also sought to undermine backing for President Washington, while the French commissioning of privateers sailing from American ports harmed relations with Britain. In the event, opposition by the American government and the impact of political instability in France combined to end these schemes, which also suffered from impracticability and only limited French interest.[49] The British were also concerned about French subversion in Canada.[50]

In America, there were profound differences over foreign policy, specifically relations with France and Britain, differences that played a prominent role in domestic politics. To many American politicians, the response to the French Revolution had to be vigilance, vigilance against domestic radicals who might support France and be inspired by it, and vigilance against French power projection. American foreign policy was republican, not radical.[51]

The situation became more serious, and was magnified by rumor, once France forced the defeated Spain and conquered Dutch into alliance in 1796, as this development greatly altered the naval situation: the world's second, third, and fourth naval powers were now aligned against the first. Indeed, the newly vulnerable British withdrew their fleet from the Mediterranean and the French were able to attempt invasions of Ireland and Wales, although they failed. This situation exposed the extent to which America still relied on the cover of the Royal Navy, and also led to concern in America both about the consequences of French hostility and about the possibility of France gaining Spanish colonies, notably Louisiana and Florida.

Rumors also focused on Saint-Domingue and French plans about slavery. These were of great significance to the South as the role of slavery in the North was becoming increasingly marginal. Slavery was slowly abolished in the states of the North, although, with the exception of Massachusetts, this did not involve the emancipation of slaves but rather, as in New York under legislation of 1799, the freeing of slave children born thereafter once they reached maturity.[52] Nevertheless, the bulk of the black population, which was 19.3 percent of the national population in 1790, was in the South. The legal changes in the North were at the state level, but the argument was very much more wide ranging.

Mangourit had planned that Florida would become a pro-French republic with slavery, a way to win support in the American South, but the freedom given slaves in Saint-Domingue worried the government of South Carolina in late 1793 as they feared that it would affect their state. More generally, the radicalism seen in France and Haiti, both radical popular sovereignty and its implications at this stage, was not welcome in America, and especially not in the South.[53]

Hamilton's sense of a menacing international system and his more specific concerns about France gave reason to his drive to develop America's public finances and national economy, and to anglophilia. Relations between Britain and America improved for a while. Jay's Treaty of 1794 settled, or at least eased, commercial and territorial disputes, thus improving American access to trade with the British West Indies.[54]

The treaty also led to the abandonment of Britain's North American allies, and, as a result both of heavy defeat by the Americans, in the shape of the Legion of the United States under Anthony Wayne at Fallen Timbers on 20 August 1794, and of this abandonment, the Native Americans agreed to the Treaty of Greenville with the United States in 1795, which ceded much of Ohio to the Americans.[55] This development underlined the extent to which American relations with the Native Americans could not be separated from the real, or possible, role of Britain. So also with relations with Spain. Spain, in 1795, accepted the 31st N Parallel as the northern border of West Florida, opening the way for American penetration into the lands of the southeastern tribes. Spain's willingness to do so reflected the Anglo-American treaty of 1794, Jay's Treaty, which left Spain more exposed, and also the Spanish wish to limit the number of potential enemies at a time of conflict and confrontation in Europe. However, this treaty reversed the buffer policy of Charles III and his local governors, and put the Floridas on the slippery slope to eventual American control.

Moreover, in 1796, Britain handed over the seven bases in America, including Detroit and Fort Niagara, that it had retained after the 1783 treaty. This action was seen as very important in the establishment of America's position west of the Appalachians. Yet, this was still a vast prospect open to international competition, as could be seen with the career of French traders. Jean Baptiste Truteau, who explored the Missouri valley in 1794, did so for the American Missouri Company, part of the process by which the French, left behind by the end of imperial control in 1760, 1763, and 1803, facilitated American expansion,[56] but in 1786 Pierre Vial opened a trail from San Antonio to Santa Fe and in 1792 from there to St. Louis, as Don Pedro Vial in Spanish service. Imperial competition, however, also threatened activity. In 1806, the Canadian traders of the North-West Company complained to the British envoy that their trade "with the Indian tribes up the River Missouri" had been obstructed by American action.[57] The Americans also used the bases handed over in 1796 to limit British trade with America and the lands it claimed, ignoring British diplomatic complaints on this point.[58]

If one dynamic was that of international challenges, another was provided by domestic discontent within America. Shays's Rebellion in Massachusetts in 1786–87, followed by the Whiskey Rebellion of 1794 in Pennsylvania, were the most prominent instances of a widespread unrest, also seen for instance in New Jersey, Virginia, Maryland, and South Carolina. The causes were varied, not least economic problems and a strong localism, but the focus was a conviction, notably but not only in the western frontier areas, that political élites were using taxation for their own interests. As these taxes, which were largely motivated by the need to pay the debts left by the war, also meant a transfer of money, they exacerbated the liquidity crisis in frontier areas, and, indeed, one key aspect of the geopolitics of this period was the movement of money, both within America and internationally. This movement was enforced through debt collection and repossessions, and the process helped give a violent character to the dispute over taxation.

The risings also exposed the problems with reliance on militia, a decentralized practice that was fundamental to the geopolitics of military power. Indeed, Shays's Rebellion posed a problem in that Congress did not have the troops to suppress the rising, and this encouraged Edmund Randolph to open the Constitutional Convention in 1787 by calling for the federal government to have the power to suppress rebellions.[59] The Whiskey Rebellion found the federal government reasonably powerful, but still in jurisdictional disagreements with the state about control over responding to the rebellion and the militia. These disagreements spilled over into disagreements in Congress about the militia. Rebel success in taking over Pennsylvania's militia exacerbated the situation, and the seven thousand armed men who converged on Pittsburgh represented a fundamental challenge to established power. Four state militias – those of Maryland, New Jersey, Pennsylvania, and Virginia – were consequently federalized, and an army of 12,950 men was assembled, and it suppressed both the rebellion and draft riots. Washington, Hamilton, and Henry Lee all played a role in this suppression.[60]

In 1797, France and America began what was known as the Quasi War, a naval conflict in which attacks on American merchantmen were used by France to try to force the United States to accept French views on America's role in the global trade system. The conflict also reflected France's anger with the Anglo-American Jay Treaty: America had to be brought into the French camp as Spain and the Dutch had been. That this, America's first war with a European power, was very much limited in scale and scope – concentrated in the Eastern Caribbean – did not make it less serious, not least because it was unclear where the war might lead, especially if French forces were reestablished in North America and regained possessions in the West Indies. Moreover, war with one European power might leave America vulnerable to another one.

To Hamilton and others, the necessary response was clear: America had to take specific defensive measures, to align with Britain, following up Jay's Treaty, and to strengthen its political system. Hamilton saw Britain as an essentially liberal state and therefore less of a threat than France, and the British ministry saw the Quasi War as an opportunity to improve relations,[61] while noting reports that the Americans were concerned about the possibility of peace between Britain and France.[62] Indeed, Grenville was concerned that any peace should leave Britain able to maintain good relations with America.[63]

Strengthening America entailed, for Hamilton, a shift of power from the states to the federal government, and from regions to the national level, and thus was unwelcome to many not only in specific terms but also because of the opposition to distant government already seen in the American Revolution. Key elements were the size of the military and the provision of a national bank. Rejecting the views of those who felt that the militias were more effective than regulars,[64] the governing Federalists expanded the army in 1798, during the Quasi War, with Washington as commander in chief and Hamilton as senior ranking major general, although the army was not required for combat during the conflict. Hamilton sought to develop the force as a powerful permanent body able to unite America against internal subversion and foreign threat, but his intentions were suspect to many Americans and he was accused of having authoritarian aspirations. Nevertheless, the Federalists built up a professional army, although it was also both politicized and greatly affected by personality-based factionalism.[65] Hamilton's emphasis on a strong army as a defense against foreign attack and domestic subversion was to be matched by Simón Bólivar, the president of Gran Colombia (Venezuela, Ecuador, and Colombia) from 1819 to 1830.

Benefiting from a vigor and popularity stemming from the Quasi War, the Federalists linked foreign and domestic policies closely to military preparedness. "Millions for defense, but not one cent for tribute" (to a foreign state) became their slogan after the XYZ affair, a French attempt, when Washington's successor as president, John Adams, sought to settle differences, to make the Americans buy them off. The limiting consequences of federal financial weaknesses ensured, however, that the construction of ten frigates during the Quasi War was financed by subscriptions raised in the major ports, such as Philadelphia.[66] By 1798, in an undeclared war, France and the Americans were pursuing hostile policies, notably in the Caribbean, while the British government was prepared to lend or sell warships in return for American seamen for the Royal Navy, and acceded to an American request to loan cannon from the base at Halifax.[67] The following year, Hamilton suggested using the army to gain Louisiana and the Floridas from France's ally, Spain, an idea Grenville supported while also pointing out the benefit to the Americans of the British conquering Saint-Domingue.[68]

The Federalist government also passed the Alien and Sedition Acts in order to strengthen against internal opposition, a major step in the process of "constitutionalising politics and politicising the Constitution" seen in the 1790s.[69] This, however, proved a divisive step, for, in response, while asserting states' rights in their Resolutions, Kentucky and Virginia denounced the acts as violations of the American Constitution and thus, in effect, pressed the role of state governments in deciding the constitutional character of federal actions. Adams's son, the diplomat John Quincy Adams, called the Resolutions a "tocsin of insurrection," and Thomas Jefferson, the vice president under Adams (1797–1801) and an opponent of Hamilton, thought rebellion in Pennsylvania a possibility. A small-scale rising, Fries's Rebellion, was played up by Hamilton in order to justify a display of federal power and to expand the army.[70] Hamilton considered moving the army into Virginia in order to overawe opposition and prevent Virginians from preparing for resistance.

In practice, hostility to the Acts was widespread and took forward the hostility seen earlier in the decade to the assumptions and policies of the Federalists and that were associated with them, assumptions and policies that had a counterrevolutionary character insofar as they sought to contain the radical aspects and implications of the American Revolution.[71]

Regional and other tensions led to reports of the imminent dissolution of the Union, such as that sent to Robert, Viscount Castlereagh, the British Foreign Secretary, by Francisco de Miranda, the Venezuelan revolutionary, in 1807.[72] Alongside these tensions, there was a more general localist hostility to the payment of taxes, and notably for the national government. That the latter's army provided a force that could enforce taxation amplified the problem. Differences over the size and organization of the military reflected contrasting assumptions about the nature of America as a state and about American society. A rift in the latter was discerned by foreign commentators, such as Thornton, who contrasted "a commanding aristocratic influence which pervades their system of government" with "a strong principle of democracy among the common people."[73]

There were also clashing conceptions of the international system. Hamilton advanced a pessimistic interpretation of competing states and of the need, in response, for governmental and military preparedness.

In contrast to Hamilton's views, critics felt that a benign international system was possible or that America could distance itself from the European powers by an appropriate conduct. Thomas Jefferson, who served as envoy in France, secretary of state, vice president, and president (1801–1809), generally favored diplomatic initiatives over warfare and/or coercion, and Liston linked him to the idealistic Girondins of the French Revolution, writing of "that visionary philosophy derived from the school of [Jacques] Brissot which Mr Jefferson carries to its utmost."[74] Alongside his insistence that American diplomats not dress grandly, Jefferson was concerned that American diplomats might be corrupted by living among the wicked Europeans, while he felt the need to defend and reenact the revolution in order to protect it from the Federalists, who were seen as aristocrats in disguise and as keen to anglicize American politics. To Jefferson, Hamilton's interest in money, notably the creation of the Bank of America, and his alliance with the growing financial interest,[75] was part of his drive to establish an aristocratic élite of moneyed men, based in the national capital, and seeking to create a new centralized power.

In short, the struggle that had given rise to the revolution was to be repeated, but with the threat based in America, although looking to Britain. Jefferson thus domesticated and politicized the European anti-aristocratic discourse and the suspicion of finance and credit, and linked them to an account of public virtue and a narrative of American history, that he indeed sought to shape, not least through arranging his papers for publication and through the use of gossip and rumor.[76] Both of these means were related to the concern for honor and reputation that were so important to American politicians,[77] as well as to counterparts elsewhere, for example in Colombia.[78] The emphasis on honor made compromise more difficult, as did the impassioned rhetoric of leading politicians when they additionally sought to rally support.

The racial refraction of American history ensured that Jefferson could present himself as a democrat while being the second biggest slaveholder in Albemarle County, with eight hundred slaves, extensive cash holdings, and an aristocratic consumption pattern. To Jefferson, who had to withstand Lafayette's bitter criticisms of slavery when he visited Monticello in 1824 and 1825,[79] a revived America meant an America that had defeated at home its leading foe, with democracy the means and result of victory. In practice, John Adams, whom Jeffersonians attacked as an aristocrat, was a product of the highly democratic culture of New England,[80] while Jefferson's political legacy was initially to be carried forward by Southern landowners who were slave-owning aristocrats, rather than the autonomous family farmers whom he idealized. A similar process can also be seen in Latin America, where republicanism was in practice linked to the racial discrimination it had in theory overcome.[81]

Force came close to playing a role in the bitterly contested election of 1800 in which Jefferson beat Adams, and Liston warned of the possibility of a civil war.[82] The governors of Pennsylvania and Virginia, McKene and Madison, were prepared to march their militias on Washington to prevent the Federalists from, as they saw it, stealing the election. In May 1800, a prominent Jeffersonian, fearful, when four hundred troops camped near Richmond, that they intended to remove the federal arms stored in Virginia, made plans to have the state militia seize these arms.[83] Such concerns, like those about politics after the Civil War, led to pressure for a small army, which affected America's capacity for power projection. Jefferson and the Democratic-Republicans who gained power after the election rejected Hamilton's military plans. They were not interested in what they saw as an authoritarian army of imperial size, nor, indeed, in a European-style military, being opposed to the taxes maintaining such an army entailed and the dependency this taxation was believed to give rise to, and suspicious of the existing army, not least because most of the senior officers were Federalists and because they saw the army as a threat to liberty, both republican and individual.[84]

Indeed, Jefferson limited the peacetime army establishment to 3,284 men and sought to rely on a citizen soldiery organized in the militia and supposedly committed to a republican view of America. As president, he preferred to rely on national unity, which was an example of the comforting illusion that virtue would necessarily prevail. This view led him, in his inaugural address in 1801, to claim that America's republican form of government was the strongest in the world. Yet, subsequently, confronted by the difficulties of using the militia,[85] Jefferson realized that he could not do without any national army, and he came both to strengthen this army and to make it, in his eyes, a more reliable part of the polity by replacing Federalist officers with Republicans and by creating the United States Military Academy at West Point (where he is memorialized) as a means to ensure both professional education and political reliability, through recruitment and training.[86]

More generally, Jefferson sought to downplay the federal government by emphasizing a national political community that took its dynamic from popular, not institutional, energy, and that was decentralized. Independence was seen to depend on liberty. Jefferson's concern for farming meant that land was the measure of national health as well as power, and this encouraged his lack of sympathy with the occupation of land by Native Americans, who were uncivilized in his eyes as well as failing to use the land productively. It was claimed that, if the Natives moved from hunting to farming, as in the conventional stadial scheme of human development, they would require less land as well, freeing it for new settlers, while the Natives themselves would become more civilized and more open to Christian proselytism.

The Federalist plan to build up the navy, which they reconstituted in 1794, was stopped when the Jeffersonians took power and demobilized part of the fleet. Only thirty-six naval lieutenants were retained. Albeit within what he sought as a balanced navy, including ships of the lines, frigates, and floating batteries, Jefferson favored coastal gunboats rather than the more expensive frigates with their oceanic range and their capacity for power projection and trade protection. Indeed, timber stockpiled for the construction of ocean-going ships was used for other purposes. He sponsored the construction of 180 gunboats with crews of twenty and cannon mounted in the bow and stern. This emphasis on gunboats conformed to the militia tradition of American Republicanism,[87] and was a stark contrast to the determination of the French revolutionaries and, later, Napoleon to use their ships of the line against Britain. Gunboats could be commanded by stout Republicans while the officers' quarters of frigates were seen as Federalist gathering places.

Jefferson, however, was obliged to confront an unwelcome reality when the Barbary pirates of the North African states attacked America's Mediterranean trade. Hitherto, American trade had been protected as part of the British imperial system, with the Royal Navy providing an effective cover, not least because it had a local base in Gibraltar and drew on the strength of the largest navy in the world. From 1784, however, the Barbary states launched attacks on American ships, the sailors of which were enslaved. In response, the American government, like some others, paid to protect their ships. A delay in the tribute to Algiers, however, led the angry Dey to oblige the USS *George Washington* to carry passengers and goods for him to Constantinople, threatening otherwise that the ship would be fired on. This bullying constituted a humiliation that led Jefferson, rather than paying more tribute, to determine to send three frigates and a schooner to the Mediterranean. He felt that this deployment, which was linked to effective consular representation in the Mediterranean, would cost scarcely more than keeping the warships in American waters (a mistaken conviction), and that it would also provide useful training. Jefferson's action also tested the Constitution, which had reserved the right to declare war to Congress, only for the president in 1801 to inform Congress that he was sending a squadron against the Barbary states.

From 1801, the American navy blockaded Tripoli, a major center of privateering, but, in October 1803, the frigate *Philadelphia* ran aground and was captured. The captured ship was set on fire in a daring raid by Stephen Decatur the following year, but the blockade failed to achieve its goals. Instead, a force of American Marines, Arabs, and mercenaries under William Eaton acting on behalf of the brother of the pasha of Tripoli captured the city of Derna, having marched overland, and this step led the pasha to settle terms in June 1805. American prisoners were ransomed, a humiliation, but the annual tribute came to an end.[88]

The war with Tripoli, and, suggested the British envoy, a desire to win over the "Eastern states," led Jefferson to support a navy capable of force projection and to back the plan for a large dry dock in Washington.[89] The resulting American navy was operationally inadequate for war with Britain, but was strategically in line with the degree to which Americans did not see their revolution as for export throughout the European world. Contrasting with the views of the French revolutionaries, this attitude arose from the powerful sense of a culture and society separate from those of Europe, a disengagement encouraged by the unwelcome turmoil of the French Revolutionary period. The sense of distance helped ease relations with European powers, although it also fostered a degree of unreality in responding to their real or supposed policies. This unreality was taken further by Jefferson's animus against Britain (an animus he denied)[90], so that he judged British actions without considering the pressures created for Britain by its conflict with France. Britain was primarily concerned with preventing the neutral Americans from trading with France, and thus circumventing the British blockade, which was designed to weaken the French economy. As with Britain against Germany in 1940–41, this blockade was seen as the key way to strike at the power that dominated the European continent; but, to the American government in the 1800s, this control over trade, including grain supplies, was unacceptable, as was the impressment of sailors of British origin.

The French ban on British exports to countries in its sphere of control and influence was designed to trump the British blockade as a form of economic warfare, and it led in Britain to a greater emphasis on exports to the Americas, both Latin America and the United States. The share of British exports going to the United States rose from 18.8 percent in 1803–1805 to 23.6 percent in 1806.[91] Jefferson, in turn, sought, in a reprise of the struggle in the 1760s and early 1770s that had made it easier to imagine independence[92] and, indeed, had climaxed in independence, to use trade as a weapon, following a nonimportation law in 1806 with an Embargo Act in 1807 that was intended to settle the commercial issue by ending most if it: as well as blocking imports, American ships were banned from trading with Europe; the export of American goods there was also prohibited.

This legislation reflected the expansion-minded Jefferson's mistaken conviction that Europe was dependent on American agricultural exports, and thus that the United States could use the economic weapon to force compliance to its will. This legislation, however, played through American politics in a divisive fashion, leading to a determined effort to force economic and sectional interests to heed the wishes of the federal government, and thus involved contentious and divisive issues of enforcement within the United States. Indeed, the recalcitrant attitude of the militia to attempts to stop smuggling led Jefferson to deploy regular troops in upstate New York in 1807. In addition, trade was intertwined with domestic politics, not only in terms of policy, but also with reference to political ideology.[93] In 1805, Jefferson had complained about "the influence gained by the commercial towns on public opinion, and their exclusive possession of the press."[94]

Directing admonition and coercion against trade with Europe did not work, while the policy also caused great damage to the American economy and to public finances as the latter were dependent on import duties. Indeed, to adopt an ahistorical comparison, the defiance of the outside world that the measure reflected was suggestive of the Chinese approach during the Cultural Revolution of the 1960s. The Embargo Act also led to a marked revival in support for the Federalists, support that was to be shown in the Congressional elections of 1808. The confused policy of the government thus not only reflected a failure to appreciate America's relative position, both diplomatic and economic, but also a lack of understanding of the domestic consequences of such a mishandled policy.

As a result, after the end of Jefferson's presidency, a Non-Intercourse Act, which banned trade with Britain and France (rather than Europe as a whole), replaced the Embargo Act in March 1809. This legislation, in turn, resulted in large-scale evasion and also encouraged the West Indies to turn to Canada for supplies, which was not the American intention. Damaging economically, "non-intercourse" was abandoned in 1810, to be replaced by an act that established restrictions on Britain or France if the other agreed to respect America's rights. This legislation, however, was cleverly manipulated by Napoleon in order to turn America against Britain. Far from altering the terms of the Atlantic economy, America was becoming a player, if not a tool, in the struggle between Britain and France.

That, indeed, was an aspect of the Louisiana Purchase of 1803, a measure that reflected the failure of Napoleon's Western Design, an attempt to create a major empire in the west that would include Louisiana, Florida, Cayenne, Martinique, Guadeloupe, and Saint-Domingue. His plans had focused not on Louisiana but on Saint-Domingue, which had always been far more important in the French imperial economy, but Louisiana was regarded as a crucial source of food for the French West Indies, just as Britain treated the Atlantic seaboard as a source of food for its sugar colonies. The Western Design would, therefore, have led to an expansion and strengthening of slavery.[95] In 1802, Napoleon sent 20,000 troops to Saint-Domingue, under the command of his brother-in-law, Charles Leclerc. Amphibious forces landed at numerous points, including Fort Dauphin, Cap Français, Port-de-Pais, and Port-au-Prince, and, combined with rapid subsequent advances by land, this ensured that the defenders, under Toussaint L'Ouverture, lacked any strategic depth. Indeed, French forces converged on the Crête-à-Pierrot area, forcing battle on Toussaint, who was seized and deported to France. Most of his generals defected to Leclerc. In Guadeloupe, which was a smaller island, French authority had been more rapidly asserted against the resistance of former slaves in May 1802.

However, resistance continued in parts of Saint-Domingue and, in the autumn of 1802, it was joined by many of the officers who had fought under Toussaint. These took the initiative and the French forces, hit hard by yellow fever, were reduced to isolated ports. Moreover, in 1803, the resumption of war with Britain led to a British blockade of Saint-Domingue, cutting the food supplies of the French forces and greatly weakening their position in the face of the revived opposition by the black population, which owed much to opposition to reenslavement.[96] The French abandoned the island with British cooperation and, on 1 January 1804, the independence of Saint-Domingue as the new state of Haiti was proclaimed.

As a result of their failure in Saint-Domingue, Louisiana became apparently worthless to the French, and Napoleon sold it to Jefferson in order both to stop it being a target for British attack and to gain money for operations in Europe. For sixty million *louis*, or $15 million, America gained over eight hundred thousand square miles, with no clear borders. The money was raised in part thanks to the British bank of Barings Brothers, and notably the efforts of Alexander Baring,[97] the second son of the head of the firm, Sir Francis Baring. His elder brother was in the service of the East India Company, with which Sir Francis had important links, but Alexander spent many years in America, marrying, in 1798, Anne Bingham, daughter of Senator William Bingham. As Lord Ashburton, Alexander Baring was to negotiate the Ashburton treaty with America in 1842, settling frontier disputes. The following year, Barings became the sole financial agent of the American government in London.[98]

The lands covered by the Louisiana Purchase were not mapped, and were to be defined by the Transcontinental Treaty with Spain in 1819. In the event, the Purchase brought America all or much of the future states of Montana, North and South Dakota, Minnesota, Wyoming, Colorado, Nebraska, Iowa, Kansas, Missouri, Oklahoma, Arkansas, and Louisiana, while the United States also claimed the Oregon Country (which included the modern states of Oregon and Washington as well as part of Canada) as part of the Purchase. In practice, most of the territory gained was under Native American control. Indeed, as a result of the problems in mobilizing the militia, the Americans had only been able to assemble a small force at Natchez on the Mississippi in order to overcome any resistance in Louisiana that might arise on behalf of Spain. The Senate ratified the treaty on 21 October 1803, by a vote of twenty-four to seven, the Federalist opponents being concerned about the dangerous implications of such an expansion.

The different possibility that Louisiana would be the basis of a separate federal state was considered by Jefferson, although he was not troubled by it, as he thought that common values would bind the two federal states (Louisiana and America) together. This issue captured the sense, expressed from independence, that the West might become a different state, a scheme plotted in the mid-1800s by Aaron Burr, Jefferson's first-term vice president and, in some respects, a would-be *caudillo* or strong-man on the Latin American model.[99] Burr approached Anthony Merry, the British envoy, telling him that Louisiana wanted independence, but needed the protection of a foreign power and a link to Trans-Appalachia for which he also sought independence. Putting on pressure, Burr said that if British protection was refused, he would turn to France. Telling Merry that an independent Louisiana would provide Britain with commercial advantages as it was a growing market, Burr initially sought two or three British frigates and the same number of smaller vessels off the mouth of the Mississippi in order to stop the Americans blockading the river. Burr also sought a loan of £100,000 and the support of a British consul at New Orleans.[100]

By the end of 1805, Burr had increased his needs, to two or three ships of the line as well as the ships already asked for, and also the opportunities apparently on offer. He told Merry that West and East Florida would also make themselves independent, and that he thought that parts of Latin America would follow. As a result, Burr argued, France would win greater benefits if Britain turned down the opportunity to intervene. He claimed that conflict between America and Britain was likely anyway, as Jefferson was determined to resist the British blockade of France. Merry saw the possibility of a very different geopolitics: he thought that if the west split off, the east would separate from the Southern states and "thus the immense power which is now risen up with so much rapidity in the western hemisphere" would be wrecked by division.[101] Burr, however, complained about a lack of British response, and Merry feared, instead, that France and Spain were sending help, and that Burr's plans had expanded to include a filibustering invasion of Mexico.[102]

In the event, Burr failed, because he exaggerated his strength and was unable to maintain secrecy. Instead, one of the drives behind American policy, both before and after independence, was to link the west to the earlier, Atlantic, territories. This aspiration was not, as yet, troubled greatly by the question of slavery.

The American gain of Louisiana, including the crucial port of New Orleans, ensured that the Spanish stranglehold on the Gulf of Mexico was broken, challenging the Spanish position to east and west: in West Florida and Texas. Arguing that France had not complied with the conditions under which it had obtained Louisiana from Spain in 1800, the Spaniards delivered a memorial against the Purchase, but it had no effect. The Spanish hope that Louisiana in French hands would serve as a barrier against American expansion toward Spain's other colonies had been cruelly exposed. Indeed, in 1803, Jefferson told Edward Thornton, the British envoy, that he would press for Louisiana's eastern limits before it had been ceded to Spain in 1763 when Britain gained Florida; namely to include part of what had become British West Florida in 1763. Jefferson regarded the Rio Perdido east of Mobile Bay (now the western border of Florida) as the appropriate frontier, a challenge to the Spanish position in West Florida as a whole.[103] Two years later, Jefferson told Merry that Spain was hostile to America and that, if there was war, he would invade first Florida and then Cuba, the last, as the key to the Gulf of Mexico, necessary for the defense of Louisiana and Florida.[104] Jefferson indeed attempted to gain Florida in 1806, his successor, James Madison, pursued the same objective,[105] and, in 1811, Spain unsuccessfully sought British help against American expansion into West Florida.

More generally, Jefferson pressed to define and claim Louisiana as hugely as possible, despite historical evidence, and Madison followed suit. The dispatch in 1804 of the Corps of Discovery, an expedition under Meriwether Lewis and William Clark that had been planned before the Louisiana Purchase, asserted American interests across the new possessions to the Pacific. They also sought to establish an overland route there, a goal for which it was important to discover the headwaters of the Columbia and then follow it to the Pacific, which they reached at the close of 1805. The expedition, on which the British envoy reported,[106] was also seen by Jefferson as a way to thwart the possibility that the British would develop the potential for transcontinental routes shown by Alexander McKenzie, who had crossed the continent in Canada in 1793,[107] and it helped focus attention on the Pacific Northwest as a key

area of American interest. National assertion through cultural competition was displayed in the instructions to find proof to discredit Buffon's
theory of New World degeneracy. Further south, the Red River Expedition of 1806 provided valuable knowledge, including a map of the river,
that was to help subsequent American expansion.

There was a clear racist dimension to Jefferson's policies, in his
treatment of the Native Americans, who were acceptable only if they
discarded their culture, and of the blacks, the latter seen as a "captive
nation." The Louisiana Purchase enabled the spread of American slavery,
and created the possibility for further expansion, which exacerbated
New England's concerns about the Southern domination of the federal
government. Slavery was also a challenge politically as the apportion-
ment of representation in the House of Representatives and the Electoral College by the Constitution counted each slave as three-fifths of a
freeman,[108] a provision that the Federalists at the Hartford Convention
in 1814–15 were to resolve to remove. A racist agenda was also seen with
the limited efforts initially made to enforce the ban on the slave trade,
which, in 1807, with effect from 1808, was prohibited by the United States.

Jefferson's attitudes were displayed by his refusal to extend diplomatic
recognition to the independent black state of Haiti, the product of the
Saint-Domingue revolution once France failed there in 1803. Whereas the
Adams government had responded favorably to Toussaint L'Ouverture's
interest in diplomatic and trade links with the United States, and had
sought to normalize relations with Saint-Domingue, a policy in full accord with the Quasi War with a France that threatened both, Jefferson
would have none of this. Friendly relations with France were more important to him, but there was also a racist dynamic. A black state proved
too much for the influential slaveholding interests, for black republicanism was perceived as a threat to the racial order in America. During the
revolutionary stage in Saint-Domingue, this view was also expressed by
Lord Grenville, the British foreign secretary, when seeking to find shared
interests with America: slave rebellion there and in the West Indies was
presented as a threat that could be exploited by the French.[109]

In Haiti, ironically, the plantation economy producing for European
markets survived black independence. Slavery had gone, but the black
élite who ran the state used forced labor to protect their plantations

from the preference of people to live as peasant proprietors. Thus, the pressures of the global economy and the attractions of cash crops selling into international markets triumphed over the potential consequences of independence.[110] These sales were, in turn, affected by competition from the products of Caribbean colonies.

It was not until most of the slave states had disenfranchised themselves by their rebellion in the Civil War that the independence of Haiti and Liberia were recognized: in April 1862, Congress authorized the dispatch of American envoys. Opposition to recognition then was led by Senator Garrett Davis of Kentucky, who claimed to be able to imagine no sight so dreadful as that of "a full-blooded negro" in Washington society. Diplomatic relations with Santo Domingo, the Dominican Republic, which had declared independence from Spain in 1821, become part of Haiti in 1822 and gained a precarious independence from Haiti in 1844, did not follow until 1866.[111]

As a result of the Louisiana Purchase, America now had a far longer frontier with Canada. This increased the potential American challenge to the British position there, although the stability of Canada had been enhanced by the adroit British handling of the Québecois. From the conquest in 1760, government-sponsored anglicization was tempered by sensible concern for the position of the Catholic Church, while the anticlericalism and then atheism of the French revolutionaries encouraged local support for Britain.[112] More generally, Jefferson and others overestimated American power after the Louisiana Purchase, which can therefore be seen as partly responsible for the deterioration in relations with Britain. Jefferson understood the potential of the American west and was correct in his long-term appraisal that America would become a world power. Yet, he exaggerated America's future potential, as in November 1801 when he speculated that Americans would multiply and spread to "cover the whole northern if not the southern continent." More seriously, in the short term, Jefferson mistook America's marginal leverage in the threatening bipolar dynamic between Britain and France[113] for a situation in which all three were major powers, which was not to be the case until the 1860s. Madison, who had been Jefferson's secretary of state and a long-time friend and ally,[114] followed this reasoning reflexively when he became president in 1809.

This attitude ensured that, at a time when sensitivity to supposed British hostility in Trans-Appalachia was increased by the development, in fact separate, of anti-American pan-Native religious revivalism,[115] American policymakers saw little reason to compromise with Britain over the regulation of trade. Manipulated by Napoleon, Madison foolishly thought he had won concessions from France that justified his focusing American anger and the defense of national honor on Britain, whereas, in practice, French seizures of American shipping continued. Moreover, Madison had departed from Jefferson's principles in foreign policy. Crucial to these were an attempt to maintain neutrality in great-power confrontation, which Jefferson presented as the way to avoid dangerous entanglements.

This departure was to have a serious consequence for America in that the War of 1812 did not work out as intended. However, as so often occurs, the domestic context was crucial in leading to war. The pressures on Madison were serious and led Jeffersonians to fear for the survival of the republic, and certainly of the Republican Party. Unsuccessful as a tool of foreign policy, nonimportation had also resulted in major economic strains, and this was increasing opposition to the government. Indeed, having become much weaker, Federalist support was rising, while Britain, which was seen as the opponent of republicanism, was not yielding over trade or impressments, and the Royal Navy clearly remained the dominant force at sea.[116]

Madison in 1812 thus appeared to have the choice of backing down in order to assuage domestic pressures, or of forcing Britain to back down, in part by extending commercial warfare in the shape of a conquest of Canada that would deprive the British of a key source of the naval supplies necessary for maritime activity. Canada's development was thus a threat to America, but one that could be cut short by expansionism.[117] Irrespective of Madison's failure to anticipate Napoleon's journey in 1812–14 from imperial conqueror to exile, he underestimated the risks of trying to force Britain to yield and failed to appreciate the prudence of backing down, taking America into the crisis of a war it could neither win nor end. Yet, obliging Britain to provide unequivocal recognition of American sovereignty seemed not only nonnegotiable[118] but also a clear destiny for both party and nation.

# 9

## FLORIDA BUT NOT CANADA: FROM THE WAR OF 1812 TO THE MONROE DOCTRINE 1812-23

The key event in this period occurred south, not north, of the Rio Grande. The end of Spanish power meant that the European imperial presence in the New World went from being the norm for those lands not still run by the indigenous population to becoming the less common option, and notably so on the continental land mass to the south of the United States. Moreover, the collapse of the Spanish Empire left the fate of its former territories unclear, as far as spatial organization, form of government, stability, and international alignments were concerned. This uncertainty offered major prospects (although less than anticipated) for American expansionists, not least because of the weakness of the empire during its dissolution. Nevertheless, there were also risks that other powers, notably Britain, France, or a revived Spain, would move into the vacuum, creating a formal or informal empire, and that the successor states in Latin America might have a territorial energy and expansionist agenda of their own.

Thus, the Latin American wars of independence were of key importance not only for Iberia and Latin America, but also for wider systems of power in the Americas and the Atlantic world. The political factors that shaped these wars were different from those prevalent in the American War of Independence, although, in contrast to the Haitian revolution, there was a shared background between the American and Latin American conflicts in terms of assertion by colonial élites against metropolitan control. In Spanish America, the *criollos,* locally born but of European descent, felt themselves to be the victims of discrimination, but the key initial step in the Latin American wars of independence took place in Europe.

Given the significance of these wars for America, this point serves yet again as a reminder that the geopolitics of North America spanned the Atlantic as part of a system that owed much of its development to European politics, albeit without any suggestion that the Americans were therefore passive recipients, or respondents without initiative. The combination of Charles IV of Spain (r. 1788–1808); Manuel de Godoy, his leading minister; Napoleon; and Ferdinand VII of Spain (r. 1808, 1814–33) rendered that empire a second- or third-class power. Napoleon's seizure of power in Spain in 1808 led not only to lengthy and bitter resistance there, in what was the most significant of the Latin wars of independence, one that lasted until 1814, but also to a breakdown of structures of authority and practices of power across the Spanish Empire, and to a subsequent struggle for control there. Moreover, the departure of the Portuguese royal family for Brazil in the face of French invasion in 1807 also had a destabilizing effect. Spanish weakness helped explain the feebleness of the response to American pressure on Florida, especially West Florida, notably the seizure of Mobile in 1813 and its retention.

The situation became more complex in 1814, when, with the fall of Napoleon, Ferdinand VII, freed from French captivity and returned to power in Spain, chose to use force in order to restore royal authority to the Spanish Empire on his terms. This attempt was initially successful, except in the distant estuary of the River Plate, which was not part of the North American system; but Ferdinand's cause faced many difficulties. The royalists in Spanish America were badly divided, and their divisions interacted with contradictions within Spanish policy. Finances and logistics formed a related set of severe problems, with the royalist army obliged to rely on the unpopular measures of forced loans and seizing local supplies.

Yet, as with the American War of Independence, there was no inevitable course of events and no inherent superiority of the insurgents over the counterinsurgency forces,[1] and this point from military history has relevance for the political history of these struggles: a teleology of insurgent success in war or politics should not be employed to demonstrate the inevitability of the other. For example, the Mexican rising of 1810 was thwarted in 1811 by successful counterinsurgency policies, both military and political.[2] Led by Father Miguel Hidalgo, who appealed to the rural bulk of the population, the rising was defeated by General Calleja, outside Mexico City (1811) and at the Battle of the Bridge of Calderón (1812), battles that deserve consideration alongside the contemporaneous struggles involving the United States. Moreover, insurgents who had captured Texas in 1812–13, proclaiming its independence in April 1813, were defeated on 18 August 1813 by Spanish forces at the battle of Medina. In Mexico, the rebellion was continued by Father José María Morelos, a *mestizo,* but he was defeated in 1815 by Calleja, now viceroy of New Spain, and executed. Guerrilla action, however, continued, led by Vicente Guerrero.

More generally, the Central American royalists enjoyed considerable success in 1811–15, being assisted by the ethnic character of the opposition, which sets up an instructive comparison with the United States, and yet also draws attention to the extent to which the American South in particular had a similar potential for division. The ethnic complexities of Latin America restricted the appeal of radical ideologies and movements: while many *criollos* resented European control, others were concerned about the possibility of risings mounted by the mixed-blood and native populations. Largely supported by *mestizos,* the Mexican rising was seen as a threat to *criollos,* as well as to Spanish authority. Worry about popular rebellion led the *criollo* élites of Mexico, Cuba, and Peru to side with Spain, and the royalists were able to use local militias against the rebels.[3] This racial inflection serves as a potent reminder of the need to consider geopolitics in terms of more than space and economic links. Moreover, the attitude of the Mexican *criollos* helps underline the possibility that the Southern colonies would have taken a loyalist path during the War of American Independence.

Yet, although the royalists were victorious in Mexico in 1815, as in Venezuela in 1806, 1812, 1816, and 1818; Bolivia in 1811 and 1815; and Chile in 1814, they failed to understand the degree to which the situation had changed as a result of the Napoleonic era and found it impossible to bring the struggle to a close. Local and regional dimensions were crucial, to an even greater extent than was manifested during the tensions between Patriots and Loyalists during the War of American Independence. In Mexico, these dimensions provided the context for a fragmentation of the insurrection,[4] but the same was true of the royal army. Its units engaged in counterinsurgency operations with little central supervision, while their commanders tried to build up local power bases.[5]

The conflict showed the difficulty of sustaining a revolutionary struggle, but also of mounting effective counterinsurgency action. The royalist forces found it possible to win on the battlefield, but counterinsurgency action was more difficult. A new generation of active royalist officers from Spain, who had gained experience in counterinsurgency conflict against the French, arrived in Latin America in the mid-1810s and were more successful, not least with using light cavalry columns, but they faced difficulties in winning cooperation from regional commanders, while the insurgents withdrew to more isolated regions from which resistance continued.[6]

To take the case of the Papantla region near Veracruz in Mexico, which had rebelled in 1812, the royalist reconquest of the towns by 1818 did not end the rebellion. Instead, it changed into a guerrilla war, with royalist garrisons in the towns unable to control rural hinterlands. In the summer of 1820, a change of strategy under a new royalist commander, José Rincón, altered the tempo of the war. Whereas previously the rainy season had served as a break in campaigning, providing the rebels with an opportunity to recover, Rincón planned no such break. In a campaign against the rebel stronghold of Coyusquihui, he circled the area with forts and kept campaigning, which hit the rebels; but the royalists were badly affected by disease, which was a frequent fate of campaigning in Central America. Both sides agreed to a settlement in 1820.[7] More generally, by 1820, helped by numerous pardons, the guerrilla war was nearly over in Mexico.

The royalist effort, however, was weakened by the liberal constitutional revolution in Spain in 1820. Viewed as an unwelcome development by *criollo* conservatives and by those who wielded power in Mexico, this revolution led to a declaration of independence. In November 1820, the viceroy had ordered Augustín de Iturbide to destroy what was left of the rebellion, but, in February 1821, Iturbide, searching for a solution based on consensus, agreed with the rebels on a declaration of independence, the Plan of Iquala.

As this was widely acceptable, the new regime gained power with very little fighting, and none at all in the provinces from California to Texas: a situation very different to that in much of Spanish South America. Liberalism in Spain thus encouraged conservatives in Mexico to support independence, in contrast to the case of the War of American Independence, as the ministers pressing in the 1760s and 1770s for new governmental arrangements did not offer a convincing liberalism. Under great pressure elsewhere, Spain accepted the situation with the Treaty of Cordoba of August 1821. The new regime was dominated by army officers, one of whom, Iturbide, declared himself Emperor Augustin I in 1822, although he was forced to abdicate in March 1823 after the army turned against him.[8]

The war had a traumatic impact on Mexican society, not least with the loss of about one-tenth of the population, but it also resulted in a political system that was to prove much less successful in harnessing national energies than that of America, reflecting as it did the longstanding social inequality and linked racial divisions of colonial rule, and the consequent hostility of the élite to democracy. Mexican civil society proved weaker, in part because the independence struggle encouraged a militarism that subverted constitutional practices, the rule of law, and the functioning of politics. However, the victory, in the Mexican-American War of 1846–48, of one state over the other, initially of comparable strength, was due to more factors than political structures and culture. Military quality, notably Scott's adroit command, was crucial. It was certainly important for America that the warfare of the 1810s, notably the War of 1812, did not lead to a social or political crisis comparable to that in Mexico. Again, there was nothing inevitable about this, as had the conflict lasted for longer, it would have caused greater strain, not only in terms of fiscal pressure, economic problems, and regional political separatism, but also because it might have opened up the complex racial mix of the South.

Comparisons and contrasts remind us of the problematic nature of deterministic analysis. For example, as well as key differences, notably that American independence was not at stake in the 1810s, there was a curious, important, and instructive parallelism between the War of American Independence (1775–83) and the War of 1812 (1812–15), and both differences and parallels suggest the problem with focusing on geo-

politics in a determinist fashion. Each war indicated the problems facing an oceanic power when confronted by a continental one, although,
alongside the inherent limitations of naval strength in this period, it is
necessary to devote due weight to the difficulties created by other commitments as well as to mistakes in British policy.[9]

At the same time, repeated American failures in 1812–14 to conquer
Canada indicated grave limitations in American war-making, notably
(initially) command quality,[10] a lack of preparedness, serious logistical fog and friction,[11] as well as the resolve of the defense and the lack
of support for the Americans in Canada. These failures were highly significant to the geopolitics of North America because they helped ensure that the British authorities in Canada could repel attack. Thus, the
survival of Canada as a separate polity was not dependent, instead, on
British oceanic power and its ability to gain countervailing benefits from
America that could be exchanged in a peace treaty. These attacks were
also America's last attempt to conquer Canada, although that was only
clear in hindsight.

As far as the conflict on land was concerned, both the War of Independence and the War of 1812 started in the north and ended further
south after the British had adopted a Southern military and political
strategy in 1778, in an attempt to counter their difficulties in achieving
their goals further north and in 1814–15 because Britain's northern goals
had largely been met. This parallelism invites a number of reflections,
not least concerning the way in which, in another variation of the dependence of geopolitics on demographics, the British came to seek local
support as a way to compensate for their numerical problems in army
size, so that people and space were linked, but in a different way to that
which we have considered elsewhere, for example over slavery. Thus, in
the War of 1812, the British were seeking a force multiplier comparable
to that found in Continental Europe with subsidized alliance forces,
in Britain and the colonies with militia and other volunteer units, in
India with local troops, and in the West Indies with slave units. This
move to the South and search for local support was significant because,
while American ambitions for Canada and maritime rights led to the war
which the British government did not want, the British largely shaped
the conflict by 1814.[12]

The South, therefore, posed a wider political and military challenge facing the Americans, as well as providing a particular racial mix that was a potential cause of instability.[13] The region, for example, provided opportunities for the British use of amphibious power, another product of the geostrategic interaction of Continental and oceanic, as well as a key aspect of British effectiveness, but one again that required appropriate implementation and effort. In the War of American Independence, this amphibious potential meant operations on Long Island Sound, the Chesapeake, the Delaware, the Ashley, and the Cooper, near Charleston, providing the British with opportunities to strike at Philadelphia and Charleston. In the War of 1812, the British could strike at Pensacola, New Orleans, and Mobile, and, at the close of the conflict, could plan attacks on Charleston and Savannah. This potential looked toward subsequent American fears of British attack.

Parallels and contrasts between the two wars can be understood by appreciating the constant nature of strategy, namely that the military dimension of what is termed strategy is, in fact, the operationalizing of strategy that, instead, is a profoundly political process. In the War of American Independence, the crucial point was that the Southern strategy was a response to a wider political problem, that of British isolation, in the face of an international coalition at a time when the American Patriots could neither be knocked out of the war militarily or persuaded to negotiate. Seeking support in the South, and to attack the Patriots there, was an attempt to level the playing ground at the operational level, and thus to counter the strategic pressure being brought to bear on Britain by the intractability of the struggle and, even more, once France had joined the Patriots in 1778.

In the War of 1812, in contrast, Britain, by the summer of 1814, no longer faced conflict with Napoleon; but the political situation, unlike in 1778, when the Southern strategy was launched with the capture of Savannah, was one that demanded a swift end to the war, and, in the meantime, an inexpensive conflict. In 1814, the British government, which had been at war, with a brief gap in 1802–1803, since 1793, faced an unprecedented national debt and pressure, from within and without, for a peace dividend, including the ending of the income tax. Indeed, this fiscal position was to play a key role in affecting British options toward America, and more generally, for the remainder of our period.

Moreover, the European situation in the summer of 1814 was increasingly uneasy. The war had ended with the abdication of Napoleon in April and with the Allies dictating peace terms to France on which they could agree. However, the Sixth Coalition, the alliance of powers arrayed against France, had been divided from the outset. In particular, there were major tensions between Austria and Britain, and also between Russia and Britain. From 1813, the British government had correctly discerned a lack of support from its allies for its territorial and security interests, both insofar as the retention of transoceanic conquests was concerned and with specific reference to the future of the naval dockyards at Antwerp, dockyards which the British, unlike the Austrians, wished to keep out of French hands.

Yet again, the struggle for mastery in North America involved crucial issues in Europe, where victory over Napoleon was not alone the issue in Europe for Britain. Moreover, there was an important chronological dimension, for Britain was not only in difficulties in 1812, at the outset of the war, when Napoleon's alliance system was very much the strongest and, indeed, the American Democratic-Republicans could be seen as largely aligned with it. Instead, Napoleon's very failure in Russia in 1812, a failure that totally undermined American strategy against Britain, followed by the Russian advance into Poland in 1813, created additional problems for Britain as well as representing advantages. This dimension has to be considered alongside the more conventional tendency to focus solely on the question of British (and other) military dispositions when considering the link between the two spheres, Europe and North America.

The same situation was true of 1814. Napoleon's abdication led President Madison to lower his terms for peace and freed up some British military resources, on land and at sea, for operations against America, although there were still other requirements, including a force for Belgium, designed to secure the position of Britain's ally, William I of the Netherlands in his newly acquired territory. Moreover, there was demand in Britain for a measure of demobilization. In addition, the deterioration in the cohesion of the Sixth Coalition, as the weak cement of alliance against Napoleon frayed, created a major problem for Britain.

In 1814–15, as antagonistic alignments developed among the allies, they focused on a particular issue, the future of Saxony, a kingdom that had remained closely allied to Napoleon until late 1814. Prussia sought to acquire most of neighboring Saxony, a step that was particularly unwelcome to Britain as its ruling house derived from Hanover, a North German state that had long competed with Prussia. This competition had become more serious from the early 1800s as Prussian ambitions in northern Germany became more prominent. In turn, in 1814–15, the ambitions of Frederick III, King of Prussia, were supported by Tsar Alexander I of Russia, for whom, in contrast, Russia's North American empire was a very minor issue and one that he was not really to address until 1821 when the European situation was very different.

In opposition over Saxony in 1814–15, Britain allied with Emperor Francis I of Austria, and they were joined by Louis XVIII of France, who was keen to secure reintegration into the European system. The inability of diplomats to settle this issue led to the possibility, first, of confrontation and, then, of conflict. Indeed, the tension was to remain until after the War of 1812 ended, and was only resolved by the return of Napoleon to power in France in March 1815, which resulted in the re-creation of an alliance pledged to overthrow him, the Seventh Coalition. As an aspect of this new order, the Saxony issue was settled with a compromise, in which Prussia gained 58 percent of Saxony.

Prior to this settlement, the international situation in Europe was unsettled. Britain was a principal in a contentious situation, one that threatened to deteriorate. This position ensured that the possibility of sustaining conflict in North America was unclear. In short, the British "surge" of 1814, as more troops were sent to North America, might be sustainable and repeatable, but that, too, was uncertain. This international context, specifically Britain's wider international commitment and entanglements, tends to be forgotten by those who focus on particular operational, even tactical, issues, asking, for example, whether, had different moves been made in 1814 or 1815, it would have been possible for Britain to defeat the Americans; for example, "What if Prevost had not ordered the retreat at Plattsburg in 1814?" or "What if British tactics at the battle of New Orleans in 1815 had been more appropriate?" or "What if the war had continued in 1815, not least with attacks on Savannah and Charleston and/or with more successful attempts to win support from Native and African Americans?"

In some respects, these arguments are reminiscent of attempts to rewrite American failure in the Vietnam War. The latter neglect the wider and prime strategic requirement, namely not to lead to World War Three with Soviet and/or Chinese pressure elsewhere, and also to assume that there was a total war objective on the part of the Americans, with all means being justified accordingly. This situation was not the case, for either the British or the Americans, in the War of 1812 (although the situation was very different as far as American policy toward Native Americans were concerned), nor, indeed, was it the case for the Americans in the Vietnam War.

Domestic goals came first: the British, by 1814, wanted an end to the War of 1812. They did not want any process of negotiation to be intertwined with European power politics, and were therefore especially keen that the Russian attempt to mediate a settlement of the war should fail and not be revived. This desire was a clear aspect of the international dimension of the war. The British did not want their erstwhile allies to sit in judgment on their war effort, no more than they had wished to allow them to determine the results of Britain's transoceanic conflict with France. Thus, the British sought not an equivalent to the later Monroe Declaration, but a situation in which bilateral negotiations with the United States were not to be subject to international scrutiny. The collectivist solutions represented in the Congress of Vienna, and indeed the negotiation of the Sixth and Seventh Coalitions, were not to apply in North America as far as the British government was concerned. The American response to the attempt by Alexander I of Russia to mediate in the War of 1812 was not to be encouraged, although Russia was to act, after the war, as mediator over American claims on Britain arising from the shelter provided to escaped slaves.

Ironically, this British opposition to outside mediation was eventually to become that of the United States, notably of the Union in the American Civil War, and for similar reasons: namely the advantages of being the stronger power as well as a public politics suspicious of out-

siders and collectivist solutions. Yet, in 1813–14, it was America that was
the weaker power and, as the weaker power, therefore the one keener
about the assistance of an outside mediator.

Turning to another perspective, the potential impact of the War
of 1812 on the wider regional situation was cut short by the rapid termina-
tion of the conflict, but the Napoleonic wars had left a number of players
in the Caribbean. These included not only Britain and the United States,
but also France, which regained control of Guadeloupe and Martinique
with the peace treaty in 1814; Spain, where Bourbon monarchy had been
reestablished in 1814 with Napoleon's failure; the rebels against Spain
(themselves far from united); and Haiti. It was far from clear what the
future held in store in the region. Haiti was unstable, Spanish America
faced serious rebellions, and, in the summer of 1815, the return of Napoleon was to lead to swift and successful British amphibious action against
Guadeloupe and Martinique. This success indicated Britain's continued
amphibious capability in the region, as well as the primacy of the political dimension, as the latter helped ensure that the British were far more
successful against the French islands than they had been earlier that year
at New Orleans.

In one respect, therefore, whereas British forces based in Canada
could not be readily used elsewhere other than to invade America, the
forces deployed in the Gulf against the United States could be employed
in other parts of the region, not least indirectly, by diverting American
forces. Conversely, war with the United States challenged the British
ability to act effectively in pursuit of these other interests. The overlap
was most pronounced with British (and American) intervention in West
Florida and, to a lesser extent, East Florida, but there were other possible
consequences of the options facing Britain. For example, it was important to consider the possible implications for British slave colonies, or
for British relations with the Spanish colonies, of any British attempts
to secure Native and African American support against the Americans.

The extent to which these factors affected, let alone determined,
policy is unclear. The nature of decision making was that a small group
of individuals set policy, and usually as a result of face-to-face discussions in London. This process was not government by memoranda, and,
instead, as is more generally the case with strategic culture, it is neces-

sary for the scholar to infer the factors that played a role. In one respect, this process is frustrating as far as scholarly precision is concerned, and can lead to excessive weight being placed on documents that do exist, but the need to rely on inferences also returns us to the realm of implicit assumptions that set policy at the time.

The British government's need for peace and its relative lack of interest in the Gulf region ensured that even had New Orleans been taken, there were no plans to dominate the Mississippi Valley and link up with Canada as the French had sought to do from the 1680s to the 1750s. The stance of the British ministry contrasted with its far greater concern for the West Indies, as well as with both the bold interest in the Gulf shown by some of the local British agents and would-be agents, and the American conviction that Britain had continued designs on the South. The latter was always Andrew Jackson's justification for taking Florida and Native American territory, in order to secure American security against Spain and, particularly, Britain.

To a certain extent, Jackson's view was one from the periphery, a view that the decentralized and representative nature of American politics was to make important at different stages of his career. There were comparable views from the periphery in the British system, but they lacked political traction or governmental weight. The loss of the Floridas was certainly a sore spot for some in the empire, especially in the Caribbean, after 1783. Many of these people had lived in the Floridas, including those who ran Panton, Leslie and Company, a key British trading company, and had economic ties to the Creek. Thus, some British citizens sought to regain a Florida foothold while, in contrast, the home government (a body with relatively few bureaucrats) had no real interest, a situation repeatedly also seen with the British role on the Caribbean coastlands of Central America, especially East and West Florida, which had been handed over to Spain in 1784 and the Mosquito Coast of Nicaragua, where the British abandoned their position in 1787, although they were subsequently to resume their presence.

This lack of interest in Florida was demonstrated after the War of 1812 in Josiah Francis's pitiful reception in London. Francis was a Red Stick (the name given to those Creeks who opposed acculturation with the Americans) who went to London after the war to garner support for the continuing Creek fight in Florida, with the hope that Britain would be interested in regaining the Floridas. However, Francis was ignored while in London and returned to North America, only to be captured and executed by the remorseless Jackson.[14]

The number of "players" involved underlines the complexity of the international implications of the War of 1812. The latter also serve as a reminder of the need to impact our understanding of the operational dimension of the war in its multiple political contexts. Conversely, the end of our story, in 1871, reflects the manner in which developments had led by then to a fall in the number of participants, and thus contexts.

The War of 1812 and, even more, its consequences played a central role in the geopolitics of North America. The war did not lead to the hoped-for conquest of Canada by America, nor to a settlement of commercial issues on American terms, as some critics of the Madison government pointed out, but it concluded with an important perception of American success against Britain, notably as a result of the repulse of the British advance on Lake Champlain[15] and the attacks on Baltimore and New Orleans.

Moreover, major American victories over the Native Americans, especially the battles of the Thames over Tecumseh (5 October 1813) and of Horseshoe Bend over the Creek (27 March 1814), gravely weakened the latter east of the Mississippi. In addition, the divided Iroquois suffered as a result of their role in the defense of Canada.[16] American victories also shattered the movement for intertribal unity based on the call for a restoration of sacred power,[17] a nativist religiosity that can be profitably contrasted with movements in Christian America from the mid-eighteenth to the mid-nineteenth century.

The collapse of successful British–Native American cooperation during the war, and the end of any real cooperation as a consequence of the peace settlement, were important to the changing relationship of Britain and America, each clearly empires as far as the Native Americans were concerned. In 1815, the Americans obliged tribes that had been allied to the British to agree to new treaties that accepted American dominance.

The domestic dimension was also significant, as America had divided over going to war. These divisions became more serious during its course. In the event, however, the war was too brief and limited to lead to major changes in the governmental system or to a transformation in the American military. Yet the end of the Federalists as an effective force was a key political development, one that also reflected important changes in the geography and culture of American politics, as well as specific events. Federalist opposition to the War of 1812, which was exacerbated by the weakness of the national defense effort in the face of British threats and the concomitant reliance on state-level expedients,[18] had led to a New England Convention at Hartford (15 December 1814–5 January 1815) that proposed changes to the Constitution designed to lessen the influence of the South and to insist on a two-thirds Congressional mandate for war.[19]

The convention, and extremist talk of secession by a minority in New England (and notably not the convention), compromised the Federalists, who disappeared as a national party.[20] They were not only on the wrong side of the myth of American victory, but also seemed redundant in an age of peace that rendered superfluous an opposition to the Jeffersonian policy of hostility to Britain and commercial sanctions.[21] Also, the Federalists increasingly were seen as a party contemptuous of the common man.

Despite trade with New England during the conflict, Federalist opposition to the war was not taken to the point of effective cooperation with Britain, and this helps explain the contrast between India and America. The British had also been under great pressure in India, notably in 1778–82, but, whereas they did not recover their position in America in the 1800s and 1810s, they defeated their opponents in India between 1798 and 1818, in part because they were able to fight them sequentially and to benefit in doing so from considerable local support, for example from the Marathas and Hyderabad against Mysore.

American military capability was enhanced postwar not only by the defeat of the Natives but also by establishing the army at ten thousand men, the largest American standing army so far, as well as by the Naval Expansion Act of 1816 that led to a marked increase in the size of the navy, and by the launching of the "Third System," a systematic program of coastal fortification and the establishment of arms depots.[22] The war also left an appreciation of the limitations of the militia, notably when units refused to cross into Canada.[23] Moreover, there was anxiety that another conflict, most likely with Britain, might be less fortunate,[24] and this had led the government to press for an army of twenty thousand. Yet, the War of 1812 also encouraged a confidence that fed through into expansionism. This was commented on by British observers. William Hamilton, the Undersecretary of State for Foreign Affairs from 1809 to 1822, noted in December 1815, "Seeds of unlimited expansion . . . have taken root in that country."[25]

Finally, it is instructive to contrast America's repeated failure to conquer Canada and its need, postwar, to manage relations with Britain carefully, with the very different character of relations with Spain. Indeed, the greater ability of America to expand at the expense of Spain ensured that the geopolitics of North America changed considerably, both in the 1810s and in subsequent decades. This change arose not only because Spain proved weaker, but also because Britain was no longer willing to help protect Spain's position.

As before, this crucial development was not simply, or even largely, due to the situation in North America, but, rather, to a wider political reconfiguration. Having been allied with the Spanish crown during the Peninsular War against Napoleon in 1808–14, the British government, though still governed by a conservative administration under Robert, 2nd Earl of Liverpool who had been Prime Minister from 1812, moved to support (albeit less than fully) the rebellions in Spanish America, a movement associated in particular with George Canning, foreign secretary from 1822 to 1827. In so doing, the British government parted from its former allies against France, especially Austria and Russia, the powers now linked in the Holy Alliance, although it also responded to the unwelcome rapprochement between Spain and France, both now ruled by branches of the Bourbon dynasty.

Thus, factors specific to North America interacted with wider diplomatic currents, while the British government's need to reduce expenditure was also a major factor and one linked not only to concerns about fiscal stability but also to the desire to assuage domestic discontent. Indeed, after 1815, as earlier during the War of 1812, an important pattern was set, one in which successive British governments were wary of North American entanglements not only for the prudential reasons posed by likely American opposition but also as a result of straightforward issues of cost and worth. The American Question was not worth the cost to governments seeking to spend little.

Much of this restraint was domestic and, indeed, the phrase *night-watchman state* has been coined to describe the limited role that was sought. Abroad, there was a drive to maintain Britain's status as the world's leading naval power and a willingness to pursue international goals by conflict, if necessary, but the central concern was to avoid the recurrence of a major war both because of anxiety about the cost and due to worry about the consequences for trade and industry. This pattern was to be seen at the time of Anglo-American crises in mid-century, notably in the 1840s, and was also at play in the determination to contain costs in defending Canada, an issue that was important to support if there was to be a federation of the Canadian colonies.

Avoiding the recurrence of a major war was also the goal of the United States, although the greater military and naval expenditure that followed the War of 1812 reflected the extent to which it was no longer deemed appropriate to rely on the Jeffersonian panaceas of the 1800s. This expenditure was essentially directed against Britain, so that America would be better able to resist Britain in a future conflict. This policy was seen in particular in the significance of coastal fortifications in the American force structure, and indeed in the military education offered at West Point that focused heavy on fortress engineering and ballistics, the latter necessary for officers who were to command fortifications designed to repel British naval attack.

However, the territorial expansion, both of the war years and postwar, were obtained at the expense of the Native Americans and Spain. Yet, again, the British position was important, as the Peace of Ghent ending the War of 1812 obliged the Americans to restore the Native Americans to their prewar situation and to negotiate treaties with the tribes. There was no British guarantee that their position would be maintained and, in practice, nothing was done to support the Native Americans. The British government took care not to challenge American claims over Natives within their jurisdiction, and also to deny reports that traders from the Hudson's Bay Company were involved in opposition to American power.[26]

The War of 1812 led, on the American frontier, to squatters claiming Native American lands and, in 1815–18, as American troops were deployed to the west, to a series of treaties that in effect curtailed Native independence and led to the American government seeing itself as akin to a trustee. In military terms, the activity of the American government could be seen in occasional expeditions, notably up the Missouri Valley in 1818–19 and, more successfully, 1825, and, more insistently, in the building of forts, such as Forts Armstrong, Crawford, Dearborn, and Howard as the army moved north in 1816; Fort Smith on the western border of the Arkansas Territory in 1817; Fort Snelling, where the Minnesota and Mississippi rivers meet, in 1819; Fort Jesup near Natchitoches in 1822; and the construction of roads. In turn, forts were abandoned in areas now considered under control, notably in the Ohio and Wabash valleys.

In already-settled territories, the war strengthened anti-Native American attitudes in the United States, not least because politicians who had played a prominent role in the conflict and were hostile to the Natives, such as Jackson, rose to power. The Native Americans were not to be part of the new country, except on terms that destroyed their cultural integrity, a policy already seen in the attitudes of Jefferson, who had envisaged a choice between assimilation in an American agrarian order and being driven away into remote fastnesses, a choice that he believed had been made easier by the lands gained through the Louisiana Purchase. His attitudes were widely shared, for example by Benjamin Lincoln, the Federal Commissioner to the Shawnee in 1793. Even those who had helped the (European) Americans suffered, such as the Choctaw, who lost their land under treaties of 1816 and 1830.

In contrast, although power and authority in Mexico were dominated by those of Spanish origin, the Native population was proportionately more important than in America and could not be excluded from the new state, although it was to be oppressed. For 1810, the population of Mexico has been estimated at about 6,121,000, consisting of 3,676,000 Natives, 1,107,000 Spaniards (whether born there or immigrants), 704,000 *mestizos* (mixed), and 634,000 *pardos* (wholly or partly black).[27]

In Canada, treaties with Natives led to the creation of reserves that provided security but limited hunting and seasonal movement. As a result, fatalities from starvation became frequent among Natives in the Maritimes, while winter food shortages were more generally a problem in what became Quebec and Ontario. The relatively low numbers of Natives in these colonies, compared to the situation in America, made control easier, but the expansion of European settlement posed problems. Visiting Halifax en route to Washington in December 1822, the British diplomat Henry Addington showed that Jefferson's views were very much those of the mainstream when he wrote,

> The Indians are fast disappearing, as uncivilised tribes must always yield to the tide of civilisation. This is a necessary consequence and according to nature, no less desirable than necessary. Sentimentalists weep over deserted wigwams and the mouldering tombs of barbarian ancestry, but the man of sense hails the substitution of comfort and contentment and Christianity, flocks, cornfields, the sound of the hammer, the shuttle and the Church-bell for the scalping knife, war-whoop, and the idolatry of the savage.[28]

In the Mississippi Valley, the process of expansion at the expense of Native Americans was recorded with the establishment of new states: Indiana in 1816, Illinois in 1818, and Missouri in 1821. Further south, the American position in the hinterland was consolidated when Mississippi and Alabama became states in 1817 and 1819 respectively, which was also a culmination of the Spanish failure to maintain their position in West Florida.

Indeed, the War of 1812 was crucial to the course of American–Spanish relations, and, as such, the war was situated firmly in the course of American territorial expansionism.[29] The conflict enabled the United States to consolidate its pre-1812 gains and to add more along the Gulf coast east of the Pearl River. The conquest of Mobile and West Florida from the Pearl to the Perdido River in April 1813, the sole American territorial gain from Spain (or Britain) during the conflict, was particularly important as it made Spain fearful of further American steps and thus more amenable. The Americans seized the town without being at war with Spain, but the latter was too weak during the Peninsular War to prevent it or to respond. Holding Mobile as well as New Orleans increased the challenge to British planning and amphibious power during the War of 1812. Moreover, the British presence in Florida during the war, which led to inaccurate rumors that Spain had ceded it to Britain, encouraged American sensitivity and interest in its acquisition, as Florida was seen as crucial to the defense of the South.

The War of 1812 was followed by aggressive American operations in Florida, an inchoate world that weak Spanish authority made possible, and that Americans both exploited and sought to order. Thus, the Negro Fort on the Appalachicola River was destroyed on 27 July 1816 by an American amphibious force, with those blacks not killed enslaved.[30] An American base, Fort Scott, was established on the Appalachicola that year. The Florida Republic, created by a multinational revolutionary force under the quixotic Sir Gregor MacGregor on Amelia Island off the Atlantic coast in June 1817, defeated Spanish attempts to regain the island, but was overcome that year by American forces who saw the republicans as pirates. MacGregor, who had served both Miranda and Bolívar as a general, went on, in 1821, to establish a colony on the Mosquito Coast of Nicaragua, but it failed both as an economic proposition and because MacGregor had fallen foul of George Frederick, the leader of the Mosquito Coast Natives.[31] In contrast to America's southern borderlands, Canada was far more ordered and under greater imperial control, although in 1815–19 there was conflict between the North West Company and both Lord Selkirk's settlement of Scottish Highlanders on the Red River and the Hudson's Bay Company, with Selkirk raising a force of German and Swiss mercenaries.

Britain was now the most important player not only to America's north, but also to its south. There was particular concern when Viscount Castlereagh, the Foreign Secretary, told the American envoy in January 1816 that American expansion at the expense of Spain would lead Britain to take steps, a message he underlined in November 1817 when replying to Adams's request for clarification on rumors that Britain was to gain Florida. Castlereagh disavowed the report and said that, as long as America did not encroach on neighboring states, Britain would not seek such possessions, but he saw this as "a warning to America if she did not wish to see us on her southern boundary not to provoke any change in our existing policy."[32] In what was a key instruction, Castlereagh outlined a policy of restraint. Spain had pressed Britain for help in settling its differences with America, which would have acted as a powerful restraint on the latter, but the British government, as later during the Civil War, took the view that such action depended on both parties wishing it. He added:

> Were Great Britain to look to its own interest alone, and were that interest worth
> asserting at the present moment, at the hazard of being embroiled with the
> United States, there can be no question that we have an obvious motive for de-
> siring that the Spaniards should continue to be our neighbours in East Florida,
> rather than that our West Indian possessions should be so closely approached
> by the territory of the United States; but this is a consideration that we are not
> prepared to bring forward in the discussion at the present moment, in bar to a
> settlement between Spain and North America.... The avowed and true policy
> of Great Britain being, in the existing state of the world, to appease controversy,
> and to secure, if possible, for all states a long interval of repose, the first object to
> be desired is a settlement of these differences upon reasonable terms.[33]

American pressure on both the Natives, in what was to be the First Seminole War, and on Spain culminated with Jackson's invasion of Florida in 1818.[34] Heavily committed to the defense of its endangered position in Mexico and South America, Spain had no power to push him out or to prevent a repeat attack, and, following the Anglo-American settlement of 1818, no ally to back it. As a result, by the 1819 Transcontinental Treaty (also called the Adams-Onís Treaty after the negotiators, John Quincy Adams and Don Luis de Onís), Spain relinquished claims to Florida to the United States even though Jackson had already removed his forces. Adams thereby removed the last European outposts from what was now an American coastline running uninterrupted from Maine to Louisiana, a coastline moreover that, with Florida, extended into the Caribbean, particularly toward a more important Spanish colony, Cuba.

The conflict with Spain had not expanded to include American military intervention in the Latin American wars of independence, as Henry Clay in Congress had suggested might happen. American warships were sent to South American waters in 1818 and 1819, in large part to display naval capability, but these were small squadrons. These wars vastly increased the pressure on Spain, and thus provided a significant window of opportunity for American expansion, while, at the same time, creating a problem for America if this window closed. In addition, the Panic of 1819 revealed economic weaknesses in America and hit the government's finances. Spain initially refused to ratify the Transcontinental Treaty. Concluded by Adams and Onís in February 1819, the Spanish government investigated the prospects of war with America and European support, but, as the first seemed bleak and the latter failed, the treaty was ratified in October 1820.

The Transcontinental Treaty, moreover, regularized the recent American territorial settlement with Britain. The Anglo-American Treaty of Ghent of 1814 had provided for the adjustment of boundary disputes between British North America and the United States by joint commissions. Castlereagh argued that it would be best to negotiate boundaries while the region at issue was not settled, by which, typically, he meant settled by Europeans, and wrote "the great object is to remove doubts." Castlereagh suggested the negotiation of the disputed claim to the mouth of the Columbia River and then the tracing of the "intermediate boundary"[35] to where the frontier was already agreed on, but that was not to be the solution.

Instead, a convention, signed on 20 October 1818 in London, recognized American fishing rights off Labrador and Newfoundland, and extended the frontier along the 49th parallel, from the Lake of the Woods to the Rockies. This was a major extension of the frontier that entailed the abandonment of British interests with the cession of a considerable body of territory in the valley of the Red River, including much of the modern state of North Dakota, part of Minnesota, and a fraction of Montana, while the Americans ceded a tranche north of Montana.

Moreover, the Oregon Country to the west (the lands between Spanish and Russian America comprising modern Oregon, Washington, Idaho, and British Columbia), was, it was agreed, to be jointly administered by Britain and America for ten years without prejudicing existing claims. This agreement structured the American claim to a Pacific border, which had not been insisted upon at the time of the Louisiana Purchase, and gave the Americans a transcontinental presence as well as an opportunity to populate the region. Significantly, and in contrast to the situation for Britain and France after the War of the Austrian Succession ended in 1748, neither Britain nor the United States had used the unsettled state of the border after the War of 1812 as an excuse to attempt a wider revisionism, nor, indeed, to reopen hostilities, and nor were they to do so. This convention was extended indefinitely in 1827 and, in practice, until the Oregon Boundary Treaty of 1846.[36]

In addition, the Commercial Convention of 1815 sought to settle trade issues on the basis of reciprocity of tariffs, while the Rush-Bagot Agreement of 1817 limited naval armaments on the Great Lakes to those necessary for preventing smuggling. This agreement was in response to postwar tensions that included American concerns about British ship-building on the Great Lakes and with regard to alleged encouragement of Native Americans. Castlereagh supported the step as likely to "allay jealousy and diminish the chance of collision."[37]

The British were the key foreign players in the Oregon Country, as part of the major expansion of trading by both the Hudson's Bay Company and rival traders from the St. Lawrence. The latter took over networks that had been developed by the French and expanded them, initially, by 1789 to the Great Slave Lake. This activity led the Hudson's Bay Company, in turn, to expand, and, between 1774 and 1821, about six hundred western posts were established by the two companies, albeit mostly only for a few years. Ninety-nine were constructed between 1774 and 1789 inclusive, at least 323 between 1790 and 1805, and 172 from 1806 to 1821. In 1821, when the Hudson's Bay Company, with government encouragement as a way to stabilize the situation, merged with the rival Montreal-based North West Company, 125 posts were in operation.

The North West Company expanded into the northwest coastal regions from 1805, adding a new element to an area in which the Americans were a presence from 1788 and the dominant players in the maritime fur trade from 1800, replacing the British and Russians in that role.[38] Fort McLeod in the valley of the River Peace was the first North West Company base, and was followed by forts in the Upper Fraser area, notably Forts Fraser and St. James, both established in 1806, and Fort George in 1807. There was southern expansion in New Caledonia (now British Columbia), with Fort Kamloops opened in 1813, but another concentration developed on the Columbia River. This expansion brought the British into competition with the American Pacific Fur Company (owned by John Jacob Astor), which had a series of bases, notably Fort Astoria at the mouth of the Columbia, established in 1811, but also a series of inland forts, including Forts Okanagan and Spokane. These provided the Americans with routes out of the region both by sea and to the headwaters of the Missouri.

The War of 1812 brought British control. On 30 November 1813, Fort Astoria was captured by HMS *Raccoon* and renamed Fort George. The fort had, in fact, already been sold on 7 October to the North West Company. John McTavish, a company trader, had explained to the Americans that a British frigate was en route, and had successfully suggested such a purchase, but the *Raccoon*'s captain insisted on going through the motions of seizing the position. The other bases were also taken.[39]

Although the peace treaty decreed the return to prewar boundaries, the British remained dominant in the region and both New Caledonia and the Columbia District continued to be trading territories of the North West Company. Moreover, its position was enhanced with new positions, such as Fort Nez Percés on the Columbia River, founded in 1818. The company's trappers and traders also pressed south, with routes followed both to the Snake country in eastern (modern) Oregon and to the source of the Willamette River, further west.

The union of the North West and Hudson's Bay companies in 1821 enabled the latter to dominate the British presence, although it also led to a decrease in activity in the Upper Missouri Valley, as the end of competition reduced the attraction of seeking fur from areas of limited profitability, and still more of risky expansion. This decrease reduced tension with the Americans, who in 1816 had passed a law enabling the army to arrest foreigners found in Native country without American permission as well, even if there was a passport, as to seize goods used in trade with the Natives. Further west, there was still competition from American and Russian maritime traders, as well as problems posed by the extent to which this competition provided opportunities for the Native traders to maneuver with advantage. The distances involved also challenged the company. Nevertheless, thanks to their success in 1813, the British were in the strongest position in the Oregon Country, and there was no reason to anticipate that this situation would be reversed. John Melish showed the Oregon Country up to the 49th parallel as American in his *Map of the United States with the Contiguous British and Spanish Possessions* (1816), which went through seven editions in 1816 and five in 1818, and copies of which were owned by five presidents – both Adamses, Jefferson, Madison, and Monroe, but his decision to extend the frontier line from the Rockies to the Pacific did not correspond to the reality on the ground.

The 1818 Convention excluded Russia (in Alaska) and Spain, and its successor Mexico, from the Oregon Country: these were the other two European powers that bordered the Oregon Country. In September 1821, Tsar Alexander I issued a rival proclamation claiming that his possessions stretched to the 51st parallel and pressing Russians to settle in the region, but he was not in a position to give substance to these aspirations and the American government did not accept them, especially the Russian claim to exclude foreign shipping from neighboring seas and thus to prevent trade. The British response was not robust, part indeed of a pattern of responding cautiously to Russian advances in the North Pacific,[40] but it did not need to be. Russia had many other commitments, threatening to send troops into Germany to counter radicalism in the late 1810s, annexing the lands of the Middle Kazak Horde in 1822, fighting Persia in 1825–28, and Turkey in 1828–29, providing help in the Greek War of Independence from Turkish rule, and suppressing a large-scale Polish rebellion in 1830–31. In 1823, Adams suggested joint Anglo-American negotiations with the Russians over the issue, which was a diplomatic means to attempt to solve the problem of Russian unilateralism. In the event, the Americans were to counter with their own type of unilateralism, the Monroe Doctrine.

Britain claimed that Spain had no standing in the matter because it had effectively surrendered title with Nootka Sound when that crisis had ended. Spain protested against Anglo-American presumptions, but might made right, and in 1819, by the Transcontinental Treaty, Spain recognized the 1818 Anglo-American Convention. The status of Texas, however, became a point of contention, as Southern Democrats, and Northern sympathizers such as James Buchanan, the future president, charged Adams, then and, far more, later, with giving away Texas in 1819 for, as part of the treaty, the American government had to surrender its claims to Texas, abandoning what Buchanan in the Senate on 8 June 1844 termed "our natural limits," and leading four senators to vote against the treaty's ratification on 19 February 1821.

Instead, defining the Louisiana Purchase, the Sabine, Red, and Arkansas rivers became the agreed-upon border between America and Spain as far as the 42nd parallel, which was then to be the border until the Pacific, a frontier Buchanan decried as "a mere arbitrary line." Such lines were to be adopted by Americans when they suited and were decried at other times. A similar point could be made about other Western imperial powers, which underlines the extent to which American exceptionalism is not a helpful concept. In a process of allocating territory that neither possessed, the Spanish negotiators had sought a border as far north as the Missouri River, but also on the 43rd parallel, and the Americans as far south as the Rio Grande, but also on the 41st. Spain would have preferred a frontier on the Mississippi. In the event, Spain's relinquishing, by the Transcontinental Treaty, of any claim in western North America north of the 42nd parallel removed one of the three European powers with claims to the Oregon Country. At the time, the price paid to obtain this concession and, even more, Florida, was regarded as minimal: relinquishing $5 million of American claims against Spain and relinquishing American claims to Texas. In contrast, the first American envoy to Mexico, Joel Poinsett, was to arrive bearing instructions from Adams to ask if Texas was for sale, but he found the Mexicans unreceptive.

Partly as a result of his success in the Transcontinental Treaty and in the 1818 Convention with Britain, Adams deserves to be considered among the most important of the republic's diplomats. He transformed the American desire for a continental presence from a probability into a reality and also moved his nation far closer to the goal of establishing North American dominance.[41] In the event, the Transcontinental Treaty was scarcely mentioned in the contentious 1824 election. Every candidate thought it a good development, although the acquisition of Florida was the focus and not the precise western boundary with Spain, and relatively little was said about giving up Texas until years later.

The new frontier with Spain was challenged in June 1819 when American filibusters under James Long seized Nacogdoches, declared an independent republic (with Long as president of the Supreme Council and commanding general), and established outlying posts that were designed to become the focus of Native trade, and thus to ensure profit. Later that year, however, Spanish troops regained the territory, although Long maintained a presence in Galveston Bay where the Republic of Texas was declared anew in 1820 at the aptly named Bolivar Point. Sensing an opportunity in 1821, when Mexico declared independence, Long invaded Texas in September, only to be captured by a larger Mexican force. Texas, instead, became a frontier part of an independent Mexico. The 1819 treaty came into effect when ratifications were accepted in February 1821, and, succeeding Spain, Mexico did not try to overturn the treaty. The Native Americans were not consulted, and swiftly suffered. For example, the Moultrie Creek Treaty of 1823 left the Seminole of Florida only four million acres of poor land.

Better Anglo-American relations did not only ease the territorial situation for the Americans, although frontier disputes continued along the Canadian border, for example with the Detroit River.[42] There was also an important improvement in the commercial situation, with the British in 1815 offering to reduce the heavy duties on American shipping under the Navigation Act as long as the Americans offered similar concessions. This agreement led to a marked increase in American shipping in British ports, an increase that was an aspect of the increasing economic links between the two countries. Thus, American development was an aspect of the growing British-dominated Atlantic economy,[43] albeit one that involved considerable tensions between the two in the Caribbean and over other issues. There were disagreements, for example, over American duties on British iron,[44] and British restrictions on foreign trade to its West Indian colonies.[45] The expansion of the British Empire led to new issues, for example duties on South African wine,[46] but relations were markedly better than they had been during the Jefferson and Madison administrations. In January 1824, Henry Addington felt able to write to George, 9th Earl of Dalhousie, Captain-General and Governor-in-Chief of Canada, that "the harmony and good understanding which subsist between the two governments and nations are so perfect as to fear very little cause for apprehension of any disagreeable occurrences arising which may have a tendency to resuscitate the feelings of jealousy and animosity heretofore but too prevalent, but now happily laid asleep."[47] In the 1824 election, Anglo-American relations were discussed only in relation to the tariff and the need to encourage greater economic independence from Britain.

James Monroe (1758–1831), was a Virginian who had been a prominent member of Madison's government as secretary of state (1811–17) and acting secretary of war in the War of 1812. Easily winning the 1816 and 1820 presidential elections, Monroe is most famous in international terms for a statement of American intentions that threatened greatly to extend national commitments. On 2 December 1823, in his annual message to Congress, Monroe announced that attempts by European powers to establish or reestablish colonies in the New World would be seen as "dangerous to our peace and safety." This declaration, which was, as John Clayton, the former Secretary of State, pointed out in the Senate on 20 February 1855,[48] a recommendation, and not a measure sanctioned by Congress, has been seen as a key moment in American foreign policy, one offering a major expansion in geopolitical aspirations. Moreover, Monroe's meaning was clear, as the background was not only that of Alexander I's ambitions for Russian America but also of the threat that the Latin American wars of independence would fail and that Spanish authority would be restored in Latin America. Thus, Monroe offered, at once, a bold geopolitical prospectus and a pledge to defend republican independence and therefore, in American terms, political liberalism.[49] Adams, indeed, saw an "impending conflict between autocracy and parliamentary government."[50]

At the same time, American commercial and political interests were pushed hard in the new states. British and American commentators noted Anglo-American competition in Latin America.[51] Commercial opportunities were linked to the hopes of Latin American states, especially Mexico, repaying loans that their leaders sought and international creditors proved overly eager to offer.[52] Treaties of commerce with Guatemala and Colombia were negotiated by the Americans in 1825, and there was British concern about American plans for building a canal across the Isthmus of Panama and British interest in the same idea.[53]

There were also worries that American recognition of the new republics would lead to political intervention designed to produce a hostile new order. The Earl of Orford wrote in 1826, "I am not at all surprised to see Yankee send an envoy to Panama; it is with the view (*not unlikely to succeed*) of becoming the head and leader of the Confederacy."[54] Indeed, Henry Clay, the American secretary of state, wanted America to act as leader of the Western Hemisphere. In some respects, this prefigured the idea of PanAmerika, one of the pan-regions designated by Karl Haushofer, the leading German geopolitician of the 1920s and 1930s.[55] The context was very different, however, and Clay offered a liberal ideological account very different to Haushofer's focus on security, control, expansionism, and independent endeavor. Adams had stressed that, in recognizing the independence of Latin American states, America did not seek any exclusive advantage.[56]

Yet, at the same time, what became known as the Monroe Doctrine was, like the Nootka Sound Crisis of 1790, more significant both for what it might have led to and for what it showed about America's relative powerlessness as an independent state. There was, indeed, concern that Spain would be backed by the conservative regimes of Europe: Austria, Russia and, in particular, France. French forces were sent into Spain in a full-scale invasion alliance with King Ferdinand to suppress liberalism in 1823, as Austrian troops had also successfully moved into Naples and Piedmont in 1821, and there was little reason to assume that they would not try to extend this policy. Adams was worried that French intervention and the related conflict in Spain might spread to the New World and lead to the conquest or cession of territories there. This threatened all ideas of American separateness from European power politics, and Adams told Stratford Canning, the British envoy, "The policy of their government as well as the force of circumstances had hitherto excluded the United States from any immediate connection with the general system of European affairs. With respect to the vast continent of the west, the United States must necessarily take a warm and decided interest in whatever determined the fate or affected the welfare of its component members."[57]

The crisis, therefore, encouraged the idea that the Americas were one continent that defined the geopolitical security of the United States, and, in doing so, led to an engagement with a wider Atlantic politics. Thus, aside from unfounded anxieties that Britain had its eyes on Cuba and that Spain was willing to cede the island temporarily as a means to retain long-term control,[58] an immediate international crisis was a background to the Monroe Doctrine, although Adams convinced Madison to delete condemnations of existing European interventions from his nascent doctrine. This allowed Adams to present the Doctrine as one assuring Europeans that America would not intervene in their conflicts of empire if they did not expand their holdings or try to reconquer lost territory in this hemisphere.

In subsequent discussions, Adams argued that the president should underplay the threat from the Holy Alliance on the grounds that the public felt so secure and unthreatened by outside powers that overstatement would spread a sudden panic. In practice, there was not much perception outside the cabinet of the threat from the Holy Alliance in late 1823. Indeed, despite earlier British fears that electoral considerations would direct the policy of the American government,[59] foreign affairs played a surprisingly small role in the presidential election of 1824. Some partisans argued that, in a potentially dangerous world, there was a lot to be said for a skilled diplomat like Adams, but this argument had little independent traction. This was a good example of élite awareness of higher things not mattering in an election driven, ultimately, by popular concerns in the wake of a persisting depression. Most popular attention had been given to the case for Greek independence from Turkish rule, but there were few complaints after Monroe made clear that there would be no American intervention. Recognition of Latin American independence effectively ended public concern in America.

Hemispheric developments meant that there was certainly a serious potential threat to America, even though the avoidance of crisis with Russia helped ensure a settlement in 1824 that removed the second of the three European contenders for title to the Oregon Country. Although Britain was the leading naval power throughout, there was a major expansion in the French navy after 1815, in particular in frigates, and France launched warships with a displacement tonnage of 73,000 in 1816–25. Such a buildup was no longer restricted by the impact of war with Britain. In his annual messages to Congress, Monroe announced the deployment of permanent American naval forces across the world, but, in reality, they were overshadowed, although the decline in the Spanish navy was such that the American one had passed it by 1825 to become the fourth largest naval power after Britain, France, and Russia, a position it then consistently held to the Civil War.[60]

Nevertheless, with the far greater, second-largest navy in the world, France was in a position to support the restoration of Bourbon authority in Latin America. Spain's alliance with France from 1796 to 1808, which included action against America during the Quasi War, underlined the danger to America of cooperation between the two states. In 1825,

France deployed twelve warships in support of its harsh and nonnegotiable terms for the recognition of Haitian independence: an indemnity of 150 million francs, later reduced to 90 million, which compared to the 60 million for which Louisiana was sold. The debt swallowed up much of the country's budget and was only paid off in 1947.

Thus, the Monroe Doctrine was, in many respects, foolish. It was to have meaning after the Civil War, when America was a powerful and more united state, but far less so earlier. Spanish forces seeking to regain Mexico were defeated by the Mexican general Santa Anna at Tampico in September 1829: the Americans were in no position to determine the struggle, nor to deter the French from real and rumored pressure on Colombia in the late 1820s and early 1830s, including a blockade mounted in 1833 by warships from the French colony of Martinique,[61] and, secondly, a blockade of, and then attack on, Veracruz in order to force Mexico to observe the financial interests of France and its citizens.[62] It was fortunate for the local powers, including America, as well as for France, that the latter never devoted to the New World, including in Mexico in 1861–67, the resources it expended in conquering Algeria from 1830. Indeed, by 1846, France had 108,000 effectives in Algeria.

Britain, not America, was the key power in the New World, and, in practice, provided the basis of the Monroe Doctrine. Indeed, the British government, which had played no role in the decisions reached by the leading European conservative rulers at Carlsbad (1818), Troppau (1820), and Laibach (1821), obtained assurances that France would not support Spain. In addition, in 1826, Mexico turned to Britain, not America, for assistance. The intimidatory strength of the Royal Navy deterred Spain from persisting in attempts to regain its Latin American colonies, although other factors also played a role.

Moreover, it was to be the Royal Navy later in the 1820s that played a role in the power politics linked to Brazilian independence from Portugal and, subsequently, to Brazil's struggle with Argentina over what became Uruguay.[63] Britain's commitment to free trade in Latin America benefited the United States, as Castlereagh pointed out.[64] Furthermore, although, with the Monroe Doctrine, they wanted to speak independently of the British, the Americans could put forward their new policy toward Latin America with confidence that the British would enforce it.

American policymakers understood that they could not do everything implied in it themselves, but they knew that the British would do much the same, with some of the same effect. Later, in the 1840s and 1850s, America was able to advance its interests in China as a result of British military action there. While disclaiming British methods, the Americans sought to obtain rights to trade on equal terms.

Britain was not only a shield for Latin America. In addition, Britain was probably the only state that was economically strong enough and had a fleet large enough to sustain power projection against America. However, if France or Spain were not in a state to threaten America significantly, equally the American ability to thwart French or Spanish power projection elsewhere in the New World was limited. Furthermore, a combination of the (British) Royal Navy, distance, American ideology, and the nature of the American military ensured that America could not figure significantly in European power politics and was therefore not treated as an important participant in the international order or an equal by the European powers. The American ability to project naval power into the Mediterranean and to defeat Barbary states made little impact on Austria or Russia.

Yet, the aftermath of the War of 1812 was not such as to encourage a critical debate about American capability, and thus its proper geopolitical span. Despite the efforts of British writers,[65] a partial American reading of the last year of the war, with focus on the successful defense of Fort McHenry against British bombardment and amphibious attack on 13–14 September 1814, the naval victory on Lake Champlain on 11 September 1814, and the triumph at New Orleans on 8 January 1815, encouraged confidence. Independence had been reasserted and interests defended.

Moreover, the acquisition of Florida, the replacement of imperial Spain by a weaker Mexico that lacked the stability and strength to sustain its imperial ambitions, and the ability to settle differences with Britain, whatever the tensions between the two states,[66] greatly eased American geopolitical concerns by 1821. So also did the rapid growth of American society, with a booming population and an expanding economy. British commentators were concerned about migration, especially skilled migration, to America rather than within the British empire.[67] There was also considerable British investment. It was scarcely surprising that this situation encouraged a marked degree of American assertiveness, and the British government was worried about reports that America was after Cuba.[68]

Political divisions linked to an assertive regionalism were soon to make this American expansionism part of the cause of a growing sense of instability in America. Yet perceptive observers were already looking ahead to an international system in which America was very powerful, and were linking this to the profound demographic and economic trends focused on it. In 1816, Napoleon told Lieutenant-General Sir Hudson Lowe, the governor of the British colony of St. Helena, where he was being held prisoner: "The high price of all articles of prime necessity is a great disadvantage in the export of your manufactures ... your manufacturers are emigrating fast to America. . . . In a century or perhaps half a century more, it will give a new character to the affairs of the world. It has thriven upon our follies."[69]

# 10

# EXPANSIONISM AND
# ITS PROBLEMS
# 1823-43

America was the most dynamic society in the Western world, with its population rising rapidly prior to the great territorial expansion of the 1840s, from 9.6 million in 1820 to 17.1 million in 1840, whereas Mexico's population, which had been similar to that of America in the late eighteenth century, rose from 1820 to 1840 by little to 7 million. Moreover, a sense of national destiny became more pronounced in America during these years and also seemed within grasp. This sense was seen in the engagement with American landscape as sublime and morally uplifting, a view clearly demonstrated by the enthusiastic response to the self-consciously national Hudson River school of painters. Regarded as more vigorous and unspoiled than those of Europe, the American landscape also appealed to British visitors such as Henry Addington, Richard Cobden, and Charles Dickens. Addington found more grandeur and beauty in the Hudson Valley than in those of the Rhine, Elbe, or Oder, sites of awe for European Romantics. Cobden was enthralled by the sight of the Hudson Valley in 1835, and Dickens by the sublimity of Niagara Falls in 1842.[1]

Similarly, transcendentalist thought, combining Romanticism and Deism and associated with writers such as Ralph Waldo Emerson and Henry David Thoreau, reflected a strong American optimism and was seen as a declaration of independence from Church control and traditionalism. Emerson presented America as a visionary poem, a country of young men, who, in 1775, had fired at Lexington on 19 April "the shot heard round the world." A Romanticism of national vision affected many individual Americans, and public culture as a whole, and, in doing so, discredited the earlier theory of New World degeneracy.[2]

The sense of national destiny had consequences within the country, in relations with America's neighbors, and also as far as the wider world was concerned. It was inscribed in America's future not only as rhetoric but also with the increasing number of pioneers who trekked west to Oregon and California, and with the growing sense that they represented the nation's future.[3] Yet, expansionism also posed problems not least because it interacted with growing sectional differences and greatly exacerbated them by threatening the regional balance between these sections. In particular, expansion helped shape the growing divide between North and South and gave it both fresh issues and a spatial dynamic.

Expansionism, however, was also intended by some as a way to overcome this north–south divide by developing a contrary west–east alignment. In this, a prosperous interior was to be linked to the Atlantic littoral by new transport links, notably canals, such as the Erie Canal opened in 1825,[4] river improvements,[5] steamships, railways, and telegraphs, as well as by other measures of economic nationalism, including tariffs to protect nascent industries and markets, the spread of banking, and the acceptance of paper currency.[6] Henry Clay proved a keen protagonist of this view of America's future, presenting it as a national solution to problems and a source of strength. Charles Vaughan reported in 1827 that "the Adams' administration is attempting to turn a popular tide in its favor, by vaunting itself, as the avowed support of what has been lately termed 'the American system.'"[7] Population growth matched this system, with settlers moving westward into Trans-Appalachia, the cotton-producing southwest, Texas, and, for the first time, along the Overland Trade. Settlers divided up by land, so that, by the mid-1820s, Illinois, for example, was increasingly distributed between white farmers. The rate of increase in these areas was much greater than further east,[8] a process that was important to the reconceptualization of America as a continental power as well as to the development of the political significance and voting strength of Trans-Appalachia. This significance, however, did not extend to sectionalism, and certainly not in comparison with those of North and South, let alone to separatism.

Geopolitics involves control over credit as well as territory and people. British investment played a significant role in American growth, especially in the development of railways, notably the Baltimore and

Ohio. Moreover, leading British exporters and banks mobilized capital to extend lengthy credits to American purchasers and borrowers. Yet, such dependence led to tension on the part of Americans, providing another example of a difficult relationship that looked back to colonial times. Separately, economic growth was also seen as a key way to resist Britain in any future war, as it would lessen economic reliance on foreign trade and the place of customs revenue in public finances, both of which were vulnerable to British naval action. Moreover, such growth would reduce the accumulated debt burden. The American army played a role in the economic development of the west, with the General Survey Act of 1824 providing a context for canal and railway surveys, which remained significant until 1838. There was no equivalent energy or growth in Mexico, in part because the serious and violent divide there between centralization and federalism acted as a barrier to good government.

American expansionism was primarily encouraged by two features already present prior to 1823. First was the weakness of the Native Americans, a weakness that was particularly apparent without any countervailing support for them from Britain, and with the British government, in addition, keen to reassure its American counterpart that reports to the contrary, even of action by traders of the Hudson's Bay Company, were groundless.[9] Secondly, the replacement of the powerful Spanish Empire of the eighteenth century by two weaker states, Mexico and the much reduced Spanish Empire, each of which themselves risked dissolution, was important in encouraging expansionist ideas. These two features were related, as the ability of the United States to threaten to exert power in the former Spanish Empire owed much to the lessening of the sense of American vulnerability to Native Americans and, albeit far more equivocally, Britain. Increasingly, the U.S. continental power therefore was also better placed to appear powerful (in the New World) in comparison with the great world empire, Britain, and certainly so by the 1840s.

Yet, the worldwide expansion of the British Empire concerned American commentators, notably those anxious to develop American trade, while a fear of British intervention in the New World also greatly influenced American policy, for example in preferring in the 1820s that Cuba remain Spanish rather than be attacked by Mexico and Colombia, which might have led to European intervention.[10] Moreover, exaggerated notions of a continued British threat stoked the fires of American nationalism, and, alike, among Democrats and Whigs (in effect, the successors to the Federalists), although with radically clashing assessments of risk and with differing conclusions as far as policy was concerned. In part, the difficulties the United States had encountered in the War of 1812 shaped a generation of policy making so that, despite continuing population expansion to the west, the United States gave up serious western territorial expansion until 1845, although it still achieved more than Mexico. This uncharacteristic hesitation on its part reflected domestic political divisions, notably sectional tensions that, for example, affected the appointment of diplomats,[11] but also a fear of being roughly handled by Britain if it took umbrage at America's acquisitive ways. The impact on military expenditure of the (economic) Panic of 1819 was also significant and interacted with longstanding concerns about the size of government.[12]

More than American hesitation played a role in the avoidance of renewed conflict. In addition, tension was reduced by the way in which British ministers understood national interests in terms of wider-ranging liberal causes,[13] and, so long as there was no fundamental challenge, were willing to accept or seek compromise with American views. In 1835, a serious dispute between France and America over damages for depredations on American commerce during the Napoleonic period led Britain to seek to accommodate differences, rather than to exploit them for their own advantage.[14] Indeed, British policy was so accommodating, especially that of George, 4th Earl of Aberdeen, foreign secretary from 1841 to 1846 and prime minister from 1852 to 1855, that it has been described in terms of appeasement.[15] Such compromise was far less in evidence in British policy in Asia and Africa, a factor that underlines the racist inflection of the providential destiny affecting British attitudes toward imperial expansion, a destiny also seen by Americans as at work in their own case.

As far as disputes with the latter were concerned, there was a clearly discernible trend on the part of Britain to resort to arbitration, notably over the Maine boundary, in large part because war with America was now recognized as undesirable, costly, and too problematic, but also because of the different attitudes taken as far as America were concerned.

The resulting neutralizing of America's northern frontier, which was seen in the limited expenditure on fortifications on that frontier,[16] played a role in preparing the way for American territorial expansion elsewhere. Thus, Britain helped make it feasible for Americans to see the possibility of their country becoming a great nation.

At the same time, the absence of conflict with America over Canada and Latin America greatly helped British imperialism at the global level by aiding concentration on the possibilities and problems posed in particular by South and East Asia. Moreover, in North America this absence of conflict with America ensured that Canada became well grounded as a viable entity within the British Empire, despite the absence of large native forces that could be called upon, as in India, to provide assistance to the imperial power, and despite the presence, unlike with Australia and Cape Colony in southern Africa, of a threatening neighbor in the case of America. As so often, demographic factors were crucial, for, between 1815 and 1850, nearly a million immigrants arrived in Canada from the British Isles, in large part due to demobilization after the Napoleonic War, economic depressions, and social disruption linked to large-scale urbanization and economic transformation.[17] This migration strengthened the British presence by enhancing the importance of Upper Canada, which, in 1851, had 38 percent of the population of the area of modern Canada compared to only 4 percent in 1800, and lessening the dominance of Lower Canada (Quebec) by people of French origin. There was high natural growth in Lower Canada, but nearly no immigration from France: the respective percentages of the population of what is now Canada in Lower Canada were 35 (1851) and 60 (1800).

The power of the American state was qualified: it was seen not in any expansion into Canada but in the fate of Spain. This power was also readily apparent in the removal of Native Americans to distant reservations, an important aspect of the relationship between people and space that can be considered alongside that posed by the distribution of slavery. Championed by the Democrats and by advocates of states' rights, notably in Georgia and Alabama, and opposed by the Whigs, the removal policy, which would now be described by most non-Americans in terms of expropriation and ethnic cleansing, was driven by demands of settlers for land and was pursued explicitly from 1830, when the Indian Removal Act was passed. Natives lost their homelands in return for land west of the Mississippi that, from 1834, meant the Louisiana Purchase minus Louisiana, Arkansas, and Missouri, which already had been established as states.[18] The Chickasaw, for example, signed a removal treaty in 1832, and they and the Choctaw were moved in 1832–34. In 1834, the Topographical Bureau produced a "Map of the Western Territory" designed to help plan the separation between the settlers and the Native Americans, a policy of separate development that provided land for American settlers and removed to what were regarded as lands too arid for cultivation, the Natives who were seen as unwelcome. The latter was an important element, as land itself was not the sole issue: much of the cleared land remained unsettled, although it was now allocated to American owners.[19]

Having sought to expel white intruders, supported by Georgia and Alabama, from Native lands in the 1820s and early 1830s, the army, which devoted the largest share of its manpower to frontiers where Natives were the main challenge,[20] was responsible for supervising the removal policy and, if necessary, enforcing it. Many officers disliked the policy, and clashed with the civilians, especially frontiersmen, who pressed hardest for removal, this disagreement being a theme that could be traced back to the early days of the republic and into colonial times. Nevertheless, officers enforced the policy.[21] Force was employed against the Creek in 1836, in order to make those of the Creek who had not already moved west of the Mississippi in 1834, in accordance with the implications of the Treaty of Cusseta of 1832, do so. The fairly well-assimilated Cherokee had fruitlessly declared their independence as a nation in 1827, but in *Cherokee Nation v Georgia* in 1831, the Supreme Court declared the indigenous nations "wards" of the American government, which opened the way to harsh treatment. The Cherokee were forcibly moved in 1838–39, with about 4,000 people out of the 14,000 moved dying as a result of the hardship, disease, and disruption, now known as the Trail of Tears. The Trail of Death of that year was that along which Potawatomi were forced by Indiana militia. The Winnebago of Wisconsin, who had been brought under control in 1827 in a "war" that involved no military conflict, were moved by the army to Iowa in 1840, a key part of the process by which most of Wisconsin had been cleared of Natives by 1848 without any large-scale resistance. West of the Mississippi, the Texans, once independent, were to try to drive the Natives from east Texas.

Removal completed the disruption of Native American society east of the Mississippi, a process begun by commercial pressures and desires, cultural syncretism, and white intimidation. Removal also led to conflict between Natives, for example Osage versus Cherokee, as they competed in areas now under ecological pressure.[22] Removal, moreover, was even more menacing because it was clearly intended by most whites as a stage that was to be followed by the seizure of the land into which the Natives had been moved.

The removal policy was divisive within America. It enjoyed less support in New England than in frontier regions and the South, in each of which there was far more hostility to the Native Americans and far more concern with land. Indeed, the presence in the South of the Creek, Cherokee, and Seminole helped give a frontier consciousness to Southern life.

From the Native perspective, there was no doubt of the pressure of American advance and aggression, but the Americans had a capacity to fear Natives, or at least to employ such fears in order to justify action. In 1830, the British envoy reported, "It appears that the Indians upon the South-western and North-western borders of the United States, excited the fears of the government during the last year, which required detachments of troops to be sent to those points."[23] In practice, there was scant need for American concern. The defeat of Black Hawk and his band of 1,000–2,000 Sauk and Fox in the Black Hawk War in Illinois and Wisconsin in 1832 reflected the vulnerability of tribes east of the Mississippi, especially when they received no assistance from foreign powers. Moreover, Black Hawk's attempt to revive the pan-Native activity seen with Pontiac and Tecumseh fell foul of the weakness of this cause, not least due to the strength of rival tribal identities in the Upper Mississippi region. Indeed, there was considerable Native military support for the American cause, as was frequently the case. Looking toward the Civil War (1861–65), Captain Abraham Lincoln and Lieutenant Jefferson Davis both took part in a campaign in which the Americans deployed larger numbers with relative ease. The war itself was an accidental conflict in that, in trying to remain in the Rock River Valley, Black Hawk and his followers did not seek a struggle that was falsely represented as an "invasion." Instead, the war began when troops attacked Sauk carrying a white flag.[24] Subsequent attempts to surrender were ignored or misunderstood. Heavy losses to American firepower in the battle of the Bad Axe on 2 August brought the conflict to a close.

In Florida, a more intractable environment, the Seminole rejected the government's removal policy and the Second Seminole War (1835–42) began when a number of Seminole chiefs agreed to resist the removal to Oklahoma extorted in the Treaty of Payne's Landing of 1832. The American determination to end slave flight from Georgia to Florida was a powerful factor in causing the war, as the Seminole provided refuge for escaped slaves.[25] More than 40,000 troops, 30,000 volunteer militia, and 10,000 regulars, although never more than 5,000 regulars at a time, were eventually deployed, especially after the Seminole, whose total population was only about 5,000, won several battles in the initial stages. Their guerrilla tactics caused problems to a number of American commanders, as did the racial politics of the conflict. An armistice came to an end in 1837, and Seminole resistance revived when the Americans allowed slavers to enter Florida and to seize Seminole and African Americans.

In contrast, in 1838, the racial politics of the struggle changed when African Americans who abandoned the Seminole and joined the Americans were offered their freedom, which cost the Seminole dearly: they lost about four hundred fighters.[26] By 1842, the Seminole had been driven into the more inaccessible parts of the Florida Everglades, many had agreed to move west, and the government then felt able to wind the war down. There was no formal peace treaty. The war also saw opposition among the northern Whigs to the removal policy toward Native Americans.

The Seminole War led in 1838 to the adding of an eighth infantry regiment to the army, but the main change in the army was the introduction of the Battalion of Mounted Rangers in 1832 and mounted (dragoon) regiments in 1833 and 1836. There had been none since the War of 1812, and this change reflected the experience of the Black Hawk War, and, more generally, the need to adapt both to greater distances and to the advance beyond wooded terrain into the Plains, as well as the desire to avoid dependence on mounted frontier volunteers and militia who had a tendency to inflame relations with the Natives.[27]

Yet, in the 1830s, military strategy focused on the idea of an essentially stable frontier, rather than on supporting far-flung expansion, not least because it had become clear that the British from Canada were not, as had been feared, a challenge to American power in the Mississippi and Missouri valleys. Moreover, British traders were not supplying the Sioux who dominated the Upper Missouri with arms and ammunition in any quantity.[28] The problems the army encountered in the Upper Missouri Valley over the previous decade, as well as concern about funding and costs, encouraged caution and also suggested a more general limitation in military operations against Native Americans.[29] Having advanced there to assert national sovereignty, and to keep British power at a distance from the Natives, the military withdrew from the Upper Missouri Valley in 1827, abandoning Fort Atkinson, built in 1819 in the Council Bluffs area of modern Omaha, and falling back to Fort Leavenworth. The focus of expansion in American power was not the Central Plains, but the Upper Mississippi Valley in Wisconsin and Minnesota, as well as modern Oklahoma, which was used as a Native reservation.[30] In contrast, after Joel Poinsett became Secretary of War in 1837, there was a marked upsurge in support for army exploration as a way to understand America's geography. The Topographical Bureau was expanded in size and made into a corps in 1838.

The frontier that was most unstable was that to the southwest, but there the issue became that of Texan independence, rather than solely American expansion. Texas had continued troublesome after Mexico declared independence. Indeed, in December 1826, there was an attempt to create a Republic of Fredonia around Nacogdoches that was rapidly put down in early 1827. Significantly, militia from Austin's Colony joined Mexican troops from San Antonio as the rebels angered important American settler interests as well as the Mexican government. The failure of the filibusters then, and earlier, was notable despite the peripheral character of Texas within Mexico and the need for the Mexican army to focus on dissidence in more central regions within Mexico. It was possible to threaten Spanish and later Mexican control of the eastern borderlands near the Sabine River, but the heart of Texas lay beyond the reach of the filibusters.

Meanwhile, Mexico was challenged by the aftermath of the war of independence, where turbulence certainly did not end with the severing of Spanish metropolitan control. Indeed, because the government of Mexico was "extremely unsettled," no American envoy was appointed in early 1823.[31] The war of independence had seen the disruption of the colonial state, with its emphasis on bureaucracy, and the rise, instead, of *caudillos:* regional chieftains who used control over land and armed clients to seek a form of power that was personal rather than institutional.[32] Similarly, guerrilla bandits became more prominent, ensuring another form of instability.[33] The rise of *caudillos* was a key element in the turbulence of the period in Latin America, as was widespread tension between federalism and local forces. In Mexico, the federalist government of General Anastasio Bustamante overcame and disbanded several state-based militias in 1830. As elsewhere in Latin America, force was commonly used for the pursuit of domestic power, with military action proving a key means for the transfer of governmental authority.

As so often in the history of North America, demography proved a crucial factor in Texas. Its population grew rapidly in the 1820s and early 1830s as a result of immigration from America. People were seen as a source of strength, and this immigration was initially encouraged by the Mexican government, with colonization laws passed in 1824 and 1825 as a way to protect northern Mexico from the attacks of the powerful Comanche as well as to foster economic growth and thus produce revenues for Mexico. In the event, this rise in population, which owed much to Southern land hunger and the potential for expanding cotton cultivation, made the situation volatile and led to Mexican concern about the degree of central governmental control in Texas. As a result, American immigration was stopped from April 1830. Moreover, the government's attempts to prevent the import of slaves into Texas aroused ire among the settlers: slavery had been abolished by Mexico in 1824 and 1829, although Texas was exempted. There was also the question of the implication for America of Americans settling outside its boundaries.

The central issue in Texas was that of control, which had also been the main problem in the American War of Independence. In 1832 and

1833, Texan conventions called for separate statehood within Mexico, as well as the freedoms and liberties they regarded as their due. Richard Pakenham, the British envoy in Mexico, complained to Vaughan about the uncontrolled and undisciplined state of the Texans and noted the report that the Americans had encouraged Native attacks on Mexico, which, he pointed out, had been damaging, not least because the frontier defenses were decayed.[34] The Texans, in turn, complained that Mexico was failing to provide protection against Comanche attack.

Fighting between Mexicans and Texans began in October 1835 when troops from San Antonio sought to take back a cannon they had provided for the town of Gonzales in 1831 to help it deter attack by Native Americans: as with the American War of Independence, issues of "frontier" security played a role in increasing tension. The following month, a convention, known as the Consultation of All Texans, created a provisional state government that was designed to negotiate with Mexico, but the Mexican strongman, General Antonio López de Santa Anna, characteristically tried to deal with the situation by force. The abrogation in 1835 of the 1824 constitution, under which the Americans had settled in Texas, and the claim that their failure to convert to Catholicism meant that their land grants were void, were unacceptable to the Texans.

It is understandable that Santa Anna's policy is generally discussed in American popular accounts with reference only to Texas, but, in practice, it was part of an authoritarian, centralist drive directed against federalism and liberalism that he saw as causes of national weakness. This policy was resisted by liberals across Mexico, but the radical administration was overthrown in 1834 with Congress closed, while, in May 1835, the anticentralist provincial government of Zacatecas was crushed by Santa Anna.[35] The centralist policy was resisted in Texas not only by most of the Anglo colonists but also by many Texans of Hispanic origin, and they initially opposed Santa Anna in the name of the 1824 constitution. This cooperation was an aspect of the fluidity of loyalties and identities in the region, as American and Mexican interests and beliefs cross-fertilized.[36] The Texans were also concerned about Comanche attacks, which would have become more serious had Santa Anna succeeded in his goal of ending state militias and focusing power on the army. As with the Thirteen Colonies in 1775, control over local military forces was a key aspect of the developing crisis. The Texans also wished to maintain economic links with America.

On 23 February 1836, Santa Anna and his army reached San Antonio, where, instead of withdrawing, an outnumbered Texan force defended the poorly fortified Alamo mission until it was stormed in the early hours of 6 March, the surviving defenders being slaughtered. Meanwhile, on 2 March, the Texans had declared independence. Santa Anna then pressed on further east, while Sam Houston tried and failed to win Comanche support. However, having divided his forces, Santa Anna, operating without reliable information and, in practice, beyond the bounds of safe campaigning, was surprised, outfought, and rapidly beaten at San Jacinto on 21 April by a smaller army under Houston that successfully took the initiative, and he was captured the next day.

On 14 May 1836, the captured Santa Anna signed agreements bringing peace, withdrawing the Mexican army, and recognizing Texan independence, with the border at the Rio Grande. Although the remaining Mexican forces in Texas far outnumbered the Texan army and, indeed, the force defeated at San Jacinto, their commanders obeyed Santa Anna's order to retreat, and Texas was evacuated. In some respects, there was a parallel with the fall of Quebec in 1759 in that, although Montcalm's army was defeated outside that city, Quebec itself did not fall that day while other French forces were marching to join Montcalm, and thus to the city's relief. Nevertheless, the defeat and death of Montcalm led to a crucial collapse of French will, and the city surrendered. Unlike in the case of Quebec, however, there was to be no attempt in 1836 to regain the position: in 1760 the French advanced, defeated the British outside Quebec, and besieged the city, which had to be relieved by a British squadron, whereas, in 1836, there was to be no second Mexican advance in Texas. Moreover, the Mexican advance that was to be made at the outset of the Mexican-American War in 1846 was far more limited.

The inability of Mexico to sustain the struggle, which in part arose from the limited number of Mexican settlers in the northern provinces, was an important element of the geopolitics in 1836, one that reflected also the military consequences of the political limitations of the Mexican war effort. In contrast, Santa Anna was more successful in suppressing a federalist revolt in Tampico in northeast Mexico in 1839: the rebels were defeated at the battle of Acajete. Another federalist revolt, in Mexico City, was suppressed in 1840.

The Texan cause benefited from American volunteers, but the American army had been ordered to patrol the Texas border during the revolution and did not intervene against Santa Anna when he invaded in 1836. In 1834, Vaughan had sent information to his counterpart in Mexico City about possible American military action against the Comanche within Mexican territory, information that was to be used to put the Mexican government on its guard.[37] However, Jackson favored restraint and did not wish to internationalize the crisis, although that policy risked an outcome unwelcome to America, notably a new stability based on the strengthening of Mexico. In the event, the crisis ended not with an expanded America, but with an American state outside the United States. This had not arisen due to separatism, as had occurred in Latin America (now including Texas), the fate foretold for the United States by many commentators, but rather because Americans had created a state outside the bounds of the country. In part, this development was a culmination of the filibustering seen from the outset of the American republic, and notably at the expense of Spain. As an instance of this process, the Hudson's Bay Company reported in 1836 that a party of American adventurers, the Indian Liberating Army, wanted to persuade Native Americans to act against British and American encroachments so as to become an independent nation under this army.[38]

The establishment of Texas also reflected a fissiparous tendency that was latent within the United States with its strong regional differences. As a result, Texas posed a serious challenge. It suggested that American expansion might well lead to a series of states that would both weaken the United States, by creating potentially strong neighbors, and, despite hopes of a federation of such states, could also provide a challenge as to how these states should cooperate with each other and with the United States. Texan independence posed the challenge of a model that might spread within the United States, in the aftermath, in particular, of the Nullification Crisis, and one that could, more plausibly, be employed in other areas outside the country, such as California, or as part of the result of the Oregon Question. In California, a revolt in 1831 by Pio de Jesus Pico, a wealthy landowner, led not to independence but to Pico becoming governor for the Mexican government.[39] The Nullification Crisis in South Carolina was very different in its character, but there was a common theme of regional distinction.

Yet, if Texas was to be incorporated within the United States, this outcome posed the danger (and opportunity) that the balance of interests there, notably over slavery, would be greatly altered, not least if Texas entered as several states. As a result, the Texan issue threw the issues of Southern distinctiveness and the consequences of future American expansion harshly into the limelight. In May 1844, James Buchanan was certain that Martin Van Buren would not be chosen as Democratic candidate for the presidency because he had come out against the immediate annexation of Texas, which was rejected by the Senate on 8 June by thirty-five to sixteen in large part as a consequence of its being presented as a means to protect slavery. As Buchanan noted, the South, in contrast, was united in favor of such annexation: "the Texas question has absorbed the Anti-Tariff feeling there."[40] Indeed, the economic interests and regional concerns that had been focused on opposition to the tariff regime were, instead, focused, with greater intensity and more divisive effect, on slavery. In the event, James Polk beat Van Buren to the Democratic nomination on the ninth ballot and then, with the solid support of the South, won the presidency against Henry Clay, who, like Van Buren, was against immediate annexation, although the margin in the popular vote was only 38,181.

Texas did more than accentuate American political divisions, because, as a sovereign republic, it raised the issue of America's international position in a volatile fashion. Texas was able to pursue its own policies, but also attracted the interest of other states, notably Britain and France. With a clear preference for paranoia, American politicians were soon concerned that Texas would become a protectorate for one or both, and that this would challenge American interests in the West and more generally. Slavery played a role in this issue, as in so much else, as British policy toward recognition of Texas was affected by its reintroduction of slavery, which had been abolished by Mexico. In turn, pro-slavery Southerners, especially from 1843, saw Britain as having ruined its West Indian colonies by emancipation and as now intent on wrecking the competitive economies, notably the South, by making them abolish slavery.[41] Moreover, American politicians saw Texas as the base for the expansion of British and French interests in neighboring areas, so that they might become active players in the future of the western part of North America. Alarmist American commentators linked Canada, Oregon, and Texas as aspects of a British determination to control the future.

Texas was also very much an unfinished issue in international relations, as the Mexican Senate refused to accept its independence. There were expeditions and raids by both sides, but full-scale conflict between Mexico and Texas was avoided, in part because western Texas was dominated by Native Americans, particularly Comanche. Texas was more exposed to Native raids than other frontier areas and, in turn, sought to enforce its control over the Natives, which led to campaigns against them. On 12 August 1840, the Great Comanche Raid down the Guadalupe River to the Gulf of Mexico was intercepted at Plum Creek near Austin, and the Comanche thereafter did not raid settled communities east of San Antonio, but the war exhausted Texans as well as the Comanche and peace was agreed to in October 1844.[42] Further east, the Texans faced opposition from rebellious Natives and Mexicans near Nacogdoches in 1838, in part because the Texans sought to drive out Native refugees from east of the Mississippi who had settled in east Texas.

The shape of Texas was also unclear and attempts to advance goals reflected the volatility of the situation. Aside from disputes with Mexico over the frontier to the south, with Texas claiming a frontier on the Rio Grande, whereas the land from there to the Nueces River was seen by Mexicans as in the state of Coahuilla, there was also the problem caused by Texan interest in gaining New Mexico, which, like the frontier on the Rio Grande, was claimed under the Treaty of Velasco of 1836 by which Texan independence had been acknowledged. It was hoped that a show of force would lead the New Mexicans to reject the authority of Mexico City and, instead, join with Texas. Mirabeau Lamar, the president of Texas, and an ardent advocate of its continued independence, was a keen supporter of this idea and in 1841 sent an expedition to Santa Fe. This is not an episode that tends to be discussed in general accounts of American history. Disasters are not usually part of the American account, with the prominent exception of Lieutenant General George Custer and much of the Seventh Cavalry Regiment at Little Bighorn in 1876.

Nevertheless, the failure of the 1841 expedition is instructive. First, the expedition was a disaster, in large part because of a lack of knowledge, both about the route and about watercourses. In addition, the expedition was harassed by Native Americans and ran short of food. As a result, the Texans surrendered to Mexican troops without fighting. Their subsequent mistreatment inflamed relations and contributed to the picture of the Mexicans as inhuman, one that owed much to the Texan revolution, notably the execution of prisoners at Goliad in 1836. Secondly, the episode is instructive because it raises the question of what would have happened had Texas been successful and indicates the extent to which geopolitics was in flux. A fourth, far-flung empire in North America might have arisen, following the United States, Britain (in Canada), and Mexico; and this empire could have expanded to the Pacific. If so, it would have blocked or affected American expansion.[43]

Counterfactuals are only so far useful, and Texas was greatly weakened by its lack of settlers, the factor common to all these empires in the west, but that problem would have been lessened with time. Indeed, the possibility of Texan expansion was one that worried American politicians, while continued conflict in the area and the prospect of more large-scale warfare were also of concern. In 1842, when Mexican forces twice briefly captured San Antonio, there were reports of plans for Native–Mexican cooperation against Texas, and orders to American commanders to try to limit Native–Texan hostilities. American forces in the region were increased. American newspapers in favor of Texas joining the Union inaccurately reported that the invasion had been financed by Britain. Cross-border incursions continued. There was a particularly serious defeat for the Texans on 26 December 1842 when an attacking Texan force was forced by Mexican regulars to capitulate at Mier on the Rio Grande: some of the prisoners who escaped and were recaptured were shot by firing squad, the victims chosen by drawing beans from a covered jar while blindfolded.[44] In February 1844, an armistice was signed, only to be repudiated by Santa Anna when he became president that June, as he was committed to reconquering Texas.[45]

There were, however, also tensions between Texan and American interests. For example, in 1842, Jacob Snively, the Texan inspector general, won support for a retaliatory strike against Mexican caravans on the

Santa Fe route, in an operation that revealed the complexity of North American geopolitics. In 1843, Snively's 177-strong "Battalion of Invincibles" moved into modern Kansas near Dodge City, defeating a Mexican force sent to seize them, but, in turn, was overawed and forced back by American army dragoons under Captain Philip St. George Cooke, who was convinced that the Texans were on American territory. As a result, the opportunity to capture a Mexican caravan was lost. Cooke's action led to an official protest by the Texan government, but a court of inquiry cleared Cooke. In army circles, there was a lack of sympathy for independent military initiatives, and Texan operations were seen as a form of independent American military initiative, akin to that of the filibusters, notably, for these years, those supporting the Canadian Patriots (rebels).[46]

As a reminder of the range of conflict, and also of the potential influence of the great naval powers, Mexico and Texas clashed not only on the frontier but also in the Gulf of Mexico. Texan warships raided Mexican shipping and also supported rebels in the Yucatán, for any weakness of Mexico elsewhere, or indeed the collapse of the state, would not only help protect Texas but also enable it to expand. A center of opposition to Mexico, the Yucatán, was also an aspect of the more widespread failure of the states of Central America to control their coastlines, a process particularly seen with Honduras and Nicaragua. Without good ports, the Yucatán, however, was of limited value to maritime powers.

On 16 May 1843, there was a full-scale battle off Campeche, in which Texas sail vessels, the sloop *Austin* and the brig *Wharton*, fought off the *Moctezuma*, a Mexican paddle steamer that, to American concern, had been purchased in Britain the previous year and was armed with shell guns (artillery firing explosive shells as opposed to shot), and officered and manned by Britons. The Mexicans had the technological lead, and theirs was the first warship to fire shell guns in a ship-to-ship action, but Tomas Marin, the Mexican commander, did not provide adequate leadership in this case.[47]

The situation was highly volatile, and, indeed, British attempts to mediate between Texas and Mexico collapsed in early 1844. The anxieties of American commentators were increased by uncertainty over the future of Texas at the same time that opportunity beckoned in the shape of Texas joining the Union. Sam Houston, the Texas president, wished to join, but there was opposition in America from abolitionist interests.

America's other frontiers were also unsettled, but not with the same degree of volatility or concern. The frontier settlement with Britain left both the general question of the future of Oregon and more specific border disputes, especially over the boundaries of New Hampshire, Minnesota, and, most particularly, Maine, the state government of which actively supported the frontier claims. This list of points in dispute was far from exhaustive. Thus, in 1822, there were disagreements over the status of islands in the Detroit River, with the British envoy fearful of the consequences if the Americans gained and fortified the islands, while Adams made it clear that any compromise under which the islands they claimed were unfortified would not be ratified by Senate, and that, even if a reciprocal agreement was reached to leave all disputed islands unsettled, this was an impractical provision as far as the Americans were concerned. The last was a sensible point on Adams's part, and one that captured the subordination of diplomatic schemes to the drives of American expansionism, but the issue drove the British envoy to despair.[48]

An enormous amount of diplomatic effort was devoted to the Maine boundary. British politicians and commentators were certain that the issue was significant, as they were concerned that, if America succeeded in its claims to a frontier near the St. Lawrence, then it would be impossible to provide an adequate winter link between, on the one hand, the Atlantic and the Maritime provinces and, on the other, the Canadian interior: the water route up the St. Lawrence was closed by ice in the winter. Henry Addington, who had served in Washington, and who remained influential thereafter in British policymaking circles, was convinced of the need to make a stand on the issue and referred in 1827 to "the fierce question of the North East boundary."[49] Vaughan remarked that year that "our interminable negotiations upon points which two wars have left unsettled and which the tenacity of the people seems inclined to leave to be decided by future wars makes one hopeless of seeing the relations between the two countries put upon a good footing."[50]

There were periodic crises as the dispute rose to a height, notably in the late 1830s. Thus, in February 1839, the movement of an armed body from Maine into territory it disputed with the colony of New Brunswick, a movement seen by the British as a military incursion and by the Americans as an escorted land agent's party, led the Americans to threaten action if New Brunswick responded. The language in the House of Representatives was particularly strong. On 2 March, Congress authorized the president, Martin Van Buren, to resist any British attempt to enforce the claim to exclusive jurisdiction in the disputed territory by raising 50,000 volunteers and a loan of $10 million to cover the cost of preparations. The latter were to include armed steamboats on frontier lakes and rivers to resist invasion, as well as the repair and arming of seaboard fortifications.

Henry Stephen Fox, the British envoy, thought the discussions in Congress showed "an extreme asperity against England" arising from a sense of guilt over what he had earlier termed "the American crusade against Canada," but he was also confident of Van Buren's "prudent and pacific nature." Indeed, the president's attitudes helped lessen tensions. Adopting the familiar tone, Fox argued that populism was at fault: "the statesmen of America are trained up in helpless and blind obedience to the worst passions of the multitude."[51] In the event, Fox and John Forsyth, the secretary of state, negotiated a provisional agreement, which Van Buren urged Maine to accept. Van Buren also recommended that Maine stand down its militia and promised not to move regular troops to the area, while Fox suggested to Lieutenant-General Sir John Colborne, a Waterloo veteran who was governor-general and commander-in-chief in Canada, that the regiment already en route be kept out of the disputed territory. Finally, Maine and New Brunswick reached agreement.[52]

In 1838, Alexander Macomb, the American commanding general, toured the Vermont border, a marked departure from his usual practice, while, in 1839, there was planning for war, but the American government was keen to avoid conflict. Anxieties over Britain, however, played a role in American domestic politics, with Democratic expansionists seeing Britain as a threat, both in terms of America's foreign interests and also with reference to its domestic situation, which was regarded as closely linked to these interests. There was also longstanding concern about what was seen as British wide-ranging commercial imperialism and its implications for American trade and thus the economy.[53] Economic concerns were accentuated by the serious problems linked to the Panic of 1837, problems that included bankruptcies and unemployment.

Moreover, as in the 1790s, the idea of republican engagement played an international role, with many Americans supporting those Canadians who rebelled in 1837–38. The rebels protested against oligarchic government and a shortage of land for settlement,[54] but, given that most adult males in Upper Canada had the vote (the property qualifications were very low), and given the absence of slavery, the colony was pretty much as democratic as the American state. Lower Canada (Quebec) was a different case, and one probably inspired more by the French Revolution than anything the United States did, which was why the rebellion there was serious while the one in Upper Canada fizzled out quite soon.

The rebellion was backed by raids from America mounted by Canadian refugees and American sympathizers. The latter, who styled themselves Patriots, were more numerous than is generally appreciated, and saw themselves as finishing the work of the American Revolution.[55] These raids were wide-ranging, with attacks on the Niagara frontier in December 1837, from Cleveland and from Detroit in January, February, and December 1838, and the Prescott invasion from Oswego and Sacket's Harbor in November 1838. While American involvement prolonged the crisis, it also undermined the rebels' putative support, as the Americans were not mistaken as liberators by most in Upper Canada. For all their claims of benignity, American activities amounted to irredentism, akin to what happened in Texas at the same time, not idealism.

Palmerston pressed for action by the American government, threatening that, if not, "force will be repelled by force." Indeed, these raids raised the prospect of war between Britain and America over Canada, but in the event the British government was pleased with the stance of the American government.[56] Loyalists, a key military resource and more significant than they had been in 1775–83, took a major role in suppressing opposition in Canada, but the oceanic and maritime complement to continental power was also shown in the interconnected nature of British military power. The Royal Navy played a key role in moving troops within British North America, from Halifax to St. John's, New Brunswick and Quebec. The navy also moved troops there from the West Indies, Gibraltar (units en route home from Corfu in the Ionian Islands), and the British Isles. The vessels used as troop ships included large warships, while warships also carried specie for the Commissariat.[57]

The rebellion whetted the appetite of American expansionists who, in particular, saw the southwesterly axis of Canada to the north of Lakes Ontario and, especially, Erie as blocking the natural westward growth of New York. This issue took forward the commitment to gaining Canada seen in the War of 1812, but more closely focused it on land rather than, as earlier, the British role in using Canada to support Native Americans. At a more minor scale, American fishermen used force to encroach on Canadian fishing grounds off Nova Scotia and to drive away Canadian fishermen.[58]

The agenda of expansionism into Canada, let alone that of international republicanism, however, did not rise to the fore for American policymakers. In part, this failure reflected the salience of other issues in American politics, but the extent to which Britain could be seen by some as taking part in the same advance of progressive reform was also significant to some Americans. This was the Britain in which George Canning, foreign secretary in 1822–27 and prime minister in 1827, sought to harness public opinion for his policies, notably the cause of Catholic emancipation,[59] while the Britain of the Great Reform Act of 1832 was one that was explicable in terms of American politics. Three years earlier, Henry Clay had sent Vaughan a Kentucky rifle as well as congratulations on Catholic emancipation, specifically, and significantly, that of the Irish Catholics.[60]

However, there were also powerful cross-currents in Anglo-American relations, not least because, whatever the Whig revival, for the late 1810s and much of the 1820s, the Tory-dominated Liverpool government had resisted reform. Moreover, the many Irish Catholics who settled in America tended to oppose Britain and support the Jacksonians (and later the Democrats), which, in turn, encouraged the Whigs, as a key element of adopting and defining the nativist cause, to criticize the Catholics. This stance encouraged the Jacksonians, in tapping the breadth of anglophobia, to label their opponents "British Whigs."[61] The idea that British policy was inherently sympathetic to political reaction was also seen in the American treatment of Latin America. Thus, in 1831, Thomas Moore, the envoy in Bogota, falsely informed the government of Colombia that the British were seeking to reinstall a military dictatorship,[62] while American attitudes to the Mexico Question were characterized by a suspicion of British intentions in domestic Mexican politics.

In turn, Britons' views of America were not simply an extrapolation of their political allegiances. Some liberals and radicals, such as Richard Cobden, who visited America in 1835, John Bright, and the Unitarian utilitarian Harriet Martineau, who published *Society in America* (1837), saw aspects of the country as a desirable model,[63] but there was also concern about American long-term support for slavery and racism, although William Thackeray returned from his second lecture tour sympathetic to slavery.[64] British commentators opposed to reform were particularly hostile to American populists such as Jackson,[65] a theme that was subsequently taken up by commentators such as Walter Bagehot.[66] There was also opposition to what was seen as American hypocrisy. Captain Basil Hall, who had already commented from Canada on the difficulties made by American negotiators, wrote from Fayetteville, North Carolina in 1828, "Democracy and Slavery a preposterous medley." In 1830, he published his *Travels in North America in the Years 1827 and 1828*. The high degree of anglophobia British visitors experienced first hand colored their views of America, while American politicians frequently spoke on the stump about their right to Canada, which annoyed British visitors, including Frances Trollope and Frederick Marryat.[67]

More perceptively, Alexis de Tocqueville, a French lawyer who visited America in 1831, described in *De la démocratie en Amérique* (1835) a new type of society and political culture that was different from that of Europe, a mass society organized on the basis of an equality that ignored the aristocratic ethos of honor and threatened to create conformism but that also helped ensure that America would, with Russia, be one of the great powers of the future. At the same time, de Tocqueville regarded the real transition as that from the old to the new with the reforming monarchies of Europe, such as France after the 1830 revolution, which were also opposed to privilege. Able to harness developments in a fast-changing world, these states could prove a threat to America.[68]

Both these states and America faced instability in the period 1816–71 (as in other periods) as they sought to direct and respond to change. To European commentators, populism made America appear particularly unstable, and it certainly could be difficult to negotiate international disputes with America. Indeed, Addington, like many other British diplomats, complained about the impact of the Congressional ability to overturn agreements negotiated by the executive. Yet, compared with France and Spain, America appeared much more stable until the close of the 1850s. In Spain, there were violent transfers of power, while President Louis-Napoleon of France, behaving like a *caudillo* when he seized power in a coup d'état on 2 December 1851, went on to become Emperor Napoleon III. For example, America in the early 1830s was less unpredictable than France, where Charles X was overthrown in 1830, or Belgium, where there was a successful rising against Dutch rule the same year. As not only the world's leading naval power, but also a state that managed transitions of power without conflict, and that faced little serious domestic radicalism, Britain was a more challenging power to America than France.

The lack, despite frequent remarks by politicians, of governmental support for expansion into Canada and of any commitment on the part of American commanders to meddling in Canada, was not simply a case of the American army not being up to the task of conquering Canada. In addition, the British willingness, alongside defensive precautions, to avoid provocative steps and to make concessions, helped keep the temperature low. Concern about Britain, nevertheless, led to a major program of coastal fortifications, although these tied up much of the army in garrison positions. Brigadier-General Edmund Gaines, a veteran of the War of 1812 and a critic of such fortifications, pressed, instead, from 1826, for a rail and canal system financed by the federal government, able to move militia from the hinterland to oppose any British invasion, as well as for the construction of large ironclad warships. Yet, there was no real official pressure for proactive policies to weaken Britain by destabilizing Canada, still less conquering it.[69]

In 1837–38, the use of the American army to suppress filibustering on the Canadian border led to tensions with civilians, including militiamen, as the army was ordered to enforce the Federal Neutrality Acts of 1818 and 1838. American officers thus served as representatives of an unpopular national policy. Indeed, in marked contrast to the earlier situation over Florida, there was a willingness to accept that the principles and culture of international law should shape the Canadian–American situation, rather than any commitment for republican enthusiasm or territorial expansion on all frontiers. British commentators, such as Henry

Stephen Fox, the envoy, praised the policies of the American army commanders, especially Scott, who was seen as helping defuse tensions in the late 1830s, as he was again to do at the time of the Pig War in 1859 (see p. 281).[70] In 1842, the American government provided notice of a planned attack by Canadian rebels on British warships on Lake Erie.[71]

Quebec separatists unsuccessfully sought the assistance of the American government, criticizing its abandonment "of the cause of American liberty." In response, Jackson proved uncommunicative, while Clay, described by Fox as "the most openly declared enemy to England of all American statesmen," expressed the hope that Britain would no longer hold any portion of the continent "in colonial subjection," but said that opposition in Canada would receive no help unless war broke out for some other cause.[72] The French government also steered clear of Quebec separatists.[73]

The threat that local disputes would lead to conflict was demonstrated anew by the Canadian frontier in 1840–41, and the dispute played an instructive role in helping to account for tension with Britain over Texas. In an instance of anticipatory self-defense that is of interest to more modern commentators,[74] an American ship, the *Caroline,* gunrunning to Canadian rebels, had been intercepted by loyal Canadians on 30 December 1837 on the Niagara River in American waters by Navy Island, and one of the Americans on board, Amos Durfee, was killed before the ship was set on fire. In November 1840, Alexander McLeod, Deputy-Sheriff to the Niagara District, was arrested in New York State and charged with the murder, even though he had probably not been there, while the British government had already informed the Americans that the interception was an official act, and not one for which individuals could be held responsible.

The refusal of the American government to intervene in the judicial action of New York State led to bitter complaints in the British press. Henry, 3rd Viscount Palmerston, the experienced Whig Foreign Secretary, issued instructions to the envoy to leave if McLeod was executed, and his successor, Aberdeen, followed suit with similar instructions. In October 1841, senior British ministers discussed the possibility of war, a prospect reported by the American envoy, but, in the event, McLeod was acquitted. Moreover, William Seward, the governor of New York, had told Daniel Webster, the secretary of state, that McLeod, if convicted, would be pardoned.[75]

Oregon raised different issues from the Canadian frontier further east, in part because its future status was open. Contrasting interests and attitudes were readily observable. Thus, George Canning saw the Oregon Country as a key advantage for the British Empire, opening the way for the economic development of Canada as a springboard for trans-Pacific trade with China, to the benefit of the British Empire. American politicians and commentators had rival ambitions, but self-interested prudence was never far from their pursuit of the gains and prospects temptingly offered by Manifest Destiny.[76]

Distance ensured that the situation in the Oregon Country was followed with less attention than that on the northeast frontier, but there was British concern about American interest in the Columbia River throughout the period.[77] This interest became more acute from the late 1830s. In 1836, Jackson sent William Slacum to the Pacific coast to gather information about the area, and his highly optimistic report, laid before Congress in December 1837, led to pressure to hold the area south of the 49th N Parallel and the introduction of a bill to create the Oregon Territory as part of America.

The British, however, were already taking the dominant role in the region. Aside from the Hudson's Bay Company consolidating what it already had after the 1821 merger with the North West Company, there was also activity by the company south of the Columbia River, including large-scale trapping of beavers and the establishment of positions at Fort Boise (now the state capital of Idaho) and at Fort Umpqua on the river of that name in modern southwest Oregon. Supplementing its position in the interior, the company also developed a stronger coastal presence, notably with Fort Vancouver on the Columbia River (across from modern Portland), which was established in 1825, and Fort Simpson, founded in 1834, the major trading post north of Vancouver Island.

These positions were linked to trading vessels, and thus became part of a commercial system in which Britain was the center, while both San Francisco and the Sandwich (Hawaiian) Islands were important staging posts. In 1836, a steamer, the *Beaver*, was added to the company fleet. This commercial system proved much stronger than that of the

Americans and by 1841 their maritime trade to the region had essentially disappeared. Moreover, by the 1820s, the Russian sea otter and seal catch off North America had fallen dramatically as animals were hunted to near extinction.

In 1824, Alexander I of Russia had discarded his earlier claim to the Pacific coasts, instead asserting that 54'40" N would be the boundary to his claim. Alexander also granted American ships ten years' access to Alaskan waters. Yet, it was the British who benefited: an 1839 agreement with the Russian-American Company, the key player in Alaska, ensured that, from 1840, the Hudson's Bay Company gained access to the Alaska panhandle, establishing bases at Forts Stikine and Taku. In contrast, a Russian warship, the *Chichagoff*, and a Russian redoubt at what became Fort Wrangel, had blocked a company attempt to establish Fort Stikine in 1834.[78] The Hudson's Bay Company's bases became key nodes in the Native trading systems, which enhanced their value.

A fur-based economy might seem to have limits, and the number of beavers traded from the region fell in the late 1830s, but attention profitably switched to other furs, including marten, bear, mink, and fox, while the economic base diversified as the Hudson's Bay Company took an interest in timber, agriculture, and fish: salmon, in particular, was exported. Thus a dynamic economy underwrote a presence that increasingly seemed a strategic challenge to American commentators concerned about the West and tempted by the Pacific. Reflecting, however, a difference in the character of the two imperialisms, one that was to be of growing importance, the crucial element that the British lacked was people. Yet, whatever their disadvantages, the British presence scarcely conformed to American notions of Manifest Destiny. Moreover, growing British commercial links with San Francisco created the danger that California would look to Britain, whether as a province of a weak Mexico, or as an independent state, or, indeed, as a colony.

British diplomats could be very critical of the populism of American politics. They also argued that this populism challenged the possibility of good relations. Thus, Vaughan, the son of a physician who had been educated at Rugby and Oxford, complained in 1827, "they have introduced into all our political transactions with them a miserable spirit of bargain and sale which belongs to the counting house."[79] Two years later, he informed John Backhouse, the under-secretary of state for foreign affairs, not only that the tariff question had divided America but also that "the administration formed by General Jackson carries with it but little weight of talent or character – as it is at present constituted it has disappointed general expectations."[80] Sir Charles Bagot, envoy from 1816 to 1818, the son of a peer who had also attended Rugby and Oxford and who had come into Parliament for a rotten borough (a constituency with few voters), was not keen on Washington society, nor on the climate, a common complaint, but he took steps to make himself popular.

Addington, who was sent as secretary of legation in 1822, was taken with Jackson's inaugural speech, which he thought "extremely judicious, sensible and temperate, and from my knowledge of the man I have little doubt that his general conduct will conform to the spirit of his speech, although I would not answer for the control which he might be able to exercise over his temper in irritating circumstances."[81] Charles Bankhead, however, was less impressed by American politics, noting in 1832 its contentiousness and commenting that nothing was done. He added five years later about a Congressional dispute: "epithets of villain, liar, blackguard used without end. Oh the blessings of Democracy! Why don't you send some of the theorists over here – their cure would be instantaneous I will venture to say."[82] Moreover, Vaughan's American connections had contempt for populism.[83]

The views of some British diplomats reflected a disdain for American politics that could be seen in terms of a conviction that British politics were better, as well as an opposition to the extension of the franchise in Britain, and a professional dislike for unpredictability. Henry Stephen Fox, who was sent to America in 1836, came from a famous Whig family, but he did not like his American posting and became reclusive. His Eton and Christ Church background and his interest in London's fashionable world did not provide points of contact with American political society.[84] In contrast, Addington, the son of a Tory prime minister who was close to George III, but a member of a family that was not socially grand, found much to praise in America, particularly among the women, and fell in love there. He took care not to be perceived as "an insolent aristocrat."[85]

Alongside unease about American populism, if not contempt, there were linked concerns about the nature of American politics, although these concerns were moderated by an awareness of the need to respond to American moves. In 1825, Canning told the House of Commons that, the previous year, the American government had proposed a mutual and limited right of search designed to end the slave trade, a goal the British had been pursuing for several years and that had been presented as a way to help preserve relations.[86] The British government agreed and the Americans drew up a treaty accordingly. Canning added: "By the constitution of the United States, the confirmation of treaties is vested, not in the Executive only, but in the Senate and Executive jointly. This was an inconvenience of which we were certainly aware, and therefore we have no right to complain, when we found that the treaty, regularly negotiated and ratified by His Majesty, was refused to be ratified by the American Senate, unless on conditions to which we could not accede."[87] In the event, the Senate altered the treaty to end the reciprocity: Britain had conceded the right to search in the West Indies and the Americans off their coast, but the Senate, concerned with the domestic political resonances of "No Search," struck out the latter.[88] In 1833, a British government memorandum on frontier negotiations commented, "it is especially essential that His Majesty should be previously assured that the President of the United States will possess the power of carrying into full effect his part of any engagements which may be concluded betwixt the plenipotentiaries of the two governments."[89]

Attitudes toward American politics appeared more relevant during the years of the Jackson presidencies (1829–37), because Jackson had embraced a populism that included an explicit criticism of Britain and of aspects of British policy and politics. He bore the personal and psychological scars of British mistreatment during the War of Independence, and had made his name defeating Britain at New Orleans in 1815. Addington had already commented in 1823 that "it was considered anti-American to display a conciliatory tendency towards Great Britain."[90] Yet, in office, Jackson proved willing to ameliorate his stance, and could also make himself agreeable, as when in 1835 he responded to William IV's message about an assassination attempt that, if successful, would have propelled the vice president to office.[91] Vaughan felt able to write in 1834, "in the whole course of my communications with the American administration under the present President, [I found] an entire abandonment of any suspicious angry feeling growing out of ancient animosities which sometimes marked the conduct of the party attached to his immediate predecessor in office, Mr Adams."[92]

In the event, disputes were settled or handled without conflict: the Americans did not support the Canadian rebels, while the Ashburton-Webster Treaty of 1842 settled disputes over the boundaries of Maine, and Minnesota. To Fox's chagrin, the Peel government, concerned about his hostility to America, had sent the more pragmatic Lord Ashburton to settle these frontier disputes. Ashburton, formerly Francis Baring, had an American wife and was a banker with important American interests: he had represented the family bank in America from 1794 to 1801. The treaty brought a conciliatory close to a longstanding dispute. Although Britain ceded much of its claim over the Maine frontier, the drawing of a line further from the St. Lawrence than the Americans had claimed helped provide for the security of the water route.[93]

The treaty was criticized by some British commentators, including Palmerston, as a weak step that failed to support the balance of power in North America or guarantee Canada's security. Nevertheless, Palmerston's criticisms did not find favor with his Whig colleagues, notably Lord John Russell, their leader in the House of Commons. Palmerston was keen to discredit Aberdeen's policy and diplomacy, having been replaced by him in 1841 when the Tories, under Robert Peel, regained power. Palmerston and Aberdeen were old rivals, and Palmerston saw Aberdeen as weak and conciliatory, notably toward both France and America. However, he failed to kick up a parliamentary storm in 1843. On 2 May, the Commons passed a vote of thanks by 238 to 96.

As colonial secretary from 1839 to 1841, Russell had been responsible for Canada. His successor until 1844, Edward Stanley, later, as 14th Earl of Derby, prime minister in 1852, 1858–59 and 1866–68, was one of the few prominent British politicians who had extensive firsthand knowledge of both America and Canada. During 1824–25, while a young MP, he undertook an extensive tour of North America over a period of eight months. He traveled through New England, New York, Philadelphia, west through Pennsylvania to Kentucky, down the Mississippi to New

Orleans, then through Alabama, Georgia, and South Carolina en route back to Washington in time for the close of the presidential contest. The tour also included Upper and Lower Canada.[94]

Thus, Stanley knew American politics and culture more directly and intimately than most of his contemporaries. Though he became highly suspicious of America,[95] he drew on his experience, referring to his first-hand knowledge of American politicians, their values, character, and attributes, in responding to issues that arose in Anglo-American relations. His experience of Canada was equally important, especially with reference to difficulties arising with Canadian internal politics and the vulnerability of the Canadian border with America during the 1830s to the 1860s. Stanley's experience informed his responses to the Canadian revolt in 1837, the Durham mission of 1838 on Canada's future, the diplomatic crisis with America while he was colonial secretary, the Ashburton-Webster Treaty, the issue of Canadian corn tariffs, and, later on, his views on the Civil War and Canadian federation. Significantly, Derby sent his eldest son, Edward, Lord Stanley, off on an American tour in 1848, feeling it important for British politicians to possess direct knowledge of "the Great Republic." He, in turn, became foreign secretary.

The settlement of the Maine issue in 1842 was reflected in the disposition of the American army, with the Hancock Barracks in Maine, which opened in 1828 and closed in 1845. Instead, America was increasingly active further afield, as part of an expanding geopolitics of interest. Opportunity and a sense of need played a role. The first was provided by the navy, which had been built up during the War of 1812. Postwar plans to expand the navy, notably with Congress in 1816 voting $1 million per annum for eight years to construct nine 74-gun ships of the line, twelve 44-gun frigates, and three steam batteries, were not sustained, but the navy was stronger than had been the case prior to the War of 1812 and, in the event of conflict, could raise the burden for any European fleet blockading America. Moreover, naval administration improved as a result of the establishment of the Board of Navy Commissioners in 1815. Power projection was aided not least when a naval base was established at Pensacola in Florida, a move reported on by Vaughan.[96]

Naval strength provided opportunities for America as long as Britain was willing to allow them, for Britain by far remained the leading naval power, and was able to use its navy for intimidation, as in 1831–32 over Belgium and in 1833 in deterring Russia. At times, British interests prevailed at the expense of America. Thus, in 1831–32, the USS *Lexington* sought to protect American interests in the Falkland Islands, where American sealers had been captured, only to find that the British thwarted both Argentina, which had inherited Spain's claims, and the United States, and, instead, established control in 1833. The British government was concerned about the potential threat that the Falklands in other hands might pose to British seaborne and political interests in South America and the southern oceans, while the American government was reluctant to cooperate with Argentina against Britain.[97]

Elsewhere, Britain and the United States were able to accept each other's role, if not cooperate, notably in operations against pirates and slavers. For example, in 1827 American warships in the Mediterranean sent landing parties against pirate bases in the Cyclades Islands in the Aegean. This activity was a product of what became a regular naval presence in the Mediterranean, which assisted America's commercial and diplomatic interests, not least by encouraging Britain and Spain to an awareness of American capability.[98] The Greek War of Independence against Turkish rule made neutral rights an issue, and thus led the American navy to protect national interests,[99] and the same process occurred in Latin America.[100]

In 1815, peace with Britain enabled the Americans to resume the pressure on the Barbary states they had exerted in the 1800s. Stephen Decatur was dispatched to the Mediterranean with ten warships, a force larger than that deployed by Jefferson, and one that reflected the military value of involvement in the War of 1812, as that had led to investment in the navy. The Algerians were defeated and forced to release American prisoners and to accept the end of American tribute. This victory was followed by successful demonstrations by the squadron off Tunis and Tripoli.

Closer to home, there was extensive activity against pirates and slavers in the Caribbean, with operations offshore and onshore at Cuba, Puerto Rico, Santo Domingo, and the Yucatán, operations that were politically significant given concern that the Spanish colonial authorities in Cuba and Puerto Rico were not being cooperative.[101] In 1822, for example, Commodore James Biddle commanded a squadron of fourteen

American ships in the Caribbean, and in 1823 David Farragut won notice in command of a shore party in Cuba while on antislavery duties.[102] Such activity was also important to the training of officers and crew.

A marked degree of assertiveness was shown. In 1824, Captain David Porter, commander of the West Indies Squadron and a veteran of the War of 1812, landed armed sailors, spiked Spanish cannons, and threatened to destroy the port of Foxardo unless local authorities apologized for arresting Charles Platt, one of his lieutenants, who had made representations on behalf of an American merchant in the Virgin Islands; the goods of the latter had been taken, probably to Foxardo where the local government had links to pirates. This action resulted in an apology, although the American government disavowed Porter's actions as they were seen as contrary to the American policy of nonintervention; comparisons with Jackson's invasion of Florida in 1818 were not welcome to the administration. In 1825, Porter was suspended and court-martialed. An angry Porter entered Mexican service until Jackson became president in 1829.[103]

The 1830s witnessed a relative obsolescence for the American navy, as earlier construction programs were not sustained.[104] Nevertheless, new ships were built[105] and there was an active use of the navy to protect American trade and interests, for Jackson sent the navy to respond to attacks on Americans on Sumatra, and also to the East Indies and the Middle East to negotiate trade agreements. This stance was the key aspect of a more powerful assertion of American overseas interests, one that gathered pace in the 1840s.

The Americans were also active in South America. Marines were landed at Buenos Aires in 1833, and at Callao and Lima in 1835–36, to protect American interests during insurrections. America, moreover, was more assertive in the Pacific. In 1826, the USS *Peacock*, under Thomas ap Catesby Jones, commander of the Pacific Squadron, became the first American warship to call on Tahiti before sailing to Hawaii, where he drew up a treaty with King Kamehameha III, the first treaty signed by the Hawaiians. The protection of American interests during insurrections, as well as attacks on Americans, led to the landing of forces not only on the Pacific coastline of South America, but also on Fiji (1840), Drummond Island (1841), Samoa (1841), and Canton (1843).

Such activity was related to another form of power projection, exploration. In 1838, Lieutenant Charles Wilkes was placed in command of the Depot of Charts and Instruments, and also given command of a six-ship expedition to explore the Pacific, which led to the first human sightings of the Antarctic Continent. Wilkes, moreover, explored the Pacific coastline of North America, a means of asserting American interests. Returning in 1842, he publicized his work and ambition with a multivolume narrative appearing in 1844.[106] British humanitarians who objected to his brutal treatment of the islanders in Fiji, Samoa, and elsewhere took a bleaker view. Wilkes's expedition was related to greater American interest in the Pacific, with the Hawaiian Islands proving a focus of interest. Abel Upshur, who became secretary of the navy in 1841, proposed the establishment of a naval base there, while Daniel Webster, as secretary of state, announced the so-called Tyler Doctrine in 1842: that America would oppose their annexation by any European power, which was, in part, a response to British and French expansion in the Pacific.[107]

A limited commitment to Africa was shown with Liberia, which was originally established by an antislavery group, the American Colonization Society, as a home for freed American slaves. A recommendation by the British government to the governor of the neighboring British colony of Sierra Leone proved important.[108] The first settlers were landed in Liberia in 1821 and the colonists were transported by American warships. There was also activity elsewhere in Africa, although not on the scale of Liberia. In the Webster-Ashburton Treaty with Britain in 1842, America agreed that a squadron would help Britain try to stamp out the slave trade in African waters. In 1843, sailors and mariners from four American warships landed on the Ivory Coast in West Africa in order to discourage the slave trade and to act against those who had attacked American shipping.[109]

Meanwhile, the changing nature of slavery within the United States was altering the geopolitics of racial control and oppression as well as affecting the political atmosphere. The development of cotton production led to major internal slave trade, from the Chesapeake colonies to the Deep South, accentuating the already strong contrast between the racial composition of the two areas. This trade provided the slave labor that could not be obtained from 1808 when the import of slaves from outside America became illegal, and provided a parallel to the situation in Brazil, where sugar planters of the northeast sold slaves to coffee planters further south, who were expanding west into the province of São Paulo, using the railway to create new links and opportunities.

Abolitionists had hoped that the end of the international slave trade, combined with the high death rate among American slaves, would lead to an extinction of slavery by natural causes, as the extension of settlement made Native American society less viable by reducing land for hunting. However, this death rate declined in this period and the American slave population increasingly sustained its numbers and then grew rapidly. As a consequence, abolitionists became more convinced that slavery had to be ended by state action, a belief encouraged by its abolition in the British Empire in 1833. This belief affected the political atmosphere in the North, contributing to the conviction that beneficial change could, and should, be introduced. Conversely, the greater centrality of slavery to the expanding cotton economy led its Southern advocates to become more vocal and to add a conviction of potent economic need to the arguments they offered for sustaining their sociopolitical world. That these arguments were directed against fellow American politicians was readily apparent. Racial exclusion was presented as both form and focus of Southern cultural identity.

Identity interacted with economic factors to ensure that slavery was not an issue of the fading past. The slave economy was transformed as a result of the major expansion of cotton cultivation, which owed much to Eli Whitney's invention in 1793 of the cotton gin, a hand-operated machine that made it possible to separate the cotton seeds from the fiber. This machine, which was subsequently improved, encouraged the cultivation of "upland" cotton, a hardy variety that could be widely cultivated across the South but which was very difficult to de-seed by hand. In contrast, the Sea Island cotton hitherto grown could be de-seeded by hand, but was largely restricted to the Atlantic coastlands. As a result of the change, annual cotton output rose from three thousand bales in 1793 to over three million in the 1850s, and American cotton became the key source for British cotton manufacturers, who, in turn, were a major force in the British economy, notably in Lancashire.

The profitability of the cotton economy greatly affected American internal and external trade and communications.[110] This profitability was also a key instance of geopolitics in terms of people (rather than primarily territory) and of the geopolitical consequences of economic developments: the profitability of cotton both encouraged the removal of Native Americans and was important to the continued appeal of slavery in the South. As tobacco became less well capitalized, slaves from the tobacco country were sold for work on cotton plantations. Moreover, the prevalence of slave hiring in the South ensured considerable geographical mobility among slaves, which helped keep slavery responsive to the market, and thus an effective economic system. Without a trade in slaves, there would have been little room for such entrepreneurship, nor for the interaction with capital that purchase and hiring offered.[111]

Although slaves became less important in the Chesapeake states, the success of the cotton economy and the ability to boost the birth rate of American slaves were such that Southern apologists did not regard the slave system as anachronistic. The earlier support of Jefferson and others for ending what he saw as the slave problem by expatriation (sending slaves abroad, essentially to West Africa) now seemed anachronistic. Indeed, the number of slaves rose considerably in the nineteenth century until the Civil War, providing an economic dimension to ideological debates about slavery.[112] That this economic dimension cannot be separated from racism was shown by the increasing marginalization of mulattoes, who were more frequently treated as black.[113]

With other topics more prominent, the issue of slavery was in abeyance as far as most politicians were concerned in the second decade of the nineteenth century, but the consequences of expansionism, specifically the Louisiana Purchase of 1803, threw the issue to the fore in 1819 when part of this purchase, the Missouri Territory, applied for statehood. The proposals of James Tallmadge, a New York congressman, for the gradual ending of slavery in the territory (by prohibiting the entry of new slaves and freeing all existing slaves born after admission to statehood once they turned twenty-five), won extensive support in the North, but was seen in the South as a threat to its identity and existence. By April 1820, Jefferson was expressing his concern at the prospect of division.

In the event, the Missouri Compromise of 1820 allowed Missouri to enter the Union as a slave state in 1821, but banned slavery elsewhere above the 36°30' N Parallel, which ran along Missouri's southern boundary. This measure, which left most of the Louisiana Purchase free from slavery, was scarcely an authentic compromise. Instead, it was seen as a challenge by Southerners opposed to Northern interference, notably by means of federal power over the sovereign authority of the states. As a result, the Missouri Compromise led to an increase in support for slavery,[114] while the resulting geopolitics encouraged Southerners to press for expansion to the west and also to develop an interest in Mexico and the Caribbean.

Moreover, as a sign of continuing division there were bitter remarks in Congress as to whether Missouri was to have a voice in the presidential election while its admission as a state was as yet undecided, with talk of an "appeal to the sword" if not. In 1822, the British envoy thought that interest in creating a new state out of West Florida was related to the wish to establish more Southern states, and the following year he noted pressure for slavery in Illinois in order to cut labor costs and raise land values.[115]

The geopolitics expressed in the choice between free and slave labor was to become increasingly important in American politics, but it was not simply a matter of the use of labor. There was also a conviction among Southern slaveholders that territorial expansion was necessary to protect their position in both political and economic terms. Fear of soil exhaustion played a part but so did a concern that slaves, as well as poor whites, would become too numerous for the stability of the South unless it could gain new territories in Mexico and the West Indies. The mental space of the South thus expanded to include Texas, other parts of Mexico, Cuba, and Haiti.

Organized opposition to slavery by the slaves was limited in large part due to the coercive context in which slaves were held and the difficulties of coordinating opposition. Thanks largely to the power of planters, but also to measures, such as state-sponsored and large-scale slave patrols,[116] control over the slaves was maintained by coercion without the need for any full-scale suppression of slave activity. Nat Turner's rebellion in Virginia in 1831 was the most prominent slave rising, and Turner presented himself as deploying his men like soldiers. However, the rebellion was swiftly suppressed. Nine years earlier, a planned rebellion, Denmark Vesey's in Charleston, was betrayed and preempted. Evidence for the plans has been questioned on the grounds that they were devised to give credence to the idea of a slave revolt.[117] From that point of view, it is instructive to note that such a rising did not occur.

Slavery was the underlying issue, though not the overt one, when South Carolina attempted to nullify a new tariff in 1832–33, on the grounds that it was unconstitutional as well as unfair, and that individual states could protect themselves from such acts by interposing their authority, and thus nullifying the federal law. This was an attitude already seen when, after the Vesey trials, South Carolina endorsed a Negro Seaman Act and enforced it in the face of the contrary provisions of federal law and despite the Act creating problems for British diplomats who were not prepared to see black British sailors treated like criminals and detained while their ships were in Charleston. The issue became a longstanding problem in British governmental relations with South Carolina and an issue in those with the American government.[118] In November 1832, the South Carolina convention passed an ordinance of nullification, and the state raised an enthusiastic army of more than 25,000 men and purchased arms. The nullifiers threatened secession from the Union if the federal government sought to enforce the tariff.

The federal government did not give way, and Charleston's garrison was reinforced by Winfield Scott, who then proved an adept manager of local sensitivities. Moreover, unsupported by the other Southern states and also facing opposition to nullification from within, South Carolina had to back down, to abandon the threat of nullification and to accept a settlement of the tariff issue that did not meet its goals. The dispute indicated the fragility of political and constitutional conventions, the clash between Southern notions of the Union as a voluntary compact among independent states and Northern views of the indivisibility of the one American nation,[119] and the possibility of conflict. Moreover, aside from this dispute, diplomats reported frequently on fiscal weaknesses and political divisions.[120]

At the same time, there was still truth in Addington's observation in 1823 that "like well-boiled rice, they remain united, but each grain separate."[121] The Nullification Crisis certainly revealed America as much stronger politically than the states of Latin America. There was no equivalent to the situation in Mexico, nor in Brazil where rebellions included the *Cabanos* in Pernambuco in 1832–35 and in Pará in 1835–36, the *Sabinada* in Bahia in 1837–38, the *Balaida* in Maranhá in 1839–40, and the *Farrapos* in Rio Grande do Sul and Santa Catarina in 1835–45, nor in Argentina, nor in Colombia, from which Venezuela successfully rebelled in 1829–30. Instead, like the Federalist plotting in 1800 and 1814–15, talking about disunion in 1832–33 proved an alternative to conflict. The situation was to be very different in 1861 when South Carolina, again the focus of disobedience, took the lead in moving to civil war.

# 11

# FROM THE OREGON QUESTION
# TO THE GADSDEN PURCHASE
# 1844-53

*It can be no longer disguised that this question has become a British and an American question ... whilst England is using every effort of skilful diplomacy to acquire an influence in Texas, to be used notoriously to our prejudice.*

James Buchanan left the Senate in no doubt on 8 June 1844 that a struggle with Britain was the key element for American foreign policy, and, with that pronounced passive aggressive stance so typical of many American politicians of that generation, he presented Britain as the aggressor because Texan annexation was "necessary to our defense, peace, and security." A former Jacksonian, who, indeed, had unsuccessfully spoken in February against the ratification of the Ashburton-Webster Treaty, Buchanan was chosen as secretary of state when James Polk, a protégé of Jackson and the Democratic candidate, became president after the bitterly contested 1844 election.

That election epitomized much that foreign governments and commentators found alarming about the United States. There was a conflation of populism with bold calls for territorial expansion, calls that reflected the changing nature both of the country and of its self-perception. The development of the railway and of steamships made it easier to think of a potential that could, and thus should, be realized.[1] Far from the Rockies being a boundary to effective control, let alone to an integrated nation, they were now seen as a barrier to be overcome as America expanded more clearly to the Pacific and beyond. The key issue coming to a head was the Oregon Question, and that, rather than the possibility of war with Mexico, dominated attention during the 1844 election campaign. The end of the 1818 Anglo-American agreement over Oregon appeared inevitable, not least as it now more obviously approximated to a postponement, and this apparently imminent change led to contrasting demands, demands that reflected the differing requirements of the two powers. The United States sought territory in bulk, land in short, and not so much because this land was required for settlement, although that was important, but, rather, because the acquisition of land was a key theme of American politics. This theme was one in which local drives could be extrapolated onto the national scale and as part of an economy in which agriculture was a key source of output and the flow of produce from the West important to growth,[2] while white settlement was seen as a way to avoid overpopulation in the East and, instead, to ensure that a fairly egalitarian society could be maintained there and expanded westward.[3]

There was also a conviction that a wide-ranging position on the Pacific would benefit America, both as far as the hinterland was concerned and with regard to opportunities for activity across the Pacific. In terms of the continuum of interests and motivation seen with America, and, with a different emphasis, Britain, the trans-Pacific was viewed in terms of trade, rather than land, and there was a powerful sense that East Asia would provide new opportunities for American commerce and industry, not least as Britain's victory over China had encouraged a belief in new possibilities there.[4] President John Tyler, who was in office from 1841 to 1845, sought to develop commercial links with China, sending the Cushing mission that led to the Treaty of Wanghsia in 1844, by which America gained commercial rights at five ports. Citizens, a loosely defined category, could only be tried by their consuls, while Chinese subjects who wished to bring legal claims against them had to turn to consular courts. These measures were intended to ensure that America obtained concessions comparable with those gained by Britain and France.

Links with China were seen as an aspect of, and possible solution to, the serious and longstanding political tensions over tariffs, and as a way to settle the sectional interests bound up in these tensions, notably Southern agriculture and Northern industry. In particular, the South felt that its economic, and thus political, interests were not consulted. As a result, the attempt after the War of 1812 at a wide-ranging economic policy of national renewal had not only ceased to pay political dividends but had become politically destructive, and this at a time when slavery was becoming a more divisive issue.[5] Thus, expansion was regarded as the cure for atomistic, fissiparous tendencies in American politics, and as the redress for regional pressures.

Debates and negotiations over the future of Oregon[6] were very much located in the world of American politics, and seen as highly sensitive as a result. Bills authorizing the occupation of the Oregon Country had been advanced since the early 1820s. They were rejected by the Senate in 1838 and 1841, but the issue was coming increasingly to the fore, not least as a result of the development of American settlement in the region. The American Society for Encouraging Settlement in the Oregon Territory, founded by Hall Jackson Kelley in 1829, had failed in its effort to establish a New England settlement in the Colombia Valley, and Nathaniel Wyeth's attempts to organize expeditions in the early 1830s also failed, but a settlement was established in the Willamette Valley. More followed, with the Great Reinforcement, of fifty settlers, in October 1839.

The political pace also intensified. In 1840, Senator Lewis Linn of Missouri, a noted Western expansionist, spoke in the Senate in favor of a chain of military posts designed to help emigration, and in February 1843 the Senate passed his bill both to occupy the Oregon Country and to establish a chain of posts from the Missouri and Arkansas Rivers to the best pass for entering the Oregon Country and on to the mouth of the Colombia. This was despite Henry Stephen Fox, the British envoy, lobbying leading senators, including John Calhoun and William Archer, against the measure, a skill that British diplomats found increasingly necessary and in which language and political culture gave them a marked advantage over their diplomatic colleagues. However, the House Committee on Foreign Affairs found against the bill, so that it was not discussed. Nevertheless, this Congressional activity increased the diplomatic pressure to settle the issue.[7] As the Maine boundary dispute had indicated, an official presence on the ground, in the shape of forts and road building, was important in supporting claims.[8]

Meanwhile, the Oregon Trail developed, with the energetic John Frémont, as part of the widespread activity of the Topographical Corps, surveying it as far as South Pass (Wyoming) in 1842. Frémont planted an American flag on Frémont's Peak in the Wind River Range, which he (wrongly) thought the highest peak in the Rockies, and in 1843–44 traveled to the Oregon settlements and crossed the Sierra Nevada to California. A keen publicist, well connected through his father-in-law, Senator Thomas Hart Benton of Missouri, himself a prominent expansionist who opposed European links and loudly called for western expansion,[9] Frémont greatly increased interest in Oregon and helped end the idea of the Rockies as a barrier.[10] He also exceeded instructions by entering Mexican territory without authorization.[11]

In 1843, American settlers in the Willamette Valley decided to establish a provisional government and petitioned Washington for Territorial status. Nothing was done, but interest in the region was further spurred in 1844 by the publication of the report of Charles Wilkes's expedition that had reached Puget Sound in 1841. This report greatly extolled the Sound's value as a commercial base while, correctly, noting that the bar at the mouth of the Colombia River, further south, ensured that it was not a viable alternative.[12]

In late 1842, the British had pressed the Americans to negotiate a settlement, and, in late 1843, George, 4th Earl of Aberdeen, the British foreign secretary, was in no doubt that the settlement of the Maine frontier by the Ashburton Treaty had left Oregon as the key issue. As Fox's relations with the American government were poor, he was replaced by Richard Pakenham, who was informed that "the issue is growing daily in importance."[13] The decision was taken in November 1843, and Fox presented his recall in February 1844, but he remained in Washington, in part in order to pursue his enthusiasm for botany. Fox died there from an overdose of morphine in October 1846.

In the spring of 1844, Aberdeen was worried about the room for maneuver, writing to Pakenham, "I hope you will find the Oregon fever a little subdued, compared with its violence at the opening of the Congress. It is very likely, however, that you will not be long, when once you open the negotiation, before you are brought to the end of your concessions." A concerned Aberdeen suggested that, if existing negotiations failed, new terms should be sought. Although the Hudson's Bay Company was well established south to the Columbia River, he proposed a more northerly frontier on 49°N, with Britain also having Vancouver

Island, and with additional benefits to the south that showed the concern of British policymakers with trade when considering North American developments. Thus, Aberdeen sought free trade rights in ports from the 49° Parallel to the Columbia River inclusive, as well as free navigation on the Columbia which was believed to be a key link between the Pacific and the interior, and was certainly important to the regional presence of the Hudson's Bay Company. The supposed benefits to be derived from rivers were a major theme in European plans for exploiting the wider world, a theme that was to be largely superseded in the second half of the century by an emphasis on railways. In a reminder that domestic constraints did not only operate for the Americans, a situation that was to be seen more clearly during the Civil War, Aberdeen stressed that these terms were subject to Cabinet agreement.[14]

Richard Pakenham was more concerned about American politics, writing, in June 1844, that "recent events in this country have tended to diminish in some degree the confidence which I then felt in the continuance of a good understanding with the American government." Pakenham was not so much worried about a "violent or irritating measure . . . by either House on the subject of Oregon," as fearful that President Tyler might think that war with Britain would assist him to reelection, a concern voiced periodically throughout the period, as in 1860 and 1865 when British envoys were concerned that unity might be pursued by means of war with Britain. Pakenham linked the prospect of Tyler's bellicosity to the political struggle over the cause of American expansionism: "The failure of his Texan Treaty, and the check which he has received in his electioneering schemes by the appointment of another candidate on the annexation interest [Polk], have reduced him [Tyler] to the situation of a desperate man without sense or shame or principle to control him." Pakenham noted that he would not be surprised at anything until the election was "at an end."[15] More soberly, he reported that the Americans would not accept a border on the Columbia, which was the formal British position, and, instead, clung to the 49th Parallel.[16]

Meanwhile, reports that America was increasing its naval forces on the Great Lakes, in breach of the 1817 agreement, led Aberdeen to order Pakenham to tell the American government that Britain would match such action and do everything necessary to protect Canada.[17]

By November 1844, a gloomy Aberdeen, mindful of the domestic pressures "so prevalent in the United States" and their capacity to paralyze government, suggested a sounding of the American government on the prospect for arbitration and, if not, the renewal of the existing agreement for another ten years.[18]

Polk's election brought a marked increase in concern, as America now appeared pledged to a far bolder and more northerly frontier, with Polk taking possession of the slogan of "54°40' or fight," 54°40'N being the southern boundary of Russian America. Sir Robert Peel, the British Tory (Conservative) prime minister, was moved to complain in February 1845 that "the point of honour is now brought into the foreground." He wished to avoid national humiliation, which was a potent issue in British foreign policy, as had been shown by the decision to go to war with China in 1837. There was also a public interest in Britain in the Canadian west, one shown most clearly in 1845 when the *Erebus* and the *Tower* under Sir John Franklin were sent by the Admiralty to conduct investigations linked to the impact on navigation of Magnetic North. This expedition was to come to a deadly end when stranded in the Arctic ice, and its fate and the relief attempts were followed with great attention.

Concerned about the possibility of an American infraction of the 1818 treaty as a result of pressure in the House of Representatives for the annexation of the Oregon Territory, Peel remarked, "We have as much right under the existing treaty to occupy and to fortify as the Americans have." This was correct, but hardly helpful as a means to secure a settlement. Peel, however, was ready to consider the dispatch of more forces to the region, notably a stout frigate carrying marines and artillerymen.[19] Positioned at the mouth of the Colombia, this frigate would have been able to exert force similar to that seen in the War of 1812 when Fort Astoria was brought under British control, but the situation was very different, and there was a need to appreciate this changing context in order to plan most effectively: military operations in the west were not going to have political outcomes comparable to those in the second decade of the nineteenth century. The successful use of naval power for deterrent purposes and as a force multiplier had to be very mindful of the political context, a linkage at which Palmerston was particularly adept.

In April 1845, Aberdeen thought that Polk's inaugural speech offered a very different approach to Oregon than that of his predecessor; Aberdeen feared that there was no chance of a settlement: "Judg-
ing from the language of Mr Polk, I presume we must expect that the
American government will denounce the Treaty without delay. In this
case, unless the question be settled in the course of the year, a local
collision must speedily take place, which may too probably involve the
countries in the most serious difficulty, and finally lead to war itself."
Aberdeen argued that it was necessary to be prepared for every contingency, adding "our naval force in the Pacific is ample, and Sir George
Seymour [Rear-Admiral; Commander-in-Chief in the Pacific] has been
instructed to show himself in the neighbourhood of the Columbia."
Aberdeen pressed for "a temperate, but firm language," writing that "we
are perfectly determined to cede nothing to force or menace . . . there is
a good spirit in Parliament and the public," and that, the previous week,
40,000 seamen and marines had been voted by the Commons without
opposition.[20] Temperate, but firm was the note the British were repeatedly to try to cite, not least during the Civil War, although this goal, an
obvious one, did not necessarily mean that they calibrated the means
successfully.

In a successful use of deterrence over the Oregon Question, the dispatch of a substantial force of warships to Halifax had a sobering effect
on the Americans, especially those on the seaboard, but, in line with its
general fiscal stance, the government, especially Peel, did not want to
have to spend heavily on defense.[21] There was a concern, however, about
the deficiencies of the Canadian militia, deficiencies that owed much to
the unwillingness of the legislature to cooperate.[22] Aberdeen, nevertheless, was encouraged by the feeling that British preparations and moves
were having an impact, and wrote, in April 1845: "It would not appear
that Mr. Polk's inauguration speech had produced such an effect on the
public of the United States, as it has done in this country. . . . I hope the
very serious manner in which it has been regarded here, whether necessary or not, will be attended with a good effect." Aberdeen now clearly
favored the 49th Parallel, Vancouver, free ports and the navigation of the
Columbia, rather than a frontier on the Columbia.[23] Pakenham was also
convinced that British firmness had played its role:

The declarations of Her Majesty's Ministers in Parliament on the Oregon question have made Mr President Polk look very foolish. He is afraid to go forward, and ashamed to go back – but when the first smarting of the rebuke has passed away, I think the good effects of what has happened will become more apparent. In the mean time all reasonable people blame him, as they did before, for those words so foolishly introduced into his inaugural address; although I feel bound to say that notwithstanding their obvious impropriety it was never imagined here that they would attract as much attention as has been created by them in England. There has not yet been time to hear of the effect produced in the more distant parts of the country by your Lordship's and Sir Robert Peel's declarations but except in the remote Western districts which are beyond the reach of warlike operations. I have no doubt that the result will be the same as it has been at Boston, New York and Philadelphia, that of salutary alarm and apprehension.

Luckily Congress is not sitting, or in the heat of the moment something disagreeable might have occurred which could not afterwards be so easily remedied.[24]

Warlike preparations were at issue, including in Washington, when Pakenham discussed the matter with Sir George Simpson who was responsible, on behalf of the Hudson's Bay Company whose interests he managed in Canada,[25] for defensive precautions in the Oregon Country. Simpson spoke of constructing a fort at the mouth of the Columbia at the expense of the company, but finally agreed with Pakenham that it would be best to avoid the appearance of forcible occupation as that would provoke American action. In a reminder of the impact of the simultaneity of commitments, a simultaneity seen in the Americas as well as spanning the Atlantic, such action now seemed unlikely because, as Pakenham correctly suggested, the Americans were more concerned about Texas.[26] That August, Polk noted "the strong probability" that a Mexican army was on the western borders of Texas and would cross the Rio Grande, a danger such that the Oregon Question had to be settled.[27]

Anglo-American negotiations continued in late 1845, albeit with difficulties,[28] and "flaming" speeches in Congress were noted in Britain.[29] The American approach was condemned by Palmerston in February 1846 when he pressed the importance to Britain of a Pacific harbor.[30] That month a report from Louis McLane, the American envoy in London, that Aberdeen had mentioned recourse to "thirty sail of the line" if America became too aggressive on Oregon and the issue became one of national honor for Britain, apparently scared Polk into backing off; until then, his *modus operandi* had been to "look John Bull in the eye." However, by May 1846, when agreement had virtually been reached on the 49° N parallel as a frontier, excluding Vancouver Island which Britain was to receive, Aberdeen could write with growing optimism about prospects, not least that the Senate would "essentially be conciliatory."[31] Aberdeen was still concerned about the uncertainty of American politics: "where so much is done under the influence of popular excitement, and with a view to produce some effect in domestic policy, we can never be quite certain of the principle upon which the President may ultimately act."[32]

Aberdeen, however, added that the situation was the same in Britain, as Peel's government was "very precarious." He claimed that, if it fell, the next one would not be more conciliatory over Oregon, and that this should encourage the Americans to settle, although Pakenham was told to say nothing about this.[33] Indeed, the danger that a Whig government would result in Palmerston becoming Foreign Secretary, and that he might lead to war with America, played a role in tensions among the Whig leaders in December 1845 when they unsuccessfully sought to form a new government, with Charles, 2nd Earl Grey being unwilling to serve if this was likely. As a result, having resigned on 9 December, Peel resumed office on 20 December.

In June 1846, Pakenham reported that the growing Mexican crisis, stemming from Texan admission to the Union on 29 December 1845, would lead Polk to wish the Oregon issue settled, but he warned that Britain should not try to profit from their combination:

> It seems to me that it would be neither politic nor worthy of a country like England to make any difference in our manner of dealing with the Oregon question on account of the existing state of things between Mexico and this country. Not politick, – because as we can never calculate with anything like certainty on what may be likely to happen in such a context. Any further success which may attend the operations of the invading force would, under such circumstances tend to make the American government more impracticable than ever on the Oregon question. . . . England is, and ought to appear to the world to be able to defend her own rights and interests without the assistance of any such complication.[34]

In turn, McLane reported, correctly, that the Peel government was in a precarious state, which led James Buchanan, the secretary of state, to feel that the opportunity should be taken to settle the Oregon Question. Pakenham was convinced that confidence in the conciliatory views of the Peel ministry was an important factor in American politics. Buchanan regarded the Columbia navigation as the most important difficulty, but was encouraged to settle as the Hudson's Bay Company license to trade there would expire in 1859.[35]

On the evening of 12 June 1846, the Senate agreed, by thirty-seven votes to twelve, to recommend the 49° N compromise. "All of Oregon," in contrast, had been demanded in the Democratic platform of 1844, but the South was solidly opposed to such an extension of the free territories, while the Northern Whigs, unwilling to shatter their party on the issue, also opposed the policy. On the morning of 13 June, Polk and Buchanan told Pakenham that they were accepting the terms. That day, he reported that "the positive impatience shown by Mr. Buchanan to sign and conclude convinces me that the fear lest any complication should arise out of the Mexican war, has done a great deal in inducing the American government" to accept.[36]

The news reached London on the morning of 29 June, and Parliament was very pleased. Aberdeen observed, "I am not aware that we leave any question behind us which is likely to grow up into a serious cause of quarrel with the United States."[37] The extension of the 49th Parallel boundary line to the Pacific provided a mutually favorable resolution. America, crucially, received the long-sought Pacific coastline and anchorages.

By then, the Anglo-American agenda was being set for the new British government by the Mexican question, which was to provide America with a much-extended Pacific coastline and already developed ports. What Oregon had shown in the meantime was the complexity of Anglo-American relations when they were in the public eye. Some British commentators were very hostile to America. William Peter, the consul in Philadelphia, passed on reports that reflected almost paranoid concerns, notably that the vociferous Missouri senators, Benton and Linn, were being stirred up by Russia to oppose Britain over Oregon. Fox had earlier forwarded reports of Russian influence.[38] Peter also offered a hostile account of Pennsylvania politics, as corrupt, and excessively democratic, the two being seen as linked. This political culture was then related to hostility to Britain:

> There prevails but too much of a war spirit in this country – not indeed among educated and respectable men, but among those who, as unfortunately for the honour and interests of their own, as for the peace and goodwill of other nations, form a much more numerous and influential body, – viz – low editors of newspapers and their rabble-readers. One great evil here is the little expense at which a newspaper may be established. Every ignorant democrat is enabled to start one; and the consequence is that the greater portion of the press has fallen into the most unworthy and incompetent hands, whose one object apparently to excite and pamper the popular appetite, and to mislead the great body of the nation as to everything that is going forward in other countries, and more especially in England. . . . The Vulgar are, in most parts of the Union, complete Lords of the Ascendant.

Peter indeed saw democracy as a failure, as it had "degraded the standard of education, morals and government," and presented this situation as a warning to the Old World. The members of the House of Representatives were described as "the mere creature of an ignorant and conceited Mob."[39] Pakenham was more measured, although he also regarded public opinion as playing a role and greatly complicating the nature of interest politics, writing to Aberdeen in March 1844,

> The Americans are much more afraid of a rupture than we are and I am convinced that the bare probability of such a result would cause such a demonstration on the part of the leading interests in this country in favour of peace as would speedily lead to the removal of all difficulties.
>
> Nor are the mischievous declamations of Congress which at a distance appear to argue so warlike a disposition to be taken at their literal import. A great deal of all this is nothing more than electioneering manoeuvre, to make, what they call, Political Capital, in this country. Even in this sense the subject appears to have become nearly exhausted, and the becoming attitude assumed by the Senate has put an end to all apprehension of any violent proceeding, at least while the negotiation is in progress.

Yet Pakenham was concerned that British concessions would seem insufficient: "A government so dependent on popular opinion as this government is must always be difficult to deal with in such matters, because on their side a case of success must always be made out."[40] Aberdeen also saw American domestic politics as crucial, as he thought "the President and his government more afraid of the Senate than they are of us . . . Mr Polk may well doubt his power of obtaining the sanction of two thirds of the Senate to any convention which he could conclude with us." At the same time, Aberdeen was convinced that material factors would sway

American opinions: "The access of Indian corn [maize] to our markets would go far to pacify the warriors of the Western States." Twelve years later, western interest in foreign agricultural markets for maize and meat was presented by Napier as leading to support for plans for the American purchase of Cuba.[41]

Returning to Aberdeen's observation, the repeal of the protectionist Corn Laws by Peel's government, its central policy, was seen as likely to create a shared community of interest, with American farmers and British workers both benefiting from the end of any restraint on trade, the former getting larger markets and the latter lower prices, and thus becoming less vulnerable to radical ideas. Free trade, moreover, was believed by Peel to offer moral as well as prudential benefits by ending interference with Providence. In 1842, Peel had significantly reduced the Corn Laws, and by 1845 he came to believe that they would have to go completely. He resigned over the failure of the Cabinet to support him, but Lord John Russell, the Whig leader, was unable to form a new government, and Peel returned to power and, in 1846, carried repeal. However, repeal, which ended the protected British market for Canadian exports, split the Tory Party and Peel fell from power, being replaced by Russell who was prime minister from 1846 to 1852 and then again from 1865 to 1866.

Domestic affairs took precedence over foreign policy in Britain, but, in the United States, although there was a longstanding support of free trade with Latin America, this did not extend to the extensive northern parts of Mexico. Instead, a marked pressure for expansionism came to the fore with Polk, and an important and vocal section of American opinion, which was keen on gains from Mexico and, specifically, on gaining a wide Pacific coastline. Already, in February 1843, Webster had suggested a solution to the two major territorial issues confronting America by means of a tripartite agreement between America, Britain, and Mexico, with America gaining San Francisco thanks to British good offices while Britain, in turn, benefited from a satisfactory settlement to the Oregon issue. A laconic Fox doubted that Mexico would agree.[42] San Francisco and, even, San Diego were sought by the Americans as bases for the exploitation both of the Pacific and of the western littoral of North America.

Moreover, in October 1842, American warships under Commodore Thomas ap Catesby Jones, the commander of the Pacific Squadron,[43] who had been ordered to protect American interests in California and who erroneously believed that war had begun with Mexico, briefly seized Monterey and San Diego. This was reported as done to preempt their occupation by the Royal Navy.[44] The autonomous role of naval commanders also caused problems in 1845 when Robert Stockton, a friend of Andrew Jackson, tried to provoke war between Texas and Mexico, which was in keeping with his career of barely-contained independence.[45]

The 1844 presidential campaign had committed Polk to the goals of advancing to the Pacific, to the "reannexation" of Texas, as well as the "reoccupation" of Oregon. In 1845, Percy Doyle suggested that California would become American territory, whereas he thought that the Oregon Country had little to offer settlers.[46] California was a separate issue but also an adjunct to that of Texas. The unresolved nature of disputes over Texas provided the opportunity for the American government to move to force with Mexico once diplomacy had failed. Texas was an issue for Britain as well, and, expressing his concern in February 1845, Peel claimed that Britain might have to intervene over the issue.[47]

The British sought to mediate a settlement between Mexico and Texas in order to help maintain Texan independence from America, which was regarded as a way to limit American expansion and to provide an independent source of cotton imports from outside the American tariff system. Free trade as a British goal was sometimes accompanied by pressure. Britain negotiated free-trade agreements with Turkey in 1838, Egypt, Persia, and Showa (part of Abyssinia/Ethiopia) in 1841, and China in 1842. Texas was seen as part of this prospectus, with America, in contrast, as a rival, protectionist system. A treaty of amity and commerce with Texas was ratified by Britain in June 1842.

British abolitionists, moreover, hoped that Texas could be persuaded to abolish slavery. In 1839, Daniel O'Connell floated the idea of no recognition without abolition and, in addition, of negotiations with Mexico for the creation of a British protectorate in its territory that would be a safe haven for free blacks.[48] Trade and abolitionism were linked in British government policy, an instance of the fusion of materialist and idealist drives, not least as slave economies seemed a threat to the economic viability of the British West Indies where slavery had been ended in the 1830s, although, as a sugar producer, Cuba was more of a rival than the cotton lands of America. In 1842, Aberdeen described the attempt to end the slave trade as a "new and vast branch of international relations."[49] In 1839, reporting on the Texan wish to borrow $4 million in London to be spent on paying Mexico to recognize Texan independence, with $2 million to be paid to British holders of Mexican bonds in order to obtain British governmental support, Fox commented that Britain could neither recognize Texan independence nor obtain Mexican recognition as Texas had reestablished slavery. However, if slavery was abolished, Fox was in favor of recognition: "All risk of the incorporation of Texas with the United States would be averted; and a new cotton growing country would be brought into execution which in a very few years might render British commerce, for that article of importation, independent of the Southern States of the American Union."[50]

In the event, Texan independence was recognized by Britain in 1840 in return for agreeing to suppress the slave trade, an issue on which the American government was seen as unhelpful,[51] and correctly so. France backed British opposition to Texas becoming American, while Charles Elliot, the British envoy there, advanced the idea of an independent pro-British Texas partly reliant on free black labor, and thus a suitable ally for Britain. However, the British government did not wish to offend the Americans by formally opposing annexation,[52] and, aside from failing to encourage Elliot, Aberdeen was to deny that Texas had been offered a loan tied to emancipation. These reassurances were ignored by the American government.

In 1845, Charles Bankhead, the British Minister-Plenipotentiary in Mexico, helped persuade Mexico to recognize Texas, a step it had refused to take for nine years. Texas, however, did not fulfill British hopes, as it preferred union with America that year, despite Elliot's effort (backed by his French counterpart) to persuade it to preserve its independence on the basis of Mexican recognition. In contrast, the American government was willing to provide the offers of assistance against Mexican invasion that the Texas government sought, and American troops were ordered into Texas in June accordingly, landing at Aransas Bay in late July. The decision for union was the key step, with a Texas convention voting on 4 July to accept the invitation by Congress that February[53] to enter the Union. The vote led to strong pressure in Mexico for war as this union was seen as a threat to Mexican national honor and as sealing the Texas Revolution. Texas was admitted to the Union as the twenty-eighth state on 29 December 1845.[54]

In addition, there was continuing disagreement over the Texan frontier, with Mexico refusing to accept the Rio Grande, the border extorted from the captured Santa Anna as part of the Treaty of Velasco in 1836. Particular controversy attached to the Nueces Strip, the territory between the Rio Grande and the Nueces River, which was seen by the Mexicans as in the Mexican state of Coahuilla, while, further north, Santa Fe and the land to the east of the Rio Grande were part of the province of New Mexico. Aberdeen's repeated reluctance to take a role in the crisis had included his turning down a Mexican idea that Britain receive the Nueces Strip.[55] Despite Polkite claims, the Strip was not part of Texas, as Lincoln understood, when he dared Polk to prove the claim. American Whigs generally supported Lincoln's position.

Believing that Mexico would back down, and keen to show America as a resolute supporter of Texan interests, Polk proved willing to press for the Rio Grande as the border. He authorized the deployment of troops south of the Nueces River to provide security for Texas, and tried to purchase the disputed territory, New Mexico and California, for $35 million, but there was to be no second Louisiana Purchase. The Mexican government rejected the offer and also refused to receive John Slidell, the American envoy. Polk tried to increase pressure by sending an army under Zachary Taylor to the Nueces, but the Mexicans responded by sending their own army to the Rio Grande. For a while, both sides stayed out of the Nueces Strip, but the failure of negotiations led Polk to order Taylor to the Rio Grande, which was an invasion as far as Mexico was concerned. He moved south from Corpus Christi in March 1846.

The result of the subsequent war might seem foreordained, in part as a result of the contrast in political culture and resources between the two sides, as well as through reading back from the eventual result, but this is a problematic approach. Mexicans hoped that the Americans would be weakened by internal political divisions, slave insurrection, Native American opposition, and British hostility arising from the Oregon issue, as well as by the deficiencies of a small army and low-quality volunteers. They were also sure of the strength of their own military. The wife of the British envoy was less hopeful, writing of Mexico, "everything about it is hopeless – no money – and no energy."[56] Waddy Thompson, the American minister plenipotentiary, claimed in the early 1840s:

> I do not think that any commander could perform a tactical revolution with five thousand Mexican troops. I do not believe that such a one – a manoeuvre in the face of any enemy – ever was attempted in any Mexican battle; they have all been more melees or mob fights, and generally terminated by a charge of cavalry, which is, therefore, the favorite corps with all Mexican officers.[57]

This account may reflect prejudices, but many engagements do appear to have been mob fights, and few of the battles entailed sophisticated stratagems. Moreover, few of the engagements were major battles or part of carefully thought-out campaigns. The exceptions include Acajete in 1839 as well as the battles in the civil war of 1832, especially Rancho de Posadas, which led eventually to the overthrow of Anastasio Bustamente and to the election of Santa Anna as president, and the battle of Guadalupe in 1835, in which a revolution was suppressed. These were more than Thompson's mêlées ended by a cavalry charge.

In early 1846, there was a widespread expectation in America and among its army, many of whom were bored in Texas,[58] that a weak Mexico would back down, an expectation in which Polk was encouraged by Colonel Alejandro Atocha, a representative of the exiled Santa Anna. British commentators were less sure, and, indeed, in late December 1845, the government of José Joaquin de Herrera was overthrown by General Mariano Paredes and his army, in part because the government was discredited by reports that it was yielding to the Americans by proposing to sell the disputed territory, as well as New Mexico and California. Pakenham reported in May 1846 that

> the Americans greatly underrate the difficulty and expense of a war with Mexico. Unless the Mexican character has undergone a great change since I left that country, I think the Americans will meet if not with a gallant resistance at least with a sullen and a dogged resolution to protract the struggle to the utmost, were it only for the sake of the expense and embarrassment which such a contest must occasion to this country.[59]

He was also unconvinced about the strength of the American
military:

> Numerous bodies of volunteers have been forwarded to Matamoros from New
> Orleans and other places, but apparently in a hasty and confused manner, and, as
> far as I can discover, without any attempt at discipline or organisation. It seems
> difficult to imagine how a campaign undertaken under such circumstances in
> an enemy's country can be successful, however low an estimate may be formed
> of the resistance to be encountered.[60]

Conflict had begun on 25 April 1846, when an American patrol on
the north bank of the Rio Grande was ambushed by Mexican cavalry
seeking to challenge the American presence, but both governments had
already determined on war. The Mexican government had decided that
Taylor's advance meant that a state of "defensive" war existed, and, on 8
March, Paredes told Bankhead, the British envoy, that America was an
"indefatigable and powerful neighbour" and that he did not want Mexico
to become her prey.[61]

Claiming the need to repel invasion, Polk falsely told Congress that
he had tried to avoid hostilities, and secured a declaration of war, a course
of action that attracted criticism at the time and has been commented
on more recently in the context of misleading presidential statements
helping lead to war, not that such action is possible in modern times.
Following approval of his war bill by the House of Representatives on 11
May by a vote of 174 to 14, and by the Senate the following day by a vote
of 40 to 2, Polk signed the measure on 13 May.

Britain was Mexico's major trading partner and leading source of
capital investment, and there was (unfounded) concern that Britain
would support Mexico.[62] This concern was longstanding, and, in June
1845, Buchanan expressed his view that a Mexican invasion of Texas
would be instigated by foreign nations: Britain and France.[63] Furthermore, the Peel government had shown in 1843 that it was willing to resort
to coercion in the New World. Allied with France, a blockade of the Plate
estuary was mounted in order to coerce Rosas, the Argentine dictator,
and ensure the independence of Uruguay and the free navigation of the
Parana–Plate river system. Support for Uruguay's independence had
been a British goal since the 1820s, and there was no reason why an effort should not have been made over Texas, a larger state, although, in

practice, the crisis of the 1840s in Anglo-Argentine relations revealed that the British navy could only achieve so much.[64]

In fact, the British had pressed Paredes to negotiate with Slidell, but without success. A more significant foreign presence in Mexican politics was that of Spain. General Ramón Narváez, Duke of Valencia, the head of the Spanish government from his successful rebellion in 1843 until 1851, was a supporter not only of Paredes's coup but also of the plan to bring stability to Mexico by restoring the monarchy in the shape of a Spanish prince. This plan had the additional potential benefit of thwarting American expansionism and thus protecting the Spanish position in Cuba, which had been under threat from America since the 1820s. Buchanan, however, made clear in March 1846 that America would resist any attempt to install European monarchy, a position that looked toward the opposition to Emperor Maximilian in the 1860s. In 1846, the monarchist plan was destroyed by the impact of American victories on the prestige of the Paredes government.[65]

Having used his superior artillery to push back a larger, but poorly led, advancing Mexican army at Palo Alto on 8 May 1846, Taylor defeated the Mexicans anew at Resaca de la Palma the following day. In these two battles, the Mexicans lost 10 percent of the men deployed, compared to 4 percent for the Americans. Once war was declared, Taylor was ordered south of the Rio Grande and fought his way into Monterrey, the capital of the province of Nuevo Léon. On 24 September, Taylor secured his achievement by signing an eight-week armistice under which the Mexicans were to withdraw. Polk, however, regarded this as a failure to ensure a decisive victory and abrogated the armistice.

In light of the degree to which the conflict shaped the geopolitics of North America, it is worth considering this point, for Taylor was aware of the problems of advancing further with his limited manpower and supplies. Taylor pressed on to capture Saltillo, the capital of the province of Coahuilla, on 16 November, but he thought San Luis Potosí too far. Saltillo is about 550 miles from Mexico City. These distances were part of Mexico's natural defenses, and underlined the marginal character of operations in Mexico's northern provinces as far as Mexico's center of power was concerned. Canada was far more vulnerable to American attack, although not Halifax.

American successes in 1846 did not lead the Mexicans to negotiate peace. Instead, the government wished to see the national honor
redeemed, and all the lost territory recaptured. The room for political maneuver in Mexico was lessened by internal disaffection, which included
the Federalist Revolt in August 1846 and the Revolt of Los Polkos in February 1847; the latter led to street fighting in Mexico City between regulars and the militia.[66] There was similar tension between the army and
the National Guard in France, and the latter played a central role in the
successful revolutions there in 1830 and 1848. Santa Anna was summoned
back from exile in Cuba and reached Mexico City in September 1846, becoming both commander of the army and, in 1847, provisional president.
This return was seen by conservatives as a way to avert revolution and
secure victory, but Santa Anna proved both divisive and unsuccessful.[67]

The bold stroke of a strike at the Mexican center was deemed necessary by Polk and Winfield Scott, the commanding general of the American army, an effective and fastidious commander known as "Old Fuss
and Feathers." Already, on 14 November 1846, the American navy had
captured the port of Tampico on the Gulf of Mexico, and this provided
a base for the attack, further south, on Veracruz, Mexico's major port
and the gateway to Mexico City. To support this expedition, troops were
transferred from Taylor's army, which, for Polk, had the beneficial consequences of weakening a Whig who was likely to be the presidential candidate in 1848: as a war leader, Polk was intensely political throughout.

Scott landed 15,000 troops near Veracruz on 9 March 1847, meeting
no resistance. This reflected a force-projection capability that had not
been there in the War of 1812, not least in the Gulf of Mexico. This was
one aspect of a more general naval capability, as the American navy not
only dominated the Gulf but was also important in Pacific waters. This
would not have been the case had Britain been involved, as the Royal
Navy was more powerful in the Pacific.[68] Indeed, Peel observed in March
1846:

> Every speech made in the American Congress – every letter which I see from
> the United States contains an admission that our state or preparation for naval
> hostilities is far more advanced than theirs. I think it probable that a deep con-
> viction of the executive of the United States that such is the case will facilitate a
> settlement of our present differences with that country – but at any rate I see no
> such danger of hostilities.[69]

Commodore John Sloat's problems were complicated by the presence of a strong British squadron in Mexican Pacific waters.[70]

Britain faced a more propitious international context than when it had gone to war with America in 1812, as relations with France were initially good.[71] In 1843, accompanied by Aberdeen, Queen Victoria made a successful visit to King Louis-Philippe of France, the beneficiary of the 1830 revolution in France. His royal liberalism was compatible with British governmental assumptions, while Aberdeen's support for what was termed the *entente cordiale* led to his being called "the Under-Secretary to Guizot," the French prime minister and foreign secretary.

In December 1845, Henry Reeve, leader writer on foreign affairs for *The Times,* had a conversation with Guizot that he reported to Russell. Guizot told him that he had transformed French foreign policy for, whereas France had backed America against Britain for fifty years, he supported Britain over Texas and that, while he held office, he would maintain Britain's North American policy of opposing American expansion and maintaining a form of balance in the New World.[72] This cooperation was as much a challenge to America as the idea of limiting American power, while the ambiguous idea of the balance of power ensured that it could be adapted against America if judged necessary. The potential for joint action was to be shown in 1847 when Britain, France, and Spain successfully intimidated the Oporto-based junta into ending its rebellion against the Portuguese Crown. However, as a reminder of the need to consider the wider context, and to appreciate the extent to which options for North America were shaped by more potent concerns elsewhere, the Anglo-French entente was greatly harmed in 1846 by a dispute over French marriage plans for the Spanish Crown. More generally, by the end of the 1840s, the hopes of the 1830s that an alliance between constitutional governments in Britain and France could spread peace and liberalism throughout Europe had been dashed.[73] Britain itself was engaged in the hard First Sikh War (1845–46), with difficult victories at Mudki (1845), Forozshah (1845), and Sobraon (1846). The Second Sikh War followed in 1848–49.

The Royal Navy could have destroyed America's use of naval power and forced the Americans to rely on the overland campaigning blazed by Taylor, rather than on Scott's amphibious thrust, but it did not do so.

The closest parallel was the use of British naval and amphibious action against Mehmet Ali of Egypt in 1840 – the blockade of Alexandria, the occupation of Beirut, and the bombardment and capture of Acre, which blocked Egypt's northward advance against the Turks in Palestine and Syria. The Royal Navy was indeed to be used in an ambitious fashion against Russia in the Crimean War (1854–56), but already, by the 1840s, the pattern of the 1860s was increasingly apparent, with the navy as a deterrent force linked to the avoidance of war,[74] rather than an asset to be compromised by action.

British capability helped explain the costly "Third System" of coastal forts developed by the Board of Engineers created in 1816, a system that became more pressing with rising population density on the American littoral and with the American failure to sustain their post-1815 naval plans. Forts protected New Orleans, especially Jackson and Macomb, founded in 1822 and 1827 respectively, and New York, notably Fort Hamilton, established in 1831. The protection of the North Carolina coast with the foundation of Fort Macon on an offshore island in 1834 was clearly designed against European attack, though the key fear that year was of France. This system grew with American expansionism. Fort Brooke was established in Florida in 1824 and the Presidio of San Francisco in 1847. In total, $41 million was spent, a substantial proportion of federal expenditure.[75] In turn, the British upgraded the defenses of Bermuda in the late 1840s.

In the highly likely absence of British entry into the Mexican War, the Americans at sea were in a position comparable to that of Britain, not their forbears, in the War of 1812. The naval task, however, was greater than that facing the British then, in that there was a requirement on America to operate in the Pacific as opposed to the pattern of discretionary use of naval power that had been tried in the War of 1812; although in the Mexican-American War that was also a distant theater with no relationship to naval capability in the Gulf. American ships in the Pacific and from the Far East were joined by others that had sailed round Cape Horn. Guaymas and Matzatlán on the west coast of Mexico were captured by the navy in October and November 1847 respectively.

American naval attacks served to make the entire Mexican littoral feel threatened, and also degraded the Mexican infrastructure. American naval power in the Gulf of Mexico emulated that of Britain in the latter's imperial campaigns of the period: the littoral could be overawed, blockaded, interdicted, and bombarded.[76] American forces landed along the Gulf across a broad front, including at Tuxpan, Alvarado, Tabasco, Frontera, and Carmen. The 84-gun *Ohio* took part in the heavy bombardment of Veracruz, which surrendered on 29 March 1847.

Scott then advanced inland, away from the yellow fever and malaria of the coastal lowlands, on the National Road toward Mexico City. Defeating Santa Anna at the pass of Cerro Gordo on 18 April, by outflanking his strong position, Scott thwarted the Mexican attempt to confine the Americans to the lowlands and destroyed Santa Anna's force. Yet, having captured the city of Puebla on 15 May, Scott was affected by the need to release his volunteer regiments whose period of enlistment was coming to a close. This blow meant that he had to stay in Puebla while new volunteers arrived, and, during that time, Santa Anna rebuilt his army.

On 7 August 1847, Scott advanced anew, and forced Santa Anna to defend Mexico City, winning, in high-tempo operations, a series of battles from 19 August, before storming the capital on 14 September. These operations were supported by an advance in July under DeRussey from Tampico toward Mexico City. In response, the suspicious and vindictive Polk, whose executive power increased in wartime,[77] became concerned about Scott's political ambition. Scott had sought the Whig presidential nomination in 1840, 1844, and 1848 and gained it in 1852, only to be defeated.[78] Having initially made scant use of Scott in the war, Polk backed him when Taylor was seen as a greater threat, as a potential Whig candidate for the presidency, but then, much to the anger of fellow officers,[79] Polk recalled Scott on groundless charges of misconduct, on which Scott was subsequently acquitted.

In contrast, Polk backed Democrats, and was keen to commission and promote civilians irrespective of a lack of suitability. Franklin Pierce, later president, was one of his political appointees. Another, Gideon Pillow, Polk's law partner, mishandled the battle of Cerro Gordo, leading to a costly frontal attack rather than relying on the flanking movement that Scott favored, while Polk sought to have the powerful Senator Thomas Hart Benton, Frémont's father-in-law and a keen expansionist, made a lieutenant general.

Further afield, American forces had overrun Mexico's northern possessions. The American way of war in the South (displayed for example in Andrew Jackson's ambitious offensive campaigns of the 1810s) combined with a racist conviction of superiority over the Mexicans to encourage boldness. Troops under Colonel Stephen Kearny, commander of the Army of the West, rapidly advanced in June 1846 from Fort Leavenworth to Santa Fe, which was evacuated by the Mexicans and captured without firing a shot (18 August), and then moved to San Diego (12 December). The problems of crossing the desert were very serious, but Mexican opposition was also an issue.

Meanwhile, California had been lost to Mexico. In 1845, Paredes had suggested that it be sold to Britain. This was an option already raised in Britain in 1841,[80] one widely believed in America in 1842–43 to be a done deal,[81] and one that, in 1845, Lord Ellenborough, the First Lord of the Admiralty, wished to accept, while Aberdeen was interested. Four years earlier, however, Edward, Lord Stanley, the secretary of state for the colonies, later, as 14th Earl of Derby, prime minister, had turned down a proposal that Upper California be occupied by adventurers or filibusters who would establish British sovereignty. Stanley, instead, argued that Britain did not seek new and distant territories,[82] although that did not prevent the acquisition of Hong Kong on the other shore of the Pacific in 1841.

The British government made clear in the mid-1840s that it did not want another major power to replace Mexico in California, but the American government was determined to seize California once war broke out and to thwart Britain from acting there. The American navy was given instructions accordingly, while American settlers launched the Bear Flag Revolt, helped by American military support, notably by "explorers" under Colonel John Frémont, and encountering little opposition.[83] The Pacific Squadron, under first John Sloat and then Robert Stockton, played a major role. It occupied Monterey, San Francisco, San Diego, Santa Barbara, and Los Angeles. Stockton appointed himself governor of California.

Paredes told Bankhead that the settler movement was unexpected and that the government was unable to repress it.[84] On 13 August 1846, Bankhead wrote that the fall of California had "long been expected, but I own I did not think it would be accomplished in so short a period. Misgovernment and internal strife have done much to aid them in this enterprise, and to place in their power one of the most valuable posses- sions in the habitable globe, and whose resources are as yet most imper- fectly known."[85]

Yet, as a reminder of the extent to which American expansion de- pended on conquest, the Mexican inhabitants in southern California rebelled against American control in September 1846, while there was also an uprising in New Mexico that December. These risings, however, were defeated in December–January and February 1847 respectively. Meanwhile, the new conquests had no obvious southern border. Indeed, dispatched by Stephen Kearney, a force of Missouri volunteers under Colonel Alexander Doniphan marched south from New Mexico into the state of Chihuahua, where they captured Chihuahua City on 1 March 1847, having defeated Mexican forces en route at El Brazito north of El Paso and at the Sacramento River on 25 December 1846 and 28 February 1847. Doniphan then pressed on to join Taylor's army at Saltillo.[86]

The distances involved contrasted with those seen in the War of 1812 and indicated that a different type of war was occurring. Canada had also represented a challenge of distance and scale, but the Americans had not fought a high-tempo conflict. Instead, especially in the Niagara and Champlain theater (*fronts* would be a misleading term), the war- fare in 1812–14 had been both episodic and in a restricted area. In part, climate and logistics were responsible, but the lack of determination on the part of many American commanders and troops was also at issue.

In contrast, in the Mexican War, there was a greater determination to fight on the part of the Americans and this helped overcome the chal- lenge of distance and the problem of logistics. Not all the fighting was across a broad canvas. Indeed, there was urban fighting in both Monter- rey and Mexico City. Yet, bold advances both achieved key strategic outcomes and captured public attention. The professionalization of the American officer corps from the latter stages of the War of 1812[87] yielded significant benefits, both tactically and operationally in the Mexican- American War.

Bankhead had suggested in October 1846 that the process of trans- fer of protection that he saw at work in New Mexico, with the Mexican population offering loyalty to their conquerors in return for protection against Native Americans and commercial benefits, might well be followed in the provinces of Chihuahua, Coahuila, and Nuevo Leon.[88] This would have meant a significant southward extension for the United States, and the Americans were helped initially in their advances and subsequent control by the limited extent of hostile guerrilla warfare, which was, in part, a testimony to the skillful management of the situation by the Americans, especially Scott, who avoided relying on a logistics of depredation or turning to a politics of brutality.[89] Furthermore, California was lightly populated, while some of those who were conquered welcomed American trade; indeed, Santa Fe had been drawn into the commercial range of the United States prior to the conflict thanks to the opening of the Santa Fe trail in 1823. The absence of large-scale guerrilla warfare, which Percy Doyle, Bankhead's successor, saw as a missed opportunity for the Mexicans, also reflected the grossly non-egalitarian nature of Mexican society and the state and doctrine of the Mexican military, and contributed to the apparent character of the war as a series of set-piece engagements between regulars, a conflict the Americans could win.[90]

However, the situation became less favorable after the initial stages of occupation. Opposition and guerrilla activity increased, with frequent attacks on American convoys. There was particular opposition in the northeast of Mexico near Monterrey. The Americans responded with firmness, including with the use of summary punishments, staging both executions and the burning of the villages of those suspected of having helped them. Mexican atrocities against American prisoners and the mutilation of the wounded and corpses were used to justify the shooting of prisoners taken with arms.[91] The conduct of the American soldiers also caused problems. Scott ordered his troops to respect the religion and customs of the Mexicans, although they often did not, especially the militia, who had hoped for fame and loot and who found the realities of being an occupying force difficult. This situation led to atrocities that, in turn, exacerbated relations. Scott responded with severe punishments against those who committed crimes against civilians.

American campaigning was what would be subsequently described as "high tempo." Its aggressive and fast-moving character was necessary for political as well as military reasons, as American domestic support for the war was seen to be fragile. The Americans were helped by stronger credit and naval superiority, as well as by better artillery, which made a major difference in battle. American battlefield quality owed much to the caliber of the junior officers who helped to turn recruits and volunteers into effective soldiers. In addition, Scott's effective generalship displayed strategic insight, a skillful transfer of this insight into effective operational direction, and an ability to gain and retain the initiative. He always favored attack, and this preference underlines the need to relate operational practice to strategy when discussing geopolitics. Scott showed daring when, in his advance in Mexico, he cut away from his lines of communication in order to reduce vulnerability to any insurrection,[92] and pressed on despite being in hostile country. Size–supply ratios were one factor in the American success, as small forces could take their supplies with them and/or seize them en route. Of the American Civil War generals, Robert E. Lee, Ulysses S. Grant, George McClellan, P.T. Beauregard, and James Longstreet served under Scott, and Lee in particular learned from his training.[93]

On the American side, there was pressure for filibustering against Yucatán, which was a rebellious part of Mexico where the brutal Caste War had broken out in 1847,[94] as well as against Spanish-ruled Cuba, which would have been a major extension of the conflict. In a dangerous sign of independence, William Worth, an ambitious general who had fallen out with Scott, was ready in 1848 to resign and to command an invasion of Cuba, but he abandoned the idea under pressure from Polk.[95] From another direction, there was also talk of the prospect of war with Britain, with an attempt to conquer Canada once the war was over.[96] This was just talk but it also reflected the strong animus against Britain seen in expansionist circles, an animus that had helped propel America into war with Mexico, and that repeated assurances by Aberdeen when he was foreign secretary from 1841 to 1846 could not assuage.

There was contention in America over how much of Mexico should be seized and retained in the war, but the Americans benefited from the possibility of a ready exit strategy. Despite serious divisions within Mexico, including a civil war in February 1847 and disorder in the states,[97] defeat did not lead to the disintegration of Mexico. Thus, a peace could be negotiated with a Mexican government that, in turn, could end the fighting on the Mexican side. This situation made the Americans sensitive to divisions within Mexico, notably over whether peace terms were acceptable. In January 1848, the pronouncement (defiance) of the state of San Luis Potosí against the government hit the peace party as the government had no money and could not put down the rebellion. On 18 January, Scott told Percy Doyle, the British envoy, that "he was determined to march upon San Luis, and defend the General Government," but, as Doyle reported, this step might prove fatal to the government as its existence "would then be guaranteed by the Americans."[98] The problems of stabilization were readily apparent, and increasingly linked both the American forces and the Mexican government in a common interest.

The Americans were helped, however, because, despite their major gains in the fighting and bold talk of annexing all or much of Mexico, they did neither that nor attempt to annex all that they occupied. Indeed, despite the longevity of Hispanic settlement in New Mexico, the United States did not appropriate any real core areas of the Mexican state. In the face of Mexican opposition, Nicholas Trist, the American negotiator, dropped his proposal for a secret clause stipulating that the Mexican government declare its support for the 1824 federal constitution and that American troops support this by occupying key positions for five years. Trist pressed Doyle to recommend this clause to the Mexican government, as he said that stable government would help foreign economic interests. Doyle, however, thought that there were too many objections. The Mexicans were also against discussing the idea of an Atlantic–Pacific communication by the Isthmus of Tehuantepec, where Mexico is at its narrowest,[99] a route that would rival those across Nicaragua and Panama, then part of Colombia.

Yet, despite the dropping of these issues, it proved difficult to negotiate a settlement because the Mexican élite did not wish to accept the loss of much of their country, a loss that was the consequence of all the American demands. As a result, it took longer to negotiate peace than the Americans wished, or had anticipated after the fall of Mexico City. Indeed, there was an anticipation of the problems facing Prussia when it invaded France in 1870–71: it proved easier to defeat French armies in 1870 than to force France to peace, or indeed to end resistance in conquered areas.

The social politics of the situation in Mexico made a key difference to the outcome, as the war threatened the position of the Mexican élite and, in particular, their dominance of the indigenous population, that which was descended from the peoples conquered by the Spaniards from 1519. In the end, concern about this factor took precedence over the failure bound up with accepting American demands. At the same time, a degree of American restraint was important in both the politics and the military dimension of the conflict.

Concerned that the Mexicans were simply trying to gain time, Trist pressed Doyle to speak to the Mexican commissioners to facilitate the peace, and the latter did so, a course that Palmerston entirely approved as conforming to the wishes of the British government and Doyle's instructions.[100] The eventual peace treaty of Guadalupe Hidalgo, signed there on 2 February 1848 because the Mexican commissioners did not wish to sign in the nearby capital, Mexico City, left the United States with what were to become California, Nevada, and Utah, as well as most of Arizona, and parts of New Mexico, Colorado, and Wyoming. By the 1848 treaty, the Rio Grande was recognized as the border between Texas and America. The American government agreed to provide $15 million for the territories gained as well as to pay another $3 million as the claims of American citizens against Mexico.

These terms were thought insufficiently beneficial by Polk and the Democrats[101] and, conversely, as leading to the gain of too much territory by the Whigs. Contributing to the "vigour of anti-imperialist movements" in American history,[102] the Whigs had earlier been critical of the annexation of Texas and were suspicious about the likely consequences of increasing the number of slave states. All the twenty-five senators who voted on 27 February 1845 against Texas becoming a state were Whig, while the twenty-seven who voted for this included all twenty-four Democrats and three Southern Whigs.[103] Texas's entry as a single state, rather than, as had been feared, and indeed proposed by Senator Benton, a number of (slave) states, was significant. As in the War of 1812, the northeast was particularly hostile to the conflict, although in the case of the Mexican War, this was primarily due to the slave issue.

Information about the Mexican War is usually followed by a discussion of the consequences for America, but those for Mexico were more immediate. Moreover, they contribute to the geopolitical theme of this book, because the important result was that the country did not regain its strength, and this failure provided a context for the subsequent history of the North American Question, enabling the United States to enjoy strength and then to cope with the crisis of the Civil War without fearing Mexican *revanche*.

While the Americans were still in Mexico, its Congress in May elected José Joaquin de Herrera as president, an office he had held from 1844 until he was replaced by Paredes. Herrera was seen as compliant, and thus suitable, to the United States, but he only held office until 1851 when he was succeeded, until 1853, by Mariano Arista, who had been defeated by Zachary Taylor in 1846. The succession of Mexican administrations in the 1850s was a clear sign of crisis, with 1853, 1855, and 1858 in particular being years of several presidents. Structural features, such as the hostility between Congressional authority and presidential power,[104] were exacerbated by the absence of a strong practice and widespread belief that the peaceful and stable alteration of power was normal and desirable. Conflict was involved, including both violence in the streets of Mexico City and provincial risings. In 1854, Santa Anna failed to suppress rebels at Acapulco and in 1855 a rebellion in the province of Michoacán that he could not suppress led to his fall.

The situation collapsed completely in 1858–61 as the War of Reform pitched the liberal government of Benito Juárez against conservative opponents. Alongside political strife, the longstanding social tensions continued reflecting the grossly unequal distribution of property, wealth, and opportunity, shot through with racial prejudice by those of Spanish descent against the Native (Indian) majority.

Already, in February 1848, Doyle had noted the multiple challenges to Mexico's stability, especially the fear of a military revolution, and the extent to which America could be seen as a panacea, with annexation to some radicals "the only means to prevent its falling into a complete state of anarchy," while property holders were dismayed by the departure of American troops as they also feared chaos. Indeed, the Mexican government sought American support against "Indians" and "revolutionists." The American military provided help, notably by selling surplus weaponry cut price, but the last American soldier left Mexico on 6 September 1848.[105]

Knowing the option of American help to be impossible, Doyle pressed Mexican commissioners on the need for "every person of property and influence" to resist military coups and, in radical Jeffersonian style, criticized the army, which indeed had been the basis of Santa Anna's power, and, instead, urged the establishment of a National Guard. Pessimistic about the chance of such action, Doyle noted that another remedy, that of monarchy, had "gained ground," although he reported that it required European support and was unacceptable to the United States. In 1846, the Spanish envoy had floated such a scheme, for the Infanta Don Enrique, but Spain lacked the necessary funds and influence. Two years later, Doyle thought the idea of monarchy enjoyed more support, "not only from the idea that it would prove the best security for property, but from its being the surest means of preventing this country becoming a prey to the United States."[106]

Thus, Doyle located the monarchical option in the geopolitics of greater American pressure, a reminder that the linkage between politics and foreign policy was not restricted to America. This option was frequently raised in political and diplomatic circles, although the nature and basis of such a monarchy was presented in a variety of lights, with a clear contrast between the European preference for a member of a European ruling family, the method used with new states such as Greece, and a Mexican tendency to look to a local savior. In 1857, General Robles, the Mexican envoy in Washington, told his British counterpart that Mexico's stability and welfare depended on the overthrow of the democratic constitution "and the election under a universal popular reaction of a dictator."[107] Doyle's analysis looked toward the 1860s when domestic political strife in Mexico became linked to the foreign-backed attempt to impose a new constitution, and the possibility of American intervention became significant, adding a powerful element of uncertainty to the geopolitics of North America.

The Mexican War of 1846–48 brought a whole series of new security issues for America. It was necessary to secure the new territories from internal disturbance and external challenge, to define their borders, and to decide how best to rethink military tasks in response to the new gains. The American state now ruled about 60,000 Mexicans, as well as about 150,000 Native Americans whose relations with Mexican authority had frequently been poor, if not hostile. In addition, with the cession of Utah, the Mormon nation had been brought under American rule, although not yet under control as developments in the late 1850s were to show.

Last, it was unclear how far it would be possible to secure the border with Mexico, not least to prevent both continued Mexican influence, and also Native American attacks on Mexico. In the peace treaty, the Americans had promised to prevent these and, more generally, they had an interest in doing so in order to reduce the volatility of the region and to ensure stability. Fortifications were rapidly erected, including in Santa Fe as well as Forts Craig, Defiance, Massachusetts, Stanton, and Utah. These fortifications were essentially designed to provide security against the Native Americans rather than the local Mexicans, which was a response to the shift that rapidly occurred from regarding the latter as a possible challenge to seeing, instead, the new territories as another aspect of longstanding security concerns over Native Americans.

Kearny had met no Native opposition on his march to the Pacific, and, at Santa Rita del Cobre in 1846, he met Mangas Coloradas and other Apache leaders who swore allegiance to the United States and offered help against Mexico. However, many Natives saw no reason why their profitable raiding of Mexican settlements should cease, and in 1849 and 1851, partly as a result, the American army mounted expeditions against the Navajo.

The weakness of revanchist tendencies within Mexico was also important to the political and security situation in the new conquests, although the key element was the recent experience of American success and the scale of new settlement, notably in California. The weakness of revanchism was to be further demonstrated by the Gadsden Purchase of 1853, named after James Gadsden, the American envoy in Mexico, a railway promoter who had had himself appointed to that post in order to further his transportation plans. The purchase for $10 million of 45,535 square miles of land, mostly uninhabited, south of the Gila River, provided a route for the Southern Pacific Railroad, which was completed from New Orleans on its own lines in 1883. Like interest in acquiring Cuba, this purchase was an indication of the growing pressure of sectional politics, as the route was sought by Southern politicians seeking rail links that would serve their interests and provide an alternative to northern links focused on Chicago. This was an instance of a more general relationship between rail routes and both national and international politics.[108]

The status of slavery in the newly acquired territories became a key topic of controversy. Southern politicians thwarted the argument that it should be illegal and, instead, a compromise in 1850 left California, a new state, free, like the recently created states of Iowa (1846) and Wisconsin (1848), while the Oregon and Minnesota territories were also free. However, the western border of Texas was also settled in 1850, with New Mexico established as a territory that included land east of the Rio Grande purchased from Texas by the federal government. Some of this land also became part of the Utah Territory. As a consequence, what became Texas's iconic shape was established.[109] Alongside the slave states accepted in 1845, Florida and Texas, slavery was to be legal in the New Mexico and Utah territories, subject to popular sovereignty in the shape of the settlers, as well as in the as-yet-unorganized territory that in 1907 became Oklahoma.

The fate of slavery in the west remained highly contentious, with extensions to the lands opened to slavery provided by the Kansas-Nebraska Act of 1854 and the Dred Scott decision of the Supreme Court in 1857, which determined that slave owners could take their slaves into any territory. Southern advocates of slavery, such as Jefferson Davis, saw it as a way to guarantee a labor force in the West that would bring prosperity, notably by making irrigated agriculture feasible, and thus overcoming the constraints of geography and providing the security of continuous settlement. These were themes in his speech to the Senate on 14 February 1850 and his annual report as Secretary of War in 1853.[110]

At his inaugural in 1845, Polk had told his rain-drenched audience that "the bonds of our Union" would become stronger as it expanded. Instead, success in the Mexican War both increased regional tensions within the United States, helping to lead toward the Civil War,[111] and was also responsible for an increase in strife with Native Americans, especially because settlers began to enter the new territories in substantial numbers. Yet the situation was not restricted to these territories. Further north, in Oregon, there was pressure from the settlers to move the Natives from the valleys of the western Cascades to eastern Oregon, and to that end, the Willamette Valley Treaties were negotiated in 1851.

Meanwhile, American national self-confidence had been greatly boosted by success, a success underlined by Europe's instability. In the Year of Revolutions, 1848, when the monarchy was overthrown in France, there were rebellions and conflict in Italian and German principalities, Austria and Hungary, and, less seriously, large-scale Chartist demonstrations in London. Charles Sumner observed from Boston, "America now seems to be *terra firma* compared to the volcanic earth of Europe." American commentators, characteristically, praised the liberalism, but not the radical violence, of the European revolutions.[112]

Victory over Mexico boosted the Jacksonian Democrats who pressed for expansion as a means to spread their populist vision of a Protestant, democratic, and individualistic America. Yet, like the War of 1812, the Mexican War, however divisive, also strengthened the sense of America as a potent country. In the West, it was scarcely any more the case of two competing republics and a rival empire. The grip of the war on the American imagination was enhanced by the extent to which it was covered in developing media, notably photography and lithography, while the press also benefited from war reporters.[113] The war left America with a greatly extended coastline and, combined with the California Gold Rush that began in 1848, led to much excitement about the future.

This self-confidence, part of the "Young America" nationalism of these years, resulted in a more assertive international position. Within a month of the treaty with Mexico, Buchanan wrote to John Mason, secretary of the navy, to inform him that disturbances in Venezuela, where the conservative *caudillo* and former president José Antonio Paez unsuccessfully rebelled against the liberal president José Tadeo Monagas, threatened American citizens, and to request that he "direct one or more of our ships of war, of sufficient capacity for the purpose, to proceed to Venezuela at the earliest practicable period, and to render all necessary protection to our citizens and interests in that republic." A year later, Buchanan instructed Charles Eames, commissioner to Hawaii, to secure a treaty similar to those negotiated by Britain and France.[114] That was now the standard.

In 1850, Congress decided that the National Observatory should be the official prime meridian for the United States. Moreover, in 1853, an American squadron entered Tokyo Bay, and the Crystal Palace was constructed in New York for the Second World's Fair on the design of London's Crystal Palace built for the Great Exhibition of 1851. The latter had "created great interest" in America, which sent 1,023 exhibits and won five council medals including for the Virginia Reaper. America's role in the Great Exhibition reflected its status in manufacturing, using notably cutting-edge technology.[115]

The decision to hold the Second World's Fair reflected America's confidence in its own economic development, status, and future. The 1860 census was to reveal a population of 31.5 million, with one-third of the population supported directly or indirectly by the manufacturing industry. American confidence seems well-judged in hindsight. The solution of the Oregon Dispute and, more successfully and dramatically, victory over Mexico, meant that America became a "new kind of country," with a coastline on both the Atlantic and the Pacific, a position that was to be of major value both economically and in power politics.[116] Yet the 1850s were to reveal that, whatever the potential, there were still serious challenges, both domestic and international, challenges that were to become far more acute in the 1860s.

# 12

# A GREAT POWER IN
# THE MAKING? AMERICA
# 1853-61

The People have learnt, even more than ordinary minds in general
do, to attach the idea of national greatness to extensive territory.

*Lord Lyons, British ambassador, 1862*

Success over Mexico, combined with the settlement of the Oregon Question, led to bold plans for further expansion and activity. The range was
dramatic, and notably so in the Pacific. Both the experience of the value
of deployment there during the Mexican War, and the new interests and
possibilities that followed the annexation of California, led to greater
interest in the Pacific, and this interest was not restricted to the eastern
Pacific. Indeed, after the war, when the USS *Ohio* made its final cruise,
it visited both Hawaii and Samoa. More significantly, on 8 July 1853,
a squadron of four ships under Commodore Matthew Perry anchored
at the entrance to Tokyo Bay in order to persuade Japan to inaugurate
relations. After presenting a letter from President Millard Fillmore
(1850–53), Perry sailed to China, declaring that he would return the following year. Having wintered on the Chinese coast, itself an important
display of naval capability, and made naval demonstrations in the Ryuku
and Bonin Islands, which secured a coaling concession from the ruler
of Okinawa, competing with British interests there,[1] Perry returned to
Japan with a larger squadron of eight warships and negotiated the Treaty
of Kanagawa of 31 March 1854, providing for American diplomatic representation, coaling stations, the right for American ships to call at two
ports, and humane treatment for shipwrecked American soldiers.[2] This
"unequal treaty" left deep grievances, but it reflected the extent to which

force underlay America's advancing merchants' frontier around the Pacific with the developing Pacific trade system seen as a particular national opportunity.[3] Perry then returned to the United States, but, in 1854–55, another American naval expedition, the North Pacific Surveying Expedition, greatly expanded hydrographic knowledge of Japanese waters. In the southwest Pacific, American warships had rarely ventured west of the Sandwich (Hawaiian) Islands prior to the 1850s, but Commodore William Mervine, who took command of the Pacific Squadron in August 1854, was keen to champion American commercial interests and instructed his captains accordingly.[4]

Fillmore's successor, Franklin Pierce (1853–57), was interested in acquiring Alaska, Cuba, and Hawaii, albeit without success. In a context of mounting international competition, the British helped thwart the last.[5] Moreover, the protection of American interests led to the landing of forces in East Asia and the Pacific: in Shanghai in 1854, 1855, and 1859; Canton in 1856; and Fiji in 1855 and 1858. In 1856, Andrew Foote destroyed the barrier forts on the Pearl River near Canton,[6] although in 1859 the American envoy, John Ward, was willing to travel to Beijing in traditional tribute style, unlike his British and French counterparts.

Economic interest was believed to play a key role in American expansionism, which was called for in speeches and newspapers, not least by senators more prominent later in the 1860s, such as William Seward, who was to be secretary of state from 1861 to 1869, and Charles Sumner, chairman of the Senate Committee on Foreign Affairs from 1861 to 1871. Both were interested in northward expansion to Canada and Alaska, and it was widely assumed that Canada would gradually move to independence from Britain and then possibly to form a union with the United States.[7] However, the issue of slavery led them to be ambiguous about Southern expansionism, for example over the gain of Cuba, unless slavery should cease. Seward was also interested in America becoming a great economic power in the Pacific and Asia.

Cuba, however, was the goal of many Southerners. In 1851, Joseph Crawford, the British consul in Havana, had reported that Southern cooperation would lead to revolution against the unpopular Spanish government.[8] Alliance with the slaveholding South would provide safety for the slaveholders who dominated Cuban society and, in 1844, had helped repress a slave rebellion that had broken out in western Cuba the previous year. The Ostend Manifesto, a claim, in 1854, by the American envoys in Britain, France, and Spain that America could seize Cuba if Spain refused to sell it,[9] increased international tension over the island. America was Cuba's foremost trading partner, taking most of Cuba's sugar and being the major source of its imports. In the event, Spain rejected Pierce's offer, just as it had that of Polk in 1848. Moreover, America lacked the necessary military to conquer Cuba as long as Spanish forces remained in a good state.[10] The filibustering expeditions against Cuba in 1850 and 1851 by Narciso López failed, and López, a former Spanish officer and provincial governor, and his force were executed. The hopes of Pierce and others that Cuba could be gained[11] were unavailing, in addition, in part because the free states did not wish to see an extension of the slave states.

Race also played a role in American policy toward Haiti, Sir Henry Bulwer, the British envoy, noting in 1851 that the Spanish envoy had told him that he had been informed by the Secretary of State, Clayton, "that the United States government did intend to interfere in the quarrel between the Haitians and Dominicans in favor of the latter, and put down completely the black population of Haiti, in which enterprise he said that he should meet with no opposition from France or England." Bulwer added that he suspected that Clayton would have "commenced a policy which in all probability would have ended in the annexation of St Domingo and a large portion, to say the least, of Haiti to this republic."[12] In the event, the Americans did not act.

In addition, reports that America would expand south in Mexico, notably by gaining Sonora, the province to the south of the Gadsden Purchase, as well as other areas, especially Lower California and Chihuahua, were unfounded, although Pierce made a major effort to acquire them in 1856, while James Buchanan, as president, (1857–61), repeatedly pressed Mexico on this issue,[13] and was also very interested in acquiring Cuba. Interest in the development of a route across Central America also proved unavailing, although the major growth of California as a result of the Gold Rush led to much consideration of the idea as the route round Cape Horn was long and hazardous, while there was no rail route across America. In 1853, Percy Doyle, the British envoy, was concerned that American interest in a route across Mexico would lead to American intervention in Mexican affairs, and the president of Mexico shared this worry.[14]

Reports in 1854–55 of a treaty with Ecuador giving America a protectorate over the Galapagos Islands and the privilege of buying guano in return for a loan of $3 million led to a protest from the representatives of Peru, Spain, France, and Britain, but the treaty was not communicated to the Senate, and the report circulated that the dealing was a stock fraud.[15] Guano was also the key issue in tension with Venezuela over uninhabited islands off the coast of the latter that Americans saw as eligible for acquisition.[16] The protection of American interests led to Fillmore sending naval expeditions to the Amazon and the Plate and to the landing of forces in Buenos Aires in 1852–53, Nicaragua in 1853, Uruguay in 1855 and 1858, and Panama, then in the Republic of New Granada or Colombia, in 1856. The dispute with Colombia over the New York-backed Panama Railway Company escalated the following year, reflecting the importance of trans-isthmus routes.

A major deployment to South America occurred in 1858, one that was far distant from the Caribbean. As a result of disagreements with Britain and France over the treatment of their citizens in Paraguay, its dictator, Carlos Antonio López, closed the Paraguay and Paraná Rivers to all foreign warships but, in enforcing this policy, his forces in 1855 fired on the *Water Witch*, a lightly armed naval steamer that had ascended the Paraná on a mapping expedition. The Americans did not respond rapidly, but, when they did, it was with force. In 1858, Commodore William Shubrick cruised up the Paraná with a squadron led by the *Sabine* and the *St Lawrence*, two 50-gun sailing frigates. López apologized, paid an indemnity, and let the mapping expedition proceed. By early 1859, the American navy had eight ships deployed on the rivers of Paraguay, while the *Sabine* and *St Lawrence* remained nearby, assigned to the South American station off the Brazilian coast. All the warships were recalled after the Civil War began.[17] Also in 1859, the threat of a naval bombardment of the Pacific port of Guaymas led to the release of Captain Ewell, the commander of Fort Buchanan, New Mexico, who had been imprisoned by the Mexicans when, in accordance with instructions from the Secretary of War, he protested about Mexican reprisals for real and rumored American filibustering.[18]

Naval effectiveness was linked to a conscious attempt to improve organizational structures and practices, as in the Naval Efficiency Board established in 1855. A larger navy was not necessary for the major expansion in American foreign trade, which rose from $286 million in 1848 to $687 million in 1860. Indeed, Latin America was more in the shadow of the Royal Navy, but, by mid-century, American trade there had grown significantly. For example, although the 1828 trade treaty with Brazil had lapsed in 1843, America was Brazil's biggest market, and therefore an indirect beneficiary of the continuation of slavery there. A larger navy, however, was believed to give support to America's maritime position, for example in 1857, according to Lewis Cass, the secretary of state, with the prospect of action against Colombia and China and in the event of war between Spain and Mexico.[19] Naval support was certainly important against the piracy that became more of a problem as American trade to Asian waters increased, because there was much piracy in Chinese and East Indian waters.[20] However, the most important naval support to American trade was provided by British operations against these pirates.

Alongside disputes among its politicians over goals as well as over military means, there was a growing American presence and role in much of the world, although neither compared to those of Britain and France, in part because America lacked the drive for overseas colonies but also because it did not have the military infrastructure. There was no equivalent to the local forces, officered by Europeans, deployed most successfully by Britain, notably in South Asia. The United States also lacked the bases and tradition of interest in particular areas, while the Napoleonic warfare that had left Britain with possessions around much of the world was not matched for America. Therefore, in many respects, the United States was a continental power despite its naval capability for power projection.

To an extent, Latin America provided opportunities comparable to those the British pursued elsewhere, with, for example, the decline of the Spanish Empire matching the crises of Mughal and Manchu power in India and China, respectively. Yet, alongside the constraints posed by the character of the American state and by its politics, the nature of Latin American independence, as well as a power politics dominated by the offshore presence of the Royal Navy, limited opportunities for expansion by the United States, other than in overthrowing the Mexican empire, which was unique in being contiguous. This overthrow was taken a long way forward in 1846–48, although major American territorial gains did not also lead to the collapse of Mexico. Moreover, despite ambitions for further acquisitions from Mexico, both then and subsequently, not least by Polk, there was a contrary wish to preserve its stability, and this wish was seen in the American army's support for the Mexican government as the occupation came to a close in 1848. Thus, ironically, but in practice in keeping with important earlier elements of American policy, other than the Gadsden Purchase of 1853, there were no further territorial gains from Mexico. As a result, contiguous territorial expansionism both flourished mightily in the 1840s and came to an end shortly thereafter.

While America played a more active role abroad, there was nothing to compare with Anglo-French policy in the mid- and late 1850s. There had been ministerial uncertainty in Britain and political instability in the early 1850s: the government of the Earl of Aberdeen formed in Britain in December 1852 was a coalition of political groups borne out of the failure of both Liberal and Conservative governments to sustain a parliamentary majority in 1852, while, in December 1851, Louis Napoleon carried out what in effect was a coup d'état in France. Yet, whatever the problems of these governments, the power projection the British and French displayed in the Crimean War (1854–56) with Russia was formidable. Moreover, the Arrow or Second Opium War (1857–60) led to the Anglo-French occupation of Beijing in 1860 and to the expansion of the treaty ports system, a move for exclusive control that threatened America's "Open Door" policy toward China, and that overshadowed America's own deployment of force in the region.[21] However, American cooperation had been sought by Britain, and Napier had lobbied American politicians, including Seward, as well as chambers of commerce, to that end. The American government refused support, although it approved of the initial British objectives.[22]

In terms of warships and manpower, the Crimean War was a far greater projection of power than that shown by the United States in the Mexican War. In addition, the range of British operations indicated a capacity to bring the United States within range if necessary as, during the Crimean War, Russia had been attacked by the British on its Pacific and White Sea coasts, as well as in the Black and Baltic Seas. Indeed, British commentators contemplated the prospect that a blockade of Russia would bring America into the war against Britain. Moreover, the British were angered by what they saw as pro-Russian attitudes in America,[23] attitudes that led to reports of an anti-British alliance,[24] and the Americans were angered by the British attempt to recruit Americans (and others), which infringed the American Foreign Enlistment Act of 1818. John Crampton, the British envoy who had served in Washington from 1845, was recalled as a result of American pressure over this issue, as Pierce broke off relations with him in May 1856.[25]

In the event, the Crimean War did not broaden out, and the Americans, emphasizing a strict neutrality, did not push the idea of mediating[26] and turned down Russian suggestions that America provide bases for privateering against Britain. Moreover, discussion of an American purchase of Alaska in order to preempt a British attack was not followed up. The discovery in 1848 by Thomas Roys of whaling grounds in the Bering Strait had led to a marked increase in American activity in Alaskan waters. In the event, the British did not attack Alaska nor the Russians the Hudson's Bay Company.

While cross, Palmerston and Clarendon restrained their anger over the treatment of Crampton,[27] and the American envoy, George Dallas, was not sent home, although Palmerston's favor for Crampton led to his being rewarded with a knighthood and sent, successively, to Hanover, St. Petersburg and, eventually, to be a long-serving ambassador in Madrid. Neither power sought to push matters. In the spring of 1856, there was much criticism in Britain of the government for endangering relations with America, a view also held within the ministry, notably by William Ewart Gladstone, the Chancellor of the Exchequer, speaking in the House of Commons on 4 April. The key point was that America did not seek to exploit British commitments, whether with the Crimean War or the Indian Mutiny.[28]

In the 1850s, the British also operated not only in China but also in India, Persia (Iran), and New Zealand, so that the British government found American diplomatic approaches to Persia unwelcome.[29] Furthermore, the Americans paid close attention to British activities. These were extensively covered in the press while the Americans also sent a military mission under Major Richard Delafield to report on the Crimean War, one that included George McClellan, the leading Union general in 1862. This mission had been criticized for encouraging American officers to accept the value of a European paradigm of war, rather than developing an American doctrine useful in America.[30] Delafield was a fortification expert and the Fortification Board took from the war the need for more harbor fortifications,[31] at a time of arguments that fast steamships with shell guns made the traditional masonry forts of the "Third System" redundant.[32]

If, in the meanwhile, the Americans focused on seeking to control their recent acquisitions, this task did not match that faced by the British, nor the major effort the French made not only in the Crimean War and in their colonies, especially Algeria, but also in defeating Austria in 1859 in a full-scale war in northern Italy. Nevertheless, given the extent of the acquisitions and the limited American military resources – the army was increased to only 17,867 men in 1855 and had fewer effectives[33] – the task was still a formidable one. Whether it was worth it was unclear. For example, in 1851, Colonel Edwin W. Vose Sumner, commander of the Department of New Mexico from 1851 to 1853, had to campaign against the Navajo, although Sumner doubted the value of controlling the barren territory. The region proved troublesome for the Americans, as they sought to enforce their authority in a region that had not been under the control of the Mexicans. In 1854, the Jicarilla Apache were defeated; in 1854–55, the homelands of the Mescalero Apache were invaded; and, in 1855, the Ute were quelled. Conflict against the Apache rose to a height again in 1859.[34]

The government tried to lessen disputes with the Natives by moving the Indian Bureau, with its responsibility for relations with the Natives, from the War to the Interior Department in 1849. However, the problems caused by the arrival of substantial numbers of white settlers, and their desire for land, ensured that the army found itself forced to take up armed constabulary duties in the 1850s on an hitherto unprecedented scale. Methods of pacification varied. By the Treaty of Fort Laramie of 1851, Arapaho, Cheyenne, Crow, and Sioux chiefs agreed to restrict their hunting grounds to designated lands, and also not to hinder the Oregon Trail. In return, the government provided annual payments.

This attempt to keep the peace, however, was not an adequate response to the pace of American migration and the nature of American activity. In particular, depredations on the bison that the Natives relied upon for food were a real threat to their livelihood, as the Natives had no real alternative to that food source. The resulting conflicts were wide-ranging, including on the Plains and in both the northwest and southwest, for example warfare with the Cheyenne, Comanche, and Kiowa in West Texas. It also proved difficult to bring hostilities to a close. For example, the Comanche were defeated in 1859, but conflict continued.

Such a situation encouraged brutality. In response both to more difficult opponents and to a sense that Manifest Destiny required that the Natives be driven from the land, far more violence was used against women and children after 1848 than in earlier warfare, and there was also a greater willingness to massacre Natives. Certain operations were particularly brutal. The Plains Indian Wars were touched off by American aggression in the Grattan Massacre in Fort Laramie on 19 August 1854, in which Conquering Bear, the Sioux leader, was killed. General William Harney refused to take male Brulé Sioux as prisoners in 1855 and permitted the killing of their women and children at Ash Hollow, although this was the only massacre by regular troops as opposed to volunteers. Harney killed Chief Little Thunder at the battle of Blue Water Creek on 3 September 1855, and the Sioux submitted the following spring.[35]

The fame of opponents, especially the Apache, Cheyenne, Comanche, and Sioux, ensures that some wars became well known.[36] Others, such as the Rogue River uprising in southwestern Oregon in 1855–56 and the Spokane War on the Upper Columbia Plateau in 1858, are far less familiar. These conflicts were touched off by the pressures of American settlement, the policy of forcing tribes into reservations in Oregon and Washington, and the failure of the authorities to protect the Natives, if not their aggressive desire to expropriate them. As elsewhere, the Natives in this region benefited from their skill in fighting from cover and from their knowledge of the terrain, but were disunited. Converging columns of regulars and expeditions of volunteers led to the Native surrender that ended the Rogue River uprising, while, in 1858, the tactical skill of Colonel George Wright and the superior capabilities of the new

1855 Springfield .58 caliber rifled muskets, which outranged the Native weapons, brought victory in the Battles of Four Lakes (31 August) and Spokane Plains (5 September). The slaughter of Native horses and the hanging of prisoners helped to terrify the Natives and lead them to terms. Moreover, Native hopes of British assistance were ended when the Hudson's Bay Company and James Douglas, the governor of Vancouver Island, sent arms and ammunition to the Americans. Thanks to these campaigns, American control of the northwest was established.[37]

Further south, the Native population of California was brutally reduced in the 1850s by conflict as well as disease. The federal army did not control the situation there: instead, as in the northwest, local volunteer forces inflicted great damage, for example slaughtering the Yahi and Yana – men, women, and children alike.[38] They were in a position to do so there as, due to large-scale immigration, the American population in California rose greatly in the 1850s (the state population rising from 15,000 in 1840 to 380,000 in 1860), while the Natives lacked unity or a strong military tradition. In Florida, the small number of remaining Seminole waged the Third Seminole War, a guerrilla struggle, in 1855–58, before agreeing to move to the Indian Territory.

Whether by conflict or pressure, land was cleared in a process marked by treaties such as that of 1854 by which the Miami lost nearly 80 percent of their reservation in Kansas. This cession was a result of the pressure on Native land in Kansas from land speculators, settlers, and railway companies after it became a territory under the Kansas-Nebraska Act of 1854, pressure that was facilitated by the weakness of the federal government and by the willingness of some Natives to cooperate for their own benefit in gaining property from the allocation of tribal land, which had been held in common. When Kansas became a state in 1861, taxation was used to take land from the Shawnee. Under pressure in Kansas, many Natives moved south to the Indian Territory which, in 1907, became the state of Oklahoma.[39] Although violence did not play a comparable role in Canada, the government there favored a policy of assimilation that would justify the end of the reservations. The Act for the Gradual Civilization of the Indian Tribes in the Canadas was passed in 1857. The intention was to turn them into farmers with an individual title to their land. In the meanwhile, reservations were to continue.

More generally, the Natives suffered from a lack of unity. The Plains Natives were not tribes, but bands, although various groups could be fitted under a general designation, such as Sioux or Comanche, which was linguistic rather than organizational. From mid-century, the Natives in the United States also suffered from the impact on their divisions of the replacement of the weak nature of Mexican control (and the deliberately accommodating views of the British in the Oregon Country) by the more insistent territorial demands and military activity of the burgeoning American state. Rather than simply lack of unity, there was also active and longstanding rivalry between Natives.[40] On the northern and central plains, the Lakota Sioux, allied to the Cheyenne and Arapaho, used the mobility given by their embracing of a nomadic horse culture to dominate and, at times, brutalize, sedentary agricultural tribes such as the Pawnee and Arikara, who had the horse but had not become nomadic. The Sioux, an alliance of linguistically similar tribes, fought to obtain territory for hunting bison to feed their growing population, which reached about 32,000 by 1870. With weaponry and military means similar to those of their opponents – firearms and horses – the Sioux benefited, from the 1780s on, from smallpox epidemics that weakened tribes, such as the Crow, Pawnee, and Shoshone, that had blocked their westward move from Minnesota. The large farming villages of these tribes made them particularly vulnerable to smallpox, and whites' diseases struck particular tribes at different times. The Sioux had been exposed and partially immunized earlier than other tribes. The Sioux also benefited from their combination of constant small raiding parties and occasional large war parties, which destroyed entire villages. The ability of the Sioux alliance to hold their own different tribes together was also important to their success.[41]

Sioux domination encouraged many of the other Native tribes to look to the Americans. Their willingness to do so emphasizes the degree to which any discussion of relations in terms of conflict alone would be incomplete. Instead, military, political, economic, cultural, and religious ties crossed American–Native divides, turning them into zones of interaction in which symbiosis, synergy, and exchange occurred alongside, and, often, instead of, conflict and war. Moreover, much of the violence also involved an important measure of collaboration between Americans and Natives. In the Plains Indians' Wars which began in 1854, Crow and Pawnee cooperated with the Americans against the Lakota Sioux. The Ute, Crow, and Pawnee provided the army with scouts.

The process of conflict was less significant to American expansion in the West, however, than systemic factors including, as so often indicated in this book, the key element of population. The demographic weight of the Americans, or rather the European Americans, was crucial in combination with their willingness to migrate and force their way into regions already settled by Natives. Rapid and continuous American population growth encouraged significant levels of migration within America, as new cohorts sought opportunities. The linked processes of economic growth and improved infrastructure were also significant. The interior had been transformed by a series of changes, including the introduction of steel ploughs, which permitted the working of the tough soils of the Midwest and were displayed at the Great Exhibition of 1851, as well as railways, grain elevators, and flour mills. As a result, commercial agriculture made the vast spaces of the interior a source of profit rather than a problem of distance. Technology was not the sole issue: political economy and political culture, alongside resources, helped explain why northern industrial development was far more extensive than that in the South, not least why, of the coal-rich states, Pennsylvania did better than Virginia.[42]

The railway played a major role in the western expansion, not only in speeding American troops, but also in developing economic links between coastal and hinterland America, and thus integrating the frontiers of settlement with the exigencies of the world economy. Such improvements in communication were particularly significant for the spread of mining and of ranching, with cattle being driven to railheads. Linked to railways at river and coastal ports, steamships also aided integration. These were important on the great rivers, in the Gulf of Mexico, and, especially, on the Pacific coast. The settlers' ability to derive production and profit from the land made the Native American way of life appear increasingly anachronistic, and, indeed, a threat to American strength. In the stadial view of human progress, hunting was seen as a primitive form of economic activity reflecting a limited society.

As elsewhere with expansion by Western powers, American advances were in part expressed through the building of forts. Although these could be bypassed by Native raiders, they were difficult to take, and both helped to control communication routes and were a solid sign of American power. Thus, the annexation of Texas, the Oregon Settlement, and the Mexican War were each followed by a major extension of the imprint of federal fortifications. This extension was not a matter of random building, as the forts reflected a series of politico-strategic objectives. In particular, the 1848 peace treaty with Mexico included, in article 11, an obligation on the Americans to prevent Natives raiding Mexico from the newly annexed lands, from which it was indeed highly vulnerable. This obligation encouraged a series of border fortifications that also served to define the boundary and to mark a federal presence there, including Camp Ringgold at Rio Grande City (1848), Fort Bliss at El Paso (1848), Fort Duncan near Eagle Pass (1849), and Fort Drum at Zapata (1852). Nonetheless, the Americans were unable to implement this article, which was abrogated with the Gadsden Purchase in 1853. Instead, wide-ranging Native attacks, especially by Comanche, Kiowa, Apache, and Navajo, played an important role in the devastation of the Mexican north, as they had also done prior to the Mexican-American War, and thus contributed to the weakness of Mexico in the face of American power.[43]

Forts were also built along the edge of settlement within America in order to protect it from Native attack. Thus, the Mexican War was followed in Texas by the establishment under General George Brooke of Fort Worth (1849), Fort Graham (1849), Fort Gates (1849), Fort Croghan (1849), Fort Martin Scott (1848), Fort Lincoln (1849), and Fort Inge (1849). In turn, westward moves of the line of settlement led to new forts and to the closure of many earlier ones. Thus, in Texas in the early 1850s, new forts included Fort Merrill (1850), Fort Belknap (1851), Fort Chadbourne (1852), Fort McKavett (1852), Fort Terrett (1852), Fort Ewell (1852), and Fort Clark (1852), as well as camps such as Joseph E. Johnston (1852) and Elizabeth (1853). A double line of forts was considered the best way to address Texan concerns about Comanche attacks and deter Native raids, but strategic and operational thinking developed in favor of using forts as a base for offensive campaigns against Native homelands.[44] The general desire to control the Native Americans led to the construction of forts in west Texas, for example Davis (1854), Lancaster (1855), Quitman (1858), and Stockton (1859).[45]

Forts were also built further north. The Santa Fe Trail was guarded by Forts Atkinson (1850) and Union (1851). On the northern plains, Forts Kearny and Laramie on the River Platte in 1849 were followed by Forts Randall and Pierre on the Missouri in 1855. Troops entered the Yosemite Valley in 1851 in order to protect miners from Native attacks. In Minnesota, Fort Snelling, the first American fort there, built in 1819, was followed in 1848 by Fort Marcy (renamed Fort Ripley in 1850), which was designed to establish government authority and, in particular, to keep the Winnebago peaceful. In the 1850s, the American presence in Minnesota was consolidated by a network of roads that were surveyed and built through the War Department. The onward movement of the frontier of concern led to the foundation in 1853 of Fort Ridgely on the Sioux reservation on the upper Minnesota River, and, in 1856, to an expedition to the Red River valley in Minnesota and the establishment of Fort Abercrombie. Fort Ripley was evacuated in 1857, although that led the Chippewa to an outbreak of violence, which caused the reoccupation of the post. The Chippewa lands in northern Minnesota had been opened to settlement in 1855 and the Winnebago had again been moved that year. The fort was not finally abandoned until 1877.[46]

The net effect for the army of the gains in 1848 was a policy of dispersal, as the new territories, which were further enlarged by the Gadsden Purchase of 1853, were secured by forts. There was no equivalent enlargement of the army to reflect the lands gained, but, instead, a transfer of forces from east of the Mississippi. New commands, such as the departments of the Pacific and of Texas, reflected this new military reach,[47] and underlined the continental nature of American power. The establishment of garrisons in forts met the needs of settlers for reassurance, but the War Department preferred to see troops concentrated in large forces, which were regarded as the best means of maintaining discipline and training, and also to intimidate opponents. There was, thus, a tension between military and political interests.[48] A comparison of the distribution of regulars in 1843, 1850, and 1860 shows a movement of troops into garrisons beyond the Mississippi and, by 1860, the end of most garrisons on the Canadian border, on the Atlantic coast, in Florida, and in the Mississippi valley. This process was accentuated in the 1850s, as more garrisons were established in the west,[49] and reflected the extent to which, from the 1840s, Americans were no longer interested in pushing the Natives back and, instead, now sought total control of the whole of America. The construction of railways reflected the same process. The multiple facets and results of U.S. activity ensured that the geopolitical perspective of American weakness in 1857 offered by Francis, 9th Lord Napier, the British envoy, was mistaken, it not self-deluding: "The intercourse of the central government with California, its most precious dependency, still hangs on a single thread, which is liable to be severed by the marauding expedition of a party of savages or Spaniards."[50]

The redistribution of garrisons was also a product of greatly eased relations with Britain, and of a renewed American confidence, linked to a longstanding critique of a stress on coastal fortifications.[51] Thus, the redistribution reflected the strategic consequences of a major geopolitical shift. Tensions certainly continued with Britain, notably in Latin America where the United States continued to refer to the Monroe Doctrine to justify opposition to activity by European powers, as in 1849 when E. George Squier, the envoy to Nicaragua, opposed British pretensions there.[52] The previous year, the Nicaraguans, who had occupied Greytown on the Mosquito (Caribbean) Coast of Nicaragua, a center of British influence in what was claimed as a protectorate, were expelled with British help. The Americans were concerned as the river on which it sat was likely to be part of the route for a canal across the isthmus. Moreover, the deployment of British warships in Cuban waters was intended to protect the island from American intervention, which became a more pressing prospect from 1848.[53] Other issues in dispute between Britain and America included the stopping and searching of American ships to establish whether they were carrying slaves, an aspect of Britain's attempts to end the international slave trade. This was not a side issue, but a serious diplomatic dispute and, given Britain's antislavery treaties with other major powers, a genuinely international issue. In 1858, a public outcry in America over this practice led to an ultimatum that caused a war scare, only for the British to back down.[54]

Nevertheless, in comparison with the decades from independence to the end of the Oregon Question and the Mexican War, Anglo-American relations were much more equable, despite greater American activity in the Pacific. British claims in Central America were drawn in, and the Clayton-Bulwer Treaty of 19 April 1850 reflected the attempt to lessen Anglo-American tensions in the area as well as to reach agreement on a canal across Central America by accepting that it should not depend on the prior settlement of contentious territorial issues, such as the status of the Mosquito Coast. The following January, the Americans responded positively to a British complaint that the American flag still flew on Tigre Island off Honduras.[55] British investment in any canal was seen as a benefit by American interests and entrepreneurs, such as Cornelius Vanderbilt.

However, tensions remained, in part because of ambiguities in the treaty and contrasting interpretations. Frederick Chatfield, Britain's determined Consul in Guatemala from 1834 to 1852,[56] angered American policymakers and politicians, including Daniel Webster and Henry Clay, and was seen as overbearing. Indeed, on 17 January 1851, the Senate discussed the matter and complained of the British naval blockade of El Salvador in response to the debts of the latter. The recall of Squier and not of Chatfield was also a matter of complaint.[57] In 1853, Buchanan pressed Pierce on the British position in Central America, especially in the Bay Islands in the Caribbean to the north of Honduras, a British colony from 1852 that he presented as a valuable naval and commercial station near the isthmus commanding the Caribbean. Naval bases were seen by him as the currency of competition. In 1854, in pursuit of the interests of the Accessory Transit Company (a U.S. American company transporting passengers and goods across Nicaragua), an American warship and marines destroyed Greytown,[58] a case of hostilities without Congressional sanction.[59] Crampton complained[60] and the British reinforced the West Indies fleet, but the government did not respond with the use of force and pressed only for compensation for personal losses and not for any indemnity.[61] Also in 1854, and contributing to an impression of spreading power, American interests persuaded Honduras to agree to their railway schemes.

In general, despite pronounced and often vitriolic Congressional concern, as with the Senate debates on 20 February and 31 December

1855 and 24 January 1856, about supposed British and French ambitions in Latin America and, more specifically, Central America,[62] American ministers noted the more accommodating British position. In turn, Britain, seeking to minimize the number of its opponents, benefited greatly from the lessening of its ambitions for, and commitments in, Central America. Thus, in March 1851, Bulwer and Webster agreed on the need to use their influence to contain differences between Nicaragua and Costa Rica and, more generally, to avoid being drawn into differences between Central American states.[63] Five years later, Sir Charles Wood, the First Lord of the Admiralty and a former Chancellor of the Exchequer, pressed Palmerston, who had become prime minister in 1855, on the lack of key British interests in Central America, a view shared by Lord John Russell, as colonial secretary (1838–41, 1855) and, later foreign secretary (1852–53, 1859–65). Back in Washington, Bulwer had taken great pains to try to influence what he saw as a prejudiced anti-British populism by winning over the press. An experienced diplomat, Bulwer had shown marked liberal sympathies in his postings in Paris and Madrid in the 1840s, and was well-suited to the Washington embassy. He was a popular after-dinner speaker in America, and helped lessen tensions.[64]

Nevertheless, it proved difficult to settle differences over Central America. Terms for a treaty revising and expanding Clayton-Bulwer were agreed in London on 17 October 1856 by George Dallas, the American envoy and George, 4th Earl of Clarendon, the Foreign Secretary, but they encountered problems with Senate ratification. Lewis Cass, a Democratic expansionist with a military background and an anglophobe who became Buchanan's secretary of state, told Napier that he had thought Clayton-Bulwer ended the British territorial presence in Central America, and that the frontier of British Honduras and the future of the Mosquito Indians were key issues. Cass argued that the rights of the latter should be guaranteed, but under Nicaraguan sovereignty. That indeed was a modification insisted on by the Senate which, on 12 March 1857, adopted the treaty if these modifications were accepted. The treaty, which also stipulated that Greytown was to be a free port in Nicaragua, was carried by the efforts of John Mason, the chairman of the Committee on Foreign Relations, Jefferson Davis, and Seward, but the Democrats were more dubious. Nevertheless, Buchanan ratified the treaty subject to the changes, a course Napier thought reasonable.[65]

Subsequently, the status of the Bay Islands became a breaking point. Britain and Honduras had negotiated a treaty over them in 1856, but, aside from this not having been ratified, the Senate was unwilling to support the provision that these islands should be a free territory under Honduran sovereignty. Such a provision was overly sensitive given American divisions over slavery. Honduras, in fact, rejected the treaty in 1857. Buchanan told Napier that Britain had no rights to the islands, and Clarendon's wish for a new Anglo-American treaty excluding any discussion of them was judged unacceptable.[66] Clarendon's proposal was declined.[67] This failure threw attention back onto the Clayton-Bulwer treaty, which Buchanan criticized and Cass warned might be abrogated.[68] Yet, the key point was that Buchanan wanted a settlement, not least in order to provide an agreed basis for "interoceanic communications," and agreed on the need to preserve territorial borders between the Central American states and to open a transit route.[69]

By 1860, "a rapprochement with the United States seemed close at hand."[70] The previous year, a boundary controversy over the San Juan Islands in Vancouver Sound had been contained: the Pig War, which arose from an American settler shooting a pig belonging to the Hudson's Bay Company, led General William Harney, the military governor of the Washington Territory, to send troops to the island, without authorization from Washington, but lessening the chance of a speedy settlement.[71] In turn, the British deployed forces in the archipelago. However, thanks in large part to the restraint of British naval officers on the spot, the British did not use force. Palmerston suggested a vigorous response, but most of the Cabinet, including prominently Gladstone, did not wish to push the issue. Instead, although concerns about American attitudes led Palmerston in 1861 to press for the dispatch of troops,[72] the issue was shelved by being left open as an aspect of the larger realization that settlement through incomplete treaties was more important than tying up negotiations. Ultimately, the dispute was settled by arbitration following the Treaty of Washington of 1871.[73]

Restraint of a type was also shown by the American government, although it tended to be accompanied by a public critique of Britain that was less welcome. Thus, in 1856, Crampton suggested that Senate speeches critical of Britain had encouraged the operations of the Irish associations that sought to incite rebellion in Britain. Clarendon was certain that there was "an inveterate animosity to England." At the same time, Crampton noted that the district attorney for Massachusetts had been ordered to repress anything likely to be hostile to Britain, and regarded these associations as essentially designed for domestic political purposes, notably opposition to the Know Nothings.[74] In 1859, Scott was sent to the northwest to lessen the tensions created by Harney, and succeeded in doing so.[75]

Better relations with America were not a policy driven by the exigencies of European politics as, despite concerns over French plans for Belgium in 1852, the British Tory government under Edward, 14th Earl of Derby, which very much sought to maintain the peace, established an entente with Napoleon III that year. Nevertheless, cooperation was not sustained, and, despite their relationship as allies during the Crimean War (1854–56), relations deteriorated as Napoleon III's determination to overthrow the 1815 Vienna settlement was increasingly mirrored by Russia's determination to end the neutralization of the Black Sea it had been obliged to accept in 1856. There was an Anglo-French war scare in 1858–59, as well as more lasting suspicions of Napoleon III.[76] Napoleon III was not an attractive alternative to most Americans, and, for many American commentators, Britain appeared the sole major plausible guardian of liberty in Europe, at the same time that the liberal image of the British state was strengthened by domestic developments there. Yet, Napoleon's rise affected the European (and global) balance of power to Britain's disadvantage, which affected British options for unilateral intervention in the New World. However, as its government did not seek to pursue such options, Britain shared with America a policy of isolationism that was at once essentially expansionist toward non-Western powers and peaceful toward other Western states. "Essentially," however, is a matter of definition and emphasis, as the Mexican-American and Crimean wars clearly demonstrated.

Falling Anglo-American tension was linked to the settlement of the American west. Unlike in Africa and South Asia, where rivalry between European states acted as a prompt for their territorial expansionism, there were no problems from competing Western powers, and no need to preempt them. Britain did not challenge American sovereignty in areas gained from 1803 to 1853, and disputes instead focused on frontier details. Indeed, the allocation of the future territory of the United States between powers that recognized each other's sovereignty was complete by 1820, which greatly altered the situation as far as the Native Americans were concerned. This situation worked both ways. Success against Native Americans transformed the wider geostrategic situation. There was no longer any need for Americans to fear the Anglo-Native axis, and therefore American aggressiveness, active in so many other directions, was not aimed in any major way against Canada after the War of 1812. Instead, it was possible to take a different attitude to Britain's position in Canada, one that more closely moved to the rhythm of Anglo-American relations. Similarly, there was far less danger that Mexico would be able to undermine America's position. Once the two nations got over the hostility stemming from the Mexican War, Mexico indeed rendered the United States considerable assistance in overcoming the Apache.

Had Britain remained an ally of important Native tribes and been willing to provide them with support, then it is likely that there would have been far more pressure within America to annex Canada. A failure to settle differences with the Natives would have encouraged a search for scapegoats and solutions, and Canada would have provided both. There were, indeed, examples of Western assistance helping non-Western powers resist expansionism by Western rivals, but these instances were of powers, such as Mysore in India in the 1780s or Ethiopia in the 1890s, with considerable forces at their disposal. The Native Americans were not in the same position. Were they to resist successfully, they required not advisers or arms, but more manpower, and this was no more on offer from Canada than the former. There was suspicion and anger on both sides. J. Savile Lumley reported from Washington that the United States, both government and people, was determined to expel Britain from North America, as a central element in its "fixed . . . policy of expansion." More specifically, John Pope, later a Civil War general, but at this stage a captain who had led a surveying party on the Red River in Minnesota, complained that the Hudson's Bay Company trade with American Natives served to encourage their opposition, while Bulwer alleged that American attempts to trade with the Métis on the Red River and, via them, the Natives in Canada, disrupted the British policy of settling the latter as farmers.[77] Yet, it is the rarity of such complaints in the 1850s that is striking. The replacement of the company's men by public officials similar to the Americans on the other side of the border had been pressed by Napier in 1857.[78]

A key precondition of the new geopolitics of the 1850s was that British restraint, a restraint already seen earlier, was now much better understood and appreciated all around, once the crises of the 1840s had passed. The British stance was defensive, but with this defensiveness focused on consolidation, as in 1848 when Sir Edmund Head, the governor-general of British North America, announced support for a policy of confederation for the Canadian colonies. Even so, consolidation was conceived of in cautious and prudential terms. Thus, in 1859, Henry, 4th Earl of Carnarvon, under-secretary at the Colonial Office, noted the unsympathetic response when Canadian ministers came to Britain to ask for completion of the Intercolonial Railway: this "practically amounted to the demand for a large pecuniary contribution from the funds of this country to a great speculation, which however useful and comprehensive in its objects was hardly worth £1,500,000 at our hands."[79]

There was also concern to avoid becoming involved in Mexican politics, as in 1852 when Doyle rejected a Mexican request that the crew of two warships who had "pronounced" against the government be treated as pirates, which would justify intervention by the Royal Navy that Doyle said was unacceptable. When the Mexican government allegedly claimed otherwise, thus seeking to associate its authority with British power, Doyle used the press to deny that Britain would act.[80]

As already indicated (see p. 283), British restraint enabled America to pursue a new geography for its military power, although that geography was to be totally overthrown by the Civil War. Moreover, American growth depended in part on foreign credit, most of it supplied by Britain. By not investing greatly in military strength or activity, the Americans ensured that there was a good rate of return on these investments.[81]

Yet, Britain and the Native Americans were not the sole issues in furthering U.S. control of the west. There were also difficulties with Americans who defied government control. In particular, the Mormons were pledged to struggle in order to achieve the Kingdom of God on Earth or, at least, eventually, in Utah. Joseph Smith formally organized the later Church of Jesus Christ of Latter-day Saints in 1830, and communities were established, first in Kirtland, Ohio, and then in Independence, Missouri. The frontiersmen drove them initially from Independence and then from the state, and the Mormons moved to Illinois, where they established the theocratic city of Nauvoo in 1839. The Mormons had, in 1841, organized a large private militia, the Nauvoo Legion, and a secret society, the Sons of Dan, that was like a secret police, and their willingness to resist by force of arms helped them survive. Although the Nauvoo Legion was organized under Illinois law and under the nominal authority of the governor, it was led by Smith and largely composed of Mormons. Thousands served in the legion and, with its uniforms and parades, it had a prominent character, while military operations, including pretend battles, developed its prowess and led to local opposition.[82] Smith and his brother Hyrum were murdered in 1844, a reminder of the extent to which violence served political ends. Local opposition led state authorities to say that they could not protect the Mormons and to revoke the Nauvoo Charter, which ended the legal status of the Legion as a city militia, a step that encouraged the Mormons to move west.

Having done so, Smith's successor, Brigham Young, established Salt Lake City in Utah in 1847, and it initially proved possible to reconcile Mormon ends with the lightness of federal control in the vast lands of the West. Young, indeed, became governor of the Territory of Utah, a territory (covering much more than modern Utah) organized in 1850, but there were tensions over his bold hopes for the territorial extent of what he termed, in 1847, with reference to the honeybee, the "state of Deseret," which Young originally envisaged as including most of southern California as well. Furthermore, as so often, population issues were linked to territorial control. Young sought to prevent non-Mormons from arriving, only to find this goal fall victim to the development of the west and to Utah's position on the Oregon Trail. In addition, Mormon claims, both political and other, especially the public endorsement of polygamy in 1856, a means of increasing Mormon numbers, and the hostile treatment of non-Mormons, proved incompatible with federal pretensions, a clash that led to claims by federal officials that the Mormons were in a state of rebellion. Mormon firmness was strengthened by a religious revival, but the Republican Party condemned polygamy in 1856, declaring it a "barbarism" equal to slavery, and in 1857 President James Buchanan decided that the Mormons were in rebellion.

This decision led, that year, to the appointment of a non-Mormon to succeed Young as governor, and to the dispatch, under General William Harney and, subsequently, Colonel Albert Sidney Johnston, of 2,500 troops to provide necessary support. Although this number might seem a small force, it represented much of the army that could be used for an expedition once the numbers deployed linked to fortifications were taken into account. Young presented this as "a hostile force who are evidently assailing us to accomplish our overthrow and destruction," and prepared a response including a withdrawal from northern Utah into the mountains, a step that would have exposed another geographical dimension of the limits of government power. Mormon militia burned three of the army's supply trains in early October 1857, although they were instructed not to take life. This move helped to delay Johnston's force, which had at any rate been sent too late in the year. Captain Stewart Van Vliet, who was sent to Salt Lake City in September, in order to demand supplies for the army, reported that the Mormons would not help and that they would fight to stop the army entering Utah, if necessary responding with a scorched earth policy and taking refuge in the mountains where they had stored food and could destroy American forces. Winfield Scott had claimed in May 1857 that it was already too late that year to send the expedition. Scott warned that the Mormons could deploy four thousand men, and argued that such a challenge, and the need to protect supply lines, would require a very large American force. This warning was not heeded, and the first American troops did not depart from Fort Leavenworth for Utah until 18 July. Johnston failed to occupy Utah, as planned, in the autumn of 1857 and, instead, had to spend the winter near Fort Bridger. Meanwhile, one Mormon group slaughtered 120 migrants en route to California at Mountain Meadows. War, however, was avoided as the result of an agreement in 1858, in which Young lost the governorship, the Mormons were pardoned, and the army stayed outside Salt Lake City. Instead, it established Camp Floyd nearby, and this position helped support emigrant trains on the Oregon Trail. In 1861, Utah lost territory to Colorado and Nevada, although conflict was avoided and plans to partition Utah were abandoned.

The willingness to send an expedition against the Mormons, combined with the dispatch of a naval squadron to Paraguay in 1858–59, indicated the readiness of the Buchanan administration to use force, not least to employ the army for political purposes against countries and people on the margins of American society. This situation looked toward the use of troops under Lincoln to preserve the Union, although Buchanan's employment of force against South Carolina, if it can be considered as such, during the secession winter of 1860–61 was limited to the resupply of Fort Sumter. Lincoln attacked the notion of state sovereignty as an answer to the slavery question by asking whether Utah was to be admitted into the Union if its constitution tolerated polygamy.[83] Utah did not become a state until 1896, and only after polygamy had been abandoned as an essential doctrine in 1890. War with the Mormons was avoided in 1858 and, as president, Lincoln had other concerns than Utah. Nevertheless, the tension from 1857 on was a reminder of the potential that frontier regions offered for conflict, although other would-be frontier utopias did not produce comparable problems, for example the romantic socialist one that the French radical Victor Considerant tried to create in West Texas, only to fail in 1855 due in part to his poor leadership.[84]

Another aspect of frontier resistance is seen in the Kansas Territory in the 1850s, as disagreements over extending slavery escaped government control and became bloody. Protagonists for the two sides sought to terrorize their opponents in order to ensure a majority for their view, which was the consequence of the Kansas-Nebraska Act of 1854, the basis for the establishment of Kansas as a territory in 1854. This act allowed the people in the territory to decide on slavery rather than settling the question at the federal level. Hence, rival governments were established in Kansas in 1855 and, in May 1856, conflict broke out. On the other hand, opposition in both Kansas and Utah was constrained by the arrival of the army. In Kansas, which Crampton thought "may be made the battleground upon which an actual contest upon the subject of slavery may be commenced," troops successfully lowered the temperature.[85]

As one of the central functions of a military is preserving the authority of the state, one of the major might-have-beens in American military history relates to the likely consequences had there been what was seen as a major internal challenge prior to 1861. Such a challenge would have been very different in scale to the Confederacy, but might still have posed an important military problem, not least because of the small size and limited preparedness of the army. Politics played a major role in avoiding such a crisis, in that the federal structure of America made it easier to accommodate differences within states, as many governmental and political functions were both the prerogative of the latter and reflected local wishes, not central government instructions. There were also surprisingly few examples of attacks on troops. In the Kansas disturbances, only one soldier was killed in action, although about two hundred civilians died.

Alongside problems on the frontiers, difficulties were still created by filibusters. Indeed, one of the most prominent filibusters, William Walker (1824–60), came to prominence in the mid-1850s, which were also the years of John Quitman's plans to seize Cuba (in 1854–55),[86] Henry Kinney's pursuit of the Mosquito Coast (in 1855),[87] and Henry Crabb's invasion of the northwestern Mexican province of Sonora (in 1857).Crabb's men marched from Sonoita to the Gulf of California, where they launched hostilities, only to be captured and shot. Quitman, a governor of Mississippi and general, who led the military contingent at Buchanan's inauguration on 4 March 1857, was the best connected, but Walker made the most splash.

A Tennessee-born doctor, Walker studied in Europe, where he was influenced by radical nationalist writers. Having switched from being a physician in Philadelphia to a lawyer in New Orleans, Walker became a newspaper editor in San Francisco, a city of apparently boundless prospects. There he conceived the idea of a Central American state that was to fulfill his views of manifest destiny for white men and himself. Indeed, Walker sought to create a state ruled by whites and resting on a slave-based agriculture, a transposed South. Walker's first step was an invasion of Lower California in 1853, a step taken after efforts at San Francisco to thwart him from violating the neutrality laws were blocked by Democratic Party politicians.[88] Capturing the capital, La Paz, Walker declared that it was independent, as was the neighboring province of Sonora, and he put the new "Republic of Lower California" under the laws of Louisiana, which provided a legal basis for slavery, although Louisiana's law was more liberal than that of other slave states, including in its presumption that all mulattoes were free unless the contrary could be proven, while, until 1857, Louisiana also had the most liberal of the Southern states' emancipation laws.[89] Walker also proclaimed free trade with all the world. Although the capture of La Paz had been eased by the small size of the population of Lower California, the Mexican army swiftly drove Walker's band out.[90] Once back in America, Walker was charged with breaking the neutrality laws, but, supported by Democratic Party politicians, he was not convicted.

In May 1855, Walker tried again, this time seeking to exploit the civil war in Nicaragua. The collapse of the United Provinces of Central America, the state that had governed Guatemala, Honduras, Nicaragua, and Costa Rica from the end of union with Mexico in 1823 until separation in 1838, had left a series of small states, each close together, and their bitter rivalries interacted with domestic conflicts. Walker acted with the support of the railway tycoon Cornelius Vanderbilt, who was trying to develop a route across the country as the key link between the Atlantic and Pacific coasts of America, avoiding the lengthy journey round Cape Horn. Walker defeated the Nicaraguan army at the battle of La Virgen on 4 September and captured the capital, Granada, in October.

Despite earlier condemnation of Walker,[91] in May 1856, the new government, much to the anger of Clarendon,[92] was acknowledged by Pierce, the American president, who hoped to increase American influence in Central America. That July, Walker declared himself president of Nicaragua. The Emancipation Edict of 1824, forbidding slavery, was annulled, and Walker encouraged the idea that Nicaragua would be a key partner of the South, as well as a fulfillment of its hopes. Immigration to Nicaragua from the South was encouraged. The British government was convinced that its American counterpart was behind Walker,[93] and that his activities, which included the annexation of Greytown on the Mosquito Shore, breached the Clayton-Bulwer treaty, but, despite a minor war scare, Palmerston refused to intervene. As Clarendon pointed out, both Nicaragua and Costa Rica, which was threatened by Walker and had also sought British and French help, had poor relations with Britain,[94] which, moreover, was at war with Russia from 1854 to 1856. Britain, however, did agree to sell arms to Costa Rica.[95]

The situation was inherently unstable, with both Nicaragua and Central America unsettled. Thus, in 1856, Nicaraguan forces invaded the Guanacaste region of Costa Rica to which Walker lay claim, only to be defeated at Santa Rosa by a larger Costa Rican force financed by coffee exports. Moreover, Walker's relations with American interests were fraught. His seizure of the properties of the Accessory Transit Company, Vanderbilt's enterprise, led the latter to turn against Walker in what in part was a quarrel between rival speculators over controlling the transit route.[96] In 1857, Vanderbilt's agents persuaded the governments of the two neighboring countries, that of Juan Rafael Mora Porras in Costa Rica and José Santos Guardiola in Honduras, that Walker planned to conquer their states in order to create an empire based on slavery and governed by Americans. Vanderbilt recruited and paid for an army for Costa Rica, and Walker's forces, hit by cholera, nearly surrounded by their opponents, and increasingly reluctant to fight, were defeated. That May, Charles Henry Davis, commander of the USS St Mary's, arranged the surrender of Walker and his followers, and they were shipped to safety outside the region. José Maria Estrada resumed his position as president of Nicaragua.

Walker, however, did not give up. Later that year, he landed at Punta Arenas in Nicaragua, but, in turn, American warships under Commodore Hiram Paulding landed marines who arrested Walker. This action, however, was disapproved of by Lewis Cass, the secretary of state. Walker was acquitted in an American court on the charge of violating the neutrality laws, and Paulding was forced to retire.

Support for Walker declined[97] and his last expedition, to Honduras in 1860, ended in disaster. He seized the town of Trujillo, but won no backing and his men deserted him. Walker then sought to place himself under the protection of a British warship, but he was turned over to the Hondurans, who shot him.[98] The British had taken a consistent stand against filibustering, cooperating with Spain in seeking to discourage it against Cuba,[99] a cooperation that extended to the threat of naval action in 1851.[100] In 1855, Americans suspected that British warships visiting

Havana were connected to the crisis linked with Quitman's plan for an invasion. Crampton told Pierce that Britain was "an American power" and that it had a legitimate interest in the fate of Cuba.[101]

The nature of opportunity in Central America and the Caribbean was changing, for states as well as filibusters. Thus, Britain and France acted in 1851 to achieve, by coercion, a settlement between Haiti and St. Domingo.[102] Imperial ambitions were in flux, with Britain becoming less active, although France was to be far more so in the 1860s. British claims on the Mosquito Coast became more modest in the 1850s. Suzerainty had been claimed there until 1850, but the British protectorate came to an end with the recognition of Nicaraguan sovereignty in 1860. The northward extension of this protectorate in Honduras was recognized as coming under Honduran sovereignty in 1859, as were the Bay Islands in the Caribbean to the north of Honduras. This was the outcome recommended by Napier in 1857,[103] while in 1859, with reference to China, Russell had noted his concern about the health of island bases in the Tropics.[104]

These British withdrawals, which reflected a lack of political and public commitment to a longstanding part of Britain's informal empire,[105] and certainly no wish to extend British influence or possessions,[106] did not open the way for American occupation, for, despite the ambitions of some speculators, such an occupation was not the intention of the American government, which was well-satisfied with the British withdrawal. Cass had told Napier in March 1857 that America only wanted clear independence and neutrality for Central America, free from any exclusive influence or ascendancy.[107] As Napier predicted, a British abandonment of the Bay Islands would not lead America to try to annex them.[108] British accommodation, however, did not extend to governmental support for the American purchase of Cuba, although Napier backed the idea in 1857, seeing American control as beneficial to British economic interests and strategically acceptable.[109] Cuba, however, took second place to Central America in Anglo-American relations in the late 1850s. Although the British disengagement from the Mosquito Coast and Bay Islands was not free from American suspicion and accompanying tensions, it was a measure that eased relations. Richard, 2nd Lord Lyons, the new envoy in Washington, saw it as a sacrifice for the sake of the latter.[110] The Anglo-American rapprochement, to which active diplomacy contributed, helped greatly when relations were placed under pressure during the Civil War, and thus made intervention in that conflict less probable. There was no comparable improvement in the case of Franco-American relations.

Walker's career showed the impact that an individual could achieve. So, more dramatically, did John Brown's seizure of the federal arsenal at Harpers Ferry on the night of 16 October 1859. Intended to terrorize slaveholders and as the first stage of a war on slavery, to be achieved in large part by armed slaves, this rising by twenty-one men, however, was rapidly suppressed by Colonel Robert E. Lee and a force of Marines who stormed the building on the morning of 18 October, but it helped raise tension greatly in the South, leading Lyons to complain about racism there, notably toward blacks and abolitionists.[111] Many Southerners were convinced that the insurrection revealed the true intentions of abolitionists, and this view proved a troubling background to the election campaign in 1860, as well as helping to accentuate the regional character of the contests.

# 13

# AMERICA DIVIDED
# 1861-63

The admission of California as a free state in 1850 gave the free states a majority in the Senate, and the minority status of the South in the Union was a key feature of the sectional controversy of the 1850s, a feature that created problems for the South. Minnesota and Oregon followed as free states in 1858 and 1859 respectively. A sense of being under challenge ensured that Southern secession was frequently threatened in the 1850s, before it finally triumphed in 1860–61. British envoys noted this development. Already, in 1851, Bulwer had written of "the but half suppressed excitement which the Southern states have lately been exhibiting," and in 1859 Lyons observed "after making due allowance for the tendency to consider the 'present' crisis as always the most serious that has ever occurred, I am inclined to think that North and South have never been so near a breach."[1]

The alternative to secession was to seek to make the Union safe for the South and slavery, in part by reeducating Northerners about the constitution, or by acquiring more slave states, or by somehow addressing the vulnerabilities of the slave system in the South. The Southerners' failure to do so was compounded by the difficulties posed by the slaves' desire for freedom, although the latter did not have a scale nor disruptive consequences comparable to the situation in Brazil in the 1880s.

The 1860 election gave victory to Abraham Lincoln of the Republican Party, who wished to prevent the extension of slavery into the federal Territories. This was understood by Lincoln and others as a step that threatened Southern interests and identity. The election of Lincoln, "a man almost unknown, a rough Western, of the lowest origin and little education,"[2] reflected the refashioning of politics by the slavery issue, which had led, first, to pressure on the Whigs, as with the rise of Liber-tyites and the Free Soil Party,[3] subsequently, to the disintegration of the Whigs in the aftermath of the Kansas-Nebraska Act of 1854, and the related rise of the Republicans as a Northern sectional party focused on the restriction of slavery, and, then, to the division of the Democratic Party, "the only remaining bond between north and south,"[4] between Northern and Southern wings.

In 1856, James Buchanan, the Democratic candidate, had won the South but also Pennsylvania, Illinois, and Indiana, showing a winning national appeal; but, in 1860, Stephen Douglas, the Northern Democrat, competed with John Breckinridge, the Southern Democrat. This compe-tition allowed Lincoln, the Republican, who carried the Northern states but none of the Southern ones, to win on fewer than 40 per cent of the votes cast. National politics were no longer being contested by effec-tive national parties, and, partly as a result, American mass democracy could not generate a consensus. Compromise was on offer, but no longer seemed sufficiently acceptable in the North and South to gather impetus. Lincoln rejected the proposal by Senator John Crittenden of Kentucky that the 36–30' line of the 1820 Missouri compromise accepting slavery for the Arkansas Territory be run toward the Pacific, a line that would include the New Mexico Territory in the world of slavery.

Lincoln's election led to the secession of the South, beginning with South Carolina on 20 December 1860, and the formation of the Con-federate States of America. Yet, as a reminder of the significance of geo-graphical factors and also at the same time of their uncertainty, and thus of the volatility of geopolitics, the Confederacy did not equate with the slave states. Only the Lower South seceded at first and Montgomery, Alabama, was the initial capital of the Confederacy. Moreover, much of the Upper South, including Virginia, Tennessee, and Kentucky, had voted for John Bell of Tennessee, the candidate of the new Constitu-tional Union party pledged to back "the Union, the Constitution and the Laws,"[5] rather than for Breckinridge.

Although Lincoln was willing to back a constitutional amendment prohibiting the federal government from interfering with slavery, seces-sion was unacceptable to him and the Republicans; and Lincoln was very concerned about the consequences of his actions for his party.[6] They argued both that the maintenance of the Union was essential to the purpose of America as well as to its strength and that it was necessary to understand that the superiority of the federal government over the states was critical to the idea of the American nation. This superiority was demonstrated when Lincoln refused to yield to demands for the surrender of the federal position of Fort Sumter in Charleston harbor: the reality of national power in the face of a forge of Southern consciousness and separatism. On 12 April 1861, Confederate forces opened fire, and the beleaguered fort surrendered the following day after more than three thousand shells and shots had been fired, setting fire to the wooden buildings in the fort.

Far from intimidating him into yielding, as Southern leaders had hoped, this clash led Lincoln to determine to act against what he termed "combinations" in the South. He went to war to maintain the Union, and not for the emancipation of the slaves. Lincoln's call for 75,000 volunteers, and his clear intention to resist secession with force, by invading the Lower South, played the major role in leading Arkansas, North Carolina, Tennessee, and Virginia to join the Confederacy, as they did not intend to provide troops to put down what Lincoln termed an insurrection.[7]

This subsequent secession of the Upper South greatly altered the demographic and military context of the war: political events reshaped the geography and thus the geopolitics of the war. Arkansas was not able to contribute much to the Confederacy, but Virginia, Tennessee, and North Carolina were each more important in economic and demographic terms than any state in the Lower South. In order, they were the leading states in white population in the Confederacy, while, together, they were to field close to 40 percent of the Confederacy's forces, provided half of its crops, and more than half of its manufacturing capacity. South Carolina's ability to win over Virginia was important to the geopolitical definition of the South.

In military terms, the location of this productive capacity in frontier areas was a problem for the Confederacy, as they were vulnerable and thus rewarded Union attack while compromising the idea of a defense in depth. However, while the gain of the four states ensured that there was more territory to defend, it transformed the military potential of the Confederacy. The Union no longer had a common frontier with every seceding state bar Florida, and thus the Lower South became less vulnerable. It also became easier to think of the Confederacy as a bloc of territory that could be defended in a coherent fashion and that therefore required a coherent strategy in order to bring it down. In particular, the secession of Virginia and North Carolina greatly altered the location of the likely field of operations in the east as, militarily, the front line of the secession was no longer on the northern border of South Carolina. Had that been the case, Columbia and Charleston would have been readily vulnerable to Union attack, just as Atlanta in Georgia would have been from Chattanooga in Tennessee.

Conversely, the Union was able to gain control of an important bloc of slave states: Delaware, Maryland, Kentucky, Missouri, and those parts of Virginia that, in 1863, became the state of West Virginia. Had these states joined the Confederacy, as Missouri and Kentucky sympathizers did, leading to their being seated in the Confederate Congress, then the situation would also have been very different. Instead, the Union consolidated its superiority in resources, blocked invasion routes into the North, and exposed the South to attack. As Maryland stayed in the Union, the central battleground of the war lay between Washington, which remained the capital of the Union, and Richmond, Virginia, which became the capital of the Confederacy in May 1861.

Their proximity helped give a geographical focus to the conflict, one that reflected the political importance of the two capitals, and also cut across the potential expansiveness of the conflict arising from the extent of the area in rebellion. Indeed, this proximity offered the prospect of the rapid end to the war that Northerners sought. Moreover, these states in Union hands affected the offensive capability of the Confederacy. Given Lee's willingness to march north across the Potomac in 1862 and 1863, it is instructive to consider the military impact, had the frontier been on the northern border of Maryland. There was also a key demographic dimension in terms of the manpower available to both sides.

The Civil War, furthermore, was a civil conflict within the states that seceded. In the latter, the prevalence of slavery varied greatly, with, for example, few slaves in Appalachia. Conversely, fears of an abolitionist plot in Texas in late 1860, a major instance of the sequence of panics following John Brown's attempt on Harpers Ferry, helped lead to vigilante action and encouraged backing for secession.[8] The variation in the prevalence of slavery was linked to the degree of support for the war, though it was not the sole factor involved. Some 104,000 white Southerners fought in the Union forces,[9] a major addition to the latter and cause of Confederate weakness, and the degree of opposition to secession underlined the degree to which chance factors played a considerable role in ensuring that it occurred.[10] Yet, alongside a commitment to slavery, many who fought for the South did not own slaves and were more motivated by a sense of the need to defend communities, cultures, and the states' rights that were believed to protect both. These states' rights, however, were defined in part in terms of the defense of slavery. There were many northern "dough faces" willing to accept slavery, including Pierce, a recent president, but they did not provide a military support for the South equivalent to that of Southerners who fought against separation.

The extent of different beliefs in the South serves as a reminder of the complexity of the issues at stake, and thus of the geopolitics and strategy of the war. Initially unprepared for the difficulty of the struggle, both militarily and politically, Union forces had to try to shift the political balance within the South in order to lead to its surrender, and that indeed occurred in 1865. The military alternative of the conquest of the entire South was not viable given the size of the Confederacy. The latter's political option appeared clearer. There was the hope that success in the conflict would lead the Union to change policy by abandoning the war, and, secondly, that success would bring the British and French into the war, and thus ensure that the Union had to change policy. There was considerable weight in both ideas, and if the playing out of the war revealed that neither was viable, that was not readily apparent to contemporaries in America and abroad until well into the conflict.

The prospect of Confederate success in these respects helps provide a chronology that is linked to the chapter division. In 1861–62, a possibility of outcomes left a distinct South as an option, but, from 1863, this possibility receded. Lincoln's victory in the 1864 presidential election both cemented the political coherence of the North and, as a consequence, created the basis for a political settlement that would entail not only victory over the Confederacy but also a postwar American order able to intimidate other powers in the New World. That the Civil War particularly invites counterfactuals testifies to the geopolitical volatility of this conjuncture and, with it, of the trends and developments that had led to it. The two most significant counterfactuals focus on the possibility of the Confederacy doing better in the conflict and on that of foreign intervention. The two were linked, but separate. Each raises important questions about the relationship between agency and structure, as well as concerning the determinism bound up with the argument from the availability of greater resources on one side. The purpose of dwelling on each here rests not only on their inherent significance but also on the extent to which they draw attention to issues and questions during the period of this book as a whole. A brief and selective discussion of the campaigning in 1861–62 will be followed by a consideration of the resource issue and then of the counterfactuals.

The impact of politics on strategy was shown at the outset when political pressure in the North for a rapid advance on Richmond, to destroy the Confederacy by seizing the capital, led to a departure from the plan drawn up by Winfield Scott, the general-in-chief. He, instead, had called for an advance down the Mississippi, to bisect the Confederacy, combined with a blockade. Termed the "Anaconda Plan" by the press, this was intended to save lives and, by increasing support for a return to the Union, to encourage the Confederacy to make peace or, failing that, to put the Union in the best state for further operations. However, Scott's emphasis on planning, as well as on the indirect approach, training, and a delay in the offensive until the autumn of 1861, fell foul of the pressure for action. He unsuccessfully opposed the proposal of Brigadier-General Irvin McDowell, the field commander in the Washington area, to attack the Confederates at Manassas Junction, Virginia, that July. Scott sought strategy in "a war of large bodies," but, instead, what he termed "a little war by piece-meal" prevailed. Any hopes that the war would be rapidly brought to a close were ended by failure on 21 July in what became the First Battle of Bull Run or First Manassas. Neither commander behaved adroitly, and the fate of the battle hinged not on planning, but on the arrival of fresh troops. In that, the Confederates benefited from operating on interior lines, and their reinforcements from the Shenandoah Valley decided the battle with an attack on the Union flank. The battle ended with the flight of the Union forces, who suffered heavier losses, although the Confederates failed to exploit their victory, in large part because they had been exhausted and disorganized by the fighting.

In contrast, a verdict had been delivered in 1860 in the Ecuadorian civil war between the rivals Guillermo Franco, president from 1859, and the Conservative Gabriel Garcia Moreno, based in the rival centers of Guayaquil and Quito, when Juan José Flores, a former president and commander of the Conservative army, won a decisive victory at Bodegas. Flores then advanced on Guayaquil, Franco went into exile, and Moreno was president until 1865.

From before the American Civil War started, the British government was determined not to intervene. However, at the outset, there was a playing out of the possibility of international intervention, not least because of the war's consequences for international trade, the freedom of which was a matter of ideological commitment for British politicians as well as economic interests. While permeable by small, fast steamships until late in the conflict, the blockade of the Confederate states, organized by the Union's Blockade Board established in 1861, indicated the potency of economic warfare by limiting Southern exports, and also led to a host of disputes with commercial states, among which Britain was most prominent. The amount of time spent on quarrels over the fate of individual ships is very striking in the diplomatic archives.

The blockade, which drew on American experience against Mexico in 1846–48, also helped to limit the Confederates' efforts to build up their own fleet. Even before the blockade became effective, the Confederacy had made insufficient efforts to import rolled iron and machinery,[11] a serious factor because they were so short of iron that they had to pull up railway tracks and could not adequately maintain their transport system, including by relaying track.[12] Had Britain fought the Union, such factors would have limited the ability of the Confederates to provide support.

In May 1861, Richard, 2nd Lord Lyons, the British envoy, noted, in his confidential correspondence with Rear-Admiral Alexander Milne, the commander of the North America and West Indies station, that nonintervention was the order of the day for Britain: "The present policy of the government at home is to keep entirely aloof from the quarrel which is raging in this country, to show neither favour nor disfavour to one side or the other." Although obliged to protect British subjects and property, Milne was not to interfere with the Union blockade, a key advantage for the North, nor with Southern privateers.[13] However, America's legal position vis-à-vis Britain was affected by the unilateralist American refusal in 1856 to sign the Declaration of Paris, an international agreement codifying practice over blockade and privateering.

Britain did not use the crisis in America as an opportunity to "meddle," let alone to press its claims over the San Juan issue (the basis of the Pig War of 1859), despite tension over the issue in the winter of 1860–61,[14] and issued a neutrality proclamation on 13 May.[15] However, evenhandedness was unacceptable to the Union because, by treating both sides as belligerents, the British and French, whom the British government was keeping informed,[16] did not present the Confederates as rebels. The Union proved reluctant to accept the constraints posed by this stance, and, later in May, Lyons noted, "I am seriously alarmed at the recklessness and imprudence of this government in their treatment of foreign powers,"[17] a point more generally true of American attitudes and European responses. He added in June: "I do not regard a sudden declaration of war against us by the United States as an event altogether impossible at any moment," an anxiety to which he was to recur on other occasions.[18] If he believed the danger imminent and could not telegraph in cipher, he would send the message "Could you forward a letter for me to Antigua."[19]

Lyons did not think that Bull Run would affect the British line of conduct, but, by ensuring that the war would continue, it made his hope that the Union would not try to close the Southern ports to international trade less plausible. For him to point out that Britain had faced a comparable issue in Colombia was unhelpful, as the Union would not let itself be treated in a similar fashion,[20] although, throughout the Civil War and thereafter, comparisons were to be drawn as all sides struggled to gain advantage in debate. Russell observed in September 1861: "The great question of all is the American, and that grows darker and darker every day. I do not expect that Lyons will be sent away, but it is possible. [Secretary of State] Seward and Co. may attempt to revive their waning popularity by a quarrel with Great Britain; but if we avoid all offence, I do not see how they can do it."[21] The danger of war for popularity was to be returned to repeatedly by Lyons, but there was no real basis for his fear.[22]

Palmerston's suggestion in June that naval reinforcements be sent to American waters was not followed up, in part because of concern about tensions with France, and Anglo-American relations did not deteriorate in late 1861 until 8 November. Then a Union frigate, the *San Jacinto*, named after Houston's victory over the Mexicans in 1836, fired across the bows and stopped the British packet (mail) steamer RMS *Trent*, in the Old Bahama Channel en route from Havana to Nassau with an onward voyage to Southampton. Acting without orders, the *San Jacinto* took two prominent Confederate politicians off the *Trent*, James Mason and John Slidell, who were being sent to Europe to try to win formal recognition of independence, and their two secretaries, and they were confined in Fort Warren, Boston. The blockade thus compounded the weaknesses of Confederate diplomacy.[23] Congress voted Captain Wilkes the thanks of the nation.

"It is not lawful to take passengers out of a neutral vessel going from a neutral port to a neutral port," commented Russell.[24] This clear breach of British maritime rights was exacerbated by the assurance from Charles Adams, the American envoy in London, that the ship would not be stopped, an assurance given in good faith as Wilkes had acted without orders. Informed of the incident on 27 November, the British government, after a Cabinet meeting on the 28th, demanded the return of the men and an apology. Concerned that the American government, to win support through conflict with Britain, would not agree (a longstanding fear on the British part), the British prepared for war. Edward, 12th Duke of Somerset, the First Lord of the Admiralty, ordered Milne to concentrate naval forces, so that no ship would be left isolated and vulnerable to attack. Benefiting from the naval buildup stemming from concern about French plans in 1859 and subsequently,[25] Somerset planned the dispatch of "our most effective ships and also smaller vessels to operate in shallow waters" and, in the meanwhile, dispatched warships from both the Home and Mediterranean fleets, in part to protect steamships hired to transport troops.[26] Russell was confident on the naval side but fearful for an unprepared Canada, rather as Palmerston had been when fearful of war earlier in the year.[27] From 29 November, reinforcements were sent to Canada and Bermuda, both troops and *matériel,* while the export of munitions to the Union, notably crucial saltpeter from India for gunpowder, were suspended on the 28th. The British imperial system came into play with its multiple interconnections. Coal was sent to the West Indies to support a larger naval presence,[28] while Canadian Volunteer units gained recruits. In response to the prospect of war, the New York stock market fell.

British ministers speculated about the likely international consequences, and about the possibility that the Union's options would be constrained by domestic circumstances aside from their leaders seeking war with Britain, both points made by Palmerston.[29] Presenting Britain as having no other options, Russell observed on 6 December 1861: "I cannot imagine their giving a plain yes or no to our demands. I think they will try to hook in France, and if that is, as I hope, impossible, to get Russia to support them in some plausible philo-neutral proposition. Their government has all the genius of a country attorney," a remark, frequently made, that reflected social disdain and also a sense that the Americans preferred narrow interests to statecraft. On 16 December, Russell added, "The President's message is prudent.... But the Congress will, I fear, intercept any rational solution," while, expressing optimism, Lyons wrote on 28 December, "the only present danger seems to lie in the surrender causing so violent an outburst of public wrath, as to drive the government to some highhanded proceeding in order to satisfy the American populace."[30]

On 17 December, Adams communicated Seward's letter of 30 November to Russell; the letter stated that Wilkes had lacked authorization. Four days later, the French envoy made it clear to Seward that France would not help America and, instead, urged compliance with British demands. Subsequently, the Union government, after a Cabinet meeting on 25 December, apologized, disavowed Wilkes, and released the envoys, a settlement, of which news reached London on 8 January 1862, that was a great relief to Russell.[31] His letter of 10 January announcing that the government was satisfied by these steps was communicated by Lyons to Seward on 30 January.[32] Russell had pointed out that the Union's best chance in the Civil War was to keep Britain and France neutral, but he also linked policy to American politics, expressing the hope that George B. McClellan, the commander of the main Union field army, whom he had been told found the seizures unjustifiable, "could be made Dictator."[33]

Counterfactuals come into immediate play, as both sides could have taken a different line. Indeed, the draft for the initial British protesting dispatch that was to be sent to the Union government was softened according to the advice of the dying Prince Albert, as he felt it would endanger relations. Submitted to the queen for consideration on the night of 30 November, the draft was countered the following day by a memorandum from Albert urging modifications that were approved by Palmerston and adopted by Russell.[34] Albert himself died from typhoid on 14 December, an event seen in the North as a loss to America. His views had influenced those of Victoria, while the Prince of Wales's visit to America in 1860 had revealed a degree of anglophilia[35] alongside the willingness to cheer on the Russians against Britain in the Crimean War. Yet, the strength of the British naval challenge was a more important source of continued peace than Albert's intervention, as it acted as a potent restraint on American policy.[36]

The *Trent* crisis and its resolution might seem to have drawn the sting on both sides of the Atlantic by showing the danger of conflict, but it also revealed the highly dangerous nature of relations. The outcome of the crisis, public support in Britain for Prime Minister Palmerston, a politician who had long cultivated public opinion as a means to advance and protect policy and his own position,[37] and a rapid close to the crisis on British terms, encouraged Palmerston. He had consistently been ready to use sea power as an integral aspect of his foreign policy of supporting British interests, and, personally, disliked America as an unpredictable force in international relations. However, his conduct in the *Trent* crisis was less belligerent and risky than that of Seward.

Rather than criticizing Palmerston for risky belligerence, it is worth noting the views of the opposition (Conservative) leader, Derby. Like Lyons, Derby always felt that the most effective way of dealing with America was with forthright directness as, otherwise, popular enthusiasm and democratic agitation would run unchecked. Over the *Trent* crisis, Derby advised Henry, 5th Duke of Newcastle, the colonial secretary, who had met Seward earlier in the year while visiting America, and George, 2nd Earl Granville, the lord president of the council, accordingly. Derby shared in the patriotic anger but did not want war, and supported Palmerston's policy of recognizing the South as a belligerent but not as independent. Palmerston, indeed, was a cautious realist as far as policy was concerned.[38] He had no great desire to confront America, because he focused on Europe. He read the disputes with America partly in European terms, in the sense of wanting to use assertiveness in North America to underpin policy closer to home, at least in giving that impression, although the material limitations of British power influenced the shape of policy in terms of the extent to which that policy would ever be pushed in practice.

Successfully pressing the Union to back down in the *Trent* case did not satisfactorily address the problems created by a blockade that Britain accepted as legal, which was a key basis for the maintenance of relations with the North. Moreover, the argument that military preparations, especially the maintenance of a considerable force in Canada, were the best way to get America to be reasonable[39] was not without risk, as they could have encouraged Britain to pursue a policy that might have led to an unwanted war, although British policy tended to be cautious. Lyons also pointed out the risks created by the willingness of Union subordinate officers to commit acts of violence on their own account,[40] risks that were enhanced as Britain clarified its position on trade with the South. Indeed, Lyons greeted the news of the safe arrival of Mason and Slidell at Bermuda by fearing that another dispute might soon arise.[41]

Meanwhile, European observers followed the war with attention, but it was difficult to understand developments in distant parts, and still harder to get a grip on the relationship between the different fronts. There were also the problems of the accuracy of the information available. The European envoys were in Washington, and communications with Richmond, while possible, under a flag of truce via Norfolk, were such that it was more difficult to understand the situation there. Lyons noted on 27 February 1862 that the Union government expected the fall of New Orleans and Savannah within days; in fact, the first occurred on 1 May 1862 and the second on 22 December 1864. Thinking Seward "always excessively sanguine,"[42] Lyons nevertheless explained the difficulty of assessing the situation, a point that can be made more generally, and also speculated on the contrast between output and outcome:

> The United States have recently had a series of successes – not perhaps any one taken simply of very great military importance – but taken all together they constitute a great advantage morally and materially. The impression produced by the surrenders at Roanoke Island and Fort Donelson certainly is that the Southern Men do not manifest in action the desperate valour to which they lay claim in speech. . . . If this is a specimen of the spirit which prevails generally among them, they will hardly make any effective resistance to the Northern armies, which are greatly superior in numbers, and still more so in arms and equipment. . . . The fall of Fort Donelson and Fort Henry has given the Federals the command of the Cumberland and Tennessee Rivers – They expect to be thus enabled to occupy the Western part of Tennessee, to obtain possession of Nashville and the railroads which united at that point, and in this way to interrupt the communication between Virginia and the South through Tennessee. The communication by General Burnside's expedition; and the Confederate army at Manassas being thus isolated, is to be compelled either to retreat or to accept a battle under unfavourable circumstances.
>
> The month of May is to see the Federal armies in undisputed possession of Missouri, Kentucky, Virginia and Tennessee, and of the seaboard of the other states.
>
> This is going very fast indeed, as all that has been done yet is to take two small river forts. . . . Nevertheless, if the Southerners do not recover their military superiority by gaining a battle on a large scale, or some other great success, the state of affairs may not be unlike what the ardent Northern partisans expect. But will this end the war? If the South acts with the determination and possesses the endurance to what it lays claim, the contest may be maintained for years in the interior of the Gulf states. . . . At this moment the North is full of confidence and spirit.[43]

Palmerston was also uncertain of the future and, as a result, was disinclined to record guesses.[44] Mason, who met Russell on 10 February 1862, found the latter unwilling to commit the government, and his reports offered scant grounds for optimism. Slidell encountered a similar response in Paris. The following month, parliamentary speeches on behalf of the Confederacy, in a debate claiming that the Union blockade was ineffective, and therefore invalid, were refuted by the solicitor-general, Roundell Palmer.

By May 1862, the war seemed won by the Union, which serves as a reminder of the multiple uncertainties of the conflict. Nashville, New

Orleans (the most populous city in the Confederacy), which fell on 25 February and 1 May respectively, and most of Tennessee had all been captured, and, on 6–7 April, Ulysses Grant defeated a surprise Confederate counterattack at Shiloh. This bitter battle had initially seemed likely to end in Southern victory, but the death of the Confederate commander, Albert Sidney Johnston, and the arrival of Union reinforcements changed the situation. Moreover, the Confederate expedition under Brigadier General Henry Sibley sent to capture Santa Fe, and which hoped to overrun Arizona and open a way to the Pacific, was defeated in February 1862, ending plans for a Confederate hegemony in the southwest. Such a hegemony would have ensured a very different postwar America to one simply focused on the Confederacy from Texas east, although these plans faced a formidable logistical challenge.[45] Furthermore, the Confederate coasts were threatened by Union naval superiority. After the fall of Norfolk on 10 May, Lyons (wrongly) anticipated that of Savannah and Charleston.[46]

Union forces continued focused on Richmond. That which was intended as the decisive blow was launched against it. Control of Virginia was economically and industrially, as well as politically, crucial, as the Tredegar Iron Works, in Richmond, was the Confederacy's sole large-scale foundry. Instead of attacking overland from the north, McClellan, commander of the Army of the Potomac, advanced on Richmond along the James River after a landing to the east of the city and the lengthy siege of Yorktown. He was no Moltke (the Elder), the Prussian chief of the general staff: rather, McClellan organized for battle, but could not win it. In so far as he was termed the "Young Napoleon," this pertinent comparison was with Napoleon III, who was to be defeated by Moltke in 1870, and not with the famous Napoleon I. In particular, McClellan lacked Moltke's fixity of purpose and ability to give rapid operational effect to strategic planning, and also greatly overestimated Confederate strength, which led him to accentuate his natural caution.

McClellan's campaign initially seemed promising, with the Confederate forces retreating in the face of their numerous but ponderous Union opponents. Lyons predicted that McClellan would reach Richmond before the end of June, although, with an instructive reference to the international context, he thought that the South would fight on, so as to make it unlikely that the Union could spare many forces to act against any other power.[47]

In the event, helped by the disruptive consequences for Union force-allocation of Stonewall Jackson's successful diversionary campaigning in the Shenandoah Valley, Robert E. Lee reversed the pattern of Confederate retreat set by Joseph Johnston, when he replaced him in command after Johnston was wounded on 31 May at the battle of Seven Pines. Indeed, Lee succeeded in blocking McClellan's cautious advance in the Seven Days battles (26 June–2 July 1862), thwarting the approach toward Richmond, and went on to regain the initiative. This strategy involved costly attacks that can be criticized, such as Lee's decisions at Malvern Hill (1 July), where frontal attacks led to five thousand casualties without inflicting serious harm. Battles that ended with the opponent retreating after frontal attacks on their positions, as with the Confederate attacks at Mechanicsville (26 June) and Malvern Hill, should not necessarily be seen as vindications for those attacks, as the Union forces did not need to retreat in either case.

Nevertheless, the Seven Days battles started a series of Southern advances and victories in the east that affected the political as well as the military development of the struggle. Lee was a figure around whom the Confederates could rally, and this was important in helping to create a Confederate "nation" from people who stood for states' rights. He understood that Confederate public opinion had a preference for taking the initiative, not responding to Northern moves, that it sought offensive victories, and that control of Virginia was politically crucial.

Appreciating the implications of large-scale conflict between democratic societies, Lee fostered a strategy designed to hit Northern popular will,[48] at a time when Union strategy was still unfocused. In particular, Lee's advance across the Potomac River into Maryland in September 1862 not only obliged the Union forces to follow, and thus reduced the threat to Richmond, but was also designed to shock Union opinion by carrying the war to the North and inflicting defeat there, as well as to convince foreign opinion of Confederate strength, and perhaps to encourage Maryland to secede. Thus, the tide of the war was turned, but to a political as much as a military end. In autumn 1862, there was a possibility that Democrats might capture the House of Representatives and press for peace, and, indeed, they were to make gains in the elections.

Russell wished the Democrats success,[49] and reports of their victories in the elections in late 1862 were keenly noted.[50] Moreover, recognition of the Confederacy was pushed hard by Napoleon III, which reflected his hostility to the Union. There was a more general trend in French policy toward keeping other states small, notably seen in efforts to keep Italy and Germany divided into a number of kingdoms. This policy was regarded as a way to maintain French power and, in December 1861, Palmerston was concerned about the possibility of a forthcoming French attack on Austria and Prussia. Aside from backing Southern secessionism, there was also a rumor that French diplomats supported the separation of Texas from the Confederacy "in order to further the supposed ambitious designs of the Emperor Napoleon upon this continent."[51]

A similar view was to be taken later by Robert, 3rd Marquess of Salisbury, the Conservative prime minister of Britain in 1885–86, 1886–92, and 1895–1902. He was to argue during the Venezuela Crisis in 1895 that Britain should have supported the Confederacy so as to make American power more manageable. Furious with American aggression, Salisbury wished Britain had taken this earlier opportunity to break up the United States. Then, as Lord Robert Cecil, he had pointed out that Britain recognized both Brazil and Spain, each of which accepted slavery: Spain in Cuba. In a less considered tone, Cecil was a critic of American democracy, who saw Lincoln as a despot, compared Sherman to Genghis Khan, and argued that there was much Native American blood among the Northern population.[52] Some of the press, for example the *Oldham Standard* of 30 May 1863, was even more scathing.

The British government's emphasis was not on divisiveness for America. Lyons, for example, wrote in November 1862: "The immediate and obvious interest of Great Britain as well as of the rest of Europe, is that peace and prosperity should be restored to this country as soon as possible. The point chiefly worthy of consideration appears to be whether separation or reunion be the more likely to effect this object."[53] Recognition of the South enjoyed influential support in Britain, not least because a war fought to preserve or overthrow the Union did not seem too different to other struggles, notably that for Italian unification, in which Britain had supported the cause of self-determination.[54] Indeed, in 1863, Britain ceded the Protectorate of the Ionian Islands, which it had gained in the Vienna peace settlement, to Greece, which was a concession to Greek nationalism. British commentators compared the Confederate cause to the Italian and Polish struggles for independence, but that did not mean that they necessarily favored intervention by Britain.

After news of Confederate success at Second Manassas/Bull Run on 30 August 1862 reached London, Palmerston suggested that Britain and France recommend a peace agreement on the basis of separation if the Confederacy won more battles. The Confederacy appeared not only to enjoy the firm backing of the majority of its (white) citizens, but also to be able to persist in the struggle with reasonable success.[55]

The linked issues of recognition of the Confederacy and Anglo-French mediation of the war came to the fore. Indeed, on 2 October 1862, Palmerston wrote to the foreign secretary, "The condition of things which would be favourable to an offer of mediation would be great success of the South against the North. That state of things seemed ten days ago to be approaching."[56] Russell and W. E. Gladstone, the Chancellor of the Exchequer, both supported mediation.

Had Lee's invasion of Maryland maintained its initial dynamic that September, and Lee outmaneuvered McClellan, instead of dividing his army in the face of the Union forces who had managed to acquire a copy of Lee's orders, a prospectus that would have been underlined had Braxton Bragg's simultaneous operations in Kentucky been successful; then the midterm elections might not have gone for the Republicans. Instead, in a confused battle that abundantly reflected the friction of war,[57] both sides fought each other to a costly draw at Antietam on 17 September 1862, the Confederate defenders taking heavy casualties because they were not entrenched. McClellan's command of the larger Union forces was woefully poor. He did not coordinate the attacks on the Confederate left, right, and center. As a result, McClellan failed to implement his plan for hitting the Confederate flanks before breaking the center. Instead, a series of piecemeal attacks were unable to provide mutual support, and this failure exacerbated their costly character as frontal assaults. The attack on the Confederate left was mounted before that on the center, let alone the right. The eventual Union breakthrough, on the Confederate right on Antietam Creek, came too late to determine the flow of the battle, and McClellan failed to develop his victory.[58]

Lee's generalship had brought a reversal in the flow of the war, but at Antietam he failed to sustain his success. Moreover, the heavy losses of his Army of Northern Virginia forced Lee to a cautious exploitation of the battle. He withdrew from Antietam two days later. Antietam both ruptured the run of Confederate success and also suggested that the war would be longer and more costly than had been anticipated. It was clear, moreover, that success in an individual battle was not going to bring the destruction of the opponent's military strength. This outcome was extremely important for the international situation, as it discouraged those who advocated recognition of the Confederacy. From a different direction, however, a longer struggle directed attention to the role of the great powers because it made the blockade more important to Union success as the best means to hit the Confederate economy. Only the great powers were in a position to end the blockade. Not only did the blockade prevent exports that could finance foreign purchases including munitions, but it also stopped Southern coastal transport, which was an important means of trade.[59] This stoppage helped push up prices in the South, as an aspect of a more general difficulty in obtaining goods, and the shortages and inflation hit civilian morale hard.[60]

Napoleon III's policy toward the American Civil War was part of a very active French stance in the New World, although one that centered on Mexico, not America. This stance can be seen as a continuation of the competition between America and European powers for control over the Caribbean, Mexico, and Central America already potent in the 1840s, although there was a related upsurge of political disorder in these areas, focusing on tensions between liberalism and conservatism.[61] In 1858–61, the War of Reform in Mexico pitched the liberal government of Benito Juárez against conservative opponents. The difficulty of achieving a lasting settlement there reflected the complex interplay of sectional advantage and regional power bases, although, in December 1860, liberal forces regained Mexico City. In 1861, in turn, political instability and a default on international debts by the Mexican Congress on 17 July led to the breaking of diplomatic relations on 27 July and to coordinated intervention by Britain, France, and Spain, "for the purpose of coercing Mexico" to fulfill its obligations.[62] This was a highpoint in the long-term difficulties made by the Mexicans in repaying loans. Defaults and restrictions ensured that there was no final settlement of large loans raised in London in 1824 and 1825, in what was very much a loan bubble, until 1888, and, in Britain, the Committee of Mexican Bondholders became a vocal lobby group with their own agent in Mexico, a lobby that affected bilateral relations.[63]

Allied forces occupied Mexico's leading port, Veracruz, in 1861, in effect imposing a takeover of the country's trade that was designed to seize customs revenue that could be used to help repay the loan. The British, however, decided to send no troops: marines provided the forces they landed. Somerset's instructions were wide ranging in that the cooperation of British warships on Mexico's Pacific coast was envisaged, but Milne was also ordered to be cautious: "the number of marines being limited will not enable you to send any force inland. As however it may be requisite that the marines should occupy some position onshore," and, in light of the danger of disease, notably yellow fever which was a particular problem in Veracruz, "you have a discretion so that you can order them to any more healthy position in the neighbourhood which it may be convenient to occupy. . . . Our wish of course is to bring the operation to a close as speedily as may be . . . I am well aware of the difficulties that may arise in dealing with the rulers of a country which has been so long distracted by hostile parties."[64]

Russell made it clear that the marines were not to march inland, even though the French and Spanish forces would probably do so. Moreover, a Spanish request for command over the marines was rejected.[65] Milne was informed that although France and Spain were probably to back the establishment of monarchy in Mexico, Britain could not take any part: "We abstain from all interference in constitutional changes, assisting to secure tranquility for all foreigners resident in Mexico, and to secure the performance of the engagements into which the government of Mexico had entered with us by treaty."[66]

This careful delimitation was challenged by Sir Charles Wyke, the British envoy to Mexico, who was at Veracruz, and the commander, Commodore Hugh Dunlop, who were readier to cooperate with France and Spain. In terms reminiscent of modern "mission-creep," Milne was "much afraid we are gradually creeping into a state of war, which if not at once checked, must inevitably lead to the necessity of sending large reinforcements."[67] Concerned about the deviation from British policy, Somerset was worried by the possibility of needing to maintain "a large British force for an indefinite period." He also provided a clear account of the need to match policy to national interests, whatever the pressures from allies or for the stabilization of the local situation. Again the modern parallels are instructive: "Our allies may now intend measures different from those originally proposed or they may have found that the first measures were inadequate for the attainment of the legitimate objects of the Convention [of 31 October 1861 defining Allied intervention], and may therefore feel themselves constrained to adopt other plans. With all such changes of policy we can have no connexion, and must stand aloof, only taking care that British property and British subjects are not injured by any course which may be adopted." Milne was ordered not to support "measures, which may or may not be beneficial to Mexico, but which are at all events beyond the purposes intended by the British government."[68]

British caution was also indicative of a wider concern to avoid provoking America if possible. In September 1861, Russell wrote to the Queen, explaining the need to dispatch a naval force to destroy Veracruz's defenses, but adding that not only was it undesirable to send troops to occupy the city, but also that it was necessary to invite American cooperation and to declare that Britain had no intention of interfering in the internal government of Mexico: "To do so would be to meddle in a bitter struggle between two violent factions, equally cruel, unjust and unprincipled; to depart from the principle of non-intervention which is our usual rule of conduct; to offend not only the government but the whole people of the United States, who are opposed to any intervention in the internal affairs of America."[69]

In 1862, longstanding American plans for a loan to Mexico to enable a repayment of foreign debts, the basis for a convention the British had signed in Mexico, failed due to opposition in the Senate.[70] The French took the intervention further, and the other powers withdrew, Lyons assuring Seward that the British government would not interfere in Mexico's internal affairs,[71] a stance shared by Spain[72] and supported for the opposition Conservatives in a parliamentary speech on 6 February by Benjamin Disraeli, their leader in the House of Commons. Mexico therefore showed the possibility of foreign intervention in the American Civil War, and also indicated the contrast between British and French policy, a contrast that was also to be (differently) seen in the case of the Civil War. This contrast raises a series of counterfactuals of which two are most instructive. First, the plausible counterfactual relates to how far the response to the American Civil War would have been different had there been no Mexican intervention; although there might have been no such intervention had America been more powerful.

Secondly, it is worth asking how far foreign intervention in the Civil War would have been more likely had France been stronger than Britain. This question raises the issue of the dependence of American developments on wider international events, or at least the close relationship between the two. The obvious conclusion is that, just as American independence owed much to the configurations of politics, in North America and more widely, in 1754–83, so the Union's success in 1861–65 rested in part on the earlier failure of Napoleon I to defeat Britain and/or to leave a European system in which France was the leading power, and therefore able to limit Britain's naval and colonial position. Such a system might have left his successors more influential in the New World, and, although Napoleon's seizure of the Spanish throne for his brother Joseph in 1808 was such that the relationship between Napoleonic power and the Latin Wars of Independence would have been problematic, a stronger France would have been better able to support power projection.

The extent to which, far from being exceptional, America was part of a wider international situation, however, made foreign intervention in the American Civil War less likely. France was already heavily involved in Mexico in 1862, and, with its leading military commitment being the longstanding one to Algeria, was also active elsewhere. In 1862, for example, the port of Obok in what became French Somaliland was acquired. France also conquered part of Indochina in 1858–63, a hard-fought campaign. Action against missionaries led to a Franco-Spanish expedition that seized Danang in 1858 and Saigon in 1859. Cochin China and Cambodia became French protectorates in 1863. Indeed, the range of French commitments, as well as the difficulties posed by supporting substantial forces in Mexico and at that distance, contributed to the situation in which too few troops were deployed in Mexico.

Spain under General Leopoldo O'Donnell, who had seized power in 1856 and held it until 1863, was already involved from 1859 in a series of imperial episodes that were intended to ensure public support, but which left few resources available for additional commitments. O'Donnell was an interventionist with a strong penchant for dramatic gestures on the international stage. Aside from intervention in Mexico in 1861, there was participation in French operations in Indochina. On its own, Spain was involved, with French[73] encouragement, in a campaign in Morocco in 1859–60, a conflict that concerned Britain,[74] as well as the resumption of control of Santo Domingo (now the Dominican Republic) in 1861 in order to help the president resist domestic opposition, and naval action in the Pacific against Bolivia, Chile, and Peru. The success in Morocco, which led to the capture of Tetuán and Ifni in 1860, brought patriotic support, but the cumulative pressure of these commitments was too great, and O'Donnell was affected by a rise in opposition from both radical and progressive directions. Support for the Confederacy, at any rate, was too great a task unless offered as part of a European coalition.

Britain was not committed in Mexico, but the French pressed Britain to repeat over America the diplomatic and military cooperation already seen in the previous decade against Russia and China. However, although Anglo-French relations were based on an understanding of the value of cooperation,[75] the volatile Napoleon III, with his opportunism and machinations, repeatedly posed a problem for the British. Palmerston was particularly suspicious of France, and his correspondence was full of his conviction of French enmity[76] as well as of suspicion of particular French steps, for example in Syria,[77] and rumored moves, such as reports of attempts to take over Iceland, Sardinia,[78] and an island in the Cape Verde Islands, the last as a naval coaling station.[79] Leaving aside Palmerston's concerns, there was a danger that Napoleon, who wished to direct British policy in the New World as well as Europe, would fight America to the very last Briton. Seward, indeed, told the Russian envoy that he had no fear of intervention because he was convinced that Britain and France would not agree on the subject.[80] An Anglo-French *entente,* however, also offered the prospect of a measure of security from

Union anger, and that also led to suggestions that a bigger coalition be assembled. In considering Union anger, Palmerston put military and diplomatic factors together, beginning with the seasonal geopolitics of North America:

> we should have less to care about their resentment in the spring when communi-cation with Canada opens, and when our naval force could more easily operate upon the American coast than in winter, when we are cut off from Canada and the American coast is not so safe.
>
> But if the acknowledgement were made at one and the same time by England, France and some other powers, the Yankee would probably not seek a quarrel with us alone, and would not like one against a European Confederation. Such a quarrel would render certain and permanent that southern independence, the acknowledgement of which would have caused it.

Palmerston thought it best not to offer mediation but, rather, to suggest direct talks between North and South; although he noted that if there was an armistice it would have to be accompanied by the end of the blockade or it would help the North: "the whole matter is full of difficulty, and can only be cleared up by some more decided events between the contending armies."[81]

The correspondence of the British ministers was perceptive about these difficulties, not least the incompatible preconditions of the two sides. Antietam definitely had an impact in leading to a stress on the problems involved in any negotiations, Palmerston cautiously observ-ing on 22 October 1862 that he was "inclined to change the opinion on which I wrote to you when the Confederates seemed to be carrying all before them, and I am very much come back to our original view of the matter, that we must continue merely to be lookers-on till the war shall have taken a more decided turn."[82] Napoleon III proposed to Britain and Russia that they recommend an armistice, a step that lent urgency to the ministerial discussions in Britain. Different scenarios were sketched out, including the North rejecting the Allies' good offices, which would have entitled the latter to recognize the South,[83] a course that Lyons saw as pointless unless the blockade was ended.[84] Conversely, there was the fear that Britain might be exposed to trouble if the North won,[85] an argument that the Americans were to use toward foreign powers.[86]

On 11 November, the Cabinet met and rejected the French proposal of joint intervention, a measure also urged by Belgium. Pope Pius IX's support for the Confederate cause was scarcely going to recommend it to Britain. As Gladstone, who argued at a public dinner in Newcastle on 7 October that the South "had so made a nation," and who had produced a paper advocating joint intervention, noted, Russell had "given up *the* point."[87] Somerset thought that raising the issue of an armistice might lead the American navy to become troublesome, and plans for naval reinforcements were therefore in hand. The four available ironclads were sent out to Lisbon from which they could be readily deployed to Bermuda, the key point from which to threaten the Chesapeake.[88] Had Gladstone been prime minister, the situation might have been more serious, but, as it was, he had infringed convention by speaking about another minister's brief and Adams was told by Russell that Gladstone's speech was not government policy, although Palmerston was more sympathetic.[89] Subsequently, Gladstone disavowed the position he had taken and spoke in favor of strict neutrality. Other ministers who supported mediation nevertheless felt that the moment was not yet opportune, in part because of the state of the campaigning, but also due to hopes that the midterm elections would see Democrat successes, and that then would be the time to suggest peace.[90]

European intervention would certainly have altered both the resource issue and pushed the question of naval power to the fore, not least as the blockade of the South was regarded as the key point.[91] Although the Confederacy contained about 30 percent of the country's wealth, the Union's advantages were formidable, not only in this wealth but also in the ease with which it could be employed. It had a 4:1 edge in manpower, which was significant in tactical, operational, and strategic terms. The Union also had a formidable advantage in manufacturing plant, railway track, and bullion resources, the gold and silver of the west being particularly important. The North had six times as many factories as the Confederacy and ten times its productive capacity, producing 97 percent of America's firearms, 94 percent of its pig iron, and 90 percent of its boots and shoes. The disparity was accentuated by the economic and financial dislocation of the Confederacy stemming from the Union blockade.

The Union also had a marked advantage in agricultural production, even though the South was more agricultural in character. The North had 800,000 draught animals to the South's 300,000, and the North's agricultural strength also rested on an ability to respond to new possibilities, specifically with agricultural machinery. As a consequence, wheat crops rose in 1862 and 1863, and wheat, corn, beef, and pork exports rose, even though about a third of the agricultural workforce served in the army and indeed had to be fed there. Supply problems in the Confederacy were far more serious and encouraged Lee to march into the North in 1862 and 1863: he hoped to gain food, shoes, and other supplies.

Helped by a wartime prosperity that impressed foreign observers,[92] the North also had a far greater capacity to raise both tax revenues and loans, and thus to finance what was, for America, a conflict of unprecedented expense and one that Lyons thought posed very serious financial problems. War bonds provided about two-thirds of the cost of the conflict, and the financial strength and stability of the North permitted the issue of close to $457 million of Treasury notes, which held their value well. Income tax and paper currency were introduced, although the latter had to be supported by government action. Union resources made it easier to equip the large numbers of troops that were raised. For example, nearly 1.5 million Springfield rifles were manufactured, a total that reflected the capacity of contemporary industry, and one that could not be matched in the Confederacy.

In April 1865, in his Farewell Address to his soldiers, Lee argued that they had been "compelled to yield to overwhelming power," a theme that was to be taken up often, as by Jubal Early, a Confederate general, in an 1872 address at Washington and Lee University. This argument, which was to contribute to the nostalgic "Lost Cause" view of Southern war making, was also employed, to a different purpose, by Union representatives seeking to explain to foreign powers why the North was bound to win and therefore the Confederacy should not receive support. Thus, reviewing the 1862 campaign in November of that year, William Dayton, the envoy in Paris, told the French foreign minister that the Confederacy was running out of men and money and that the Union's superiority in both was linked to its success.[93]

Yet, resources do not explain conflict, first because a host of factors affect their use and effectiveness and, second, because more than resources are involved in war. Thus, Lee's defeat owed much to the effectiveness of his opponents, especially from 1863.[94] As with World War I and II, there is a tendency to explain why one side lost, when the emphasis should rather be on why the other side won.

Generalship required the coordination and deployment of resources so that mass could be brought to bear, although this faced major problems. There were impressive aspects of planning and organization. For example, in 1861, in response to reports that the Confederates were building an ironclad warship, the Union navy created a board that called for ironclads and recommended the building of experimental vessels, so that effectiveness could be assessed. This, indeed, prompted a focus on ironclads, on the model of the *Monitor*.[95] More generally, such responsiveness drew on the resources of society, including patterns of associational behavior, high rates of literacy, and the ability to comprehend, tap, and organize productive resources, not least the capital investment required for the large-scale manufacture of weapons. These factors were important to the North's ability to overcome problems of military inexperience, logistics, and the size of campaigning area, to take war to the South and force it to surrender.[96]

Yet, it is necessary not to overestimate the sophistication of the organization on either side. They cannot be described as war machines, if that is intended to suggest predictable and regular operating systems that could be readily controlled and adapted, while the possibilities and problems created by the changing nature of war led to additional issues.[97] Resource strength was applied through logistical systems that could not cope adequately, while it proved difficult to make an effective use of resources on the battlefield. Moreover, despite the role of West Point and other military institutions in the prewar training of many future commanders on both sides, much of the command culture and many of the techniques were amateurish, specifically the limited ability to coordinate widely spread operations and the absence of high-grade general staff work. Poor command and staff work repeatedly helped throw away the chance of more striking victories,[98] which explains the importance of overcoming these problems.

As a result of this and other factors, the Union lacked an advantage equivalent to that which it had in overall resources. For example, superiority in manpower did not readily translate into trained troops on the battlefield, let alone the right battlefield. There was also an asymmetry of grand strategic aims, an asymmetry that helps explain international support for the idea of mediation: the Confederacy, ultimately, had only to fend off the Union, which did not require its conquest; whereas the Union had at least to crush Confederate military power and probably to occupy considerable swathes of the Confederacy in order to force it back into the Union. Thus, the weaker power was helped by having the more modest goal, while, for the Union, the failure of conciliation as a means to end the conflict was eventually linked to the definition of more radical war goals by Lincoln. These goals put even greater premium on military victory, while, in turn, this premium made the issue of warlike ardor and political determination in the North of importance.[99]

There was a parallel with the Mexican War of 1846–48, in that the Mexican unwillingness to negotiate forced the Americans both to defeat their armies, repeatedly, and to overrun more of Mexico than originally intended. However, the Confederacy was more united than Mexico, mounted a more sustained effort, and was in a position to inflict blows on core Union areas.

There was much still to fight for as 1862 came to its close. The elections had revealed the strength of support for the Democrats, as they took New York, New Jersey, Pennsylvania, Ohio, Indiana, Illinois, and Wisconsin, all bar New Jersey having voted for Lincoln in 1860. Yet, Lincoln's dismissal of McClellan after Antietam was taken as a defiance of the Democrats,[100] and, in returning to Washington from London via New York, Lyons noted that the Democrat leaders he met in the latter had had their hopes dashed that Lincoln would become more moderate and seek an end to the war. In a dispatch endorsed "For the Queen," he reported that these leaders were concerned that a "premature proposal" of foreign mediation would be used by the Radicals to revive the war spirit, and thus to thwart the Democrats. Lyons agreed and argued that the present was an inopportune moment to offer mediation, but that there might be a change of mood after Congress ended in March 1863 if no great military success had been obtained by then. Lyons also noted that any offer would be best made by Britain, France, and Russia jointly, and certainly not by Britain alone,[101] as he thought Britain uniquely unpopular.[102] Drouyn de l'Huys, the French foreign minister, told the American envoy that Britain's stance affected French options.[103]

Lyons reported that, for political reasons, McClellan's replacement, Ambrose Burnside, had been told to cross the Rappahannock River at Fredericksburg and march on Richmond, despite the winter season.[104] Antietam, however, did not end foreign attention to the possibility that the campaigning would lead to an outcome other than that of Northern victory. Indeed, Gladstone responded on 27 December to the news of Southern victory at Fredericksburg a fortnight earlier by writing, "surely this will end the madness," by showing the North that it could not win.[105]

The wider international context was scarcely defined by the American crisis. Sir Frederick Grey, the First Naval Lord of the Admiralty, noted "we have an insurrection in Greece or rather a revolution and little quarrels of our own both with Brazil and Chile so our hands are full."[106] In Greece, King Otho was deposed in 1862, the crisis, which involved a British naval deployment,[107] ending in 1863 when George I was elected by the Greek National Assembly. In 1863, the Polish crisis was to focus European attention, dividing Russia from France and leading Palmerston to fear Napoleon III's ambitions. This division was taken forward into the Schleswig-Holstein crisis of 1863–64. Important developments in North America were to attract less attention than they might, and this separateness of America from the European system provided the Union with a vital margin of opportunity.

# 14

## WINNING THE WAR
## 1863-65

"If there be a decided victory one way or the other, it will be an event of very great importance, but drawn battles seem the rule in this war." Lord Lyons began 1863 by reporting on "a great battle" then going on at Stones River in Tennessee.[1] To foreign observers, there appeared no obvious end to the conflict. The battle of Antietam had ended expectations of such a result through Southern victory, but the opposite still seemed far distant. Instead, there was a belief that the North would focus on making secondary theaters the deciding places. Indeed, Lyons had reported on 24 November 1862 that Charleston was seriously threatened with attack, and he added, "The real object of this government now is their campaign on the Mississippi and their attacks on the Southern ports. The Grand Army of the Potomac will do as much as is wanted, if it protect Washington."[2] Seward told Lyons that success would lead to control over the cotton that could be marketed yielding valuable funds.[3]

Yet, this strategy had only a limited impact on European observers, in part because the ports did not fall as anticipated. Lyons, indeed, reported on 5 December 1862 that he did not think that Charleston would be attacked, and it only fell on 18 February 1865. Without army support, naval attack could prove unsuccessful, as Union warships discovered at Charleston in April 1863, a failure that Milne thought likely to lead to "some change in the operation of the war."[4] Similarly, on 14 January 1863, Lyons reported that the Union forces would probably attack Wilmington, which, in the event, also fell only in January 1865.[5] Moreover, the Mississippi campaign, although eventually successful in 1863, took a while, and, in early January, Lyons reported a severe Union repulse at Vicksburg.[6]

There are problems with applying modern notions of strategic clarity and planning, because the Union army lacked an equivalent to the navy's Blockade Board that, newly established in 1861, laid down coherent strategic recommendations that remained valid for the rest of the war.[7] Contemporaries were uncertain as to how the geography of the war worked, in terms of the relationships between spheres of operations, and this uncertainty affected discussion of strategy. These relationships, in turn, became a matter of scholarly discussion and encouraged a concern with the role of geography in the planning and conduct of the war.[8] Yet, this role was less apparent to contemporary foreign commentators than with the benefit of hindsight.

Alongside the problem at the strategic level were serious deficiencies at the operational one. The Americans conformed more to the French system of muddling through than to the Prussian practice of training staff officers. The extent to which many officers gained positions through volunteering and political influence,[9] and the absence of effective command structures, meant that mediocrities were not tested adequately before being entrusted with independent command, nor removed sufficiently rapidly thereafter. Histories of particular armies and studies of individual generals are frequently an account of squandered opportunities.[10]

In early 1863, Lyons was clearly convinced that the North was in difficulties not only in its military operations but also on the Home Front, with political opposition matched by problems in recruiting new troops and continuing existing ones, a view shared by the French and Russian envoys. On 1 February, he suggested that "the war must come practically to an end for want of men and money," adding, a fortnight later, that news from Charleston and Vicksburg was important to the politics of the struggle within the North: "There is no doubt that the mass of the people are heartily tired of the war and the army not less tired than the rest – but have not yet made up their minds to separation [Southern independence], and they see that peace at this moment means separation."[11]

The possibility that external intervention would affect this situation was raised in America and abroad. On 9 February, the House of Representatives was warned that "unless some success in a short time crowns our arms, does not every man in this House feel that the nations of Europe will essay to intervene in our affairs," and, indeed, in early 1863, the French government pressed the Union to negotiate directly with the Confederacy without suspending hostilities, only to have the approach rejected by the Union, which insisted on unconditional surrender.[12] Aside from opposition to such negotiations, France's position was compromised by anger about the policy of Napoleon III in Mexico, and indeed, on 3 February, critical resolutions about the latter were introduced in the Senate.

Convinced that independence for the Confederacy was best, Henri Mercier, the French envoy, saw foreign action as a necessary precondition. He complained to Lyons: "American politicians are timid. They sought to sail with the current – they followed public opinion, they did not attempt to lead it. Now separation was an idea too repugnant to the pride of the people to be willingly admitted, and those Americans who themselves entertained it were afraid to announce it boldly. 'Impulsion' from abroad might be eminently useful in such a case." Mercier argued that the war might end if Britain and France recognized the Confederacy, and that Russian support was worth seeking, but Lyons retorted that the failure of the French proposals had compromised the idea of European mediation, and Britain was against interfering by force.[13] Moreover, that July, meetings of the Conservative leadership confirmed that the opposition was opposed to recognition of the South.[14]

The French attitude helped draw suspicion and unpopularity in the Union away from Britain,[15] and Lyons became more confident that he could finesse disputes. The most dangerous seemed to be that the Union would, as threatened, issue letters of marque for privateers, enabling them to detain neutral ships on charges of breaches of blockade, and that the activities of the privateers would lead to clashes.[16] As a consequence, Lyons was glad that Milne abandoned the idea of a cruise in Caribbean waters, a deployment that would make it harder to bring the threat to bear of the prompt use of force against the Union.[17]

Relations, however, were put at risk by the *Alabama* affair.[18] This was a commerce raider built at Birkenhead on the Mersey for the Confederacy, and the British government's role in permitting the construction of this large (990 tons) and fast ship became a matter of great controversy, as it seemed to present a serious linkage of British industry with the Confederate cause. Sailing from the Mersey on 15 May 1862, the *Alabama* collected its armament outside Britain in the Azores, but there was little doubt of its intention, and the ship captured (numbers vary) between sixty-nine and seventy-one merchantmen before being sunk off Cherbourg on 19 June 1864 by the Union warship *Kearsage,* an event seen from shore and thus recorded on canvas by Edouard Manet. The *Florida,* which had sailed in March 1861, was another successful raider.

While the *Alabama* was at Birkenhead, the Union made representations to the British, which the government referred to its law officers for advice, but the ship was not detained pending their report, and it was able to set sail on 29 July 1862. On 27 March 1863, Lyons wrote: "There is so violent an exasperation now against England, on account of the proceedings of the 'Alabama' and of the rumours that other such ships are fitting out in our ports for the Confederates – that it is more than usually necessary to be careful not to give our susceptible friends any just cause of offence."[19] Subsequently, he noted an increase in anger, and the danger that letters of marque would be issued if Britain did not adopt a satisfactory policy.[20] Lyons was also concerned about the actions of American warships, and feared that because many naval officers wanted war with Britain, they ignored conciliatory instructions.

Populism also played a role: "The universal exasperation in the country against England makes the government unwilling and afraid to do anything which looks like a concession to us."[21] The Democrats had failed to derive the anticipated benefit from the 1862 elections.[22] The floating in London of a loan for the Confederacy also angered Union opinion, although Lyons pointed out that business transactions with belligerents were acceptable in international law.[23]

The crisis leads us to consider likely outcomes. Naval confrontation with Britain would have led to the risk of an escalation of conflict, and there was the danger that any clashes might result in full-scale war. At sea, British entry into the conflict would have transformed the Civil War. In part, British strength was a product of European power politics. The threat of French naval power had encouraged heavy British investment in the navy in order to ensure security and thus maintain diplomatic freedom, and the two powers took part in an ironclad naval race in 1859–65 that was won by Britain with its greater resources and commitment.[24]

The French had the infrastructure to build a few big iron ships, but not a new fleet, while the British had been building large iron ships for some time and also benefited from superior-quality iron plate. In contrast, the Americans faced problems arising from the lack of capability for rolling iron plates of this quality. The British had the experience of the merchant marine, of skilled shipbuilding, and of ambitions and innovative naval architects such as Isambard Kingdom Brunel on whom to draw. Moreover, greater number of British naval bases capable of servicing warships by mid-century created a more visible presence in the North Atlantic and thus contributed to a deterrent capability.

However, the extent to which steam power and iron ships might have changed the nature of naval warfare by 1865 was unclear, owing to the paucity of naval battles over the previous decade. In part, the Union developed ironclads in order to be able to resist the danger of British intervention, and both built up its confidence in the event of war and reduced Britain's political leverage by doing so.[25] However, aside from the problems of acquiring coal when America lacked colonial bases,[26] American ironclads were designed for coastal service and were not really suitable for long-range service on the high seas or, indeed, service in heavy seas.[27]

Yet, the overall strategic rationale for the American navy facing the threat of a foreign war was to use coastal ironclads for defense and commerce raiders for offense, possibly coupled with military operations against Canada and perhaps even against British imperial bases in the Atlantic and Caribbean. The navy assumed that a few marked repulses to any British offensives along the eastern seaboard, as well as mounting losses to the British merchant marine worldwide, would eventually dampen any British mandate for war against the Northern states.

Much of this was due to developments at the tactical level. American monitor-ironclads were designed to fight at close quarters; 1,000 yards or less. As these vessels were largely submerged below the waterline, offering only a concentrated armor protection scheme along the exposed (18-inch) hull and especially the gun turrets, it was quite reasonable to assume that enemy fire would not be effective against this target profile until the 15-inch guns of the monitors began to tell in response. Naval combat before, during, and after the Civil War confirmed that reliable naval gunnery was still in the "Age-of-Sail," despite the advent of rifled heavy cannon. Battle was still confused – noisy, clouded with smoke – and accuracy was always at the mercy of the slightest pitch and roll of the vessel. As a result, the raft-like feature of the monitors, as gun platforms, made them much more stable than the high-freeboard, broadside iron-clads of the European variety.

As for the hitting power of the American 15-inch Rodman (Army) or Dahlgren (Navy) guns themselves, Civil War ironclad engagements proved time and again that at effective combat ranges, no armor afloat could possibly resist a 450-pound shot propelled by 50–60 1b. service charges. In 1863, the CSS *Atlanta* was reduced to surrender after three hits from the 15-inch gun of the monitor USS *Weehawken*, one of which blasted a 3-foot-wide hole in her casemate armor. True, this armor was "laminated" with two layers of 2-inch iron plates. But these were rolled, wrought-iron plates, backed by 24 inches of wood, and angled at nearly 40° to the horizon on point of impact. Furthermore, the shot in question struck at a compound angle, meaning that even more armor and backing was offered to resist the shot, a cored shot of 330 1bs. The same experiment was demonstrated against the 5- and 6-inch thick armor of the CSS *Tennessee* (at Mobile Bay, 1864) and the 6-inch armor of the CSS *Virginia II* (at Trent's Reach, 1865) with similar results, demonstrating the effectiveness of the American ordnance.

The primary concern for Union ironclad designers, especially John Ericsson, however, was the 4- and then 6-inch armor plating of ocean-going British ironclads, from *Warrior* to *Bellerophon*, the Reed-designed "central-battery" broadside-and-sail ironclad. While the *Warrior's* armor, for example, consisted of solid rolled plates of 4.5-inch thickness backed by 18 inches of teak and a thin iron inner "skin," the sides of the vessel were vertical; deflection would not assist, as in the case of Confederate casemates. *Warrior's* plating was also defective at the joints. To confirm by firsthand experience themselves, the American navy, in 1862–63, procured rolled iron plates from the same British and French companies producing armor for their own nations' ironclad fleets. These were then backed by up to 3 feet of wood – and the targets packed against a solid hillside bank of clay. Nevertheless, 15-inch smoothbores tore ragged holes through these structures, not only penetrating the iron and wood but also leaving the plates themselves "shattered" and "brittle" around the point of impact.

All of this, however, argued little for actual British ironclads afloat during the American Civil War; namely *Warrior* and her sister-ship *Black Prince*, the *Defence* and *Resistance*, *Achilles*, and a few wooden ironclad conversions – all protected with 4.5-inch iron armor plates. By 1864, the U.S. Army and then Navy had already produced 20-inch guns that packed approximately double the hitting power of the 15-inch varieties. Rates of fire were reduced, but this mattered little when lighter-caliber weapons could effect no appreciable damage in the meantime against the turret armor of the American monitors, by 1864 up to 15 inches in thickness. Armor plates arrayed in a turret structure were also found to be innately stronger overall to resist the force of impact and therefore penetration than thick slabs bolted onto the broadside. Monitor turret armor proved impervious at even point-blank ranges to Confederate 10-inch Columbiads firing shot weighing 168 1bs, as opposed to the 68-pound smoothbores of *Warrior* and her sisters. Moreover, the monitor form of ironclad at least enabled upgrades without requiring an entirely new design of ship to float the armor of equal weight.

Thus, any European ironclad would have done well to stay clear of Union monitors, and a blockade would have been too hazardous for Britain sensibly to risk capital ships. In order to be any real threat to the Union, the Royal Navy needed to invest in a Brown Water ironclad force to operate effectively in North American coastal waters.[28] In addition to the problems posed by the American monitors, the fast wooden-screw steamers authorized by Congress in 1864 would, it was feared, act as "a chain across the great lines of commerce,"[29] and this concern led to the British building fast, unarmored iron-hulled warships in response.

There was also the Canada issue, notably the danger that, as in 1775, 1812, 1813, and 1814, war would be accompanied by an American invasion, an invasion that greater American economic and demographic strength, as well as the improvement in communications, and potentially large numbers of battle-hardened troops, made more threatening. British sensitivities led to defense planning, although vulnerability on the Canadian frontier would have been reduced by the Union's acute need for troops against the Confederacy, and the problems the Union forces faced in the key campaign zone of Virginia were underlined by their defeat at Chancellorsville on 1–4 May 1863, even if this battle failed to produce positive strategic consequences for the Confederacy. There was also a tendency in Europe for armies and commentators to underrate the Civil War, treating it as a conflict waged by amateur militia.[30]

In November 1861, Captain William Noble of the Royal Engineers produced a memorandum on the situation on the Canadian lakes and the assistance that could be provided by the Royal Navy. He argued that once war broke out, the British needed to act speedily to capture the fort at Rouses Point at the upper end of Lake Champlain, both in order to protect Montreal and to cut a key link between New York and Ogdensburg, the main American town on the St. Lawrence River. Noble pointed out that the American presence on that waterway was a threat to British communications, and, indeed, the only railway from Montreal to Kingston and points further west went along its north bank. Noble also saw an American threat to the Welland Canal on the Niagara peninsula, the key link between Lakes Ontario and Erie and one close to the frontier. Indeed, the Trent affair led Lyons to fear a filibustering expedition of Irish Americans to attack the canal.[31] In addition, Noble called for a British naval squadron on Lake Huron.[32] There were worries about reported American intentions to establish a naval station and dockyard in Michigan,[33] while the defenses of Bermuda were upgraded.[34]

Another memorandum, from December 1861, suggested that six lines of battleships, eleven frigates, twenty-three sloops, and twenty gunboats would be necessary to blockade the Union's Atlantic ports, a number endorsed by Milne as "entirely inadequate."[35] That such action would entail cooperation with the Confederacy was recognized by the memorandum's observation that coal could be obtained from its ports if the blockade were raised.[36] Indeed, the following month, Milne pointed out that "the *daily use of steam* would be a matter of necessity" in any blockade.[37]

In 1863, concern increased as the Americans discussed enlarging canals to enable warships to move from the Atlantic and Mississippi to the Great Lakes, although, ultimately, Congress decided that it was more appropriate to build up its naval facilities on the lakes.[38] Lieutenant-Colonel William Jervois, a key individual as deputy director of fortifications, who visited Canada in the autumns of 1863 and 1864, presented the Royal Navy as a means to help defend Canada. He noted that "although, owing to the length and nature of the frontier of Canada, it was impossible to protect it throughout its whole extent, an enemy must nevertheless acquire possession of certain vital points before he could obtain any decided military advantages; – that there are only a few small points." Jervois regarded these as chiefly Montreal and Quebec and the river between, which were to be protected by iron-plated vessels, and argued that, if these were held, there could be "a successful resistance ... so long as Great Britain had command of the sea." He argued that 90,000 troops would suffice to defend Canada from Kingston to Quebec inclusive, whereas the United States would require 250,000 to 300,000 to mount a successful attack, and that, at the same time, it would be necessary to protect the coast.[39]

Thus, British naval capability had both an interior/continental aspect, in the shape of warships on rivers and lakes, and a key oceanic component. The defense of Canada therefore conformed with the British strategic culture outlined in 1856 by Sir John Burgoyne, inspector-general of fortifications, who noted that Britain needed to rely for its defense on its navy and fortifications because "the peace establishment of its land forces is insignificant as compared with those by which it may be assailed; and we may assume that the feelings of the country, its policy, and perhaps its real interests, render it impossible to vie, in its standing military establishments, with the continental powers."[40] Indeed, Burgoyne commented that year on the threat posed by an oceanic power in a way that threw light on a potential clash later during the Civil War:

> The progress in the state of gunnery and steam navigation renders it necessary to reconsider from time to time the principles of attack and defence of coasts and harbours. Whatever improvements may be made in land batteries, their entire adequacy for the purpose of defence cannot be certain against the rapidity of steamers and the facility of their manoeuvring power ... but they may be powerful in combination with ... the floating batteries with their sides coated with thick iron plates.[41]

During the Civil War, the Confederacy also used torpedoes and mines to protect its coastal waters. Nevertheless, the fate of coastal positions showed the vulnerability of masonry forts to large rifled guns,[42] and, indeed, on 23 April 1856, the American envoy in London had been one of the diplomats treated to a display of the new coastal-assault force of steam gunboats and mortar vessels.

The limited nature of the rail system posed a problem to the reinforcement of Canada by sea, because troops landed at Halifax could only cross as far as the Bay of Fundy and Moncton by rail. The rail route to the St. Lawrence was not completed until 1876, although from Rivière-du-Loup on that estuary there was were tracks to Montreal from 1859. The Victoria Bridge across the St. Lawrence at Montreal, an impressive feat of engineering officially opened in 1860, was the final link to the Grand Trunk Line on to Sarnia on Lake Huron, and an important demonstration of imperial capability. Yet, given the ferocious debates in Parliament over Palmerston's forts to protect southern England against French attack, it was difficult to see where the money would have come from to refortify Canada adequately.

Canada's defenses appeared at issue because of a number of issues, including Confederate attempts in 1863 and 1864 to organize attacks thence on Union territories, notably the capture of Union ships on Lake Erie and a raid on St. Albans, Vermont, on 19 October 1864 in which three Americans were killed. Nevertheless, despite government and popular complaints, the American response was not bellicose while the British helped to thwart other attempts.[43] The British also tried to stop the supply of arms and ammunition to hostile Native Americans, for example the Sioux in Minnesota in 1863.[44] In 1865, the Canadian Parliament passed an Alien Act aimed at Confederate activists.

Neither government took provocative steps over, or after, the *Alabama* affair. For example, Seward reassured Lyons about rumors that preparations in California were intended to threaten British Columbia,[45] while most of British public opinion remained unwilling to enter the Civil War. Few Britons, outside of the cotton-manufacturing centers of Lancashire and a few radicals such as John Arthur Roebuck, William Schaw Lindsay, and George Reynolds, were ever in favor of entering the war, although that did not mean that there was wider agreement over the merits of the war and concerning British policy.[46]

Although British exports to America were hit by the protectionist Morrill Tariff passed in 1861, affecting British attitudes to the North,[47] Canada itself benefited greatly from the economic opportunities opened up by the large-scale growth in U.S. government expenditures made necessary by the war. Agricultural and industrial goods, such as Montreal boots, flowed south, while immigration was encouraged by the introduction of the draft in America, although Canadian industry was badly affected by the American ban on exports of anthracite coal, an issue that testified to the linkages provided by economic growth.[48] Moreover, the U.S. Senate refused to renew the Fisheries Reciprocity Treaty of 1854, and Congress considered the repeal of the act allowing free transit rights for goods to and from Canada.

The British ministry pursued a policy of careful, but conciliatory, vigilance. Russell noted in March 1863: "I do not apprehend anything unless our naval forces on the American station and our troops in Canada are diminished."[49] The following month, Somerset instructed Milne accordingly: "The irritation on the part of the Federals on account of the *Alabama* and probably also of the numerous deceits which have been practiced upon them by the assumption of the British flags renders Lord Russell anxious that you should still continue in a central position from which you may be able to watch and to advise on the innumerable questions which arise and which cannot be foreseen."[50] At the same time, the British government took the necessary steps to prevent the construction of further warships for the Confederacy, being careful to block the risks posed by the use of intermediaries. A key instance arose later that year, again at Birkenhead, and Russell, anxious to avoid a repetition of the *Alabama* case, acted more swiftly, and with a willingness to test the law, albeit cautiously, that was a pale shadow of the policies of the Lincoln government, driven as they were by the exigencies of war:

> The conduct of the gentlemen who have contracted for the ironclads at Birkenhead is so very suspicious that I have thought it necessary to direct that they should be detained. The Solicitor-General has been consulted and concurs in the measure as one of policy though not of strict law. We shall thus test the law, and if we have to pay damages we have satisfied the opinion which prevails here, as well as in America, that this kind of neutral hostility should not be allowed to go on without some attempt to stop it.[51]

Charles Adams, the American envoy, sent a note to Russell on 5 September that threatened war if the ships were allowed to leave the harbor. The pragmatic Palmerston recommended that Britain buy the two ships, "Laird rams" equipped with "rams" intended to smash in the wooden hulls of Union warships, in question,[52] and that was done for £220,000 each but only after they had been detained, blockaded, and boarded, a clear demonstration of the primacy of policy of state over legal complexities. Seward was secretly informed in advance. Moreover, pro-Confederate lobbying was again defeated in Parliament, a call for recognition of the Confederacy failing in the Commons on 30 June, and on 10 August Russell rejected Mason's request to alter Britain's stance on the blockade. The government's position was supported by the Conservative opposition.

The purchase of the "rams" was scarcely the action of ministers seeking war, and there was also restraint on the American side, albeit also a significant clash between Seward and Gideon Welles, the Secretary of the Navy. The U.S. government needed to stop Britain providing a navy for the Confederacy, but, in searching for a way to avoid war, Lincoln focused on expedients that would preserve the peace. These were more important to him than either legal interpretations or public anger. Lyons noted, "There is a want of firmness in checking individual officers who transgress international law, but certainly a strong desire on the part of those highest in authority here that no transgressions should take place."[53]

Charles Sumner, the chairman of the Senate Committee on Foreign Affairs, was convinced that any war with Britain would be wide-ranging and not restricted to North America. He warned John Bright, a radical Liberal politician, that the Irish would take the opportunity to rebel against British rule, and suggested that Russia would fight France. To Sumner, American Anglophilia was at risk and "western civilization" at stake.[54] In practice, Sumner was a notorious anglophobe who, relying on Cobden and Bright's alarmist correspondence, misunderstood Britain's position. Cobden passed on Sumner's warnings to Russell.[55] The possibility of war, nevertheless, eased after the *Alabama* crisis, despite the fact that in a dispatch of April 1864 printed for the benefit of the Cabinet, alongside the detailed accompanying naval report, Lyons warned of bitter anglophobia and American willingness to consider an attack on Britain.[56] In part, the easing of tensions reflected the gradual working out of a form of modus vivendi between the two powers, so that, for example, Lyons advised that if a warship be sent to Charleston he hoped that the captain would be "conciliatory and cool headed."[57] In January 1864, the American government took care to reassure the British that no warships would be supplied to Japan until its differences with Britain were over.[58]

Yet other factors also played a role. The defeat of Lee's second march north at Gettysburg was important. In June 1863, Lyons observed, "A battle, a great slaughter, and no result has hitherto been the end of such a meeting between the armies as seems to be imminent,"[59] but that scarcely described Gettysburg, fought from 1 to 3 July. Lee retreated after the battle and this combined with Grant's success at Vicksburg on the Mississippi, which surrendered on 4 July, to suggest that a major shift in the balance of advantage had occurred. Lee's army fought again, but at Vicksburg the Confederacy lost an army, while the western Confederacy in effect shrank as the Trans-Mississippi ceased to be an integral part of the war effort.[60] Any European intervention on behalf of the Confederates now appeared less plausible.

Moreover, France's primary interest in the Americas was in Mexico. Napoleon III was also concerned about Russian-ruled Poland, where the suppression of a large-scale, but poorly organized, Polish rebellion[61] maintained the territorial order created in the late eighteenth century and reinforced in 1814–15, an outcome unwelcome to Napoleon. France, supported in part by the British ministry, was interested in the idea of an independent Poland; but this idea was unwelcome to Russia, whose government took the view that the insurrection was simply an internal affair, a view that was directly pertinent to the American Civil War.

The Polish crisis was important to European international developments, both then and subsequently, and, as a result, also greatly affected the situation in North America. The crisis led to the end of the Franco-Russian alliance and also weakened relations between France and Britain, the Cabinet of which rejected, on 24 June 1863, the French proposal for a joint declaration on Poland by Britain, France, and Austria. The failure to agree on this made any later joint declaration on America unlikely and throws light on the earlier lack of such action. Parliamentarians also took a controversial view on the crisis, with Gladstone having to speak in the Commons on 20 July 1863 in defense of Palmerston's conduct in it. Again, this underlined the risk of action.

Separately, relations between Britain and Russia were tense because of British concerns about Russian expansionism in Central Asia, while Alexander II was also seeking an opportunity to recover prestige from the blow to Russia's international position suffered as a result of the Crimean War of 1854–56. Already, in 1859, Russia had offered to sell Alaska to America, a step seen as challenging Britain's position in the Pacific, while, in 1860–61, the Russian navy had played a role in the Middle East. In 1863, six Russian warships were sent to New York and others to San Francisco, in part to benefit from any tension between Britain and the Union. Aside from uneasy relations with Britain, Alexander II's emancipation of Russia's serfs in 1861 led to a degree of sympathy from Union abolitionists. Congressional interest in early 1862 in surveying a telegraph route across the north Pacific from San Francisco to the Amur estuary as a key link between American and Russian communication systems testified not only to American interest in East Asia, including the Philippines and Australia, but also a belief in the value of good relations with Russia.[62]

The Polish Crisis looked toward later international tensions. Prussia gained more freedom for maneuver in European power politics as a result of the new tensions between Britain, France, and Russia, while, by the end of the crisis, Austria had alienated both sides, which helped Prussia further.[63] The Polish crisis led into that over Schleswig-Holstein, duchies with large German populations that were joined to the Crown of Denmark by a personal union. Frederick VII of Denmark sought to strengthen this link by incorporating Schleswig into Denmark, a step that led the German Confederation to threaten military action. Palmerston recommended that Frederick withdraw this constitution, but on 23 July 1863 he told Parliament that if any power tampered with Danish independence, "it would not be Denmark alone with which they would have to contend." The recent marriage of the Prince of Wales to Alexandra, the daughter of Frederick's heir, Christian of Glücksberg, a marriage that had attracted enormous attention in Britain,[64] was a significant complication, but it was unclear how Britain should respond. In

September, Russell withdrew from a draft the pro-Danish remark that Britain would regard foreign intervention in Holstein as an act of international hostility.

That November, the Danish parliament ratified the incorporation of Schleswig, but this step was unacceptable to the German Confederation, which invaded to give effect to its demand for the abrogation of this constitution. Danish refusal led to the outbreak of fighting on 1 February 1864, and to an Austro-Prussian invasion of Schleswig. In response to the Danish request for assistance, Russell, without Cabinet approval, proposed a joint naval demonstration in the Baltic to France and Russia, but Gladstone complained and, on 24 February, the Cabinet refused to send a British squadron to Copenhagen. Palmerston was against joint action, as he did not trust Napoleon III's intentions.

American pressure on Denmark not to seize postal steamers sailing to America from Bremen led to an instructive discussion about the changing nature of the public context of foreign policy. Seward told Colonel Raasloff, the Danish envoy, that the government "felt it impossible not to do something towards satisfying the German population of the United States." Raasloff told Lyons that this approach posed a serious problem:

> that if a large portion of the population regarded themselves not merely as citizens of the United States but also as retaining a distinct European nationality which entitled them to impose a policy inspired by that nationality upon the government of this country, the political relations between Denmark and the American government must be very much disturbed.

Such "hyphenation" was a theme that would be developed later in American history. Raasloff was also concerned that this issue would become more significant as the election approached.[65] Similarly, in response to calls from the New York-based Board of Delegates of American Israelites, Seward pressed Lyons on the treatment of Jews in Morocco.[66] An awareness of such pressures broadened out British concerns, apparent since the 1830s, about the role of Irish Americans in populist politics, concerns that remained strong in the 1860s.[67]

In Cabinet on 30 April 1864, Russell proposed the dispatch of a British squadron to the entrance of the Baltic, with instructions to stop the Adriatic-based Austrian fleet from entering it, but the Cabinet rejected the idea. In a situation of great fluidity, Napoleon sought an agreement with Prussia, while the British Cabinet on 25 June again debated the dispatch of a fleet, agreeing, only on Palmerston's casting vote, to decide not to do so. Defeated, the outnumbered Danes were driven to accept an armistice in July, and, three months later, by the Treaty of Vienna, to surrender Schleswig and Holstein to joint Austrian and Prussian control. Palmerston lost a motion of censure over his conduct in the Lords and only narrowly survived it in the Commons.[68]

This was not the background for unilateral or joint action in America, and thus the international situation greatly improved for the Union side. This improvement was taken further by serious French problems in Mexico. Napoleon III's attempt to take over the country was mishandled and met a strong nationalist response. Unlike in the American Civil War, and, again, indicating the range of possible outcomes, there was a long guerrilla war led by Benito Juárez, a war with few conventional battles. Despite deploying forty thousand troops at the peak and enjoying additional Austrian military support, as well as deploying Egyptian and Belgian contingents, the French had insufficient forces to defeat Juárez. They had naval strength on both coastlines, enabling them for example to capture Guaymas in March 1865 and to thwart an attack on Matamoros that spring by reinforcing it by sea; but on land, despite successful counterinsurgency policies in some areas, the French were unable to progress from seizing positions to stabilizing the situation. Advances led to the fall of positions, as when Puebla was successfully besieged in 1863, falling on 17 May, or when the French successfully besieged Oxaca in February 1865, having built roads in order to bring up their siege guns and cut the garrison off from water supplies. However, it then proved difficult to consolidate control. Guerrilla resistance helped compensate the Liberals/Republicans for failures in battle, as at San Luis Potosí in 1863.[69] Using classical references that made his bias readily apparent, Peter Scarlett, the British envoy, reported in February 1865:

> Fresh bands of guerrillas seem to start up everywhere like the heads of the hydra as often as others are put down, and partly from the natural and habitual love of a plundering life on the part of a lawless and ruffianly population, and partly from the inadequate and insufficient number of foreign troops, especially cavalry, to deal with this evil, the eradication of it is indeed a labour of Hercules.[70]

Contemporary speculations and contingency planning in the American Civil War (as well as later counterfactuals) ceased to be those of foreign intervention, although Britain remained anxious about Canada's defenses, while Mexico continued to be a central issue in relations between France and the Union. In 1863, Lincoln became concerned about the buildup of French forces in Mexico, their capture of Mexico City, the stage-managed offer in 1863 of the crown to Archduke Ferdinand-Joseph Maximilian of Austria (he was crowned Emperor of Mexico in 1864), the subsequent move of French units toward the American border in order to suppress opposition in northern Mexico where Juárez's support was concentrated, and the nature of French intentions. The major failure of the Union's Red River Expedition, an attempt to invade Texas in the spring of 1864, revealed Union weaknesses in the Trans-Mississippi. It was reported that France saw its presence in Mexico as a bar to American dominance of the region, and Napoleon III was certainly opposed to the Monroe Doctrine.[71] There were also reports in 1865 that France was seeking a territorial position in Mexico, and these were linked to French interest in colonization by Confederate supporters, in part in order to ensure that mines were worked successfully and revenues raised to reimburse French loans.[72] Lincoln had long been anxious about French moves there, and, during the American Civil War, Juárez received covert support from Union forces. Lincoln's concern led him to clash in 1863 with Halleck, the general-in-chief of the army. Lincoln wanted Union forces built up on the Texas coast in order to address the threat he saw posed by the French army in Mexico, but Halleck circumvented these instructions because he did not share this concern and, in contrast, saw deployment to Texas as part of the strategy for action against the Confederacy.[73]

Affected by Congressional pressure, Seward, although cautious about appearing to dictate the nature of Mexico's government,[74] protested French policy, while in 1864 Lincoln pressed successfully for the dispatch of a Union force to the Texas coast. That April, the House of Representatives unanimously passed a resolution that it would not acknowledge "any monarchical government erected on the ruins of any republican government in America under the auspices of any European power," a position very much contrasting with Palmerston's view that Mexico needed a monarch.

By 1864, the Union was taking a more active international stance in which they sought to elicit cooperation as well as to display strength. In May, Seward, in pressing Lyons about Spanish conduct toward Peru and Santo Domingo, suggested that the two states cooperate in order to settle the dispute. The possibility of Spanish action against Haiti was a matter of concern the following month.[75] That September, the U.S. corvette *Jamestown* cooperated with British, French, and Dutch warships in Japanese waters, in acting against batteries erected by the Prince of Nagato that threatened the international use of the Straits of Shimonoseki by foreign shipping.

As the international situation became more benign, so counterfactuals, instead, came to focus largely on operations within America. The possibility that Confederate success would lead to a change of government in the North was voiced in both 1862 and 1863, and, indeed, became more of an issue as Union goals became more radical. In November 1862, the North's envoy in Paris told the French foreign minister that "neither principle nor policy will induce the United States to encourage a 'servile war' or prompt the slave to cut the throat of his master or his master's family,"[76] a clear reference to deep-seated racial anxieties. Nevertheless, war goals and military methods changed in response to the difficulty of the conflict, changes that again underline the limitations of a geopolitical account, but that indicated the extent to which a difficult conflict could help radicalize the situation. Whereas McClellan opposed attacks on private property, Grant pressed it from the spring of 1862 in order to hit Confederate supplies and, thus, war-making ability. Similarly, Major-General John Pope, commander of the Union's Army of Virginia in 1862, agreed with the Republicans, not McClellan, and claimed that it was legitimate to confiscate rebel property and move civilians who refused to take the oath of allegiance. His army destroyed a large amount of property and thus made its presence unwelcome. Union forces responded harshly to opposition by becoming more destructive, and especially by living off the land.[77] Moreover, there were significant pressures on the home front, where frustration with the intractability of the struggle led to an abandonment of conciliation toward Southerners in late 1862.[78]

This change was an instance of political parameters being affected by military factors. McClellan had pursued a quick victory by means of a victorious advance in Virginia alongside a conciliatory strategy to undermine Southern support for the rebellion, but this plan was wrecked by failure. McClellan, who had advocated modest war goals as part of a general conciliatory Union approach, a policy that reflected his political engagement as a Democrat,[79] was replaced by Lincoln after Antietam. Instead, as hopes of a quick war faded, the emphasis came to be on how best to win a long conflict, an emphasis that led to a greater concern on securing control of the Mississippi Valley, while conciliation ceased to be the political goal,[80] and the conduct of the war became more brutal, although not in comparison with the contemporary conflict in Mexico or with the hostilities involving Native Americans.[81] Moreover, the Union's insistence that Southerners were still American citizens affected their treatment.[82]

Initially, the Union had made no attempt to abolish slavery, both because Lincoln feared the impact of emancipation on sections of Northern opinion, especially in loyal border states such as his native Kentucky, and because, like many others,[83] he hoped that avoiding a pledge to support emancipation would weaken Southern backing for secession. After Antietam, in contrast, Lincoln heeded radical Republicans, many of whom were linked to the Congressional Joint Committee on the Conduct of the War,[84] and the Union became committed to the emancipation of the slaves in those parts of the South still in rebellion.[85] This was seen as a way to weaken the Southern economy, and thus war effort, as well as providing a clear purpose to maintain Northern morale and a means to assuage the sin that was leading a wrathful God to punish America. The international audience was also in Lincoln's mind, and international law on war influenced the Emancipation Proclamation.[86] When, in 1862, the government agreed to a search treaty that would hit the illegal slave trade under the American flag, a measure for which the British had long been pressing, this pleased British opinion, including that of the ministry.

Emancipation, like conscription, another radical step, was also linked to the need for troops. In the second half of the Civil War, the recruitment of blacks for the Union army (a step encouraged by the French use in Mexico of black troops supplied by Egypt from Sudan) was a symbol to and for the Confederacy of what was a total war. Moreover, the recruitment of all-black regiments for the army, numbering more than 120,000 men, was also a major operational help to the Union. Black troops were frequently employed as labor, but were also given combat jobs, the action at Fort Wagner in July 1863 proving a key watershed. Sometimes blacks made up the bulk of a force. The force under John Newton that landed south of Tallahassee and advanced into Florida, before being defeated at Natural Bridge on 6 March 1865, was mostly black. The symbolic power of black troops was shown in February 1865 when the forces that occupied Charleston, the site of the outbreak of the war, included black troops recruited from former Carolina slaves.[87]

Yet, leaving aside the murderous treatment of black Union soldiers by the Confederates, as at Fort Pillow in 1864, which reflected the way in which the war became more brutal,[88] prejudice continued in the Union forces. Black soldiers were paid less while, faced with the pressure of creating large armies willing to fight, discipline became harsher during the Civil War, and the Union army staged many public executions. There was a racist dimension, as more black soldiers were executed, and usually by hanging, while whites were shot by firing-squad, which was seen as more dignified.[89] Nevertheless, Congress maintained the concept of all-black regiments after the war, with Congress establishing specific cavalry and infantry regiments in 1866.

During the war, claims of necessity were employed to justify the extension of governmental power, a process eased by the absence of Southern representatives in Congress and the weak position of the Northern Democrats. Moreover, radical Republicans claimed that, by their secession, the Southerners had forfeited their constitutional rights.[90] The power of the federal government was enhanced at the expense of the states, and a host of measures including conscription and the establishment of a national banking system were important in themselves and for what they signified. To Democrats and Palmerston, the Lincoln administration seemed tyrannical, as with the suspension of *habeas corpus* in Maryland, and action against critical newspapers. Moreover, in the Congressional elections of 1862, the Democrats won the Indiana state legislature, only to find the Republicans refuse to attend the session and the governor, Oliver Morton, governed without it.[91]

Conscription, which was agreed by the Senate on 20 February 1863, greatly increased federal power[92] and led to anger, evasion, and riots. The Democratic presidential platform, agreed on 29 August 1864, declared that "under the pretence of a military necessity, or war power higher than the Constitution, the Constitution itself has been disregarded in every part."

The difference between Democrats and Republicans led to predictions of change if Lincoln fell, predictions made by foreign commentators, such as Lyons, as well as domestic counterparts. In the 1864 election, McClellan, the Democratic candidate, wanted reunion as the price of peace, but his running mate, George Pendleton, was a Peace Democrat, and the platform pressed for an armistice. The Democrats were also against an emancipation amendment for the Constitution, which was a policy supported by the Republican Convention.

Another aspect of division was provided by attitudes toward Latin America. When, in the House on 4 April 1864, a Democrat praised Monroe, the Republican riposte was a call to a more ideological policy:

> The Democratic policy in dealing with our republican brethren in South America and in Mexico has been that of the wolf to the lamb. Their growl was to frighten foreign wolves from the prey they marked for their own; they hectored, bullied, and plundered them without even stretching out the hand of republican sympathy to appease their dissensions or consolidate their power. . . . We wish to cultivate friendship with our republican brethren of Mexico and South America, to aid in consolidating republican principles, to retain popular government in all this continent from the fangs of monarchical aristocratic power, and to lead the sisterhood of American republics in the path of peace, prosperity, and power.

Like much of the radical program, this aspiration was only realized in small part, at least in the short term.

Contemporaries were sure that the 1864 election would be decided by the campaigning,[93] and it was also seen as important to the success of conscription.[94] In 1864, Lincoln had found a war-winning general with Grant, but this result was not apparent at first. Appointed general-in-chief of the Union army in March 1864, Grant made the decision to take field command, rather than act as military adviser to the government. His choice can be queried, but he added strategic purpose, and impetus to Union military policy. Moreover, in the Overland Campaign, Grant subordinated the individual battle to the repeated pressure of campaigning against the Confederates. Attacking their army became the key, and not capturing particular positions. Indeed, the near-continuous nature of the conflict from his advance in May 1864, which led, initially, to the battle of the Wilderness, combined with heavy casualties to give the war in the Virginian theater an attritional character, which indeed was Grant's intention. In the long term, although repeated attacks failed to destroy the smaller Confederate army, Grant's attrition ground it down.

Yet, in the short term, the heavy casualties suffered by Grant's army hit civilian morale, as did Sherman's initial failure to capture Atlanta. Moreover, the Red River Expedition, which was intended to secure cotton for the textile industry in New England, failed. Faced by a range of bad news, Lincoln feared that he would not be reelected. However, Sherman's capture of Atlanta turned morale round.[95] Lincoln also benefited from Northern successes in the Petersburg campaign and the Shenandoah Valley,[96] while these campaigns exacerbated Confederate supply shortages, increasing the reliance on blockade runners, which, in turn, the steadily more effective Union blockade thwarted.

The election saw Lincoln, who drew on Republican Party organization and patronage, win by 212 to 21 electoral votes, but the popular vote was far less unfavorable to McClellan than this figure suggests. The Republicans also won a substantial majority in Congress. Lincoln was helped by the backing of the War Democrats and by the army's support: 78 percent of the Union soldiers who voted in the presidential election did so for him. This backing reflected the strong sense of religious mission that helped empower the Union soldiers and encouraged them to prefer war for victory to negotiations. Having denied God's support by supporting sectional interests, America was to be made new, an affirmation of faith that reflected broad chords in American, and indeed British, culture.[97] McClellan, the former general, did not attract this emotional commitment.

Lincoln's victory encourages a benign view of the continuance of the political process during the war, but, again, in part, this view is an instance of the broad-brush approach of hindsight, for, at the time, the politics of the war, both at the national and the state levels, and between and within the parties, had proved highly disruptive. Moreover, this divisiveness had absorbed much political effort, posing problems for the direction of the war.[98] Diplomats seeking signs of opposition were able to find them in plenty.

Lincoln's reelection, however, ended the political options for counterfactual speculation as far as the North was concerned. Northern morale affirmed Lincoln's position, just as his leadership helped ensure the resilience of this morale. The reelection provided the background for the pursuit of a strategy designed to stop Southern support for the war by crippling morale and destroying infrastructure, a goal shared by his troops.[99] Although Sherman's devastation of the Confederate hinterland increased the resolve of some Southern soldiers, the ability to spread devastation unhindered across the Southern hinterland exacerbated the already serious tendency to desertion, helped destroy civilian faith in the war, and made the penalty for and limitation of guerrilla warfare apparent.[100] The slave basis of Southern society collapsed as Union forces advanced, with thousands of slaves using the opportunities of Sherman's advance to escape their masters, although, in doing so, they also clogged Union lines with "contraband" as they were known.

By making territory his objective, Sherman moved beyond the unproductive nature that that goal and method frequently entailed. Instead, he used the occupation of territory to fulfill his aim of focusing on the psychological mastery of Southern society. This mastery was a goal that proved more productive than that of seeking the chimera of victory in battle,[101] and one that matched the desire (on both sides) to achieve such mastery through humiliation and vengeance.[102]

Sherman's advance also threatened Lee's rear in Virginia, and was to be praised by Basil Liddell Hart accordingly as an instance of the indirect approach. Columbia, South Carolina, was occupied on 17 February 1865; North Carolina was entered the following month; Raleigh was occupied on 13 April; and this advance contributed to the situation in which Lee was defeated without his army being destroyed. The home front was literally collapsing, and this collapse was closely linked to the failure of the Confederate armies.[103]

In their different ways, Sherman and Grant ensured that the uncertainty of war undermined the Confederacy, for they managed risk and uncertainty while their opponents came, in 1864, to experience it. The tempo of Union operations exploited the uncertainty of conflict and directed it against the Confederacy's military as well as its sociopolitical underpinning. Sherman's advance was also the culmination of the long series of Union triumphs in the western theater. In 1862 and 1863, these had not prevented Lee from advancing in, and from, Virginia and, to a considerable extent, it had been possible to trade space in the west for time with which to attack in the east. This potentially war-winning Southern formula had failed, in the east, not across the Appalachians, but it was only after that the Union forces were able to exploit their success in the west in order to attack what could otherwise have been a defense in depth in the east.

This exploitation of Northern success was in part a matter of a psychological shift. Grant brought a conviction that victory could be won, a confidence that reflected the repeated Union successes in the west. This conviction replaced the earlier hesitation of many Union commanders in the east, a hesitation born of a caution, if not a lack of confidence, that had been seen with McClellan's deliberative generalship and been encouraged by Lee's attacks.[104] Conversely, Grant's reputation benefited from the usually poor Confederate generalship he faced in the west.[105]

A very different American geopolitics to that which was created in 1865 was presented by Jefferson Davis, who was determined to fight on after Lee's surrender to Grant at Appomattox Court House on 9 April. The previous July, Davis had responded to the terms offered in Lincoln's amnesty proclamation of December 1863 by declaring "We are fighting for Independence – and that, or extermination, we will have.... You may emancipate every Negro in the Confederacy, but we will be free. We will govern ourselves ... if we have to see every Southern plantation sacked, and every Southern city in flames."[106] To that end, Davis headed for the Trans-Mississippi region, only to be captured in Irwinville, Georgia, on 10 May 1865. In the event, greatly influenced by Lee's surrender, there was to be no fighting on by the other armies. Joseph E. Johnston, commander of the other major Confederate force in the field, in North Carolina, had already surrendered to Sherman, at Durham Station, North Carolina, on 20 April, a step that increased the vulnerability of Lee further north. On 4 May, Richard Taylor, who commanded the last Confederate force east of the Mississippi, surrendered at Citronelle, Alabama, while, in the Trans-Mississippi, Kirby Smith's army surrendered on 26 May. The last clash, the Battle of Palmetto Ranch, had occurred near Brownsville, Texas, on 13 May. The Confederacy's currency had collapsed with its government, and the prospects for continued resistance by this army were terrible.[107]

The prospect of further conventional operations therefore came to an end, but there was also to be no guerrilla war such as the one anticipated in 1862 by the French envoy after a trip to Richmond, and proposed by Davis in a proclamation after the fall of Richmond that very much suggested a new spatial understanding of the South and of the war zone:

> Relieved from the necessity of guarding cities and particular points . . . with an army free to move from point to point . . . operating in the interior of our own country, where supplies are more accessible, and where the foe will be far removed from his own base . . . nothing is now needed to render our triumph certain but the exhibition of our own unquenchable resolve.[108]

This was not an alien concept, as guerrilla warfare had already been seen in areas, notably southern Appalachia, where terrain was difficult and the number of regulars limited,[109] while the last stages of the Mexican-American War had shown the problems the American occupying forces confronted due to continued opposition.[110] The same was even more true for the French in Mexico.[111] Yet, despite the Partisan Ranger Act of 1861, the Confederate political and military leadership had proved largely unwilling to encourage guerrilla warfare that, while particularly important in Appalachia and in the Missouri–Kansas region, was not so in the crucial war zones. Furthermore, some of what is now termed guerrilla warfare, with the misleading implication that it was not waged by regulars, can better be described as irregular warfare by regulars, particularly engaged in raiding activities. The Union forces were able to counter these methods, both by defensive means, especially blockhouses and patrols, and by action designed to provide the exemplary threat of retribution and/or to find and engage those directly involved.[112]

Lee and his fellow generals ignored Davis's call. Such a policy was antipathetic to their understanding of military and social order, and unacceptable under both heads. As a result, the most bitter conflict in

American history came to a more abrupt end than might have been anticipated, although it could be argued that it subsequently reerupted in areas such as Mississippi through Reconstruction with the actions of white militia in the Colfax massacre and street fighting in New Orleans. At any rate, in 1865, the Union forces were able to stage a Grand Review at Washington on 23 May.[113]

The end of the war settled the issues of slavery and secession and left to commentators the question of why the war had occurred, a conflict that was to be refought endlessly, from bars to seminars. It became a political issue, redolent with questions of and for American identity and Southern culture, and also (and not always separately) a matter of discussion for military specialists. The very sites of the war served to highlight disputes. Thus, in 2000, in response to discussion of the Interior Appropriations Bill, the National Park Service submitted to Congress a report assessing the educational information at Civil War sites and recommending that much be updated, not least to illustrate the "breadth of human experience during the period, and establish the relevance of the war to people today." Representative Jesse Jackson, Jr. and other members of Congress had complained that many sites lacked appropriate contextualization and, specifically, that there was often "missing vital information about the role that the institution of slavery played in causing the American Civil War."[114]

Explanations of the causes and significance of the war were the key issues in dispute, as they reflected the American interest in righteousness and concern to explain a key traumatic episode, but there was also much room to discuss the reason for Northern success, although some of the discussion was elliptical in that it arose from narrative accounts of the conflict. The value of a broader canvas is apparent because there are many parallels between the discussion of the American Civil War and other conflicts, notably the First World War (1914–18). For both, there was an emphasis on the failure of the home front of the defeated power, particularly as a consequence of the pressures and privations of the war (including, in each case, the results of blockade), but also with reference to the weakness of the nationalism and political coherence of the society that surrendered. In each case, however, this approach underplays the strength of the victor, both of their own home front and of their ability to create an effective, confident, and triumphant military system that eventually outfought its opponent. As the latter account is unwelcome in many quarters, it tends to be underplayed, and there is a comparison between Confederate arguments of the Lost Cause and the German presentation of the "stab in the back" in 1918. Nevertheless, this military theme pulls together the motivation of the Union soldiers, which continued strong throughout the conflict[115] with the availability of resources, and links this combination to improvements in command.

These elements played out across America and raise issues about the geopolitics of the Civil War. This question does not so much refer to the spatial contexts and dynamics of military operations, with Mexican liberal positions "pointed out to me on a map" by Marshal Bazaine in June 1865,[116] as to the geographical relationships between the major players. As the last two chapters have indicated, these spanned the Atlantic, while, in addition, the Congressional Committee on Military Affairs in 1862 supported the subsequently unsuccessful development of a trans-Pacific telegraph route able to link America to Russia, with which relations were friendly.[117] In the event, trans-Atlantic relations did not collapse into conflict which, in turn, was highly significant both for the Civil War and for American relations with Canada.

As throughout this book, the relationships between agency and structure, the short- and the long term, pose a significant analytical problem. The conclusion here is that British caution reflected the long-term trend in policy seen for decades, but was crucially assisted by a comparable degree of caution and restraint on the part of Lincoln's government.

As also elsewhere in this book, there is the argument that people and ethnicity are a central aspect of geopolitics. This aspect had many facets, and the audience on 20 January 1864 at a pro-Emancipation meeting at Chorlton Temperance Hall in Manchester listened to a speech tracing the Civil War to that between Plymouth Rock and those who landed at Jamestown.[118] In 1857, Lewis Cass mentioned "the obstinacy and unreasonableness of the governments of Spanish extraction,"[119] while ethnic issues were also raised in the case of the Mexican Civil War, with *Estafette,* the French newspaper in Mexico City, pressing in 1865 for new immigration to protect Mexican independence from the aggressive and self-appropriating tendencies of the Anglo-Saxon race in North America.[120] The son of a peer, Peter Scarlett, the British envoy, agreed on the need for immigrants, but his approach was very different, as he adopted another ranking:

> The future regeneration and progress of Mexico are eminently associated with a well-directed system of foreign immigration. A population so sparse as this is, and so incapable, both physically and morally, of undertaking the development of resources which require abler and more numerous hands, renders it imperative that the Emperor Maximilian should turn his serious attention to the subject of immigration.

Scarlett added that Maximilian's intentions were "too frequently frustrated by the old-rooted prejudice of the Spanish Mexican race against the admission of foreigners" and linked this to a reactionary social stance, notably an opposition to free trade: "the attachment with which all classes cling to a corrupt and exclusive policy in preference to more enlarged views and legitimate ideas in commercial matters."[121] His dispatches worried the British government and a draft seen by the Queen noted the hope that some Mexicans might "be found capable of governing their own country" in order to forestall the need for "a perpetual foreign intervention."[122] Such comments rested on an understanding of territory in terms of the tension between the character of its people, generally seen as an inherent, and thus structural, element, and the play of external forces whether political, military, demographic, or economic, for example the role of external trade, all usually presented as contingent.

The American and Mexican civil wars were inscribed by outsiders in part in terms of such dynamics, with the crucial difference that "Mexicanness" was seen as a characteristic shared by the people as a people, while its American counterpart was more readily divided in terms of the two combatants. The clear geographical division between the two helped in this process, but it also tended to exclude African (let alone Native) Americans other than as minor players on whom history was visited. The mapping of territory in physical terms thus sat alongside vitalist assumptions about national characteristics that were often based on crude ethnic stereotyping. Such stereotyping was to play a major role in the postwar politics of America, with the revival of Southern racism helping ensure that the South was increasingly viewed as a backwater outside what was clearly a national mainstream.[123] In the case of Mexico, a different form of value by attention played a role, as the end of the Franco-Imperial episode in 1867 ensured that the country was largely ignored. As for the American Southerners, especially African-Americans, and also for the Natives of the American west, this neglect was a key aspect of a geopolitics that helped define and reflect their condition.

# 15

## SETTLING THE NORTH AMERICAN QUESTION 1865-71

The war left the Union with a massive and well-honed military, just over a million men strong at the start of 1865, and with the second-largest navy in the world: 671 warships, including seventy-one ironclads, in commission, as well as the prospect of further growth in the number of ships. This force appeared to offer options for expansion, or at least activity, notably against Canada and Mexico. Concerns about the former led Britain to press ahead with plans for Canadian unity through confederation, but the possibility of conflict focused on Mexico. After the war, American pressure for the departure of the French troops increased, and America's nonrecognition of Maximilian's government became more significant. There was an important popular dimension, with volunteers going to fight for Juárez. Sir Frederick Bruce, the British envoy in Washington, was being naïve, when he reported in January 1866:

> As soon as the temper of this country allows the Mexican question to be discussed on its merits, it can be conclusively demonstrated that the Mexican people are at present incapable of appreciating a republican form of government, and the United States have the most direct interest in seeing a firm and orderly government substituted for the anarchy which has hitherto prevented the development of the resources of Mexico.
>
> With a practical people these considerations cannot fail to have great weight, and I should not be surprised if a feeling gradually grows up that the Emperor Maximilian should be allowed fair play in attempting to carry out the difficult task he has undertaken.
>
> This hostility to him is chiefly due to the impression that his appearance in Mexico was part of a hostile design entertained by the Emperor of the French [Napoleon III] against this country.[1]

Bruce's implication that the end of such an impression would lead to American acceptance of the situation was unwise, not least as Seward had made clear the previous November that America was against a foreign and imperial government in Mexico and did not regard the French army there as having any authority. Bruce's argument was of a piece with his criticism of Monroe's "dicta," the Monroe Doctrine,[2] a view that, however well grounded, made little sense in terms of the power politics after the Civil War. Bruce was, by background, scarcely sympathetic to American policy. The son of an earl, he had been attached to Ashburton's mission to America in 1842, but his diplomatic experience in the New World, in Bolivia (1847–51) and Uruguay (1851–53), did not lead him to sympathize with American pretensions. The same was true of his other post in the New World, as lieutenant-governor of Newfoundland (1846–47), a colony where American fishing activity had long proved a serious irritant. Other posts, colonial secretary at Hong Kong, Agent and consul-general in Egypt, and envoy to China, were not the best preparations for an American embassy, although Bruce befriended the American envoy, Burlinghame, in China. Bruce was willing to let rip about American politics, especially "the pernicious influence exercised by demagogues on the excitement and disorderly elements that abound in the great cities,"[3] although he was to die in 1867 with Sumner at his side. Despite the self-conscious professionalism of the British diplomatic service,[4] the radical John Bright, a correspondent of Sumner, complained in 1858 that "foreign policy . . . is neither more nor less than a gigantic system of outdoor relief for the aristocracy,"[5] and, as Lyons's comments showed, aristocratic envoys had limited sympathy for American democracy.

Bruce's assumptions, which reflected the continuing distaste for American populism in the official diplomatic "mind,"[6] help explain the clash between European and American views on Mexico, a clash that involved far more than the stability of that country. From another perspective, both America and France had exploited Mexico, America by launching a war of aggression and seizing territory, and France by trying to turn it into a satellite state. In the late 1860s, French failure was to leave America with the option of deciding how far and how best to exploit the country.

As a separate issue, Mexico in 1865 became a possible base for Confederate *revanche*, with several prominent Confederates finding shelter there. John Bankhead Magruder became one of Maximilian's major-generals that year. However, the risk that the Mexican situation would hamper the pacification of the South was averted. U.S. pressure was significant in ensuring a satisfactory outcome from the American perspective. This pressure included both diplomatic moves and the transfer of troops to the Rio Grande. Appointed commander of the military division of the Gulf in May 1865, Major-General Philip Sheridan was sent with more than 40,000 troops to overawe the forces of Maximilian, a stance that entailed staging provocative maneuvers on the Rio Grande border.[7] Sheridan also engaged in a massive resupply operations for the Juárista army, writing later, "During the winter and spring of 1866, we continued covertly supplying ammunition and arms to the Liberals – sending as many as 30,000 muskets from the Baton Rouge arsenal alone."[8]

Grant favored pressure, as he saw Napoleon III, Maximilian, Mexican conservatives, and Southern exiles as the key elements in a far-ranging geopolitical and ideological combination directed against liberal progress in Mexico, and, therefore, against American interests. With the more cautious Seward opposed to full-scale military intervention, war, however, was avoided and fears of American filibustering, for example by disbanded troops against Canada or Mexico, proved groundless.[9] Nevertheless, the belief that Napoleon III had to increase his commitment to Maximilian in order to counteract the possibility of American action, Marshal Bazaine mentioning 50,000 more troops if necessary, placed considerable pressure on him.[10] American actions and the threat of more action played a role in helping lead Napoleon III in January 1866 to decide to withdraw his forces.[11] The *Corps Législatif* were informed that Maximilian was now strong enough not to need French assistance, which Napoleon III knew was untrue.

Although American pressure was significant, it is also necessary to devote due weight to the problems that France faced in Mexico, as well as to the developing crisis in Germany. The unsettled nature of the Austro-Prussian condominium of Schleswig-Holstein (created after the defeat of Denmark in 1864), and of the political situation within Germany, were causes of dispute between Austria and Prussia, while domestic problems in each country encouraged their rulers to make war. This conflict did not break out until June 1866, but, already, Napoleon III was having to consider how best to respond to Prussian strength, a strength made more of a challenge as a result of Prussia's alliance with Italy which threatened Austria. Indeed, the Prussians were to be keen on a rapid victory over Austria in order to forestall a hostile French entry into the war. They succeeded in this objective, while Britain remained more determinedly aloof despite the fact that the war led to the conquest of Austria's ally Hanover, ruled by Victoria's first cousin, and its absorption into Prussia. Continuing the pattern seen with the Italian *Risorgimento* (movement for liberation and unification) and the American Civil War, both the Russell government, which was the continuation of the Palmerston ministry after his death in 1865, and the succeeding Conservative Derby ministry, in office from 1866 to 1868, were resolute on standing aside, even though the war was to lead to a major change in the European system, and one that in the end threatened both the global balance of power and British security.

Similarly, British governments were unwilling to get involved in the Mexican issue, even to the extent of responding to Maximilian's request for advice,[12] although there was a determination to support specific British interests. Thus, the case of British firms exposed to pressure for forced loans to help the impoverished Imperialist cause was taken up,[13] while there were also complaints about the Mexican failure to respect the borders of British Honduras.[14]

In contrast to Britain, Napoleon III responded to Prussia's success against Austria in 1866 by preparing for confrontation with Prussia, not least in a competition for primacy that owed much to contrary interests in both southern Germany, which Prussia was absorbing into its system of power, and Spain. This situation encouraged Napoleon to end his Mexican commitment, whatever the cost to his prestige, and the change of policy was an instructive linkage of New World and European politics. Prussia had been pro-Union during the Civil War.

The last French troops left Mexico City on 5 February 1867 and Veracruz on 16 March 1867. Already, the Liberals/Republicans had proved successful in conventional operations against Franco-Austrian forces and their conservative Mexican allies, winning a victory at Tacámbaro on 11 April 1865, three days before Lincoln's assassination. In 1866, the Liberals/Republicans under Porfirio Diaz besieged an Imperial force at Oaxaca, repulsed an Austrian relief column at La Carbonera, and then received the surrender of Oaxaca. The following year, the Liberals/Republicans were victorious. Puebla, Querétaro, and Mexico City were successfully besieged by the Liberals, while Imperial-Mexican forces were defeated in battle, as at San Lorenzo. Refusing to leave, Maximilian was defeated when Querétaro was successfully besieged, and he was executed on 19 June 1867 alongside two of his generals, providing Manet with an epic subject. Such executions of prisoners helped underline and secure victory.

Conflict in Latin America in the 1860s provides both instructive contrasts with the American Civil War, contrasts that throw important light on the latter, and also permits consideration of the degree to which America was able to dominate the New World after the war. The major effort expended by the participants in the Paraguayan War of 1864–70 was atypical, but indicated the damaging nature of conflict for the societies of the period, as well as the potent impact of foreign intervention in domestic struggles, in this case in Uruguay: Paraguay, Brazil and Argentina all became involved in the war. The Americans were spared such intervention in their civil war, and the rumor that the quixotic President Francisco López of Paraguay had placed Paraguay under American protection[15] was fanciful, but foreign intervention was the norm elsewhere, not least as Conservatives and Liberals both looked for support from foreign colleagues. In 1863, for example, Guatemalan forces invaded El Salvador, only to be beaten at Cotepeque, after which Salvadoran forces intervened in Nicaragua in order to back a Liberal rising. Gerardo Barrios Espinosa, the president of El Salvador, was defeated at San Felipe by Tomás Martinez, the president of Nicaragua, and then faced a renewed Guatemalan invasion backed by Nicaragua. Besieged in his capital, Barrios surrendered, and Guatemala installed a new president, Francisco Dueñas. Guatemala and Nicaragua also succeeded in ensuring that their client prevailed in Honduras. These conflicts were important because of continuing American interest in routes across Central America, which, for example, played a major role in the treaty with Honduras concluded in July 1864 and ratified the following March.

Hostilities, however, continued. In 1870, an attempt to overthrow President Vicente Cerna of Guatemala, who had played a major role in Central American warfare in 1863, was defeated, but he was overthrown in 1871 by the Liberals in renewed conflict, and one of their commanders, Miguel Garcia Granados, then became president. The political culture was very different from that in America, where Grant was peacefully elected president in 1868 and was peacefully reelected in 1872. Honduras and El Salvador went to war in 1871, each concerned that the other was backing internal disaffection. Supported by Honduras, the Salvadoran rebel Santiago González defeated the Salvadoran president, Dueñas, and became president himself, only to attack Honduras successfully the following year.

There was also warfare elsewhere. At Pavón in 1861, Bartolomé Mitre and the army of Buenos Aires defeated Santiago Derqui, president of Argentina, which paved the way for Mitre to become president until 1868. In turn, in 1867, while at war with Paraguay, Argentina was affected by a rising in the west.

As Mexico showed in the 1860s, such political practices, and the instability they reflected and sustained, made long-term foreign intervention difficult. The conflicts in Latin America helped ensure that, although it took only an indirect role at most, the United States was to be the most successful of the New World powers, and the one that benefited from the opportunities provided by western expansion and globalization, more so than Argentina and Brazil. In particular, there was an obvious contrast between America and Mexico, as far as the strains of civil war in the 1860s were concerned. America was hit much less, in large part because the bulk of the North, the economic core of the country, did not directly experience conflict. Moreover, after the war, America returned more readily to constitutional politics, whereas, in Mexico, there was politics as usual. Unwilling to accept defeat in the presidential election of 1875, Porfirio Diaz, a veteran of the Mexican-French war, rebelled that year and seized power after a series of battles. Had France been more successful in Mexico in the 1860s, then it would still probably have found itself committed to maintaining stability there, or at least resisting long-term guerrilla activity, as Bazaine admitted to Scarlett.

Like France, Spain was in no position to pursue its New World ambitions in the late 1860s, and, again, it is necessary to explain American pressures while considering the situation in Europe. In May 1864,
Seward had taken a tough tone about Spanish policy: "It might be impossible for the government of the United States to restrain the indignation
of the country."[16] American pressure in 1866 helped lead Spain to end
hostilities with Peru and Chile, while Spain also abandoned its attempt
to control the Dominican Republic, which, as a result of local opposition,
had indeed turned out to be a fruitless commitment.

Yet, as with France, it is important, in discussing causes, also to note
developments in Europe. There was a high level of instability in Spain,
which made it difficult to sustain an active foreign policy, and this instability reflected both acute divisions between key political groups and
also important rivalries within them. Governments were repeatedly put
under pressure by *pronunciamientos,* or declarations of intention to act,
and these could lead to a *golpe del estado,* the equivalent of a French *coup
d'état.* In 1866, General Juan Prim, a liberal, tried to seize power in Madrid, but this revolution was suppressed by Leopoldo O'Donnell, Duke
of Tetuán, who, in 1844, had suppressed the slave revolt in West Cuba.
His successor as prime minister, Ramón Narváz, was backed by the more
conservative elements in the army, but, following the death of Narváz
in 1866, Prim and Francisco, Duke de la Torre, seized power in a military coup in 1868, ousting Queen Isabella II, after loyalist troops were
defeated at Alcolea on 28 September. The throne was declared vacant,
contributing to French ambitions that helped lead to war with Prussia
in 1870, and a new king, Amadeo I, a son of the King of Italy, was chosen
that year; but instability, including army mutinies, led him to abdicate
in 1873. Fresh instability under the first Spanish Republic led to a new
coup under Brigadier Martinez Campos in 1874 – a coup that restored
the Bourbon dynasty in the shape of Isabella's son, Alfonso XII.

This instability was not the best basis for power projection, and that
is as important a context as American action, indeed far more so, for the
abandonment of Spain's New World pretensions. Indeed, a similar lack
of expansion was shown by Spain elsewhere, notably in Africa where
Rio Muni in West Africa and Ifni in southern Morocco, occupied in 1843
and 1860 respectively, did not serve as the basis for additional expansion.

Instead, the next initiative did not occur until 1884 when a protectorate was established on the Rio de Oro, which subsequently became the
Spanish Sahara.

The 1868 coup in Spain led to an insurrection against Spanish rule
in Cuba. As in Mexico during the century, the course of this struggle
strongly reflected the role of ethnic and social divisions. In particular,
from 1870 on, the Spaniards, in resisting the insurrection, were helped
by ethnic tension, as Cuban whites increasingly rejected what they now
saw as a black-run rebellion. The conflict also indicated the problematic
choices that might have been posed in the American South had Reconstruction been sustained in the face of large-scale violent opposition. In
Cuba, Spanish forces employed harsh measures, including the forced
relocation of the rural population so as to create free-fire zones and to
prevent the rebels from gaining access to civilian aid, as well as the killing of rebel families. In turn, the rebels waged economic warfare, destroying sugar mills and plantations.[17] A combination of military action
and conciliatory promises led to a settlement in Cuba in 1878.

Grant, American president from 1869 to 1877, faced liberal pressure
to support the Cuban insurrection, pressure that reminded the British
of the controversy over their conduct in the Civil War.[18] This pressure
looked toward the situation in 1898 when America intervened in a second Cuban insurrection that had begun in 1895, but, earlier, Grant was
unwilling to provide such support, although he favored the annexation
of the Dominican Republic if its people backed the proposition. Congress, crucially, did not, with Sumner taking a major role against Grant,
which helped lead the latter to displace him from his chairmanship of the
Senate Foreign Affairs Committee. The annexation treaty was dropped
in 1870.

The American acquisition of Alaska and the Aleutian Islands from
Russia in 1867 was scarcely the product of American pressure. The
Americans were in no position to exert such pressure and, instead, for
$7,200,000, bought the territory, which the Russians were keen to sell,
not least because the Russian-American Company, the finances of which
had long been precarious, was close to bankruptcy. Critics condemned
both the idea and the expense, referring to the episode as "Seward's
Folly," although only a small minority of the American press used this

term or even criticized Seward for making the purchase, which was generally supported as another large expansion of territory.[19]

The gain certainly preempted the possibility of British acquisition,
although that was scarcely an option, and also placed British Columbia
and Vancouver Island, which had become British Crown Colonies in
1858, between two areas of American territory. Indeed, disputes over the
boundary of the Alaskan Panhandle were only settled in 1903. Further
north, Fort Yukon, at the confluence of the Yukon and Porcupine Rivers,
had been established by the Hudson's Bay Company in 1847, but, in 1869,
the American army expelled the British traders from what was clearly
now American territory. The new American territory created other issues in relations with Britain, including the transit of cattle through
British Columbia en route for the American garrison.[20] In December
1867, the Foreign Office instructed the governor of British Columbia to
help America's authorities in Alaska in their relations with Natives if required.[21] There was no wish to sow or exploit problems for the Americans.

At Novo Archangel'sk, the Russian headquarters in 1799 to 1802 and
from 1804, the American flag replaced the Russian one on 18 October
1867, when sovereignty was officially transferred. At the time, there were
only 2,000 white settlers in Alaska. Novo Archangel'sk was renamed
Sitka and the Americans rapidly established forts in order to assert their
control. The coastal location of these forts reflected the distribution
of population, the possibilities for trade, and the extent to which any
attack by other powers would come by sea. The forts included Fort Ton-
gass, on Portland Channel facing British territory, Fort Kodiak, Fort
Wrangel on an island at the mouth of the Stikine River (where British
efforts to penetrate had been blocked in 1834), and Fort Kenay near the
head of Cook Inlet. In 1868, the Alaska force rose to 21 officers and 530
men, but, in 1870, all the posts except Sitka were abandoned, and only
two artillery companies were left there. It was decided that ships would
be more effective than troops in maintaining order in a territory without
roads. The garrison of Sitka itself was withdrawn in 1877. Drink had been
a major problem affecting discipline,[22] while the need for troops was
more pressing in the American west.

Alaska was scarcely going to be the basis for expansion into northeast Asia, where the continental land mass was under the authority

of Russia, which was also expanding its power offshore into Sakhalin: northern Sakhalin in 1853 and southern in 1875. The Kurile Islands only came under Japanese control in 1875, but it would have required a particularly dynamic and risky American policy to have taken preemptive steps in the Kuriles or southern Sakhalin. Such a step would have been a challenge for American capabilities, although in May 1871 two warships and a small marine force attacked Korea in revenge for the burning, five years earlier, of an armed merchant schooner, the *General Sherman*, that had sought to open up Korea to American trade. In 1871, about 650 Koreans were killed, but the American use of force, particularly superior firepower, yielded them no benefit and their force sailed off.[23]

Russian policy was the key factor in the northern Pacific. Rather than being pushed out by the Americans, the Russians did not wish to retain Alaska and also had accepted the organization, with successive measures in 1859, 1862, and 1863, of British control nearby in what became Canada. Instead, the Russians were far more interested in the China question. The Arrow (or Second Opium) War between China and an Anglo-French alliance provided Russia with the opportunity to make territorial gains, first the Amur region to the north of the River Amur in 1858 and, subsequently, the Ussuri region between there and the Sea of Japan in 1860, the port of Vladivostok being founded that year. This expansion did not encourage Russia to take an interest on the opposite shores of the Pacific, where the Crimean War had suggested that Russia was overextended, nor indeed in the ocean itself. Instead, other than the Far East and, increasingly, the Chinese province of Manchuria, Central Asia was the key area for Russian expansion in the 1860s–90s, with Tashkent acquired in 1864 and Samarkand in 1868, while, in the Caucasus, control over the Circassians was gained in 1864. Later, the Pacific power that was to be of most concern to Russia was Japan, not America.[24]

Seward had plans for areas other than Alaska. The Midway Islands were annexed in 1867, providing a mid-Pacific base on the way to East Asian waters. Seward also suggested gaining Hawaii, the Dominican Republic, and the Danish West Indies, and building a canal across Central America. Such plans, some of which had been considered prior to the Civil War, did not seem unrealistic in its aftermath, and all of these, bar the gain of the Dominican Republic, were to be realized. The Danish

Virgin Islands became the American-ruled Virgin Islands by purchase in 1917. The Danish legislature had agreed to sell them in 1868, but its American counterpart was less prepared to spend the money at this stage, and in April 1870 the Senate decided not to proceed with the purchase.[25] German submarines changed the situation in 1917, although Greenland, which Seward had also sought to gain, remained Danish, albeit with American air bases established there in 1941.

Diplomatic correspondence conveyed a sense of restless American energy and extensive prospects. Indeed, Seward was omnivorous and had been talking up empire-for-commercialism since the 1840s. Thus, in January 1870, the British government noted the inaccurate rumor that Ecuador would cede the Galapagos Islands to America.[26] Two years earlier, interest in Brunei was recorded, and in 1869 there was a rumored sale of "one of the Malay islands."[27] Rumors also spread about American territorial interests in Macao and Japan.[28] In January 1867, Bruce reported that America was considering the establishment of a naval base on the Samana peninsula in the Dominican Republic (a site of interest for several years), adding that this might be attractive to America as a form of security blanket: "The ill-judged expedition of the Spaniards may reconcile the Dominican government to the arrangement, as a security against any such pretensions in future."[29] Thus, America, with its powerful navy and determination to achieve goals, was now in a position to give force to the Monroe Doctrine, a concept that was seen as a possible source of "violent assertion."[30] Bruce also noted Seward's wish to negotiate with Nicaragua "for the cession of one of her Pacific ports," a measure that would have greatly increased American influence in Central America and the Pacific,[31] providing also a forward base from which to exert pressure if necessary on Mexico and Colombia.

Paradoxically, Bruce suggested that European weakness might act to limit America, a reversal of the situation a few years earlier, for he argued that if European powers maintained friendly relations with the states of Central America and respected their independence, the latter would not be anxious to provide the United States with a footing: "They resent their [American] patronizing and at the same time overbearing tone."[32] As a result, Bruce reported that the withdrawal of France from Mexico would be useful in strengthening Central American hostility to the American presence. American reluctance to take a joint role with the Europeans had already been signaled in 1865: in March, Spain and France had agreed to provide a guarantee of the independence of the Dominican Republic that was also to be given by Britain and the United States, but the Americans, in August, had refused to participate.

Bruce reported a "disposition, at least on Mr. Seward's part to acquire naval stations abroad." Their conversation suggested to Bruce that Seward wanted to acquire the Sandwich Islands (the Hawaiian Islands), but Seward told him that reports that the United States was seeking an island or station in the Mediterranean were untrue and, in light of the British position at Gibraltar and the strength of the French fleet in the Mediterranean, such reports did seem absurd, although the Americans did show an interest in the disturbed situation in Crete in 1867–68. There was a proposal among the insurgents there against Turkish rule to place the island under American protection,[33] but it did not lead to anything.

America was not to pursue a major naval buildup until the early 1880s, nor overseas ambitions on a bold scale until the 1890s, by which time the international situation was very different. Instead, the Civil War was followed by political stabilization to the north and south, which helped ensure a shift in American military priorities in the late nineteenth century. Like Britain and Japan, the United States was not threatened over land, and so all three could concentrate more of their defense spending on their navies than powers such as France. The shift to becoming more of a naval power from the 1880s has been related to changing political priorities within the United States, but contingent circumstances also played a role, specifically the ability to win the Civil War without going on to create long-term military commitments in the U.S. South or in Mexico or Canada. Furthermore, as yet, the Americans had not developed the practice of sustained, large-scale military interventions in Central America or the Caribbean. The army was only forty-thousand strong by 1866, while, as a result of a cut in expenditure, the navy, which was still in a good shape at the close of 1867, declined rapidly thereafter.

High levels of debt restricted America's ability to act and also encouraged a dependence on British financial markets and a wish to see economic growth through trade with Britain.[34] Similarly, debt had limited Britain's willingness to act after 1815, but, unlike Britain then, the United States was not affected in North America by the neighboring presence of an expansionist power. In the late 1860s, when Seward would otherwise have been free to act because of the end of the Civil War and the nullity of President Andrew Johnson, he was restrained, except in the case of Alaska, by the huge war debt overhanging America. Hardly any money was free for other purchases, and the appropriation for Alaska just passed the House of Representatives in 1868.

The lack of a long-term military commitment in the South was important not just to the American army but also to American politics. In March 1863, the French envoy, ever looking for evidence of American weakness, had suggested to Lyons that the war would end with the independence or subjugation of the South, adding "either event would make so great a change on this Continent as to amount to a revolution." If the result was subjugation, he predicted that "the hatred between the two sections of the country could never now be appeased. The North could govern the South only by force, and by establishing a rigid despotism there. This would at once destroy all the elements which had produced the strength and the prosperity of the Americans. It was freedom – the 'spontaneity of individual action' which had made the Americans what they were."[35]

Many of the Southern white males by 1865, however, were dead, wounded, or had personally experienced defeat. Moreover, most of the war had occurred in the South, and it had been ruinous even without the specific attempts to spread devastation. These factors weakened the former Confederacy and helped ensure that its capacity for further resistance was lessened. Once defeated, the Confederacy underwent a militarized occupation, and the structure of the latter was rapidly created. Given the current American experience over the last sixty-five years of being an occupying power in Germany, Austria, Japan, and Iraq, it is instructive to consider the earlier episode.

As had been the case in Cromwellian England in the 1650s, the army was the agency for the new order, much of it high-minded, as a major effort was made to unite the nation, and thus help make America a world power, by remolding the South in the image of the North. Thus, in Galveston, a center for occupation forces, Major-General Gordon Granger announced emancipation for Texas slaves on 19 June 1865. The army played an important role in the Bureau of Refugees, Freedmen, and Abandoned Lands, which answered to the War Department. Its commissioner from 1865 to 1872 was Major-General Oliver Otis Howard, who had played an important command role throughout the Civil War, losing an arm at the Battle of Seven Pines. He was responsible for looking after the freed slaves, and also for dealing with confiscated and abandoned properties. The army also played a major role in restoring infrastructure, building bridges, and running railways. Reconstruction literally occurred and achieved much, although there was later a strong tendency to forget this.

The political situation soon ensured that this task was greatly enlarged. Lincoln's vice president and successor, Andrew Johnson, president from 1865 to 1869, a Democrat who had been a slave owner and senator from Tennessee, sought conciliation, a rapid return to normality, at least in the shape of Southern self-government and reentry into the Union,[36] but the Republican majority in Congress disagreed and pushed through the Reconstruction Acts of 1867. The following year, the House of Representatives impeached Johnson, although he was acquitted by the Senate. A guide to Johnson's attitudes and his view on the conditional nature of whites and blacks sharing space was provided by his reply to the National Theological Institute for Coloured Ministers, in which he declared that "the free negro must work or seek a dime where he can live apart from the white man."[37]

Potentially, military control and activity were departures not only for the South but also for America as a whole, and would have added an entirely novel dimension to its geopolitics, one of an occupation zone sustaining a new political order. This order was ethnic as well as territorial, reflecting the overthrow of the previous system of exclusion, subordination, and oppression. In 1865, the Thirteenth Amendment to the Constitution led to the freeing of about four million slaves. Slavery was ended in the loyal as well as the Confederate states. In 1866, over Johnson's veto, Congress passed the Civil Rights Act, giving full citizenship to all born or naturalized in the United States, and voting rights to all male citizens. Blacks thus gained legal equality. The provisions of this legislation became the Fourteenth Amendment, which was ratified in 1868. These amendments reflected the extent to which the radicalizing nature of the war, and the issues to which it had given rise, made it possible to envisage improvements on the provisions decreed by the Founding Fathers.

Moreover, the Reconstruction Acts of 1867 dissolved the Southern state governments, which, in 1865, as Bruce had anticipated,[38] had passed racist "black codes" designed to limit the effect of slave emancipation, and, instead, reintroduced federal control, which gave the army the potential task of preserving this control against local opposition. The difficulty of this task was exacerbated by the unpopular nature of the new state governments that were created on behalf of the "carpetbaggers": Northern adventurers; at least unpopular as far as the bulk of the white population was concerned. In the face of this opposition, the army was expected to support the new governors and the new order, which entailed protecting government buildings, polling places, and blacks as a whole.

The South, bar Tennessee which had ratified the Fourteenth Amendment, was divided into five military districts, each under the command of a general, a technique employed in England under Oliver Cromwell in 1655–57 but abandoned because of its unpopularity. The army was not simply a latent presence in the South; it was responsible for a range of functions, mostly civil, but including the military tasks of disarming local militia and preserving order. The latter was particularly necessary in some areas, notably Appalachia, where guerrilla warfare had left a legacy of vendettas and feuds.[39] The troops were also a restraint on any attempt to mount organized resistance or to resort to low-level seditious behavior.

The army was confronted by the strength of white Southern belief in white superiority,[40] and the military burden of Reconstruction acted as a restraining factor on American behavior elsewhere, for example Canada. The foundation of the Ku Klux Klan, a Confederate veterans' movement, in 1866, was followed by several thousand lynchings, although not all were by the Klan.[41] In 1866, the army intervened to prevent a pogrom, if not massacre, of the black population of New Orleans, while white militias that had been created after the Civil War were disbanded by the government in 1867. However, whites clashed with the militias recruited by Radical Republican state governments, militias that included blacks, as bodies such as the White Brotherhood and the White League challenged Reconstruction. Thus, in Tennessee, the role of the army was complemented by the State Guard, which included some black soldiers and provided crucial protection against the Klan and gangs of former Confederates.[42]

There was a danger that, fulfilling wartime warnings, for example by the French envoy,[43] the army would become a long-term occupation force, with a task focused on controlling civilians and, possibly, even low-level counterinsurgency work. The commanding general in each district had the authority, if his actions were approved by the U.S. attorney for that district, to arrest any civilian in state government, the governor included. The establishment of the districts, in March 1867, prompted the creation of the "invisible empire" of the Klan in April, with the Klan restructured for political combat: states as realms in the Klan empire, and Congressional districts as dens.

Military support for the new political program was modest, amounting to only about 20,000 troops in the South from 1867. As a consequence, even had it been willing, the army was not in a position to support Reconstruction once it was challenged by widespread violence against blacks. As with the potential for foreign expansionism, this situation was a critical product both of postwar demobilization by the heavily indebted federal government and of related and subsequent political decisions. The two should not be separated, although there was a different logic to, and context for, each. When President Johnson considered using the army against Congress in early 1868, the military proved unwilling to accept his plan for creating a sizeable new unit based near Washington.[44] The army was then cut to 28,000 men, compared to 16,000 at the start of 1861, at which strength it remained until the Spanish-American War of 1898. The army might be small, and certainly was compared to its European counterparts, but it was no longer required to hold the country together, and it was not necessary to employ force in order to ensure that the United States would be dominated by Northern capital and industry.

As with the American War of Independence, there was no possibility of using force in a comparable fashion to that employed by the French revolutionaries. Partly for that reason, the 1871 closure date for this book is pertinent, even though Reconstruction and the related military pres-

ence still had several years to run, because, although the Klan was out-
lawed that year, it was abundantly clear by 1871 that Reconstruction
would not be sustained by a large military presence. For example, the
previous year, troops were moved from supporting Reconstruction in
Florida to the Montana Territory, where they acted against hostile Native Americans.

After 1871, clashes continued, with the White League trying to seize
control of New Orleans. By 1877, the Republican governments in the
South had been overthrown, in part by the threat of mob violence, in
every state except Florida, Louisiana, and South Carolina. It was only
in these states that the troops sent to support Reconstruction remained,
and these were now very few.

This situation was resolved as a result of political developments
at the national level. The 1876 presidential election led to disputed returns, and, in the centennial year of the United States, the army indeed
made contingency plans to keep the peace.[45] The disputed returns from
Florida, Louisiana, and South Carolina were crucial, and, as a result
of complex political maneuvers, a compromise awarded the presidency
to the Republican candidate, Rutherford B. Hayes, a volunteer who
had risen to be a major-general in the Union army, but only in return
for withdrawing the troops from the three states, which occurred in
1877. This withdrawal, welcomed by those concerned with civil–military
relations and the federal system of government, led to the fall of the
three Republican state governments.[46] The new, more limited role for
the army was underlined by the Posse Comitatus Act of 1878 which
banned the use of the military in law enforcement, a major restriction
on federal power.

Hayes was one of four Union generals (Grant, Garfield, and Harrison were the others) and one major (McKinley) who became president,
ensuring that veterans held the post from 1869 to 1881, 1889 to 1893, and
1897 to 1901. All were Republicans, as the party used their role in the
war to justify their claim to guide the nation. Thus, the memorialization of the war was politically loaded. Union victory was also marked
with the erection of monuments, so that Washington was filled with
equestrian statues of generals, as well as with the celebration of an-
niversaries, especially Memorial Day, when graves were decorated and

speeches listened to.[47] Yet, this civic memorialization did not lead to militarism.

The end of the occupation suggested a degree of return to normality, but the spatial order of America had been transformed since 1861. Aside from the devastation of much of the South, the war had brought economic growth to the North as resources had been unlocked, and the vast military machine had been mobilized. Thereafter, the contrast in economic and demographic development continued, although the consequences of the Civil War for the American economy have been a source of debate among economists.[48] Immigration focused on the North and the railway system was densest there. This economic growth was intended to encompass the South. In May 1865, Bruce noted the hope that economic transformation would yield benefits for both South and North alike with trade permitting growth: "the introduction of Northern capital and energy will give employment to the Southern people who are now starving, and it is hoped will tend to develop the resources of the states, and thus promote the restoration of tranquility."[49]

However, the political, economic, and social disruption brought to the South by defeat, occupation, and emancipation, had a potent psychological impact, not least in leaving a backward-looking bitterness that contributed to a failure to engage with the possibilities of development within a strong America orientated on national grounds. This failure to engage also arose from a decision of many of the remaining Southern élite to maintain a smaller and poorer agricultural society with oppressive labor relations in which they remained at the top of the socioeconomic pyramid,[50] rather joining the newer industrial order whose urbanization and mechanization would threaten their superiority in the South.

These attitudes and policies led to both absolute and relative underdevelopment as agriculture, as well as industry, elsewhere responded to the economic opportunities created by large-scale population growth, improved communications, and industrialization. Looked at differently, national grounds and criteria were now understood very much in terms of the values of the North. In particular, scant investment was devoted to the South, both from within America and also internationally, and it remained very short of capital and credit.

The North's victory, paradoxically, was to be confirmed, in a fashion, by the theme of "reconciliation" that became stronger from the 1890s. This theme entailed the idea of some sort of moral equivalence between the combatants, and, in doing so, meant underplaying slavery and ignoring the role of blacks in the Union victory. Reconciliation, therefore, made many, and excessive, allowances for Southern views, but it also rested on a willingness by much of a North, triumphant in their dominance of present and future, not to be overly troubled about the past, an outcome that proved beyond many Southerners who preferred the identity of collective grievance. However, there were always major American historians, such as James Ford Rhodes in 1913, who repudiated this moral equivalence between North and South, and, whereas the South largely won the day when it came to the historical narrative about Reconstruction, it was less successful about the causes of the war.

If occupation of the South was restrained in comparison to what could have occurred, and to how it would be remembered by Southern Democrats, no such restraint was to be shown in the West. Indeed, the number of troops in the South had been considerably reduced in the 1870s, prior to 1876, as securing the West became the central issue for the army. Already, as with the War of Independence, although for very different reasons, conflict with Native Americans continued during the Civil War, although, initially, the gathering crisis led to a decline in hostilities. Thus, plans for a winter campaign against the Navajo in 1860–61 were abandoned. However, the customary tensions over settlement and control remained, and, as American activity remained incessant, so the Native response was frequently hostile. Moreover, the Civil War encouraged a response to force on the part of government by lessening peacetime restraints. Attacks may have been inspired by rumors of Native support for the Confederacy. There was, indeed, some support, and a number of treaties were signed, although, in each of the Five Civilized Tribes, loyalists also rallied to the Union and fought for it.[51]

As a result, there was conflict across much of the west, conflict that interacted, often indirectly, with the Civil War.[52] In some areas, the Americans were under pressure, notably in Texas, where, despite some success, the Confederates were unable to protect their western settlements, and an outnumbered Ranger force was routed by Kickapoo at Dove Creek in January 1865.[53]

More commonly, it was the Natives who were defeated. In Minnesota and Colorado, the extent of American settlement was the key provocation. This was certainly an issue in the Minnesota rising of 1862, which also affected the Dakota Territory. Eastern Sioux attacked American settlements in Minnesota, although they failed to capture the forts, while other Sioux attacked Americans, en route to gold workings in Montana, crossing their lands on the Bozeman Trail. The army responded by driving the Eastern Sioux back from Minnesota, and, then, during the summers of 1863, 1864, and 1865, launched columns under Brigadier Generals Henry Sibley and Alfred Sully against the Sioux in Dakota and Montana. Sully beat Sioux opponents at Whitestone Hill on 3 September 1863 and defeated Sitting Bull at Killdeer Mountain, North Dakota, on 28 July 1864. In 1863, the British turned down an American request to be allowed to pursue hostile Natives into Canada, a prewar issue, but, in January 1864, Seward returned to the charge, claiming that the Canadian authorities were feeding Sioux who had taken refuge.[54]

In Colorado, violence between settlers and the Arapaho and Cheyenne led to an increasingly tense situation. In June 1864, the governor of the Colorado Territory, John Evans, instructed "friendly Indians" to present themselves at army posts, but also prepared a military response. In August, Evans was given governmental permission to raise the Third Colorado Cavalry, a regiment of volunteers to be commanded by Colonel John Chivington, head of the army military district in Colorado. Native Chiefs sought to negotiate a settlement and thought they had done so with Evans and Chivington at Camp Weld on 28 September.

As a consequence, Arapaho and Cheyenne moved to Fort Lyon in accordance with Evans's proclamation of June and what they believed to be the Camp Weld agreement. However, Evans was preparing to destroy the tribes. At dawn on 29 November, Chivington's men attacked the Native encampment, killing many both there and a mile further on where the fleeing Natives adopted a defensive position, only to be bombarded by 12-pounder mountain howitzer guns. In the Sand Creek Massacre, at least 150 and as many as 200 Natives, mainly women, children, and the elderly, were slaughtered. Ten soldiers were killed. Chivington's men were applauded in Denver, but the massacre, which helped to touch off a major bout of fighting across the Plains, was swiftly condemned in Washington.[55]

There was also conflict further west, with California troops defeating Shoshone in Idaho and Ute in Utah in 1863. That year, treaties were negotiated with Native tribes in California and Oregon. Further south, federal columns forced the Navajo to agree to move to reservations in 1864, a bland description of the use of scorched earth policies and of the subsequent forced march of the Navajo and their confinement in the bleak reservation of Bosque Redondo. The Comanche, meanwhile, were hit hard by smallpox and by drought, the latter greatly affecting bison numbers.

The pace of expansion at the expense of Native Americans resumed after the Civil War, with the Powder River Expedition launched into Wyoming in the summer of 1865 against the Sioux, Cheyenne, and Arapaho,[56] but much of the preparatory work had been done during it, and, indeed, there was continuity in the case of that expedition, which was a reprisal for raids earlier that year. The notion that it was Civil War veterans, notably Sherman (Commander of the Division of the Missouri from 1865) and Philip Sheridan (Commander of the Department of the Missouri from 1867), who inaugurated a harsher, exterminatory, approach to Plains warfare requires qualification as, aside from assuming a misleading consensus in frontier warfare, Harney before the war and Carleton during it both advocated wiping out their Native enemies and practiced this to the best of their ability.[57] Moreover, during the Civil War, the useful tactic of winter campaigning got its start.

Nevertheless, there were serious problems for the army. Many commanders from the 1850s were dead or had lost their commissions by serving the Confederacy; and their replacements, trained in, and from the Civil War, with its emphasis on commanding and fighting large numbers of regulars, were not adept at dealing with the very mobile Natives. Moreover, the sharp reduction of the army in the aftermath of the Civil War ensured that there were few troops available for frontier warfare. When, in 1867, Sheridan took command of the Department of the Missouri, which covered much of the frontier, he had only 6,000 troops.

Aside from the problem that the show of force helped provoke further resistance, as General Winfield Scott Hancock's expedition of 1867 demonstrated with the response of the Cheyenne,[58] in operational and tactical terms it proved difficult to force the mobile Natives to battle, not least because they knew the terrain and were adept at surprise. The Sioux showed this in 1866–68 in their successful campaigning against the army in Montana and Wyoming in the Bozeman Trail War, also known as Red Cloud's War. The Sioux surrounded and besieged American forts, forcing their abandonment.

As a consequence, the army developed techniques that focused on winter campaigning, employed in late 1868 in attacks in north Texas. Native settlements were particularly vulnerable in the winter; those who escaped risked starvation and death by exposure. This method was employed on 26 November 1868 at the battle of the Washita when Lieutenant-Colonel George Armstrong Custer annihilated a southern Cheyenne village led by Black Kettle, killing women and children as well. The destruction of crops and villages and the confiscation of pony herds, none a new tactic, also brought misery,[59] and the British envoy deplored such methods as "unnecessary" and "wholesale slaughter."[60] The coordination of independently operating columns advancing from different directions was also important to American success.

There was an important shift in government policy after Grant became president in 1869. Believing in "conquest by kindness," in which Natives moved to reservations where Christian education and agriculture were intended to make them "good" neighbors who were civilized and Christianized, Grant followed what has been seen as a peace policy from 1869 to 1874. He was opposed to the previous treaty system by which tribes were viewed as domestic, dependent nations with which America must negotiate. In 1871, the Senate acceded to an act abolishing the treaty system, although the House was opposed to it as they did not participate in the conclusion of treaties by the executive or their ratification by the Senate.[61]

As a result of the shift in policy, the pace of hostilities declined at the close of the 1860s, although the situation deteriorated in the early 1870s with the peace policy discredited in 1871. That autumn, Sherman sent troops against the Comanche, who were seen as putting Texas under excessive pressure. The inexorable nature of this adversary placed the Comanche in unprecedented difficulties.[62] Moreover, Colonel George Crook forced Cochise, the head of the Arizona Apache, to surrender in 1871, although he soon resumed hostilities.[63]

Whatever the pace of conflict, Native American resistance had been largely broken, and a successful military methodology to that end had evolved. Its focus on wrecking civil society, or, rather, on the notion that there was no civil sphere separate to the military, had been seen in the conflict between North and South in the latter stages of the Civil War. In the west, this system was made especially effective against Native Americans thanks to the mobility of the regulars and their ability, through a good logistical system, to stage winter campaigns. This success indicated the army's potential to adapt its military style and methods, and its mobility was an important legacy to subsequent American military culture and doctrine.[64] Industrial capacity underlay this mobility as the railway was used to move troops against opponents.

Yet, other factors also continued to play a role. The Americans were still able to obtain local support because of Native American rivalries. In the Sioux Wars (1854–77), most of the other Plains tribes joined the Americans against the Sioux, as they saw the latter as a far more immediate threat to their safety than the more distant Americans. The American army used Pawnee and Crow scouts in the major battles of the 1860s and 1870s, as well as Shoshone warriors as auxiliaries.[65] The Sioux, in turn, viewed the Americans as merely one more tribal enemy for much of the time, and alternated attacks on American units and forts with raids against Crow and Shoshone.[66] The same was true of the Comanche.

The Sioux suffered from the army's adoption of breech loaders in 1867, which provided a crucial firepower advantage. On 21 December 1866, Captain William J. Fetterman, a Civil War veteran, and eighty troops armed with muzzle loaders were taken unawares outside Fort Philip Kearny, Wyoming, in a matter of minutes by about 2,000 Northern Cheyenne, Northern Arapaho, and Lakota Sioux, a force far larger than they had anticipated. By the following August, the army had new single-shot breech loaders with copper cartridges able to fire twelve shots a minute compared to the muzzle loaders' three. On two different occasions, on 1–2 August, the Wagon Box fight and the Hayfield fight, three dozen soldiers held off several thousand warriors.[67] The Native American attempt to counter this by acquiring the same technology, not least from defeated opponents, could be deadly, as at Little Big Horn in 1876, but suffered from their lack of access to ammunition supplies. Moreover, there were major limits to the changes in Native war making, notably away from the style of individual fighting that stressed bravery and yet also tried to avoid casualties. In particular, the Sioux did not attempt to institute anything like military discipline or coercive leadership, and the seasonal nature of their warfare could not be altered.

Red Cloud and his warriors came to the bargaining table for peace shortly after his fighting power had been greatly reduced by the American use of breech loaders. This usage also had an impact in episodes of European expansion in the period, as well as with the case of expansion elsewhere in the New World; although, as in the United States, a range of factors played a role.[68] By 1867 on the southern plains (Treaty of Medicine Lodge) and by 1868 on the northern plains (Treaty of Fort Laramie), most tribes had been sent to reservations. Those who left without permission were deemed hostile. Although the Fort Laramie treaty created a large Lakota Sioux reservation centered on the Black Hills and not under military supervision, this meant a new geography of power and control.

It was also a geography in which the army positioned the West into America not solely by enforcing the reservation policy and maintaining security but also by playing a major role in supporting economic integration, notably by building roads and encouraging the building of railways. Sherman was particularly involved in this process.[69] These policies were part of a wider program by which the railway fostered public policies that encouraged the stabilization of civil society, including public relief and law enforcement, while the reservations were intended to clear threatening Natives from the rail routes, notably from those along the Platte and Kansas valleys, the routes for the Union Pacific and Kansas Pacific lines.[70] In addition, military expenditure was important in bringing a measure of prosperity.[71]

In Canada, the federal government created by Confederation on 1 July 1867 was made responsible for "Indians and Lands reserved for the Indians." There was the same pressure of settlement as in the United

States, but not the same violence, in large part because the pace of settlement was less intense.[72] Nonetheless, with the participation of the Plains Crees, the mixed-blood Métis staged the unsuccessful Red River rebellion in 1869–70 in Manitoba in response to the division of the land by government surveyors. British troops suppressed the rebellion without American intervention.[73]

The American grasp of the West had renewed the question of Canada's future. Again, it is very easy to discuss this largely in terms of a response to America's strength and the danger of U.S. expansion. British envoys stressed American support for annexation,[74] and the defenses of Canada were a matter of government concern.[75] In 1865, although most of those who spoke in the House of Commons in the Canada debate on 13 March argued that relations with America were friendly, there was concern about the possibility of American filibustering in Canada,[76] and about the construction of American gunboats for the Great Lakes.[77] Yet, Bruce, Gladstone, and others noted the speed with which America demobilized its army, while Seward informed Bruce that the gunboats were for revenue purposes.

Nevertheless, Fenian activities in the late 1860s, stigmatized in *Punch's* caricature "The Fenian Pest" on 3 March 1866, underlined the possibility that America might be the basis for pressure on Canada.[78] In September 1866, an (in hindsight) overly alarmed Charles, Lord Monck, the governor-general of Canada, called for reinforcements against a threatened Fenian invasion from America, and fears of such an invasion continued thereafter. The crisis of the late 1830s had shown that pressure on Canada could best be countered with American support, but the American attitude appeared more expansionist in the late 1860s.

British anxieties about the extent to which Canada could be defended were important to the government's encouragement of Confederation. In 1840, Lower and Upper Canada had been joined together in the Province of Canada, a step taken in large part in response to the revolts of 1837 and the subsequent Durham Report of 1839 by John, 1st Earl of Durham, the recent Governor-General. Similarly, the tension linked to the Civil War encouraged Confederation in 1867, which brought together Canada and the provinces of New Brunswick and Nova Scotia. As part of the new system, enacted by the British North America Act, the two parts of Canada, Canada East (Lower) and West (Upper), were separated and given the names of Quebec and Ontario.

Confederation linked the economically weak Maritimes, notably a hesitant Nova Scotia, to the more dynamic interior, and, in strengthening an east–west axis of mutual dependency, provided a key basis for the new state, the Dominion of Canada. As in the United States, an economic dynamic was provided by the export of agricultural goods from the prairie west, but the scale was very different as the Canadian population in 1871 was 3.7 million, compared to 39.3 million in the United States in 1870. Confederation was linked to the development of intercolonial trade and was a response to the rival possibilities created by trade with America. It also helped Canada cope with the beginning of a serious depression in 1873, one that lasted until the late 1890s.

Confederation was not the full extent of the changes in British North America. The following year, 1868, Rupert's Land Act authorized the acquisition of Rupert's Land and the North-Western Territory from the Hudson's Bay Company, and, in 1870, an Order in Council transferred these lands to Canada and renamed them the North-West Territories. Also in 1870, an Act of Dominion established Manitoba as a fifth province, while on 25 July 1871, by another Act of Dominion, British Columbia entered Canada as the sixth province: British Columbia and Vancouver Island had been united into one colony in 1866. Other provinces were to follow, Prince Edward Island in 1873.

Concern about American intentions continued after Confederation. Edward Thornton wrote to the foreign secretary in January 1870, "I have often spoken to you of the great hankering felt by Americans for our possessions on this continent. This feeling seems to be growing every day." Hamilton Fish, Grant's secretary of state, told Thornton that nine-tenths of the Canadian population would vote for annexation "if they were not coerced by the government, their adherents, and capitalists interested in the maintenance of the present state of things," and he also asked whether Britain would use force to oppose Canadian separatism.[79] Uncertainty over the possible direction of American pressure encouraged the British government to seek a settlement to Anglo-American disputes, not least because they were aware that American politicians linked Canada's "evident destiny" with the *Alabama* claims,[80] and were concerned that a failure to end the dispute might encourage what they saw as a latent tendency in American democracy toward demagogy.

On 8 May 1871, after high-level negotiations, the signature of the Treaty of Washington settled Anglo-American differences, including fishing rights, access to the St. Lawrence River, and the San Juan boundary dispute between Vancouver Island and the United States, which was submitted to arbitration by Wilhelm I, the newly created emperor of Germany. Moreover, Britain expressed its regret for the actions of the *Alabama,* and arbitration in Switzerland was agreed to. The settlement, in 1872, was largely to America's satisfaction, bringing to a close demands for compensation that had vexed relations since the Civil War. America was awarded £3.2 million, although the potentially unlimited claims for indirect damage by the *Alabama* and other ships raised by the Americans in December 1871 were rejected. Passed by the Senate on 24 May 1871 by fifty votes to twelve, this was a treaty that, by and large, Americans liked much and the British accepted grudgingly, as the price to be paid for easing into the new geopolitics of American dominance in North America and a greater American role in the wider world.[81] However, the settlement's rejection of the indirect claims caused anger and the Republicans suffered political reverses as a result.

Thereafter, the British withdrew their armed forces, with the exception of the well-fortified Atlantic naval base at Halifax and the Pacific naval base at Esquimalt, which was just opposite San Juan Island.[82] In turn, the American military presence in the Great Lakes was reduced, with Fort Wilkins closed in 1870 and Fort Gratiot in 1879. In Vancouver Sound, the American camp on San Juan Island was closed in 1874. Decrepit frontier bastions became national parks.

The American government did not trouble Canadian confederation (although the House complained), and this has been traced to an implicit bargain made when Britain withdrew its garrisons, as with the claim that "Britain was using confederation to disclaim a military presence . . . confirming that it – and Canada – would not challenge American preeminence on the continent. On these terms, the Americans accepted the existence of a transcontinental Canada."[83] This approach, however, is all too typical of a certain type of geopolitical argument in that it is instrumentalist rather than based on evidence. There are indeed powerful contrary arguments. First, the importance of European power politics again emerges, for the rapprochement between Britain and America was, to a degree, a reflection of France's failure to divide the two and, moreover, in part a product of France's relative decline, notably from 1866 and, most clearly, in 1870–71. Secondly, rather than treating the British military withdrawal solely as an aspect of the North American Question, it is necessary to note the extent to which it conformed to the more general trend in British colonial and military policy. From the late 1850s, "colonial reformers" in the Westminster Parliament had pressed for the recall of British troops from the colonies, a cause supported both by the Treasury, which was mindful of costs, and by the War Office, which wished to maintain fighting effectiveness and did not see colonial garrison duty as the way to achieve this.[84]

The consequences of the army's initially poor showing in the Crimean War was accentuated by anxieties about French intentions in the late 1850s and 1860s,[85] and, more generally, by continuing concern about British military capabilities; which, indeed, led in 1871–73 to maneuvers held in response to the Franco-Prussian War. Indeed in 1864, three battalions were withdrawn from Canada, in part as a measure of economy but also linked to the Schleswig-Holstein crisis.

The report by the Defence Committee on colonial defense, printed in January 1863, only recommended the maintenance of fortifications at imperial cost in positions where they involved an imperial interest. The maintenance of Quebec as a "first-class fortress" was recommended as all help to Canada had to go via it.[86] As secretary of state for the Colonies from 1864 to 1866, Edward Cardwell (who on 1 January 1862 told the annual dinner of the Oxford Druids' Lodge that war with America would be like a civil war)[87] withdrew regular troops from the colonies for which the latter were not willing to pay. A politician for whom financial issues were important and who was linked to Gladstone,[88] Cardwell pressed hard for Canada to take a greater burden, arguing that otherwise it could not be defended. Palmerston's support for a greater commitment to Canada was sidelined. Cardwell and Gladstone also backed Confederation and tied financial support for the fortification of Quebec to this issue.

The last British soldiers in Australia left in 1870, a policy seen as Fortress England by critics, and the colonies were encouraged to develop their forces, a process that bore fruit with the assistance they provided to Britain in the Boer War of 1899–1902.[89] The process of disengagement can also be related to a focus on Russian expansionism as the key threat to British imperial interests.[90]

It is also possible to put the emphasis not on British withdrawal but on Confederation as a clear sign of a readiness to unite and a will to survive. Indeed, on 11 October 1864, John A. Macdonald, at the start of a conference held in Quebec to decide whether to create a new government for all of Canada, declared, "The great security for peace is to convince the world of our strength by being united,"[91] a sentiment Hamilton and, despite his commitment to states' rights, Jefferson would have applauded for America. Charles Sumner, the chairman of the Senate Committee on Foreign Affairs, told the Republican state convention on 22 September 1869 that he regarded Canada's union with the United States as an appointed destiny, but that it had to come as a peaceful process and with the consent of its people, a route that developments in Canada were ruling out.

Continuing the policy seen in the late 1830s, in response to rebellion in Canada and the dispute on the New Brunswick–Maine border, and despite British concern that America would support disaffection,[92] American governments neither sought nor wished greatly to disrupt the consolidation of authority and power in British North America. As a result, the latter was stabilized without intervention. Fish might suggest that separatism be allowed in Canada,[93] but nothing was done, and opponents of British/Canadian authority were overcome. British gunboats enforced control on the coast of British Columbia, destroying canoes and villages in punitive action.[94] Moreover, in 1885, the Canadian government mobilized more than four thousand militia, deploying them by means of the Canadian Pacific Railway to suppress the Métis, the mixed-race population of the Canadian west, when, angered by their poor treatment in land allocation, they formed their own government.

Such action by the Canadian government scarcely challenged American interests, although it indicated the extent to which international frontiers now constrained American overland expansionism as they had not done to the same extent in the first half of the century, albeit with the important exception of the Canadian frontier after 1815. Exceptionalism as an explanatory device is inappropriate, as such a situation was increasingly the case across the world in the second half of the century when leading powers came to share out direct or indirect control, while other states lessened opportunities for these powers by defining their territorial boundaries.[95] However, more than constrained territorial expansion was involved in the case of America. Instead, as with Britain, there was a commitment to other goals, and, as with Britain, there was a shift in emphasis that can be linked to the displacement of a key governing group and its assumptions.[96]

That the Civil War represented a triumph for the urban and industrial society of the North over its agrarian-based Southern counterpart had implications for foreign policy. Seward proclaimed that "the nation that draws the most materials and provisions from the earth, fabricates the most, and sells the most of productions and fabrics to foreign nations, must be, and will be, the great power of the earth."[97]

This definition of the future growth of American power excluded both the original Jeffersonian concept of an agrarian state whose farmers constituted the basis of economic and political power and the Southern manifestation of that concept in which land investors from Washington to Jackson and Quitman sought an uninterrupted march westward. Seward's vision, indeed, required the subjugation of the agrarian alternative society of the South.

Once the North accomplished that end in a civil war started by the South in pursuance of its requirements for social and political development, there was the mistaken hope that the new economic and political order in the South would share Northern values. Nevertheless, the geopolitical policies of the United States reflected Seward's vision. Rather like Britain's longstanding policy in Latin America,[98] the priority became access to markets and the securing of routes to those markets, rather than the conquest of land. Most obviously, the United States no longer sought to annex Mexican territory, but, instead, gained access to the Mexican market. The Americans eventually controlled all the major extractive industries there, and foreigners, led by Americans, owned slightly less than a quarter of Mexico's land. The turn away from territorial expansion was demonstrated by the substantial public relations campaign Seward undertook to persuade Congress to fund his purchase of Alaska.

Looking ahead, Cuba was not annexed after Spain was defeated there in 1898. Instead, the Americans retained control of the naval anchorage at Guantanamo and the power to control sea lanes that came with such a base. In 1912, the Americans sent marines into Cuba in order to protect American property in the face of a large-scale, mostly black, peasant uprising motivated by the strains of economic change, social pressure, and political discrimination. Annexation was no longer an option, but, as in Nicaragua, the disruptive consequences of American activity remained acute.[99]

By 1871, the geopolitical struggle for North America had evolved into a geoeconomic struggle for markets, one that the Americans were increasingly to conduct not only in Latin America and East Asia but also on a world scale. Limits were scarcely the concluding theme. America had emerged from the maelstrom of civil war and the international volatility of the 1860s as the most powerful state in the New World and as one clearly on a path toward an even greater future.

# 16

## POSTSCRIPT
## 1871-2010

The year 1871 saw not only the Treaty of Washington, which ended, or, at least, greatly eased, Anglo-American differences in North America, but also the declaration of the German Empire. Initially, this might have seemed benign to America, as in 1872 Wilhelm I arbitrated the Anglo-American dispute over the San Juan Islands boundary essentially in line with American claims. Moreover, in 1870, Fish had told Thornton that he "hoped some day to see Germany, England and the United States, the three great Protestant and progressive Countries, in the most friendly alliance with each other."[1] However, in the long term, German power was to pose a major challenge to America. In part, this challenge reflected specific issues, but there was also a more serious cultural disdain for America on the part, first, of Imperial Germany and, subsequently, of Nazi Germany, a disdain that was stronger and more significant for policy than anything stemming from Britain. Moreover, Germany was to project its ambitions, although not its power, into the New Hemisphere, seeking to challenge American influence in Mexico in 1917 and in Latin America as a whole in the early 1940s.[2]

Yet, in 1871, these concerns lay very much in the future. Instead, the United States experienced a major burst in economic growth, a burst that reflected not only international opportunities and the strengths of the American economy, including plentiful resources, but also the consequences of the politics of the 1860s, in particular the strengthening of national cohesion and effective government as a result of Union success in the Civil War. The specific circumstances of that outcome, combined with the civic culture and religion established from the American War of Independence, ensured that America did not share in the counterrevolutionary mood that the 1848 revolutions had helped provoke across much of Europe.

A stark division between America and Europe would be inappropriate, not least because the abandonment of Reconstruction and the shelving of its potential implications can be seen as counterrevolutionary, as well as a conciliatory (or appeasing) abandoning of the prospect of a new America and a different civic culture free of discriminatory racial governance and based on a powerful national state directing the South. In addition, far from Europe being a uniform counterpoint, Britain scarcely shared the counterrevolutionary direction of Prussia/Germany. Rather than being a case of strong or weak governance, simply defined, a key element in America was the ability, once wartime exigencies had been put aside, to return to a large margin of self-government by the states, while Germany, in contrast, came to symbolize the linkage of a bureaucratic powerful state to a strong army.

Germany and America both saw significant economic growth, but there were distinctive features to the American economy, which became more self-sufficient, with much less of a dependence on supply and demand factors focused on Europe. As a result, an independent dynamic developed in the American economy, encouraging specialization, investment, and growth.[3] By the start of the twentieth century, American economic output was equivalent to that of the whole of Europe, and, by 1918, with America both a major creditor state and benefiting from large-scale wartime growth, it had the capital to match. The American economy benefited from substantial natural resources, including coal, iron, copper, silver, and timber, a large domestic market, extensive immigration, an openness to foreign investment, a legal code that protected property, a governmental system that supported economic growth, and a political practice at the national level that avoided extremism. America's innovatory ethos derived in part from the shortages of skilled labor throughout the nineteenth century, whereas the plentiful supplies of cheap, skilled labor in Britain militated against maximizing technological inputs.

Albeit against a weak empire, America demonstrated its power in a war with Spain in 1898 that reflected wide-ranging geopolitical interests and capabilities.[4] The conquest of Cuba and Puerto Rico and the arrival of American troops in the Philippines followed rapid and decisive naval victories. The peace treaty with Spain left Puerto Rico, Guam, and the Philippines to the United States, but, in the last, control was enforced only after nationalist opposition was suppressed in a bitter counterinsurgency war. These difficulties underlined the value of not having had to face a guerrilla war in the South from 1865, for, in the Philippines, the Americans found it hard to fix their opponents for combat, and, while they were ultimately successful, their methods were often brutal.

The American achievement against Spain was thrown into greater prominence by the problems Britain encountered in defeating the Boers in South Africa in 1899–1902, and by the serious defeat Russia suffered at the hands of Japan in 1904–1905, although, of course, these wars were far from comparable. President Theodore Roosevelt's successful mediation of the Russo-Japanese War, for which he won the Nobel Peace Prize, was a testimony to America's importance and influence, and both were demonstrated in 1907–1909 when the sixteen battleships of the "Great White Fleet" sailed round the world in a major show of strength, albeit one that in practice depended on British help with coaling. By 1914, America was a major power in the Pacific, with Hawaii, Midway, Johnston, Palmyra, Tutula, and Wake islands, as well as Guam and the Philippines, and was also increasingly assertive in Central America and in the Caribbean.

American power was dramatized in the new geopolitics of the Panama Canal, which provided a link for warships and merchantmen between the eastern and western seaboards of the United States. A project originally and unsuccessfully begun with French capital had ended in 1914 as a triumph for American engineering and influence, for, in 1903, Panama became an independent state carved out from Colombia under American protection, and, under the Hays-Bunau-Varilla Treaty, the United States gained control over the canal zone, providing a parallel to British control over the Suez Canal. The construction of the canal owed much to the American army, which played a major role in its planning and organization, as well as in providing protection from disease.[5] The Panama Canal, over which America handed over control in 1999, was a key indicator of the extent to which the struggle for mastery in North America had ended on American terms, and also of the degree to which the struggle entailed influence in Central America.

Another indicator was provided by the settlement of the Alaskan frontier dispute between Canada and the United States largely on American terms, because Britain was more conciliatory over this and over seal fishing rights in the Bering Sea than the Canadians would have liked.[6] A different testimony to America's importance was provided by the extent of immigration from Canada,[7] while trade with Canada had been encouraged by the dismantling of British imperial preference from the 1840s.

Anglo-American relations improved in part on the basis of Britain managing its disputes with the United States skillfully and accepting American hegemony in the Western Hemisphere; for example, Britain adopted a largely compliant approach to American policy during the Mexican Revolution of 1910–17.[8] In turn, the United States did not seek to overthrow the British Empire, not, for example, exploiting the Indian Mutiny of 1857–59 or the Boer War in order to challenge the British position in Canada, although by the 1920s there was talk of possible war.

A more critical tone is struck if a different vocabulary is employed, as with Michael Howard writing of the rivalry being "appeased" by Britain,[9] although such language has also been used of British relations with other powers, for example France in 1858–59.[10] There was a parallel to the British treatment of American policy in the willingness of British politicians in 1866–67 to accept Canadian confederation, despite the doubts of the Colonial Office and colonial governors, and opposition in Nova Scotia. As a result of British management and American policy, the Committee of Imperial Defence and the Foreign Office concluded in 1908 that the possibility of war with the United States was remote.[11]

The likely development of closer relations between Canada and the United States led to concern in Britain, where it helped to lend support to calls from the 1900s, especially from Joseph Chamberlain, the Colonial Secretary, for imperial preference linked to a tariff reform predicated on the abandonment of free trade and the embrace of protectionism. Yet relations were easier than those between the United States and Mexico, where insurrections and civil wars in 1910–11 and 1913–17 appeared to suggest an inherent instability that the United States could only respond to with a clear demonstration of greater power. The situation was part of a more general instability in Latin America that included coups, such as that in Venezuela in 1908, civil wars, for example in Venezuela (1898–1900), Colombia (1899–1903), Uruguay (1904), Ecuador (1911–12), and Paraguay (1911–12); and the international conflicts with which civil wars were often intertwined, for instance the Central American wars of 1906–1907 involving Guatemala, El Salvador, Honduras, and Nicaragua.

The United States found itself increasingly drawn into Latin America in order to protect its growing economic interests. Moreover, the American understanding of the Monroe Doctrine as an argument to deny European powers the right to intervene in Latin America, whether Venezuela in the 1890s and 1900s or Mexico in the first decade of the twentieth century, further encouraged action, as did the changing strategic place of the Caribbean and Central America in American naval plans following the opening of the Panama Canal in 1914.[12] America's diplomatic role in Venezuela's 1895–96 dispute with Britain over the border of British Guiana was important,[13] and in 1902–1903 American intervention led Britain, Germany, and Italy to end their blockade of Venezuela in pursuit of unpaid debts. This activity looked toward longstanding American interventions in Haiti, the Dominican Republic, and Nicaragua between 1915 and 1934, a policy, however, that proved more difficult than anticipated due to resistance from popular guerrilla movements.

Throughout, America benefited from the absence of any real need to consider its northern frontier. This situation continued during the two world wars, although the Fall of France to German invasion in 1940, and the apparent danger that Britain might follow, led to concern in America about the consequences for Canada, not least the threat that Vichyist tendencies would thrive in Quebec where Catholic conservatism was strong. By allying with Britain in 1917 and 1941, the United States automatically allied with Canada and with the world's largest navy, and both greatly increased American security. In going to war, the United States constructed national interest in terms of the freedom of international trade from the unrestricted submarine warfare declared by Germany, a construction that aligned the United States with Britain as the two powers committed to running the Atlantic in particular as a protected zone for trade and transport.

Britain became of lesser relative consequence during the Cold War, but Britain was still America's leading ally and the United States was joined to both it and Canada as founding members of NATO (the North Atlantic Treaty Organization), which was established in 1949. Practical cooperation was demonstrated by the construction of early-warning radar stations across Canada in order to provide the United States with advance warning of a bomber or missile attack from the Soviet Union across the Arctic, notably with the Pinetree Network in 1954 and the Distant Early Warning Line in 1957. A North American Air Defense Command followed in 1958, and this system was strengthened after the terrorist attacks on New York and Washington in 2001.

The alliance became less warm as Canada moved from supporting America, notably in the Gulf Wars of 1990–91 and 2003, but it continued (and continues) to provide the United States with a strategic depth that contrasted with growing anxieties about instability on, or near, its southern borders, and with related threats from hostile powers, notably Cuba from the 1960s, Nicaragua in the 1980s, and Venezuela in the beginning of the twenty-first century. The American attempt to stabilize Mexico under the North American Free Trade Agreement (NAFTA) of 1994, which was followed by the Central American Free Trade Agreement of 2005, was hindered by persistent problems with corruption and drug-linked crime, and the recession of the early 2010s greatly exacerbated the situation. Popular anxieties in America focused on Mexico, not Canada, notably with Ross Perot, an independent presidential candidate in 1992 and 1996, who claimed that, as a result of NAFTA, there was a "giant sucking sound" of jobs moving to Mexico. In contrast, the key trading partnership between America and Canada is generally seen as bringing mutual benefit.

It is possible that concerns about Central America and the Caribbean will affect America's wider geopolitical situation, although the experience of the 1980s and 2000s suggests otherwise. The centrality of the Middle East, South Asia, and the Far East in American policymaking will probably continue and, like America's earlier participation in the two world wars and the Cold War, will provide a clear testimony to the beneficial consequences of its success in winning the struggle for mastery in North America.

# CONCLUSIONS

The silver sparkled and there were toasts aplenty on 1 January 1862 when Edward Cardwell MP, Chancellor of the Duchy of Lancaster, rose in Oxford Town Hall, at the annual dinner of the Oxford Druids' Lodge, to reply to the toast for the MP of Oxford. He offered a panegyric to friendship across the ocean, one, according to the newspaper reports, that was greeted by acclamation in the hall:

> We saw with sorrow a civil war break out between two parts of one great country – the inheritors of our blood, of our literature, and of our glory – and we should regard it as little less than a civil war among ourselves if an unhappy circumstance should arise to involve us in hostilities with the people of America.

Cardwell then pressed on to address the highly topical *Trent* episode:

> We have sustained an injury – one that has been such as we could not possibly pass by, if we meant to retain the name and the position which England has heretofore enjoyed among the nations of the world.[1]

The interplay of contexts and events as much concerned contemporaries as later observers, and geopolitics sits astride the longstanding tension between, on the one hand, the facts of territory and territorial power, and, on the other, the complex and often tangible processes by which humans shape their understandings and interests and then seek to devise and execute policy. As a subject, it has been affected by the linked crises of materialist explanations of motivation, structuralist and systemic presentations of power, and determinist accounts of development. Yet, despite the limitations of geopolitical approaches, there is still a need to consider the question of space and its implications.

Unfortunately, many historians underplay this question and, more particularly, the frictions of distance. Moreover, once removed from the specifics of historical contingency, the discussion of national development is apt to embrace abstractions and to reify nations, and this process can involve a serious downplaying of spatial factors, not least those linked to regional politics. Thus, Robert Kagan, in one of the most perceptive broad-brush accounts, argued that the War of 1898, in which America conquered Cuba, Puerto Rico, and the Philippines and became a transoceanic power, was consistent with his central themes:

> The war was the product of deeply ingrained American attitudes toward the nation's place in the world.... It reflected Americans' view of themselves, stretching back to before the nation's founding, as the advance guard of civilization, leading the way against backward and barbaric nations and empires.[2]

In practice, as Kagan's book indeed indicated, it is appropriate not to simplify American attitudes and politics in order to offer a misleading consistency and, notably, one that depoliticized the national space. There is a well-established practice of doing so, including, but not only, by geopoliticians and by others looking at international relations in a systemic fashion. The reality, instead, was of very different views, as, in the case of America, in the 1812, Seminole, Mexican, and Spanish-American wars, and over Native American removal in the 1830s, and there was often political opposition to territorial expansion. Moreover, such differences over foreign policy were linked to contrasting views of American development and, in turn, to domestic political images and alignments. The perception that America could, and should, be a united expression of free and independent people joined in a common enterprise added to the tensions linked to these divisions.

Differences over policy also underline the role of contingency, an aspect of the challenging not only of the conventional geopolitical approach but also of systemic notions of international relations.[3] Thus, the highly contentious presidential election of 1800 seemed likely to lead to a political breakdown, if not possibly civil war,[4] which indeed was to happen sixty years later. Fixing contingency to American policy is doubly important because it prevents an account in which the Americans had consistent goals that were brought to fruition by circumstances, in the shape of events, with the latter understood largely in terms of American success in implementing their policies. Instead, the role of uncertainty and the extent of risk are underlined by an appreciation that contingency related to America, including its goals, to other powers, and to their interaction. This book has discussed some of these contingencies, but the examples can be multiplied.

Two major conclusions emerge before we reconsider the methodological points. First, the struggle for mastery in North America was, for long, far more uncertain than posterity has imagined. Indeed, there were not only key episodes that indicated the possibility of very different outcomes, such as the Louisiana Purchase in 1803, and conflicts, for example the War of 1812, but also periods of uncertainty, notably the mid-1840s and the early 1860s.

Secondly, the North American Question depended to a greater extent on European power politics and the views of European powers than is sometimes appreciated, notably in American public myth. Thus, Spain's collapse under Charles IV, particularly during the Napoleonic occupation of 1808–1813, was highly important to America as Spain bordered it to the south and west. Crucially, American expansionism was helped by the extent to which the Question was usually a secondary one for European powers, a point that does not generally emerge in studies of bilateral relations which, necessarily, tend to exaggerate the importance of this bilateralism. This situation was particularly the case because of the extent to which Europe's Atlantic powers were closely involved in relations not only with each other but also with other European powers. Indeed, whatever the suggestions of Atlanticists, there was no separate Atlantic system. For example, the attention that George III and his ministers could devote to America in 1772–73 was greatly lessened by the international crises surrounding the First Partition of Poland in 1772 and Gustavus III's coup in Sweden also in 1772. These crises involved Austria, Prussia, Russia, and France, and led George to consider a rapprochement with France to which extra-European disputes would have been subordinated. Moreover, in 1803 Napoleon was focused on European power politics rather than on the New World; in the 1840s there were important crises involving Britain and France in the Near East, and also across Europe in the Year of Revolutions (1848); while, in 1863–64, the Polish and Danish crises, not the Civil War, dominated governmental concerns in Europe.

The political culture of the European powers was also important to America. Thus, the extent to which British policy in Europe after 1815 was "generally status quo-oriented"[5] also influenced attitudes taken in North America. There, the status quo was greatly challenged by American expansionism, but, after the War of 1812, the status quo also meant peace between Britain and America, and British ministers sought to maintain this. Thus, rather than fight to maintain the interests of other powers in North America, as with George Canning's dispatch of an expeditionary force to Portugal in 1826, Britain did not support Spain in Florida, nor Mexico, and, whereas the cause of Greek independence profited in the late 1820s from military backing by Britain, France, and Russia, these powers did not act to preserve Texan independence nor the interests of the Native Americans, and did not intervene in the Civil War.

British policy in these issues reflected the dynamics of European power politics, notably, but not only, in the case of relations with Spain and France in the decade after the War of 1812, but also with ideological factors, especially the support for liberal causes, particularly Latin American independence, and the extent to which there were powerful constraints on British behavior in the shape of military capability and financial exigency. Only so much could be achieved with naval deployment and amphibious operations,[6] as had been amply demonstrated in the New World by British failures at Cartagena in 1741,[7] Louisbourg in 1757, Charleston in 1776, and, far more clearly, Buenos Aires in 1807 and New Orleans in 1815.

This situation might appear to suggest that Britain was the classic oceanic power confronted with the problems of a continental foe, and, as such, anticipated much of the geopolitical literature of the twentieth century, both Halford Mackinder for the British empire,[8] and the geopolitics of the Cold War.[9] However, aside from the risks of the ahistorical application of later ideas, the United States, while expanding across the continent with the rail links that impressed Mackinder and others, was also very much an oceanic economic power, albeit not yet at the scale that influenced Alfred Thayer Mahan's call later in the century for America to develop its naval strength. From independence, transoceanic trade was very significant for the United States, leading to vulnerability to Britain[10] which encouraged the development of a large navy from the

1810s. Moreover, the terms on which America was an oceanic economic power were important for the domestic as well as international politics of the situation, not least because the American economy was dependent on European markets and capital. Indeed, this heavy dependence encouraged strong interest in other areas with which America could trade, notably Latin America from the 1820s and East Asia from the 1840s. In light of the dependence on Europe, the Jeffersonian view that trade challenged national integrity was apposite, but an agrarian self-sufficient economy was not a viable proposition in economic, social, or political terms.

America was thus both interested in global power politics and vulnerable to other powers, even as war with the United States was scarcely a welcome prospect for them. This situation set up a balance of possibilities that were part of the context when European policymakers considered how best to respond to specific issues in relations with America. In the case of Britain, and with influential foreign parallels in particular policymaking circles, they did so within the context of liberal values that made conflict with America unwelcome as, however selfishly, America either appeared to support liberal themes or, with the important exception of slavery, could be seen as less reprehensible than those European states presented as reactionary, notably Russia.[11]

In particular, reformers in Britain who supported the extension of the franchise (right to vote) could incorporate America into their assessment of benign politics, although, conversely, conservatives were appalled by American populism, and aspects of this populism also disturbed reformers. Indeed, the British attitude toward America was ambivalent, and vice versa.[12] Many prominent Victorians wrote about the country, including Dickens, Dilke, Trollope (both mother and son), and James Bryce, all of whom were taken by its energy and drive, yet were often shocked by its "vulgar" (populist) politics. Britons, whatever their political beliefs, were not simply ambivalent in their views of America because of populism but also because of slavery, racism, protectionism, anglophobia and constant threats to Canada.[13]

Yet, it was the fundamentals of British policy that were more significant. In September 1865, these were outlined when Earl Russell, the Foreign Secretary, replied to a dispatch from Peter Scarlett, the envoy in

Mexico, in which the latter had observed that it was fortunate for Britain that it had been able to withdraw in 1862 from the onerous task of stabilizing Mexico. In a draft endorsed as being seen by both the Queen and Palmerston, Russell wrote

> You do not seem to be aware that the principles upon which the government of England have for a long time acted, forbid their intervention in the domestic affairs of other countries. Sir Charles Wyke acting upon these principles was able to decline the proposal of his French colleague to set the affairs of Mexico in order. That refusal was not a fortunate circumstance but a settled policy.[14]

These attitudes greatly affected British policy toward both Mexico and the United States in the key decade of the 1860s and were also significant earlier, in both cases as any attempt to determine a new direction for relations necessarily entailed implications in terms of the domestic politics of these states and, to be well-grounded, required affirmation by them. British policymakers and, even more, diplomats, had preferences in terms of both American and Mexican politics, but they had to respond to developments in them. Moreover, as conquest was not an option for Britain, and a large-scale military commitment was unwelcome, there was no intention to treat force other than as a last resort. Given American expansionism, the end result was a politics of management on the part of Britain.

To argue that British compliance, even unwillingness to spend seriously on the military, were preconditions of American success and "the myth of the weak American state,"[15] not least as part of a process by which British hegemony adjusted to American power,[16] would be going too far. The argument underplays the mutual dependence of the two powers, including the degree to which the British world system required American acceptance.[17] More positively, an emphasis on compliance captures an important element of the extent to which the wider geopolitics depended on attitudes and policy choices. Britain and the other major powers coped not only with the aspirations of each other, but also with both new entrants to the great power stakes, Germany, Italy, Japan, and the United States, and minor powers, such as Portugal, as a result of the normative character of imperial expansion, the sheer range of opportunity, and the willingness to accept notions such as equivalent gains (which, in effect, happened for Britain and the United States in North

America), or to share in open access. Free trade was an important political and ideological aspect of the latter.

This point leads to the key methodological conclusion, in that geopolitics emerges as most useful as a sphere for consideration and not as a formal analytical doctrine. Linked to this comes the need to be aware of contingencies, and thus the pertinence of counterfactual discussion, not least because such discussion helped frame the contemporary response to contingencies.[18] Yet, if Manifest Destiny appears neither manifest nor destiny, and American exceptionalism does not appear exceptional, that does not lessen the significance of the development of the North American Question, nor its long-term importance for the world.

The application of classical geopolitical thought for this study is valuable in one respect and flawed in another. As far as the former is concerned, geopolitics provides a way to interrogate the idea of a struggle for mastery in North America by showing repeatedly that North America was part of a wider world, in political, strategic, economic, demographic, and ideological terms, and that its development was influenced accordingly, either by commission or omission. The flow of influences and pressures was two-way, but that did not lessen the extent to which this wider scale is the appropriate one for consideration. Indeed, the two-way flow of influences was an expression of this wider conspectus, and that is the case whether classical notions of geopolitics are at stake or others, relating for example to economics.[19]

Geopolitics provides a way to study these influences and pressures, but also risks a serious ahistoricism unless sufficient weight is placed on contemporary understandings of these processes. The spatial awareness of the outside world, particularly oceanic and transoceanic, held by Native Americans was limited, and notoriously so when the Aztecs sought to fit the Spaniards into their mental picture. The Aztec resort to the idea of the Spaniards as sacral or semi-sacral beings reflected the extent to which human and divine space were not separated in Native American thought.

The absence of such a separation could also be true for European and European Americans: their knowledge of the outside world might be greater, because the Atlantic had become a means of communication, not a perimeter to knowledge, but sacral space was also an issue for them. Far from being made redundant by change, this concept linked the Spaniards advancing Christianity and the Puritans looking both ways across the Atlantic in the seventeenth century, to the close relationships between British and American abolitionists.[20] Thus, *Clotel; Or the Presidents Daughter: A Narrative of Slave Life in the United States* (1853) by William Wells Brown, a former slave, the first novel published by an African American, was published in London and aimed at a British audience, and sought to deploy religious arguments of the universality of divine and Christian benevolence. This relationship rose to a height during the Civil War, with abolitionists seeing their cause as a universal one. Thus, the British abolitionist George Thomas, who was very well received when he lectured in Massachusetts in September 1864 on behalf of the cause, wrote: "On the side of the North the battle must be fought upon the very highest moral grounds and with the most uncompromising fidelity to the principles of equal absolute impartial, universal liberty."[21]

Such a universal quality was central to Christian ideas of political action, because they were moralized as issues of the human condition. As with those Enlightenment strands that were more secular in character, the universalism was heavily qualified in practice, but it still remained important as a way to analyze the world. In a different form, a universalism centered on supposed Anglo-American values has proved important to modern commentators advocating a particular set of policies.[22]

These issues require further discussion but help explain the flaw referred to above. Not only is there a risk of ahistoricism, due to the failure to understand contemporary notions, but there is also the linked problem of underplaying the nature of agency. This is important whether or not geopolitics are embraced as a means of analysis. In the former case, agency provides a way to explain how geopolitical forces came into play, but, in the latter, agency suggests that these forces should not be exaggerated. The idea of the balance of power provides a good instance for, if it is descriptive, it raises the question of how the balance operated in practice. If this operation is explained by arguing that it was normative, then there is the question of how norms were understood and how far they influenced discussion over policy. Thus, the mechanistic understanding of international relations, in terms of a system akin to those being popularized for Newtonian physics,[23] was inappropriate.[24]

The balance of power is particularly important in this light because the idea played a role in the response to Britain in the Atlantic world in the late eighteenth century and also to America in the context of North America in the mid-nineteenth century. In each case, it is possible to see the language needing to avoid an over-mighty state, and the argument of needing to avoid such a state can be presented as underlying geopolitics, but also as an expression of geopolitical thought. Yet, aside from the confusion between descriptive and normative, the extent to which ministers were guided by such ideas is far from clear. Obviously, they had an understanding of the world, and clearly it had a spatial component. Indeed, the fascination with maps and globes ensured that such a component was regarded as an aspect of proper knowledge, and thus genteel behavior. Ministers were pictured with globes, as with the portrait of Count Tessin, the influential Swedish envoy to Paris in the mid-eighteenth century.[25] This idea was taken forward in the nineteenth century, as an understanding of space was seen as a demonstration of knowledge and competence and as part of an application of knowledge that was regarded as important in policymaking.[26] Diplomats referred to maps in dispatches.[27]

Power and profit were involved, and the advancing of territorial claims, as well as the demarcation and allocation of territories and land, all ensured that spatial considerations were pushed to the fore. In some cases, a radical ability to rethink space was displayed, as when Jefferson in 1784 drafted a plan for the division of America east of the Mississippi among a number of new states (within the United States), with geometrical regularity playing a key role. Spatial considerations were therefore important and can be readily seen in terms of geopolitics because such considerations reflected political assumptions and had political consequences.

Yet it is striking how often such considerations were subordinated to exigencies reflecting other political narratives. If, for example, French policy after 1763 can be seen in part as an attempt to restore the balance, with the American War of Independence called into play to do so, and thus to help the Old World, that account has to be put alongside other pressures affecting French policy. Moreover, both the Falklands crisis, which led to the fall of Choiseul in 1770, and differences, in 1775–78, over the response to the American War of Independence, reflected ministerial divisions that underplay any sense of consistency, let alone inevitability. The same point emerges from divisions among French ministers over how best to respond to the Bavarian Succession issue in 1777–78, and that was directly pertinent to America, as the ability to act against Britain there and/or in India was related to the policy France followed in Europe: neutrality was maintained in the War of Bavarian Succession of 1778–79.

Similarly, British policy toward America was subordinated to concerns about European power politics. France tended to be the prime issue, which helps explain why the British sought to avoid war with America in 1812, but this issue remained important thereafter, even though Britain and France were continually at peace from 1815. Indeed, this book shows that, whatever its crucial importance from the 1910s on, American independence made only limited difference to a European system organized around clashes between European powers,[28] and this situation remained the case up to and including the early stages of the First World War.

A systems analysis might discuss this clash in terms of the limitations of a multipolar Europe as far as focusing attention and resources on relations with the outside world were concerned. Alternatively, it would be more pertinent to see the once-European colonies as part of this multipolar system, and to argue that, as relatively minor players from the perspective of European governments, they did not become a dominant question, and, instead, were seen as a semidetached and subordinate part of the system, with Central America in particular being largely inconsequential.

Geopolitics thus succumbs to perception. Propinquity was a key element in the latter, which provides a somewhat limited take on geopolitics. There is room for considerable skepticism in assessing geopolitical influences and in drawing conclusions. Yet the story was played out across both space and time, and their interaction was an important element.

# NOTES

**PREFACE & ACKNOWLEDGMENTS**

1. Canning to Robert, Viscount Castlereagh, Foreign Secretary, 28 Jan. 1821, NA. FO. 5/157 fols 35–43, quote fol. 41.

2. Choiseul, French Foreign Minister, to Ossun, French envoy in Spain, 9 Jun. 1761, AE. CP. Espagne 532 fol. 373; *Monitor* [London newspaper], 11 Sept. 1762.

3. In Canada they are known as First Nations. Some scholars favor the term *Indians*, but that term is unhelpful in a book dealing with British military commitments as a whole, and such a consideration is an appropriate context when approaching North American developments at a global scale.

4. Charles H. Brown, *Agents of Manifest Destiny: The Lives and Times of the Filibusters* (Chapel Hill: University of North Carolina Press, 1980).

5. Claudia L. Bushman, *America Discovers Columbus: How an Italian Explorer Became an American Hero* (Hanover, N.H.: University Press of New England, 1992); F. Fernández-Armesto, "Columbus: Hero or Villain?" *History Today* (May 1992), reprinted in *PastMasters*, ed. D. Snowman (London, Sutton Publishing, 2001), 366–74.

6. Jeremy Black, *The Curse of History* (London, Social Affairs Unit, 2008), 184–89.

7. Jorge Canizares-Esguerra, *How to Write the History of the New World: Histories, Epistomologies and Identities in the Eighteenth-Century Atlantic World* (Stanford, Calif.: Stanford University Press, 2001), v.

**INTRODUCTION**

The epigraph comes from the anonymous work published in London in 1765, p. 23.

1. For the intellectual and practical background, see Daniel R. Headrick, *When Information Came of Age: Technologies of Knowledge in the Age of Reason and Revolution, 1700–1850* (Oxford: Oxford University Press, 2000).

2. Martin W. Lewis and Kären E. Wigen, *The Myth of Continents: A Critique of Metageography* (Berkeley: University of California Press, 1997).

3. Felipe Fernández-Armesto, *Continuity and Discontinuity in the Sixteenth-Century New World* (Minneapolis: Associates of the James Bell Ford Library, 2001), 19.

4. Benjamin Franklin, "Narrative of Negotiations in London," *The Diplomatic Correspondence of the United States*, II (Washington, 1889), 11.

5. Harriet Wanklin, *Friedrich Ratzel: A Biographical Memoir and Bibliography* (Cambridge: Cambridge University Press, 1961); David Livingstone, *The Geographi-*

cal Tradition: Episodes in the History of a Contested Enterprise (Oxford: Blackwell, 1992), 196–202; Mark Bassin, "Imperialism and the Nation State in Friedrich Ratzel's Political Geography," Progress in Human Geography 2 (1987): 473–95.

6. S. Holdar, "The Ideal State and the Power of Geography: The Life and Work of Rudolf Kjellén," Political Geography 2 (1992): 307–323; B. Haggman, "Rudolf Kjellén and Modern Swedish Geopolitics," Geopolitics 3 (1998): 99–112.

7. R. Peet, "The Social Origins of Environmental Determinism," Annals of the Association of American Geographers 75 (1985): 309–333.

8. Henry Clifford Darby et al., The Relations of History and Geography: Studies in England, France, and the United States (Exeter: University of Exeter Press, 2000), 191; I. M. Keighren, Bringing Geography to Book (London: I. B. Tauris, 2010).

9. Frederick Turner, The Frontier in American History (Huntington, N.Y.: R. E. Krieger Publishing Co., 1920); Ray A. Billington, Frederick Jackson Turner (New York: Oxford University Press, 1973).

10. Newsletters cited in Newcastle Courant, 14 Jan. (os) 1744.

11. Cynthia Radding, Wandering Peoples: Colonialism, Ethnic Spaces, and Ecological Frontiers in Northwestern Mexico, 1700–1850 (Durham, N.C.: Duke University Press, 1997).

12. Fernand Braudel, The Mediterranean and the Mediterranean World in the Age of Philip II, 2 vols. (London: Harper & Row, 1972).

13. Braudel, Mediterranean, I, 16, 21.

14. H. Mackinder, "The Geographical Pivot of History," Geographical Journal 23 (1904): 421–37; Brian Blouet (ed.), Global Geostrategy: Mackinder and the Defence of the West (London: Frank Cass, 2005).

15. Colin S. Gray, The Geopolitics of the Nuclear Era: Heartland, Rimlands, and the Technological Revolution (New York: Crane, Russak, 1977); Geoffrey Sloan, Geopolitics in United States Strategic Policy, 1890–1987 (Brighton: Wheatsheaf Books, 1988).

16. Martin Brückner, The Geographic Revolution in Early America: Maps, Literacy, and National Identity (Chapel Hill: University of North Carolina Press, 2006). For a similar emphasis on cohesion through the culture of print, see Charles E. Clark, The Public Prints: The Newspaper in Anglo-American Culture (Oxford: Oxford University Press, 1994).

17. Carolyn Eastman, A Nation of Speechifiers: Making an American Public after the Revolution (Chicago: University of Chicago Press, 2010).

18. John J. McCusker and Russell R. Menard, The Economy of British America, 1607–1789 (Chapel Hill, University of North Carolina Press, 1991); Trish Loughran, The Republic in Print: Print Culture in the Age of United States Nation Building, 1770–1870 (New York: Columbia University Press, 2007).

19. Stephanie Kermes, Creating an American Identity: New England, 1789–1825 (New York: Palgrave Macmillan, 2008).

20. Jackson to Henry, 3rd Earl Bathurst, Foreign Secretary, 22 Jan. 1810, NA. FO. 5/69 fol. 5.

21. Bruce to John, 1st Earl Russell, Foreign Secretary, 14 Apr. 1865, NA. FO. 5/1017 fol. 165.

22. John Crampton to Henry, 3rd Viscount Palmerston, Foreign Secretary, 6 Oct. 1851, NA. FO. 5/530.

23. B. H. Rodrigue, "An Album in the Attic: The Forgotten Frontier of the Quebec–Maine Borderlands during the Revolutionary War," Journal of the Historical Society 3 (2003): 67.

24. Francis, 9th Lord Napier to George, 4th Earl of Clarendon, Foreign Secretary, 26 May 1857, NA. FO. 5/671 fols 192–94.

25. That of British North America.

26. Canada East (Quebec from later in 1867) and Canada West (Ontario) were the key provinces on this transport route.

27. The North-Western Territory covered the extensive tracts not included in British Columbia or Rupert's Land.

28. The Last Spike was driven in at Craigellachie in the Cordillera on 7 Nov. 1885.

29. The province of Manitoba was established in 1870.

30. Bruce to Edward, Lord Stanley, Foreign Secretary, 12 Jan. 1867, NA. FO. 5/1104 fols 40–42.

31. Eg., Lord Lyons, British envoy to Lord John Russell (from 1861 John, First Earl Russell), Foreign Secretary, 14, 22 Nov. 1859, NA. PRO. 30/22/34 fols 46, 55.

32. F. O. Adams, British Legation Washington, to Hon. J. Elliot, 16 Oct. 1865, NA. PRO. 30/22/38 fols 367–68.

33. Bruce to Stanley, 12 Jan. 1867, NA. FO. 5/1104 fols 44–45.

34. Thornton to Clarendon, 8 Jan. 1870, Bod. MS. Clar. Dep. C. 481 fols 8–10.

35. Jeremy Black, Geopolitics (London: Social Affairs Unit, 2009), 21–106.

36. Paul W. Schroeder, The Transformation of European Politics, 1763–1848 (Oxford: Oxford University Press, 1994).

37. Jeremy Black, What If? Counterfactualism and the Problem of History (London: Social Affairs Unit, 2008).

38. Nancy L. Rhoden (ed.), English Atlantics Revisited (Montreal: McGill-Queen's University Press, 2007).

39. John H. Elliott, Empires of the Atlantic World: Britain and Spain in America, 1492–1830 (New Haven, Conn.: Yale University Press, 2006).

40. Crampton to Palmerston, 8 Sept. 1851, NA. FO. 5/530.

41. Napier, to Clarendon, 7 Jun. 1857, NA. FO. 5/672 fols 25, 32.

42. B. Vandervort, "Remembering the Empire of France in America," Journal of Military History 74 (2010): 196–97.

43. Daniel K. Richter, Facing East from Indian Country: A Native History of Early America (Cambridge, Mass.: Harvard University Press, 2001); Pekka Hämäläinen, The Comanche Empire (New Haven, Conn.: Yale University Press, 2008).

44. G. M. Lewis, "First Nations Map-making in the Great Lakes Region in Intercultural Contexts: A Historical Review," Michigan Historical Review 30 (2004): 33.

45. Richard White, The Middle Ground: Indians, Empires and Republics in the Great Lakes Region, 1651–1815 (Cambridge: Cambridge University Press, 1991); Erick Hinderaker, Elusive Empires: Constructing Colonialism in the Ohio Valley, 1673–1800 (Cambridge: Cambridge University Press, 1997); Frederick Cooper and Ann L. Stoker, Tensions of Empire: Colonial Cultures in a Bourgeois World (Berkeley: University of California Press, 1997); Kathleen Du-Val, The Native Ground: Indians and Colonists in the Heart of the Continent (Philadelphia: University of Pennsylvania Press, 2006); Timothy J. Shannon, Iroquois Diplomacy on the Early American Frontier (London: Viking, 2008), 80–81.

46. Donald Stoker, The Grand Design: Strategy and the U.S. Civil War (Oxford: Oxford University Press, 2010).

47. Elisabeth Glaser and Hermann Wellenreuther (eds.), Bridging the Atlantic: The Question of American Exceptionalism in Perspective (Cambridge: Cambridge University Press, 2002).

48. E. H. Gould, "The Making of an Atlantic State System: Britain and the United States, 1795–1825," in Britain and America Go to War: The Impact of War and Warfare in Anglo-America, 1754–1815, ed. Julie Flavell and Stephen Conway (Gainesville: University Press of Florida, 2004), pp. 259–60.

49. For example, Kenneth J. Hagan and Ian J. Bickerton, Unintended Consequences: The United States at War (London: Reaktion Books, 2007), esp. 10–17, 188–93.

50. Key works in reviving this long-standing thesis, included Andrew J. Bacevich, *American Empire: The Realities and Consequences of U.S. Diplomacy* (Cambridge, Mass.: Harvard University Press, 2002), esp. 244, and *The Limits of Power: The End of American Exceptionalism* (New York: Metropolitan Books, 2008); David Harvey, *The New Imperialism* (New York: Oxford University Press, 2003); Niall Ferguson, *Colossus: The Price of America's Empire* (New York: Penguin Press, 2004); Chalmers A. Johnson, *Blowback: The Costs and Consequences of American Empire* 2nd ed. (New York: Metropolitan Books, 2004); Charles S. Maier, *Among Empires: American Ascendancy and its Predecessors* (Cambridge, Mass.: Harvard University Press, 2006).

51. The frequently used term chosen in 2009 alone as a title for David Reynolds's history of the United States and for Gordon Wood's history of America from 1789 to 1815.

52. American Council of Trustees and Alumni, *Losing America's Memory: Historical Illiteracy in the 21st Century* (2000).

53. Frank Ninkovich, *Global Dawn: The Cultural Foundation of American Internationalism, 1865–1890* (Cambridge, Mass.: Harvard University Press, 2009).

### 1. SIXTEENTH-CENTURY BACKGROUND

1. Louise Levathes, *When China Ruled the Seas: The Treasure Fleet of the Dragon Throne, 1405–1433* (New York: Simon & Schuster, 1994).

2. Peter C. Perdue, *China Marches West: The Qing Conquest of Central Eurasia* (Cambridge: Belknap Press of Harvard University, 2005).

3. Robert McGhee, "Contact between Native North Americans and the Medieval Norse: A Review of the Evidence," *American Antiquity* 49 (1984): 4–26; Anne Stine and Helge M. Ingstad, *The Norse Discovery of America* (Oslo: Norwegian University Press, 1986).

4. David Beers Quinn, "The Argument for the English Discovery of America between 1480 and 1494," *Geographical Journal* 127 (1961): 227–85.

5. Ross Hassig, *Mexico and the Spanish Conquest* (London: Longman, 1994).

6. Eleanor Wake, *Framing the Sacred: The Indian Churches of Early Colonial Mexico* (Norman: University of Oklahoma Press, 2010).

7. Patricia Lopes Don, *Bonfires of Culture: Franciscans, Indigenous Leaders, and the Inquisition in Early Mexico, 1524–1540* (Norman: University of Oklahoma Press, 2010); Martin Austin Nesvig, *Ideology and Inquisition: The World of the Censors in Early Mexico* (New Haven, Conn.: Yale University Press, 2009).

8. Charles Gibson, *The Aztecs under Spanish Rule: A History of the Indians of the Valley of Mexico, 1519–1810* (Stanford, Calif: Stanford University Press, 1964); James Lockhart, *The Nahuas after the Conquest: A Social and Cultural History of the Indians of Central Mexico, Sixteenth through Eighteenth Centuries* (Stanford, Calif: Stanford University Press, 1992).

9. Inga Clendinnen, "'Fierce and Unnatural Cruelty': Cortés and the Conquest of Mexico," in *New World Encounters*, ed. Steven. Greenblatt (Berkeley: University of California Press, 1993), 12–47.

10. Thomas Symons, Stephen Alsford, Chris Kitzan, *Meta Incognita: A Discourse of Discovery: Martin Frobisher's Arctic Expeditions, 1576–1578* (Hull, Quebec: The Canadian Museum of Civilization, 1999).

11. Philip Wayne Powell, *Soldiers, Indians and Silver: The Northward Advance of New Spain, 1550–1600* (Berkeley: University of California Press, 1952).

12. Grant D. Jones, "The Last Maya Frontiers of Colonial Yucatán," in *Spaniards and Indians in Southeastern Mesoamerica: Essays on the History of Ethnic*

*Relations,* ed. Murdo J. MacLeod and Robert Wassertrom (Lincoln: University of Nebraska Press, 1983), 64–91.

13. Patricia Seed, "Taking Possession and Reading Texts: Establishing the Authority of Overseas Empires," *William and Mary Quarterly,* 3rd ser. 49 (1992): 207. See also Jonathan Locke Hart, *Comparing Empires: European Colonialism from Portuguese Expansion to the Spanish-American War* (Basingstoke: Palgrave Macmillan, 2003).

14. Barbara E. Mundy, *The Mapping of New Spain: Indigenous Cartography and the Maps of the Relaciones Geográficas* (Chicago: University of Chicago Press, 1996).

15. Karen Ordahl Kupperman, *Roanoke: The Abandoned Colony* (Totowa, N.J.: Rowman & Allanheld, 1984).

16. Peter C. Mancall, *Hakluyt's Promise: An Elizabethan's Obsession for an English America* (New Haven, Conn.: Yale University Press, 2007).

17. Allan Galley, *The Indian Slave Trade* (New Haven, Conn.: Yale University Press, 2002); Brett Rushforth, "'A Little Flesh We Offer You': The Origins of Indian Slavery in New France," *William and Mary Quarterly* 60 (2003): 777–808.

18. Lesley Byrd Simpson, *The Encomienda in New Spain: The Beginning of Spanish Mexico,* 3rd ed. (Berkeley: University of California Press, 1966); William L. Sherman, *Forced Native Labor in Sixteenth-Century Central America* (Lincoln: University of Nebraska Press, 1979); O. N. Bolland, "Colonization and Slavery in Central America," in *Unfree Labour in the Development of the Atlantic World,* ed. Paul E. Lovejoy and Nicholas Rogers (London: Frank Cass, 1994), 11–25.

19. Peter Gerhard, "A Black Conquistador in Mexico," *Hispanic American Historical Review* 58 (1978): 451–59; Matthew Restall, "Black Conquistadors: Armed Africans in Early Spanish America," *The Americas* 57 (2000): 171–206.

20. Colin A. Palmer, *Slaves of the White God: Blacks in Mexico, 1570–1650* (Cambridge, Mass.: Harvard University Press, 1976), 28.

21. Murdo J. MacLeod, *Spanish Central America: A Socioeconomic History, 1520–1720,* 2nd ed. (Austin: University of Texas Press, 2008), xxvii.

## 2. CREATING NEW FRONTIERS, 1600–74

1. Peter Bakewell, "Spanish America: Empire and Its Outcome," in *The Spanish World: Civilization and Empire, Europe and the Americas, Past and Present,* ed. John Huxtable Elliott et al. (New York: H.N. Abrams, 1991), 74.

2. Jonathan Israel, *Race, Class and Politics in Colonial Mexico, 1610–1670* (London: Oxford University Press, 1975).

3. Rudi Matthee, "Exotic Substances: The Introduction and Global Spread of Tobacco, Coffee, Cocoa, Tea and Distilled Liquor, Sixteenth to Eighteenth Centuries," in *Drugs and Narcotics in History* ed. R. Porter and M. Teich (Cambridge: Cambridge University Press, 1995), 38–46; James Walvin, *Fruits of Empire: Exotic Produce and British Taste, 1660–1800* (London: Macmillan, 1997).

4. Cynthia Jean Van Zandt, *Brothers among Nations: The Pursuit of Intercultural Alliances in Early America, 1580–1660* (Oxford: Oxford University Press, 2008).

5. Alfred A. Cave, *The Pequot War* (Amherst: University of Massachusetts Press, 1996).

6. Adam J. Hirsch, "The Collision of Military Cultures in Seventeenth-Century New England," and R. D. Karr, "'Why Should You Be So Ferocious?': The Violence of the Pequot War," *Journal of American History* 74 (1988): 1187–1212; 85 (1999): 876–909.

7. James Axtell and William C. Sturtevant, "The Unkindest Cut, or, Who Invented Scalping?" and Andrew Lipman,

"'A Means to Knitt Them Together': The Exchange of Body Parts in the Pequot War," *William and Mary Quarterly* 37 (1980): 451–72; 65 (2008): 1–28.

8. Donald Worcester and Thomas F. Schilz, "The Spread of Firearms among the Indians on the Anglo-French Frontier," *American Indian Quarterly* 8 (1984): 103–115.

9. Geoffrey J. Matthews and R. Cole Harris, *Historical Atlas of Canada. I: From the Beginning to 1800* (Toronto: University of Toronto Press, 1987), plate 35.

10. Virginia DeJohn Anderson, "King Philip's Herds: Indians, Colonists, and the Problem of Livestock in Early New England," *William and Mary Quarterly* 3rd ser. 51 (1994): 602.

11. Edmund S. Morgan, "The First American Boom: Virginia 1618 to 1630," *William and Mary Quarterly* 3rd ser., 28 (1971): 169–98, esp. 197.

12. Carol Gardina Pestana, *The English Atlantic in an Age of Revolution, 1640–1661* (Cambridge, Mass.: Harvard University Press, 2004), 225.

13. Gijs Rommelse, *The Second Anglo-Dutch War, 1665–1667* (Hilversum, Netherlands: Verloren, 2006), 103.

14. William Shea, *The Virginia Militia in the Seventeenth Century* (Baton Rouge: Louisiana State University Press, 1983).

### 3. BRITAIN, FRANCE, AND THE NATIVES, 1674–1715

1. Gerald S. Graham (ed.), *The Walker Expedition to Quebec, 1711* (Toronto and London: Champlain Society, 1953).

2. K. A. J. McLay, "Wellsprings of a 'World War': An Early English Attempt to Conquer Canada during King William's War, 1688–97," *Journal of Imperial and Commonwealth History* 34 (2006): 155–75.

3. Dudley to John, Duke of Marlborough, 28 Dec. 1703, BL. Add. 61306 fol. 144.

4. Thomas, Duke of Newcastle, Secretary of State for the Southern Department, to James, 1st Earl Waldegrave, envoy in Paris, 12 Jun. (os) 1740, NA. SP. 78/223 fol. 111.

5. Ian K. Steele, *The English Atlantic, 1675–1740: An Exploration of Communication and Community* (Oxford: Oxford University Press, 1986).

6. William, 4th Duke of Devonshire, First Lord of the Treasury, to John, Fourth Duke of Bedford, Lord-Lieutenant of Ireland, 7 Jan. 1757, London, Bedford Estate Office, Russell Manuscript Letters vol. 33.

7. Daniel K. Richter, *The Ordeal of the Longhouse: The Peoples of the Iroquois League in the Era of European Colonization* (Chapel Hill: University of North Carolina Press, 1992); Gilles Harvard, *The Great Peace of Montreal of 1701: French-Native Diplomacy in the Seventeenth Century* (Montreal: McGill-Queen's University Press, 2001); Jon Parmenter, "After the Mourning Wars: The Iroquois as Allies in Colonial North American Campaigns, 1676–1760," *William and Mary Quarterly* 3rd ser., 64 (2007): 39–82.

8. Jill Lepore, *The Name of War: King Philip's War and the Origins of American Identity* (New York: Knopf, 1998); James David Drake, *King Philip's War: Civil War in New England, 1675–1676* (Amherst: University of Massachusetts Press, 1999).

9. James S. Pritchard, *In Search of Empire: The French in the Americas, 1670–1730* (Cambridge: Cambridge University Press, 2004), 420–42.

10. William J. Eccles, *Canada under Louis XIV, 1663–1701* (Toronto: McClelland and Stewart, 1964); Jennifer Brown, ed., *The Fur Trade Revisited* (East Lansing: Michigan State University Press, 1994).

11. D. R. Farrell, "Private Profit and Public Interest: Individual Gain, State Policy and French Colonial Expansion," *Proceedings of the Western Society for French History* 14 (1987): 70–77.

12. Neal Salisbury, "The Indians' Old World: Native Americans and the Coming of Europeans," *William and Mary Quarterly* 3rd ser; 53 (1996): 458.

## 4. MULTIPLE CURRENTS, 1715–53

1. Orcoutt William Frost, *Bering: The Russian Discovery of America* (New Haven, Conn.: Yale University Press, 2003).

2. David J. Weber, *The Spanish Frontier in North America* (New Haven, Conn.: Yale University Press, 1992), 204–212; Jack Jackson (ed.), *Imaginary Kingdom: Texas as Seen by the Rivera and Rubí Military Expeditions, 1729 and 1767* (Austin: Texas State Historical Association, 1995).

3. French memorandum, Feb. 1730, A E. C P. Ang. 370 fols 89–94; Horatio Walpole, envoy in Paris, to Thomas, Duke of Newcastle, Secretary of State, 10 Jul. 1728; Waldegrave, envoy in Paris, to Chauvelin, French Foreign Minister, 13 Jun.; Waldegrave to Newcastle, 27 Jun. 1732, BL. Add. 32756, 32777 fols 283–86; Thomas Robinson, diplomat in Paris, to Charles Delafaye, Under Secretary, 4 Mar. 1730, NA. SP. 78/187.

4. Joseph M. Hall, *Zamumo's Gifts: Indian-European Exchange in the Colonial Southeast* (Philadelphia: University of Pennsylvania Press, 2009).

5. Marcel Giraud, *A History of French Louisiana, V: The Company of the Indies, 1723–1731* (Baton Rouge: Louisiana State University Press, 1991), 317.

6. Edward J. Cashion, *Guardians of the Valley: Chickasaws in Colonial South Carolina and Georgia* (Columbia: University of South Carolina Press, 2009).

7. Patricia D. Woods, *French-Indian Relations on the Southern Frontier, 1699–1762* (Ann Arbor, University of Michigan Press, 1980), 111–46.

8. Carl J. Ekberg, *French Roots in the Illinois Country: The Mississippi Frontier in Colonial Times* (Champagne: University of Illinois Press, 1998).

9. John Tate Lanning, *The Diplomatic History of Georgia: A Study of the Epoch of Jenkins' Ear* (Chapel Hill: University of North Carolina Press, 1936).

10. Cynthia Radding, "Forging Cultures of Resistance on Two Colonial Frontiers: Northwestern Mexico and Eastern Bolivia," in *New World Orders: Violence, Sanction, and Authority in the Colonial Americas,* ed. John Smolenski and Thomas J. Humphrey (Philadelphia: University of Pennsylvania Press, 2005), 169.

11. Ernest J. Burrus, *Kino and the Cartography of Northwestern New Spain* (Tuscon: Arizona Pioneers' Historical Society, 1965).

12. Harry W. Crosby, *Antigua California: Mission and Colony on the Peninsular Frontier, 1697–1768* (Albuquerque: University of New Mexico Press, 1994), 29–39.

13. Grant D. Jones, *The Conquest of the Last Maya Kingdom* (Stanford, Calif: Stanford University Press, 1998), 300–335.

14. Christopher Storrs, *The Resilience of the Spanish Monarchy 1665–1700* (Oxford: Oxford University Press, 2006).

15. William S. Coker and Robert Right Rea, eds., *Anglo-Spanish Confrontation on the Gulf Coast during the American Revolution* (Pensacola, Fla.: Gulf Coast History and Humanities Conference, 1982).

16. James Merrell, *The Indians' New World: Catawbas and Their Neighbors from European Contact through the Era of Removal* (Chapel Hill: University of North Carolina Press, 1989).

17. Alan Gallay, *The Indian Slave Trade: The Rise of the English Empire in the American South, 1670–1717* (New Haven, Conn.: Yale University Press, 2002), 337; William L. Ramsey, *The Yamasee War: A Study of Culture, Economy, and Conflict in the Colonial South* (Lincoln: University of Nebraska Press, 2008).

18. Geoffrey Plank, *An Unsettled Conquest: The British Conquest against the Peoples of Acadia* (Philadelphia: Univer-

sity of Pennsylvania Press, 2001); John Grenier, *The Far Reaches of Empire: War in Nova Scotia, 1710–1760* (Norman: University of Oklahoma Press, 2008).

19. Cambridge, University Library, Cholmondeley Houghton papers, Mss. 84/75.

20. Julian Gwyn, *Frigates and Foremasts: The North American Squadron in Nova Scotia Waters, 1745–1815* (Vancouver: University of British Columbia Press, 2003).

21. Philip Yorke MP to Joseph Yorke, 1 Aug. (os) 1745, BL. Add. 35363 fol. 91.

22. Paris, Archives Nationales, Archives de la Marine, B 63, 10 May 1735.

23. Wayne E. Lee, «Fortify, Fight or Flee: Tuscarora and Cherokee Defensive Warfare and Military Cultural Adaptation,» *Journal of Military History* 68 (2004): 713–70.

24. Daniel Beattie, "The Adaptation of the British Army to Wilderness Warfare, 1755–1763," in *Adapting to Conditions: War and Society in the Eighteenth Century*, ed. Maarten Ultee (Tuscaloosa: University of Alabama Press, 1986), 56–83; Ian K. Steele, *Warpaths: Invasions of North America* (New York: Oxford University Press, 1994).

25. Peter E. Russell, "Redcoats in the Wilderness: British Officers and Irregular Warfare in Europe and America, 1740 to 1760," *William and Mary Quarterly* 35 (1978): 629–52.

26. Armstrong Starkey, *European and Native American Warfare, 1675–1815* (Norman: University of Oklahoma Press, 1998); Guy Chet, *Conquering the American Wilderness: The Triumph of European Warfare in the Colonial Northeast* (Amherst: University of Massachusetts Press, 2003).

27. John Grenier, *The First Way of War: American War Making on the Frontier, 1607–1814* (New York: Cambridge University Press, 2005).

28. Nancy Shoemaker, *A Strange Likeness: Becoming Red and White in Eighteenth-Century North America* (Oxford: Oxford University Press, 2004).

29. Peter Bakewell, "Spanish America: Empire and Its Outcome," in *The Spanish World*, ed. John Huxtable Elliott (New York: H.N. Abrams, 1991), 74.

30. AE. CP. Ang. 429 fol. 15.

31. Julie Anne Sweet, *Negotiating for Georgia: British–Creek Relations in the Trustee Era, 1733–1752* (Athens: University of Georgia Press, 2005).

**5. WAR FOR DOMINANCE, 1754–64**
The epigraph comes from Andrew Mitchell, British envoy in Prussia, to Robert, 4th Earl of Holdernesse, Secretary of State for the Northern Department, 14 May 1756, NA. SP. 90/65.

1. President of the Council of the Marine to Rouillé, French Foreign Minister, 16 Sept. 1754, Paris, Archives Nationales, Archives de la Marine, B100.

2. Alt, Hessian envoy, to Landgrave of Hesse-Cassel, 25 Oct. 1754, Marburg, Staatsarchiv 4f England 255; William, 2nd Earl of Albemarle, British envoy in Paris, to Sir Thomas Robinson, Secretary of State for the Southern Department, 14 Sept. 1754, BL. Add. 33027 fol. 276.

3. M. H. Edney, "John Mitchell's Map of North America (1755): A Study of the Use and Publication of Official Maps in Eighteenth-Century Britain," *Imago Mundi* 60 (2008): 63–85.

4. Lawrence C. Wroth, *An American Bookshelf, 1755* (Philadelphia: University of Pennsylvania Press, 1934), 132–42.

5. Bob Harris, *Politics and the Nation: Britain in the Mid-Eighteenth Century* (Oxford: Oxford University Press, 2002).

6. For example, *Journals of the Board of Trade and Plantations* vol. 61, 14 Nov. 1753, noting the Order of Council of 10 August 1753; as well as prewar British interests in mapping British land claims.

7. Kathleen Wilson, *The Sense of the People: Politics, Culture and Imperialism in England, 1715–1785* (Cambridge: Cambridge University Press, 1995).

8. Murray to Thomas, Duke of Newcastle, First Lord of the Treasury, 7 Sept. 1754, BL. Add. 32736 fol. 438.

9. Pitt to Loudoun, 4 Feb. 1757, HL. Loudoun papers no. 2765A; *London Chronicle*, 5 Mar. 1757.

10. Cabinet minutes, 20, 28 Jul. 1756, BL. Add. 51376 fols 73–75; Pitt to Charles Lawrence, Governor of Nova Scotia, 22 Dec. 1756, HL. Loudoun Papers 2381A; William, Duke of Cumberland to Henry Fox, – Jul. 1757, Earl of Ilchester (ed.), *Letters to Henry Fox, Lord Holland* (London, 1915), 116.

11. Kilkerran to John, 4th Earl of Loudoun, commander in North America, 2 Dec. 1756, HL. Loudoun papers 8884.

12. John, 3rd Earl of Bute to William Pitt the Elder, 12 Aug. 1758, K. Schweizer, "Unpublished Letters from Lord Bute to William Pitt, 1757–58," *Archives* 23 (1998): 166.

13. Pitt to Loudoun, 22 Dec. 1756, HL. Loudoun Papers no. 2383.

14. Pitt to colonial governors, 4 Feb. 1757, HL. Lo. 2764A.

15. Charles Townshend, Treasurer of the Chamber, to William, 4th Duke of Devonshire, 30 Jul. 1757, Chatsworth, Derbyshire, papers of the Fourth Duke of Devonshire, 574.4.

16. David Syrett, *Shipping and Military Power in the Seven Years War: The Sails of Victory* (Exeter: University of Exeter Press, 2008).

17. Ossun, French envoy in Spain, to Choiseul, 6 Nov. 1759, AE CP. Espagne 526 fols 13–14.

18. Dobbs to Bute, 2 Jun. 1762, Mount Stuart, papers of John, 3rd Earl, 2/73–74.

19. John Grenier, *The First Way of War: American War Making on the Frontier* (New York: Cambridge University Press, 2005).

20. Lieutenant-General Charles, 3rd Duke of Marlborough to his wife, 29 Aug. 1758, BL. Add. 61667 fol. 43.

21. Richard Lyttelton MP to his brother George, Lord Lyttelton, 7 Mar. 1758, Worcester CRO. Hagley papers 705: 104 BA 5806.

22. *Monitor*, 2 Sept. 1758.

23. Matthew C. Ward, *Breaking the Backcountry: The Seven Years' War in Virginia and Pennsylvania, 1754–1765* (Pittsburgh, Pa.: Pittsburgh University Press, 2003).

24. Richmond to Lord George Lennox, 21 Jan. 1758, BL. Bathurst MSS 57/103 fol. 124.

25. Richard Cox, Secretary to the Master General of the Ordnance, to Weston, 19 May, 7 Jun. 1759, Farmington vol. 3.

26. Journal, possibly by Henry Fletcher, Providence, John Carter Brown Library, Codex Eng. 41.

27. Stephen Brumwell, *Redcoats: The British Soldier and War in the Americas, 1755–1763* (Cambridge: Cambridge University Press, 2002).

28. Philip, 4th Earl of Chesterfield to Newcastle, 4 May 1758, BL. Add. 32879 fol. 413.

29. Newcastle to Hardwicke, 17 Sept. 1758, BL. Add. 35418 fol. 21. Thomas, 8th Earl of Kinnoull was Chancellor of the Duchy of Lancaster.

30. Bussy to Choiseul, 11 Jun., 9 Jul. 1761, AE. CP. Ang. 443 fols 182, 339.

31. Bussy to Choiseul, 26 Jun. 1761, AE. CP. Ang. 443, fol. 286.

32. Viry to Charles Emmanuel III of Sardinia, 19 Aug., 26 Sept. 1760, 31 Mar. 1761, AST. LM. Ing. 65–66.

33. Choiseul to Bussy, 4 Jul. 1761, AE. CP. Ang. 445 fols 21–22.

34. Nivernois, French envoy, to Praslin, French Foreign Minister, 23 Nov. 1762, AE. CP. Ang. 448 fol. 87.

35. Jonathan R. Dull, *The French Navy and the Seven Years' War* (Lincoln: University of Nebraska Press, 2005).

36. Pitt, memorandum for Thomas, Duke of Newcastle, 10 Apr. 1761, BL. Add. 32921 fol. 381.

37. Viry to Charles Emmanuel, 24 Apr. 1761, AST. LM. Ing. 66.

38. David Syrett, *The Siege and Capture of Havana* (London: Navy Records Society, 1970).

39. Bussy to Choiseul, 26 Jun. 1761, AE. CP. Ang. 443 fols 289–90.

40. John Oliphant, *Peace and War on the Anglo-Cherokee Frontier, 1756–63* (Baton Rouge: Louisiana State University Press, 2001).

41. Bussy to Choiseul, 11, 19 Jun. 1761, AE. CP. Ang. 443 fols 190, 248–50; AE. CP. Espagne 537 fol. 258.

42. Doris M. Ladd, *The Making of a Strike: The Mexican Silver Workers' Struggles in Real Del Monte, 1766–1775* (Lincoln: University of Nebraska Press, 1988).

43. Charles Townshend to brother George, 13 Mar. 1759, Bod. Eng. Hist. d 211 fol. 5.

44. Viry to Charles Emmanuel, 23 Jun. 1761, AST. LM. Ing. 66; Bussy to Choiseul, 19 Jun. 1761, AE. CP. Ang. 443 fol. 258.

45. Colin G. Calloway, *The Scratch of a Pen: 1763 and the Transformation of North America* (New York: Oxford University Press, 2006).

46. David Dixon, *Never Come to Peace Again: Pontiac's Uprising and the Fate of the British Empire in North America* (Norman: University of Oklahoma Press, 2005); Richard Middleton, *Pontiac's War: Its Causes, Course, and Consequences* (New York: Routledge, 2007).

47. James Titus, *The Old Dominion at War: Society, Politics, and Warfare in Late Colonial Virginia* (Columbia: University of South Carolina Press, 1991); Fred Anderson, *Crucible of War: The Seven Years' War and the Fate of Empire in British North America, 1754–1766* (New York: Alfred A. Knopf, 2000).

48. Peter Way, "The Cutting Edge of Conflict: British Soldiers Encounter Native Americans in the French and Indian War," in *Empire and Others: British Encounters with Indigenous Peoples, 1600–1850,* ed. M. Daunton and Rick Halpern (Philadelphia: University of Pennsylvania Press, 1999).

49. Kathryn E. Holland Braund, *Deerskins and Duffels: The Creek Indian Trade with Anglo-America, 1685–1815* (Lincoln: University of Nebraska Press, 2008).

50. James Hart Merrell, *Into the American Woods: Negotiators on the Pennsylvania Frontier* (New York: Norton, 1999).

## 6. BRITAIN TRIUMPHANT TO AMERICA INDEPENDENT, 1765–76

The epigraph comes from the anonymous work published in London in 1765, p. 66.

1. Stephen Hornsby, *British Atlantic, American Frontier: Spaces of Power in Early Modern British America* (Hanover, N. H.: University Press of New England, 2005), 232–33.

2. Kevin Kenny, *Peaceable Kingdom Lost: The Paxton Boys and the Destruction of William Penn's Holy Experiment* (New York: Oxford University Press, 2009).

3. Michael McConnell, *Army and Empire: British Soldiers on the American Frontier, 1758–1775* (Lincoln: University of Nebraska Press, 2004).

4. Colin G. Calloway, *White People, Indians, and Highlanders: Tribal Peoples and Colonial Encounters in Scotland and America* (Oxford: Oxford University Press, 2008).

5. Eric Hinderaker, *Elusive Empires: Constructing Colonialism in the Ohio Valley, 1673–1800* (New York, Cambridge University Press, 1997).

6. Paul Benjamin Moyer, *Wild Yankees: The Struggle for Independence along Pennsylvania's Revolutionary Frontier* (Ithaca, N.Y.: Cornell University Press, 2007).

7. Charles Loch Mowat, *East Florida as a British Province, 1763–1784* (Berkeley: University of California Press, 1943), 68.

8. Douglas Stewart Brown, "The Iberville Canal Project: Its Relation to Anglo-French Commercial Rivalry in the Mississippi Valley, 1763–1775," *Mississippi Valley Historical Review* 32 (1946): 499–516.

9. Carla Gardina Pestana, *Protestant Empire: Religion and the Making of the British Atlantic World* (Philadelphia: University of Pennsylvania Press, 2009).

10. Philip Lawson, *The Imperial Challenge: Quebec and Britain in the Age of the American Revolution* (Montreal: McGill-Queen's University Press, 1989).

11. Mark Williams, *The Brittle Thread of Life: Backcountry People Make a Place for Themselves in Early America* (New Haven, Conn.: Yale University Press, 2009).

12. Stephen Conway, "Empire, Europe and British Naval Power," in *Empire, the Sea and Global History: Britain's Maritime World, c. 1763–c. 1840,* ed. David Cannadine (Basingstoke: Palgrave Macmillan, 2007), 22–40.

13. Woody Holton, *Forced Founders: Indians, Debtors, and Slaves and the Making of the American Revolution in Virginia* (Chapel Hill: University of North Carolina Press, 1999); Cathy Matson, "'Damned Scoundrels' and 'Libertisme of Trade': Freedom and Regulation in Colonial New York's Fur and Grain Trades," *William and Mary Quarterly* 3rd ser., 51 (1994): 414–17.

14. Parliamentary Committee on Petitions for importing iron from North America, 1757, papers of Sir Roger Newdigate MP, Warwick, CRO. CR. 136 B 2534.

15. James B. Bell, *A War of Religion: Dissenters, Anglicans and the American Revolution* (Basingstoke: Palgrave Macmillan, 2008).

16. Fred Anderson, *A People's Army: Massachusetts Soldiers and Society in the Seven Years' War* (Chapel Hill: University of North Carolina Press, 1984) and *Crucible of War: The Seven Years War and the Fate of Empire in British North America* (New York: Alfred A. Knopf, 2000).

17. Thomas J. Fleming, *1776: Year of Illusions* (New York: Norton, 1975); Peter David Garner Thomas, *Tea Party to Independence: The Third Phase of the American Revolution, 1773–1776* (Oxford: Oxford University Press, 1991).

18. Daniel A. Baugh, "The Atlantic of the Rival Navies, 1714–1783," in *English Atlantics Revisited,* ed. Nancy L. Rhoden and Ian Kenneth Steele (Montreal: McGill-Queen's University Press, 2007), 227.

19. Adrian J. Pearce, *British Trade with Spanish America, 1763–1808* (Liverpool: Liverpool University Press, 2007).

20. Nicholas Tracy, "The Falkland Islands Crisis of 1770: Use of Naval Force," *English Historical Review* 90 (1975): 40–75; Hamish M. Scott, *British Foreign Policy in the Age of the American Revolution* (Oxford: Oxford University Press, 1990), 141–55.

21. Robert Walpole, envoy in Lisbon, to Thomas, 2nd Lord Grantham, envoy in Madrid, 21 Jun. 1774, BL. Add. 24160 fol. 78.

22. G.N.D Evans, *Uncommon Obdurate: The Several Public Careers of J. F. W. DesBarres* (Salem, Mass.: Peabody Museum, 1969). See also Margaret B. Pritchard and Henry G. Taliaferro, *Degrees of Latitude: Mapping Colonial America* (Williamsburg, Va.: Colonial Williamsburg Foundation, 2002).

23. Colonel James Montresor to General Jeffrey Amherst, Commander-in-Chief in North America, 18 Oct. 1760, NA. War Office papers 34/83 fols 120–21.

24. Freeman M. Tovell, *At the Far Reaches of Empire: The Life of Juan Francisco de la Bodega y Quadra* (Vancouver: University of British Columbia Press, 2008).

25. Daniel H. Usner, *Indians, Settlers, and Slaves in a Frontier Exchange Economy:*

*The Lower Mississippi Valley before 1783* (Chapel Hill: University of North Carolina Press, 1992).

26. John H. Elliott, *Empires of the Atlantic World*. For comparative work at another level, Mariana Dantas, *Black Townsmen: Urban Slavery and Freedom in the Eighteenth-Century Americas* (Basingstoke: Palgrave Macmillan, 2008).

27. Jacques Léon Godechot, *France and the Atlantic Revolution of the Eighteenth Century* (London: Collier-Macmillan, 1965); Robert R. Palmer, *The Age of the Democratic Revolution*, 2 vols. (Princeton, N.J.: Princeton University Press, 1959–64); Jaroslaw Pelenski (ed.), *The American and European Revolutions, 1776–1848: SocioPolitical and Ideological Aspects* (Iowa City: University of Iowa Press, 1980); Franco Venturi, *Settecento riformatore. IV. La caduta dell' Antico Regime, 1776–1789*, 2 vols. (Torino: Giulio Einaudi, 1984).

28. David Armitage and Michael J. Braddick, eds., *The British Atlantic World, 1500–1800* (Basingstoke: Palgrave Macmillan, 2002); Eliga H. Gould and Peter S. Onuf, eds. *Empire and Nation: The American Revolution in the Atlantic World* (Baltimore: Johns Hopkins University Press, 2005).

29. David Armitage and Sanjay Subrahmanyam, eds., *The Age of Revolutions in Global Context, c. 1760–1840* (Basingstoke: Palgrave Macmillan, 2010).

### 7. BRITAIN DEFEATED, 1775–83

1. Edward Gibbon, *Decline and Fall*, ed. J. B. Bury, 7 vols. (London, 1896–1900), IV, 166.

2. Pitt, now Earl of Chatham, to Charles, 2nd Marquees of Rockingham, leader of the Rockinghamite Whigs, 18 Nov. 1777, Sheffield, Archives, Wentworth Woodhouse papers R151–56.

3. Michael Roberts, *Splendid Isolation, 1763–1780* (Reading: University of Reading, 1970); Scott, *British Foreign Policy in the Age of the American Revolution*.

4. Brendan Simms, *Three Victories and a Defeat: The Rise and Fall of the First British Empire, 1714–1783* (London: Allen Lane, 2007), 677.

5. Hal T. Shelton, *General Richard Montgomery and the American Revolution* (New York: New York University Press, 1994).

6. Jonathan R. Dull, *A Diplomatic History of the American Revolution* (New Haven, Conn.: Yale University Press, 1985).

7. Kenneth, Nebenzahl, *A Bibliography of Printed Battle Plans of the American Revolution, 1775–1795* (Chicago: University of Chicago Press, 1975).

8. Mary Sponberg Pedley, *The Commerce of Cartography, Making and Marketing Maps in Eighteenth-Century France and England* (Chicago: University of Chicago Press, 2005).

9. Gerald Saxon Brown, *The American Secretary: The Colonial Policy of Lord George Germain, 1775–1778* (Ann Arbor: University of Michigan Press, 1963).

10. J. William Harris, *The Hanging of Thomas Jeremiah: A Free Black Man's Encounter with Liberty* (New Haven, Conn.: Yale University Press, 2010).

11. Woody Holton, "Rebel against Rebel: Enslaved Virginians and the Coming of the American Revolution," *Virginia Magazine of History and Biography* 105 (1997): 157–92.

12. Judith L. Van Buskirk, *Generous Enemies: Patriots and Loyalists in Revolutionary New York* (Philadelphia: University of Pennsylvania Press, 2002).

13. Michael S. Adelberg, "An Evenly Balanced County: The Scope and Severity of Civil Warfare in Revolutionary Monmouth County, New Jersey," *Journal of Military History* 73 (2009): 9–47.

14. Charles P. Neimeyer, "The British Occupation of Newport, Rhode Island, 1776–1779," *Army History* (Winter 2010): 35.

15. Charles Toth, *The American Revolution and the West* (Port Washington, N.Y.: Kennikat Press, 1975).

16. David K. Wilson, *The Southern Strategy: Britain's Conquest of South Carolina and Georgia, 1775–1780* (Columbia: University of South Carolina Press, 2005); Jim Piecuch, *Three Peoples, One King: Loyalists, Indians, and Slaves in the Revolutionary South, 1775–1782* (Columbia: University of South Carolina Press, 2008).

17. PCC. 172; NA. PRO. 30/11/74.

18. Paul Hubert Smith, (ed.), *Letters of Delegates to Congress, 1774–1789*, vols. 10–11 (Washington, D.C.: Library of Congress, 1983–84).

19. John Ferling, "John Adams, Diplomat," *William and Mary Quarterly* 3rd ser., 51 (1994): 251.

20. James H. Huston, *John Adams and the Diplomacy of the American Revolution* (Lexington: University Press of Kentucky, 1980); Dull, *A Diplomatic History of the American Revolution*.

21. John D. Grainger, *The Battle of Yorktown, 1781: A Reassessment* (Woodbridge, UK: Boydell Press, 2005); Thomas Fleming, *The Perils of Peace: America's Struggle for Survival after Yorktown* (New York: Collins, 2007).

22. Orville T. Murphy, *Charles Gravier, Comte de Vergennes: French Diplomacy in the Age of Revolution, 1719–1787* (Albany: State University of New York Press, 1982), 252–60.

23. Sylvia R. Frey, "Between Slavery and Freedom: Virginia Blacks in the American Revolution," *Journal of Southern History* 49 (1983): 396–98; Jörg Nagler, "Achilles' Heel. Slavery and War in the American Revolution," in *War in an Age of Revolution, 1775–1815*, ed. Roger Chickering and Stig Förster (New York: Cambridge University Press, 2010), 285–97.

24. Glenn F. Williams, *Year of the Hangman: George Washington's Campaign Against the Iroquois* (Yardley, Pa.: Westholme, 2005); Claudio Saunt, *A New Order of Things: Property, Power, and the Transformation of the Creek Indians, 1733–1816* (New York: Cambridge University Press, 1999).

25. Edward J. Cashin, *Lachlan McGillivray, Indian Trader: The Shaping of the Southern Colonial Frontier* (Athens: University of Georgia Press, 1992).

26. George Smith McCowen, *The British Occupation of Charleston, 1780–1782* (Columbia: University of South Carolina Press, 1972), 10–13.

**8. FLEXING MUSCLES, 1783–1811**

1. John R. Short, *Representing the Republic: Mapping the United States, 1600–1900* (London: Reaktion, 2001).

2. Françoise Furstenberg, "The Significance of the Trans-Appalachian Frontier in Atlantic History," *American Historical Review* 113 (2008): 647–77.

3. Peter S. Onuf, *Jefferson's Empire: The Language of American Nationhood* (Charlottesville: University Press of Virginia, 2000), 18–52, quotation on p. 51.

4. Anthony F. C. Wallace, *Jefferson and the Indians: The Tragic Fate of the First Americans* (Cambridge: Belknap Press of Harvard University Press, 1999).

5. *Report*, 1 Mar. 1865, p. 7.

6. Robert Liston, British envoy, to William, Lord Grenville, Foreign Secretary, 13 Dec. 1799, 2 Feb. 1800, NA. FO. 5/25A fol. 479, 5/29A fol. 114.

7. Peter S. Onuf, "Liberty, Development, and Union: Visions of the West in the 1780s," *William and Mary Quarterly* 3rd ser., 43 (1986): 212.

8. Jack P. Greene, *The Intellectual Construction of America: Exceptionalism and Identity from 1492 to 1800* (Chapel Hill: University of North Carolina Press, 1993).

9. Jacques Roger, *Buffon: un philosophe au jardin du roi* (Paris: Fayard, 1989); Lee A. Dugatkin, *Mr. Jefferson and the Giant Moose: Natural History in*

*Early America* (Chicago: The University of Chicago Press, 2009); Keith Thomson, *A Passion for Nature: Thomas Jefferson and Natural History* (Chapel Hill: University of North Carolina Press, 2009).

10. James Belich, *Replenishing the Earth: The Settler Revolution and the Rise of the Anglo-World, 1783–1939* (Oxford: Oxford University Press, 2009), 56.

11. Anthony Merry, British envoy, to Lord Mulgrave, Foreign Secretary, 3 Nov. 1805, NA. FO. 5/45 fol. 313.

12. Max M. Edling, *A Revolution in Favor of Government: Origins of the U.S. Constitution and the Making of the American State* (New York: Oxford University Press, 2003).

13. Edward Thornton to James Bland Burges, Under Secretary at the Foreign Office, 31 Oct. 1791, Bodl. BB. vol. 44 fol. 6.

14. Jefferson to Marquis de Chastellux, 3 Sept. 1785, J.P. Boyd (ed.), *The Papers of Thomas Jefferson*, 8 (Princeton, N.J.: Princeton University Press, 1953), 468.

15. David Waldstreicher, "Rites of Rebellion, Rites of Assent: Celebrations, Print Culture, and the Origins of American Nationalism," *Journal of American History* 82 (1995): 47–61; Albrecht Koschnik, "Political Conflict and Public Contest: Rituals of National Celebration in Pennsylvania, 1788–1815," *Pennsylvania Magazine of History and Biography* 118 (1994): 209–248.

16. Eden to Francis, Marquess of Carmarthen, Foreign Secretary, 6 Jun. 1786, Carmarthen to Duke of Dorset, envoy in Paris, 12 Nov. 1784, NA. FO. 27/19 fol. 116, 27/13 fol. 175.

17. Montmorin, *American Historical Review* 8 (1903): 713.

18. Dorset to Earl Gower, Lord President of the Council, 29 Jul. 1784, NA. PRO. 30/29/1/15 no. 47.

19. Adams, Franklin and Jefferson to Dorset, 28 Oct. 1784, NA. FO. 27/13 fols 147–48.

20. Pitt to Carmarthen, 16 Dec. 1785, BL. Egerton manuscripts, 3498 fol. 155.

21. Hämäläinen, *The Comanche Empire*, 135.

22. Anthony Merry, Consul in Madrid, to Leeds, 17 Sept., 29 Oct., Leeds to Merry, 9 Oct., 25 Dec. 1789, NA. FO. 72/15 fols 178–80, 270, 232, 375–86.

23. Eden to Lord Sheffield, 26 Feb. 1789, BL. Add. 45728 fol. 99.

24. H. M. Majors, "The Hezeta-Bodega Voyage of 1775," *Northwest Discovery* 1 (1980): 208–252; Henry R. Wagner, "The Last Spanish Exploration of the Northwest Coast and the Attempt to Colonize Bodega Bay," *California Historical Society Quarterly* 10 (1931): 311–45.

25. Donald C. Cutter, *Malaspina and Galiano: Spanish Voyages to the Northwest Coast, 1791 and 1792* (Seattle: University of Washington Press, 1991) and *California in 1792: A Spanish Naval Visit* (Norman: University of Oklahoma Press, 1990); Robin Inglis (ed.), *Spain and the North Pacific Coast: Essays in Recognition of the Bicentennial of the Malaspina Expedition, 1791–1792* (Vancouver: Vancouver Maritime Museum, 1992).

26. John M. Norris, "The Policy of the British Cabinet in the Nootka Crisis," *English Historical Review* 70 (1955): 572–75.

27. *Parliamentary Register*, 27, 564–65.

28. William S. Robertson, *The Life of Miranda* (Chapel Hill: University of North Carolina Press, 1929), I, 97–112.

29. Charles R. Ritcheson, *Aftermath of Revolution: British Policy towards the United States* (Dallas: Southern Methodist University Press, 1969), 98–106, 111–15, 154, 160–63; J. Leitch Wright, *Britain and the American Frontier, 1783–1815* (Athens: University of Georgia Press, 1975), 50–65.

30. Grenville to Lord Hawkesbury, 14 Jan. 1791, BL. Add. 38226 fol. 42.

31. Leeds to Fitzherbert, 16 May 1790, NA. FO. 72/17.

32. Norris, "Policy," 580.

33. Arthur P. Whitaker, *The Spanish-American Frontier, 1783–1795: The Westward Movement and the Spanish Retreat in the Mississippi Valley* (Boston: Houghton Mifflin, 1927).

34. Harold C. Syrett (ed.), *The Papers of Alexander Hamilton, VII* (New York: Columbia University Press, 1963), 70–74; Julian P. Boyd, *Number 7, Alexander Hamilton's Secret Attempts to Control American Foreign Policy* (Princeton, N.J.: Princeton University Press, 1964), 4–13; Charles Ritcheson, *Aftermath of Revolution*, 103–104, 112–15.

35. John Sugden, *Blue Jacket: Warrior of the Shawnees* (Lincoln: University of Nebraska Press, 2000).

36. A E. C P. Etats Unis 35 fols 135, 188.

37. Leeds to Fitzherbert, 17 Aug. 1790, N A. F O. 72/18.

38. G. Williams, *The British Search for the North West Passage in the Eighteenth Century* (London, Longmans, Green, 1962), 221–26, 235–45; David Mackay, *In the Wake of Cook: Exploration, Science and Empire, 1780–1801* (London: Croom Helm, 1985), 83.

39. Bern Anderson, *Surveyor of the Sea* (Seattle: University of Washington Press, 1960); Daniel R. Clayton, "On the Colonial Genealogy of George Vancouver's Chart of the North-West Coast of North America," *Ecumene* 7 (2000): 392; and *Islands of Truth: The Imperial Fashioning of Vancouver Island* (Vancouver: University of British Columbia Press, 2000).

40. Liston to William, Lord Auckland (earlier William Eden), 14 Sept. 1790, B L. Add. 34433 fol. 117.

41. Robin Fisher, *Contact and Conflict* (Vancouver: University of British Columbia Press, 1977); James R. Gibson, *Otter Skins, Boston Ships, and China Goods: The Maritime Fur Trade of the Northwest Coast, 1785–1841* (Seattle: University of Washington Press, 1992).

42. John Scofield, *Hail Columbia, Robert Gray, John Kendrick and the Pacific Fur Trade* (Portland: Oregon Historical Society Press, 1993).

43. Luzerne to Montmorin, 21, 28 Sept. 1790, A E. C P. Ang. 574 fols 282, 294–95.

44. John R. Bockstoce, *Furs and Frontiers in the Far North: The Contest among Native and Foreign Nations for the Bering Strait Fur Trade* (New Haven, Conn.: Yale University Press, 2009).

45. Alexei V. Postnikov, "The Search for a Sea Passage from the Atlantic Ocean to the Pacific via North America's Coast: On the History of a Scientific Competition," *Terrae Incognita* 32 (2000): 31–52.

46. Richard A. Pierce, *Russia's Hawaiian Adventure, 1815–1817* (Berkeley: University of California Press, 1965).

47. David Armitage, *The Declaration of Independence: A Global History* (Cambridge, Mass.: Harvard University Press, 2007).

48. Morton J. Frisch, (ed.), *The Pacificus-Helvidius Debates of 1793–1794* (Indianapolis: Liberty Fund, 2007).

49. Harry Ammon, *The Genet Mission* (New York: Norton, 1973); E. R. Sheridan, "The Recall of Edmund Charles Genet: A Study in Transatlantic Politics and Diplomacy," *Diplomatic History* 18 (1994): 463–88.

50. Grenville to Liston, – Jun., – Dec. 1798, N A. F O. 5/22 fols 32, 65.

51. Alexander DeConde, *Entangling Alliance: Politics and Diplomacy under George Washington* (Durham, N.C.: Duke University Press, 1958).

52. Arthur Zilversmit, *The First Emancipation: The Abolition of Slavery in the North* (Chicago: University of Chicago Press, 1967).

53. Robert J. Alderson, *This Bright Era of Happy Revolutions: French Consul Michel-Ange-Bernard Mangourit and International Republicanism in Charleston, 1792–1794* (Charleston: University of South Carolina Press, 2008).

54. Lawrence S. Kaplan, *Colonies into Nation: American Diplomacy, 1763–1801*

(New York: Macmillan, 1972); John L. Harper, *American Machiavelli: Alexander Hamilton and the Origins of U.S. Foreign Policy* (Cambridge: Cambridge University Press, 2004); Marie-Jeanne Rossignol, *The Nationalist Ferment: The Origins of U.S. Foreign Policy, 1789–1812* (Columbus: Ohio State University Press, 2005).

55. Alan D. Gaff, *Bayonets in the Wilderness: Anthony Wayne's Legion in the Old North-west* (Norman: University of Oklahoma Press, 2004).

56. Jay Gitlin, *The Bourgeois Frontier: French Towns, French Traders, and American Expansion* (New Haven, Conn.: Yale University Press, 2010).

57. Merry to Lord Mulgrave, Foreign Secretary, 31 Jan. 1806, NA. FO. 5/48 fol. 25.

58. Merry to Mulgrave, 31 Jan. 1806, NA. FO. 5/48 fols 25–28.

59. Robert W. Coakley, *The Role of Federal Military Forces in Domestic Disorders, 1789–1878* (Washington D.C.: Center of Military History, U.S. Army, 1988); Leonard L. Richards, *Shays's Rebellion: The American Revolution's Final Battle* (Philadelphia: University of Pennsylvania Press, 2002).

60. Thomas P. Slaughter, *The Whiskey Rebellion: Frontier Epilogue to the American Revolution* (New York: Oxford University Press, 1986); Terry Bouton, *Taming Democracy: "The People," the Founders and the Troubled Ending of the American Revolution* (Oxford: Oxford University Press, 2007).

61. Grenville to Liston, 15 Jan., 8 Jun. 1798, NA. FO. 5/22 fols 16–17, 38.

62. Grenville to Liston, 8 Jun. 1798, NA. FO. 5/22 fol. 41.

63. Grenville to Pitt, 8 Oct. 1797, NA. PRO. 30/8/140 fol. 107.

64. Paul D. Nelson, "General Charles Scott, the Kentucky Mounted Volunteers, and the Northwest Indian Wars, 1784–1794," *Journal of the Early Republic* 6 (1986): 220–22. For problems with the militia in 1790, see Michael S. Warner, "General Josiah Harmar's Campaign Reconsidered: How the Americans Lost the Battle of Kekionga," *Indiana Magazine of History* 83 (1987): 45–47.

65. Richard H. Kohn, "General Wilkinson's Vendetta with General Wayne: Politics and Command in the American Army, 1791–1796," *Filson Club Historical Quarterly* 45 (1971): 361–72; and *Eagle and Sword: The Beginnings of the Military Establishment in America* (New York, 1975); Robert Gough, "Officering the American Army, 1798," *William and Mary Quarterly* 43 (1986): 460–71.

66. Fredrick C. Leiner, *Millions for Defense: The Subscription Warships of 1798* (Annapolis, Md.: Naval Institute Press, 2000).

67. Alexander DeConde, *Entangling Alliance Politics and Diplomacy under George Washington* (Durham, N.C.: Duke University Press, 1958); Michael A. Palmer, *Stoddert's War: Naval Operations During the Quasi-War, 1798–1801* (Columbia: University of South Carolina Press, 1987); Gregory E. Fehlings, "America's First Limited War," *Naval War College Review* 53 (2000): 101–144; Grenville to Liston, 8 Jun., – Oct. 1798 NA. FO. 5/22 fols 39, 54.

68. Grenville to Liston, 8 Jun. 1798, NA. FO. 5/22 fol. 42.

69. Jack N. Rakove, "Thinking Like a Constitution," *Journal of the Early Republic* 24 (2004): 22.

70. Paul D. Newman, *Fries's Rebellion: The Enduring Struggle for the American Revolution* (Philadelphia: University of Pennsylvania Press, 2004).

71. For a gender dimension, see Barbara C. Smith, "Food Rioters and the American Revolution," *William and Mary Quarterly* 3rd ser., 51 (1994): 34.

72. Miranda to Castlereagh, 10 Jun. 1807, BL. Loan manuscripts, 57/107 fol. 165.

73. Thornton to Burges, 31 Oct. 1791, Bodl. BB. 44 fol. 7.

74. Liston to Grenville, 27 Dec. 1800, NA. FO. 5/29A fol. 361.

75. Robert E. Wright, *The First Wall Street: Chestnut Street, Philadelphia, and the Birth of American Finance* (Chicago: University of Chicago Press, 2005).

76. Joanne B. Freeman, "Slander, Poison, Whispers, and Fame: Jefferson's 'Anas' and Political Gossip in the Early Republic," *Journal of the Early Republic* 15 (1995): 25–57.

77. Joanne B. Freeman, *Affairs of Honor: National Politics in the New Republic* (New Haven, Conn.: Yale University Press, 2001); John A. Schutz and Douglas Adair, eds., *The Spur of Fame: Dialogues of John Adams and Benjamin Rush, 1805–1813* (Indianapolis: Liberty Fund, 2001).

78. Matthew Brown, "How Did Rupert Hand Get out of Jail? Colombia and the Atlantic Empires, 1830–1833," *History* 95 (2010): 30.

79. Gary B. Nash, "Sparks from the Altar of '76: International Repercussions and Reconsiderations of the American Revolution," in *The Age of Revolutions in Global Context, c. 1760–1840*, ed. David Armitage and Sanjay Subrahmanyam, 18.

80. Joseph J. Ellis, *Passionate Sage: The Character and Legacy of John Adams* (New York: Norton, 1994).

81. Marixa Lasso, *Myths of Harmony: Race and Republicanism during the Age of Revolution, Colombia, 1795–1831* (Pittsburgh: University of Pittsburgh Press, 2007).

82. Liston to Grenville, 27 Dec. 1800, NA. FO. 5/29A fol. 303.

83. Michael A. Bellesiles, "'The Soil Will Be Soaked with Blood': Taking the Revolution of 1800 Seriously," in *The Revolution of 1800: Democracy, Race, and the New Republic*, ed. James Horn et al. (Charlottesville: University Press of Virginia, 2002), 75.

84. Lawrence D. Cress, *Citizens in Arms: The Army and Militia in American Society to the War of 1812* (Chapel Hill: University of North Carolina Press, 1982).

85. Mark Pitcavage, "Ropes of Sand: Territorial Militias, 1801–1812," *Journal of the Early Republic* 13 (1993): 481–500.

86. Theodore J. Crackel, *Mr. Jefferson's Army: Political and Social Reform of the Military Establishment, 1801–1809* (New York: New York University Press, 1987).

87. Gene A. Smith, *"For the Purposes of Defense": The Politics of the Jefferson Gunboat Program* (Newark: University of Delaware Press, 1995).

88. Joshua E. London, *Victory in Tripoli: How America's War with the Barbary Pirates Established the U.S. Navy and Built a Nation* (Hoboken, N.J.: Wiley, 2005); Richard Zacks, *The Pirate Coast: Thomas Jefferson, the First Marines, and the Secret Mission of 1805* (New York: Hyperion, 2005).

89. Thornton to Lord Hawkesbury, Foreign Secretary, 28 Dec. 1802, NA. FO. 5/35 fol. 366.

90. Thornton to Grenville, 7 Mar. 1801, NA. FO. 5/32 fols 73, 76.

91. A. J. Pearce, "The Hope-Barings Contract: Finance and Trade Between Europe and the Americas, 1805–1808," *English Historical Review* 124 (2009): 1352.

92. T. H. Breen, "'Baubles of Britain': The American and Consumer Revolutions of the Eighteenth Century," *Past and Present* 119 (1988): 104.

93. Burton Spivak, *Jefferson's English Crisis: Commerce, Embargo and the Republican Revolution* (Charlottesville: University Press of Virginia, 1979).

94. Jefferson to Joel Barlow, 14 Aug. 1805, BL. Add. 39908 fol. 13.

95. Seymour Drescher, *Abolition: A History of Slavery and Antislavery* (Cambridge: Cambridge University Press, 2009), 75 n. 60.

96. P. R. Girard, *"Liberté, Égalité, Esclavage:* French Revolutionary Ideals and the Failure of the LeClerc expedition to

Saint-Domingue," *French Colonial History* 6 (2005): 69–70.

97. Thornton to Lord Hawkesbury, Foreign Secretary, 28, 31 Oct. 1803, N A. F O. 5/38 fols 305, 322.

98. Ralph W. Hidy, *The House of Baring in American Trade and Finance: English Merchant Bankers at Work, 1783–1861* (Cambridge, Mass.: Harvard University Press, 1949).

99. Thomas P. Abernethy, *The Burr Conspiracy* (New York, 1954); F. Fernández-Armesto, *The Americas* (New York: Oxford University Press, 2003), 124.

100. Merry to Mulgrave, 29 Mar., 29 Apr., 4 Aug. 1805, N A. F O. 5/45 fols 128–32, 192–93, 259.

101. Merry to Mulgrave, 25 Nov. 1805, N A. F O. 5/45 fols 322–31.

102. Merry to Charles James Fox, Foreign Secretary, 2 Nov. 1806, N A. F O. 5/49, fols 218–24.

103. Thornton to Hawkesbury, 28 Oct. 1803, N A. F O. 5/38 fols 307–308.

104. Merry to Mulgrave, 3 Nov. 1805, N A. F O. 5/45 fol. 314.

105. J. C. A. Stagg, *Borderlines in Borderlands: James Madison and the Spanish-American Frontier, 1776–1821* (New Haven, Conn.: Yale University Press, 2009).

106. Merry to Mulgrave, 4 Aug. 1805, N A. F O. 5/45 fol. 254.

107. David L. Nicandri and Clay Jenkinson, *River of Promise: Lewis and Clark on the Columbia* (Washburn, N.D.: Dakota Institute Press of the Lewis & Clark Fort Mandan Foundation, 2009).

108. Fred Anderson and Andrew Cayton, *The Dominion of War: Empire and Liberty in North America, 1500–2000* (New York: Viking, 2005), 227.

109. Grenville to Liston, 19 Jan. 1799, N A. F O. 5/25A fols 8–9.

110. Alex Dupuy, *Haiti in the World Economy: Class, Race, and Underdevelopment since 1700* (Boulder, Colo.: Westview Press, 1989).

111. Edward L. Pierce (ed.), *Memoirs and Letters of Charles Sumner: 1860 to Death* (London: Sampson Low, Marston, Searle and Rivington, 1878), 68–69.

112. Philip Lawson, *The Imperial Challenge: Quebec and Britain in the Age of the American Revolution*; F. Murray Greenwood, *Legacies of Fear: Law and Politics in Quebec in the Era of the French Revolution* (Toronto: Osgoode Society, 1994).

113. Thornton to Hawkesbury, 5 May 1803, N A. F O. 5/38 fol. 170.

114. James M. Smith (ed.), *The Republic of Letters: The Correspondence between Thomas Jefferson and James Madison, 1776–1826*, 3 vols. (New York: Norton, 1995).

115. John Sugden, *Tecumseh: A Life* (New York: Henry Holt and Co., 1997); Alfred A. Cave, *Prophets of the Great Spirit: Native American Revitalization Movements in Eastern North America* (Lincoln: University of Nebraska Press, 2006).

116. J. C. A. Stagg, *Mr. Madison's War: Politics, Diplomacy and Warfare in the Early Republic* (Princeton, N.J.: Princeton University Press, 1983).

117. Stagg, "James Madison and the Coercion of Great Britain: Canada, the West Indies, and the War of 1812," *William and Mary Quarterly* 3rd ser., 38 (1981): 33–34.

118. Gordon S. Wood, *Empire of Liberty: A History of the Early Republic, 1789–1815* (Oxford: Oxford University Press, 2009), 662.

### 9. FLORIDA BUT NOT CANADA

1. John Lynch (ed.), *Latin American Revolutions* (Norman: University of Oklahoma Press, 1994); G. Paquette, "The Dissolution of the Spanish Atlantic Monarchy," *Historical Journal* 52 (2009): 175–212.

2. H. M. Hammill, "Royalist Counter-insurgency in the Mexican War for Independence: The Lessons of 1811," *Hispanic American Historical Review* 53 (1973): 470–89.

3. George R. Andrews, "Spanish American Independence: A Structural Analysis," *Latin American Perspectives* 12 (1985): 127; Peter Blanchard, *Under the Flags of Freedom: Slave Soldiers and the Wars of Independence in Spanish South America* (Pittsburgh, Pa.: University of Pittsburgh Press, 2008).

4. Christon I. Archer, "Insurrection-Reaction-Revolution-Fragmentation: Reconstructing the Choreography of Meltdown in New Spain during the Independence Era," *Mexican Studies* 10 (1994): 63–98; Virginia Guedea, "The Process of Mexican Independence," *American Historical Review* 105 (2000): 116–30.

5. B. Hamnett, "Royalist Counter-insurgency and the Continuity of Rebellion: Guanajuato and Michoacán, 1813–1820," *Hispanic American Historical Review* 62 (1982): 19–48.

6. C. I. Archer, "The Army of New Spain and the Wars of Independence, 1790–1821," *Hispanic American Historical Review* 61 (1981): 710.

7. Michael T. Ducey, "Village, Nation, and Constitution: Insurgent Politics in Papantla, Veracruz, 1810–1821," *Hispanic American Historical Review* 79 (1999): 471–76.

8. Timothy Anna, *The Fall of the Royal Government in Mexico City* (Lincoln: University of Nebraska Press, 1978); Timothy J. Henderson, *The Mexican Wars of Independence* (New York: Hill and Wang, 2009).

9. Wade G. Dudley, "The Flawed British Blockade, 1812–15," in *Naval Blockades and Seapower: Strategies and Counter-Strategies, 1805–2005*, ed. Bruce A. Elleman and Sarah C. M. Paine (London: Routledge, 2006), 34–45.

10. Richard Rush, Comptroller of the Treasury, to John Adams, 2 Aug. 1813, Penn. AM. 1352.

11. J. Kimball, "The Fog and Friction of Frontier War: The Role of Logistics in American Offensive Failure during the War of 1812," *Old Northwest* 5 (1979–80): 337.

12. Jon Latimer, *1812: War with America* (Cambridge, Mass.: Belknap Press of Harvard University Press, 2007); Jeremy Black, *The War of 1812 in the Age of Napoleon* (Norman: University of Oklahoma Press, 2009), 147–203.

13. Frank L. Owsley, "The Role of the South in British Grand Strategy in the War of 1812," *Tennessee Historical Quarterly* 31 (1972): 22–35; John Sugden, "The Southern Indians in the War of 1812: The Closing Phase," *Florida Historical Quarterly* 60 (1982): 273–312.

14. Frank L. Owsley, "Prophet of War: Josiah Francis and the Creek War," *American Indian Quarterly* 9 (1985): 273–93.

15. David G. Fitz-Enz, *The Final Invasion: Plattsburgh, the War of 1812's Most Decisive Battle* (New York: Cooper Square Press, 2001).

16. Carol Benn, *The Iroquois in the War of 1812* (Toronto: University of Toronto Press, 1998).

17. Gregory E. Dowd, "Thinking and Believing: Nativism and Unity in the Age of Pontiac and Tecumseh," *American Indian Quarterly* 16 (1992): 309–335.

18. Donald R. Hickey, "New England's Defense Problem and the Genesis of the Hartford Convention," *New England Quarterly* 50 (1977): 587–604.

19. Theodore Dwight, *History of the Hartford Convention* (New York: Da Capo Press, 1833), 352–79.

20. Steven Watts, *The Republic Reborn: War and the Making of Liberal America, 1790–1820* (Baltimore: Johns Hopkins University Press, 1987).

21. Donald R. Hickey, "Federalist Party Unity and the War of 1812," *Journal of American Studies* 12 (1978): 39.

22. Jamie W. Moore, *The Fortifications Board 1816–1828 and the Definition of National Security* (Charleston, S.C.: Citadel, 1981).

23. Carol E. Skeen, *Citizen Soldiers in the War of 1812* (Lexington: University Press of Kentucky, 1999).

24. Nicholas Onuf and Peter Onuf, *Nations, Markets, and War: Modern History and the American Civil War* (Charlottesville: University Press of Virginia, 2006), 240–47.

25. Hamilton to Vaughan, 5 Dec. 1815, AS, Vaughan papers, C50.

26. Castlereagh to Sir Charles Bagot, British envoy, 21 May 1818; George Canning to Addington, 15 Nov. 1823, NA. FO. 5/129 fol. 43, 5/177 fol. 15.

27. Peter Bakewell, "Spanish America: Empire and Its Outcome," in *The Spanish World*, ed. John H. Elliott (New York: H.N. Abrams, 1991), 75.

28. DRO. 152M/Box 38/Diaries vol. 7.

29. Rafe Blaufarb, "The Western Question: The Geopolitics of Latin American Independence," *American Historical Review* 112 (207): 751.

30. J. W. Covington, "The Negro Fort," *Gulf Coast Historical Review* 5 (1990): 79–91.

31. A. Hasbrouck, "Gregor MacGregor and the Colonization of Poyais, between 1820 and 1824," *Hispanic American Historical Review* 7 (1927), 438–59; T. Frederick Davis, *MacGregor's Invasion of Florida, 1817* (Jacksonville: Florida Historical Society, 1928); David Bushnell (ed.), *La República de las Floridas: Text and Documents* (Mexico City: Pan American Inst. of Geography and History, 1986); Matthew Brown, "Inca, Sailor, Soldier, King: Gregor MacGregor and the Early Nineteenth-Century Caribbean," *Bulletin of Latin American Research* 24 (2005): 51–58.

32. Castlereagh to Bagot, 11 Nov. 1817, NA. FO. 5/120 fols 76–77.

33. Castlereagh to Bagot, 10 Nov. 1817, NA. FO. 5/120 fols 58–67.

34. David S. Heidler and Jeanne T. Heidler, *Old Hickory's War: Andrew Jackson and the Quest for Empire* (Baton Rouge: Louisiana State University Press, 2003); Robert V. Remini, *Andrew Jackson and His Indian Wars* (New York: Viking, 2001); John Missall and Mary L. Missall, *The Seminole Wars* (Gainesville: University Press of Florida, 2004).

35. Castlereagh to Bagot, 4 Feb. 1818, NA. FO. 5/129 fols 21–28.

36. J. Scafer, "The British Attitude to the Oregon Question, 1815–1846," *American Historical Review* 16 (1910–11): 273–99.

37. Castlereagh to Bagot, 23 Apr. 1816, NA. FO. 5/113 fol. 16; S.L. Falk, "Disarmament on the Great Lakes: Myth or Reality?" *United States Naval Institute Proceedings* 87 (1967): 69–73.

38. Marjorie Wilkins Campbell, *The Northwest Company* (Toronto: University of Toronto Press, 1957).

39. John A. Hussey (ed.), *The Voyage of the "Raccoon": A "Secret" Journal of a Visit to Oregon, California, and Hawaii, 1813–1814* (San Francisco: Book Club of California, 1958); Barry Gough, *The Royal Navy and the Northwest Coast of America, 1810–1914: A Study of British Maritime Ascendancy* (Vancouver: University of British Columbia Press, 1971), 8–28.

40. Glynn Barratt, *Russian Shadows on the Northwest Coast of North America, 1810–1890: A Study in the Rejection of Defense Responsibilities* (Vancouver: University of British Columbia Press, 1983).

41. Samuel F. Bemis, *John Quincy Adams and the Foundations of American Foreign Policy* (New York: Knopf, 1949).

42. Stratford Canning to Castlereagh, 1, 26 Jan. 1822, NA. FO. 5/166 fols 1–4, 43.

43. Robert O. Keohane, "Associative American Development, 1776–1860: Economic Growth and Political Disintegration," in *The Antinomies of Interdependence: National Welfare and the International Division of Labor* ed. John G. Ruggie (New York: Columbia University Press, 1983), 43–90.

44. Addington to John Quincy Adams, 4 Mar. 1824, DRO. 152M/Box 34.

45. Stratford Canning to Castlereagh, 7 Feb. 1822, NA. FO. 5/166 fols 61–62.

46. Palmerston to Vaughan, 7 Apr. 1834, NA. FO. 5/288 fol. 7.

47. Addington to Dalhousie, 3 Jan. 1824, DRO. 152M/Box 34. See also Bradford Perkins, *Castlereagh and Adams: England and the United States, 1812–1823* (Berkeley: University of California Press, 1964).

48. Crampton to Clarendon, 25 Feb. 1855, NA. FO. 5/619 fol. 310.

49. William R. Manning (ed.), *Diplomatic Correspondence of the United States Concerning the Independence of the Latin American Nations* (New York, Oxford University Press, 1926); Edward H. Tatum, *The United States and Europe, 1815–1823: A Study in the Background of the Monroe Doctrine* (New York: Russell, 1967); James E. Lewis, *American Union and the Problem of Neighborhood: The United States and the Collapse of the Spanish Empire* (Chapel Hill: University of North Carolina Press, 1998).

50. Stratford Canning to George Canning, 27 Mar. 1823, NA. FO. 5/176 fol. 31.

51. Rufus King, envoy in London, to Henry Clay, 21 Feb. 1826, James F. Hopkins and Mary W. M. Hargreaves, eds., *The Papers of Henry Clay. V. Secretary of State, 1826* (Lexington: University Press of Kentucky, 1973), p. 125.

52. Frank Griffith Dawson, *The First Latin American Debt Crisis: The City of London and the 1822–25 Loan Bubble* (New Haven, Conn.: Yale University Press, 1990); Carlos Marichal, *A Century of Debt Crises in Latin America: From Independence to the Great Depression, 1820–1930* (Princeton, N.J.: Princeton University Press, 1989).

53. Vaughan to Canning, 6 Dec. 1825, 28 Aug., 2, 20 Oct. 1826, AS, Vaughan papers, H18 no 25, H27 no 65, H29 no 72,

H30 no 78; Stratford Canning to George Canning, 8 Apr. 1823, FO. 5/176 fols 67–72, re canal via Guatemala.

54. Orford to Vaughan, 12 Jan. 1826, AS, Vaughan papers, C77 no. 2.

55. John O'Loughlin and Herman van der Wusten, "Political Geography of Panregions," *Geographical Review,* 80 (1990): 2–9.

56. Stratford Canning to George Canning, 20 Jun. 1823, NA. FO. 5/176 fol. 221.

57. Stratford Canning to George Canning, 6 Jun. 1823, NA. FO. 5/176 fol. 187.

58. Stratford Canning to George Canning, 19 Mar., 9 Apr. 1823, NA. FO. 5/176 fols 24, 75.

59. Stratford Canning to Castlereagh, 3 Jul. 1822, NA. FO. 5/168 fol. 314.

60. Jan Glete, *Navies and Nations: Warships, Navies and State Building in Europe and America, 1500–1860* (Stockholm: Almqvist & Wiksell International, 1993), p. 465.

61. Christian Hermann, *La politique de la France en Amérique Latine, 1826–1850: une rencontre manquée* (Bordeaux, Temiber, 1996).

62. William A. Deplao, *The Mexican National Army, 1822–1852* (College Station: Texas A&M University Press, 1997), 67–69.

63. Gerald Graham and R.A. Humphreys, eds., *The Navy and South America, 1807–1823: Correspondence of the Commanders-in-Chief on the South American Station* (London: Navy Records Society, 1962).

64. Castlereagh to Bagot, 10 Nov. 1817, NA. FO. 5/120 fol. 72; C.J. Bartlett, 'Statecraft, Power and Influence', in Bartlett (ed.), *Britain Pre-eminent: Studies in British World Influence in the Nineteenth Century* (London: Macmillan, 1969), p. 184.

65. Andrew D. Lambert, "William James, the War of 1812 and the Origins of Naval History," in *A Naval History of Great Britain,* ed. W. James (London: Maritime Press, 2002).

66. Richard Rush, envoy in London, to Madison, 13 Dec. 1818, 15 Nov. 1820, Penn. Am. 13520.

67. Papers of Henry, 1st Viscount Sidmouth, Home Secretary, DRO. 152M/C/1815/OH/34–5, C/1816/OH/125.

68. George Canning to Stratford Canning, 11 Oct., 7 Dec. 1822, NA. FO. 5/165 fols 53–54, 80.

69. BL. Add. 57315 fol. 39.

## 10. EXPANSIONISM AND ITS PROBLEMS, 1823–43

1. Addington diary, DRO. 152M/Box 38 vol. 8. See also Bradford Perkins (ed.), *Youthful America: Selections from Henry Unwin Addington's Residence in the United States of America* (Berkeley: University of California Press, 1960) and J. Smith, "'Savages and Rattlesnakes'. Washington, District of Columbia: A British Diplomat's view 1823–5," *The Historian* (Mar. 2002): 31–36; Michael Slater, *Charles Dickens* (New Haven, Conn.: Yale University Press, 2009), 186–87. Palmerston, in contrast, was pleased that the future Victoria Falls were finer, Palmerston to Lord John Russell, 12 Apr. 1861, NA. PRO. 30/22/21 fol. 463.

2. William H. Goetzmann, *When the Eagle Screamed: The Romantic Horizon in American Diplomacy, 1800–1860* (New York: Wiley, 1966), xiii–xvi; Norman K. Risjord, *Representative Americans: The Romantics* (Lanham: Rowman and Little-fielf, 2001).

3. William Bagley, *So Rugged and Mountainous: Blazing the Trails to Oregon and California, 1812–1848* (Norman: University of Oklahoma Press, 2010).

4. Addington was impressed by the "very large" steamboats on the Hudson, Diary, vol. 8.

5. Paul E. Paskoff, *Troubled Waters: Steamboat Disasters, River Improvements, and American Public Policy, 1821–1860* (Baton Rouge: Louisiana State University Press, 2007).

6. Stephen Mihm, *A Nation of Counterfeiters: Capitalists, Con Men, and the Making of the United States* (Cambridge, Mass.: Harvard University Press, 2007).

7. Vaughan to Addington, 4 Jul. 1827, AS, Vaughan papers, C7/3.

8. Stratford Canning to Castlereagh, 28 Apr. 1821, NA. FO. 5/158 fol. 70.

9. George Canning to Addington, 15 Nov. 1823, NA. FO. 5/177 fols 15–16.

10. Robert V. Remini, *Henry Clay: Statesman for the Union* (New York: W.W. Norton, 1991), 301–303.

11. Fredrick Merk, *Slavery and the Annexation of Texas* (New York: Knopf, 1972), 21–22.

12. C. B. Smith, "Congressional Attitudes towards Military Preparation during the Monroe Administration," *Military Affairs* 40 (Feb. 1976): 22–25.

13. J. Parry, *The Politics of Patriotism: English Liberalism, National Identity and Europe, 1830–1886* (Cambridge: Cambridge University Press, 2006).

14. Palmerston to Vaughan, 27 Jun., Palmerston to Charles Bankhead, 30 Oct., 21 Dec., Vaughan to Palmerston, 20 Dec. 1835, NA. FO. 5/299 fols 9–12, 82–83, 132–33, 5/293 fols 168–69.

15. George L. Bernstein, "Special Relationship and Appeasement: Liberal Policy Towards America in the Age of Palmerston," *Historical Journal* 41 (1998): 727.

16. Samuel J. Watson, "U.S. Army Officers Fight the 'Patriot War': Responses to Filibustering on the Canadian Border, 1837–1839," *Journal of the Early Republic* 18 (1998): 493.

17. Helen I. Cowan, *British Immigration to British North America: The First Hundred Years* (Toronto: University of Toronto Press, 1961); William Van Vugt, *Britain to America: Mid-Nineteenth-Century Immigrants to the United States* (Urbana: University of Illinois Press, 1999).

18. Brian W. Dippie, *The Vanishing American: White Attitudes and U.S. Indian*

*Policy* (Middletown, Conn.: Wesleyan University Press, 1982).

19. Ronald N. Satz, *American Indian Policy in the Jacksonian Era* (Lincoln: University of Nebraska Press, 1975).

20. Francis P. Prucha, *The Sword of the Republic: The United States Army on the Frontier, 1783–1846* (New York: Macmillan, 1969).

21. William B. Skelton, "Army Officers' Attitudes towards Indians, 1830–1860," *Pacific Northwest Quarterly* 67 (1976): 124; James M. Denham, "'Some Prefer the Seminoles': Violence and Disorder among Soldiers and Settlers in the Second Seminole War, 1835–1842," *Florida Historical Quarterly* 70 (1991): 38–54; Samuel J. Watson, "'This Thankless . . . Unholy War': Army Officers and Civil–Military Relations in the Second Seminole War," in *The Southern Albatross: Race and Ethnicity in the South*, ed. Philip Dillard and Randall Hall (Macon, Ga.: Mercer University Press, 1999), 9–49; L. M. Hauptman, "General John E. Wool in Cherokee Country, 1836–1837: A Reinterpretation," *Georgia Historical Quarterly* 85 (2001): 1–26.

22. David LaVere, *Contrary Neighbors: Southern Plains and Removed Indians in Indian Territory* (Norman: University of Oklahoma Press, 2000).

23. BL. Add. 49964 fol. 11.

24. Patrick J. Jung, *The Black Hawk War of 1832* (Norman: University of Oklahoma Press, 2007); John W. Hall, *Uncommon Defense: Indian Allies in the Black Hawk War* (Cambridge, Mass.: Harvard University Press, 2009).

25. John D. Milligan, "Slave Rebelliousness and the Florida Maroon," *Prologue* 6 (Spring 1974): 4–18.

26. Kenneth W. Porter, "Negroes and the Seminole War, 1835–1842," *Journal of Southern History* 30 (1964): 427–50.

27. Louis Pelzer, *Marches of the Dragoons in the Mississippi Valley* (Iowa City: State Historical Society of Iowa, 1917).

28. David G. McGrady, *Living with Strangers: The Nineteenth-Century Sioux and the Canadian-American Borderlands* (Lincoln: University of Nebraska Press, 2006).

29. Roger L. Nichols, "The Army and the Indians 1800–1830 – A Reappraisal: The Missouri Valley Example," *Pacific Historical Review* 41 (1972): 167–68.

30. Samuel Watson (ed.), *Warfare in the USA, 1784–1861* (Aldershot: Ashgate, 2005), xxiv.

31. Stratford Canning to George Canning, 6 May 1823, NA. FO. 5/176 fol. 153.

32. John Lynch, "Bolívar and the Caudillos," *Hispanic American Historical Review* 63 (1983): 4–5, and *Caudillos in Spanish America, 1800–1850* (Oxford: Oxford University Press, 1992); Hugh M Hamill (ed.), *Caudillos, Dictators in Spanish America* (Norman: University of Oklahoma Press, 1992).

33. C. I. Archer, "Banditry and Revolution in New Spain, 1790–1821," *Bibliotheca Americana* I (1982): 88.

34. Pakenham to Vaughan, 20 Dec. 1834, AS, Vaughan papers, C85 no. 2.

35. Will Fowler, *Santa Anna of Mexico* (Lincoln: University of Nebraska Press, 2007): 158–60.

36. Andrés Reséndez, *Changing National Identities at the Frontier: Texas and New Mexico, 1800–1850* (Cambridge: Cambridge University Press, 2005).

37. Vaughan to Palmerston, 12 Jun., 20 Dec. 1834, NA. FO. 5/291 fols 71–72, 5/293 fol. 166.

38. Palmerston to Fox, 6 Feb. 1837, NA. FO. 5/313 fol. 1.

39. Carlos M. Salomon, *Pio Pico: The Last Governor of Mexican California* (Norman: University of Oklahoma Press, 2010).

40. Buchanan to Mrs. Roosevelt, 13 May 1844, John B. Moore (ed.), *The Works of James Buchanan, VI* (London: Lippincott, 1960), 2–3.

41. Steven H. Mitton, "The Free World Confronted: The Problem of Slavery and Progress in American Foreign Relations, 1833–1844" (Ph.D. diss., Louisiana State University, 2005), 133–45.

42. Donaly E. Brice, *The Great Comanche Raid* (Austin, Tex.: Eakin Press, 1987).

43. Joseph M. Nance, *After San Jacinto: The Texas-Mexican Frontier, 1836–1841* (Austin: University of Texas Press, 1963).

44. Sam W. Haynes, *Soldiers of Misfortune: The Somervell and Mier Expeditions* (Austin: University of Texas Press, 1991).

45. Fowler, *Santa Anna*, 226.

46. Joseph M. Nance, *Attack and Counterattack: The Texas–Mexican Frontier, 1842* (Austin: University of Texas Press, 1964).

47. Jonathan W. Jordan, *Lone Star Navy: Texas, the Fight for the Gulf of Mexico, and the Shaping of the American West* (Washington D.C.: Potomac Books, 2006).

48. Stratford Canning to Castlereagh, 1 Jan. 1822, NA. FO. 5/166 fols 1–4.

49. Addington to Vaughan, 22 Jun., 29 Jul. 1827, AS, Vaughan papers, C1/4, 6; correspondence between Vaughan and Sir Howard Douglas, Governor of New Brunswick, 1825–30, AS, Vaughan papers, C32–36.

50. Vaughan to Addington, 4 Jul. 1827, AS, Vaughan papers, C7/3.

51. Fox to Palmerston, 21, 23 Feb., 7 Mar. 1839, NA. FO. 5/331 fols 45, 80–84, 104–129.

52. Fox to Palmerston, 17, 23, 31 Mar. 1839, NA. FO. 5/331 fols. 199–205, 209, 237–38.

53. K. J. Brauer, "The United States and British Imperial Expansion, 1815–60," *Diplomatic History* 12 (1988): 19–37; Phillip E. Myers, "Mask of Indifference: Great Britain's North American Policy and the Path to the Treaty of Washington, 1815–1871" (Ph.D. diss., University of Iowa, 1978).

54. Richard Brown, *Three Rebellions: Canada, 1837–1838, South Wales 1839, and Victoria, Australia 1854* (Southampton: Clio Publishing, 2010), 109–172.

55. M. L. Harris, "The Meaning of Patriot: The Canadian Rebellion and American Republicanism, 1837–1839," *Michigan Historical Review* 23 (1997): 33–70; A. Bonthius, "The Patriot War of 1837–1838: Locofocoism with a Gun," *Labour* 53 (2003): 9–44.

56. Palmerston to Fox, 22 Jul. 1837, NA. FO. 5/313 fol. 27, 5/321 fols 8–9; Mary B. Fryer, *Volunteers, Redcoats, Rebels, and Raiders: A Military History of the Rebellions in Upper Canada* (Toronto: Dundurn Press, 1987).

57. J. C. Arnell, "Trooping to the Canadas," *Mariner's Mirror* 53 (1967): 143–60.

58. Palmerston to Fox, 6 Oct. 1838, NA.FO. 5/321 fols 38–39.

59. Stephen M. Lee, *George Canning and Liberal Toryism, 1801–1827* (Woodbridge: Royal Historical Society, 2008).

60. Clay to Vaughan, 18 Jun. 1829, AS, Vaughan papers, C30 no. 2.

61. Richard Carwardine, "Evangelicals, Whigs and the Election of William Henry Harrison," *Journal of American Studies* 17 (1983): 66.

62. Matthew Brown, "How Did Rupert Hand Get out of Jail? Colombia and the Atlantic Empires, 1830–1833," *History* 95 (2010): 34. For Moore's hostility to British influence in 1832, see p. 36.

63. Anthony Howe (ed.), *The Letters of Richard Cobden I* (Oxford: Oxford University Press, 2007), xxxvi; Murney Gerlach, *British Liberalism and the United States: Political and Social Thought in the Late Victorian Age* (London: Palgrave, 2001). See more generally, Kathleen Burk, *Old World, New World: The Story of Britain and America* (London: Little Brown, 2007), 277–307.

64. Clarendon to Crampton, 23 May 1856, Bod. MS. Clar. Dep. C 136, p. 91.

65. R. W. Hay to Vaughan, 28 Dec. 1829, AS, Vaughan papers, C54; David P.

Crook, *American Democracy in British Politics, 1815–1860* (Oxford: Oxford University Press, 1965).

66. James Epstein, "'America' in the Victorian Cultural Imagination," in *Anglo-American Attitudes: From Revolution to Partnership*, ed. Fred M. Leventhal and Roland Quinault (Aldershot: Ashgate, 2000), 107–123; Hugh Dubrulle, "'We Are Threatened with Anarchy and Ruin': Fear of Americanization and the Emergence of the Anglo-Saxon Confederacy in England during the Civil War," *Albion* 33 (2002): 583–613.

67. Hall to Vaughan, 15 Jul. 1827, 15 Feb. 1828, A S, Vaughan papers, C45–46; Duncan A. Campbell, *Unlikely Allies: Britain, America and the Victorian Origins of the Special Relationship* (London: Hambledon Continuum, 2007), 108–109.

68. Abraham S. Eisenstadt (ed.), *Reconsidering Tocqueville's Democracy in America* (New Brunswick, N.J.: Rutgers University Press, 1988); Jon Elster, *Alexis de Tocqueville: The First Social Scientist* (Cambridge: Cambridge University Press, 2009); Campbell, *Unlikely Allies*, 95–98.

69. Joseph M. Schweninger, "'Lingering War Must be Prevented': The Defense of the Northern Frontier, 1812–1871" (Ph.D. diss., Ohio State University, 1998).

70. Albert B. Corey, *The Crisis of 1830–1842 in Canadian–American Relations* (New Haven, Conn.: Yale University Press, 1941). For a more critical approach, see Scott Kaufman and John A. Soares, "'Sagacious beyond Praise?' Winfield Scott and Anglo-American Canadian Border Diplomacy, 1837–1860," *Diplomatic History* 30 (2006) : 57–82.

71. Fox to Aberdeen, 28 Jan. 1842, N A. F O. 5/377 fol. 7.

72. Fox to Palmerston, 12 Jan. 1839, N A. F O. 5/331 fols 7–11.

73. Fox to Palmerston, 12 Jan. 1839, N A. F O. 5/331 fols 6–7.

74. R. Y. Jennings, "The Caroline and McLeod Cases," *American Journal of International Law* 32 (1938): 82–99; L. P. Rouillard, "The Caroline Case: Anticipatory Self-Defense in Contemporary International Law," *Miskolc Journal of International Law* 1 (2004): 104–120.

75. Albert B. Corey, "Public Opinion and the McLeod Case," *Canadian Historical Association: Historical Papers* (1936), 53–64; Kenneth R. Stevens, *Border Diplomacy: The Caroline and McLeod Affairs in Anglo-American-Canadian Relations, 1837–1842* (Tuscaloosa: University of Alabama Press, 1989); Kenneth Bourne, *Britain and the Balance of Power in North America, 1815–1908* (London: Longmans, 1967), 93–96.

76. Thomas R. Hietala, *Manifest Design: Anxious Aggrandizement in Late Jacksonian America* (Ithaca, N.Y.: Cornell University Press, 1985).

77. Stratford Canning to Castlereagh, 28, 30 Jan., 7 Mar. 1821, 8 Feb., 3 Jul. 1822, and to George Canning, 5 May 1823, N A. F O. 5/157 fols 35–43, 51–53, 178, 5/166 fol. 131, 5/168 fol. 314, 5/176 fols 150–51.

78. Barry M. Gough, *Gunboat Frontier: British Maritime Authority and Northwest Coast Indians, 1846–90* (Vancouver: University of British Columbia Press, 1984), 150.

79. Vaughan to Addington, 4 Jul. 1827, A S, Vaughan papers, C7/3.

80. Vaughan to Backhouse, 28 Aug. 1829, A S, Vaughan papers, C15/1.

81. Addington to Vaughan, 14 Apr. 1829, A S, Vaughan papers, C5/7.

82. Bankhead to Vaughan, 13 Mar., 13 Apr. 1832, 17 Feb. 1837, A S, Vaughan papers, C19 nos 2, 4, 6.

83. Joseph Story to Vaughan, 7 Nov. 1837, Charles Sumner to Vaughan, 1 Sept. 1840, A S, Vaughan papers, C101 no. 3, 115 no. 2.

84. For Fox's lack of sympathy with the workings of American democracy, Fox to Aberdeen, 28 Jan. 1842, N A. F O. 5/377 fol. 2.

85. Addington, Diary, DRO. 152M/Box 38/vols 7–9. On Addington as an instance of the opportunities offered by America, see Cornelis A. van Minnen and Sylvia L. Hilton, eds., *Nation on the Move: Mobility in U.S. History*, (Amsterdam: VU University Press, 2002).

86. Stratford Canning to Castlereagh, 21 Jan. 1821, 29 Jun. 1822, Stratford Canning to George Canning, 31 Mar., 6 Jun. 1823, NA. FO. 5/157 fols 21–22, 5/168 fols 296–303, 5/176 fols 35, 189–93.

87. 15 Feb. 1825, R. Therry, (ed.), *The Speeches of the Right Hon. George Canning*, 2nd ed., 6 vols. (London, 1830), V, 325–26.

88. Addington, Diary, DRO. 152M/Box 38/vol. 8.

89. BL. Add. 49963 fol. 5.

90. Diary, vol. 7.

91. Palmerston to Vaughan, 10 Mar. 1835, NA. FO. 5/299 fol. 1; *Correspondence of Andrew Jackson*, VI, 518–19; John M. Belohlavek, *"Let the Eagle Soar!" The Foreign Policy of Andrew Jackson* (Lincoln: University of Nebraska Press, 1985).

92. Vaughan to Palmerston, 20 Apr. 1834, NA. FO. 5/290 fols 244–45.

93. Kenneth Bourn (ed.), *McLeod and Maine, 1837–1842*, Vol. I of Series C, *North America, 1837–1914*, in Part One of *British Documents on Foreign Affairs: Reports and Papers from the Foreign Office Confidential Print* (Bethesda, Md.: University Publications of America, 1986); Ronald V. Remini, *Daniel Webster, The Man and His Time* (New York: W.W. Norton & Co., 1997), 535–69; Francis M. Carroll, *A Good and Wise Measure: The Struggle for the Canadian–American Border, 1783–1842* (Toronto: University of Toronto Press, 2001).

94. Edward Stanley, *Journal of a Tour in America, 1824–25* (London, 1931); Angus Hawkins, *The Forgotten Prime Minister: The 14th Earl of Derby, Vol. 1, Ascent, 1799–1851*, 2 vols. (Oxford: Oxford University Press, 2007), I, 33–43.

95. Ibid., I, 251.

96. Vaughan to George Canning, 31 Oct. 1825, AS, Vaughan papers, H16 no. 8.

97. Barry Gough, *The Falkland Islands/Malvinas: The Contest for Empire in the South Atlantic* (London: Athlone Press, 1992).

98. Michael S. Fitzgerald, "'Nature Unsubdued'": Diplomacy, Expansion and the American Military Buildup of 1815–1816," *Mid-America* 77 (1995): 14.

99. James A. Field, *America and the Mediterranean World, 1776–1882* (Princeton, N.J.: Princeton University Press, 1969); Thomas Bryson, *Tars, Turks and Tankers: The Role of the United States Navy in the Middle East, 1800–1979* (Metuchen, N.J.: Scarecrow Press, 1980).

100. Edward B. Billingsley, *In Defense of Neutral Rights: The United States and the Wars of Independence in Chile and Peru* (Chapel Hill: University of North Carolina Press, 1967).

101. Stratford Canning to Castlereagh, 8 Feb., 6 Mar. 1822, 12, 27 Mar., Stratford Canning to George Canning, 22 Apr. 1823, NA. FO. 5/166 fols 144, 190, 5/176 fols 1, 32–33, 88–90, 100–102.

102. Francis B. C. Bradlee, *The Suppression of Piracy in the West Indies, 1820–1832* (New York: Library Editions, 1970).

103. Michael J. Birkner, "The 'Foxardo Affair' Revisited: Porter, Pirates and the Problem of Civilian Authority in the Early Republic," *American Neptune* 43/3 (1982): 165–78.

104. Andrew D. Lambert, *The Last Sailing Battlefleet, Maintaining Naval Mastery 1815–1850* (London: Conway Maritime Press, 1991), 23–24.

105. Vaughan to Palmerston, 20 Dec. 1834, NA. FO. 5/292 fols 163–64.

106. Charles Wilkes, *Narrative of the United States Exploring Expedition*, 5 vols. (Philadelphia: Lea and Blanchard, 1845); Geoffry S. Smith, "Charles Wilkes: The Naval Officer as Explorer and Diplomat," in *Captains of the Old Steam Navy*, ed.

James Bradford (Annapolis, Md.: Naval Institute Press, 1986), 64–86; Nathanial Philbrick, *Sea of Glory: America's Voyage of Discovery, The U.S. Exploring Expedition, 1838–1842* (New York: Viking, 2003); Nathaniel Philbrick and Thomas Philbrick (eds.), *William Reynolds, The Private Journal of William Reynolds: United States Exploring Expedition, 1838–1842* (New York: Penguin Books, 2004).

107.  Fox to Aberdeen, 27 Jan. 1843, NA. FO. 5/391 fol. 44.

108.  Stratford Canning to Castlereagh, 5 Feb. 1821, NA. FO. 5/157 fol. 78.

109.  George M. Brooke, "The Role of the United States Navy in the Suppression of the African Slave Trade," *American Neptune* 21 (1961), 28–41; Donald L. Canney, *Africa Squadron: The U.S. Navy and the Slave Trade, 1842–1861* (Washington D.C.: Potomac Books, 2006).

110.  Aaron W. Marrs, *Railroads in the Old South: Pursuing Progress in a Slave Society* (Baltimore: Johns Hopkins University Press, 2009).

111.  Michael Tadman, *Speculators and Slaves: Masters, Traders, and Slaves in the Old South* (Madison: University of Wisconsin Press, 1996); Walter Johnson, *Soul by Soul: Life inside the Antebellum Slave Market* (Cambridge, Mass.: Harvard University Press, 1999); Jonathan D. Martin, *Divided Mastery: Slave Hiring in the American South* (Cambridge, Mass.: Harvard University Press, 2004).

112.  John Ashworth, *Slavery, Capitalism, and Politics in the Antebellum Republic. I: Commerce and Compromise, 1820–1850* (Cambridge, Mass.: Harvard University Press, 1996).

113.  Joel Williamson, *New People: Miscegenation and Mulattoes in the United States* (Baton Rouge: State University of Louisiana Press, 1995).

114.  Robert P. Forbes, *The Missouri Compromise and Its Aftermath: Slavery and the Meaning of America* (Chapel Hill: University of North Carolina Press, 2007).

115.  Stratford Canning to Castlereagh, 14 Feb., 6 Mar. 1821, Stratford Canning to George Canning, 22 Apr. 1823, NA. FO. 5/157 fol. 159, 5/166 fol. 196, 5/176 fol. 103.

116.  T. R. Young, "The United States Army and the Institution of Slavery in Louisiana, 1803–1835," *Louisiana Studies* 13 (1974): 209–213; Sally Hadden, *Slave Patrols: Law and Violence in Virginia and the Carolinas* (Cambridge, Mass.: Harvard University Press, 2001).

117.  Robert A. Gross (ed.), "Forum: The Making of a Slave Conspiracy," *William and Mary Quarterly* 58 (2001): 913–76, 59 (2002): 135–202.

118.  Stratford Canning to George Canning, 12 Mar. 1823, George Canning to Henry Addington, 15 Nov. 1823, George Matthew, Consul in Charleston, to Sir Henry Bulwer, British envoy, 27 Dec. 1850, Bulwer to Palmerston, 27 Jan., 10 Feb. 1851, NA. FO. 5/176 fols 13, 5/177 fol. 13, 5/527 fols 23–29, 98, 148–50, 200–203.

119.  Re Senate speeches of January 1830, Herman Belz (ed.), *The Webster–Hayne Debate on the Nature of the Union* (Indianapolis: Liberty Fund, 2000).

120.  Vaughan to Palmerston, 4 Mar., 20 Apr., 4 Jul. 1834, NA. FO. 5/289 fol. 103, 5/290 fols 236–42, 5/292 fol. 56.

121.  Diary, 152M/Box 38/vol. 7.

## 11. FROM THE OREGON QUESTION TO THE GADSDEN PURCHASE, 1844–53

1.  Thomas Crump, *Abraham Lincoln's World: How Riverboats, Railroads and Republicans Transformed America* (London: Continuum, 2009).

2.  Philip S. Bagwell and George E. Mingay, *Britain and America 1850–1939: A Study of Economic Change* (London: Routledge and Kegan Paul, 1970), 11.

3.  Drew McCoy, *The Elusive Republic: Political Economy in Jeffersonian America* (New York: Norton, 1980).

4. Fox to Aberdeen, 27 Jan. 1843, N A. F O. 5/391 fol. 42.

5. Fox to Aberdeen, 28 Jan. 1842, N A. F O. 5/377 fol. 9.

6. Fredrick Merk, *The Oregon Question: Essays in Anglo-American Diplomacy and Politics* (Cambridge: Belknap Press of Harvard University Press, 1967); William D. Jones, *The American Problem in British Diplomacy, 1841–1861* (London: Macmillan, 1974).

7. Fox to Aberdeen, 29 Jan., 4, 17 Feb., 4 Mar. 1843, N A. F O. 5/391 fols 50–53, 81–83, 89, 143–44.

8. Palmerston to Fox, 14 Oct., 2 Nov. 1839, N A. F O. 5/330 fols 124, 129.

9. Kris Fresonke, *West of Emerson: The Design of Manifest Destiny* (Berkeley: University of California Press, 2003).

10. Allan Nevins, *Frémont: Pathmarker of the West* (New York: Ungar, 1955); J. L. Allen, "Division of the Waters: Changing Concepts of the Continental Divide, 1804–44," *Journal of Historical Geography* 4 (1978): 357–70; Richard V. Francaviglia, *Mapping and Imagination in the Great Basin: A Cartographic History* (Reno: University of Nevada Press, 2005).

11. Vernon L. Volpe, "The Origins of the Frémont Expeditions: John J. Abert and the Scientific Exploration of the Trans-Mississippi West," *Historian* 62 (2000): 262.

12. Fox to Aberdeen, 20 Jan. 1843, N A. F O. 5/391 fols 8–10.

13. Fox to Aberdeen, 15 Nov. 1842, N A F O. 5/377 fols 172–76; Aberdeen to Fox, 2 Nov. 1843, Aberdeen to Pakenham, 17 Oct. 1843, B L. Add. 43123 fols 225, 229.

14. Aberdeen to Pakenham, 4 Mar. 1844, B L. Add. 43123 fols 233–34.

15. Pakenham to Aberdeen, 13 Jun. 1844, B L. Add. 43123 fol. 239.

16. Pakenham to Aberdeen, 29 Aug. 1844, B L. Add. 43123 fol. 243.

17. Aberdeen to Pakenham, 3 Jun. 1844, N A. F O. 5/403 fols 57–61.

18. Aberdeen to Pakenham, 1, 18 Nov. 1844, N A. F O. 5/403 fols 111–13, 117.

19. Peel to Aberdeen, 23 Feb. 1845, B L. Add. 43064 fols. 179–81.

20. Aberdeen to Pakenham, 2 Apr. 1845, B L. Add. 43123 fols 247–48.

21. Michael S. Partright, *Military Planning for the Defense of the United Kingdom, 1814–1870* (Westport, Conn.: Praeger, 1989).

22. N A. War Office, 6/86, pp. 300–301.

23. Aberdeen to Pakenham, 18 Apr. 1845, B L. Add. 43123 fols 249–50.

24. Pakenham to Aberdeen, 28 Apr. 1845, B L. Add. 43123 fols 253–54.

25. Frederick Merk (ed.), *Fur Trade and Empire: George Simpson's Journal* (Cambridge: Belknap Press of Harvard University Press, 1931).

26. Pakenham to Aberdeen, 28 Apr., 13 May 1845, B L. Add. 43123 fols 255–56, 259.

27. Polk to James Buchanan, Secretary of State, 7 Aug. 1845, James B. Moore (ed.), *The Works of James Buchanan*, VII (New York: Antiquarian Press, 1960), p. 223.

28. Aberdeen to Pakenham, 3 Oct. 1845, B L. Add. 43123 fol. 261.

29. G. W. Featherstonhaugh to Vaughan, 24 Jan. 1846, A S, Vaughan papers, C42 no. 6.

30. Palmerston to Russell, 2 Feb. 1846, N A. P R O. 30/22/5A fol. 107.

31. Aberdeen to Pakenham, 4 May 1846, B L. Add. 43123 fol. 286.

32. Aberdeen to Pakenham, 18 May 1846, B L. Add. 43123 fols 289–90.

33. Aberdeen to Pakenham, 18 May 1846, B L. Add. 43123 fols 290–91.

34. Pakenham to Aberdeen, 7 Jun. 1846, B L. Add. 43123 fol. 297.

35. Pakenham to Aberdeen, 7 Jun. 1846, B L. Add. 43123 fols 300–302; Buchanan to McLane, 6, 13 Jun. 1846, James B. Moore (ed.), *The Works of James Buchanan*, VII (New York: Antiquarian Press, 1960), 3, 11.

36. Pakenham to Aberdeen, 13 Jun. 1846, BL. Add. 43123 fol. 304.

37. Aberdeen to Pakenham, 30 Jun. 1846, BL. Add. 43123 fol. 308.

38. Peter to Aberdeen, 17 Jan. 1843, BL. Add. 43123 fol. 338; Fox to Palmerston, 20 Apr. 1839, NA. FO. 5/331 fol. 5.

39. Peter to Aberdeen, 20 Apr. 1842, BL. Add. 43123 fols 312–15.

40. Pakenham to Aberdeen, 28 Mar. 1844, BL. Add. 43123 fols 235–37.

41. Aberdeen to Pakenham, 3 Dec. 1845, BL. Add. 43123 fol. 273; Napier to Clarendon, 14 Jun. 1857, NA. FO. 5/672 fol. 77.

42. Fox to Aberdeen, 24 Feb. 1843, NA. FO. 5/391 fols 107–110.

43. Gene A. Smith, *Thomas ap Catesby Jones: Commodore of Manifest Destiny* (Annapolis, Md.: Naval Institute Press, 2000).

44. Fox to Aberdeen, 4 Feb. 1843, NA. FO. 5/391 fol. 77.

45. H. Langley, "Robert F. Stockton: A Naval Officer and Reformer," in *Command under Sail: Makers of the American Naval Tradition, 1775–1850,* ed. James C. Bradford (Annapolis, Md.: Naval Institute Press, 1985), 273–304.

46. Doyle to Vaughan, 29 Nov. 1845, AS, Vaughan papers, C37 no. 2.

47. Peel to Aberdeen, 23 Feb. 1845, BL. Add. 43064 fols 178–79.

48. W. J. Fitzpatrick (ed.), *Correspondence of Daniel O'Connell,* 2 vols. (London: John Murray, 1888), II, 207–210.

49. Gerald S. Graham, *Great Britain and the Indian Ocean: A Study of Maritime Enterprise, 1810–1850* (Oxford: Clarendon Press, 1967), 106–107.

50. Fox to Palmerston, 11 Jun. 1839, NA. FO. 5/331 fols 285–90.

51. Fox to Aberdeen, 12 Dec. 1842, NA. FO. 5/377 fols 199–200.

52. Aberdeen to Pakenham, 18 May 1844, NA. FO. 5/403 fols 53.

53. Signed by President Tyler on 1 March.

54. Justin Smith, *The Annexation of Texas* (New York: The Baker and Taylor Co., 1971).

55. Ephraim D. Adams, *British Interests and Activities in Texas* (Gloucester: P. Smith, 1963), esp. 79–96.

56. Mrs. Bankhead to Vaughan, 29 Oct. 1845, AS, Vaughan papers, C20 no. 3.

57. Waddy Thompson, *Recollections of Mexico* (New York: Wiley and Putnam, 1846), 170.

58. Samuel J. Watson, "Manifest Destiny and Military Professionalism: Junior U.S. Army Officers' Attitude Toward War with Mexico, 1844–1846," *Southwestern Historical Quarterly* 99 (1996): 474–75, 468.

59. Pakenham to Aberdeen, 28 May 1846, BL. Add. 43123 fol. 295.

60. Pakenham to Aberdeen, 23 Jun. 1846, Southampton, University Library, Palmerston papers, BD/US/51.

61. BL. Add. 49968 fol. 8.

62. Sam W. Haynes, "'But What Will England Say?': Great Britain, the United States, and the War with Mexico," in *Dueling Eagles: Reinterpreting the Mexican-American War, 1846–1848,* ed. Richard Francaviglia and Douglas Richmond (Fort Worth, Tex.: Texas Christian University Press, 2000), 19–39.

63. Buchanan to Andrew Donelson, envoy in Texas, 15 Jun. 1845, James B. Moore (ed.), *The Works of James Buchanan* VI (New York: J.B. Lippincott and Co., 1960), 173.

64. H. S. Ferns, *Britain and Argentina in the Nineteenth Century* (Oxford: Clarendon Press, 1960).

65. Miguel E. Soto, "The Monarchist Conspiracy and the Mexican War," in *Essays on the Mexican War,* ed. Wayne Cutler and Douglas Richmond (College Station: Texas A&M University Press, 1986), 66–84.

66. Will Fowler, *Santa Anna of Mexico,* 263–64.

67. For Robles' views of his deficiencies, Napier to Clarendon, 21 Jun. 1857, NA. FO. 5/672 fol. 144.

68. Memorandum on British and American naval power in the Pacific, 3 Mar. 1846, BL. Add. 40473 fol. 82.

69. Peel to Edward, Earl of Ellenborough, First Lord of the Admiralty, 17 Mar. 1846, BL. Add. 43198 fol. 122.

70. K. Jack Bauer, *The Mexican War 1846–1848*, 2nd ed. (Lincoln: University of Nebraska Press, 1992), 166.

71. A. B. Cunningham, "Peel, Aberdeen and the *Entente Cordiale*," *Bulletin of the Institute of Historical Research* 30 (1957): 189–206.; D. McClean, "The Greek Revolution and the Anglo-French Entente, 1843–1844," *English Historical Review* 96 (1981): 117–29.

72. Reeve to Russell, 15 Dec. 1845, George Peabody Gooch (ed.), *The Later Correspondence of Lord John Russell*, 2 vols. (London: Longmans, Green, 1925), I, 91.

73. Roger Bullen, *Palmerston, Guizot and the Collapse of the Entente Cordiale* (London: Athlone, 1974).

74. John F. Beeler, *British Naval Policy in the Gladstone-Disraeli Era, 1866–1880* (Stanford, Calif: Stanford University Press, 1997).

75. Jamie W. Moore, *The Fortifications Board, 1816–1828, and the Definition of National Security* (Charleston, S.C.: Citadel, 1981); John R. Weaver, *A Legacy in Brick and Stone: American Coastal Defense Forts of the Third System, 1816–1867* (McLean, Va.: Redoubt Press, 2001); Paul Branch, *Fort Macon: A History* (Charleston, S.C.: Nautical and Aviation Pub. Co. of America, 1999); Mark A. Smith, *Engineering Security: The Corps of Engineers and Third System Defense Policy, 1815–1861* (Tuscaloosa: University of Alabama Press, 2009). Re 1834, Samuel J. Watson, "Knowledge, Interest and the Limits of Military Professionalism: The Discourse on American Coastal Defense, 1815–1860," *War in History* 5 (1998): 294.

76. K. Jack Bauer, *Surfboats and Horse Marines: U.S. Naval Operations in the Mexican War 1846–48* (Annapolis, Md.: U.S. Naval Institute, 1969).

77. John C. Pinheiro, *Manifest Ambition: James K. Polk and Civil–Military Relations during the Mexican War* (Westport, Conn.: Praeger Security International, 2007).

78. Paul H. Bergeron, *The Presidency of James K. Polk* (Lawrence: University Press of Kansas, 1987).

79. William B. Skelton, "Officers and Politicians: The Origins of Army Politics in the United States before the Civil War," *Armed Forces and Society* 6 (1979), 22–48.

80. Memorandum on British Trade, 31 Dec. 1841, NA. FO. 97/284.

81. Fox to Aberdeen, 4 Feb., 24 Mar. 1843, NA. FO. 5/391 fols 77, 234–35.

82. Angus Hawkins, *The Forgotten Prime Minister: The 14th Earl of Derby*, 2 vols. (Oxford: Oxford University Press, 2007), I, 252.

83. BL. Add. 49968 fols 52–54.

84. BL. Add. 49968 fol. 42; N. Harlow, *California Conquered: War and Peace on the Pacific, 1846–1850* (Berkeley: University of California Press, 1982).

85. BL. Add. 49668 fol. 75.

86. J. G. Dawson, *Doniphan's Epic March: The First Missouri Volunteers in the Mexican War* (Topeka: Historical Society of Kansas, 1999).

87. William B. Skelton, "Professionalization in the U.S. Army Officer Corps during the Age of Jackson," *Armed Forces and Society* 1 (1975), 443–71; and "High Army Leadership in the Era of the War of 1812: The Making and Remaking of the Officer Corps," *William and Mary Quarterly* 3rd ser., 51 (1994): 523–74; Wayne Wei-Siang Hsieh, *West Pointers and the Civil War: The Old Army in War and Peace* (Chapel Hill: University of North Carolina Press, 2009).

88. BL. Add. 49968 fol. 177.

89. David A. Clary, *Eagles and Empire: The United States, Mexico, and the Struggle for a Continent* (New York: Bantam Dell, 2009), 290.

90. Irving W. Levinson, *Wars within War: Mexican Guerrillas, Domestic Elites, and the United States of America, 1846–1848* (Fort Worth, Tex.: Texas Christian University Press, 2005).

91. Doyle to Palmerston, 13 Jan. 1848, NA. FO. 50/219 fols 5–7, 9–10; Brian Linn, *The Echo of Battle: The Army's Way of War* (Cambridge, Mass.: Harvard University Press, 2007), 75.

92. Timothy D. Johnson, *A Gallant Little Army: The Mexico City Campaign* (Lawrence: University Press of Kansas, 2007).

93. Kevin Dougherty, *Civil War Leadership and Mexican War Experience* (Jackson: University Press of Mississippi, 2007).

94. Michael W. Williams, "Secessionist Diplomacy of Yucatán," *Spanish American Historical Review* 9 (1929): 33–43; W. Gabbert, "Of Friends and Foes: The Caste War and ethnicity in Yucatán," *Journal of Latin American Anthropology* 9 (2004), esp. 98–102.

95. Tom Chaffin, *Fatal Glory: Narciso López and the First Clandestine U.S. War Against Cuba* (Charlottesville: University Press of Virginia, 1996).

96. Dr. Bartlett, editor of the *Albion* in New York, to Vaughan, 30 Aug. 1847, AS, Vaughan papers, C21 no. 1.

97. Pedro Santoni, "A Fear of the People: The Civic Militia of Mexico in 1845," *Hispanic American Historical Review* 68 (1988): 269–88, "The Failure of Mobilization: The Civic Militia of Mexico in 1846," *Mexican Studies* 12 (1990): 169–94; and *Mexicans at Arms: Puro Federalists and the Politics of War, 1845–1848* (Fort Worth, Tex.: Texas Christian University Press, 1996); Timothy J. Henderson, *A Glorious Defeat: Mexico and Its War with the United States* (New York: Hill and Wang, 2007).

98. Doyle to Palmerston, 19 Jan. 1848, NA. FO. 50/219 fols 95–97.

99. Doyle to Palmerston, 14 Jan. 1848, NA. FO. 50/219 fols 72–79.

100. Doyle to Palmerston, 1 Feb., Palmerston to Doyle, 12 Mar. 1848, NA. FO. 50/219 fols 101–111.

101. Wallace Ohrt, *Defiant Peacemaker: Nicholas Trist in the Mexican War* (College Station: Texas A&M University Press, 1997).

102. Gary Gerstle, "A State Both Strong and Weak," *American Historical Review* 115 (2010): 780.

103. M. A. Morrison, "The Westward Curse of Empire: Texas Annexation and the American Whig Party," *Journal of the Early Republic* 10 (1990): 221–49; and "Martin Van Buren and the Partisan Politics of Texas Annexation," *Journal of Southern History* 61 (1995): 695–724; J. M. Schroeder, "Annexation or Independence: The Texas Issue in American Politics, 1836–1845," *Southwestern Historical Quarterly* 84 (1985): 137–64.

104. Doyle to Malmesbury, 2 Feb. 1853, NA. FO. 50/258 fol. 266.

105. I. W. Levinson, "A New Paradigm for an Old Conflict: The Mexico-United States War," *Journal of Military History* 73 (2009): 413–15.

106. Doyle to Palmerston, 13 Feb. 1848, NA. FO. 50/219 fols 166–74.

107. Napier to Clarendon, 21 Jun. 1857, NA. FO. 5/672 fol. 143.

108. Thomas G. Otte and Keith Neilson (eds.), *Railways and International Politics: Paths of Empire, 1848–1945* (London: Routledge, 2004).

109. Roger V. Francaviglia, *The Shape of Texas: Maps and Metaphors* (College Station: Texas A&M University Press, 1995).

110. J. G. Dawson, "Jefferson Davis and the Confederacy's 'Offensive-Defensive' Strategy in the U.S. Civil War," *Journal of Military History* 73 (2009): 595.

111. John H. Schroeder, *Mr. Polk's War: American Opposition and Dissent, 1846–1848* (Madison: University of Wisconsin Press, 1973).

112. Sumner to Vaughan, 15 May 1848, AS, Vaughan papers, C116 no. 3; Bradford Perkins and Warren Cohen, *The Cambridge History of American Foreign Relations. I. The Creation of a Republican Empire, 1776–1865* (Cambridge: Cambridge University Press, 1993), 13.

113. Robert W. Johansen, *To the Halls of the Montezumas: The Mexican War in the American Imagination* (New York: Oxford University Press, 1985); Martha A. Sandweiss et al., *Eyewitness to War: Prints and Daguerreotypes of the Mexican War, 1846–1848* (Washington D.C.: Smithsonian Institution Press, 1989); Ronnie C. Tyler, *The Mexican War: A Lithographic Record* (Austin: Texas State Historical Association, 1973); George Wilkins Kendall, *Dispatches from the Mexican War*, ed. Lawrence Delbert Cress (Norman: University of Oklahoma Press, 1999).

114. Buchanan to Mason, 1 Mar. 1848, Buchanan to Charles Eames, 16 Feb. 1849, Moore (ed.), *Buchanan*, VIII, pp. 1, 333.

115. Bulwer to Palmerston, 24 Feb. 1851, NA. FO. 5/527 fol. 248; Robert F. Dalzell, *American Participation in the Great Exhibition of 1851* (Amherst, Mass.: Amherst College Press, 1960); J. E. Findlay, "America at the Great Exhibition," in *Die Weltausstellung von 1851 und ihre Folgen: The Great Exhibition and Its Legacy*, ed. Franz Bosbach (Munich: Saur, 2002), 197–204.

116. Bruce Cumings, *Dominion from Sea to Sea: Pacific Ascendancy and American Power* (New Haven, Conn.: Yale University Press, 2009), quotation on p. 92.

12. A GREAT POWER IN THE MAKING? AMERICA, 1853–61
The epigraph is from Lyons to Earl Russell, Foreign Secretary, 8 Apr. 1862, NA. PRO. 30/22/36 fol. 64.

1. R. S. G. Fletcher, "'Returning Kindness Received?' Missionaries, Empire and the Royal Navy in Okinawa, 1846–57," *English Historical Review* 125 (2010): 599–641.

2. Peter B. Wiley, *Yankees in the Land of the Gods: Commodore Perry and the Opening of Japan* (New York, Viking, 1990); John H. Schroeder, *Matthew Calbraith Perry: Antebellum Sailor and Diplomat* (Annapolis, Md.: Naval Institute Press, 2001); David M. Pletcher, *The Diplomacy of Involvement: American Economic Expansion across the Pacific, 1784–1900* (Columbia: University of Missouri Press, 2001).

3. James P. Delgado, *Gold Rush Port: The Maritime Archaeology of San Francisco's Waterfront* (Berkeley: University of California Press, 2009).

4. Jane Samson, *Imperial Benevolence: Making British Authority in the Pacific Islands* (Honolulu: University of Hawaii Press, 1998), 51.

5. R. W. Van Alystyne, "Great Britain, the United States, and Hawaiian Independence, 1850–1855," *Pacific Historical Review* 4 (1935): 15–24.

6. David F. Long, "A Case of Intervention: Armstrong, Foote, and the Destruction of the Barrier Forts, Canton, China, 1856," in Craig L. Symonds (ed.), *New Aspects of Naval History* (Annapolis, Md.: Naval Institute Press, 1981), 220–37.

7. Donald F. Warner, *The Idea of Continental Union: Agitation for the Annexation of Canada to the United States, 1849–1893* (Lexington: University of Kentucky Press, 1960).

8. Crawford to Bulwer, 8 Jan. 1851, NA. FO. 5/527 fol. 83.

9. Amos A. Ettinger, *The Mission to Spain of Pierre Soulé, 1853–1855: A Study in the Cuban Diplomacy of the United States* (New Haven, Conn.: Yale University Press, 1932); Frederick M. Binder,

*James Buchanan and the American Empire* (Selinsgrove, Pa.: Associated University Presses, 1994).

10. Crampton to Clarendon, 18 Jun. 1855, Bodl. MS. Clar. Dep. C. 43 fol. 317.

11. Basil Rauch, *American Interest in Cuba, 1848–1855* (New York: Columbia University Press, 1948); Robert E. May, *The Southern Dream of a Caribbean Empire, 1854–1861* (Baton Rouge: Louisiana State University Press, 1973).

12. Bulwer to Palmerston, 27 Jan. 1851, NA. FO. 5/527 fols 90–91.

13. Napier to Clarendon, 26 Mar. 1857, NA. FO. 5/670 fol. 260; Joseph A. Stout, *The Liberators: Filibustering Expeditions into Mexico, 1848–1862, and the Last Thrust of Manifest Destiny* (Los Angeles, Westernlore, 1973).

14. Doyle to James, 3rd Earl of Malmesbury, Foreign Secretary, 2 Jan., 2 Feb. 1853, NA. FO. 50/258 fols 147–58, 263.

15. Crampton to Clarendon, 29 Jan., 10 Mar. 1855, NA. FO. 5/619 fols 243, 372–73; *New York Herald*, 4 Mar. 1855.

16. Henry Hervey to Clarendon, 2 Feb. 1857, NA. FO. 5/670 fols 24–73.

17. Clayton R. Barrow (ed.), *America Spreads Her Sails: U.S. Seapower in the 19th Century* (Annapolis, Md.: Naval Institute Press, 1973); John H. Schroeder, *Shaping a Maritime Empire: The Commercial and Diplomatic Role of the American Navy, 1829–1861* (Westport, Conn.: Greenwood, 1985).

18. R. E. May, "Young American Males and Filibustering in the Age of Manifest Destiny: The United States Army as a Cultural Mirror," *Journal of American History* 78 (1991): 866–67.

19. Napier to Clarendon, 13 Apr. 1857, NA. FO. 5/670 fol. 370.

20. James D. Phillips, *Pepper and Pirates; Adventures in the Sumatra Pepper Trade of Salem* (Boston: Houghton Mifflin, 1949); John K. Fairbank, *Trade and Diplomacy on the China Coast: The Opening of the Treaty Ports, 1842–1854* (Cambridge, Mass.: Harvard University Press, 1969).

21. C. A. Bain, "Commodore Matthew Perry, Humphrey Marshall, and the Taiping Rebellion," *Far Eastern Quarterly* 10 (1951): 258–70.

22. Napier to Clarendon, 30 Mar., 13, 15 Apr. 1857, NA. FO. 5/670 fols 288–92, 355, 379.

23. Crampton to Clarendon, 15 Jan. 1855, Bod. MS. Clar. Dept. C 43 fol. 21.

24. J. S. Lumley to Clarendon, 3 Nov. 1856, Bod. MS. Clar. Dep. C 65 fol. 101.

25. F. A. Golder, "Russian-American Relations during the Crimean War," *American Historical Review* 31 (1926): 462–76; Alan Dowty, *The Limits of American Isolation: The United States and the Crimean War* (New York: New York University Press, 1971).

26. Crampton to Clarendon, 15 Jan. 1855, Bod. MS. Clar. Dept. C 43 fol. 12.

27. Clarendon to Crampton, 4 Jan., 30 May, 6, 13 Jun. 1856, Bod. MS. Clar. Dep. C. 135, p. 68, 136, pp. 126, 162–64, 184–86.

28. J. B. Conacher, "British Policy in the Anglo-American Enlistment Crisis of 1855–1856," *Proceedings of the American Philosophical Society* 136 (1992): 533–76 and "Lessons in Twisting the Lion's Tail: Two Sidelights of the Crimean War," *Policy by Other Means: Essays in Honor of C. P. Stacey,* ed. M. Cross and R. Bothwell (Toronto: Clark, Irwin, 1972).

29. Clarendon to Crampton, 16 May 1856, Bod. MS. Clar. Dep. C. 136, p. 48.

30. Matthew Moten, *The Delafield Commission and the American Military Profession* (College Station: Texas A&M University Press, 2000), 86, 209–210.

31. Brian M. Linn, *The Echo of Battle: The Army's Way of War* (Cambridge, Mass.: Harvard University Press, 2007), 25.

32. Mark A. Smith, *Engineering Security: The Corps of Engineers and Third System Defense Policy, 1815–1861* (Tuscaloosa: University of Alabama Press, 2009).

33. Napier to Clarendon, 26 May 1857, NA. FO. 5/671 fols 195–97.

34. F. D. Reeve, "The Government and the Navaho, 1846–1858," *New Mexico Historical Review* 14 (1939): 92–114; Lynn R. Bailey, *The Long Walk: A History of the Navajo Wars, 1846–68* (Los Angeles: Westernlore, 1964); Frank McNitt, *Navajo Wars: Military Campaigns; Slave Raids and Reprisals* (Albuquerque: University of New Mexico Press, 1992).

35. Ray Mattison, "The Harney Expedition against the Sioux: The Journal of Captain John B. S. Todd," *Nebraska History* 43 (1962), 89–130; R. L. Clow, "Mad Bear: William S. Harney and the Sioux Expedition of 1855–56," *Nebraska History* 61 (Summer 1980): 133–51; George R. Adams, *General William S. Harney: Prince of Dragoons* (Lincoln: University of Nebraska Press, 2001).

36. William Y. Chalfant, *Cheyenne and Horse Soldiers: The 1857 Expedition and the Battle of Solomon's Fork* (Norman: University of Oklahoma Press, 1989), and *Without a Quarter: The Wichita Expedition and the Fight at Crooked Creek* (Norman: University of Oklahoma Press, 1991).

37. R. C. Clark, "Military History of Oregon, 1849–1859," *Oregon Historical Quarterly* 36 (1935): 14–59; W. N. Bischoff, "Yakima Campaign of 1856," *Mid-America* 31 (1949): 162–208, and "Yakima Indian War, 1855–1856: A Problem in Research," *Pacific Northwest Quarterly* 41 (1950): 162–69; R. I. Burns, "Pere Joset's Account of the Indian War of 1858," *Pacific Northwest Quarterly* 38 (1947): 285–314; Francis P. Prucha, *Broadax and Bayonet: The Role of the United States Army in the Development of the Northwest, 1815–1860* (Madison: State Historical Society of Wisconsin, 1953); Carl P. Schlicke, *General George Wright, 1803–1865: Guardian of the Pacific Coast* (Norman: University of Oklahoma Press, 1988).

38. W. H. Ellison, "The Federal Indian Policy in California, 1849–1860," *Mississippi Valley Historical Review* 9 (1922): 37–67.

39. John P. Bowes, *Exiles and Pioneers: Eastern Indians in the Trans-Mississippi West* (Cambridge: Cambridge University Press, 2007).

40. Anthony McGinnis, *Counting Coup and Cutting Horses: Intertribal Warfare on the Great Plains, 1738–1889* (Evergreen, Colo.: Cordillera Press, 1990).

41. Richard White, "The Winning of the West: The Expansion of the Western Sioux in the Eighteenth and Nineteenth Centuries," *Journal of American History* 65 (1978): 319–43.

42. Sean P. Adams, *Old Dominion, Industrial Commonwealth: Coal, Politics, and Economy in Antebellum America* (Baltimore: Johns Hopkins University Press, 2004).

43. Brian DeLay, *War of a Thousand Deserts: Indian Raids and the U.S.-Mexican War* (New Haven, Conn.: Yale University Press, 2008).

44. G. D. Harmon, "The United States Indian Policy in Texas, 1846–60," *Mississippi Valley Historical Review* 17 (1930): 377–403; R. Wooster, "Military Strategy in the Southwest, 1848–1860," *Military History of Texas and the Southwest* 15, no. 2 (1979): 5–15.

45. Jerry Thompson (ed.), *Texas and New Mexico on the Eve of the Civil War: The Mansfield and Johnston Inspections, 1859–1861* (Albuquerque: University of New Mexico Press, 2001).

46. Francis P. Prucha, "Fort Ripley: The Post and the Military Reservation," *Minnesota History* 28 (1947): 205–224.

47. Robert M. Utley, *Frontiersmen in Blue: The United States Army and the Indian, 1848–1865* (New York: Macmillan, 1967).

48. Francis P. Prucha, "The Settler and the Army in Frontier Minnesota," *Minnesota History* 29 (1948): 233.

49. See the maps in Prucha, "Distribution of Regular Army Troops before

the Civil War," *Military Affairs* 16 (1952): 172–73.

50. Napier to Clarendon, 26 May 1857, N A . F O . 5/671 fol. 196.

51. Samuel Watson, "Knowledge, Interest and . . . American Coastal Defense," *War in History,* 292–307.

52. Guillaume-Tell Poussin, French envoy to the United States, to Alexis de Tocqueville, French Foreign Minister, 17 Oct. 1849, Aurelian Craiutu and Jeremy Jennings, eds., *Tocqueville on America after 1840: Letters and Other Writings* (Cambridge: Cambridge University Press, 2009), 445.

53. Andrew D. Lambert, *Trincomalee: The Last of Nelson's Frigates* (London: Chatham Publishing, 2002), 54–59.

54. R. D. Fulton, "The London *Times* and the Anglo-American Boarding Dispute of 1858," *Nineteenth-Century Contexts* 17 (1993): 133–34. On the *Times,* see Martin Crawford, *The Anglo-American Crisis of the Mid-Nineteenth Century: The 'Times' and America, 1850–1862* (Athens: University of Georgia Press, 1987).

55. Bulwer to Palmerston, 13 Jan., Webster to Bulwer, 10 Jan. 1851, N A . F O . 5/527 fols 15, 19.

56. Mario Rodriguez, *A Palmerstonian Diplomat in Central America: Frederick Chatfield Esq.* (Tucson: University of Arizona Press, 1964).

57. Bulwer to Palmerston, 28 Feb., 10 Mar. 1851, N A . F O . 5/527 fols 109–114, 528 fol. 47.

58. Robert E. May, "The United States as Rogue State: Gunboat Persuasion, Citizen Marauders, and the Limits of Antebellum American Imperialism," in *America, War and Power: Defining the State, 1775–2005,* ed. Lawrence Sondhaus and A. James Fuller (London: Routledge, 2005), 29–31. For the danger of an American filibuster attack and the need to keep a naval force near Greytown, Bulwer to Palmerston, 10 Mar. 1851, N A . F O . 5/528 fols 79–80.

59. Napier to Clarendon, 23 Mar. 1857, N A . F O . 5/670 fol. 252.

60. Crampton to Clarendon, 15 Jan. 1855, N A . F O . 5/619 fols 76–77.

61. Crampton to Clarendon, 12 Mar. 1855, N A . F O . 5/620 fol. 53.

62. Crampton to Clarendon, 25 Feb. 1855, 14, 28 Jan., 18 Feb. 1856, 22 Jun. 1857, N A . F O . 5/619 fols 306–313, 5/640 fols 22, 136, 5/641 fol. 15, 5/672 fol. 155.

63. Bulwer to Palmerston, 10 Mar. 1851, N A . F O . 5/528 fols. 45–47, 79.

64. Bulwer to Palmerston, 19 Jun. 1851, N A . F O . 5/529 fols 24–26.

65. Hervey to Hammond, 16, 23 Feb., Napier to Clarendon, 12, 16, 17, 23 Mar. 1857, N A . F O . 5/670 fols 93–94, 114, 135–40, 163–69, 188, 249.

66. Napier to Clarendon, 1, 3 May 1857, N A . F O . 5/671 fols 5–6, 29–30.

67. Napier to Clarendon, 7 Jun. 1857, N A . F O . 5/672 fol. 13.

68. Napier to Clarendon, 3, 6 May 1857, N A . F O . 5/671 fols 32–33, 41, 43.

69. Napier to Clarendon, 6 May, 18 Jun. 1857, N A . F O . 5/671 fol. 41–43, 5/672 fols 118–19.

70. Ronald Hyam and Doanld Low, *Britain's Imperial Century, 1815–1914,* 2nd ed. (London: Macmillan, 1993), 65.

71. Lyons to Russell, 13 Sept. 1859, N A . P R O . 30/22/34 fol. 24.

72. Palmerston to Russell, 18 Feb. 1861, N A . P R O . 30/22/21 fol. 432.

73. James O. McCabe, *The San Juan Water Boundary Question* (Toronto: University of Toronto Press, 1964); Michael Vouri, *The Pig War: Standoff at Griffin Bay* (Friday Harbor, Wash.: Griffin Bay Bookstore, 1999); Scott Kaufman, *The Pig War: The United States, Britain, and the Balance of Power in the Pacific Northwest, 1846–72* (Lanham, Md.: Lexington Books, 2004).

74. Crampton to Clarendon, 28 Jan., 12 Feb. 1856, N A . F O . 5/640 fols 111, 115, 217–20; Clarendon to Crampton, 23 May 1856, Bod. MS. Clar. Dep. C. 136, p. 91.

75. Lyons to Russell, 19 Sept., 28 Nov. 1859, NA. PRO. 30/22/34 fols 25, 58.

76. Geoffrey Hicks, "An Overlooked *Entente:* Lord Malmesbury, Anglo-French Relations and the Conservatives' Recognition of the Second Empire, 1852," *History* 92 (2007): 187–206; and *Peace, War and Party Politics: the Conservatives and Europe, 1846–1859* (Manchester: Manchester University Press, 2007); J. P. Parry, "The Impact of Napoleon III on British Politics, 1851–1880," *Transactions of the Royal Historical Society* 6th ser. 11 (2001), 157. For a more positive view, see D. Brown, "Palmerston and Anglo-French Relations, 1846–1865," *Diplomacy and Statecraft* 17 (2006): 675–92.

77. Lumley to Clarendon, 11 Nov. 1856, Bod. MS. Clar. Dep. C. 65, f. 118; Bulwer to Webster, 3 Jun. 1851, NA. FO. 5/529 fols 7–9.

78. Napier to Clarendon, 26 May 1857, NA. FO. 5/671 fol. 228.

79. Peter Gordon (ed.), *The Political Diaries of the Fourth Earl of Carnarvon, 1857–1890* (London: Cambridge University Press, 2009), 104.

80. Doyle to Malmesbury, 2 Jan. 1853, NA. FO. 50/258 fols 51–55.

81. Jay Sexton, *Debtor Diplomacy: Finance and American Foreign Relations in the Civil War Era, 1837–1873* (New York: Clarendon, 2005).

82. Richard E. Bennett, Susan Easton Black, and Donald Q. Cannon, *The Nauvoo Legion in Illinois: A History of the Mormon Militia, 1841–1846* (Norman: University of Oklahoma Press, 2010).

83. Norman Furniss, *The Mormon Conflict, 1850–1859* (New Haven, Conn.: Yale University Press, 1960). For a map of Deseret and Utah, see Donald W. Meinig, *The Shaping of America: A Geographical Perspective on 500 Years of History. III. Transcontinental America* (New Haven, Conn.: Yale University Press, 1998), 97.

84. Jonathan Beecher, *Victor Considerant and the Rise and Fall of French Romantic Socialism* (Berkeley: University of California Press, 2001).

85. Crampton to Clarendon, 18 Feb. 1856, NA. FO. 5/641 fol. 28; Tony R. Mullis, *Peacekeeping on the Plains: Army Operations in Bleeding Kansas* (Columbia: University of Missouri Press, 2004).

86. Robert E. May, *John A. Quitman: Old South Crusader* (Baton Rouge: Louisiana State University Press, 1985).

87. Nicaraguan envoy in America to Crampton, 22 Dec. 1854, NA. FO. 5/619 fols 152–58.

88. D. Ball, "Filibusters and Regular Troops in San Francisco, 1851–1855," *Military History of the West* 28 (1998): 168–70.

89. Judith K. Schafer, *Slavery, the Civil Law, and the Supreme Court of Louisiana* (Baton Rouge: Louisiana State University Press, 1995).

90. Charles H. Brown, *Agents of Manifest Destiny: The Lives and Times of the Filibusters* (Chapel Hill: University of North Carolina Press, 1980), 194–218.

91. William Marcy, Secretary of State, to Wheeler, American envoy in Nicaragua, 8 Nov. 1855, NA. FO. 5/640 fol. 169.

92. Clarendon to Crampton, 30 May, 6 Jun. 1856, Bod. MS. Clar. Dep. C. 136, pp. 127, 164.

93. Clarendon to Crampton, 16 May 1856, Bod. MS. Clar. Dep. C. 136, p. 47.

94. Clarendon to Crampton, 4 Jan. 1856, Bod. MS. Clar. Dep. C. 135, p. 38, cf. 16, 23 May, C. 136, pp. 46, 89.

95. Clarendon to Crampton, 23 May 1856, Bod. MS. Clar. Dep. C. 136.

96. Hervey to Clarendon, 16 Feb. 1857, NA. FO. 5/670.

97. Lyons to Russell, 17 Oct. 1859, NA. PRO. 30/22/34 fol. 36.

98. Robert E. May, *Manifest Destiny's Underworld: Filibustering in Antebellum America* (Chapel Hill: University of North Carolina Press, 2002); William O. Scroggs,

*Filibusters and Financiers: The Story of William Walker and His Associates* (New York: Macmillan, 1960).

99. Bulwer to Palmerston, 27 Jan. 1851, NA. FO. 5/527 fols 66–68.

100. Crampton to Palmerston, 28 Sept. 1851, NA. FO. 5/530 fol. 82.

101. Crampton to George, 4th Earl of Clarendon, Foreign Secretary, 18 Feb., 15 Jan. 1855, NA. FO. 5/619 fol. 302, Bod. MS. Clar. Dept. C 43 fol. 14.

102. Bulwer to Palmerston, 24 Feb. 1851, NA. FO. 5/527 fol. 219.

103. Napier to Clarendon, 7 Jun. 1857, NA. FO. 5/672 fols 20–21.

104. Russell to Palmerston, 14 Sept. 1859, NA. PRO. 30/22/30 fol. 24.

105. Clarendon to Crampton, 25 Jan. 1856, Bod. MS. Clar. Dep. C. 135, 145–46; Robert Naylor, *Penny ante Imperialism: The Mosquito Shore and the Bay of Honduras, 1600–1914: A Case Study in British Informal Empire* (Rutherford, N.J.: Fairleigh Dickinson University Press, 1989).

106. Clarendon to Crampton, 18 Jan. 1856, Bod. MS. Clar. Dep. C. 135, p. 103.

107. Napier to Clarendon, 12 Mar. 1857, NA. FO. 5/670 fol. 141. cf. 1 May 1857, 5/670 fol. 1.

108. Napier to Clarendon, 7 Jun. 1857, NA. FO. 5/672 fol. 23.

109. Note by Clarendon fol. 206 on Napier to Clarendon, 26 May 1857, NA. FO. 5/671 fols. 181–204.

110. Lyons to Russell, 11, 19 Jul., 16, 22 Aug. 1859, NA. PRO. 30/22/34 fols 1–8, 14–15, 20.

111. Robert E. McGlone, *John Brown's War against Slavery* (New York: Cambridge University Press, 2009); Lyons to Russell, 25 Oct., 22 Nov. 1859, NA. PRO. 30/22/34 fols 40, 54.

**13. AMERICA DIVIDED, 1861–63**

1. Bulwer to Palmerston, 24 Feb. 1851, Lyons to Russell, 12 Dec. 1859, NA. FO. 5/527 fol. 237, PRO. 30/22/34 fol. 69.

2. Lyons to Russell, 22 May 1860, NA. PRO. 30/22/34 fol. 150.

3. Bruce Laurie, *Beyond Garrison: Antislavery and Social Reform* (Cambridge: Cambridge University Press, 2005).

4. Lyons to Russell, 30 Apr. 1860, NA. PRO. 30/22/34 fol. 136.

5. Peter Knupfer, "Aging Statesmen and the Statesmanship of an Earlier Age: The Generational Roots of the Constitutional Union Party," in *Union and Emancipation: Essays on Politics and Race in the Civil War Era*, ed. David W. Blight and Brooks D. Simpson (Kent, Ohio: Kent State University Press, 1997), 57–78.

6. E. S. Rafuse, "Former Whigs in Conflict: Winfield Scott, Abraham Lincoln, and the Secession Crisis Revisited," *Lincoln Herald* 103 (2001): 18.

7. Brian H. Reid, *The Origins of the American Civil War* (London: Longman, 1966); Russell McClintock, *Lincoln and the Decision for War: The Northern Response to Secession* (Chapel Hill: University of North Carolina Press, 2008).

8. Donald E. Reynolds, *Texas Terror: The Slave Insurrection Panic of 1860 and the Secession of the Lower South* (Baton Rouge: Louisiana State University Press, 2007).

9. Richard N. Current, *Lincoln's Loyalists: Union Soldiers from the Confederacy* (Boston: Northeastern University Press, 1992); Christoher J. Einolf, *George Thomas: Virginian for the Union* (Norman: University of Oklahoma Press, 2007).

10. William W. Freehling, *The Road to Disunion II: Secessionists Triumphant* (Oxford: Oxford University Press, 2007).

11. D. G. Surdam, "The Union Navy's Blockade Reconsidered," and "The Confederate Naval Buildup: Could More Have Been Accomplished?" *Naval War College Review* 51 (1998): 104; 54 (2001): 121.

12. Robert Bunch, Consul in Charleston, to Lyons, 9 Jan. 1863, NA. FO. 5/875 fol. 184.

13. Lyons to Milne, 12 May 1861, NMM. MLN/116/1a; Regis A. Courtemache, *No Need of Glory: The British Navy in American Waters, 1860–1864* (Annapolis, Md.: Naval Institute Press, 1977).

14. Palmerston to Russell, 18 Feb. 1861, NA. PRO. 30/22/21 fol. 432.

15. Russell to Palmerston, 29 Dec. 1860, Russell to Duke of Somerset, First Lord of the Admiralty, 4 May 1861, NA. PRO. 30/22/30 fols 62, 119.

16. Russell to Earl Cowley, envoy in Paris, 20 Jul. 1861, NA. FO. 27/1378.

17. Lyons to Milne, 27 May 1861, NMM. MLN/116/1a.

18. For example, Lyons to Russell, 25 Apr. 1864, NA. FO. 5/948 fol. 119.

19. Lyons to Milne, 10 Jun. 1861, NMM. MLN/116/1a.

20. Lyons to Milne, 22 Jul. 1861, NMM. MLN/116/1a.

21. Russell to Lord Cowley, 9 Sept. 1861, Gooch (ed.), *Russell*, II, 320.

22. Lyons to Russell, 13 Apr. 1863, NA. FO. 5/881 fol. 167.

23. Charles M. Hubbard, *The Burden of Southern Diplomacy* (Knoxville: University of Tennessee Press, 1998).

24. Russell to Napier, envoy at St Petersburg, 11 Dec. 1861, NA. PRO. 30/22/1/4 fol. 65.

25. Russell to Cobden, 2 Apr. 1861, NA. PRO. 30/22/32 fols 118–20.

26. Somerset to Milne, 1, 15 Dec. 1861, Milne to Somerset, 24 Jan. 1862, NMM. MLN/116/1c.

27. Russell to Napier, 27 Dec., Palmerston to Russell, 9 Jul., 25 Aug. 1861, NA. PRO. 30/22/48 fol. 69, /21 fols 503–504, 538–39.

28. K. Bourne, "British Preparations for War with the North, 1861–62," *English Historical Review* 76 (1961): 600–632.

29. Palmerston to Russell, 29 Nov., 6 Dec. 1861, NA. PRO. 30/22/21 fols 609, 622.

30. Russell to Lord Clarendon, 6 Dec., Russell to Cowley, 16 Dec. 1861, Gooch (ed.), *Russell*, II, 321–22; Lyons to Milne, 28 Dec. 1861, NMM. MLN/116/1a. For a view of war as unlikely, see Donald Stoker, *The Grand Design: Strategy and the U.S. Civil War* (Oxford: Oxford University Press, 2010), 31.

31. Lyons to Russell, 23 Dec. 1861, NA. PRO. 30/22/35 fols 360–61; Russell to Clarendon, 14 Jan. 1862, Gooch (ed.), *Russell*, II, 324.

32. Lyons to Russell, 30 Jan. 1862, NA. FO. 5/824 fol. 62.

33. Russell to Cowley, 9 Dec. 1861, Gooch (ed.), *Russell*, II, 322.

34. Palmerston to Russell, Victoria to Palmerston, both 1 Dec. 1861, NA. PRO. 30/22/21 fols 612–14.

35. F. Prochaska, *The Eagle and the Crown: Americans and the British Monarchy* (New Haven, Conn.: Yale University Press, 2008), 62–86; Elisa Tamarkin, *Anglophilia: Deference, Devotion, and Antebellum America* (Chicago: University of Chicago Press, 2008).

36. Andrew D. Lambert, "Winning without Fighting: British Grand Strategy and Its Application to the United States, 1815–65," in *Strategic Logic and Political Rationality*, ed. Michael I. Handel, Bradford A. Lee and Karl-Friedrich Walling (London: Frank Cass, 2003), 178–87; Norman B. Ferris, *The Trent Affair: A Diplomatic Crisis* (Knoxville: University of Tennessee Press, 1977).

37. David Brown, *Palmerston and the Politics of Foreign Policy, 1846–55* (Manchester: Manchester University Press, 2002).

38. Angus Hawkins, *The Forgotten Prime Minister: The 14th Earl of Derby*, 2 vols. (Oxford: Oxford University Press, 2007), II, 263–64, 279.

39. Lyons to Milne, 19, 28 Dec. 1861, NMM. MLN/116/1a, Lyons to Russell, 3, 31 Jan. 1862, NA. PRO. 30/22/36 fols 2, 24.

40. Lyons to Milne, 23 Dec. 1861, NMM. MLN/116/1a.

41. Lyons to Milne, 21, 30 Jan. 1862, NMM. MLN/116/1a. For a discussion of the crisis from an instructive perspective, see David Paull Nickles, *Under the Wire: How the Telegraph Changed Diplomacy* (Cambridge: Cambridge University Press, 2003).

42. See also, Lyons to Russell, 11, 17, 21 Feb. 1862, NA. FO. 5/825 fols 33–36, 124–25, 244–46.

43. Lyons to Milne, 27 Feb. 1862, NMM. MLN/116/1a.

44. Palmerston to Russell, 25 Apr. 1862, Gooch (ed.), *Russell*, II, 325.

45. Donald S. Frazier, *Blood and Treasure: Confederate Empire in the Southwest* (College Station: Texas A&M University Press, 1995).

46. Lyons to Milne, 12 May 1862, NMM. MLN/116/1a.

47. Lyons to Russell, 16 May 1862, NA. PRO. 30/22/36 fol. 93; Lyons to Milne, 9 Jun. 1862, NMM. MLN/116/1a.

48. Gary Gallagher, "An Old Fashioned Soldier in a Modern War? Robert E. Lee as Confederate General," *Civil War History* 45 (1999), 321; *The Confederate War: How Popular Will, Nationalism, and Military Strategy Could Not Stave off Defeat* (Cambridge, Mass.: Harvard University Press, 1997), 58–59, 115, and *Lee and his Army in Confederate History* (Chapel Hill: University of North Carolina Press, 2001); Joseph L. Harsh, *Taken at the Flood: Robert E. Lee and Confederate Strategy in the Maryland Campaign of 1862* (Kent, Ohio: Kent State University Press, 1999).

49. Russell to Sir George Grey, 28 Oct. 1862, Gooch (ed.), *Russell*, II, 332.

50. William Stuart, Chargé des Affaires, in Lyons's absence, to Russell, 17, 24 Oct. 1862, NA. FO. 5/838 fols 23–24, 84–85.

51. Stuart to Russell, 17, 27 Oct. 1862, NA. FO. 5/838 fols 37, 152.

52. Andrew Roberts, *Salisbury: Victorian Titan* (London: Weidenfeld & Nicolson, 1991), 47–50.

53. Lyons to Russell, 17 Nov. 1862, NA. FO. 5/838 fol. 308.

54. Derek Beales, *England and Italy, 1859–60* (London: T. Nelson, 1961).

55. B. H. Reid, "Power, Sovereignty and the Great Republic: Anglo-American Diplomatic Relations in the Civil War," *Diplomacy and Statecraft* 14 (2003): 64–65.

56. Palmerston to Russell, 2 Oct. 1862, Gooch (ed.), *Russell*, II, 326.

57. Marion V. Armstrong, *Unfurl Those Colors! McClellan, Sumner, and The Second Army Corps in the Antietam Campaign* (Tuscaloosa: University of Alabama Press, 2008).

58. James M. McPherson, *Crossroads of Freedom: Antietam* (Oxford: Oxford University Press, 2002).

59. David G. Surdam, *Northern Naval Superiority and the Economics of the American Civil War* (Columbia: University of South Carolina Press, 2001).

60. Robert B. Ekelund and Mark Thornton, *Tariffs, Blockades, and Inflation: The Economics of the Civil War* (Wilmington, Del.: SR Books, 2004).

61. Thomas Schoonover, "Napoleon is coming! Maximilian is coming? The International History of the Civil War in the Caribbean Basin," in *The Union, the Confederacy, and the Atlantic Rim,* ed. Robert E. May (West Lafayette, Ind.: Purdue University Press, 1995), 122.

62. Somerset to Milne, 5 Oct. 1861, NMM. MLN/116/1C.

63. Michael P. Coesteloe, *Bonds and Bondholders: British Investors and Mexico's Foreign Debt, 1824–1888* (Westport, Conn.: Praeger, 2003).

64. Somerset to Milne, 16 Nov. 1861 (quotation), 1 Jan. 1862, NMM. MLN/116/1C.

65. Palmerston to Russell, 9 Nov. 1861, NA. PRO. 30/22/21 fol. 595.

66. Somerset to Milne, 25 Jan. 1862, NMM. MLN/116/1C.

67. Milne to Somerset, 7 (quote), 19 Feb. 1862, NMM. MLN/116/1C.

68. Somerset to Milne, 15 Mar. 1862, NMM. MLN/116/1C.

69. Russell to the Queen, 27 Sept. 1861, Gooch (ed.), Russell, II, 321.

70. Lyons to Russell, 3, 28 Feb. 1862, NA. FO. 5/824 fols 116, 343; Wyke to Lyons, 4 May 1862, NA. PRO. 30/22/36 fol. 111.

71. Lyons to Russell, 28 Feb. 1862, NA. FO. 5/825 fol. 345.

72. Russell to Crampton, 23 Jan., 20 Mar. 1862, NA. PRO. 30/22/115 fols 35, 37.

73. Palmerston to Russell, 1 Jan. 1860, NA. PRO. 30/22/21 fol. 1.

74. Russell to Palmerston, 10, 14, 19 Sept. 1859, Russell to Gladstone, 16 Jan. 1861, NA. PRO. 30/22/30 fols 17, 24, 27, /31 fol. 34.

75. D. Brown, "Palmerston and Anglo-French Relations, 1846–1865," Diplomacy and Statecraft 17 (2006): 688.

76. Palmerston to Russell, 31 Jan. 1861, NA. PRO. 30/22/21 fols 416–17.

77. Palmerston to Russell, 10 Mar. 1861, NA. PRO. 30/22/21 fol. 449.

78. Palmerston to Russell, 3, 10 Jun. 1861, NA. PRO. 30/22/21 fols 490–91.

79. Palmerston to Russell, 11 Aug. 1861, NA. PRO. 30/22/21 fol. 527.

80. Lyons to Russell, 8 Dec. 1862, NA. FO. 5/839 fol. 296.

81. Palmerston to Russell, 2 Oct. 1862, Gooch (ed.), Russell, II, 326–27.

82. Palmerston to Russell, 22 Oct. 1862, Gooch (ed.), Russell, II, 328; C. F. Adams, "A Crisis in Downing Street," Proceedings of the Massachusetts Historical Society 47: 373–424; F. J. Merli and T. A. Wilson, "The British Cabinet and the Confederacy: Autumn 1862," Maryland Historical Magazine 65 (1970): 239–62; Phillip E. Myers, Caution and Cooperation: The American Civil War in British–American Relations (Kent, Ohio: Kent State University Press, 2008); Duncan A. Campbell, "Palmerston and the American Civil War," in Palmerston Studies, ed. Miles Taylor and David Brown, 2 vols. (Southampton: Hartley Institute, 2007), II: 144–67.

83. Russell to G.C. Lewis, 26 Oct. 1862, Gooch (ed.), Russell, II, 328.

84. Lyons to Russell, 14 Nov. 1862, NA. PRO. 30/22/36 fol. 292.

85. Sir George Grey to Russell, 27 Oct. 1862, Gooch (ed.), Russell, II, 331.

86. Seward to William Dayton, American envoy in Paris, 30 Nov. 1863, NA. FO. 5/877 fol. 152.

87. R. Quinault, "Gladstone and Slavery," Historical Journal 52 (2009): 376; H. Colin Matthew (ed.), The Gladstone Diaries VI (Oxford: Clarendon Press, 1978), 156, 160; draft pages, BL. Add. 44752 fol. 51.

88. Somerset to Milne, 15 Nov. 1862, NMM. MLN/116/1C.

89. Palmerston to Russell, 12 Oct. 1862, NA. PRO. 30/22/22 fol. 111.

90. Duke of Argyll to Russell, 11, 15 Oct., Lord Granville to Russell, 29 Sept., George Lewis to Russell, 25 Oct., Duke of Newcastle to Russell, 14 Oct. 1862, NA. PRO. 30/22/25 fols 55–60, 125–28, 197–204, 317–18, 362.

91. Lyons to Russell, 26 Nov.1862, NA. PRO. 30/22/36 fol. 308.

92. Lyons to Russell, 11 Dec. 1863, NA. FO. 5/898 fol. 197.

93. NA. FO. 5/877 fol. 150.

94. Ethan S. Rafuse, Robert E. Lee and the Fall of the Confederacy, 1863–1865 (Lanham, Md.: Rowman & Littlefield Publishers, 2008).

95. K. Hackemer, "The Other Union Ironclad: The USS Galena and the Critical Summer of 1862," Civil War History 40 (1994): 226.

96. Mark R. Wilson, The Business of Civil War: Military Mobilization and the State, 1861–1865 (Baltimore: Johns Hopkins University Press, 2006).

97. William H. Roberts, Civil War Ironclads: The U.S. Navy and Industrial

*Mobilization* (Baltimore: Johns Hopkins University Press, 2002).

98. Brian H. Reid, *America's Civil War: The Operational Battlefield, 1861–1863* (Amherst, Mass.: Prometheus Books, 2008).

99. Lyons to Russell, 9 Jan. 1863, NA. FO. 5/874 fol. 81.

100. Stuart to Russell, 10 Nov. 1862, NA. FO. 5/838 fols 272–73.

101. Lyons to Russell, 17 Nov. 1862, NA. FO. 5/838 fols 293–306, cf. 28 Nov., 5/839 fol. 56, 11 Nov., PRO. 30/22/36 fol. 284.

102. Lyons to Russell, 2 Dec. 1862, NA. FO. 5/839 fols 159–60.

103. Lyons to Russell, 12 Dec. 1862, NA. FO. 5/839 fol. 351.

104. Lyons to Russell, 28 Nov. 1862, NA. FO. 5/839 fols 72–73.

105. Gladstone diary, 27 Dec. 1862, Matthew (ed.), *Gladstone*, VI, 169.

106. Grey to Milne, 31 Oct. 1862, NMM. MLN/116/1d.

107. Russell to Scarlett, envoy in Greece, 2 Sept., 12 Nov. 1863, NA. PRO. 30/22/108 fols 63, 69.

**14. WINNING THE WAR, 1863–65**

1. Lyons to Milne, 5 Jan. 1863, NMM. MLN/116/1a.

2. Lyons to Milne, 24 Nov. 1862, NMM. MLN/116/1a.

3. Lyons to Russell, 27 Nov. 1862, NA. FO. 5/838 fols 376–77.

4. Milne to Somerset, 18 Apr. 1863, NMM. MLN/116/1c; R.J. Schneller, „A Littoral Frustration: The Union Navy and the Siege of Charleston, 1863–1865," *Naval War College Review* (1996): 38–60.

5. Lyons to Milne, 5 Dec. 1862, 14 Jan. 1863, NMM. MLN. 116/1a.

6. Lyons to Russell, 9, 13 Jan. 1863, NA. FO. 5/874 fols 82, 133.

7. K. J. Weddle, "The Blockade Board of 1861 and Union Naval Strategy," *Civil War History* 48 (2002): 142.

8. John Frederick Charles Fuller, *The Conduct of War, 1789–1961* (London: Eyre & Spottiswood, 1961), 102; John Keegan, *The Military Geography of the American Civil War* (Gettysburg, Pa.: The Civil War Institute, Gettysburg College, 1997); *Fields of Battle: The Wars for North America* (New York: Knopf, 1996); and *The American Civil War: A Military History* (New York: Alfred A. Knopf, 2009).

9. Lyons to Russell, 24 Feb. 1863, NA. FO. 5/878 fols 73–75.

10. Steven E. Woodworth (ed.), *No Band of Brothers: Problems of the Rebel High Command* (Columbia: University of Missouri Press, 1999); Larry Daniel, *Days of Glory: The Army of the Cumberland, 1861, 1865* (Baton Rouge: Louisiana State University Press, 2004).

11. Lyons to Milne, 14 Jan., 1, 15 Feb. 1863, NMM. MLN/116/1a; Lyons to Russell, 13, 27 Jan., 2 Feb., 9 Jan. 1863, NA. FO. 5/874 fols 144, 149, 5/875 fols 132–36, 5/876 fol. 63, PRO. 30/22/37 fol. 7.

12. *Daily Globe*, 9 Feb. 1863; Lyons to Russell, 2, 6, 16 Feb. 1863, NA. FO. 5/876 fols 52–53, 139–40, 5/877 fols. 145–46.

13. Lyons to Russell, 6 Mar. 1863, NA. FO. 5/879

14. Hawkins, *Derby*, II, 279.

15. Lyons to Milne, 5 Mar. 1863, NMM. MLN. 116/1a.

16. Lyons to Russell, 24 Feb. 1863, NA. FO. 5/878 fols 109–110.

17. Lyons to Milne, 5, 27 Mar. 1863, NMM. MLN/116/1a; Russell to Lewis, 24 Mar. 1863, NA. PRO. 30/22/31.

18. Frank J. Merli, *The Alabama, British Neutrality and the American Civil War* (Bloomington: Indiana University Press, 2004).

19. Lyons to Milne, 27 Mar. 1863, NMM. MLN/116/1a.

20. Lyons to Russell, 14 Apr. 1863, NA. FO. 5/882 fol. 61; Lyons to Milne, 8, 17 Apr., 11 May 1863, NMM. MLN/116/1a.

21. Lyons to Milne, 11 May 1863, NMM. MLN/116/1a.

22. Lyons to Russell, 11 Dec. 1863, NA. FO. 5/898 fols 195–96.

23. Lyons to Russell, 13 Apr. 1863, NA. FO. 5/881 fols 148–64.

24. Goodenough to Lyons, 9 Apr. 1864, NA. FO. 5/948 fol. 132.

25. Lyons to Russell, 13 Apr. 1863, 25 Apr. 1864, NA. FO. 5/881 fols 165–66, 5/948 fols 119–20; Howard J. Fuller, "'This Country Now Occupies the Vantage Ground': Understanding John Ericsson's Monitors and the American Union's War against British Naval Superiority," *American Neptune* 62 (2002): 91–111, and *Clad in Iron: The American Civil War and the Challenge of British Naval Power* (Westport, Conn.: Praeger Security International, 2008), 282.

26. C. I. Hamilton, *The Anglo-French Naval Rivalry, 1840–1870* (Oxford: Oxford University Press, 1993); A. Lambert, "Politics, Technology and Policy-Making, 1859–1865: Palmerston, Gladstone and the Management of the Ironclad Naval Race," *Northern Mariner* 8 (1998): 9–38.

27. *Manchester Courier*, 29 Mar. 1862. For a comparison of the *Monitor* with the British *Warrior*, cf. 5 Apr. 1862.

28. This section benefits greatly from the advice of Howard Fuller and takes a different view to that of John F. Beeler, *British Naval Policy in the Gladstone-Disraeli Era, 1866–1880* (Stanford, Calif: Stanford University Press, 1997), 199–200; William H. Roberts, *Civil War Ironclads*. On weakness of American guns, report in April 1865, NA. FO. 5/1017 fol. 226.

29. Captain James Goodenough to Lyons, 9 Apr. 1864, NA. FO. 5/948 fol. 136. See also Lyons to Russell, 25 Apr. 1864, ibid. fol. 120.

30. Jay Luvaas, *The Military Legacy of the Civil War* (Lawrence: University Press of Kansas, 1988).

31. Robert Legget, *Ottawa River Canals and the Defence of British North America* (Toronto: University of Toronto Press,

1988); Lyons to Russell, 23 Dec. 1861, NA. PRO. 30/22/35 fol. 364.

32. NMM/MLN/124/2.

33. Lyons to Russell, 15 Feb. 1862, NA. FO. 5/825 fols 80–82.

34. Roger Willock, *Bulwark of Empire: Bermuda's Fortified Naval Base 1860–1920* (Princeton, N.J.: Princeton University Press, 1962).

35. *List of Chief Points on Federal Coast of the United States . . . also how far accessible or vulnerable to an attack*, NMM/MLN/114/8 p. 14.

36. Ibid., 15.

37. Milne to Somerset, 24 Jan. 1862, D-RA/A/2A/34/7.

38. Lyons to Russell, 23 Jan., 5, 16 Feb. 1863, NA. FO. 5/875 fols 71–72, /876 fol. 112, /877 fol. 99.

39. Jervois, *Report on the Defence of Canada*, presented to Provincial Government, 10 Nov. 1864, printed Jan. 1865, NMM. LMN/114/7, pp. 5, 23. For Jervois, see Timothy Crick, *Ramparts of Empire: The Fortifications of Sir William Jervois* (Exeter: University of Exeter Press, 2009).

40. BL. Add. 41410 fol. 4.

41. BL. Add. 41410 fol. 2.

42. D. Kirkpatrick, "A Tale of Three Forts," *RUSI Journal* 152/1 (Feb. 2007): 68–73.

43. Lyons to Russell, 12, 13 Jan., Seward to Lyons, 12 Jan., 11 Mar., Lyons to Seward, 13 Mar. 1864, NA. PRO. 30/22/38 fols 3–4, FO. 5/943 fols 53, 99–101, 946 fols 78–86.

44. NA. FO. 5/875 fols 89–115.

45. Lyons to Russell, 27 Apr. 1864, NA. FO. 5/882 fol. 208.

46. Mary Ellison, *Support for Secession: Lancashire and the American Civil War* (Chicago: University of Chicago Press, 1972); Richard J. M. Blackett, *Divided Hearts: Britain and the American Civil War* (Baton Rouge: Louisiana State University Press, 2001); Duncan A. Campbell, *English Public Opinion and the American Civil War* (Woodbridge, UK: Boydell Press,

2003); Michael de Nie, "The London Press and the American Civil War," in *Anglo-American Media Interactions, 1850–2000*, ed. Joel H. Wiener and Mark Hampton (Basingstoke: Palgrave Macmillan, 2007), 129–54.

47. Palmerston to Russell, 18 Nov. 1861, NA. PRO. 30/22/21 fol. 601.

48. Lyons to Russell, 5 Aug. 1864, and extensive enclosures, NA. FO. 5/957 fols 157–201.

49. Russell to Lewis, Russell to Somerset, both 24 Mar. 1863, NA. PRO. 30/22/30 fols 89, 129.

50. Somerset to Milne, 17 Apr. 1863, NMM/MLN/116/1c.

51. Russell to Palmerston, 3 Sept. 1863, NA. PRO. 30/22/30 fol. 69. See also, Russell to Somerset, 14 Sept. fol. 131.

52. Palmerston to Russell, 23 Aug., 4, 11, 21 Sept., 13 Sept. 1863, NA. PRO. 30/22/22 fols 239, 243, 258, Gooch (ed.), *Russell*, II, 334; Russell to Palmerston, 3 Sept. 1863, 30/22/30 fol. 60.

53. Lyons to Milne, 31 Jul. 1863, NMM. MLN/116/1a.

54. Sumner to Bright, 4 Aug., 22 Sept., 6 Oct. 1863, Edward L. Pierce (ed.), *Memoirs and Letters of Charles Sumner, 1860 to Death* (London: Sampson Low, Marston, Searle and Rivington, 1893), 143–46; Howard Jones, *Union in Peril: The Crisis over British Intervention in the Civil War* (Chapel Hill: University of North Carolina Press, 1992); James J. Barnes and Patience P. Barnes (eds.), *The American Civil War through British Eyes; Dispatches from British Diplomats*, 3 vols. (Kent, Ohio: Kent State University Press, 2003–2005); Myers, *Caution and Co-operation*.

55. George Elliot to Cobden, 27 Mar. 1863, NA. PRO. 30/22/32 fol. 154.

56. Lyons to Russell, 25 Apr. 1864, NA. FO. 5/948 fols 118–125, printed version fols 145–47.

57. Lyons to Milne, 20 Aug. 1863, NMM. MLN/116/1a.

58. Lyons to Russell, 12 Jan. 1864, NA. FO. 5/943 fols 33–34.

59. Lyons to Milne, 22 Jun. 1863, NMM. MLN/116/1a.

60. Michael B. Ballard, *Vicksburg* (Chapel Hill: University of North Carolina Press, 2004), 430.

61. M. Kukiel, "Military Aspects of the Polish Insurrection of 1863–4," *Antemurale* 7–8 (1963): 363–96.

62. Lyons to Russell, 25 Feb. 1862, NA. FO. 5/825 fols 296–303.

63. R. B. Elrod, "Austria and the Polish Insurrection of 1863," *International History Review* 8 (1986): 416–31.

64. *Chester Record*, 14 Mar. 1863.

65. Lyons to Russell, 11 Mar. 1864, NA. FO. 5/946 fols 61–70.

66. Lyons to Russell, 15 Dec. 1862, and enclosures, NA. FO. 5/899 fols 140–65.

67. Lyons to Russell, 5 Mar. 1860, Palmerston to Russell, 6 Dec. 1861, NA. PRO. 30/22/34 fols 117–18, 30/22/21 fol. 622.

68. Keith A. P. Sandford, *Great Britain and the Schleswig-Holstein Question, 1848–64: A Study in Diplomacy, Politics, and Public Opinion* (Toronto: University of Toronto Press, 1975).

69. Jack A. Dabbs, *The French Army in Mexico, 1861–1867: A Study in Military Government* (The Hague: Mouton, 1963).

70. Scarlett to Russell, 27 Feb. 1865, NA. FO. 50/385 fol. 113. For his praise of Maximilian, fol. 120.

71. Michael Cunningham, *Mexico and the Foreign Policy of Napoleon III* (Basingstoke: Palgrave, 2001).

72. Scarlett to Russell, 27 Feb., 18 Mar., 10 May 1865, NA. FO. 50/385 fols 118, 203–206, 5/386 fol. 188.

73. K. Hackemer, "Strategic Dilemma: Civil–Military Friction and the Texas Coastal Campaign of 1863," *Military History of the West*, 26 (1996): 187–214.

74. Lyons to Russell, 23 Feb. 1864, NA. FO. 5/945 fol. 27.

75. Lyons to Russell, 23 May, 20 Jun. 1864, N A . F O . 5/950 fols 19–22, 5/952 fols 93–94.

76. N A . F O . 5/877 fol. 149.

77. D. E. Sutherland, "Abraham Lincoln, John Pope, and the Origins of Total War," *Journal of Military History* 56 (1992): 581–82; B. Franklin Cooling, *Fort Donelson's Legacy: War and Society in Kentucky and Tennessee, 1862–1863* (Knoxville: University of Tennessee Press, 1997).

78. Mark Grimsley, "Conciliation and Its Failure, 1861–1862," *Civil War History* 39 (1993): 335; and *The Hard Hand of War: Union Military Policy toward Southern Civilians, 1861–1865* (New York: Cambridge University Press, 1995).

79. Stephen Sears, *George B. McClellan: The Young Napoleon* (New York: Ticknor and Fields, 1988).

80. B. H. Reid, "Rationality and Irrationality in Union Strategy, April 1861–March 1862," *War in History* 1 (1994): 38; E. S. Rafuse, "McClellan and Halleck at War: The Struggle for Control of the Union War Effort in the West, November 1861–March 1862," *Civil War History* 49 (2003): 50.

81. Palmerston to Russell, 26 Sept. 1861, N A . P R O . 30/22/21 fols 567–68; Mark E. Neely, *The Civil War and the Limits of Destruction* (Cambridge, Mass.: Harvard University Press, 2007).

82. Daniel W. Hamilton, *The Limits of Sovereignty: Property Confiscation in the Union and the Confederacy during the Civil War* (Chicago: University of Chicago Press, 2007).

83. Lyons to Russell, 21 Feb. 1862, N A . F O . 5/825 fols 247–48.

84. Hans L. Trefousse, *Benjamin Franklin Wade: Radical Republican from Ohio* (New York: Twayne Publishers, 1963).

85. Allen C. Guelzo, *Lincoln's Emancipation Proclamation: The End of Slavery in America* (New York: Simon & Schuster 2004).

86. Burrus M. Carnahan, *Act of Justice: Lincoln's Emancipation Proclamation and the Law of War* (Lexington: University Press of Kentucky, 2007).

87. Joseph Glatthaar, "African-Americans and the Mobilization for Civil War," in *On the Road to Total War: The American Civil War and the German Wars of Unification, 1861–1871*, ed. Stig Förster and Jörg Nagler (New York: Cambridge University Press, 1997), 199–215; Susan M. Grant, "Fighting for Freedom: African-American Soldiers in the Civil War," in *The American Civil War: Explorations and Reconsiderations*, ed. Susan-Mary Grant and Brian H. Reid (Harlow, UK: Longman, 2000), 191–213; Gregory J. W. Unwin (ed.), *Black Soldiers in Blue: African American Troops in the Civil War Era* (Chapel Hill: University of North Carolina Press, 2002).

88. George S. Burkhardt, *Confederate Rage, Yankee Wrath: No Quarter in the Civil War* (Carbondale: Southern Illinois University Press, 2007).

89. Franny Nudelman, *John Brown's Body: Slavery, Violence, and the Culture of War* (Chapel Hill: University of North Carolina Press, 2004).

90. Lyons to Russell, 11 Dec. 1863, N A . F O . 5/898 fol. 198.

91. Mark E. Neely, *The Fate of Liberty: Abraham Lincoln and Civil Liberties* (New York: Oxford University Press, 1991); Daniel Farber, *Lincoln's Constitution* (Chicago: University of Chicago Press, 2003).

92. Lyons to Russell, 24 Feb. 1863, N A . F O . 5/878 fols 72–77.

93. Lyons to Russell, 4, 22 Mar., 19 Apr., 18, 26 Jul., 15 Aug. 1864, N A . P R O . 30/22/38 fols 19, 26, 37, 72, 79, 92.

94. Lyons to Russell, 26 Jul. 1864, N A . P R O . 30/22/38 fol. 79.

95. Lyons to Russell, 15 Aug. 1864, N A . P R O . 30/22/38 fol. 92; James M. McPherson, *The Mighty Scourge: Perspectives on the Civil War* (Oxford: Oxford University

Press, 2007), 178; Richard M. McMurry, *Atlanta 1864: Last Chance for the Confederacy* (Lincoln: University of Nebraska Press, 2000).

96. M. J. Forsyth, "The Military Provides Lincoln a Mandate," *Army History* 53 (2001), 11–17.

97. Orville V. Burton, *The Age of Lincoln* (New York: Hill and Wang, 2007).

98. Mark E. Neely, *The Union Divided: Party Conflict in the Civil War North* (Cambridge, Mass.: Harvard University Press, 2002).

99. Joseph T. Glatthaar, *The March to the Seas and Beyond: Sherman's Troops in the Savannah and Carolinas Campaigns* (Baton Rouge: Louisiana State University Press, 1995).

100. Peter S. Carmichael, *The Last Generation: Young Virginians in Peace, War and Reunion* (Chapel Hill: University of North Carolina Press, 2005); Mark A. Weitz, *More Damning than Slaughter: Desertion in the Confederate Army* (Lincoln: University of Nebraska Press, 2005).

101. A. Jones, "Jomini and the Strategy of the American Civil War, a Reinterpretation," *Military Affairs* 34 (1970): 130–31.

102. Charles Royster, *The Destructive War: William Tecumseh, Sherman, Stonewall Jackson, and the Americans* (New York: Knopf, 1991).

103. Joseph T. Glatthaar, *General Lee's Army: From Victory to Collapse* (New York: The Free Press, 2008).

104. Michael C. C. Adams, *Our Masters the Rebels: Speculation on Union Military Failure in the East, 1861–1865* (Cambridge, Mass.: Harvard University Press, 1978).

105. Thomas L. Connelly, *Autumn of Glory: Army of Tennessee, 1862–1865* (Baton Rouge: Louisiana State University Press, 1971).

106. J. M. McPherson, "No Peace without Victory, 1861–1865," *American Historical Review* (2004): 10.

107. Frederick Bruce, British envoy, to Russell, 19 May 1865, NA. FO. 5/1018 fols 159–62.

108. Lyons to Russell, 25 Apr. 1862, NA. PRO. 30/22/36 fols 74–55; Noah A. Trudeau, *Out of the Storm: The End of the Civil War, April–June 1865* (Boston: Little, Brown, 1994).

109. Michael Fellman, *Inside War: The Guerrilla Conflict in Missouri during the American Civil War* (Oxford: Oxford University Press, 1989); Sean M. O'Brien, *Mountain Partisans: Guerrilla Warfare in the Southern Appalachians, 1861–1865* (Westport, Conn.: Praeger Institute Press, 1999); Martin Crawford, *Ashe County's Civil War: Community and Society in the Appalachian South* (Charlottesville: University Press of Virgina, 2001); Daniel E. Sutherland, *A Savage Conflict: The Decisive Role of Guerrillas in America's Civil War* (Chapel Hill: University of North Carolina Press, 2009).

110. Percy Doyle, British envoy in Mexico, to Palmerston, 13 Jan. 1848, NA. FO. 50/219 fol. 7.

111. Scarlett to Russell, 28 Apr., 9 Jun. 1865, NA. FO. 50/386 fols 146–47, 210.

112. Robert R. Mackey, *The Uncivil War: Irregular Warfare in the Upper South, 1861–1865* (Norman: University of Oklahoma Press, 2004); Clay Mountcastle, *Punitive War: Confederate Guerrillas and Union Reprisals* (Lawrence: University Press of Kansas, 2009).

113. Bruce to Russell, 26 May 1865, NA. FO. 5/1018 fols 199–202.

114. See also, Dwight T. Pitcaithley, "'A Cosmic Threat': The National Park Service Addresses the Causes of the American Civil War," in *Slavery and Public History: The Tough Stuff of American Memory*, ed. James O. Horton and Lois E. Horton (New York: New Press, 2006), 169–86; Robert J. Cook, *Troubled Commemoration: The American Civil War Centennial,*

*1961–1965* (Baton Rouge: Louisiana State University Press, 2007).

115. Earl J. Hess, *The Union Soldier in Battle: Enduring the Ordeal of Combat* (Lawrence: University Press of Kansas, 1997); James M. McPherson, *For Cause and Comrades: Why Men Fought in the Civil War* (New York: Oxford University Press, 1997).

116. Scarlett to Russell, 9 Jun. 1865, NA. FO. 5/386 fol. 210.

117. NA. FO. 5/825 fols 299–303.

118. *Manchester City News*, 23 Jan. 1864.

119. Napier to Clarendon, 13 Apr. 1857, NA. FO. 5/670 fol. 371.

120. Scarlett to Russell, 1 Apr. 1865, NA. FO. 50/386 fol. 1.

121. Scarlett to Russell, 22 Jun. 1865, NA. FO. 50/386 fols 228–29.

122. Draft to Scarlett, 21 Oct. 1865, NA. FO. 50/384 fol. 165.

123. John Ashworth, *Slavery, Capitalism, and Politics in the Antebellum Republic. II. The Coming of the Civil War, 1850–1861* (Cambridge: Cambridge University Press, 2007), 648.

**15. SETTLING THE NORTH AMERICAN QUESTION, 1865–71**

1. Bruce to George, 4th Earl of Clarendon, Foreign Secretary, 4 Jan. 1866, NA. FO. 5/1062 fols 3–4.

2. Bruce to Clarendon, 4 Jan. 1866, NA. FO. 5/1062 fol. 3.

3. Bruce to Clarendon, 9 Jan. 1866, NA. FO. 5/1062 fols 16–17.

4. Raymond A. Jones, *The British Diplomatic Service, 1815–1914* (Gerrards Cross: Colin Smythe, 1983), 217.

5. James E. Thorold Rogers (ed.), *Speeches on Questions of Public Policy by John Bright* (London: Macmillan, 1898), 470.

6. William Mulligan, "Mobs and Diplomats: The *Alabama* Affair and British Diplomacy, 1865–1872," in *The Diplomats' World: A Cultural History of Diplomacy,*

*1815–1914*, ed. Markus Mösslang and Torsten Riotte (Oxford: Oxford University Press, 2008), 105–132.

7. Matt M. Matthews, *The U.S. Army on the Mexican Border: A Historical Perspective* (Fort Leavenworth, Kans.: Combat Studies Institute Press, 2007), 45. For support for the Juarists, Bruce to Russell, 2 Jun. 1865, NA. FO. 5/1019 fol. 52.

8. Philip Henry Sheridan, *Personal Memoirs of P. H. Sheridan* (New York, 1888; Wilmington, Del., 1992), 225–26.

9. Peter Scarlett to Russell, 10 May, 9 Jun. 1865, NA. FO. 50/386 fol. 186, 208, 210–11.

10. Scarlett to Russell, 10 May, 9 Jun. 1865, NA. FO. 50/386 fol. 186, 209.

11. Alfred Jackson Hanna and Kathryn Abbey Hanna, *Napoleon III and Mexico: American Triumph over Monarchy* (Chapel Hill: University of North Carolina Press, 1971); Thomas David Schoonover, *Dollars over Dominion: The Triumph of Liberalism in Mexican–United States Relations, 1861–1867* (Baton Rouge: Louisiana State University Press, 1978).

12. Draft to Middleton, 13 Mar. 1867, NA. FO. 50/404 fol. 25.

13. Draft to Scarlett, 5 Dec. 1866, and to Middleton, 22 Jan., 7, 14 Feb. 1867, NA. FO. 50/393 fol. 180, 50/404 fols 1, 11, 15.

14. Draft to Scarlett, 1 Sept. 1866, NA. FO. 50/393 fols 151, 153.

15. Draft to Edward Thornton, envoy in America, 27 Mar. 1869, NA. FO. 5/1156.

16. NA. FO. 5/950 fols 19–22.

17. Alfonso W. Quiroz, "Loyalist Overkill: The Socioeconomic Costs of 'Repressing' the Separatist Insurrection in Cuba, 1868–1878," *Hispanic American Historical Review* 78 (1998): 269.

18. Edward Hammond, Under Secretary in the Foreign Office, to Thornton, 24 Apr. 1869, NA. FO. 5/1156.

19. Richard J. Jensen, *The Alaska Purchase and Russo-American Relations* (Seattle: University of Washington Press, 1975).

20. Draft for Thornton, 15 Feb. 1868, NA. FO. 5/1126.

21. Gough, *Gunboat Frontier,* 154.

22. Robert M. Utley, *Frontier Regulars: The United States Army and the Indian, 1866–1891,* 181–83.

23. Gordon H. Chang, "Whose 'Barbarism'? Whose 'Treachery'? Race and Civilization in the Unknown United States–Korea War of 1871," *Journal of American History* 89, no. 4 (2003): 1331–65.

24. Howard I. Kushner, *Conflict on the Northwest Coast: American–Russian Rivalry in the Pacific Northwest, 1790–1867* (Westport, Conn.: Greenwood Press, 1975).

25. Draft to Thornton, 6 Feb. 1868, 27 May 1869, 31 Mar. 1870, NA. FO. 5/1126, 1156, 1187.

26. Draft to Thornton, 14 Jan. 1870, NA. FO. 5/1187.

27. Draft to Thornton, 18 Jun. 1868, 19 Jan. 1869, NA. FO. 5/1126, 1156.

28. Draft to Thornton, 23 Apr. 1869, NA. FO. 5/1156.

29. Bruce to Edward, Lord Stanley, Foreign Secretary, 8 Jan. 1867, NA. FO. 5/1104 fols 10–11. See also, Lyons to Russell, 16 Feb. 1865 and draft instructions to Thornton, 14 Jan. 1870, NA. PRO. 30/22/38 fol. 154, FO. 5/1187.

30. Lyons to Russell, 16 Feb. 1865, NA. PRO. 30/22/38 fol. 156.

31. Bruce to Stanley, 8 Jan. 1867, NA. FO. 5/1104 fol. 12.

32. Bruce to Stanley, 8 Jan. 1867, NA. FO. 5/1104 fol. 12.

33. Bruce to Stanley, 8, 14 Jan. 1867, NA. FO. 5/1104 fols 11–12, 58. For American interest in Hawaii, draft instructions to Thornton, 20 Mar. 1868, 13 Feb. 1869, and for Crete, 30 May 1868, NA. FO. 5/1126, 1156.

34. Brian Holden Reid, "Power, Sovereignty and the Great Republic: Anglo-American Diplomatic Relations in the Era of the Civil War," *Diplomacy and Statecraft*

14 (2003): 45–72; J. Sexton, "The Funded Loans and the *Alabama* Claims," *Diplomatic History* 27 (2003): 449–78.

35. Lyons to Russell, 6 Mar. 1863, NA. FO. 5/879 fols 49–50.

36. Bruce to Russell, 26 Jun. 1865, NA. FO. 5/1018 fols 169–70.

37. Bruce to Russell, 19 May 1865, NA. FO. 5/1018 fol. 130–32.

38. Bruce to Russell, 9 May 1865, NA. FO. 5/1017 fol. 54.

39. Sean Michael O'Brien, *Mountain Partisans: Guerrilla Warfare in the Southern Appalachians, 1861–1865* (Westport, Conn.: Praeger, 1999), 184–87.

40. Anne Sarah Rubin, *A Shattered Nation: The Rise and Fall of the Confederacy, 1861–1868* (Chapel Hill: University of North Carolina Press, 2005).

41. Richard Hofstadter and Michael Wallace, *American Violence: A Documentary History* (New York: Knopf, 1970), 223; Allen W. Trelease, *White Terror: The Ku Klux Klan Conspiracy and Southern Reconstruction* (New York: Harper & Row, 1971).

42. Ben H. Severance, *Tennessee's Radical Army: The State Guard and Its Role in Reconstruction, 1867–1869* (Knoxville: University of Tennessee Press, 2005).

43. Lyons to Russell, 6 Mar. 1863, NA. FO. 5/879 fol. 50.

44. Harold M. Hyman, "Ulysses Grant I, Emperor of America: Some Civil-Military Continuities and Strains of the Civil War and Reconstruction," *Revue Internationale d'Histoire Militaire* 69 (1990): 187–88.

45. Robert Wooster, "John M. Schofield and the 'Multipurpose' Army," in *The Vistas of American Military History 1800–1898,* ed. Brian Holden-Reid and Joseph G. Dawson (Abingdon: Routledge, Taylor & Francis Group, 2007), 43.

46. Vincent P. DeSantis, "Rutherford B. Hayes and the Removal of the Troops and the End of Reconstruction," in *Re-*

*gion, Race and Reconstruction: Essays in Honor of C. Vann Woodward*, ed. J. Morgan Kousser and James McPherson (New York: Oxford University Press, 1982), 417–50.

47. Stuart Charles McConnell, *Glorious Contentment: The Grand Army of the Republic, 1865–1900* (Chapel Hill: University of North Carolina Press, 1992).

48. Ralph L. Andreano (ed.), *The Economic Impact of the Civil War* (Cambridge: Schenkman Publishing Company, 1962).

49. Bruce to Russell, 26 May 1865, NA. FO. 5/1018 fols 203–204.

50. Roger L. Ransom and Richard Sutch, *One Kind of Freedom: The Economic Consequences of Emancipation* (Cambridge: Cambridge University Press, 1977); Stephen J. Decanio, "Productivity and Income Distribution in the Postbellum South," *Journal of Economic History* 34 (1974): 422–46.

51. Vine Deloria and Raymond J. DeMallie, *Documents of American Indian Diplomacy: Treaties, Agreements, and Conventions 1775–1979* (Norman: University of Oklahoma Press, 1999), Vol. I, 587.

52. Alvin M. Josephy, *The Civil War in the American West* (New York: A.A. Knopf, 1991).

53. David Paul Smith, *Frontier Defense in the Civil War: Texas' Rangers and Rebels* (College Station: Texas A&M University Press, 1992).

54. Lyons to Russell, 22 Jan. 1864 and enclosures, NA. FO. 5/120 fols 139–53.

55. Stan Hoig, *The Sand Creek Massacre* (Norman: University of Oklahoma Press, 1961); Elliott West, *The Contested Plains: Indians, Goldseekers, and the Rush to Colorado* (Lawrence: University Press of Kansas, 1998); Christine Whitacre, "The Search for the Site of the Sand Creek Massacre," *Prologue* 33 (2001): 96–107.

56. David E. Wagner, *Patrick Connor's War: The 1865 Powder River Indian Expedition* (Norman, Okla.: Arthur H. Clark Co., 2010).

57. Robert Wooster, *The Military and United States Indian Policy, 1865–1903* (New Haven, Conn.: Yale University Press, 1988).

58. William Y. Chalfant, *Hancock's War: Conflict on the Southern Plains* (Norman, Okla.: Arthur H. Clark Company, imprint of the University of Oklahoma Press, 2010).

59. Lance Janda, "Shutting the Gates of Mercy: the American Origins of Total War, 1860–1880," *Journal of Military History* 59 (1995): 26; Jerome A. Greene, *Washita: The U.S. Army and the Southern Cheyennes, 1867–1869* (Norman: University of Oklahoma Press, 2004); Gary Clayton Anderson, *The Conquest of Texas: Ethnic Cleansing in the Promised Land, 1820–1875* (Norman: University of Oklahoma Press, 2005).

60. Thornton to Clarendon, 12 Apr. 1870, Bod. MS. Clar. Dept. C. 481 fol. 75.

61. Robert M. Utley, *Frontier Regulars*, 189–90, 215.

62. Hämäläinen, *The Comanche Empire*, 333–34.

63. Charles M. Robinson, *General Crook and the Western Frontier* (Norman: University of Oklahoma Press, 2001).

64. Russell F. Weigley, "The Long Death of the Indian-Fighting Army," in *Soldiers and Civilians: The U.S. Army and the American People*, ed. Garry P. Ryan and Timothy K. Nenninger (Washington, D.C.: National Archives and Records Administration, 1987), 27–39.

65. Thomas W. Dunlay, *Wolves for the Blue Soldiers: Indian Scouts and Auxiliaries with the United States Army, 1860–1890* (Lincoln: University of Nebraska Press, 1982).

66. Anthony McGinnis, *Counting Coup and Cutting Horses: Intertribal Warfare on the Northern Plains, 1738–1889* (Evergreen, Colo.: Cordillera Press, 1990).

67. John H. Monnett, *Where a Hundred Soldiers Were Killed: The Struggle for*

the *Powder River Country in 1866 and the Making of the Fetterman Myth* (Albuquerque: University of New Mexico Press, 2008).

68. James O. Gump, *The Dust Rose Like Smoke: The Subjugation of the Zulu and the Sioux* (Lincoln: University of Nebraska Press, 1994); Bruce Vandervort, *Indian Wars of Mexico, Canada and the United States, 1812–1900* (London: Routledge, 2006).

69. Robert G. Athearn, *William Tecumseh Sherman and the Settlement of the West* (Norman: University of Oklahoma Press, 1956); Robert G. Angevine, *The Railroad and the State: War, Politics and Technology in Nineteenth-Century America* (Stanford, Calif.: Stanford University Press, 2004).

70. Michael L. Tate, *The Frontier Army in the Settlement of the West* (Norman: University of Oklahoma Press, 1999); Robert Wooster, *The American Military Frontiers: The United States Army in the West, 1783–1900* (Albuquerque: University of New Mexico Press, 2009).

71. Darlis A. Miller, *Soldiers and Settlers: Military Supply in the Southwest, 1861–1885* (Albuquerque: University of New Mexico Press, 1989); Thomas T. Smith, *The U.S. Army and the Texas Frontier Economy, 1845–1900* (College Station: Texas A&M University Press, 1999).

72. Report of Senate Committee on Indian Affairs, 1 Mar. 1865, NA. FO. 5/1018 fol. 319; Jill St. Germain, *Broken Treaties: United States and Canadian Relations with the Lakotas and the Plains Crees, 1868–1885* (Lincoln: University of Nebraska Press, 2009).

73. George F. G. Stanley, *Toil and Trouble: Military Expeditions to Red River* (Toronto: Dundurn Press,1989).

74. Edward Thornton to Clarendon, 9 Feb. 1869, 4 Jan. 1870, Bod. MS. Clar. Dept. C 480 fols 43–44, 481 fol. 3.

75. Draft to Thornton, 10 Apr. 1869, NA. FO. 5/1156.

76. Consul Archibald in New York to Bruce, 13 May, Bruce to Russell, 16 May 1865, NA. FO. 5/1017 fols 112, 118.

77. Captain John Bythesea, naval attaché, to Russell, 11 Sept. 1865, NA. FO. 5/1099 fols 386–88.

78. Brian Jenkins, *Fenians and Anglo-American Relations during Reconstruction* (Ithaca, N.Y.: Cornell University Press, 1969); Hereward Senior, *The Last Invasion of Canada* (Toronto: Dundurn Press, 1991).

79. Thornton to Clarendon, 4, 8 Jan. 1870, Bod. MS. Clar. Dept. C. 481 fols 5, 7–8

80. Thornton to Clarendon, 8 Jan., 22 Feb. 1870, Bod. MS. Clar. Dep. C. 481 fols 11, 41.

81. *History of American Foreign Policy*, 3rd ed. (1978), I, 239–64; Maureen M. Robson, "The Alabama Claims and the Anglo-American Reconciliation, 1865–71," *Canadian Historical Review* 42 (1961): 1–22; Adrian Cook, *The Alabama Claims: American Politics and Anglo-American Relations, 1865–1872* (Ithaca, N.Y.: Cornell University Press, 1975); Jay Sexton, "The Funded Loan and the *Alabama* Claims," *Diplomatic History* 27 (2003): 449–78.

82. J. Mackay Hitsman, *Safeguarding Canada, 1763–1871* (Toronto: University of Toronto Press, 1968).

83. Christopher Moore, *1867: How the Fathers Made a Deal* (Toronto: Mc-Clelland & Stewart, 1997), 241; Donald G. Creighton, *The Road to Confederation: The Emergence of Canada, 1863–1867* (Boston: Houghton Mifflin, 1965); Ged Martin, *Britain and the Origins of Canadian Confederation, 1837–1867* (Vancouver: University of British Columbia Press, 1995); W. L. Morton, "The International Context of Confederation," in *Interpreting Canada's Past*, ed. J. M. Bumsted, 2nd ed. (Toronto: Oxford University Press, 1993).

84. Peter Burroughs, "Defence and Imperial Disunity," in *The Oxford History*

of the British Empire, Vol. III: The Nineteenth Century, ed. Andrew Porter (Oxford: Oxford University Press, 1999), 327.

85. Michael J. Salevouris, "Riflemen Form": The War Scare of 1859–1860 in England (New York: Garland, 1982).

86. NMM. MLN/124/4.

87. Manchester Courier, 4 Jan. 1862.

88. Arvel B. Erickson, Edward T. Cardwell: Peelite (Philadelphia: American Philosophical Society, 1959).

89. Donald C. Gordon, The Dominion Partnership in Imperial Defense, 1870–1914 (Baltimore: Johns Hopkins Press, 1965); Donald M. Schurman, Imperial Defence, 1868–1887, ed. John F. Beeler (London: Frank Cass, 2000), 26–27.

90. C. P. Stacey, "Britain's Withdrawal from North America, 1864–71," Canadian Historical Review 36 (1955): 185–98; Kenneth Bourne, Britain and the Balance of Power in America 1815–1908 (London: Longman, 1967), 273–81, 302–305.

91. Richard J. Gwyn, John A: The Man Who Made Us (Toronto: Random House Canada, 2007), 276.

92. Thornton to Clarendon, 18 Jan., 26 Apr., 3 May 1870, Bod. MS. Clar. Dept. C. 481 fols 18–19, 85–86, 97.

93. Thornton to Clarendon, 12 Apr. 1870, Bod. MS. Clar. Dep. C. 481 fol. 73.

94. Gough, Gunboat Frontier.

95. Thongchai Winichakul, Siam Mapped: A History of the Geo-Body of a Nation (Honolulu: University of Hawaii Press, 1994).

96. Christopher A. Bayly, Imperial Meridian: The British Empire and the World, 1780–1830 (London: Longman, 1989).

97. Ernest N. Paolino, The Foundation of the American Empire: William Henry Seward and U.S. Foreign Policy (Ithaca, N.Y.: Cornell University Press, 1973), 27.

98. For Napier's views on Cuba, Napier to Clarendon, 20 May 1857, NA. FO. 5/671 fol. 182–87.

99. Michel Gobat, Confronting the American Dream: Nicaragua under U.S. Imperial Rule (Durham, N.C.: Duke University Press, 2005).

16. POSTSCRIPT, 1871–2010

1. Thornton to Clarendon, 29 Mar. 1870, Bod. MS. Clar. Dep. C. 481 fol. 59.

2. Michael J. Francis, The Limits of Hegemony: United States Relations with Argentina and Chile during World War II (Notre Dame, Ind.: University of Notre Dame Press, 1977).

3. B. R. Tomlinson, "Economics and Empire: The Periphery and the Imperial Economy," in Andrew Porter (ed.), The Oxford History of the British Empire, Vol. III, (Oxford: Oxford University Press, 2001), 57.

4. Thomas David Schoonover, Uncle Sam's War of 1898 and the Origins of Globalization (Lexington: University Press of Kentucky, 2003).

5. Jon T. Hoffman, Michael J. Brodhead, Carol R. Byerly, and Glenn F. Williams, The Panama Canal: An Army's Enterprise (Washington, D.C.: Center of Military History, United States Army, 2009).

6. Paul Gibb, "Selling out Canada? The Role of Sir Julian Pauncefote in the Bering Sea Dispute," International History Review 24 (2002): 817–44.

7. Bruno Ramirez, Crossing the 49th Parallel: Migration from Canada to the United States, 1900–1930 (Ithaca, N.Y.: Cornell University Press, 2001).

8. Peter Calvert, The Mexican Revolution, 1910–14: The Diplomacy of Anglo-American Conflict (Cambridge: Cambridge University Press, 1968); Friedrich Katz, The Secret War in Mexico: Europe, the United States and the Mexican Revolution (Chicago: University of Chicago Press, 1981).

9. Michael Howard, The First World War (Oxford: Oxford University Press, 2002), 15.

10. E. D. Steele, *Palmerston and Liberalism, 1855–1865* (Cambridge: Cambridge University Press, 1991), 252.

11. Bradford Perkins, *The Great Rapprochement: England and the United States, 1895–1914* (London: Gollancz, 1969).

12. Donald A. Yerxa, *Admirals and Empire: The United States Navy and the Caribbean, 1898–1945* (Columbia: University of South Carolina Press, 1991), esp. p. 53.

13. Paul Gibb, "Unmasterly Inactivity? Sir Julian Pauncefote, Lord Salisbury, and the Venezuela Boundary Dispute," *Diplomacy and Statecraft*, 16 (2005): 23–55.

CONCLUSIONS

1. *Manchester Courier,* 4 Jan. 1862.

2. Robert Kagan, *Dangerous Nation: America and the World, 1600–1898* (London: Atlantic, 2006). See also David Reynolds, *America, Empire of Liberty: A New History* (London: Allen Lane, 2009).

3. For a classic argument, Paul W. Schroeder, *The Transformation of European Politics, 1763–1848* (Oxford: Clarendon Press, 1994), and for criticisms, Jeremy Black and Harald Kleinschmidt, "Schroeder Reconsidered or the Limitations of the Systems Approach," *Diplomacy and Statecraft* 11 (2000): 257–70.

4. James P. Horn, Jan E. Lewis, and Peter S. Onuf (eds.), *The Revolution of 1800: Democracy, Race, and the New Republic* (Charlottesville: University of Virginia Press, 2002).

5. Thomas G. Otte, "A Janus-like Power: Great Britain and the European Concert, 1814–1853," in *Das europäische Mächtekonzert: Friedens- und Sicherheitspolitik vom Wiener Kongress 1815 bis zum Krimkrieg 1853,* ed. Wolfram Pyta (Cologne: Weimar Wien Böhlau, 2009), 153.

6. Edward Ingram, "Illusions of Victory. The Nile, Copenhagen, and Trafalgar Revisited," *Military Affairs* 47 (1984): 140–43.

7. Richard Harding, *Amphibious Warfare in the Eighteenth Century: The British Expedition to the West Indies, 1740–1742* (Woodbridge, UK: Boydell, 1991).

8. Brian W. Blouet (ed.), *Global Geostrategy: Mackinder and the Defense of the West* (London: Frank Cass, 2005).

9. Colin S. Gray, *The Geopolitics of the Nuclear Era: Heartland, Rimlands, and the Technological Revolution* (New York: Crane, Russak and Company, 1977).

10. Richard Buel, *In Irons: Britain's Naval Supremacy and the American Revolutionary Economy* (New Haven, Conn.: Yale University Press, 1998).

11. Jonathan Parry, *The Politics of Patriotism: English Liberalism, National Identity and Europe, 1830–1886* (Cambridge: Cambridge University Press, 2006).

12. Kathleen Burk, *Old World, New World.*

13. Duncan A. Campbell, *Unlikely Allies: Britain, America and the Victorian Origins of the Special Relationship* (London: Hambledon Continuum, 2007), 200–225.

14. Draft to Scarlett, 6 Sept. 1865, NA. FO. 50/384 fol. 153.

15. William J. Novak, "The Myth of the 'Weak' American State," *American Historical Review* 113 (2008): 752–72.

16. Peter Hugill, "The American Challenge to British Hegemony, 1861–1946," *Geographical Review* 99 (2009): 403–425.

17. John Darwin, *The Empire Project: The Rise and Fall of the British World-System, 1830–1970* (Cambridge: Cambridge University Press, 2009).

18. Jeremy Black, *What If? Counterfactualism and the Problem of History* (London: The Social Affairs Unit, 2008).

19. Gonzalo Pozo-Martin, "Autonomous or Materialist Geopolitics," *Cambridge Review of International Relations* 20 (2007): 551–63; Deborah Cowen and Neil Smith, "After Geopolitics? From the Geopolitical Social to Geoeconomics," *Antipode* 41 (2009): 22–48.

20. Betty Fladeland, *Men and Brothers: Anglo-American Antislavery Cooperation* (Urbana: University of Illinois Press, 1972).

21. Thomas to Elizabeth Pease, 19 Sept. 1864, Manchester, John Rylands Library, REAs/2/4/25.

22. Eg., Walter Russell Mead, *God and Gold: Britain, America and the Making of the Modern World* (New York: Alfred A. Knopf, 2008).

23. Larry Stewart, *The Rise of Public Science: Rhetoric, Technology and Natural Philosophy in Newtonian Britain, 1660–1750* (Cambridge: Cambridge University Press, 1992).

24. Jeremy Black, "The Theory of the Balance of Power in the First Half of the Eighteenth Century: A Note on Sources," *Review of International Studies* 9 (1983): 855–61.

25. Held in the National Gallery in Stockholm.

26. Mary Poovey, *A History of the Modern Fact: Problems of Knowledge in the Sciences of Wealth and Society* (Chicago: University of Chicago Press, 1998); Edward Higgs, *The Information State in England* (Basingstoke: Palgrave Macmillan, 2004).

27. J. H. Burnley, New York, to Russell, 4 Apr. 1865, NA. FO. 5/1017 fols 74, 78.

28. Paul W. Schroeder, *The Transformation of European Politics, 1763–1848* (Oxford: Clarendon Press, 1994), 574–75.

# INDEX

JEREMY BLACK is a British historian and Professor of History at the University of Exeter, and has lectured extensively in Australia, Canada, Denmark, France, Germany, Italy, New Zealand, and the United States. He is a senior fellow at the Center for the Study of America and the West at the Foreign Policy Research Institute. He is author of more than 100 books, especially on eighteenth-century British politics and international relations and on the history of warfare, and received the Samuel Eliot Morison Prize from the Society for Military History in 2008. He was made a Member of the Order of the British Empire for services to stamp design.

Lightning Source UK Ltd.
Milton Keynes UK
UKOW04f1152141114

241608UK00001B/17/P